CASSIODORUS:
EXPLANATION OF THE PSALMS

Ancient Christian Writers

The Works of the Fathers in Translation

EDITED BY

WALTER J. BURGHARDT

and

THOMAS COMERFORD LAWLER

No. 52

CASSIODORUS: EXPLANATION OF THE PSALMS

TRANSLATED AND ANNOTATED

BY

P. G. WALSH

Professor of Humanity
University of Glasgow

VOLUME II
Psalms 51–100
[Psalms 52(51)–101(100)]

PAULIST PRESS
New York, N.Y./Mahwah, N.J.

Library of Congress Cataloging-in-Publication Data

(Revised for vol. 3)
Cassiodorus, Senator, ca. 487–ca. 580.
    Explanation of the Psalms.

    (Ancient Christian writers; no. 51–
    Translation of: Expositio Psalmorum.
    Includes bibliographical references and indexes.
    Contents: v. 1. Psalms 1–50—v. 2. Psalms 51–100—v. 3. Psalms 101–150.
    1. Bible. O.T. Psalms—Commentaries—Early works to 1800.   I. Walsh. P. G.
    (Patrick Gerard)   II. Title.   III. Series.
BR60.A35 no. 51, etc. [B S1429] 270 s   90-41938
ISBN 0-8091-0441-5 (v. 1)   [223'.206]
ISBN 0-8091-0444-X (v. 2)
ISBN 0-8091-0445-8 (v. 3)

Published by Paulist Press
997 Macarthur Boulevard
Mahwah, New Jersey 07430

PRINTED AND BOUND IN THE UNITED STATES OF AMERICA

CONTENTS

Commentary on Psalm 51 1
Commentary on Psalm 52 7
Commentary on Psalm 53 13
Commentary on Psalm 54 17
Commentary on Psalm 55 30
Commentary on Psalm 56 38
Commentary on Psalm 57 45
Commentary on Psalm 58 51
Commentary on Psalm 59 62
Commentary on Psalm 60 70
Commentary on Psalm 61 75
Commentary on Psalm 62 83
Commentary on Psalm 63 90
Commentary on Psalm 64 96
Commentary on Psalm 65 106
Commentary on Psalm 66 116
Commentary on Psalm 67 121
Commentary on Psalm 68 141
Commentary on Psalm 69 161
Commentary on Psalm 70 165
Commentary on the Eight Decades that Relate to the New
    Testament 181
Commentary on Psalm 71 183
Commentary on Psalm 72 196
Commentary on Psalm 73 209
Commentary on Psalm 74 224
Commentary on Psalm 75 231
Commentary on Psalm 76 238
Commentary on Psalm 77 250
Commentary on Psalm 78 275
Commentary on Psalm 79 283

Commentary on Psalm 80 292
Commentary on Psalm 81 301
Commentary on Psalm 82 306
Commentary on Psalm 83 313
Commentary on Psalm 84 320
Commentary on Psalm 85 327
Commentary on Psalm 86 336
Commentary on Psalm 87 342
Commentary on Psalm 88 351
Commentary on Psalm 89 370
Commentary on Psalm 90 379
Commentary on Psalm 91 387
Commentary on Psalm 92 394
Commentary on Psalm 93 399
Commentary on Psalm 94 408
Commentary on Psalm 95 415
Commentary on Psalm 96 424
Commentary on Psalm 97 430
Commentary on Psalm 98 436
Commentary on Psalm 99 443
Commentary on Psalm 100 446

NOTES 455
  LIST OF ABBREVIATIONS 457
  NOTES TO TEXT 459

INDEXES 509
  1. OLD AND NEW TESTAMENTS 509
  2. AUTHORS 518
  3. GENERAL 520

CASSIODORUS:
EXPLANATION OF THE PSALMS

COMMENTARY ON PSALM 51

1–2. *Unto the end, understanding of David, when Doech the Edomite came and announced to Saul, and said to him: See, David has come to the house of Abimelech.* The case must be briefly indicated to explain the heading to us. When David was fleeing from Saul, he came to the priest Abimelech. He was received by him and obtained the loaves of proposition and the sword with which he had slain Goliath. The loaves of proposition denoted his role as priest, the consecrated sword his future rank as most powerful king. The Edomite Doech happened to be there in charge of the mules, and reported everything to king Saul. Then Saul was angry, and caused Abimelech and the other priests of the same city to be slain by Doech.[1] This Doech through whom such events occurred was called the Edomite from the name of his land. The names combined, according to the authority of the Fathers,[2] mean earthquakes. Such meaning attached to the names is rightly related to the acts of Antichrist, for Doech the Edomite was the foe of David as Antichrist will be the enemy of Christ. Doech destroyed priests, Antichrist will make martyrs. Doech through the meaning of his name denotes earthquakes, Antichrist will disturb the whole world when with sacrilegious presumption he will constrain it to worship his name.[3] So Antichrist is rightly understood by the name of Doech the Edomite, since he is seen to be similar to him in these striking parallels. So the whole of this heading is rightly to be applied to the second coming of the Lord in the time of Antichrist, for it is wholly appropriate to the appearance of Christ. So the heading seems not to be at odds with its psalm, but rather to harmonise with it.

Division of the Psalm

The prophet was enlightened by the holy Spirit, and beheld the loathsome domination of Antichrist arise before the Lord's judgment. To strengthen the hearts of the faithful, in the first section of the psalm he inveighs on a high note against him, so that Antichrist should not praise himself excessively for his wicked deeds, as a most grievous end overhung him. In the second part he continues his rebuke, saying that Antichrist is to be whisked away by a swift end without obtaining a portion of the Lord in the company of the saints. The third part tells of the emergent astonishment of the saints when the devil, who in this world has made his way with boundless audacity, will at the end be seen to be most wretched and forlorn. In the fourth part the prophet shows trust in God, and reckons that in the world to come he will have a most blessed lot with the saints. Some commentators have thought that this psalm is directed against sinners in general. But since the instruction given is that prayer be offered rather for such persons as have by no means abandoned hope of conversion, it follows that the psalm is to be interpreted as referring rather to Antichrist and his followers, for he is known to be already condemned through the harshness of his obduracy, especially since he will be destroyed at the end of the world, as is said below.

Explanation of the Psalm

3. *Why dost thou glory in malice, thou that art mighty in iniquity all the day long?* Divine Scripture says that we must not boast even in good deeds, but bids that *He that glorieth should glory in the Lord.*[4] So here the prophet angrily rebukes the wicked one who preens himself solely on his malice; he asks why he wishes to glory in his evil deeds, which ought rather to be a cause of anxiety when witnessed by his conscience. This is a feature of *enargeia,*[5] since he addresses one absent as if he were present. In the later verses after the verbal abuse he describes him in remarkably specific terms, so that he who men believe will appear a long time hence seems to be clearly visible through his manners. The one *mighty in iniquity* is he who is allowed to dwell in wickedness, and can fulfil what he attempts. But his strength in wickedness is matched by the curses which those with good manners direct at him. So that this activity may not seem to be momentary, he added: *All the day long,* which indicates the period of his whole life, so that without any interruption he both performs and meditates evil perpetually.

4. *Thy tongue hath devised injustice: as a sharp razor thou hast*

wrought deceit. With marvellous brevity he describes the behaviour of most wicked men, who do not ponder before they speak. As the most wise Solomon says: *The heart of fools is in their mouth.*[6] Here the psalmist says that the tongue, not the heart, did the devising; so the organ which usually serves the counsel of the prudent seemed to have pondered even as it spoke, and it uttered injudicious words because it did not refine them with preliminary judgment. The phrase, *the tongue has devised,* made clear both the ready inclination of a most fickle mind and a most unreflecting haste of speech, for sometimes we can devise evil things but not utter them with the tongue. Here the most wicked practice of the debased man is condemned. The psalmist added: *As a sharp razor thou hast wrought deceit.* A razor is a length of thinned-out steel made extremely sharp for shaving off hair; it crops the implanted growth of beard but leaves the flesh unharmed. So he has appropriately compared the guile of the most savage man to a sharp razor, for just as the razor does not harm a person, so the man's guile does not afflict the just man's soul, whatever the tribulation. It can shave off any external attributes like hair, but in so doing it makes the inner part of the soul more beautiful, since it strives to deprive it of worldly things.

5. *Thou hast loved malice more than kindness, and iniquity rather than to speak righteousness.* Evil never forsakes the man known to love the sin which he commits; for we wholly abandon the things which we condemn when a loathing for them makes its presence felt. This most wicked sinner is said to love his own faults; corrupted by an accursed disease, he regards as more desirable what good manners invariably condemn. To compound that man's guilt, he added: *More than kindness,* so that though kindness occasionally touched his heart, it was then rejected as a hateful vice and regarded as foul. Next comes: *And iniquity rather than to speak righteousness.* Usually when men commit sins they hide behind the elegance of ordered discourse; they do not wish those faults which they know win general condemnation and abhorrence to be detected in themselves. But this evil man proclaimed his wickedness in such a way that he did not blush to state what the aspirations of the wise reject. Observe how the psalmist in these three verses has briefly drawn attention to many things; this figure is called *leptologia*[7] or subtle discourse, when individual things are indicated piecemeal and simply.

6. *Thou hast loved all the words of ruin in a deceitful tongue.* After the break of a diapsalm he comes to the second part. Admittedly we have before our eyes some most wicked person, but whose crafty words come down as from a mountain-precipice? The reference here is indeed to Antichrist, who inverts and confuses morals and loves wickedness. He hastens to all the words of ruin, and his commands avail no-one. He utters everything with guile; his words are deemed to be of help to none.

7. *Therefore will God destroy thee unto the end. He will pluck thee out, and remove thee from his dwelling-place; and thy root out of the land of the living.* God will in this life destroy to their great advantage those whom He has decided to build up again; but he who is destroyed *unto the end* is consigned to eternal punishments. For the reasons which have been given earlier, that tyrant will at the end of the world be condemned by the Lord's words, so that such monstrous wickedness can be destroyed at the coming of the highest Judge. Daniel, too, has explained the time when His power will be in evidence, when he says: *That it should be unto a time of times and half a time, at the accomplishment of the scattering, that all these things shall be finished.*[8] Next comes: *He will pluck thee out and remove thee from his dwelling-place.* What a huge punishment and fearsome condemnation, to be plucked out from the most pleasant dwelling-house of the Lord and consigned to undying fires, where nothing is allowed to sprout or permitted to bloom, but like an aged tree torn out by the roots will lie sere in perpetual barrenness! Some may react that these words cannot refer to Antichrist, for the psalm says: *He will remove thee from his dwelling-place*, whereas that most pagan of men seems hardly to have settled there. But this can be interpreted as referring to his members, who are seen to be in the Church in body but not in mind; for just as the faithful are members of the Lord Saviour, so Antichrist gathers his confederates in a single alliance of wickedness. He added: *And thy root out of the land of the living.* The root of Antichrist will be the associates and agents of the devil, and so the psalmist says that his root will be plucked out of the land of the living in company with him; for neither the devil nor Antichrist nor their followers will have any portion of the Lord in the company of the saints. Let him who considers the

Antichrist's power as admirable examine his punishment, and he must regard as most cheap him whose dominion he must see as doomed to exstinction.

8. *The just shall see and fear, and shall laugh at him and say.* . . . He comes to the third section, in which the prophet's spirit foresaw what was now appointed to happen long afterwards. But though the just continually fear God and do not cease to harbour great thoughts of His power, on that occasion they will behold a sight making them fear more intensely than human thoughts can conceive. So *they will fear* envisages the divine glory rather than fear of punishment, for he is speaking of the blessed. Next comes: *And shall laugh at him and say.* . . . In this world the just instead lament those who they know are in error; as Paul says: *That I may mourn many of them that have sinned and have not done penance.*[9] But since at the judgment to come there will be no place for repentance, the just will rightly laugh at him, since the Lord's holy patience was scorned by that faithless man with wicked intention. Now so that we should not regard this laughter as of the very trivial kind which is often a feature in this world, the words which they will utter follow, so that the motive of the blessed can be seen to be in harmony with the Lord's judgment.

9. *Behold the man that made not God his helper, but trusted in the abundance of his riches, and prevailed in his vanity.* When *Behold* is said with hand extended, the unspeakable lot of the sinner is indicated. The outcome of those works which that most cruel one considered splendid becomes clear. We must interpret *riches* here as the entire panoply of the world in which that most wicked man will abound. As Daniel the prophet relates; *And he shall have power over hidden treasures of gold and silver, and all the desirable things of Egypt.*[10] He will be rich not only in gold but will rejoice also in abundance of nations and power over lands, and in pointing out wonders. He will vaunt in the arrogance of base distinctions, and teem with the other vices known to be embraced under the name of Egypt. But all these will be empty, for they are seen to be foreign to the Lord. *Vain* is a label given to what is empty, frail, or transient, to what is separated from the most steadfast truth. For though all worldly things are seen to be potentially subject to him, he prevailed in vain, for he gained absolutely nothing

which would be of value to him. As the teacher of the Gentiles says of him: *Puffing himself up without cause through the madness of his flesh, and not holding the head, from which the whole body by joints grows and extends into the increase of God.*[11]

10. *But I, as a fruitful olive-tree in the house of God, have hoped in the mercy of God unto eternity: yea, for ever and ever.* The prophet comes to the fourth part, in which he now delightedly rejoices at the approach of an impending event which is very long-lasting. He rightly compares himself to the olive-tree because the Lord Christ blossomed from its shoot, for He was anointed with spiritual oil before all His fellows.[12] But this most blessed olive contributed such fruit as could make the whole human race, which was dried out with sins, grow fat with the generosity of His mercy. He also added: *In the house of God,* in which the fruit of the fertile tree did indeed ripen. The reason why this wonderful fruit sprouted forth was because he hoped in the mercy of God, whereas Antichrist trusted in the multitude of his riches. The one is set against the other so that it may be clear what fruit lies in hope in the Godhead, and what death lies in the absence of hope in the Lord. This figure is termed *syndyasmos*[13] or comparison, when different things are contrasted with each other. So that this trust should not be regarded as adopted merely for the moment, he added: *Unto eternity,* which means for ever and ever. We recognise that the idea is repeated so that he may be judged to have kept his hope utterly pinned on that eternity.

11. *I will praise thee, O Lord, for ever, because thou hast done it, and I will wait on thy name, for it is good in the sight of thy saints.* When this most wholesome preacher declaimed the blessings of his confession, he revealed how we ought to behave; we have been granted the chance to confess here so as to deserve to be forgiven in the next world. He added: *Because thou hast done it;* by "done it" we must understand "performed mercy" by the figure of *ekleipsis.*[14] He earlier witnessed that he had hope in that mercy. Next comes: *And I will wait on thy name, for it is good.* He awaits His name because he believes that he will be saved at the Lord Saviour's judgment through His mercy, for he considers that the word *good* will be fulfilled in his own case. His name is rightly called good, because from it is received both hope of salvation and the palm of our entire life. There is the further addition, *in the sight of thy saints,* denoting the time when there is now general

rejoicing among the just, and the praise of the Lord will be sung unceasingly in harmonious exultation.

Conclusion Drawn From the Psalm

Following upon the happy tears of Psalm 50, and this most blessed expiation of sins which the joyful prophet poured out on the Lord's foe in his love for the Godhead, he attacks his King's enemy with the greatest devotion because he had been freed from conflict with his sins. But though in various places we find the motifs of praise and blame, which are both linked with the demonstrative type of speech,[15] in this psalm the psalmist has combined both in a most beautiful way. For from the beginning up to where he says: *Prevailed in his vanity,*[16] he achieves the aim of blame; from the next words to the end the nature of eulogy is mapped out, and thus the demonstrative genre is clearly achieved fully in both aspects. It is right for us to remember also that this is the second psalm prophesying the coming of Antichrist,[17] and the two are linked to each other in a wonderful order. Just as at the world's close Antichrist is to be destroyed by the two most holy men Elijah and Enoch, so through these twin psalms Antichrist is exposed and prevented from covertly imposing fear. So this psalm is aptly set after Psalm 50, for the son of iniquity of whom it speaks passes beyond the bounds of forgiveness, and is acknowledged to win no pardon.

COMMENTARY ON PSALM 52

1. *Unto the end, for Amalech, the understanding of David.* Though this psalm is known to harmonise to a considerable extent with Psalm 13 in resemblance of verses, understanding of them is very greatly changed through the difference between the headings. Whereas Psalm 13 has: *A psalm of David,* this has: *Unto the end, for Amalech, the understanding of David.* So without change of verses the two announce differing tidings for the future. Psalm 13 is published against the Jews; this one is shown to mount an attack on all sinners in gen-

eral. The first tells of the Lord's incarnation, whereas this will speak at the end of the psalm of the approach of the Judgment. It is a splendid type of utterance, which emerges through the figure of allegory to use the same words but to have a meaning other than the words spoken; there is found a remarkable difference in sense, though the words have not changed. Now let us clarify the words of this heading: *Unto the end, for Amalech, the understanding of David.* The meaning of *unto the end* has already become clear through frequent explanation. Amalech was a tribe extremely hostile to the people of God, warring on them in numerous struggles; the interpretation of this name is "for one in childbirth" or "for one in pain."[1] This we now aptly apply to the Lord's Church, which in its painful childbirth warns faithless people to cease from their wicked deeds that they may not perish at the divine Judgment. As Paul says: *My little children whom I again bring forth in labour, until Christ be formed in you.*[2]

Division of the Psalm

In the first section of the psalm it is the Church who speaks, rebuking those unwilling to turn their hearts to spiritual blessings, who through aping each other are polluted by foul deeds. In the second part she says that they will suffer the evils which they have inflicted on the Christian people. In the third section she warns the faithful to endure the hardships of the world with untroubled mind until the judgment of the Majesty draws near, when all the blessed will undoubtedly receive the good things which the Lord promises.

Explanation of the Psalm

The fool said in his heart, There is no God. 2. They are corrupted and become abominable in their wishes: there is none that doth good, there is not a single one. If we are willing to scrutinise this again, a categorical syllogism[3] emerges before us. Fools are corrupted and become abominable in their wishes: all who are corrupted and become abominable in their wishes say in their hearts, *There is no God:* therefore fools say in their hearts, *There is no God.* Now let us proceed to explain in more detail these statements. Speech is the function of the tongue, not the heart; but because the power of the Godhead understands our thoughts, it is stated that the fool's heart said what could reach the Lord's ears—not to make Him aware of it, but to allow Him to take vengeance for it. As the Lord says in Genesis: *I will go down and see whether they fulfil in action the cry that has come to me*,[4] and the rest. For he who on any occasion detracts from the almighty Word, and does not consent to the rules that bind Catholics, is nothing but a fool, for he has spurned the gifts of true wisdom. So in his heart this man denies God, for if he truly believed in Him he would not sin by any wickedness against Him. So that you could observe this foolish man through his manifold errors, the psalmist fittingly referred to him in the plural, saying: *They are corrupted and become abominable in their wishes*. All heretics are marked by this one word; it is corruption not to have truly believed in God, for those enmeshed in death-dealing beliefs abandon life-giving thoughts. A most just punishment attends them, so that they become *abominable in their wishes* when they obey their corrupt emotions. The Church added: *There is none that doth good, there is not a single one*. This figure is called *anaphora*[5] or repetition, when a single expression is often repeated. This is what the Church brought forth when filled with sorrows, so that in the great crowd of wicked men there was none that could do good. This must be interpreted only of those outside the confines of religion who persist in their obnoxious obstinacy. So that you may interpret this as referring to those men, she will later say of them *who eat up my people;* in that passage she points to those who pursue the faithful with gaping maw.

3. *The Lord looked down from heaven on the children of men, to see if there were any that did understand or did seek God*. The Lord did indeed look down from heaven, that is, from each of those who proclaimed Him, in whom He dwells as though in heaven. *On the children of men* describes when He caused himself to be proclaimed by apostles and prophets for men's salvation, so that through them the Gentiles could recognise with clear truth Him whom they did not know as God. He truly looked down on the children of men with great paternal love so that He might not lose those who wandered, but rescue those who repented by holy confession. Next comes: *To see if there were any that did understand or did seek God*. Though God is aware of things hidden, and knows all things before they come to be, we find here the phrase

to see; but it is with the sense of "to cause to see." A similar expression is used of Abraham; *Now I know that thou lovest the Lord thy God.*[6] This figure is called *hypallage*[7] or exchange, whenever we say that He who makes us see or know is himself seeing or coming to know. This statement is made so that unbelievers might be deprived of any excuse once it was known that the Lord Christ was proclaimed to all nations many centuries before.

4. *All have gone aside, they are become unprofitable together: there is none that doth good, there is not a single one.* She speaks of those who with hardened heart have persisted in their wicked manner of life. We can use the word *all* for a part, so that it refers only to those blinded by impious opinions. The words descend in splendid line. First they went aside: next they became unprofitable; then she appended *There is none that doth good, not a single one.* The grief of her meditations burst forth like a child at birth. She repeats the words because she could not devise a fruitful remedy for their hardened intentions. So the Church rightly issued her grief for those who afforded the faithful people no spiritual development. *Not a single one* means that all are excluded, for if she had wished us to understand that one was good, she would not have said: *Not a single one,* but "except for one." Note that she has deleted the following five verses of Psalm 13, which are fittingly applied to the Jews, so that she could transfer the entire meaning at a general level to all unbelieving people.

5. *Shall not all those who work iniquity know, who eat up my people as they eat bread? They have not called upon God.* He passes to the second section, in which the Church of God rebukes those who attack the Christian people. When she says *Shall they not know?* she maintains that they will know, for they ought not to perform what they embark upon with criminal wickedness. (The word *nonne* clearly has its syllables reversed. We must understand it as *ne non cognoscent,* "they shall not fail to know."[8] This figure is known as *anastrophe,* and in Latin as *perversio,*[9] when the words are adduced in reversed order.) Those who work iniquity are those who strive to rend the Lord's faithful, who contrary to His commands oppress widows and plunder wards, *who eat up,* that is, swallow and devour with the all-embracing impetus of their crimes. The words, *my people,* are not idle, for she wished to show that all she said earlier refers to the most wicked, when she

attests that they eat her people and thus increase their crime. But if you wish to interpret *my people*, as some do, as referring to the human race generally, this distinction will appear to have been made inappropriately.[10] So that she might demonstrate the greed with which they rend her people, she added: *As they eat bread,* a commodity always sought and obtained. Though we are satisfied by a variety of foods at any one time, bread is our regular sustenance. She further added: *They have not called upon God.* She returns here to consoling the faithful, for deeds performed by sinners against the Lord's will are vain and come to a most foul end. What is done apart from Him vanishes like smoke into the upper air.

6. *There they have trembled with fear, where there was no fear.* Sinners concentrate on the blessings of this world, and their fear is centred more on this life, in case they are robbed of the success they have gained, or enjoy less the riches they have acquired, or are deprived of the distinctions they have won. While they live here, they are fearful of losing what they know their human condition causes them to abandon. They do not ponder the things which will cause them to be tortured with a really genuine fear, when they will experience weeping and gnashing of teeth.[11] So we must understand here "where there was no fear so far as the just are concerned."[12]

For God will scatter the bones of those who are self-satisfied: they are confounded, because God has despised them. This verse is not included in Psalm 13, but is introduced here to underline the hour of judgment, whereas it does not seem at all appropriate to Psalm 13, for as has been said the heading there is different. At the future scrutiny God scatters the bones, in other words the most obdurate obstinacy, of those whose wanton behaviour has to His knowledge become harsh and hardened. She added: *Of those who are self-satisfied,* a trait known to be characteristic of wicked people. The just man is always displeased with himself, as with thoughts of heaven he disciplines the vices of his flesh; he knows that he must not nurture that part of himself which he is aware promotes the journey to eternal punishment. In the case of sinners, however, the opposite applies; they love the cause of their destruction, and long for what brings their condemnation. The evil which will cause them to endure undying punishment is pleasing to them. As Psalm 10 has already put it: *He that loveth iniquity hateth his own soul.*[13]

She added: *They are confounded, because God has despised them.* It is inevitable that such self-satisfied men be confounded, for it is certain that they are repelled from the kingdom of Christ almighty.

7. *Who will give out of Sion the salvation of Israel, when the Lord shall amend the captivity of his people?* Mother Church passes to the third section in a happier frame of mind, and returns to the words of Psalm 13, so that just as she uttered a similar exordium, so she may finish with a conclusion which harmonises with the end of that psalm. To *Who will give?* we must append: "Except thee, O Lord"; these are the words of the believer, not the doubter. *Out of Sion* refers to that blessed contemplation[14] in which the Lord is beheld and the Majesty itself is drunk in by the true light of the heart. This is what brings salvation to Israel, in other words this is what brings life to the faithful people who behold God.[15] She added: *When the Lord shall amend the captivity of his people,* that is, when the devoted people are still captive in this world to the worries of their tribulations, since they have not yet been able to attain the remedies of their promised freedom. When He frees the faithful from this world He also gives out of Sion the salvation of Israel, when by His kindnesses He brings consolation to the toils of His saints.

Jacob shall rejoice, and Israel shall be glad. This verse tells of the blessedness to come, when the Lord's faithful will rejoice in the fullest liberty. Observe that the patriarch Jacob is often cited in the context of the general resurrection, because of the words: *I have loved Jacob, but I have hated Esau.*[16] He is fittingly described as "loved" in so important a reference to the time when there is rejoicing without end. The psalmist added: *And Israel shall be glad;* we have said that the meaning of Israel is "Man seeing God."[17] This boon is undoubtedly granted to the Church when, as she has been promised, she will be set blessedly in her eternal fatherland.

Conclusion Drawn From the Psalm

We must ponder most earnestly the variations and parallels between the two psalms, since the harmony between the words and the difference in meanings are demonstrated. For the splendid majesty of divine eloquence is revealed in the most perfect sense, so that we are to grasp with faith unshaken different situations from the same words. If the colours of jewels are permitted to glow with varying light, if certain birds are allowed to gleam with diverse colours, if human eyes observe the chameleon turning now green, now blue, now rosy, now pale in one and the same body, why should not the divine utterances, so often compared to bottomless depths, possess different meanings? The sea in its waving motion gleams with varied light. This, too, explains why orthodox Fathers make differing statements about the same passage, yet all win the hearing which aids salvation. This is why one of the Fathers remarks: "The divine word is a pearl, and it can be pierced on every side."[18] It is appropriate for us to remember also that this is the second psalm[19] which has announced the chastising and conversion of the Jews. Just as they are now continually chided through the Old and New Testaments, so their remaining members will be saved at the end of time.[20]

COMMENTARY ON PSALM 53

1–2. *Unto the end. In verses, the understanding of David. When the men of Ziph came and said to Saul: See, is not David hidden with us?* It is abundantly clear that Christ is denoted by *the end. In verses* refers to the composition of this psalm, a verse being that which observes the feet of some metre, confined by its strict rules. We know that the whole psalter is fashioned in Hebrew in this way. So these verses indicate Christ's praises. *The understanding of David* tells of the Lord Saviour; David was always aware of Him to his own profit, and with boundless longing desired His coming for our salvation. Next comes: *When the men of Ziph came and said to Saul: See, is not David hidden with us?* Here once again the history of the kings is introduced, for the men of Ziph were so called from the village of Syria where Ziph dwelt. They came to Saul and revealed that David was in hiding among them.[1] But though they exercised their ill-will they could not harm the holy man in the slightest. Now let us see what people these names denote, so that the mysteries of this psalm may become more clearly known. *The men of Ziph* means "those who flourish,"[2] a condition granted to sinners in this world. David was the type of the Lord Saviour; through

him is announced the Christian people. So this allegory aptly announces that in this world traitors flourish and are free, while the
faithful are in hiding and surrounded. So now the prophet begs to be
freed from such men, so that he may not be betrayed by them and
delivered into the hands of the enemy.

Division of the Psalm

The prophet has been delivered from hazards from Saul, and
throughout the whole psalm gives thanks because betrayal by the men
of Ziph could not harm him. In the first part he prays that his very
strong enemies may not succeed in oppressing him. In the second part
he entreats that his opponents may be converted by spiritual devotion.
It befits every Christian to pray to be freed from those who flourish in
this world, so that the grace of conversion is not refused them.

Explanation of the Psalm

3. *Save me, O God, by thy name: and free me by thy strength.* This
figure of *hirmos*[3] or consistency, which occurs when the sequence of a
speech preserves its sense to the end, is seen to dominate the whole of
this section of the psalm. The prophet prays that he may be freed from
the malice of persecutors through the name of the Lord Saviour. Many
people in this world seem to obtain temporary safety for themselves
but not through the Lord's name. For example, a person may seem to
be relieved of certain immediate maladies by the use of amulets or by
sacrilegious incantations, or again a person may be freed of a crime
which he has committed by bribing the judge with a great mass of
money. But the psalmist seeks to be granted the safety which comes
from the Lord, so that by no other means than by persevering in his
most pure faith he may be rescued from the contagion of this world
through being accorded integrity of mind. Next comes: *And free me by
thy strength.* Earlier he asked that he should experience healing in this
world by the name of the Lord; now he begs that at the judgment to
come he should be freed by His strength, for just as here the Lord
came in the guise of weakness of body, so there He will appear with
the power of His majesty. So in the one verse these two aims, which

religious persons should seek before all else, are fulfilled. The words
are rightly uttered by each and every believer; they are rightly spoken
by the Christian people.

4. *O God, hear my prayer: take in the words of my mouth.* He repeats
once more the name of the Almighty, so that help may not be delayed
as God is repeatedly implored. But because God could hear even a
silent prayer, he added: *Take in the words of my mouth,* so that He
should hear not merely the impulse of his heart but also the words of
his mouth. The expression, *take in,* is notable, for the correct sense of
take in is that we store things in the hidden depths of the mind.

5. *For strangers have risen up against me, and the mighty have sought
after my soul: they have not set God before their eyes.* The reason for the
prayer earlier uttered is now explained. But since the men of Ziph are
known to have been of the tribe of Judah from which the prophet too
took his origin, why has he said that strangers have risen up against
him? He did not wish *strangers* to be understood here as men of a
foreign race, but those who have become foreign to the Lord through
their works—and rightly, because while he sought help from them to
defend him, he found instead that they were ambushing him to betray
him. By *the mighty* he wishes us to understand Saul and his agents,
inflated by royal power and armed with the malevolence of deranged
minds. Next comes: *They have not set God before their eyes.* The
psalmist sets God before his eyes, for he believes that He is present
everywhere, readily aware of what the human will strives to fulfil. But
wicked men do not set God before their eyes, believing that He is
unaware of the plans they lay with sinful intent. The devoted prayer
which he wished to be heard was that those who clearly did not keep
God before their eyes should not be allowed to gain their wishes.

6. *For behold, God is my helper: and the Lord is the protector of my
soul.* He comes to the second section, in which after the most fervent
holiness of his prayer he promises himself the Lord's help with presumption of spirit. *Is my helper,* that is, when he was in the toils so that
he was enabled to bear what those wicked men strove to heap on him.
There follows also the nature of this help: *And the Lord is the protector
of my soul.* When the Lord supports a person, He does not merely help
him in his toils, but also pities and frees him from all sins. Note that he
says: *Of my soul,* so that even if his body is exposed to hazards, the
safety of his soul is preserved unharmed. He realised that the Lord

protects it in a special way among His saints, for it is through the soul that at the Judgment He is believed to crown a person with abundant love.

7. *Turn away the evils from my enemies: cut them off by thy truth.* Since the prophet knew that he had been freed by the Lord's pity from the persecution of his enemies, he is seen to offer this sacrifice of good-will. He strives on behalf of his enemies by every means to offer the prayer which the divine love is wont gladly to accept. So he prays that ill-will be removed from his enemies, for he knew that they would be weighed down by it. Next comes: *Cut them off by thy truth.* When evil men approach the truth, they abandon their earlier intention; if a man does not forsake his wicked plan, he will not take part in goodly actions. So the psalmist prays that the men of Ziph may fail to betray his hidden person, and that Saul may fail to persecute him in his innocence.

8. *I will freely sacrifice to thee, and will confess, O Lord, to thy name because it is good.* He freely sacrifices to the Lord when he prays with pious zeal for his enemies. The person who seeks vengeance on his enemies, who desires to avenge himself because of calamities imposed by others, or who prays for other worldly needs, does not sacrifice freely to the Lord because he does not pray out of love for Him, but begs for His power because of his need for certain things. Freely sacrificing to the Lord means offering the purity of a good intention, and worshipping, fearing, loving Him only because He is known to be God the Creator, the loving Dispenser of all things. They also freely sacrifice to God who give thanks continually during hardships of sufferings, as the holy man Job is said to have done. Next comes: *And I will confess, O Lord, to thy name because it is good.* This corresponds appropriately to the earlier verses, so that he offered the sacrifice of praise to the name of Him by whose power he had been saved. *Confess* here means praise, for as we have often said the word is a homonym for praise. He added: *Because it is good,* for the desire to praise Him is a good beyond reckoning, the source both of refreshment for the devoted mind and of escape from the enmity of this world.

9. *For thou hast delivered me out of all trouble, and thy eye hath gazed upon my enemies.* Just as at the end of the first section he gave the causes for his prayer, so now he offers the reason for his confession, namely that though he seemed freely to have sacrificed to the Lord,

God had granted what He knew would avail him. For the prophet attests that he has been delivered from all his troubles by the power of the Lord; this can certainly not happen in this world save to those who are constant in the love of the Lord. The eye of the Lord gazed on his enemies, the men of Ziph, when He wholly refused to permit them to achieve their wicked plans. Often the merciful Lord does not allow us to perpetrate evil deeds so that pricked by remorse we should prostrate ourselves for our sins, just as Saul was checked when he was sent by the priests to Damascus to ravage the Church of Christ with the most savage persecution.[4] He was not permitted to attain great success, for that could have been the cause of his receiving eternal punishment.

Conclusion Drawn From the Psalm

The entreaty of the prophet and the devoted simplicity of his holy prayer afford a most useful example for our lives, so that when we are oppressed by the men of Ziph, that is, by those who flourish in this· world, we may not be roused to the most ineffectual disputes but may freely sacrifice to the Lord and by His kindnesses be freed from every hardship. Let us hasten to confess to Him most genuinely, so that even in our ignorance we may deserve to be loosed from our shackles. The form of the request is certainly impressive, so that whatever the dangers overhanging us we may make our entreaty with a trusting heart, for He can deliver us from all hardships if He thinks that it is to our advantage here. *We know not what we should pray for as we ought,*[5] for the shadows of ignorance envelop us, and harmful sins disturb us.

COMMENTARY ON PSALM 54

1. *Unto the end, in verses, David's understanding. Unto the end* has often been explained, but we shall not be ashamed to repeat it if it is capable of explanation in another way. Christ is well called the end, for whatever we perform rightly and faithfully is undoubtedly to be ascribed to Him. Alternatively it is because He comes at the end of

time; as the apostle says: *God has last of all spoken to us by his son.*[1] The
phrase alludes also to the words of Moses: *You shall kill a lamb in the
evening.*[2] *In verses* means "in praises," for he advises us to sound forth
unceasingly the Lord's praises whether in time of sadness or of joy—
this is the starting-point of the words of the psalm—and never at any
time to abandon His praise; for when He rebukes, He corrects with
fatherly affection, and when He consoles He brings refreshment. So
both are profitable to us if thanksgiving does not desert our mouths.
Next comes: *David's understanding.* It is the unshakeable understanding of David that we should speak of him in the flesh as father of the
Lord Christ; as the blind man cries in the gospel: *Son of David, have
pity on me.*[3] But let us confess that he is a servant so far as the Godhead
is concerned. As he says in Psalm 109: *The Lord said to my Lord, Sit
thou at my right hand.*[4]

Division of the Psalm

Throughout the whole psalm the words are spoken by the Lord
Saviour, with two diapsalms which are as it were twin eyes appropriately set there. He speaks in the role of a servant, and by announcing
this role without diminution of His own status He has afforded us an
example of the most salutary humility. In the first part He begs that
the prayer of one sunk in tribulation should not be despised, and asks
for a speedy release which He clearly sought through weakness of the
flesh. In the second part He begs that the iniquities of the Jews be
effaced, since they were a contradiction of the truth in their own city.
In the third section He tells of what He knew was happening to the
obdurate Jews because of their crimes. After that a kindly consolation
is introduced, so that none of the faithful would be frightened on
hearing of the harshness of the Judge.

Explanation of the Psalm

2. *Hear, O God, my prayer, and despise not my supplication.* Christ
the Lord, who has come to save us with devoted pity and grants us a
fashioning of life and salvation according to the dispensation by which
He suffered after willingly being set amidst the world's troubles, asks

in the first phrase that His prayer be heard; then He requests that His supplication be not despised. All this is uttered because, though God, He has deigned to become man. He asks first that his prayer be heard, then that His supplication be not despised, for He could have been first heard and then despised; this happens to those who long for the goods of this world, obtain what they pray for, and yet are subsequently despised because they have wholly failed to seek eternal rewards.

3. *Be attentive to me and hear me. I am grieved in my exercise and am troubled.* Attention comes first, and then hearing the voice of the suppliant. No-one hears if he has turned away, but if a gentle gaze is focussed on a person, benevolent ears are also granted him. As another psalm has it: *Gaze on me and hear me, O Lord my God.*[5] Next the reason why the prayer is uttered is given: *I am grieved in my exercise, and am troubled.* The course of the Lord Saviour's life is most beautifully expounded in the single statement. We use the word *exercise* for when we take no rest in relaxation or leisure, but earnestly persevere with continual toil in the glory of virtue. He was exercised by miracles, exercised by His sacred teaching; but most of all He was grieved because renegades clearly did not present the fruit of justice. As the evangelist says: *He was grieved over Jerusalem, and he wept.*[6] What goodness of the most devoted Creator, to say that He was grieved and troubled because that dour people in its madness did not attend to most healthy teachings!

4. *From the voice of the enemy and the tribulation of the sinner: for they have diverted iniquities on me, and in wrath they were troublesome to me.* We must understand "deliver me" after *from the voice of the enemy and the tribulation of the sinner,* so that we can preserve the verse-division according to the authority of the Hebrew.[7] He sought to be delivered from the voice of the enemy when the Jewish people said of Him: *If he be the king of Israel, let him come down from the cross, and we will believe him.*[8] So He asks that these words from those who have broken faith should be overcome by a visible resurrection. The tribulation of the sinner was when they spat on Him with sacrilegious mouths and beat Him with slaps and whips, and heaped rebukes on him in addition to the scourgings. There follows: *For they have diverted iniquities on me, and in wrath they were troublesome to me.* The onset of the raging people is described as if it were the course of a

river. They did not wish to listen to any explanation, but sought the shedding of innocent blood. Note what important matters are unfolded with each word. He says that the Jews were fired to vehemence, for burning anger swept them on to criminal action. So far as His person was concerned, He said that they were *troublesome to me;* this usually happens when we are disturbed by unnecessarily wanton attack. Let the foolish Jews hear that they have caused so much trouble to the Lord, but to themselves enduring destruction.

5. *My heart is troubled within me: and the fear of death is fallen upon me.* Here again His human humility is emphasised. Though by the law of the flesh His spirit is troubled, He overcame the griefs and tortures of His body by the protection of His divinity. If God's power achieves this in martyrs, the sharp feeling of torture could have prevailed even less in the suffering ordained for His flesh. By suffering He fulfilled the role of a true Man, but in addition by conquering such obstacles of His own accord He also showed that He was God. He added: *And the fear of death is fallen upon me.* Like is appropriately joined to like; it was logical that since His heart was troubled, the fear of death should fall upon Him. Let us examine the meaning of *the fear of death is fallen upon me.* It did indeed fall, since it came over Him, but its power was not to prevail for longer. Since the Lord's death was merely transitory, enduring death which claimed controlling power over the human race was defeated. As Paul says: *Death is swallowed up in thy victory. O death, where is thy victory? O death, where is thy sting?*[9]

6. *Fear and trembling are come upon me, and darkness hath covered me.* He describes with the most authentic significance the manner of our end. First we fear death, then we tremble at it, for this separation between body and soul cannot occur without the greatest anxiety. Next comes: *And darkness hath covered me.* The imminence of death casts its visible shadows before it, because we often discern mentally the things with which imminent fear often disturbs us.

7. *And I said: Who will give me wings like a dove, and I will fly and be at rest?* After these deadly anxieties and the needs appropriate to His most authentic humanity, it was inevitable that He should seek the deliverance which He knew would be bestowed on Him. He said: *Who will give me?* meaning; "Who except You, Father, who by leading My human nature up as far as the kingdom of heaven will set Me at Your right hand?" *Pennae* (wings) get their name from *pendere* (to

suspend), for they suspend the bodies of birds on the airy breezes with lightness on high. But note that He asks to be given wings not of an eagle or hawk or swallow (all these fly more swiftly) but of a dove. *Columba* (dove) gets its name because it is *cellae alumna*,[10] a fosterling of the cell, passing its life without oppressing its neighbour. It is an innocent, tame bird which attacks no creature with baneful intention, and does not settle happily on foul food. So the Lord Christ rightly sought a dove's wings; moreover the holy Spirit appeared over Him in the form of a dove when He was baptised. Next comes: *And I will fly and be at rest. I will fly* means "I will transport myself with the swiftest speed." He means when He escaped the molestation of the Jews to obtain peace from their wickedness, as the next verse also reveals.

8. *Lo, I have gone afar off, flying away, and I abode in the wilderness.* He is relating the incident in the gospel when by frequent miracles He roused against Himself all kinds of opposition from the faithless. Mark says: *And rising very early, going out, he went into a desert place, and there he prayed;* and a little later: *So that he could not openly go into the city, but was without in the desert places.*[11] He went far away from His persecutors so as to remove from their mad minds the opportunity for anger. He abode in the wilderness to enjoy the integrity of untroubled solitude. By this action He advises us that when downcast by the burden of some injustice we must seek tranquillity in the hidden depths of our conscience. An alternative sense is that He retired from the unfaithful Jews, and abode in the wilderness of the Gentiles. The prophet attests that the Gentiles are called wilderness when he says: *Rejoice, parched wilderness; and let the wilderness rejoice and flower like the lily, and let the wilderness of Jordan flourish and rejoice.*[12]

9. *I waited for him to save me from a pusillanimous spirit, and a storm.* He passes to the second section. After the break of a diapsalm, He has changed the form of the plea. He had stated that He had taken rest in the wilderness, but now He announces that He awaits the protection of the Father, who could save Him from the weakness of the flesh. The reason was that He did not think that He had attained safety in the wilderness; He still needed His Father's protection. He thus offers us a model of most salutary instruction, that we must presume on the help of no other, but only on deliverance by the Father. Because He had said earlier that He was troubled, He now attests that His spirit is not strong. These and similar remarks are to

be ascribed to His human nature. *Pusillum* (pusillanimous) derives from *pugillus* (a handful),[13] something very slight and small, such as the confined grasp of one hand can enclose. By *storm* He means the tempestuous disorders which the turbulent Jews stirred up like waves of the sea.

10. *Cast down, O Lord, and divide their tongues, for I have seen iniquity and contradiction in the city.* Here His prayer is usefully directed against the Jewish people, that they may not achieve the outcome of their malice by reason of the division of their tongues. This happened in the case of the tower[14] which men tried to build up high because of their fear of the recent flood; then there was first division and confusion of tongues. For in our view, earlier the world employed only Hebrew words. But we must in particular take to heart the fact that He divided tongues in anger but mercifully united them in the persons of His apostles, in the first case so that the Jews would not fulfil unnecessary vows, in the second that all nations might acknowledge the proclamation of the truth in their separate languages. He said: *Cast down,* so that they would not fortify their intentions by perverted guile, and *divide,* so that they would not merge into a unity of wickedness. Next comes: *For I have seen iniquity and contradiction in the city.* He properly demanded that they be divided, for He foresaw that they would be wicked in their sacrilegious gatherings. He rightly sought the wilderness because He recognised wickedness in their city.

11. *Day and night shall iniquity surround it above its walls: and in the midst thereof are labour and injustice.* 12. *And usury and deceit have not departed from its streets.* In these two verses the wicked morals of old Jerusalem are reasonably indicted in three ways. He says: *Day and night* (that is, at all times) *shall iniquity surround it above its walls.* The fabric of the walls could rise to a considerable height, but their wanton malice extended much further. There follows: *And in the midst thereof are labour and injustice.* He mentioned the walls first to include all the dwellers; now He speaks of the middle of the city too, pointing to the highest born and the princes, who always seek to be seen on the throne of honour set in the middle. They were controlled not by law or reason but by *labour and injustice;* labour refers to the exercise of repression, injustice to wicked judicial decisions. He appends the third way: *And usury and deceit have not departed from its streets.* Let us observe that He has not said that such things were practised in secret

but in the streets, an activity condemned by divine law. Scripture says of usury: *He that hath not put out his money to usury,*[15] and of deceit: *Keep thy limbs from speaking guile.*[16] The city practised these deceits not in secret but with intemperate wickedness; every evil becomes more abhorrent when practised with public assurance. But bear in mind the figure of speech which depicts the part as the whole,[17] for there were many known there who accepted the holy preaching with devoted hearts.

13. *For if my enemy had reviled me, I would indeed have supported it: and if he that hated me had spoken great things against me, I would undoubtedly have hidden myself from him.* In this and the next two verses the unfaithful Judas is rebuked, for if he had been a public enemy precautions could have been taken against him. How could Christ have suspected one who seemed to be a disciple? He says: *For if my enemy had reviled me, I would indeed have supported it.* One who was truly an enemy would have come to hurl rebukes, and we have to endure patiently what we clearly expect to bear. Note what a humble expression He used in saying: *I would have supported it;* usually shoes are said to be man's support, but it is not strange for Him to have used the word, since He compared Himself even with beetles and worms.[18] This figure, as has often been stated, is called *metriasmos* or self-depreciation.[19] Next comes: *And if he that hated me had spoken great things against me, I would undoubtedly have hidden myself from him.* This too affords a wonderful example of patience, for when His enemies uttered *great things,* that is, haughty sentiments, He did not break into argument or oppose them with savage altercation, but gave way to their mad words. To ensure that the views of these malicious men would not pursue His holy Spirit, He said that He was hiding, for their wanton words would inevitably cease once they had lost sight of their opponent.

14. *But thou art a man of one mind, my guide and one known to me.* This and the next verse are to be read as rebuke. But let us contemplate the degree of patience shown here. He is still called *of one mind, guide, one known to me,* though it was known that he would be an enemy and a most cruel betrayer in all that occurred. *Of one mind* refers to his place among the apostles; *guide,* because he was sent forward to hamlets and villages to acquaint ignorant minds with the proclamation of the word—we appropriately use *guide* for one who

precedes us on a journey; *one known to me,* to the fact that the betrayal by Judas is recognised not to have been secret, for the Lord Christ prophesied His betrayal at the feast of the supper, and elsewhere said: *Have I not chosen you twelve? But one of you is a devil.*[20]

15. *Who didst take sweetmeats together with me: in the house of God we walked with consent.* His guilt intensifies, for the kindnesses which he receives are reckoned as outstanding. This figure is called *emphasis.*[21] All malevolence is invariably softened when food is taken, and a man is not usually harsh if appeased by the pleasure of a sweet repast. We realise that the bodily food was fittingly allotted to that foolish man, for only that could he reckon as sweet; if he had wished to retain the food of belief of which he had earlier partaken, he would not have embarked on so great a sacrilege. Of that food the faithful were told: *Taste, and see that the Lord is sweet.*[22] Next comes: *In the house of God we walked with consent,* that is, in the temple at Jerusalem where Judas was seen amongst the Lord's disciples; he both entered when summoned and joined the Lord's circle. The consent mentioned has reference to the gatherings of the processions, not to any most constant piety in his way of life. To ensure that the words can wholly square in our eyes we must append to this and the earlier verse: "Why did you betray Me?"

16. *Let death come upon them, and let them go down alive into hell: for there is wickedness in their lodgings, in the midst of them.* Whereas He earlier spoke about Judas alone, He now turns to the Jews to utter the sentence of their communal punishment. But you may wonder why He said: *Let death come upon them,* and then added: *And let them go down alive into hell,* because it can certainly not happen that a person both dies and goes down alive to the spirits below. But we must interpret this in a more spiritual sense. After His usual fashion He demands that conversion rather than destruction be the lot of His enemies. Death is said to be the end of life, and he who is converted to a better way is rightly judged to have put an end to his earlier mode of living. In my humble opinion those who go down alive to hell are they that tremble at their own most wicked thoughts and by divine grace are converted to the path of better instruction. So we go down alive to hell, so to say, when terrified by the recollection of our wicked deeds. By understanding the passage in this way we escape from the question which we posed. He asks that they too be converted who have nur-

tured wickedness in their hearts as though in some lodging. He did well to speak of a lodging, to show that their wickedness is not innate but incurred by lending hospitality, so to say, to a stranger. As for His phrase, *in the midst,* He is pointing to their inner selves so that He could indicate the deep wickedness of the thoughts occupying man's heart.

17. *But I have cried to God, and the Lord has harkened to me.* Once He had appropriately rebuked the wicked, He returned to His own lodgings and prayers, choosing the words befitting His role as servant. He cried continually to God, who engaged Him in heavenly converse, with the result that He was listened to, for He could not be detached from His own majesty. This figure is called *prosphōnēsis,* or in Latin *exclamatio;*[23] when in the course of other conversation we suddenly direct our words to God.

18. *Evening and morning and at noon I will speak and declare: and he shall hear my voice.* Let us concentrate inwardly, for these words declare great mysteries to us. *Evening* denotes the time of betrayal when Judas is known to have betrayed Him to the cohorts who sought Him; *morning,* when He was taken to Pontius Pilate to be heard; *noon,* because at the sixth hour, as the evangelist says, He was hung on the cross.[24] *Meridies* (noon) is so called because it is *medius dies* (midday).[25] The words which follow fit these three nouns. *I will speak* refers to the evening, for it is clear that He revealed everything which the most wicked Judas planned to do. *I will declare* corresponds to the morning, when at Pilate's words, *Art thou the king of the Jews?,* He declared: *For this was I born,*[26] and the other words spoken then by the Lord. He further added: *And he shall hear my voice;* this refers to noon, when He said on the cross: *It is consummated; and he gave up the ghost.*[27] What marvellous economy! In this one short verse so great a deed is recounted, showing the condensed brevity with which that extended narration was depicted.

19. *He has delivered my soul in peace from them that draw near to me: for among many they were with me.* This is the same as His earlier statement that His voice has been heard, so that by the benefit of His resurrection His soul might be delivered in peace. He follows this by explaining from whom He was being freed, namely, *from them that draw near to me.* He means those who with feigned praises seemed to offer respect but who none the less in their hearts supported His

enemies, from whom He rightly says that His soul has been freed. It was a most oppressive type of enmity that they should oppose Him in their hearts yet with their tongues pretend to be devoted to Him.

20. *God shall hear, and He who is before the ages shall humble them.* *He shall hear* those very words mentioned earlier. *He shall humble them*, that is, make them believe, so that those who through pride had rejected the Christian faith might through humility again acknowledge the light of truth. By the additional phrase, *He who is before the ages*, the Word coeternal with the Father is denoted, so that He who created all ages should not appear to have come into existence at any moment in time. Time began when the world had its beginning. So the lunatic rashness of the Arians[28] must stop preaching that the Creator of all times is subject to time, for the only-begotten Son continues without change in the company of the holy Spirit to be coeternal and consubstantial with the Father.

For there is no change with them, and they have not feared God. After the intervening diapsalm He passes to the third part. Earlier He desired with His customary devotion that those who err be converted. But now recognising the future by the power of His divinity, He says that the thinking of the unfaithful cannot be changed because the hardness of their minds could not entertain the truth. We must interpret *change* in two senses, either that which occurs when men pass from obdurate self-will to devoted confession, or that of which Paul speaks when he says: *We shall all rise again, but we shall not all be changed.*[29] So the one who is not changed in this world cannot experience change in the next. The reason why such men as these will not be changed then follows, because *they have not feared God*. He who fears God is changed from his infidelity when he chooses to obey the Lord's commands out of fear of the Judgment and eager love. Note that in this and the next verses He speaks equally of their sinning and the vengeance which overtakes them.

21. *He hath stretched forth his hand to repay: they have defiled his covenant.* The way in which the unfaithful will be treated at the coming Judgment is now described allegorically. *Hand* here means power and action which come into play when the division between good and evil takes place. He further adds why a most just punishment attends the Jews: it is because they have debased the Lord's commands by evil deeds, and have not allowed themselves to believe what the truth of

Scripture is seen to proclaim to them. It is the person who wholly fails to obey God's commands who defiles His covenant, in so far as he is able to do so.

22. *They are divided by the wrath of his countenance: and his heart hath drawn near.* He speaks of what will happen at the Judgment. The faithless are divided from the faithful people, and the chaff is separated for burning from the wheat. *By the wrath of his countenance* expresses the time of the Judgment; wrath here expresses the vengeance which the wicked will experience for their deeds. God decrees all this without change, and in tranquillity. The psalmist added: *And his heart hath drawn near.* He is still explaining the time when the Lord's heart, that is, His will, becomes known to all. *His heart hath drawn near* states the time when all will witness most clearly what He prophesied here through the prophets and proclaimed through His apostles. He explains in the next section why He does what has been described.

They softened their words more smoothly than oil, and those words are darts. The unfaithful Jews softened their words when they said: *Master, we know that you have come from God, and teach the way of God in truth.*[30] What in the world is smoother than oil? He says in vehement exaggeration that the words of the Jews were softened more than oil. Could anything have been found comparable to such wickedness? These words were darts when they said *he is guilty of death;*[31] they are seen to have had the effect of darts. What abominable two-facedness, that men could speak soft words when they were about to perform such harsh deeds!

23. *Cast thy thoughts upon God, and he shall sustain thee: he shall not suffer the just to waver for ever.* When the heavenly Justice spoke of the Jews, He applied the most healthy regimen to our weaknesses. Worldly thinking always afflicts us, and if we do not cast it off we are ground down. As Solomon says: *As a worm harms wood and a moth a garment, so the sadness of a man harms the heart.*[32] But when thoughts are cast upon God, they not only do not consume us but they even nourish us, so that what often diminishes seems to bring us increase. Next comes: *He shall not suffer the just to waver for ever.* The decree of the Lord is true and unchangeable, but we must visualise it in the unimpaired wholeness with which it is uttered. He does not remove waverings from the just on this earth, because He tests them here for a

time so that He may ascertain whom to crown in heaven. But He does not suffer any very just man to waver for ever, as He says here, for He is known to reign with them for ever in enduring peace. In heaven there will be no sign of lashing billows, for there the harbour is utterly peaceful for ever.

24. *But thou, O God, shall bring them down into the pit of destruction.* Since He has spoken of the just, He now turns to the wicked who will be plunged into the depths of hell. A pit means a gaping hole dug out in the bosom of the earth, and containing water assigned to human uses. But so that you would not regard this as a life-giving pit, He added *of destruction.* Of this we read in another place: *Let not the pit open her mouth over me.*[33] This is a deadly pit, a fearful immersion, in which no space is granted, and wretched people are not allowed even to draw breath. Black darkness engulfs them, removing the view of the pleasant light of day. By this image of the pit He warns us to fear the torments of hell. What unprecedented kindness of the Judge! All is foretold to men so that sinning deserving of punishment is avoided.

Men of blood and deceitful men shall not live out half their days. The Latin tongue does not have a plural for *sanguis* (blood); we say that the plural is peculiar to divine Scripture.[34] Strictly speaking, the term, *men of blood,* is not restricted to those who shed innocent human blood, for sometimes just judges, impelled by the need for that discipline which keeps the population peaceful, punish the guilty. Again, the person who wards off a man of violence sheds the blood of a most savage enemy. Above all, we read that just wars were enjoined on holy men by the Lord.[35] So He added: *And deceitful men,* so that you would interpret the phrase as referring solely to guilty men who by ambush and the most wicked guile seek the destruction of another. He says that such as these do not live out half their days, for when they promise themselves a long life they meet the outcome of the swiftest death. The days of all men are known to be limited in a predestined way, but these men will not live out half their days; for them death is seen to emerge against the years assigned to them. So the word *their* is added so that you may understand that these are not the days laid down by the Lord, but self-appointed.

But I will trust in thee, O Lord. Such men as were overtaken by a most swift end undoubtedly had hope in themselves, but clearly the Lord Saviour, who speaks these words, in His role of servant put hope in the Father. He ends the psalm of suffering in the usual way by saying that He has hoped in the Lord, to show that the hearts of the faithful are always pinned upon hope in the Lord. Often the Head speaks the words which we should allot to the members. So, as we said in discussing Psalm 34,[36] we must investigate the pattern of this psalm as it is ordered beforehand. First, it was uttered by the Lord Christ. Second, it began with a prayer. Third, it recounted the events of the Lord's passion. Fourth, it harmonised with the words of the gospel in echoing truth. Fifth, it concluded with the great hope of the faithful. So there is no doubt that the present psalm accorded with the canons which were earlier laid down.

Conclusion Drawn From the Psalm

We have heard that He who gave life to creatures laid down His own life for the salvation of mortal men. We have heard that God, who is impervious to suffering, undertook suffering in the flesh on behalf of sinners. We have heard that He who is coeternal with the Father endured the punishment of death. What a price beyond measure, redeeming the human race! What a holocaust, allowing us to escape eternal flames! First there was the death which brought ruin, and then the end which brought abiding good without end; for when Satan, the dart of death, emerged against the innocent One, the result was that he rightly lost those whom he held in subjection. Hell swallowed up its own destruction like fish, and when it thought it was obtaining plunder it was deceived and obtained the plunderer instead. This is why Pope Leo, who was equal to his see, said so splendidly: "Though the death of many martyrs was precious in the sight of the Lord, the slaughter of no innocent man brought the redemption of sinners. The just did not bestow but received their crowns. From the courage of the faithful sprang exemplars of patience, not gifts of justice. Each individual experienced an individual death, and none by his own death discharged a neighbour's debt. Among the sons of men Christ alone emerged as the truly immaculate Lamb, in whom all men were crucified, all died, all were buried, and all were raised again."[37] Most devoted God, as You deigned to suffer for us in the flesh which You assumed, bestow on us a share in Your kingdom. We must also remember that this is the third psalm of those which treated the passion and resurrection of the Lord in greater breadth.[38]

COMMENTARY ON PSALM 55

1. *Unto the end, for a people that is removed at a distance from the saints, David, in the inscription of the title, when the Philistines held him in Geth.* This heading contains twin mysteries. One is a part of the gospel, up to the words: *In the inscription of the title.* The other is a part of the Old Testament up to the end of the heading. First comes: *Unto the end;* we have often explained that this points to Christ. Next comes: *For a people that is removed at a distance from the saints, David, in the inscription of the title.* We have said that the inscription of the title was not scored out at the Lord's passion because it had been prophesied long before, *Do not spoil the inscription of the title.*[1] But the Jewish people threatened Pontius Pilate, urging that the inscription of this title be changed, contrary to the inspired utterances of the prophets; Him whom they rejected in madness of mind they did not wish to be called their King. This desire set them at a distance from the saints, since the faithful eagerly seek with the whole thrust of their minds that Christ be called their King. *When the Philistines held him in Geth;* this is recounted in the text of the Book of Kings.[2] David was terrorised by attacks of Saul, and thought that he would be hidden in the city of Geth among the Philistines. But we have said that all this is to be explained as mystical allegory. Geth denotes "winepress,"[3] the squeezing which every Christian endures, but then he makes the harvest most abundant when he has been pressed by the rods of afflictions. So the Church reasonably and appropriately speaks in this heading. Though weighed down by the persecutions of the Philistines, that is, by outsiders, she pours forth the deserving merits of her saints with abundant freedom as though they were liquid nectar.

Division of the Psalm

In the first part of the psalm mother Church prays because she is burdened by various afflictions, but she trusts that she will be freed from raging enemies. In the second section she recounts her own sufferings, giving thanks that she has been rescued from numerous dangers; she says that she does not fear evils, for she knows that they will soon pass. In the third part she says that in the future state of blessedness she will continually sing praises to the Lord, for He has freed her from the enmity of this world.

Explanation of the Psalm

2. *Have mercy on me, O Lord, for man hath trodden me underfoot: all day long he hath afflicted me by warring on me.* Virgin mother Church, who begets the faithful without losing her virginity, begs her heavenly Bridegroom with devoted tears not to allow her to be afflicted by the enemy, for she is known to be still surrounded by the calamity of this world. *Hath trodden* renews the metaphor of the winepress in the heading, for the harder the grapes are trodden the more wine is squeezed out. *Man* here signifies simply the devil; as the Lord says of him in the gospel: *The hostile man who oversowed the cockle is the devil.*[4] Next comes: *All day long he hath afflicted me by warring on me.* Holy Church is describing what she suffers in this world, for we know that she endures struggles with the devil without any relief. As Paul says: *Our wrestling is not against flesh and blood, but against the principalities and powers of this darkness.*[5] This is an oppressive war because it is secret; the fighting is difficult because the struggle is with one stronger. How difficult it is to wrestle with an enemy whose nets we do not see! Moreover, our enemy does not weary of toil, nor does he at any time depart when overcome. He returns all the more oppressively if by divine grace we have been able to conquer him. We speak of war figuratively by *antiphrasis,* just as we speak of the grove without light[6] and of the fishpond without fish. So let none of the faithful complain that he is troubled by the incessant wiles of the devil, for if we wish to belong to Christ we must always endure the enmity of the devil in this life.

3-4. *My enemies have trodden on me all day long from the height of the day: for many who war on me shall fear.* To go as far as insulting people with one's feet is the harshest kind of injury, but the offering on holy altars has its origin in this way. Wine does not flow unless the grape is trodden by feet; and in the same way the enemy treads down the Church in the persons of her members, so that the glorious merits of the saints may originate from such treatment. She repeats: *All day long,* so that you may really understand that in this world no moment is wholly free from such temptations. The phrase, *from the height of the day,* points to this world, where the height of arrogance swells; just as Christ's rule enjoins humility, so the devil's way recommends the peaks of ruinous eminence. To indicate the great weight of the pressure on her, she says that she has been downtrodden from the height of arrogance, so that you may not judge as light the weight which is directed downward by such a mass. Next comes: *For many who war on me shall fear.* It is not accidental that she says that many rather than all shall fear, for of those who war on the truth very many are converted to the Lord and begin to lose their fear of eternal destruction once they join the ranks of the blessed. But those who cleave to their obduracy will all fear the penal judgment against them when the Lord's coming is announced. What a happy exchange, that here the faithful experience chaste fear for a short time, and are freed from care in the eternal joy to come! But the fate of the unhappy is the grimmest possible, for they rejoice momentarily here and are tortured in the eternity to come.

But I will hope in thee, O Lord. She gives the reason why she herself must not have the same fear as the wicked will show, for she hopes in the Lord who never deceives those who trust in Him. As Solomon says: *Who has hoped in the Lord and been confounded? Or who hath continued to fear him, and hath been forsaken?*[7]

5. *In God I will praise my words all day long, in God will I hope: I will not fear what man can do against me.* It is he who is known to attribute all his goodly words not to himself but to God's gifts who praises his words in God. We are to understand the Church's words not as those uttered by her own inclination, since these are always bad, but as those permitted by the Lord's generosity. We rightly label as ours those bestowed on us, as long as we realise that they have been granted to us by the Lord's gift. But it is clear that we must do this *all day long,* that is, during the whole of life, both when afflicted with adversity and when exalted by prosperity. There follows: *In God will I hope: I will not fear what man can do against me.* Unless this statement is carefully examined it seems opposed to what goes before. Whereas she said that

she was downtrodden and warred on by man, and in her fear of looming dangers was begging the Lord's mercy, here on the contrary she
claims that she does not fear man. Both statements are true; earlier she
feared when she looked at her present disasters in this world, but now
she has cast away fear on surveying the future. What could one suffer
at a man's hands if one has set one's hope in the reward of the Judgment? Though executioners' hands ravage her, though furnace-flames
are prepared for her, the Church in the persons of her members despises all tortures, for she awaits the gifts of God the Saviour.

6. *All day long they detested my words: all their plans were against me
unto evil.* She comes to the second section, in which in her grief she
complains that the words of her preaching are continually cursed by
faithless men, for when she spoke the truth she experienced foul
slanders. This has reference to heretics, or to those Christians lurking
with evil intent who hear the words of the Lord but despise the words
of salvation. Next comes: *All their plans were against me unto evil.*
Plans usually anticipate what is to our profit, for *consilia* (plans) comes
from *consulere* (to consult).[8] So that you would realise that their discussions had no good foundation, she added: *Unto evil,* so that you
would not think that in that deliberation they had pondered anything good.

7. *They will dwell and hide: they will watch my heel, as my soul foresaw.* So these scheming Christians are seen to dwell publicly in the
Church, and to attend the assemblies and gatherings of the people; but
they conceal the poison of their perversion, not daring openly to
mouth what they know is not contained in the rules of the apostles.
This is inner wickedness, an incurable wound, and the more it is
covered over, the wider spreads the infection with a festering beyond
healing. Next comes: *They will watch my heel.* This is the way of the
devil or of those known to be his agents, that with artful guile they
observe our heel or final end. As the Lord said to the serpent: *She shall
watch thy head, and thou shalt lie in wait for her heel.*[9] The devil knows
that our final actions are judged, and he wishes to subvert them that we
may undergo the hazards of guilt. She added: *As my soul foresaw,* that
is, "As I saw beforehand, as I was instructed, as I received the canon of
preaching from the Lord."

8. *For nothing shalt thou save them: in thy anger thou shalt break the
people in pieces, O God.* Here she promises that through the grace of the

Lord those whom she earlier labelled deceivers, hiding their attitudes with poisonous hypocrisy, will be readily saved. So she should not despair over any of those who err, even if she knows a person is blameworthy. As for her words, *for nothing shalt thou save them,* they signify that in His love He grants all things without payment; He does not demand deserving merit from any, or the attainment of salvation by our own efforts. What did the thief do to deserve that speedy entry into Paradise? What was the tax-collector's merit when he left the temple suddenly forgiven?[10] He who granted the reward bestowed also that prayer of confession. So clearly sinners are saved *for nothing,* since undoubtedly their conversion is granted by gratuitous generosity. Next comes: *In thy anger thou shalt break the people in pieces, O God.* Earlier she said that the malevolent would be delivered; here she explains how they can be saved. The Lord's justice, which is thought to be anger, breaks arrogant people in pieces. When He has shattered their hearts with afflictions and filled them with numerous diverse hardships, they are recalled from their wickedness and compelled to confess to the Lord. This appears to happen through His anger, though He is known to be equable and unchangeable as He achieves the causes of our salvation.

9. *I have declared to thee my life: I have set my tears in thy sight as in thy promise.* He who confesses his sins announces his life to the Lord, as Paul did with the words: *Who before was a blasphemer and a persecutor, and contumelious.*[11] A public proclamation of the kind of person we are, when the Lord has deigned to sustain and draw us to conversion, and when we have deserved to die through the action of our sins, is a way of giving glory to God. Notice that she says *my life,* which is known to be always blameworthy; for when do we not sin in thought or offend in words or err in wavering deeds? So the faithful declare their lives as the unfaithful conceal theirs; not to make their lives known to God (for He can be unaware of absolutely nothing), but that by condemning themselves they may merit forgiveness the more. In the words of the prophet: *Speak first thy sins, that thou mayst be justified.*[12] Next comes: *I have set my tears in thy sight.* Tears set in the sight of God are joyful, because they do not torture but deliver from tortures. So David shed devoted tears when he made entreaties for his enemies, and so deserved to get what he asked for, since he is seen to have fulfilled the Lord's command. She added: *As in thy promise.* The

Lord's promise is that He does not reject devoted tears, As He says in another psalm: *Call on me in the day of thy trouble: I will deliver thee, and thou shalt glorify me.*[13]

10. *My enemies shall be turned back: in what day soever I shall call upon thee, behold I acknowledge that thou art my God.* She says that her enemies will be turned back, lest by continuing on their journey they may be taught to perpetrate the worst of sins. He who turns back from evil abandons the guilt of his infidelity. It was in this spirit that the Lord spoke mercifully and not angrily to the apostle Peter: *Get thee behind, Satan.*[14] When this happens to persons who stray, their earlier wicked sin vanishes. Next comes: *In what day soever I shall call upon thee.* Here she proclaims the mercy and wondrous devotion of the Lord; on whatever day He is entreated He always pities and indulges her. *In what day soever* indicates satisfaction obtained at different times. One person prays to the Lord almost all his life, another is converted in middle age, another is saved at his life's end. The phrase, *In what day soever,* means that God with merciful patience awaits the hour of our conversion at any time, and so He bears with the guilty and awaits sinners with the words: *It is not my will that a sinner should die, but that he be converted, and live.*[15] The only requirement is that in this life we confess all our sinning, for here we fail through human frailty. She added: *Behold, I acknowledge that thou art my God.* Though He is the Lord common to all of us, we still speak with confidence of *my* God, because we rejoice that we can be observed by Him.

11. *In God will I praise the word, and in the Lord proclaim his speech.* We truly recognise the words of the orthodox Church; she promises that she will praise the Son in the Father, so that what is said of the Father may be felt equally of the Son. When we proclaim the eternal, almighty Father, we undoubtedly confess the eternal, almighty Son. The one praise applies to both, for the single power of both is their undivided glory; their nature is indivisible. In short, as Christ attests in the gospel: *I am in the Father, and the Father is in me.*[16] Since the Father has the nature of the almighty Son, what of the Son can He not possess? There is in truth one substance, for in Their essence nothing is found to be dissimilar or different. In Them you find nothing more and nothing less save what the Arian heresy invents for itself. This canon of unity and equality undoubtedly embraces the holy Spirit as well, for He is consubstantial with Father and Son; for the holy Trin-

ity is one God, and he who fails to understand that he has offered glory to all Three cannot bestow it on One alone. We should know the words of the most learned Augustine in *De Trinitate* 15: "The holy Spirit according to the divine Scriptures is not of the Father alone nor of the Son alone, but of both."[17] So the Spirit is the united love of Father and Son, but is also Himself perfect love. Augustine demonstrates this in many ways in his explanation of St. John's letter in Homily 7 to the Parthians,[18] where he says that he who has no love for his brother certainly does not possess the holy Spirit. Next comes: *And in the Lord I will proclaim his speech.* She turns at this point to the Lord Christ, who alone of the Trinity was *the Word made flesh, and dwelt among us.*[19] The Church rightly promises that she will praise His words or preaching, because He bestowed on the human race the rule of life and salvation. His words indeed must be proclaimed everywhere, for through them the salvation of the world could be restored through divine pity. Holy Mother Church promises that she will proclaim these two things which bestow eternal salvation on our faith, namely the power of the word and the humanity of the same Lord Christ. But so that no wicked individual should decree that these titles of God and Lord be interpreted in some separate sense so as to state that this title of Lord is not wholly appropriate to Father and to Son, the prophet bears witness in Psalm 109 with the words: *The Lord said to my Lord, sit thou at my right hand.*[20]

In God will I hope. I will not fear what man can do to me. The person who is not afraid that he is losing worldly things cannot in truth fear man. What can an enemy take from her save that which our holy mother is known to expel from her thoughts? Here, as was said earlier, we must interpret *man* as the devil, for with wicked intent he ever persecutes holy Church. This verse is the same as the last verse of the first section; it seems to have been repeated here so that a beautiful balance between sections might be made like filaments of glistening pearls.

12. *In me, O God, are vows of praise which I will pay to thee.* The psalmist comes to the third section, in which the Church is now freed from the ills of this world, and proclaims that she will praise the Lord. She says that within her are vows of praise, bestowed as they are by God's gift, which will be proffered in that eternity when the saints will perform with unwearying voices their service of praise. When

we love God we have these vows always within us, and they do not quit us at all; but we discharge them in that eternity when we always pay and owe them. What comes next shows that we must understand this verse as referring to the future, for the following lines cannot in any way accord with this world.

13. *Because thou hast delivered my soul from death, my eyes from tears, and my feet from falling.* She gives the reason why she will offer vows of praise in holy sacrifices, because He has delivered the souls of the faithful people from enduring death. This figure is called *aetiologia*, or explanation of the cause.[21] Holy mother Church well says that her soul has been delivered from death, for she rejoiced in the liberation of her sons. Next comes: *My eyes from tears, and my feet from falling.* She applies her individual members to individual situations. She says that her soul is freed from death, her eyes from tears, her feet from falling; but these three favours will be granted in the age to come when the soul will not die through sinning, the eyes will not lament their ills, and the feet will not slip. From which of the blessed does He remove tears in this world when He himself says: *Blessed are they that mourn for they shall be comforted?*[22] The feet of the just are no strangers to falling in this age, for whilst they walk in the world they are always slipping. But they are checked by divine mercy, as we read in Scripture: *The just man falls seven times, and rises again.*[23]

That I may please in the sight of the Lord, in the light of the living. The Church explains how she can please the Lord in the light of the living, which means in the brightness of the saints, amongst whom she is made beautiful, spotless and without wrinkle. Whatever befalls them shines from her face. Just as a man's healthy constitution makes his face more handsome, just as in Solomon's words: *When the heart rejoices the countenance flourishes,*[24] so the beauty of holy Church's features is diffused abroad when found in the merits of the blessed.

Conclusion Drawn From the Psalm

The words of the holy virgin, mother Church, are at an end. She begets us though remaining inviolate, she brings us forth from her chaste womb into eternal light. O that the end of this life may find us as we are when she begets us in baptism! May we not share the fate of

the most wicked people who, as the heading states, are far separated
from the saints. Rather may the winepress of this world squeeze us to
our joy, so as to produce more abundant wine. So when we are afflicted let us give thanks, when we are saddened let us utterly abandon
despair, for those pains are advantageous, since they lead us to blessed
rewards.

COMMENTARY ON PSALM 56

1. *Unto the end. Do not efface David in the inscription of the title:
when he fled from Saul into the cave.* We have often observed that the
Lord is indicated by *the end,* for it is our perfection to attain Him in
blessedness. Just as when you reach the end of a planned journey you
relax with your toil done in the place you longed for so greatly, so
when you come to the Lord you seek nothing further. *Do not efface
David.* The destruction of David by Saul was prevented, for David had
been schooled for the kingship by the will of the Lord, and clearly he
attained this. Next comes: *In the inscription of the title.* Clearly this
was relevant not to David but to Christ the Lord at the passion; the
title inscribed by Pontius Pilate was not changed.[1] David, as we have
said, took on the character of the Lord Saviour, and so what was to
take place at the Lord's passion is now recounted of him. David was
not to be effaced from the kingdom allotted to him, just as the inscription of the Lord's title could not be changed. The psalmist added:
When he fled from Saul into the cave. This incident seems to be very
similar in the cases of both David and the Lord. Just as David in
fleeing from Saul hid in a cave,[2] so the Lord Saviour's divinity is
known to have been hidden within the temple of His body from the
unfaithful Jews. In this way the individual events concerning David
and Christ are shared by them in this respect. These representations
of events in this heading have this preliminary role because the whole
psalm will speak of the Lord's passion; David endured the savagery of
Saul as the Lord endured the most wicked Jews. So we must remember that this is the fifth of the psalms which briefly recount the
passion and resurrection of the Lord.[3]

Division of the Psalm

In the first section of the psalm the Lord Christ prays in His anxiety about His passion. He prays as the Man which with love beyond reckoning He deigned to become for our sake. God was so to say made human, but even when He took on flesh He did not cease to be God. Though He assumed the form of changeable man, He remained unchangeable; He did not diminish His own nature, but exalted the condition of mortality. He is one and the same Lord Christ who both performed great miracles of power in the form of God and endured the savagery of the passion in the form of a slave. In the second section He describes the glory of His resurrection with astonishing variety. In the third He promises to sing praises to the Lord Father after His most blessed resurrection. These limbs of the psalm are further separated from each other by the insertion of diapsalms.

Explanation of the Psalm

2. *Have mercy on me, O God, have mercy on me: for my soul trusteth in thee.* Christ the Lord in His human role cries to the Father because he fears the passion to come, so that though He undertook voluntary death He announced without reservation the fear of His soul. The Son seeks God's pity; He himself takes pity on all men, for with great humility He came down to deliver us, so that you would think that it was one of the faithful crying out, for the Creator of the world makes His entreaty in the weakness of the flesh which He assumed. When He says: *Have mercy on me, O God, have mercy on me,* the repetition reveals the hazard of the death to come, so that He repeatedly demanded the miracle of the resurrection since He was to undergo the dangers of the passion. Next comes: *For my soul trusteth in thee.* This prayer is appropriate to the faithful. He who endured such treatment for our salvation wished also to instruct us as our holy Teacher by His prayers. He prayed in order to show us the right form of holy prayer; He suffered for us that none might evade a willingness to suffer for Him; He rose again so that the hope of our weak condition might reach for its own resurrection. He was not in need of these things, but He accepted them for the sake of our salvation.

And in the shadow of thy wings will I hope, until iniquity pass away.
Let us grasp the outstandingly pure holiness of this prayer. In the first
verse before all else He begged the Lord to have pity on Him. In the
second He states why He should obtain His request, and in the third
how He can be delivered from the threatening persecution. The
shadow of wings is a mother's protection both nurturing young chicks
with a show of affection and protecting them from the onset of a
storm. Because this defence reveals the great resource of a mother's
devotion, such a comparison is frequently found implanted in the holy
Scriptures. As the Lord says in the gospel: *Jerusalem, Jerusalem, how
often have I sought to gather thy children as the hen doth gather the
chickens beneath her wings, and thou wouldst not!*[4] This figure is called
parabole or comparison, and is used when things dissimilar in kind are
compared.[5] Next comes: *Until iniquity pass away.* He continued with
the comparison, asking that He rest under that same shadow while
fierce iniquity seethed.

3. *I will cry to God the most high, to God who hath done good to me.* A
great sequence of holy teaching is revealed here. He cries to the most
High, whom we reach not by strength of voice but by purity of conscience. He whom the higher creatures unceasingly entreat for aid
was crying out from the depths of the humanity which He had assumed. The words, *God who hath done good to me,* point to the preeminent mystery of the incarnation bestowed by divine grace on the
human race.

4. *He hath sent from heaven and delivered me: he hath made them a
reproach that trod on me.* The human nature united to the Son of God
confesses that He has been freed from human weakness. After the
resurrection that nature deserved to obtain the kingdom of heaven. *He
hath sent* does not indicate an angel or any creature which could of
itself merely serve and not deliver; understand with *sent* "the help of
His heavenly power." The Father delivered His Son; as Paul says: *For
which cause God also hath exalted him, and hath given him a name which
is above all names.*[6] The Son Himself attests that He too can deliver
when He says: *I have power to lay down my life and I have power to take
it up again.*[7] These statements reveal the joint working of the holy
Trinity which seeks one end and always performs the one work. He
added: *He hath made them a reproach that trod on me.* It was a reproach
to the persecutors to see the faithful rejoicing over the resurrection of

Him whom they believed they were snuffing out. An evil conscience counts it a disgrace when it appears that its purposes cannot be fulfilled.

God hath sent his mercy and his truth. He enters the gate of the second section. Though He spoke similar words in the previous verse, from here on He bursts into thanksgiving to lend strength to the hope of believers through His own success. *Sent* means sent from the Father, and this refers to the humanity He assumed. As He says similarly in the gospel: *I was not sent but to the sheep that are lost of the house of Israel.*[8] So He is mercy, because He suffers with humanity in the flesh which He has assumed, as He cries: *Saul, Saul, why persecutest thou me?*[9] and the like. He is truth, since He repays to each and all their own deeds.

5. *He hath delivered my soul from the midst of the young lions: I slept after being troubled.* He says that when His body was crucified, His soul was delivered, and He warns us to be most greatly concerned for the soul, for all is made safe when the soul is saved. The body will rise again to spiritual glory if the soul has not been stricken with the wound of obstinacy. *The young lions* points to the crowd of Jews begotten by princes and priests with their deadly intention; so the lions are those who designed evil plans for the murder of the Lord. The cubs are those who carried out the wrongful designs. He added: *I slept after being troubled.* The death of the Lord is described with remarkable aptness, for He was troubled by the din of the Jews and slept with the deepest of sleep, thus showing that the persecution by the wicked was of such total insignificance that after being slain He was transported to sleep. Sleep does not come to any troubled person, but only to Him who was set on the cross and who gave up His life of his own free will.

The sons of men whose teeth are weapons and arrows, and their tongue a sharp sword. He uses these words of the men who with wicked intent proceeded to the slaughter of the Lord. He explains who these sons of men are, whose teeth were weapons and arrows: these are the men who we read gnashed their teeth over Him. This is the fifth type of definition which in Greek is called *kata tēn lexin,* and in Latin *ad verbum.*[10] The teeth of the raging men are defined by individual words, weapons and arrows; weapons refer to their most wicked designs, and arrows to flying words discharged to effect death. He

added: *And their tongue a sharp sword.* Those words which they uttered: *Crucify, crucify,*[11] are compared to a sharp sword. Just as a sharp
blade brings death more speedily, so these words effected a swift
death-sentence. By a single onset they seemed to have dispatched
Him, just as the sharpest weapons usually cut men down. By this
description he cleverly warned us that a savage tongue too can kill. As
Solomon says: *Death and life are in the power of the tongue.*[12]

6. *Be thou exalted, O God, above the heavens: and thy glory over all the
earth.* When Christ's humanity endured such treatment on the cross,
and the Jews seemed to make a laughing-stock of the Lord of heaven,
He cried out, in the role of slave which He took up for us: *Be thou
exalted, O God, above the heavens.* Thus You who hang on the cross are
known to rule for ever in majesty. God could not be exalted above
Himself, for there is no further point to which He can grow; He was
clearly exalted among men, for the glory of His majesty appeared
before the minds of those who were converted. He spoke of *above the
heavens* because the Lord is known to have the heavenly Virtues also
subject to Him. Next comes: *And thy glory over all the earth.* Both these
statements have been fulfilled. He has been glorified over all the earth
since the Catholic Church fills the whole world. In the Church praises
are sung in harmony continually to God. As the prophet Isaiah says: *I
live, says the Lord, and the whole earth shall be filled with my glory.*[13]

7. *They prepared snares for my feet, and they bowed down my soul.
They dug a pit before my face, and they themselves have fallen into it.* He
points to the Jews as men laying ambushes, for they thought that they
were setting traps for true teachings. The evangelist charges the Pharisees with this when they brought before Christ the woman taken in
adultery, and said: *We have taken this woman in adultery. Now Moses
commanded us to stone such a one. But what sayest thou?,*[14] and further
words of this kind provoked by malicious inquiry. The *feet* of Christ
are rebukes to evil men and promises to the faithful, on which as He
preached the gospel in this world He walked as though on feet. Next
comes: *And they bowed down my soul.* Here the love and holiness of the
Lord are described. They bowed down Christ's soul when the wicked
Jews refused to believe. It was in grieving for them, as He says elsewhere, that He became destitute and barren, for His soul could not
have been bowed down by its deeds since it had no stain of sin. He
added: *They dug a pit before my face. Pit* is well used for the sentence of

death which consigns men to the pit. They said to His face: *He is guilty of death*,[15] and so they were said to dig a pit, because they were seen to consign Him to slaughter. The psalmist appended the general sentence laid on them: *And they themselves have fallen into it*. Every unjust utterance condemns those who speak it, and before it can harm another it first damns itself. Solomon says a similar thing: *He that diggeth a pit shall fall into it*.[16]

8. *My heart is ready, O God, my heart is ready: I will sing and utter a psalm to the Lord*. After mentioning the punishment due to the wicked, He now passes to the third section, in which He promises to give thanks after the resurrection. But He gives thanks in His heart, through which He rose from the dead. But the Godhead of Christ is always preeminent, being coeternal with the Father; He is always mighty, always equal with Him. Though the enemy had prepared snares, though that ungrateful one had opened up a pit, He says that He is ready to give thanks because He knew that the glory of resurrection in its totality would be at hand. The next words declare what He is ready for: *I will sing and utter a psalm to the Lord*. We have said that singing means rendering thanks with voices, and uttering a psalm means praising the Lord with action worthy of praise. These two activities are rightly seen to be joined to the earlier repetition of *ready*, for He proclaims that He is ready for both. But even as He says these things in His own name, He also instructs us how we are to confess to the Lord. The apostle too follows the Master in proclaiming that he is ready with the words: *We glory in tribulations, knowing that tribulation worketh patience, and patience trial*,[17] and what follows.

9. *Arise, O my glory, arise, psaltery and harp: I will arise at dawn*. *Arise* is used metaphorically in the sense "rise to perform a miracle"; as Psalm 11 has it: *Now will I arise, saith the Lord*.[18] These words have been transferred from His human weakness to His divine power to explain the causes of the event. He repeats Himself: *Arise, psaltery and harp*. This figure is called *epembasis* or repetition of a word;[19] He used it in the previous verse also when He said: *My heart is ready, O God, my heart is ready*. Here the nature of the humanity which He took on is being expressed. The psaltery denoted the time when His flesh performed divine commands to mingle in holy association with men; the harp denotes the glorious passion, which made the virtue of patience resound with the song as it were of the understanding, played on

stretched tendons and numbered bones. He added: *I will arise at dawn,* the time between darkness and brightness of day, the time at which a holy reading of the gospel attests that He rose again, for it says: *Very early in the morning Mary came to the sepulchre,*[20] and the rest.

10. *I will give praise to thee, O Lord, among the people: I will sing a psalm to thee among the nations.* This sentiment is expressed on behalf of His members, for it is clear that He praises the Father among the people, since He is known to be acknowledged as Head and Leader of the Church. The words, *I will sing a psalm to thee among the nations,* points to the heavenly activity of the universal Church, which in varied tongues through all the nations sings a psalmody to the Lord with devoted heart.

11. *For thy mercy is magnified even to the heavens, and thy truth unto the clouds.* This is the reason for the confession, this is the promise of the psalmody. The mercy of the Lord is magnified even to the heavens because the Son's humanity has been escorted to the kingdom of heaven. He showed His mercy to endangered man (for he was held in subjection to sins) so that by a marvellous dispensation He made out-standing the One whom wicked people in their judgment accounted despicable. Next comes: *And thy truth unto the clouds. Clouds* denotes the prophets, whom the irrigating truth of the holy Spirit filled like abundant rain. They are rightly called clouds because they are filled from the heavenly spring, and they have poured gifts of spiritual abundance over barren sinners. These two virtues are set in reverse order. Truth comes earlier in time, while mercy is later in its approach. They are reversed here so that a single glory, the single Creator, could be acknowledged without distinction in them.

12. *Be thou exalted, O God, above the heavens, and thy glory above all the earth.* He has already uttered this verse in the second section, strengthening our faith by such a promise that the glory of His name will reign over all creatures.

Conclusion Drawn From the Psalm

Who can worthily describe the power and benevolence of this psalm? Christ prays to teach us, rises again to raise us, praises the Father to instruct us. We rightly read of Him that He is our Way, our Redemption, our Advocate before the Father. So let us love this merciful Defender that we may not experience Him as harsh Judge. Clearly it goes beyond all madness that in our guilt we should not seek with all our heart Him who is known to invite us to eternal joys with such frequent admonitions.

COMMENTARY ON PSALM 57

1. *Unto the end. Destroy not David, on the inscription of the title.* Though these words are often repeated, we shall not be reluctant to make the same points at each place so that the worth of the psalms can be assessed, for we enter confidently the houses whose inner regions we identify by the external appearance. *Unto the end* points to Christ, who will be the spokesman in this psalm. *Destroy not David, on the inscription of the title:* we have often said that David denotes Christ because he was a king and his name is interpreted as "strong in hand" or "longed for,"¹ a meaning appropriately applied to the Lord as well. So Pontius Pilate is being warned not to destroy the inscribed title which declared the Lord as King, for what was known to have been written by divine command could not be rendered vain. Who could destroy the King known to be Creator of heaven and earth? This is repeated so often that those who deny it are afforded no excuse.

Division of the Psalm

The Lord Christ, who is our Saviour because of His powers and warnings, is seen to upbraid the Jews' wickedness in the first part of the psalm; whilst He is charging them with their deeds, we are being warned not to act similarly. In the second section He makes known the retribution they are to suffer, introducing most appropriate comparisons. In the third part is recounted the way in which the just receive correction from the vengeance exacted from sinners.

Explanation of the Psalm

2. *If in very deed you speak justice, make just judgments, ye sons of men.* Christ the Lord rebukes the Jews for what they were to do long

after, for those who will not judge aright interpret falsely the law's justice, whereas those who will act justly express just sentiments, for upright speech should match one's way of life. Here He rebukes those words of the Jews when they said insidiously: *Master, we know that thou art a true speaker, and teachest the way of God in truth.*[2] These words were indeed just, but they did not utter them in any way truthfully, for if they had been spoken with certainty of mind, their judgments could have been blameless, and they would not have said later to Pontius Pilate: *Crucify him, crucify him, because he maintains that he is the son of God.*[3] This[4] was their judgment, so they are proved to have uttered justice, not truly, but falsely. This manner of argument is called in the *Topics* the *ex contrario*,[5] for just speech and wicked action are opposed to each other. Some people raise a question here: they say that in this verse we are commanded to judge justly, whereas in the gospel we read: *Judge not, lest you be judged.*[6] But this statement does not deprive us wholly of our freedom to judge; the phrase, *Judge not,* is to be applied to those issues which our minds cannot fathom. There are certain open actions the motives for which we do not know. They can be done for good or evil, and it is rash for a person to make a judgment about them. Here, however, He is instructing us to judge justly matters which are clear-cut. So these statements when analysed in no sense seem opposed to each other. Father Augustine has discussed this passage with greater breadth and care in Book Two of *De sermone Domini in monte.*[7]

3. *For in your heart you work iniquity on the earth: your hands work in harmony at iniquity.* This is as if He were saying: "How could you who work iniquities in your heart pass judgment on Me? In your hearts a crime is committed before it takes place, and every wicked deed which is subject to indictment through the desire of your depraved will is subject to punishment." *On the earth* means either "In the secret depths of the heart" or "Against the people seen to be ruled by princes and Pharisees." Note that first He wrote of wickedness of heart, but next signifies actual deeds worked by hands, so that we are instructed that the crime was not merely contemplated but also carried out. *Work in harmony* at iniquities is a splendid expression; harmony implies a united wickedness agreed by many parties.

4. *The wicked are alienated from the womb: they have gone astray from the belly: they have spoken false things.* He rightly says that sinners are,

so to say, aborted, outcasts from the Church's womb, for they have not been perfected by any steadfastness of teaching. They are like the clumsy softness of young cattle, and are known to be cast out into the darkness of wickedness rather than into life-giving light. The Church is rightly said to have a womb, for by holy baptism she brings us forth into eternal light. But woe to them that come forth from her womb before their time! Next comes: *They have gone astray from the belly, they have spoken false things.* By those who have gone astray from the belly are meant people who have followed beliefs opposed to the Church, and who do not venerate with loving devotion her sacred womb. They are the ones who have spoken false things, for they have gone astray from her holy traditions.

5. *Their anger is according to the likeness of a serpent, like that of a deaf asp that stoppeth her ears.* The anger of the Jews is described in a most appropriate simile. The anger of obdurate men gets beyond control, for to avoid hearing the preaching of their teachers they make themselves voluntarily deaf. This wickedness is compared to the habit of the asp; to avoid hearing the words of the charmer and to avoid leaving its lair, it is said to block one ear by winding its tail over it, and to press the other ear to the ground.[8] The Jews are rightly compared to it, for they stopped the ears of their hearts, refusing to listen to the most salutary command of holy Scripture. The word *obturare* ('stop up') is adopted from the priests who filled their ears with incense (*tus-turis*)[9] so that their recollection of the hymns should not be disturbed and confused by the interruptions of intrusive words.

6. *Which will not hear the voice of the charmers, and the poisonous charms intoned by the wise man.* He continues to develop the simile. He speaks of the asp which will not hear the voices of charmers, because it blocked its ears and became deaf, not allowing itself to listen to the voice which could have drawn it out to the light. Alas for the human race, which is wholly blind unless enlightened by God's mercy! Though created in God's image, it seeks to be like the serpent. We label as wise this craftsman of worldly skill, who with the help of the Lord achieves the task before him with crafty endeavour. So observe that men are called wise even in the evil sense; of them we read: *Where is the wise, where is the scribe?*,[10] and the like.

7. *God has broken in pieces their teeth: in their mouth the Lord has broken the grinders of lions.* Entry is opened to the second narration. In

it are described the evils those persons will suffer who like asps have spurned salvation offered by divine preaching. First He says that their teeth will be wholly shattered, when their cunning words and crafty questions were reduced to nothing; this happened when they tendentiously asked to whom Caesar's coin was to be paid. But from the Lord they obtained such a reply as made them depart with broken teeth from the place which they had sought to bite. He said: *Render unto Caesar the things that are Caesar's, and to God the things that are God's.*[11] Next comes: *In their mouths the Lord has broken the grinders of lions.* Here He seems to exaggerate somewhat by adducing lions and grinders, doubtless indicating persons who tried with a bound to slaughter the Lord, not with crafty words any longer but with a bestial roar. They were snakes when they cunningly asked Him: *Is it lawful to pay tribute to Caesar?*[12] They were lions when with bloody maws they cried: *Crucify, crucify.*[13] So their madness is described by comparison not only with the snake's poison, but also with monstrous beasts. *In their mouth their grinders were broken* when they could not give answer to His most truthful words.

8. *They shall come to nothing, like water running down: he hath bent his bow till they be weakened.* He has spoken of asps and of lions; he now comes to cascades swollen by winter rains, which in their descent suddenly bring a deluge. They are fearsome because unexpected, dangerous because of their headlong nature. But subsequently when their violence is spent, the torrents swollen from the raining clouds abandon their harsh pride, and subside as the sky clears. This figure is called *synathroismos*[14] or collocation, when we gather together many objects or accusations in some narration. How unprecedented was the Jews' savagery! They are compared with all these great menaces from which we know monstrous dangers arise. He added: *He hath bent his bow till they be weakened.* Here the clemency of the divine power is shown; His bow is bent for men's salvation. God directs the weapons of His strength against the wicked and frightens them till they are weakened; they yield, and with heart transformed turn to salutary confession.

9. *Like melted wax they shall be taken away: fire hath fallen upon them, and they have not seen the sun.* Earlier He spoke of those who He proclaims will be converted through fear of the Lord; now He deals with those who remained pig-headed and obdurate through their infi-

delity. They are accorded the fate they deserve, so that their hardness of heart dissolves like melted wax. They shall be removed, He says, from the Lord's sight when consigned to the torments of hell. Finally comes: *Fire hath fallen on them, and they have not seen the sun.* Fire denotes the heat of an evil mind, which they have imbibed with blinded senses in this world. It darkens rather than enlightens, for it blocks rather than opens up the view. Such a fire befalls the wicked, so that they cannot see the true Sun which is the Lord Saviour. As they themselves will say at the coming Judgment: *The sun hath not risen upon us, and the light of justice hath not shined into us.*[15] Only those who behold that Sun with pure and sound minds can discern it.

10. *Before your thorns can bring forth briers: he swalloweth them up as alive, as in wrath.* A brier is a troublesome type of thorn which first grows into the softest of plants, but when it is full-grown and in its prime it sprouts forth sharp twigs, and subsequently its spikes harden into a tree-like solidity. So this is the threat which this statement makes to the Jews, that they are to be engulfed before their malevolence can wax strong in a long life. As He says of such persons in another place: *Bloody and deceitful men shall not live out half their days.*[16] Next comes the swiftness of their destruction: *He swalloweth them up as alive, as in his wrath.* His phrase, *as alive,* is good, because they seem to be alive but they are dead. Every sinner who lives in wickedness is dead to the truth; as Paul says: *The widow that liveth in pleasures is dead while she is living.*[17] His additional words: *He swalloweth them up as in wrath,* indicates that the Lord seems to afflict sinners as though in anger, but in reality He is not; of Him it was written: *But You, O Lord of powers, judge with tranquillity.*[18] The phrase, *he swalloweth them up,* denotes their sudden death, for they will be smitten at the Judgment, with a speed commensurate to the Lord's patience in enduring them. Note that as earlier He deployed climax[19] in describing their sins in two verses, so here in describing their punishment He rises to a crescendo in four verses.

11. *The just man shall rejoice when he sees revenge overtake the wicked: he shall wash his hands in the blood of sinners.* He enters the third narrative-section, in which He states that the joy of the just and the revenge exacted from the wicked occur even in this world. The just man shall see revenge overtake the wicked when he sees them do such deeds as must cause them perpetual fear. Every wicked deed on being

committed bears its own vengeance, because a man's conscience tortures him and he is seen to bring to fruition vengeance against himself.²⁰ On the other hand, the just man is happy though afflicted by a sea of troubles, for he is free in mind, and it is in the mind that true joy always arises. So both types of men endure within themselves the qualities of their own actions. Next comes: *He shall wash his hands in the blood of sinners.* How can this be, that He who has bidden us pray for our enemies maintains that the hands of the holy will be washed in the blood of sinners? If we look at this more carefully, it will afford an example of correction rather than savagery; for when the blood of a sinner is shed, the hands—in other words, the deeds—of the most just man undergo correction. When the guilty man perishes, the innocent man is warned to behave more carefully and more studiously. So it happens that the blood of the sinner cleanses the just man's hands in a holy rather than a cruel way. As Solomon says: *When the foolish man perishes, the wise man becomes more clever.*²¹

12. *And man shall say: If indeed there be fruit to the just, there is indeed a God that judgeth them on earth.* When the things mentioned earlier occur, the faithful person understands and says: "If just men obtain rewards for their good deeds also in this world, it is clear that the Lord passes judgment on them also on this earth, for He does not allow them to live their days in holiness unrewarded. He wants it to be appreciated that wicked men are not wholly free from punishments in this world, though they seem to flourish; and good men are not deprived of blessings though oppressed by the burdens of the world." This argument is called *a consequentibus,*²² for the Lord is just when rewards are conferred on the just man.

Conclusion Drawn From the Psalm

Look at the true Sun which disperses our darkness and murkiness, and reveals what our thoughts in the truth ought to be. Let none now doubt or express whispered opposition, for we are aware that God secretly judges human affairs in this world, as He is more clearly known to do in the next. So we rightly call this Sun the day most true, for He has poured the light of His truth upon us through the twelve apostles to match the number of hours in the day. As He Himself says:

Abraham desired to see my day: he saw it and was glad.[23] He is the day of sound minds, the day of the just. The darkness of clouds does not pass over Him, and shadowy night never succeeds Him.

COMMENTARY ON PSALM 58

1. *Unto the end. Destroy not David, on the inscription of the title. When Saul sent and watched his house to kill him.*[1] We have explained *unto the end* interminably. *Destroy not David, on the inscription of the title:* this too has often been explained. By this indication the Lord's passion is being announced, for the lunacy of the Jews vainly sought to destroy what divine authority so often forbade them to destroy. Through this indestructible inscription of the title, that authority reveals the unchangeable stability of the Lord's kingdom. Next comes: *When Saul sent and watched his house to kill him.* This too is fittingly associated with the Lord's passion, for *house* indicates the tomb where He rested in a three-day death. The Jews' leaders sent men to guard it, to destroy so to say the fame of His name, so that by some trick it should not be claimed that He rose again, an eventuality which Christ had been heard earlier proclaiming. It was better that His enemies should of their own accord desire to condemn this, for it allowed the whole world to acknowledge the fact more certainly. The evidence which the unwilling witness offers is beyond doubt; it cannot be called partisan when confirmed by the guilty person. So let none doubt that the matters recounted by this psalm refer to the Lord's passion. But we must carefully understand that when the Lord Christ speaks, we must interpret some of His words as emerging from the lowliness of the flesh, and some from the transcendent nature of His divinity. We must not imagine two Sons as dreamed up by the sacrilegious wickedness of Nestorius,[2] but think of the Lord Christ abiding in two united and perfect natures, as the synodal authority of the most learned Fathers of the Council of Chalcedon attests. The statement says: "We are all instructed and taught harmoniously to confess Jesus Christ our Lord in one and the same Son, perfect in His divinity and perfect in the flesh; truly God and truly Man, truly composed of rational soul and body; of one substance with the Father in divinity, and of one

substance with us in humanity, like to us in all things save sin alone. In His divinity He was born of the Father before time began, but in His humanity He was born in most recent days for us and for our salvation as God's Son from the virgin Mary, mother of God. He is to be acknowledged as one and the same Christ, Son of God, the only-begotten Lord, in two natures without confusion or change, division or separation. Nowhere do we proclaim a separation of natures through a unity wholly divided, but rather the character of each of the two natures preserved and harmonised in one Person and one substance. We confess Him not as one divided and separated into two persons, but as one and the same only-begotten Son, God, Word, Jesus Christ the Lord."[3] This is the holy faith, the unviolated truth, the proclamation to be embraced which the Catholic Church rightly proclaims is fittingly spread through the whole world by the holy Spirit.

Division of the Psalm

At the outset of the psalm the Lord Christ prays, not as one born God of the Father, but as One made man from the virgin Mary, that His enemies should not succeed in harming Him. He rises from the depths like a star of the material world, gradually mounting to the transcendent summit of His resurrection. He follows this in the second section by telling how the Jews will be converted at the end of the world, and a prayer is uttered on their behalf with wonderful devotion. In the third section He intimates what they will do after their conversion, and He attests that He rejoices among His saints. These sections are separated by the marking of a diapsalm, showing them to be considered but not precious.

Explanation of the Psalm

2. *Deliver me from my enemies, O my God, and free me from those that rise up against me.* When the humanity of the Lord Saviour demanded that He be delivered from the wiles of spiritual enemies— though He was not held in subjection to them, for as He Himself says: *The prince of this world will come, and in me he will not find anything*—[4] He showed us what we must ask for. He who is without stain of sin

begs with manifest humility that the devil or his agents the Jews be diverted from Him; whereas we ask that being imprisoned and in subjection we may by divine pity be freed from impure spirits. Our Head makes this request without being subject to the law of sin; His members ask similarly, but are subject to evil deeds. He clearly shows by this and the next verse that there are four kinds of enemies. First, He asked to be delivered from enemies merely, who might have a disposition to harm but were not showing any great eagerness to assault Him there and then. Secondly, He added: *And free me from those that rise up against me. Those that rise up* implies that they are already stirred up by the storm of their iniquity, and are prepared in mental anger to inflict future destruction.

3. *Deliver me from them that work iniquity, and free me from bloody men.* He mentions the third type, those who had risen with hardened purpose to fulfil their crime in action, to show their wickedness not only in thoughts but also in the completion of the deed itself. Next follows: *And free me from bloody men.* He comes to the fourth type; these men were seen not merely to inflict insults, but were also hastening to shed blood. Here He points to the Jews, who with their sacrilegious sin condemned the blood of the innocent One when they said: *Crucify, crucify;*[5] and again: *The blood of this man be on us and on our children.*[6] They were rightly called bloody men, for they unjustly placed on themselves the burdens of death. So in His human weakness He asks to be delivered and freed from them, yet He voluntarily endured the totality. Note that by the figure of *epembasis,*[7] the term for repetition, He repeated in these two verses: *Deliver me, free me.*

4. *For behold, they have seized my soul: the mighty have rushed in upon me. Neither is it my iniquity nor my sin, O Lord. Soul* here means physical life; no adversity could seize the soul of the Lord Saviour, which was united to God, and conducted itself with spotless behaviour. But when His soul is said to be seized, the time of the passion is being indicated. Next comes: *The mighty have rushed in upon me. The mighty* denotes the devil and his agents. As Christ Himself says in the gospel: *No man can enter into the house of a mighty one and plunder his goods, unless he first bind the mighty one.*[8] They entered into the heart of Judas so that the Saviour should be betrayed to death. They roused the people with the most wicked incitements to condemn with faithless consent the Liberator of the human race. They are called mighty

because they overcome the frail weaknesses of mortal men. But they could not be mighty so far as Christ's power was concerned; He bound them with divine strength. He added: *Neither is it my iniquity nor my sin, O Lord.* Though the devil's might rose against the Lord Saviour, now setting Him on the pinnacle of the temple and now offering Him wealth,[9] still the devil and his agents did not dare to anticipate using against Him any temptations to sinning such as they are accustomed effectively to deploy against us. *Iniquity* here is to be interpreted as malice; *sin* refers to the performance of wickedness, which we know was wholly foreign to the Lord. It was the nature of humanity, and not sin, which we know was assumed by the Lord, yet He endured the mighty Tempter because He took on the flesh of our frailty; death could justly forfeit its rights only by its attack on the Author of life. In this way grim cold melted at the onset of warmth; dark night departed when the clear, bright light came. Our Head truly says this of Himself, but the claim cannot be appropriate to His subject-members.

5. *Without iniquity have I run and was I directed: rise up thou to meet me, and behold.* A person can run without direction, like those whose lives circle on winding paths. Those guided by no truth do not attain the direct way. Christ hastened over the life of the world by a straight path; the wickedness which always twists human acts could not impede Him. Psalm 18 says of Him: *He hath rejoiced as a giant to run the way. His going out is from the end of heaven, and his circuit even to the end thereof.*[10] This was His direction, to return from where He had come. But He came from the Father without leaving the Father, and He departed from the world without abandoning the faithful. As He Himself says: *I shall not leave you orphans,*[11] and: *Behold, I am with you even to the consummation of the world.*[12] Next comes: *Rise up thou to meet me.* Here the power of the resurrection is being expressed in metaphorical allusions. He asks the Father to meet Him as He goes to Him, though in fact the Father has not at any time left Him, and the Son in his divine nature has not come to the Father in any new guise. As Christ Himself says in the gospel: *I am in the Father, and the Father is in me.*[13] The additional words, *and behold,* mean "Cause us to behold"; just as the statement to Abraham: *Now I know that thou lovest the Lord thy God,*[14] means "I have made it known." This is a metaphorical statement inserted quite regularly in the divine Scriptures.

6. *Even thou, O Lord the God of hosts, the God of Israel: attend to visit all the nations: do not have mercy on all of them that work iniquity.* These two short verses are to be explained together since they are seen to be interdependent. After the wonderful account of the resurrection, the holy Advocate intercedes for us and says to the Father: "*Even thou, O Lord the God of hosts, God of Israel* (for You are considered God of Israel alone, of a single nation) *attend* now *to visit all the nations* so that an abundance of believers may increase for You from the nations, because You have found barrenness of faith in the Jewish people." Note that He says: *All the nations,* since with the Lord's help men were to believe from all nations. As Scripture says: *And I will give thee the Gentiles for thy inheritance, and the utmost parts of the earth for thy possession.*[15] But when He returns to the Jews, He says: *Have no mercy on all of them that work iniquity.* If carefully considered, this prayer is not inconsistent with His precepts in any sense. By saying: *Do not have mercy on all of them,* He shows that those who entreat with unspotted devotion are to be shown mercy. Though all men work iniquity, undoubtedly those who are predestined and who take refuge with Him with devoted hearts will be spared.

7. *They shall be converted at evening, and shall suffer hunger like dogs, and shall go round about the city.* We have reached the second gate of the psalm, in which the future conversion of the Jewish people is announced. He shows that at the end of the world countless Jews will believe in the Lord. Paul too says this: *I would not have you ignorant, brethren, of this mystery, lest you be wise in your own conceits, that blindness in part has happened in Israel until the fullness of the Gentiles should come in, and so all Israel should be saved,*[16] and the rest. There too you see the promise that they are to be saved finally by a salutary conversion, however late, and so the end of the world is fittingly called the evening in contrast to the day. Next comes: *And shall suffer hunger like dogs.* He is indicating the intention of the Jews of that era. Just as now they have become hard in a most cruel obstinacy, so then they will suffer the most eager desires for faith. They are rightly compared to dogs, because when seized with the heat of faith they will attack with religious barking that most monstrous beast the Antichrist. *Canes* (dogs) get their name from *canere* (to sing).[17] They will be better then as dogs than they are now as men; for then they will hasten to defend faithfully that Law by which they are now sinners.

Hunger denotes greed for the heavenly word. As the prophet says: *Behold, I send hunger over the land, not hunger for bread nor thirst for water, but a hunger for hearing the word of the Lord.*[18] He added: *And they shall go round about the city.* He continued with the parallel, for it is the practice of dogs to defend the area in which they know they get nourishment. Likewise the Jews now converted defend the city (that is, holy Church) which they shall circle having corrected their declarations. The gospel-writings attest that dogs are compared to the faithful, for the Canaanite woman says: *Yea, Lord, for the whelps also eat of the crumbs from the table of their lords.*[19] This figure is called *enigma* or obscure saying, and is related to allegory;[20] for it says one thing but means another.

8. *Behold, they themselves shall speak with their mouth, and a sword is in their lips; for who hath heard it?* At that time they will clearly speak with their mouths what they do not deserve to have in their hearts now, and they will guide others to the blessings in which they themselves were earlier unwilling to believe. There will certainly be a heavenly sword in their lips, a sword which we read is two-edged,[21] striking from both Testaments and by its wounding bringing happy souls to sound health. Paul says of this sword: *And the sword of the spirit, which is the word of God.*[22] The psalmist added: *For who hath heard it?* He prefaced this well by saying that a sword was in their lips, that is, incessant preaching from their mouths, for only the occasional Gentile will listen as men stick fast to the wicked religion of Antichrist. *Who* is to be emphasised weightily, implying virtually no-one or only a quite occasional person. This monosyllable often suggests "no-one," as in, *Who is like to thee?*[23] and sometimes some individual, as in, *Who shall give out of Sion the salvation of Israel?*[24]

9. *And thou, O Lord, shalt laugh at them: thou shalt account all the nations as nothing.* He declares that those who are unwilling to listen to right preaching will be derided. As Solomon has it: *You have disregarded my rebukes and made vain my counsels, so I also will laugh in your destruction, and will be glad when death comes over you.*[25] They will be a laughing-stock when empty-handed and foolish they are banished from entry to the eternal kingdom.[26] Next comes: *Thou shalt account all the nations as nothing.* It is well known that *nations* is used in both a good and a bad sense. Here it means those who continue in their wickedness with fierce obstinacy. The Lord accounts as nothing

those who do not revere Him as the Creator of all creatures. If you were to take this statement in its full sense, from where would the Lord's Church be built up? In fact it is customary for divine Scripture to express the part as the whole. Compare that utterance of the Lord: *When the Son of man cometh, shall he find faith on earth?*[27] If you seek to interpret this verse in a general sense, who will be told: *Come, blessed of my Father, possess ye the kingdom prepared for you from the foundation of the world?*[28] So you must here understand by all nations those who will be condemned through the act of their infidelity. Some will perish from all nations, just as the just will be undoubtedly gathered from all nations.

10. *I will keep my strength to thee, for thou, God, art my protector.* We said earlier[29] that the mighty are the devil and his agents, who by ascribing their might to themselves tumbled from their eternal eminence. But the Lord Christ reveals the true shape of human ignorance, and says that the might of His humanity is to be ascribed to the kindness of the Lord. So just as we learned what is harmful to us through the guileful plotter, we know what will profit us through the true Redeemer. As for the phrase, *I will keep my strength to thee,* with the change of a syllable it connotes: "I will keep my strength *through* thee." We quite often find this in the divine Scriptures, a figure of speech called *prothēseōs parallagē,* when one preposition is expressed for another.[30] Next comes: *For thou, God, art my protector.* He rightly declares that His strength is to be ascribed to Him who He knew was His protector.

11. *My God, his mercy shall precede me: my God, reveal it to me amidst my enemies.* He is explaining His earlier words: *I will keep my strength to thee,* for the human condition offered Him nothing of worth to cause Him to rejoice at the generosity of that gift. What astonishing devotion is the Creator's! He tells us with reference to Himself what we ought to grasp and guard in ourselves. But woe to them that turn away from this prescription and think that it lies within the human will to deserve the attainment of some of the Lord's gifts! It is He who gives us our desire for blessings, and it is He who ensures that we can obtain His rewards. Paul announced this in the clearest terms: *What hast thou that thou hast not received? And if thou hast received, why dost thou glory as if thou hadst not received it?*[31] So the Pelagian heresy[32] must cease to raise its revived calumnies. We can possess nothing good of

ourselves unless we have received it from the Lord. Next comes: *My God, reveal it to me amidst my enemies.* He speaks of a second bestowal of kindness; even among His enemies the power of His majesty can be revealed, with the result that blasphemers become religious men, and after their wicked way of life become most just.

12. *Slay them not, lest at any time they forget thy law. Scatter them by thy power, and bring them down, O Lord my protector.* The message is the same as earlier: *Reveal it to me amidst my enemies.* Anger is withheld from these enemies, who by God's generosity will believe, so that they are not seen to be ignorant of the Lord's law until the end of the world, and do not begin to fade away in such a way that no good harvest can sprout from them. It is the person who does not fulfil His commands who is forgetful of the law, even if he seems to keep His words in his mind. So He prays that the race of Jews may not utterly perish, but by making heartfelt satisfaction rather admit that they have sinned. He added: *Scatter them by thy power.* The dispersion of the Jews that has taken place attests that this is said of them; they are said to be divided and scattered through almost the whole world. Though subject to Roman law, they live according to their own custom, being scattered everywhere. This is the point of *slay them not;* if they had been destroyed as they deserved, hope of their conversion would have been utterly quashed. So the Jews were scattered, either to meet the challenge of zeal for conversion, or (as some have it) so that the Church in its struggle with heretics might have testimony of the old Law adduced by enemies, for what is affirmed by an opponent's support is believed unhesitatingly. Next comes: *And bring them down, O Lord my protector.* He still continues with the same entreaties, that the Jews by being brought down may be built up for the better, and after their fall may experience a salutary rising. The apostle Paul would not have risen to salvation, had he not had the merit of falling before the voice of the Lord.[33]

13. *The sins of their mouth, the word of their lips: and let them be taken in their pride, and they shall be snatched from their cursing and lying.* The sins of their mouth, in other words, the madness of their thoughts, took place when they laid plans to betray the Lord Christ to death. *The word of their lips* too was execrable when they said: *He is guilty of death.*[34] They were *taken in their pride* when they also said: *Who hath given thee this authority? And by what power dost thou do these*

things?[35] It is clear that they were taken in their pride when they subsequently saw Him rising again, after they earlier rejected Him when He performed miracles. Next comes: *And they shall be snatched from their cursing and lying,* namely when after their conversion that shame shall be removed from them which they are now known to incur amongst all nations. They shall be snatched from lying when with true enlightenment they acknowledge the divine Scriptures, which at present they falsely interpret.

14. *In the anger of his consummation, and they shall not be: and they shall know that God will rule Jacob and the ends of the earth.* The anger of the Lord is cited in two senses. First, when He punishes to save, as in the passage: *For he scourgeth every son whom he receiveth;*[36] and second, when He consigns to eternal fire, of which another psalm says: *Lord, rebuke me not in thy anger, nor chastise me in thy wrath.*[37] The wrong sense is inferred from human habits, for when we punish some guilt we are angry at wicked deeds; but God judges all things in tranquillity, for He cannot tolerate the confusion of emotion. *Consummation* means the emotion felt by the individual when mindful of his sins, when he torments himself with inward censure.[38] *They shall not be*—supply "arrogant," for clearly they will obtain the repentance of humility. Next comes: *And they shall know that God will rule Jacob and the ends of the earth.* When the Jews have perfected their religion and have been instructed in truth, they will then acknowledge that Christ is the Lord of their patriarch Jacob, a belief which initially they did not have. *The ends of the earth* refers to the Catholic Church, which is spread through the whole world; the Jews in their hardness of heart do not now appreciate this.

15. *They shall return at evening, and shall suffer hunger like dogs: and they shall go round about the city.* After the break of the second diapsalm, He begins the third section, in which again the Jews' conversion and the Lord Saviour's resurrection are revealed. This verse has already appeared verbatim in the second section, but it is not repeated here in the same sense, which we have often observed is a feature of the divine Scriptures. The earlier passage has reference to the end of the world, this one to the Lord's passion. What follows upon each passage makes this clear; so their purpose is to be analysed according to this previously stated intention. In the earlier section we stated that *evening* denotes the end of the world, but here the beginning of the

sixth age[39] is indicated, the evening when the Lord Saviour came to bring salvation to the world. Moses says of Him: *You shall kill a lamb at evening.*[40] It was after the miracle of the resurrection that the crowd of Jews believed. Next comes: *And shall suffer hunger like dogs.* The dog is a most greedy and insistent beast, and usually defends with barking houses where it knows its hunger is satisfied by obtaining bread. The Jews are rightly compared to such animals, for stuffed with the gift of Christian faith they will hasten to defend God's Church with loud preaching, as happened to the apostle Paul. Though he previously persecuted the Christian name, through divine kindness he was subsequently joined to the apostles. He added: *And they shall go round about the city.* The city denotes Jerusalem, which is known to be universally spread throughout the world. That Paul went round this city is attested by his epistles which brought salvation to the human race, and which thundered through all the nations like sacred signals from heaven. What a blessed dog was he! He pursues the unfaithful, drives off thieves, and guards the holy sheepfolds; his barking has thundered through the whole world like a mighty trumpet.

16. *They shall be scattered abroad to eat: and shall murmur if they be not filled.* So those who have deserved to obtain true teaching are scattered abroad to eat spiritual food. Thus the nations are converted and come to the Catholic faith. As the apostle Peter was told in a vision: *Kill, and eat.*[41] Next comes: *And shall murmur if they be not filled.* The teachers are filled when they see the people longingly accept their preaching, but those who fast murmur if they do not see their words bearing fruit in the hearts of the unfaithful. So He says that those who distribute the Lord's word can murmur if they are not filled with the faith of the people. As He Himself says in Psalm 34: *They repaid me evil for good, to the depriving me of my soul.*[42]

17. *But I will sing thy strength, and will extol thy mercy in the morning. For thou art become my support and my refuge in the day of my trouble.* After He has spoken of the Jews' conversion, He suddenly directs His words to the Father. This figure is called *prosphōnēsis*, in Latin *exclamatio.*[43] He himself will sing among His saints while His members rejoice. What joy that is, always basking in the contemplation of the Lord! Just as the divine strength never fails, neither will the joy arising from contemplating it. Next comes: *And will extol thy mercy in the morning.* Morning means when the dark night of this

world passes, when the mercy of the Lord now shines out as He makes recompense to His saints. He will exult as King and Lord in the place where He sees His people rejoice in Him. He added: *For thou art become my support.* He explained why humankind exulted in Christ the Lord, because He became *my support.* He is supported when the whole Church is saved. Such is the meaning of the statement: *As long as a man did it to one of these my least ones, he did it to me.*[44] He added: *And my refuge, in the day of my trouble.* How welcome is that refuge, when afforded in time of tribulation! All flesh is under suspicion until it hears the words: *Come, blessed of my father,*[45] and the rest. But the eternal refuge is reached when these most eagerly desired words are attained. As we said in the case of earlier verses, this is to be understood as affecting His members.

18. *Unto thee, O my helper, will I sing, for thou art God, my defence: my God, my mercy.* We have stated that "psalm" refers to the active power which the Lord Saviour's flesh evinced even in this world, in His holy and revered activity. It also frequently reemphasises His kindnesses, to show us how we are to give thanks. The Helper of our humanity is the Word, who deigned to join and unite that humanity to Himself in the womb of the virgin Mary, not through any mingling or mixing of substances, but through an abiding unity which cannot be expressed or described. He added: *My God, my mercy,* a wonderful statement which we must embrace. After His many words, all had not yet been included, so He finally brought it together in a single expression. *My God* is nothing other than: *My mercy.* All kindnesses, all gifts are denoted by that phrase. What blessing is not experienced when the gift of mercy is obtained?

Conclusion Drawn From the Psalm

Lord Christ, we have understood how numerous were Your sufferings in the flesh, and that You always prayed for Your persecutors. What a truly loving Judge, beneath whose eye none of those who make confession need despair! Your kindness matches Your power. Since You pray for Your enemies, which of Your own can fear that he may perish? Grant us to do what You command, grant us to fulfil what is of benefit, for just as we are nothing save what You are, so with You we can fulfil all the good for which we strive.

COMMENTARY ON PSALM 59

1-2. *Unto the end, for them that shall be changed. On the inscription of the title to David himself, for teaching. When he set fire to Mesopotamia in Syria, and to Syria of Soba; and Joab returned and slew twelve thousand men of Edom, in the vale of the saltpits.* This heading is exceedingly diffuse, unless we attempt a summary, because of both the meaning of the names and the mention of the battles. First comes: *Unto the end, for them that shall be changed.* Those changed unto the end are persons who lay aside the sin of the old man and serve the Lord Saviour with spotless devotion of heart. Of them Scripture says: *For you were at one time darkness, but now light in the Lord.*[1] He next explains how they can be changed: *On the inscription of the title to David himself, for teaching.* The inscription of the title denotes Christ the King; so they must be changed by abandoning the devil and acknowledging Christ as their King. We have often stated that David denotes the Lord. To *teaching* add "Christian," for it is not sufficient for anyone to call Him King without being eager to obey His precepts. Next comes: *When he set fire to Mesopotamia in Syria,* and the rest. The history of the Kings recounts that David won these victories after he succeeded Saul in the kingship,[2] and it seems inappropriate to introduce them into our ordered arrangement here since they are known to be recounted *in extenso* there. But we must realise that these wars are a description in figure of the Lord Saviour's victories which He wins throughout the whole world over pagans and the faithless. It is their words which this psalm will utter, so that when truly dislodged from their old superstition they may deserve to be changed through the grace of the new man.

Division of the Psalm

The people who were in thrall to ancient errors are passing into the new grace of the holy religion. In the first section they entreat that after the affliction which they have suffered in making satisfaction, they may be refreshed by their new blessing. In the second part after the break of a diapsalm they also ask that after the hardships they have endured they may be led by the Lord into the heavily fortified city.

They ask that they may be granted aid from their affliction, the aid which God alone is known to be able to give.

Explanation of the Psalm

3. *O God, thou hast cast us off and hast destroyed us: thou hast been angry, and hast had mercy on us.* The people which had been chained by ancient errors relate that they were cast off and destroyed as graces worked upon them; in this way Christ, who is strong in hand and greatly longed for,[3] can be shown to have performed those deeds of slaughter against conquered nations which the heading proclaimed that King David carried out, as has been stated. But Christ achieved them throughout the whole world, not by the steel but by zeal for conversion, not by visible fire but by the heat of love, for this is the way in which the Godhead is wont to prevail and conquer invisibly. This people begs that being demolished in its ancient superstition, and reformed in its holy way of life, it may obtain the grace of a new rebirth. The fact that the plural is used should not trouble us; when we speak of a people, it can undoubtedly signify a plurality. When they say: *Thou hast cast us off,* they show that they have been called back by divine beneficence from their zeal for sinning, so that their lives should not end in the tenure of debased beliefs. Next comes: *And has destroyed us.* This destruction rightly occurs through the action of grace, which overturns to build up, puts down to raise up, makes lowly to lead us to the kingdom of heaven. You must interpret these words as spoken not by ungrateful persons but rather by those who rejoice. He added: *Thou hast been angry, and hast had mercy on us.* After *angry* we must understand "at those who showed resistance," those whose superstitions and vices He has laid low by the power of His justice. Quite appropriately the people says that the Lord was angry with them when they sinned, and showed mercy when they had recourse to the remedies of conversion. In this way they clarified the two situations with the separate phrases. This figure is called *emphasis*[4] or exaggeration, when it offers a wider meaning than the words themselves portray. The anger is merciful, the indignation salutary, the captivity free, the opposition fruitful. So He was angry when He destroyed their superstitions; He took pity when He led them to cultivate true religion.

4. *Thou hast moved the earth, and hast troubled it: heal thou the breaches thereof, for it has been moved.* By *earth* we must understand the sinner in general, who is moved by the coming of the Lord. As the psalmist is to say in another psalm: *The earth saw, and trembled.*[5] So sinners were moved when they realised that their forms of worship were loathsome to God, when they finally understood that their images were graven. They also became aware that riches and distinctions and the other attributes of the world which they previously thought preeminent come last in God's eyes. They were further troubled when among other teachings they heard this: *Embrace teaching, lest at any time the Lord be angry, and you perish from the just way.*[6] Observe the order of the psalm, which is organized in the most beautiful narration. First they were moved, and then they were troubled. Next comes: *Heal thou the breaches thereof, for it has been moved.* Their wounds are exposed to the heavenly Doctor, so that the appropriate remedy can help the sick in their affliction. But let us realise for how long He calls them afflicted; it is until they seem to have experienced contrition. This is the contrition which makes us stronger, this is the weakening which makes us healthier. We are contrite at heart when we descend to humility with the utmost concentration of our minds; as Psalm 50 has it: *A contrite and humbled heart God does not despise.*[7] To obtain the mercy of the most kindly Judge, the people added: *For it has been moved,* in other words, converted from its early error, so that having previously been enslaved to idols, it obeys You as Lord.

5. *Thou hast shewn thy people hard things: thou hast made us drink the wine of sorrow.* After the saving victories which the Lord had completed by grace for the renewal of the world, the people are termed *Thy people,* that is, "people subject and devoted to Thee." He showed His faithful ones *hard things* when He gained bands of martyrs through savage sufferings. He shows His just ones hard things in this transient world to make those things precious in the eternity to come. He does not bid His servants be idle, or concern themselves with extended leisure, but to be exercised with hard toils and deserve to be conducted to the palm of His mercy. This is how Paul puts it: *No man is crowned except he strive lawfully.*[8] The psalmist added: *Thou hast made us drink the wine of sorrow.* Virtue is here compared with wine; it changes the dynamic of our will towards a good end, and makes us develop a taste for right knowledge, once we have deserved to take

our fill of it through God's kindness. By contrast the cup of human wisdom dislodges sanity of mind and admits words of vanity. But the drink of which the psalmist speaks is in the mind, not on the lips; it is not prepared with human care, but bestowed by divine inspiration. As the earlier phrase has it: *And thy cup which inebriateth me, how goodly it is!*[9] The nature of this cup has been splendidly and briefly defined; it is the wine which contains no abundance of vices, but the fruitfulness of sorrow.

6. *Thou hast given a warning to them that fear thee, that they may flee from the appearance of the bow.* He gave a warning to those that fear Him when through the Scriptures He taught that His most faithful ones endure manifold sufferings. As He says in the gospel: *They will deliver you up before kings and governors, and they will scourge you in their synagogues, and you shall be hated by all nations for my name's sake.*[10] Further, the apostle Peter says: *The time is that judgment should begin from the house of God.*[11] So you see that He gave a warning to them that fear Him; these things happen so that the punishment of the judgment to come may be avoided. The reason in fact comes next: *That they may flee from the appearance of the bow.* The appearance of the bow clearly denotes the day of judgment, at which the whole people is judged beneath the two curved yokes, as it were, but the person who bends low to demonstrate humility with the devoted resolve of confession does not endure the arrow, that is, the sentence, from this bow. So let us thank the Lord, who through the warnings of His preachings has made us fear this bow, by which every uncommitted person is smitten at the Lord's judgment.

7. *That thy beloved may be delivered: save me at thy right hand, and hear me.* The faithful people, now beneath the yoke of the divine virtues, begins the second part of the entreaty, and begs that God's power may turn their afflictions into eager joy. The people do well to pray that they may be saved at His right hand, for those who are to rejoice in enduring blessedness will stand on that side. They could have begged to become safe in this world too, an entreaty sought in weaknesses and demanded in afflictions, but they beg to become safe at the Lord's right hand, where lies eternal salvation and unending joy.

8. *God hath spoken in his holy one: I will rejoice, and I will divide Sichem: and will mete out the vale of tabernacles.* God the Father has spoken in His holy One, that is, Christ, when the Word was made

flesh and the Saviour of the world appeared. *Hath spoken* points to the truth of the gospel, through which the redemption of the faithful and the blessedness of the saints came. He added: *I will rejoice, and I will divide Sichem.* The people rightly rejoiced, for the Lord had spoken profitably to them. These Hebraic names, appearing in this and the following three verses in mingled Greek and Latin forms, embody the figure called *sardismos,*[12] which is achieved by mingling different tongues. Now let us explain the words. Sichem means "shoulders,"[13] and since shoulders are aptly fitted to bear the divine burden, the people said here: *I will divide Sichem,* the burden of heavenly devotion granted to each and all by the divine apportionment. If this burden is lacking, we fall; if we bear it we are raised up. Scripture says of it: *My yoke is sweet, and my burden light.*[14] So the joyful people say that they are dividing the grace of servitude and faith on their shoulders, for they know that they bear the lightest of loads. They added: *And will mete out the vale of tabernacles.* The patriarch Jacob, who was very rich in household goods and in flocks, decided to separate from his father-in-law Laban, and came to the vale of Syria, where it is said he built a lodging and kept his sheep undisturbed, giving the place the name, *Tabernacles,* from his own abode.[15] Because Jacob's sheep are fittingly likened here to the Jewish nation, the people who are a type of holy Church say here: *I will mete out the vale of tabernacles,* that is, "from the gathering of the Jews I shall have a not inconsiderable portion"; for clearly God's Church has been fashioned from different nations like various blossoms in the single appearance of a garland. *Vale (con-vallis)* is derived from *cavata vallis* (hollowed valley).[16]

9. *Galaad is mine, and Manasses is mine, and Ephraim is the strength of my head: Juda is my king.* Let us discuss these names, since as we have already said they clearly contain meanings of events. Galaad means "heap of testimony,"[17] and can undoubtedly be referred to martyrs, which in Greek means "witnesses." So this heap of testimony, garnered from numerous heavenly grains, indicates a great assembly of martyrs. A heap starts at the bottom and rises to the top, an appropriate comparison for martyrs, since they are raised to immortal gifts and gain the summit of heaven. So the faithful people rightly call this heap their own, for it is formed from them. Next comes: *And Manasses is mine.* Manasses means "forgotten."[18] During the persecutions

of the faithful, the Church was seen to bear great reviling when any detected Christian was condemned on a capital charge by order of pagan leaders. This reviling is now seen to be abandoned and consigned to blessed oblivion, for it is now a source of glory to be a Christian in the world of Rome. So the faithful people rightly say that their forgetfulness was that which was to come with the cessation of the crimes against them. As Joseph puts it: *God hath made me to forget my pains and my father's house.*[19] He added: *And Ephraim is the strength of my head.* Ephraim means "fruitfulness,"[20] the nature of which is then explained as *the strength of my head.* What other is this but the Lord Saviour, who by dying in the flesh bestowed through His most glorious resurrection the most abundant fruit on our hope? As the Lord says in the gospel: *Unless the grain of wheat falling on the ground shall die, itself it remaineth alone. But if it die, it bringeth forth much fruit.*[21] He added: *Juda is my king.* Judah stands for Christ, who descended in the flesh from the stock of Judah. So this people do not disagree with the inscription of the title, which attests that Judah is their king, that is, their Saviour. We must say: *Juda is my king,* with exultation, for this is the splendid confession of the faithful.

10. *Moab is the pot of my hope. Into Edom will I stretch out my shoe: to me the foreigners are made subject.* The meaning of Moab is "nations,"[22] from which the psalmist foretold that the Church would gather. *The pot of hope* spells affliction, that which most holy Christians endure in this world, and which is proffered by the Lord's gift to advance hope of eternal life. As Paul has it: *We glory in tribulations, knowing that tribulation worketh patience, and patience trial, and trial hope; and hope confoundeth not,*[23] and the rest. *Pot* is used also in a bad sense, for in its debased meaning it bubbles like water boiling away. Of it Scripture says: *A boiling cauldron in the north,*[24] which has the particular sense of the devil's wiles, for he said: *I shall set my abode at the north.*[25] Next comes: *Into Edom will I stretch out my shoe.* Edom signifies "earthly things,"[26] to which the world is held in subjection. The gospel comes to them when the divine clemency lends succour to sinners. We appropriately regard *shoe* as the gospel-preaching, for just as the shoe's protection wards off troublesome thorns and other injuries from our feet, so the authority of the gospel protects our most glorious way of life, which is often compared to advancing on foot. So

fulfilled by such kind help and with the Lord's protection we can pass through the world without suffering gashes. As Scripture says: *How beautiful are the feet of them that declare peace, that declare good tidings!*[27] *And your feet are shod for the preparation of the gospel.*[28] So this shoe protects us against sinning, this is the protection which walks over the thorns of this world, so that what are known to be armed with sharp-toothed snares cannot harm us. He added: *To me the foreigners are made subject.* It is again the Christian people who speak of foreigners or strangers being subject to them, for clearly they have already made their confession of faith; but they wish these foreigners to be interpreted as false Christians who take pains to gather among the faithful but who will not reign with the Lord because they are perverted in mind.

11. *Who will bring me into the strong city? Or who will lead me into Edom?* In their longing for future blessedness, the faithful people cry out to the Lord: *Who will bring me?* They mean "None except you alone, O God." The strong city of which they speak is the future Jerusalem, which will be so strong and perfect as to be no longer shaken by persecution, or to contain mingled with it the foreigners whom the Church now patiently endures. Next comes: *Or who will lead me into Edom?* Edom, as we said earlier, means "earthly things"; *Who will lead me?* is again to be interpreted as a question implying God, of whom the people speak next. They long to have joined to them the peoples who have not yet deserved to attain perfection, so that once the number of the predestined is complete, they may together attain the joys of eternal blessedness.

12. *Wilt not thou, O God, who has cast us off? And wilt not thou, O God, go out with our armies?* By saying: *Wilt not thou, O God?* the people reveal the identity of *Who?* in the previous verse. You, O Lord, will indeed lead us to Your kingdom, for You have made us condemn images that it may avail us to have followed You, for we clearly acknowledge that You alone must be our Creator, You alone must be kindly to us. The phrase, *Who has cast us off,* means "who has prevented us doing evil," so that we might not linger in error through our own will. The Lord has cast off from the region of wickedness the people whom He deigns to guide to Christian teachings; as was said in

the first verse of the psalm: *O God, thou hast cast us off and hast destroyed us: thou hast been angry, and hast had mercy on us.* Next comes: *And wilt not thou, O God, go out with our armies?* The sense is something like this: though we rejoice because of the hope of Your mercy in the future, we do not see ourselves being helped in the present age to conquer our foes with Your aid. Since this help is not forthcoming, and since we are afflicted even more by hardships, our enemies believe that You are not going out with our armies. But this is a salutary pretence and a glorious trial; as Paul says: *For that which is at present momentary and light of our tribulation, worketh for us above measure exceedingly a weight of eternal glory.*[29]

13. *Give us help from trouble: human salvation is vain.* After the holy gathering of the Church has said that she was far from being rescued from the enemies in this world, she passes to a prayer of consolation, asking that the help of the Lord should emerge after the affliction of this world which she was constantly enduring. She knows that each individual will gain consolation in the next world in proportion to the extreme hardship endured for the Lord's name in this life. As the gospel-words have it: *Blessed are they who suffer persecution for justice's sake, for theirs is the kingdom of heaven.*[30] Next comes: *Human salvation is vain.* The one who needs salvation cannot provide it, and so he who is known to be weak in his own powers should not put hope in man. This is why the prophet Jeremiah says: *Cursed be the man that trusteth in man, and whose heart departeth from the Lord.*[31]

14. *Through God we shall do mightily: and he shall bring to nothing them that afflict us.* The congregation of the blessed, abandoning confidence in men, says that they can *do mightily through God.* They are not to battle with the devil by fire and sword, but with the virtues by which Christ Himself fought; we must conquer pride with humility, and overcome the riches of the world with poverty. Finally the people does mightily *through God,* for they have continually persevered in His commands, and through His pity have ground underfoot the temptations of the devil. Next comes: *And he shall bring to nothing them that afflict us.* What need have you, most faithful people, of arms, when you are known to have such help? He whom no man resists fights on your behalf; He whom none can turn aside presses the attack. He

brings to nothing the enemies of His faithful, for He expunges them from that book of the living in which they proudly considered themselves enrolled.

Conclusion Drawn From the Psalm

Observe the blessed contrition of this world, if only it is borne according to the Lord's command. Observe the humility which rises higher than earthly peaks, since it cannot fail as it gains aid from affliction. It obtains a benefit from that very danger which usually wears us down. Without you, O God, all the leading lights in the world are guilty. Any power whatsoever betrays anxiety in itself, whereas humility rejoices through You. Your treasures, O Lord, are hidden. The external appearance is one thing; the one within You causes to contain the truth. Who could recount Your outstanding deeds, since You can turn transient afflictions into eternal joys? What appears loathsome to wicked men in this world is precious in Your eyes.

COMMENTARY ON PSALM 60

1. *Unto the end, in the hymns of David.* The Latinity and brevity of the title clearly suggest a simple and very brief psalm. Unlike the previous one, it is not filled with obscure names and historical events, so it clearly emerges that the indications afforded by headings are truly conducive to salvation since they herald the psalms themselves. All know that *unto the end* indicates the Lord Saviour, for that has now become sufficiently clear by explanation of it. *In the hymns* is a Greek expression and means "in praises," for the whole psalm will ring forth Christ's praises. *David* denotes the Lord Saviour Himself, whose praise the Christian people, spread through the whole world, sings.

Division of the Psalm

In the first part of the psalm the faithful people from the ends of the earth begs that its prayer be heard, so that in persevering in holy

Church it may be protected by the covering of her wings. In the second part it gives thanks that the loving God of pity has bestowed His inheritance on the just, and has consecrated His name for eternal glory. Hence it promises to render continual praise to the Lord.

Explanation of the Psalm

2. *Hear, O God, my supplication: be attentive to my prayer.* The faithful people, who are members of the Lord, are fired by holy love and ask that their prayer be heard. But let us ponder the meaning of the two requests that their supplication be heard and their prayer attended to, to see if we can distinguish them in any subtle way. Supplication is a diligent and general entreaty which we often make also to men from whom we seek something; the people beg the Lord to *hear* this. But they asked that their prayer should win attention, in other words be surveyed and pitied, for they were offering it in its purest form before God's sight. Such prayer has the power, when made with faith, clearly to win a laudable request.

3. *To thee have I cried from the ends of the earth: when my heart was in anguish, thou hast exalted me on a rock: thou hast conducted me.* The holy assembly of the just which is the Lord's inheritance is depressed by the evil in the world, and groans at being set among all the nations. So they cry to the Lord because they lay subject to the needs of the flesh, and with all the longing of their hearts they hastened to abandon its vices. They cry from the ends of the earth, that is, from the whole world, in which the almighty Lord's Church is established. But the cry is raised not only from the ends but also from the inner parts, from the very navel of the earth; in the words of Psalm 18: *Their sound hath gone forth into all the earth.*[1] So the people earlier mentioned cry out: *Hear, O God, my supplication: be attentive to my prayer.* They further tell when this cry is offered with anxious hearts as a kind of sacrifice to God: it is when a cry is made to the Lord with greater urgency, at a time when necessary remedies are demanded for the soul in danger. There follows the hearing of the prayer and the unique reward of the just; *Thou hast exalted me on a rock.* Rock signifies the Lord Saviour; as Paul says: *The rock was Christ.*[2] The people declare that they were exalted on the rock on which every Christian is founded. It is clear

that they were exalted, for they were known to be established on it. The next words are: *Thou hast conducted me;* that is, to the future rest which the Lord promises to His blessed ones. As for the phrase, *thou hast conducted me,* this is the usage in prophecy by which the future is mentioned as though it were past. Compare the words of Psalm 21: *They have pierced my hands and feet, they have numbered all my bones.*[3] This figure is called *prolēpsis,* or anticipation of the future.[4]

4. *For thou hast been my hope, a tower of strength against the face of the enemy.* The reason is given why the people is guided to its reward; it is because it has made the Lord its hope, for he builds up those who trust in Him, and always exalts those who presume on Him. As Paul has it: *We glory in tribulations, knowing that tribulation worketh patience, and patience trial, and trial hope; and hope confoundeth not,*[5] and the rest. There follows a most magnificent comparison: *A tower of strength against the face of the enemy.* The Lord Saviour Himself is indicated by the simile of the tower. A tower defends the walls of its city, and from its height wounds the attacking enemy; in the same way the power of the Lord defends His people by manifestly laying low her enemy through refutation of his words. But that tower teems with virtues, not swords. It fights with words, not with conflict; it does not grapple, but lays down all its precepts. The battering-ram does not shake it, or any engine weaken it. It does not defend any single region, but protects its servants with invincible defence through the whole world.

5. *In thy tent I shall dwell for ever: I shall be protected under the covert of thy wings.* Here too a categorical syllogism[6] emerges, assembled in the same way as previously. The just man dwells in the tent of the Lord: all who dwell in the tent of the Lord for ever are protected under the covert of His wings: so the just man is protected for ever under the covert of His wings. Now let us resume the explanation of the words. The holy people[7] trusts that the kindnesses of the Lord Christ will be bestowed on her so that she may persevere in utter safety against the dangers of this world in the Lord's tent, not for a short time but until the stages of this life are completed under divine supervision. In this way the faithful people, as they live their lives and succeed each other, are kept throughout the ages in the Lord's tent. But let us study why the Lord's holy protection is often compared to the covering of wings. First, it is because the wings of birds spread out

like palm-trees, as though they were the most handsome ramparts. Second, they protect in such a way as not to be oppressive. Third, they ward off harsh heat and cold from beloved chicks with loving protection. So the Lord's shield, if only we take refuge devotedly in it, isolates us from the powers of the climate, so that its fiery rage does not harm us, and its chilly virus does not strike us down with its venomous effect. So the protection of the Lord is seen rightly to be compared with wings which do not oppress those beneath them, and which absorb the damage inflicted by any opposition.

6. *For thou, O God, hast heard my prayer: thou hast given an inheritance to them that fear thy name.* After the interval of a diapsalm, the faithful people come joyfully and gladly to the second section, boasting that their prayer is heard. By the figure called *aitiologia,*[8] they append the cause of the outcome, the reason why they rejoice in the covering and protection of the Lord's wings; and rightly, for they know that their prayer has been heard. Next comes: *Thou hast given an inheritance to them that fear thy name. Inheritance* denotes the kingdom of the future age promised to blessed servants, an inheritance not abandoned at death but possessed in company with its Donor as an enduring legacy passed to the sons yet not renounced by the Testator. This inheritance has no end; once taken up it never quits us by any change of ownership.

7. *Thou wilt add days to the days of the king: his years even to the day of this generation and to generations.* This denotes the eternity of the Lord Saviour who is truly called our King, for we are ruled by Him and made safe by His power. *Days upon days* is an expression characteristic of men; they are accounted as numerous because nights are known to succeed each of them. But in God's eternity there is but one day bounded by no end. As another psalm has it: *For better is one day in thy courts above thousands.*[9] We must also interpret *years* in the same sense, for such things are said figuratively when referred to the Lord Christ. Lastly the verse continues with: *Even to the day of this generation and to generations,* showing that in the Lord's eyes there is but a single day, for He transcends our generations. Generations *(saecula)* are so called because the seasons repeat themselves *(in se).*[10]

8. *It shall abide for ever in the sight of God: mercy and truth, which of them shall search?* Note that the eternity of the day has been clearly stated, but this is now fittingly interpreted from the standpoint of the

members as clearly expressed in many passages, for what follows cannot be appropriate to the Head. The verse reads, *It shall abide for ever in the sight of God,* and *It* is more appropriately taken as referring to the faithful people, as the following words likewise show. The psalmist added: *Mercy and truth, which of them shall search?* Why should any mercy be sought where no man is wretched? Why should truth be sought where all shall see God? None of them will be without such blessings, since they possess the kingdom of heaven for ever. As the Lord Himself says to the apostles: *Now indeed you have sorrow, but I will see you again and your heart shall rejoice. And your joy no man shall take from you. And on that day you shall not ask me for anything.*[11] So none of the saints will search for mercy and truth, since they will enjoy the priceless gift of contemplating Him.

9. *So will I hymn thy name, O God, for ever and ever: that I may pay my vows from day to day.* So means "in this way," the way which the people will declare in what follows. The blessed people say that they will hymn the everlasting name not briefly but for ever and ever, indicating that their devotion will abide unchangingly and perennially. Next comes: *That I may pay my vows from day to day.* This thought is repeated with beautiful variety. *From day to day* means the same as *for ever and ever,* that is, always. So we both pay our vows in this life and in the next sing the praises of the Lord in unending joy. The people promises to pay its vows to the Lord so that it may sufficiently discharge eternal thanks to Him. As another psalm has it: *I will pay my vows to the Lord in the sight of all his people, in the courts of the house of the Lord, in the midst of thee, O Jerusalem.*[12] So let us pay our vows on this passing day so that in the eternity to come we may deserve to sing the praises of the Lord by His gift.

Conclusion Drawn From the Psalm

Let the Donatists hear that the Church cries from the ends of the earth, and let them at once cease to say that she is bounded by place.[13] How can any of them be listened to against the voice of the world? It is most shameless to speak against the testimony of the world, yet they do not blush to take up the cudgels shamelessly against the general consensus. Why do they weary men's hearts with newly invented stories? They should certainly give ear to what they should believe, not to what they can pervert by their wickedness. The faithful people prays at the ends of the earth because the Lord has become their hope; and subsequently they give thanks with hymns of joy that they have been heard, for they will continue to be present in the sight of the Lord. What can satisfy them, if this does not give them their fill? Every day we see what He promised come to pass; we see the world coming to terms with the rules of the Christian faith. Alas, falsehood strives to hide what truth has decided to reveal. The number of this psalm is not without significance. The number sixty has reference to those who restrain their passions, and to widows; the shared attribution of the numbers indicates this. So this psalm promises sixtyfold to the Lord's faithful ones. Martyrs or virgins are not lacking in the next world who glory in the reward which is a hundredfold;[14] but in the gathering of the many, this psalm can point in a special way to certain celibates of this kind.

COMMENTARY ON PSALM 61

1. *Unto the end, for Idithun, a psalm of David.* One of the best-known titles in psalm-headings is Idithun, which is repeated here; we last spoke of it at Psalm 38. The meaning of this name always suggests something outstanding; its sense is that of "overleaping"[1] those who love this world. The soldier of Christ scorns the pleasure of this world and rises above such men. This act of overleaping seems to us to denote a blessed way of life, so a holy person is introduced here who has both renounced longings for this world and clung to the Lord with the most steadfast hope; for this man sets before us *the end*, which is the Lord Christ. Next comes: *A psalm*, that is, a praiseworthy life following the Lord's injunctions; *of David* is joined to it so that this praiseworthy life may be seen to be directed towards the Lord Christ, in whom is saving and absolute perfection.

Division of the Psalm

This man whom we described as leaping over worldly vices surveys a world full of harsh errors; some men are persecutors, others heretics, others entwined in empty desires. In the psalm's first section he proclaims that his soul is subject to God because he has obtained the gift of salvation through His only-begotten Son, and he rebukes those seeking to be called Christians only in name. In the second part he again says that his soul is subject to the Lord and Father, for through His word he has sought a wholesome patience. He strengthens the common folk with his faithful confession that he must ever hope in the Lord with all his heart's feeling. In the third section he warns the erring people to trust in God rather than in the transient happiness of this world.

Explanation of the Psalm

2. *Surely my soul shall be subject to God? For from him is my salvation.* Throughout the whole psalm one of the faithful is introduced to represent the whole body of holy men. Abandoning the vices of the world, he states that he is subject to God alone; this is what subjection to the Lord means, to empty oneself of worldly vices and to be filled with the sanctity of belief. This is a form of rebuke against those who believe that he is relaxing in considerable prosperity and idly enjoying some leisure. The word *nonne* (surely) has to be turned round to become clearer; let us say: *Ne non* ("shall not") *my soul be subject to God?* This figure is called *anastrophe* or inversion.[2] That person and no other is subject to God who always performs humbly and zealously what he knows is in keeping with His commands. He takes delight in Him, he is renewed in Him, and his blessed mind desires nothing beyond Him. *Shall be* denotes unlimited time, bounded by no end. There follows the most justified of reasons why the soul of the blessed man is subject to God the Father. He says: *For from him is my salvation,* in other words, the only-begotten Son who is salvation for those who rightly believe; the words, *from him,* point to the Son. The one God, the holy Trinity, possesses these features as its mark, that the Father is unbegotten, the Son is begotten, and the holy Spirit proceeds from Father and Son. This is the unadulterated faith, this is what the Catholic Church proclaims. So, Idithun, you do well to proclaim that you are subject to God, from whom you attest that you have gained a benefit beyond reckoning. But observe what follows, so that the holy Word may be worshipped with single and uniform reverence.

3. *For he is my God and my salvation: he is my helper, and I shall be moved no more.* He had said earlier that the Author of salvation was begotten of the Father; now he embraces in threefold confession the identity of this Saviour. First, that you may not believe that He is the lesser, he says: *He is my God,* just as earlier he called the Father God. This equality of the highest name reveals the substance and power of unity. So father Augustine in Book 15 of *On the Trinity* says: "From the reason given to those able to understand, it is clear that not only is the Father not greater than the Son in the substance of truth, but neither are both together at all greater than the holy Spirit alone; nor are any two greater than one in the same Trinity, nor all three together greater than each individually."[3] In these words he showed with marvellous truth the perfect and unique nature of the holy Trinity. He repeats: *My salvation;* for the salvation of the human race, which had perished in Adam, was renewed through the Lord Christ. Next comes: *My helper;* for He alone has afforded him help when enmeshed in the struggles of this world, enabling him to rise above the world's vices. *I shall be moved no more* is no arrogant claim, for he whose God, Saviour and Helper was the Lord Christ could not be moved. In this passage we can perhaps observe the figure called *epidiorthōsis,* or in Latin *superioris rei correctio.*[4] The appended: *No more,* indicates that Idithun had been moved at one time, when weighed down by weakness of the flesh and faltering. But once filled with the light of true teaching he could not be moved because with the Lord's help he stood firm in faith.

4. *How long do you rush in on men, and kill all of them? As though it were a leaning wall and a tottering enclosure.* After publicising his faith with that triple proclamation, he turns his words on the persecutors of Christians. He asks: "For how long will you form a column and rush in on innocent men? Fear of God does not call you back, and you rage all the more because you know that worship of demons is despised." So that you should not think that this persecution takes place without arms, or is carried out with light tortures, he added: *You kill all of them.* They sought to consign to death those who they saw were devoted to God. By *all of them* we must understand "the devoted." Most appropriate comparisons now follow: like a leaning wall which falls even without being pushed, for anything inclining from a solid base tends to fall. He added: *And a tottering enclosure.* An enclosure is a structure

of stones uncemented; they are placed without being joined together, and are built up to a height. To prevent your thinking that it was strong through being newly built, he used the word, *tottering,* so what was shaken by gales or by any other pressure would readily be levelled. These comparisons seem to indicate to us a meaning of this kind: "You sacrilegious persecutors believe that the Christian people does not have the most steadfast Defender, since you slaughter us here and there with wicked intent."

5. *But they have thought to repel my glory: I ran in thirst. They blessed with their mouth but cursed with their heart.* The previous verse refers to pagans, this one to Jews and pseudo-Christians. The Church endures two kinds of toil when attacked by pagans' error and when heretics lacerate her in wicked dispute. The glory of the holy man was the Catholic and faithful Church, Christ Himself who is both Head and Glory of His members. The unfaithful sought to repel Him when they interposed sacrilegious teachings so that He would not be worshipped with pure hearts. Then the holy man spent the course of his life in the barrenness of thirst, for he could not find the spring to drink. Thirst has the effect of a desire to enclose in one's body the liquid which is outside. So the words of the gospel say: *I thirst,*[5] and: *Woman, give me to drink.*[6] He did not ask merely to get water from her, but sought also to bestow on her a draught of faith by which she could be filled. The reason for his thirst follows: *They blessed with their mouth.* This is what people do who treat the Lord's law lightly with self-deceiving thought, and do not reflect in deeds what they declare in words. He added: *But cursed with their heart.* Those men curse with their heart who interpret the holy Scriptures with the vice of debasing novelty.

6. *But my soul will be subject to God, for from him is my patience.* After the break of a diapsalm, Idithun comes to the second section of the psalm, in which he repeats his earlier statement that his soul is subject to God. His plan is that the very repetition may implant strength of belief in our minds. But let us examine more carefully the fact that the reason for his gratitude does not seem to be similarly expressed. Earlier he said: *From him is my salvation,* but here he states: *For from him is my patience.* But though the words are different, on

deeper scrutiny we realise that the message is the same. For the Lord Christ is our patience. For Him we both gladly bear hardships and rejoice to observe the rule we have undertaken. Similarly we sing in Psalm 70: *For thou art my patience, O Lord.*[7] So that you may observe the same sense in the words here, the statement that follows is seen to make the point explicit.

7–8. *For he is my God and my salvation: he is my helper, I shall not be moved. In God my salvation and glory: he is the God of my help, and my hope is in God.* In these two verses Christ the Lord is meant, earlier described as *my patience.* Just as if he were being asked: "Who is this patience of yours?" he replied: *He is my God and my salvation,* for he really knew already that the salvation of his soul was then emerging through the Word to be made flesh. He added: *My helper,* so that he should not ascribe his rescue to his own powers. Next comes: *I shall not be moved,* that is, "from the belief to which I hold fast." As Psalm 10 already put it: *In the Lord I put my trust: how then do you say to my soul, Get thee away from hence to the mountain like a sparrow?*[8] So he says that he will not change his opinion, because he had come to realise that his tenets were beneficial to him. What he iterates is his salvation in God, not the unending death which the gods of the pagans renew. He further added: *And my glory,* so that his belief in God is not only his salvation but also his glory. He speaks also of *the God of my help,* so that human weakness should not ascribe anything to itself. Finally, so that he could round off the whole sequence, he said: *My hope is in God,* so that the holy man could both attribute to the Lord the past blessings which he had obtained, and ascribe to him in every way his future blessedness.

9. *Hope in him, all ye assembly of the people: pour out your hearts before him. God is our helper.* After announcing the sacred words of his faith, he turns to the people who were toiling in diverse empty superstitions, and warns them that they must pin their hope in the power of the Lord. He says: *Hope in him,* that is, in Him whom he has proclaimed as his God and his salvation and the rest of his earlier attributions. *All ye assembly of the people:* in thus addressing the people he does not omit the mighty ones, for it is the habit of divine Scripture to address one section without being seen to ignore the rest. He added:

Pour out your hearts before him; he who confesses his sins with most copious tears pours out his heart to the Lord. It cannot be poured out except by a most abundant shower of tears; in the words of Psalm 41: *These things I remembered, and poured out my soul in me.*[9] We reasonably regard this as one of the phrases peculiar to divine Scripture.

10. *But vain are the sons of men, the sons of men are liars in the balances: that by vanity they may deceive in this very way.* After completing a second diapsalm, he passes to the third section in which he rebukes men for their wickedness. This is the reason for proclaiming the holy content of this saving psalm, that men may change their desires for the better and abandon their debased opinions. He states a judgment which is frequently repeated, *But vain are the sons of men,* so that humanity can recognise its fault and hasten with the swiftest entreaty to the Author of salvation and truth. As Psalm 38 puts it: *And indeed all things are vanity, every man living.*[10] The sage frequently repeats this message with the words: *All is vanity of vanities.*[11] But some often wonder why we read in the psalms: *Vain are the sons of men,* but in Solomon: *All things are vanity.* Surely the things of heaven and earth, which God created and which were all very good, do not all comprise vanity? Of course not, but by comparison with better things they are accounted quite unimportant and empty. As blessed Jerome says: "An oil-lamp compared with a torch is nothing; a torch set by a star does not shine; put a star next to the moon and it is dark; join the moon to the sun and it does not glow; compare the sun to Christ and it is darkness."[12] In the same way everything becomes vain which has its brightness diminished by comparison with what is better. So men when compared with the heavenly truth can reasonably be termed vain. But the psalmist added to this defect the vice under which humanity especially labours. *The sons of men are liars in the balances* points either to those who deceive simple purchasers with fraudulent weights, or to those complacent men who wish to appear just and unflinching, but who trick their fellows by deceitful fickleness. *In the balances* denotes that since they are set over the scales of justice, they are not thought to love deceit. Next comes: *That by vanity they may deceive in this very way.* They could avoid deceiving if their wickedness could be detected, but as they are thought to be just, they deceive

more easily by cloaking their depravity. *In this very way* refers to the equity which those treacherous men are falsely thought to exercise.

11. *Hope not in iniquity and covet not by robberies.* He still advises those who he had shown were befouled by loathsome practices. He teaches them that they should not set their hope where the reward for goodly desires cannot be attained. He who puts hope in wickedness deceives himself, because nothing useful comes out of it; on the contrary, it begets eternal punishment. As has already been said in another psalm: *But he that loveth iniquity hateth his own soul.*[13] He also addresses the impoverished who aspire to theft out of their need for sustenance: he says: *And covet not by robberies.* Need cannot palliate the sin of robbery, nor can a motive of revenge be excused; rather, He who rains on the just and wicked alike, who gives meat to all flesh, restrains us. So it is very foolish to ignore the power of the Creator, and to have recourse to hope in sinning. But so that you would not imagine that only the poor were warned, he passes to the rich in the next verse to ensure that by the introduction of this salutary guidance, the poor may not embark on a round of theft, and the rich may not wax arrogant.

12. *If riches abound, set not your heart upon them.* He does not condemn abundant riches when they are dispensed with moderation. As long as the heart is not set on them and as long as they are not thought to contain a unique blessing, they are certainly necessary. Riches enable the needy to be helped, the sick to be cured, the nakedness of the poor to be covered; through riches many attain the kingdom of heaven. On the other hand, he who puts his heart in riches does not wish to spend his gold but to hide it; he seeks always to increase his inheritance. By placing his entire hope in riches, his hunger for them always increases. So Idithun rightly counsels the rich not to love what they possess. As Paul says: *Charge the rich of this world not to be highminded, not to trust in the uncertainty of riches but in the living God, who giveth abundantly all things to enjoy. Let them be rich in good works, let them give easily,*[14] and the rest.

12–13. *God hath spoken once. These two things have I heard: that the power of God belongeth, and mercy to thee, O Lord: for thou wilt render to every man according to his works.* Just as the psalm began with Father and Son, so its thread continues and ends. He says: *God hath spoken once*. If you concentrate on the literal sense, a considerable problem arises. God spoke often to our fathers Noah, Abraham, Isaac, Jacob, Job, Moses and His other holy ones. But He spoke once and in a special way to His Son, as Psalm 2 states: *The Lord hath said to me, Thou art my Son: this day have I begotten thee*.[15] Clearly the Father said this to no other. As some have sought to understand it, God has spoken once because He begot the one Word before time began as consubstantial with Himself, unmeasured, coeternal, and with equal power. True God was born of true God, Light of Light, One immortal of One immortal, One invisible of One invisible, One almighty of One almighty, and the other attributes which the one incomprehensible Unity is truly believed to possess in common. Let us investigate also what are the two things which Idithun says he has heard. After he had trodden underfoot the vices of men, he advanced to contemplation of God, and by listening with the mind's ear he came to realise that the Son has power within Himself. As the gospel says: *I have power to lay down my life, and I have power to take it up again*.[16] Next comes the second thing: *And mercy*—understand "is pleasing"—*to thee, O Lord*. Both things belong to the Godhead, who exercises power mercifully, and mercy powerfully. So that you could realise more clearly that this was said of the Lord Christ, the time of the Judgment is next mentioned: *For thou wilt render to every man according to his works*. As Scripture has it: *The Father does not judge anyone, but has given all judgment to the Son*.[17]

Conclusion Drawn From the Psalm

Let us look back at the shining statements in this psalm; they gleam as it were like candles. The faith shines out, the truth flashes forth for the Christian people to gaze upon, so that they may not be blinded by the darkness of this world and fail to follow the path of upright faith. Let pagan error depart, and the murmur of heretics be stilled; let the emptiness, the deceit of men be abandoned. We must not presume on our cleverness or on worldly doctrines, but our hope must reside in the true wisdom, which is wont to bestow doctrines such as no man can gainsay. O Lord, grant that we too may surmount vices, so that we can attain You with minds purified.

COMMENTARY ON PSALM 62

1. *A psalm of David, when he was in the desert of Edom. Psalm* and *David* often point to the Lord Christ, and often denote the Church, for Christ is in His members, and the members are contained in their Head. If the Head suffers anything, so do the members; again if the members are disturbed, the Head undoubtedly suffers with them. As Paul has it: *If one member suffer anything, all the members suffer with it; or if one member glory, all the members rejoice with it.*[1] So the words of the Church, who is to be the spokeswoman, are rightly set forth as referring to the Lord Saviour. So she dwells in *The Desert of Edom,* that is, in the aridity of this world, where she thirsts and feels longing, where she seeks the Lord's mercy eagerly until she can deserve to attain that eternal glory. Edom is the place where David in flight is known to have hid from Saul's persecution; the meaning of the name, as we have often stated, is "things earthly."[2] So we may clearly understand that this desert denotes earthly deeds wholly bereft of spiritual goods. This is why the Church at daybreak keeps vigil before the Lord, praying that she may not be enmeshed in the errors of this world.

Division of the Psalm

That spiritual bride, who embodies the limbs of the Lord Saviour, says in the first part that she is taken up with insatiable longing to be able to behold the Lord's power. She prays that her soul may be filled with the richness of all good things, so that she can be found worthy of His praises. In the second part she gives thanks because under the shelter of the Lord's wings she has escaped the storms of this world, and she asserts that her enemies will be condemned to the lower regions of the earth. She proclaims that Christ the King will rejoice with the saints in God the Father.

Explanation of the Psalm

2. *O God, my God, thee do I watch at break of day. For thee my soul hath thirsted.* The initial repetition of that venerable name reveals the

feeling behind the loving prayer. By saying *O God, my God*, she says that in a sense He is hers, so that by such longing she can reveal herself all the more as His. She added: *Thee do I watch at break of day*. For Him she is awake whenever she is asleep to worldly ambition; we obtain the first if we hasten to abandon the second. She did well to add *at break of day*, for this was when the hour of the Lord's resurrection dawned, so that she was singing His praises when He enlivened the human race with the example of His resurrection. Next comes: *For thee my soul hath thirsted*. *Thirsted* is used because of the water of which He speaks in the gospel: *Woman, if thou didst know the gift of God, and who he is that beggeth water of thee, thou wouldst have asked of him and he would have given thee living water.*[3] So the soul of the faithful thirsts for God when it longs for His commands and outstanding virtues, when it desires to see Him from whom all flowing blessings are known to emanate. So this is the soul adorned with heavenly possessions; it counts the world a desert, and it ever seethes and thirsts until it can deserve to attain the fount of divine mercy.

3. *For thee, my flesh, O how many ways! In a desert land, and where there is no way, and no water.* Earlier she said that her soul thirsted for God, and now she attests that her flesh experiences a similar longing in many ways. So just as God is Author of both, so He is sought by both. But let us note that by saying *in many ways* she states that her flesh has thirsted more for God, so that the frailer it is the more fervently it seems to have sought the loving Physician. So the soul of the blessed people thirsts for the virtues which holy Scripture commends, but the things which the flesh is known to request from God are beyond counting. Both need salvation, but the flesh further needs food, drink, clothing, transport, sleep, moderate humours, a healthy climate, expenses, and the other things which the soul does not require; the needs of the body are said to demand these. She further explained where her flesh thirsted in many ways, namely in a desert land as the heading stated, that is, in the need and barren sterility of the world. Next comes: *And where there is no way*, for the world has within it no path except the Lord Saviour, who is the Road for the blind and the direct Way of salvation for those who stray through their own efforts. She added: *And no water*, that is, in a barren and unfruitful area. We call a place watered when it has abundant irrigation; the unwatered is dry and infertile, so that her soul naturally becomes hard

there through being over-dry. So the needs of the world are being indicated by these three expressions.

In the sanctuary have I appeared before thee for this, to see thy power and thy glory. It was by enduring the thirst she mentioned of flesh and soul in a desert land where there was no way and no water, a description as we know referring to the barrenness of this world, that the Church states that she appeared in the sanctuary, that is, in her faithful manner of life when she acknowledged Christ as true God. Let us concentrate on her words. *I appeared before thee to see thy power;* for no man sees the truth unless he can first appear before God. If the sun makes us see when it shines on us with its brilliant light, how much more does the divine power, without which we cannot receive or retain anything good!

4. *For thy mercy is better than life: thee my lips shall praise. Mercy* means the rewards which He promises with generous love to His holy ones, and which are far preferable to our present life. Countless hardships take possession of our life here, whereas eternal calm accompanies that mercy, a calm as far removed from this world's light as tortures can differ from eternal peace. It is because of this that bands of martyrs gladly seek death in this world, because they know that instead of this transient death they will live happily for ever. As Paul says: *The sufferings of this time are not worthy to be compared with the glory to come that shall be revealed in us.*[4] Next comes: *Thee my lips shall praise.* After the benefits which she mentioned first, she promises the obedience of devoted praise which she knew was most welcome to God. As the Lord says in the gospel: *Were not ten made clean, and is there no one found to return and to give praise to God but this Samaritan?*[5] Her holy mind did not wish to conceal what she knew would be an accusation.

5. *Thus will I bless thee my life long: and in thy name I will lift up my hands. Thus* looks back to her earlier statement: *Thy mercy is better than life.* The word is a mere monosyllable, but the promise is mighty in scope. What greater thing can a man give than to be known gladly to offer his life to his Creator? Each individual blesses God perfectly in his life when he performs good works in the light of day. She added: *And in thy name I will lift up my hands.* The person who by concentrating on holy actions prays to the Lord lifts up his hands in the Lord's name; his very prayer fashions the image of the holy cross. We

are often advised to pray in this way. When Moses fought against the Amelekites he prayed with hands extended to heaven.[6] We also read in another psalm: *I stretched forth my hands to thee.*[7] And Paul says: *Lifting up pure hands without anger and contention.*[8] Understand that in thus extending our hands we are being counselled to perform the most holy action which our sacred faith recommends, and no foulness of deeds must disfigure them.

6. *Let my soul be filled with marrow and fatness: and joyful lips will praise thy name.* We know that the divine Scriptures often reveal heavenly mysteries by earthly analogies. Marrows are the thick coating of entrails covering and enclosing the inner parts of the liver. Fatness is the obesity of overfed cattle nurtured by foodstuffs. Such fatness was meet for sacrifices and appropriate for offerings. By citing this parallel, the Church wishes her soul to be stuffed with the fatness of virtues, so that it becomes worthy to be offered to the Lord. A soul cannot be fat unless it becomes sleek through being fed by the Lord. The fatness of the soul is in fact knowledge of things divine, upright faith, unshaken patience, and the other qualities by which the lean emaciation of the world is overcome. Next comes: *And joyful lips will praise thy name.* Lips arid through the dryness of sin could not exercise themselves with praises; as we read in another psalm: *But to the sinner God hath said, Why dost thou declare my justices?,*[9] and the rest. But once the committed mind has experienced the fatness of the Lord's mercy, it will praise His name with worthy joy.

7. *If I have remembered thee upon my bed, I will meditate on thee in the morning.* In this and the next verse a hypothetical syllogism[10] reveals itself to us in this way: "If I have remembered thee upon my bed and I also meditate on thee in the morning, because Thou hast become my Helper I will also rejoice under the covert of thy wings. But I did remember Thee upon my bed and I will meditate on Thee in the morning, because Thou hast become my Helper. Therefore I will rejoice under the covert of Thy wings." So having recounted the difficulties of the world which holy Church endured *in a desert land where there is no way and no water,* she passes to a second mode of speech in which she maintains that her untroubled life is dependent on the Lord, because under the covert of His wings she could avoid the snares of the enemy. She indicates here both that He must be sought

out in troubles and that His name is to be hymned when we are trouble-free. When she says: *If I have remembered,* she shows that she has always been mindful of the Lord, and that she was not forgetful during times of success, when human hearts are wont to forget benefits bestowed on them. By *bed* she means the rest in which we are accustomed to relax our body in sleep and to attain the joys of refreshment; it is to be associated with those situations of untroubled success when we barely keep God in mind. She is returning to the thought which she earlier expressed: *Thee do I watch at break of day.* It is right that she watches faithfully in the morning, since even in her time of success she could not forget the Creator of light. To persons such as this Paul says: *All you are children of light and children of day.*[11]

8. *Because thou hast become my helper, and I will rejoice under the covert of thy wings.* This verse contains the benefits bestowed on her through the generosity of the Lord. He was her Helper in dangers, when she was *in a desert land where there was no way and no water.* The Church rejoices under the covert of His wings when she is on her bed, that is, set in happy circumstances. She thus took in the point of the whole psalm in the brief words of a single verse.

9. *My soul hath stuck close behind thee: thy right hand hath received me.* Let us look at the Church's words in her longing: she says not that she is near to the Lord, but that she has stuck close to Him. This expression is seen to suggest a kind of gluing, so that the person sticking to the Lord never abandons his good purpose. Boundless charity and affection induce such love in us that we can always be the Lord's adherents. As Paul puts it: *He who is joined to the Lord is one spirit.*[12] She added: *Behind thee* because the apostle Peter sinned when he wished to go in front, and he was told by the Lord: *Get thee behind me, Satan.*[13] It is peculiar to divine Scripture that when the Lord wishes to free people He bids them get behind Him, where there is no chance of straying. Next comes: *Thy right hand hath received me.* The right hand of the Father is Christ the Lord, who received the Church to protect her with the covert of His wings.

10. *But they sought my soul in vain: they shall go into the lowest parts of the earth.* When she says *they,* she points to those who tried to snuff out Christ with their evil opposition. In Him, as is shown beyond all doubt, all men are healed and live. They sought her soul in vain when

by false charges they decided to shed His blood, but He was to rise again after three days into eternal glory. Next follows the punishment of sinners; *they shall go into the lower parts of the earth,* for they have not been borne to heaven, but the entrails of the earth below have sucked them in. Evil intentions head for the lowest parts of the earth, for that is their origin, and they roll again in the same foul mud. This clearly happened to the Jews when they involved themselves in blasphemies and in the blood of the innocent One.

11. *They shall be delivered into the hands of the sword: they shall be the portions of foxes.* The Jewish race was delivered into the hands of the sword when the Roman emperors Vespasian and Titus ravaged them with fire and slaughter.[14] The fox is of all beasts a wholly crafty animal, seeking its food by guile and maintaining its safety by clever deceit. Deceitful men are justly compared with such animals when they strive to achieve their wicked deeds by cunning guile. The comparison is well made with Herod, of whom the Lord said: *Go and tell that fox he shall not apprehend a prophet out of Jerusalem.*[15] And in the Song of Songs it says: *Catch us the foxes that destroy the vines.*[16] This species of small animal is often used in a bad sense, because as we have said it is extremely cunning and crafty. The Jews were unwilling to listen to heavenly tidings and became *the portions of foxes,* that is, they turned to the malice of evil deeds. Alternatively, *they shall be the portions of foxes* points to the time when during the devastation of Jerusalem the Jews' corpses were food for foxes and the other beasts. Or as others have interpreted it, the Jews are the foxes' portions when they attach themselves with debased intention to deceivers and cheats.

12. *But the king shall rejoice in the Lord: all shall be praised that swear to him.* The king denotes the Lord Saviour, for He is King for ever. The unchangeable title of His passion showed that the label is especially apt for Him. When Pilate questioned Him, He said of Himself: *For this was I born.*[17] The Church further says: *He shall rejoice in the Lord,* that is, in the Father; as Christ Himself attests: *I am in the Father, and the Father is in me.*[18] She added: *All shall be praised.* When the saints of God praise Christ, they themselves are undoubtedly praiseworthy, for only those deserving to attain the palm of mercy can worthily recount His praises. She added: *That swear to him.* She did

not say: "That swear by Him," to prevent your thinking that an oath had been enjoined, for elsewhere as we know He has forbidden it. As He Himself says: *Do not swear by heaven nor by earth,*[19] and the rest. But those who promise Him mental obedience which cannot be breached swear to Him, for elsewhere this word indicates a faithful promise. As we read in another psalm: *The Lord has sworn truth to David, and he will not make it void.*[20] The Godhead could not swear by another, for He had no peer to swear by.

Because the mouth is stopped of them that speak wicked things. She gives the cause of joy by reason of which the King rejoices in the Lord and all are praised who have faithfully fulfilled the offering of their promise to Him; it is because *the mouth is stopped of them that speak wicked things.* In this world those who evidently relish wicked words are by no means silent; but the better time of the Judgment is being indicated here, when all wickedness will be convicted generally, and will fall silent, and will no longer speak what it knows is of no profit whatever to itself. Observe that in the two previous verses vengeance on sinners and the blessedness of the saints in the Lord's company have both been recounted. This figure is in Greek called *syndyasmos,* in Latin *collatio;*[21] I think that it can be fittingly applied here, because mention is made comparatively of the good and the bad of the separate parties.

Conclusion Drawn From the Psalm

Holy Church, you are truly our mother, for you nurture those faithful to God at your sacred breasts, and you enable them to bear without grief what you maintain you have willingly borne in the struggle of this world. You further teach that thanks must always be given to the Lord so that hardship can never drown us, for you explain that there is in ourselves something worthy of our love. Next you show what can be the future of evil men and of good men, so that when all doubt has been expunged we may serve the true Prince with the whole thrust of our devotion. Eternal King, grant that we who now rejoice in the preaching of our holy mother may enjoy the future gift of Your mercy.

COMMENTARY ON PSALM 63

1. *Unto the end, a psalm of David.* The words of this heading, as has often been remarked, are wholly related to the Lord Christ, who is to speak through the entire psalm. These words are written without historical narration; the clarity of the heading seems to waft the light of the coming psalm over us. The Lord will speak of His passion, which has afforded life to the world and has poured on us the light of belief. So let us listen with eager minds, for though the theme is often repeated, we always get from it some new usefulness. This psalm is known to be the sixth of those touching briefly on the passion and resurrection of the Lord.[1]

Division of the Psalm

Our King and Head the Lord Christ, in His declaration that He will take on true manhood, initially prays that He be freed from fear of the Jewish people, as He relates their deceits and impious deeds as if they have already been performed. He teaches that they have failed in their acts of persecution, whereas He has attained the glory of resurrection. In the second place He scoffs at the savagery of the Jews, for they were the more troubled at their crimes when at the resurrection the Lord's strength was proclaimed. At that moment the joy of the just and the power of their upright faith were manifest.

Explanation of the Psalm

2. *Hear, O God, my prayer when I am in tribulation: deliver my soul from fear of the enemy.* In the human role which He has assumed and in which He was to suffer, the Lord Christ asks that His prayer uttered in tribulation be heard, since He seeks with all His strength what He feels is beneficial to Him. But let us listen carefully to what He seeks: He has subjoined the statement: *Deliver my soul from fear of the enemy.* He does not ask that He may wholly avoid the death which is for the salvation of all (so He refutes Peter when he says: *Be merciful to*

thyself, O Lord: this shall not be unto thee),[2] but that He fulfil the passion demanded by His holy dispensation, with His soul delivered from fear of the persecuting nation. This is how good plans achieve their end if the persecutor is not feared; if human weakness should yield, wickedness is not overcome but gains increase and strength.

3. *Thou hast protected me from the assembly of the malignant, from the multitude of the workers of iniquity.* Let us ponder how He says He was protected when He suffered, and let us not lament the death which the intention of wicked men sought to inflict on the Lord's faithful. He was clearly protected *from the assembly of the malignant,* because while they shared the belief that He was dying, they were found to be in confusion through the glory of His resurrection. In short, He was protected by the power of His divinity because He was the Son of man and also Son of God, one Person with two natures without a shadow of doubt, *having the power to lay down his life and to take it up again.*[3] So He was protected because He overcame the ambush of malignant men by virtue of His own power. He added: *From the multitude of the workers of iniquity;* earlier He said: *From the assembly of the malignant,* which can be applied to their designs, and here: *From the multitude of the workers of iniquity,* to relate the event of His own passion.

4. *For they have whetted their tongues like a sword: they have bent their bow, a bitter thing.* Throughout these four verses up to the division of the psalm, He indicates the Jews' persecution by various similes. But here a most just reason is offered why He was protected: *From the multitude of workers of iniquity.* The more they whetted their tongues like a deadly sword, the more their wickedness was nullified, so that the evils which they devised against the blood of the innocent One they directed instead upon themselves. This is the tendency of sinners, to harm themselves first when they hasten to oppress their neighbour. But let us examine His words: *They have whetted their tongues;* here He points to the occasion when they cried with one voice: *Crucify, crucify.*[4] The utterance is equivalent to committing the crime; it does not matter who does the slaying, if one proclaims that an innocent man is to be slain. Next comes: *They have bent their bow, a bitter thing,* that is, a hidden ambush which in their opinion went wholly undetected. With thirty pieces of silver they pressed the wicked Judas to become a traitor, though he seemed to be the Lord's

disciple. What a bitter thing, worse than any bitterness, that a table-companion should be suddenly suborned to betray, and a disciple to slay, and the treasurer by a reward of money!

5. *To shoot in secret the undefiled: they will shoot at him on a sudden, and will not fear.* This short verse is linked with the previous words, *they have bent their bow to shoot in secret the undefiled.* We must interpret *in secret* to mean "as the Jews imagined." But their action could not be hidden from Christ, and it was repeatedly foretold before it could happen. We use the word *undefiled* in two senses. There are those who are in common undefiled when they are cleansed by the Lord's mercy and made wholly pure; as Psalm 50 says: *Thou shalt wash me, and I shall be made whiter than snow.*[5] But only Christ is truly called undefiled, for He contracted no stain of sins, but being wholly clean with heavenly purity He is known to be a stranger to all sin. So he rightly said with reference to himself *To shoot the undefiled,* so that the Jews' fear would increase as they hastened to shed the blood of the innocent One. The next words are: *They will shoot at him on a sudden, and will not fear. On a sudden* is here also to be interpreted "as the most lunatic Jews imagined"; for how can we regard it as sudden when it was clearly foretold to the disciples? As we read in the gospel: *Behold we go up to Jerusalem, and the Son of man shall be betrayed to be crucified,*[6] and similar passages in which He foretold His own passion. As for His words: *They will shoot at him and will not fear,* they show the outcome of their malevolent intention, so that the crime seemed to be not only organized but also carried out.

6. *They are resolute in wicked words: they have planned to hide snares. They have said: Who shall see us?* They were resolute with wicked words when they said: *He is guilty of death,*[7] or when they proclaimed: *His blood be upon us and upon our children.*[8] *They are resolute* expresses the most hardened obstinacy with no basis on the solid stay of truth. Next comes: *They have planned to hide snares. They have said: who shall see us?* Here the practice of sinners is described, for all who plan guile think that they are deceiving a person to be able to attain their wicked ends. Thus the Jews, who were confused in their wicked minds, thought that Christ was a mere man, and did not realise that their malice was observed by Him to whom all things in heaven and on earth are more truly clear than they are known to themselves.

7. *They have searched after iniquities: they have failed in their search.*

Man comes to a high heart: and God shall be exalted. This verse is divided into these two statements. It declares how wicked plans bring turmoil on themselves, and how the malicious mind fails in the work it intends; on the other hand the good intention and the enlightened mind reveal what success they are seen to attain, so that the nearer they draw to God the more they realise that His Godhead was exalted before them. The Jews *searched after iniquities,* which was just what they should have avoided, since they could find there no fruit of their salvation. They said: *If we let him alone so, the Romans will come and take away our place and nation.*[9] They searched after iniquities also when they heard the Lord say to the man sick of the palsy: *Thy sins are forgiven thee;*[10] they at once thought that He was blaspheming, but the Lord said to them: *Why do you think evil in your hearts?*[11] They further searched after iniquities when as the gospel says they laid traps by asking diverse questions to find some pretext on which to accuse Him. Next comes the punishment of sinners: *They have failed in their search.* Men who strive to attain most evil ends always fail in their designs; of them Scripture says elsewhere: *They were weakened, and there was none to help them.*[12] The second part of the statement follows: *Man comes to a high heart, and God shall be exalted.* When He says that man comes to a high heart, He refers to those who with committed purpose seek heavenly things. The heart is high when it ponders things heavenly and shuns things of earth. Such men do not fail like one who makes a search; they wax stronger and stronger, and attain the point at which they believe in the existence of the highest, all-powerful God; not that God becomes higher, but because the Godhead when pondered in the heart of a holy man becomes great. Note that earlier the faithless Jews were described because they failed in their purpose; now the reference is to the apostles and all the faithful, in whose hearts God is exalted in so far as they have attained true and most holy reflections with pure minds.

8. *The arrows of children are become their wounds.* After detailing the wickedness of the Jews which they sought to perpetrate to achieve the slaughter of the Lord, He comes to the second section, in which He scoffs at their din and harsh plans by a most appropriate comparison. This figure is called irony;[13] what could be more trivial or empty than falsely to condemn the true Judge, to seek to kill Him who raised the dead, to hand over in bonds Him who loosed the shackles of the

world? The arrows of children are indeed empty weapons, for in their zeal for sport they often shoot canes like arrows. Likewise the aspirations of the Jews, most savage in their ineffectual malice, did not inflict lamentable death, but instead the most glorious passion. They caused such wounds as ensured the death of death itself, and the swift fulfilment of the promised salvation of the world.

9. *And their tongues against them are made weak. All that saw them were troubled.* In this verse the translation of Origen[14] is to be followed so that the general statement can make sense for us. The tongues of the Jews were indeed weakened when they said: *If he is the Son of God, let him come down from the cross;*[15] and subsequently they saw Him rising again from the tomb, though they did not believe that He could descend from the gibbet of the cross. You Jews, where is your faithlessness now? While He was still alive you said: *If he be king of Israel, let him come down from the cross.*[16] I ask your opinion and solicit your judgment: how much more marvellous is it for one dead to be able to rise again than for one still alive to seek to come down from the cross? You made a slight request, but greater events resulted. Yet your faithlessness could not be healed even by signs much stronger than you sought. Next is added: *All that saw them were troubled.* By *them* is meant the guilty and troubled men against whose tongues the glorious resurrection of Christ came forth. What a strange and remarkable obstinacy of mind! Through their confusion others became troubled; their obstinacy could not be diverted to repentance. Because of them some believers were troubled when they came to the apostles, and said: *What shall we do, men and brethren?*[17] They got salutary advice from them, and deserved to be saved from everlasting damnation by holy baptism.

10. *And every man was afraid. And they declared the works of God, and understood his doings.* We have often said that men in general are cited for a section of them. We must understand *every man* here not as the generality but as those who fear the coming judgment after weighing the power of the Lord. To realise that He speaks only of the faithful, observe what follows: *And they declared the works of God,* that is, the glory of the resurrection, the acknowledgment at the breaking of bread,[18] the ascension into heaven, the fact that the disciples spoke in different tongues, and the other signs showed by the Lord Saviour through His disciples after His resurrection. These things they an-

nounced by preaching to various people; and it is grievous to relate
that the Jews refused to heed the miracles which they had seen,
whereas the Gentiles believed them on hearsay. Next was added: *And
understood his doings.* They understood precisely that those deeds
were divine, because human frailty could not achieve such results.

11. *The just shall rejoice in the Lord and shall hope in him: and all the
upright in heart shall be praised.* Let us listen to the promise of the
Lord, to that pronouncement when He makes His most just judgment.
He says that the just man will rejoice in the time to come, for He knew
that His disciples would be weighed down by the afflictions of different sufferings; but they will rejoice when the twelve tribes of Israel
will sit in judgment. They were sad for a time, but they will rejoice for
ever, for the rewards of the Lord are greater than those known to be
offered Him by the faithful through His own kindness. So that you
would not think that these words were spoken only to the apostles,
there follows the general statement: *And all the upright in heart will be
praised.* The upright in heart are they who walk on the right paths of
the Lord. He who wishes to direct his step away from that direct
course is crooked; none can be called upright except him who is in
harmony with that truth and that proclamation. Such men are made
praiseworthy for ever because they both praise the Lord and are
praised by the Truth itself. What is more praiseworthy than to be told
by the Judge Himself in the sight of all the angels those splendid
words for which we long: *Come, blessed of my father,*[19] and the rest
which the gospel-text has taught us?

Conclusion Drawn From the Psalm

The Lord Christ in His own voice has instructed us to our great
profit. He Himself explained His own suffering, and none can refute
His statement. When we say to the Jews: "The Catholic Church
speaks," they are perhaps slow to listen. When we confront them
with their own prophet, they still have recourse to false interpretations, so that some argument can emerge out of the lie which they have
embraced to further their excuse. But what will these obdurate men
say now, when they hear their own future being proclaimed by the
Lord Himself, upon whom they presumed to inflict the most cruel
suffering? The world has acknowledged the fact of His resurrection

among them; and He promises to unbelievers their due punishment, but to the faithful eternal rewards. While there is time, you who are Jews must entreat and beg while you can to be welcomed among the lambs at His right hand, so that you may not be driven out on the left with the goats.

COMMENTARY ON PSALM 64

1. *Unto the end, a psalm of David, a canticle for Jeremiah and Ezechiel concerning the people of the captivity, when they began to go out.* The words, *unto the end, a psalm of David,* are now familiar; it remains to explain the rest. When the Jewish people because of their disobedience were led captive by the Chaldean nation, the prophets Jeremiah and Ezechiel said that they would return to their native land seventy years later, and that they would restore Jerusalem to a better state after it had been overturned by the enemy. The next words are: *Concerning the people of the captivity,* that is, the Jewish people who migrated to the city of Babylon. The spiritual sense of this is: "Whom we consigned to the power of the devil through our sins." For Babylon, as has often been stated, means "confusion,"[1] and this has obvious reference especially to the devil. So the people which after the captivity abandoned Babylon, and hastened to the Lord's city Jerusalem, represents those who have condemned the confusion of this world and hasten to join the Church of Christ. The whole of this psalm is on the authority of the Fathers to be allotted to the people who came from Babylon, because when they returned to Jerusalem Jeremiah and Ezechiel were already cut off by death.[2] We can arrange the words as follows to avoid the difficulty raised by this question: "Unto the end, a psalm of David, a canticle concerning the people of the transmigration, uttered through the prophecy of Jeremiah and Ezechiel, when the people began to set out." This word-order allows us rightly to understand that the words refer more aptly to the people than to Jeremiah and Ezechiel.[3]

Division of the Psalm

The people who have abandoned worldly sinning and returned to the Lord Saviour are liberated, and at the outset of the psalm acknowledge their Creator. They ask that their prayer be heard, and say that only he who has deserved to attain God's courts is blessed. In the second section they call the Lord the hope of all the ends of the earth. They enunciate His various praises and His power by allegorical comparison. They say that His holy ones rejoice in hymns of joy sung to Him.

Explanation of the Psalm

2. *A hymn, O God, becometh thee in Sion: and a vow shall be paid to thee in Jerusalem.* The people have returned to the Lord from the captivity of sin, and they burst forth in great exultation, maintaining that a hymn befits God alone, and not the crowds of demons as the pagans previously believed; for they had songs which they poured out to impure spirits and idols, but now they are drawn to the light of truth, and say that only He is to be praised who is clearly acknowledged as Creator of all, and only in Sion, that is in contemplation.[4] This contemplation clarifies the light of true faith, for by it a true hymn is uttered to the Lord, not with a debased shout of the tongue but in controlled song. To express this more specifically the people added: *And a vow shall be paid to thee in Jerusalem.* Vows were paid by infidels to Mars, Venus and the other demons, so if a man had been delivered from war he sacrificed to Mars Gradivus, and if he achieved foul adultery he thought that the goddess of lust should be adored. Now that the truth is recognised, the people says that a vow must be paid to God alone in Jerusalem because of His goodly works. This is a vision of peace in which blessedness remains planted and immovable.

3. *O hear my prayer: all flesh shall come to thee.* The people who had earlier said: *A hymn, O God, becometh thee in Sion,* now addresses the Lord with a hymn of supplication in the words *hear my prayer.* This was so that they themselves should do first what they had proclaimed

that the rest should do. The people described earlier asked that their prayer be heard. They knew they were to die, and they prayed to Him to whom they knew they would pass after this life, asking Him to spare them here and now so that He would not judge them hereafter. This is how the apostle speaks of that judgment: *We shall all stand before the judgment-seat of Christ that everyone may receive the proper things of the body, according as he has done whether it be good or evil.*[5] We must interpret *flesh* here as not only the saints but all men, for clearly we will all go to Him to be condemned or to be set in eternal rest. Observe that in the holy Scriptures man is often represented by the soul alone or the flesh alone, as in Genesis: *Seventy-five souls entered Egypt with Jacob,*[6] and here: *All flesh shall come to thee.* It is most useful to recall the figure of *synecdoche* here, which signifies the part for the whole.[7]

4. *The words of the wicked have prevailed over us: and thou wilt reconcile our transgressions.* The words of the wicked did indeed prevail when pagan parents pressed upon their children the old rites and sacrileges which they used to carry out, for reared from infancy they followed the practices which they adopted with inexperienced minds. *Prevailed over us* carries the idea of a very deep sea which with its overtopping waves submerges every object it meets, and allows nothing which it devours to float free. But divine love came to the rescue of these errors when it bestowed salvation on the world with the arrival of the Lord Saviour. We must however examine the sense of *reconcile.* We use this term appropriately of priests propitiating the Godhead for our sins by sacrifices which they offer; this is so that the anger incurred by faults may be transformed into the favour of salvation. So those who were most justly on trial for their deeds are absolved by the kindness of the Godhead, who in this sense was reconciled to the human race when He bestowed on us Christ Himself as Priest and Victim. As Paul says: *God was in Christ, reconciling the world to himself, not imputing to them their sins.*[8]

5. *Blessed is he whom thou hast chosen and taken to thee: he shall dwell in thy tabernacles.* Some think that this verse is to be applied to the Lord Saviour; but I say that it must refer to the blessed man in general, for earlier we had: *Thou wilt reconcile our transgressions,* and now follows: *Blessed is he whom thou hast chosen and taken to thee,* so it may

be ascertained that the reference was not to the uniquely spotless One, but to the sinner in general. So blessed is the one whom the Lord has chosen. But observe how the psalmist says: *Thou hast chosen;* none obtained the choice by his merits. As Christ says in the gospel: *You have not chosen me, but I have chosen you.*[9] The expression, *taken to thee,* means set in eternal rest, which the devoted Lord promises to His holy ones. The psalmist continues with what happens to such as these: *He shall dwell in thy tabernacles.* We say people dwell in a place when they do not change or abandon the abode they have chosen. He explains in another psalm the nature of this dwelling: *My soul hath longed and fainted for the courts of the Lord.*[10] To dwell there is already a reward, since only those whom the heavenly mercy deigns to choose can enter there.

We shall be filled with the good things of thy house: holy is thy temple. If the human mind wishes to examine clearly the good things of God's house, which is the future Jerusalem, it has not the resources to do so. Paul says of this: *Eye hath not seen, nor ear heard, neither hath it entered the heart of man what things God hath prepared for them that love him.*[11] But it is right to mention what we have heard: the good things of His house will be fruit thirtyfold, sixtyfold, and an hundredfold,[12] which the Lord promises to His faithful saints there. The good things of His house are also here, and Paul lists them: *For to one is given the word of wisdom, to another the word of knowledge, to another faith in the same spirit, to another the grace of healing, to another diverse tongues, to another interpretation of tongues.*[13] Observe that he said: *We shall be filled,* as if we shall drink as much as we can take according to our measure. This points to the words of the same apostle: *But to every one of us is given grace according to the measure of the giving of Christ.*[14] Next comes: *Holy is thy temple.* This refers either to God's house the Church, or to the Lord's incarnation. As we read in the gospel: *Destroy this temple, and in three days I will build it up.*[15] And a little later the evangelist says: *He said this about the temple of his body.*[16]

6. *Wonderful in justice. Hear us, O God our saviour.* The words, *wonderful in justice,* refer to the temple just mentioned. It can be wonderful in many ways; but he added *in justice* so that you must pay heed to His arrival when He separates the good from the evil, and renders to each what is due. So that we may understand this of Christ

Himself there follows: *Hear us, God our saviour.* For God Himself is our Saviour who has bestowed salvation on the world, and with His devotion has come to the aid of the human race.

Thou art the hope of all the territories of the earth, and in the extent of the sea. After that converted people had poured out its prayer from simple hearts, and had asserted that it was filled with the Lord's blessings, it passed to the second section, in which it describes the praises and powers of the Lord. This statement has pruned away the urgings of the Jews and the base teachings of heretics with the knife of truth; for the hope which the Lord represents is not bounded by place nor confined to one nation, but is open to all the territories of the earth when humble prayers are poured out to Him throughout the world. He is rightly called the hope of all since he promises eternal rewards to all the faithful. But so that you would not take this to mean only the land which they call the mainland, the psalmist added: *And in the extent of the sea.* This refers either to the islands which he seemed not to have included in the territories of the earth, or to the extent of sea embracing the inhabited regions of the whole world, as is described elsewhere: *This great and well-extended sea.*[17] It is extensive because its dwelling-places embrace countless nations. As for the sea, the Lord also attests that we must interpret it as the world when He says to the disciples: *I will make you fishers of men.*[18] For where are the fish especially if not in the sea? The world is justly compared with the sea for it is bitter with falsehoods, battered by the waves of the devil, and stirred up by storms of vices.

7. *Thou who preparedst the mountains by thy strength, being girded with power.* Let us examine this verse a little more carefully, for it is profound in the subtlety of its words. The expression, *preparing the mountains by strength,* does not refer at all to the height of landmasses. We use the word *preparing* only for provision by needful means for appropriate future use. So we fittingly interpret allegorically the prepared mountains as the apostles who were chosen to proclaim the word. They had strength of faith and height of sanctity; they were lowly in style of life, but deservedly ranked higher. The Lord prepared them by His strength because He performed great miracles through them, so that by the greatness of the Word they could convert unbelievers, and admiration at their deeds could soften the hardest hearts. The psalmist next explains how the Lord prepared

this. He was *girded with power*, that is, clad in His majesty. The Lord's humanity was girded with the power of the Word, so that divine strength could provide what He did not have as man. We gird ourselves with the glory of the belt, but the distinction of the belt is external to the nature of him who buckles it on. So Psalm 44 says: *Gird thy sword upon thy thigh, O thou most mighty*,[19] and elsewhere we read: *Thou hast girt me with joy*.[20] Such passages as these point to the two natures of the Lord Christ which are most full and perfect in one and the same Person, as the whole Catholic Church confesses.[21]

8. *Who troublest the depth of the sea. Who will endure the noise of its waves? The Gentiles shall be troubled.* After the psalmist has explained by the allegory of the mountains that the apostles were prepared, he now recounts what the Lord achieved through them. By the preaching of the apostles He churned up not only the surface of the sea but also its bottom, that is, the more hidden depths of the Gentiles' hearts. When they saw that their deities had fallen silent, and realised that they were eradicated, they were rightly troubled at heart since they knew that their hopes had come to nothing. Since the world is called the sea, the hearts of unbalanced men are compared appropriately with the depths of the sea, for from the depths rises all that the waves of sins churn up. So unexpected turmoil arises, which whips the innocent and wearies the holy. Next comes: *Who will endure the noise of its waves?* This refers to persecutors. Though they themselves are roused like the highest waves, their noise—that is, their cruel statements—cannot be endured by men unless their impudence is broken and defeated by permission of divine grace. *Who will endure it?* has reference to the limits of human frailty, for when God's generosity has allowed it, martyrs have been able to overcome their violence. So the Gentiles were very greatly troubled when they observed that those who were most faithful both performed deeds of virtue when alive, and in death brought to fulfilment the prayers of suppliants, whereas their own deities trembled at the power of martyrs, and refused to respond. It was then that Apollo at Delphi fell silent, then that Diana quitted Delphi, then that Venus of Cythera blushed with shame.[22] What, I ask, could the Gentiles do when they saw their deities tremble?

9. *And they that dwell in the uttermost regions of the earth shall be afraid at thy signs. Thou shalt take delight at their outgoings in the morning and in the evening.* Here the psalmist indicates the time at

which the apostles manifested diverse signs. It was necessary that the whole world, dwelling as it seemed over the whole earth, should tremble when they saw signs which their reading had not announced to them and which their eyes had not made manifest to them. The psalmist stated the likely source of such fear with the words *at thy signs.* He added: *Thou shalt take delight at their outgoings in the morning and in the evening.* The outgoing in the morning relates to when someone is converted to the Lord Saviour through happiness in this world, for the early morning is always a time of brightness and obtains the grace of illumination through the advance of daylight. The words: *Thou shalt take delight in the evening,* point to the time when it is always dark for those experiencing stern suffering; but at last they pass to the Lord Creator so that He may turn their griefs to joy. So the Lord will take delight at the outcome of both situations, because through His abundant generosity He obtains committed followers from all quarters.

10. *Thou hast visited the earth, and hast inebriated it: thou hast in many ways enriched it.* We must interpret the earth here as the human race which was filled and restored when the Lord deigned to come to it. There is another psalm which explains how this earth was inebriated: *Thy chalice which inebriateth, how good it is!*[23] It is a drunkenness which brings blessedness, a satiety which brings salvation; the more abundantly it is drunk, the more it begins to bestow satiety on men's minds. So this type of utterance is peculiar to the divine Scriptures, for the word inebriate usually has a good sense there, whereas in secular literature or in common gossip it is never found in a good sense. The psalmist adds: *Thou hast in many ways enriched it.* These words denote a mode of giving which cannot be expressed. He who enriches in many ways seems not to express the extent of his giving, but what he promises in such words extends it immeasurably. The word *locuples* ("enriching") means one who possesses several regions (*loca plura tenens*).[24] This earth He has deigned to raise up, not treading it underfoot as men do, for the earth which we wear away Scripture says will not be enriched but rather changed. In Isaiah's words: *There will be a new heaven and a new earth.*[25]

The river of God is filled with water: thou hast prepared their food, for so is thy preparation. The mercy of God is well compared to the fullest of rivers, for it cannot be lessened by any drought, and knows no diminution through frequent drinking. The world's water shows increase through rains or aridity through drought, but God's river is always full and level. Scripture says of it: *The stream of that river brings joy to the city of God.*[26] The Lord Himself says in the gospel: *He that shall drink of the water that I give him shall not thirst for ever, but it shall become in him a fountain of water springing up into life everlasting.*[27] Do not be troubled because the singular *river* appears in one place and the plural *rivers* in another. Unity has the power to embrace the many; though we speak of churches in the plural, it is clear that there is one Catholic Church which we know is mentioned on innumerable occasions.

After he spoke of drink from the river, he further mentioned spiritual food, so that the Lord's most abundant feast would not leave His friends hungry in any way. He says: *Thou hast prepared their food;* this food is not chewed with the teeth but devoured with eagerness of soul. Of it Scripture says: *He gave them the bread of heaven, and man ate the bread of angels.*[28] So the whole phrase is appropriately applied to holy communion, when we drink His blood and are filled with His body. That you might not think that this happened by chance, as pagans risibly imagine, the psalmist added: *For so is thy preparation.* All happened according to God's dispensation; as Christ Himself says in the gospel: *Are not five sparrows sold for two farthings, and not one of them will fall to the ground without the will of your Father?*[29]

11. *Fill up plentifully the streams thereof, multiply its generations: it shall rejoice in its dripping when it springs up.* Streams here denotes the apostles or other faithful who always drank of that brimming river of God. So that you would not think that their drinking was a mere sip, he says that the streams will be filled up plentifully to such fullness as to afford plenty for themselves and to benefit others. So he reverts to the singular number which we have said is appropriate to the unity of the Church; for he says: *Multiply its generations,* that is, the generations of that stream which flows from the holy river, so that through subsequent generations the blessed preaching may not fail but be multiplied, and from them the Catholic Church may ever grow. Thus those now schooled in holy doctrine may later be seen to teach others. We observe this clearly happening every day. The psalmist has spoken of *streams,* meaning those well advanced; now he speaks of *its dripping,* with reference to embryonic Christians, for the greatest

breadth of teaching cannot gain access to such confined beginnings. Paul says of these people: *I could not speak to you as spiritual but as carnal persons. As unto little ones in Christ I gave you milk to drink, not meat.*[30] Dripping consists of drops falling from roofs and piercing the soil not by weight but by repetition; the difference between drops and streams is clear even to the evidence of our eyes. So every faithful person will rejoice initially when he rises again by water and the holy Spirit, that is, when we are in truth reborn and made ready for the Lord's glory through His kindness. We feel great joy when we lay aside the senility of our old man, and are transformed to the joys of new birth. Though in one sense these kindnesses of God seem to depend on His authority, in another they seem to reveal the clearest sequence of our progress. Initially the dryness of our faith is enlivened by a few drops; next we are watered by flowing streams; finally, as the previous verse says, we attain with God's help the fullness of the river. In this way the continuing nature of God's gift is made clear through these three expressions.

12. *Thou shalt bless the crown of the year of thy goodness: and thy plains shall be filled with plenty.* *The crown of the year* appropriately denotes the whole of this world, through which the Catholic Church extends. The Lord blesses those whom He has truly made Christians through His river, stream and drops already mentioned earlier. Note what then follows: *Thy plains shall be filled with plenty.* *Plains* denotes the faithful and just, who because their hearts are so level are compared with level plains; such people are filled with plenty because through the Lord's generosity they will bring forth fruit thirtyfold, sixtyfold, or a hundredfold.[31]

13. *The desert regions shall grow fat: and the hills will be girt with joy.* The desert regions are the peoples of the Gentiles, to whom no prophet has been assigned, for all the prophets prophesied within the Jewish nation. So these desert regions became fat by the great gift of the Godhead when the holy preaching of the apostles came to them, and through the Lord's grace these peoples became handsome in faith, whereas for long previously the ghastly emaciation of unbelief befouled them. In short, the first sowing came forth through the prophets in the Jewish nation; the second was spread far and wide through the apostles among the Gentiles. But the power of the Lord sought more corn from these desert regions than came forth from the lands

which seemed cultivated. As the prophet says: *Rejoice, barren one that bearest not; burst forth with noise thou that dost not travail with child; for many are the children of the deserted one, more than of her that hath a husband.*[32] We must interpret the abundant hills as the martyrs, for they have the highest rank after the apostles. The phrase, *will be girt with joy*, indicates that by the Lord's dispensation they attain eternal joy through the endurance of sufferings.

14. *The rams of the flock are clothed, and the valleys shall abound with corn: indeed they shall shout and sing a hymn.* They are clothed: this indicates the nuptial garment in which the rams of the flock, that is, the apostles and other saints, will be clad, for they have been leaders in good teaching for the Christian people. Next comes: *And the valleys shall abound with corn.* The valleys connote humble people, for there is nothing lowlier than valleys which form a kind of hollow in the earth. These humble people shall abound with corn, like the tax-collector who did not presume even to raise his eyes to heaven,[33] or to trust in any presumption of his merits. He abounded with corn because he was a lowly valley; he was raised up because through the Lord's kindness he humbled himself. He became stronger because he confessed that his strength was weak. The psalmist added: *They shall shout and sing a hymn.* The conclusion shows that the earlier allusions are to be understood in an allegorical sense. Desert regions will not shout, nor will valleys or rams of the flock or the other things mentioned earlier; they are the persons represented by these objects in praiseworthy comparison who will shout and sing a hymn. First he said: *They shall shout*, but so that you would not think that the shouting was a babel, he added: *And shall sing a hymn*, that is, the praise known to be sweetly appropriate to rational creatures.

Conclusion Drawn From the Psalm

Let us understand the sweet rejoicing of this blessed people who come to the Lord Christ. Let us be aware of the benefit beyond reckoning which we read is celebrated with such exultation. With what varied grace the psalmist has adorned the hymn to Him which he promised in the first verse of the psalm! With remarkable brevity he has described the glory of His incarnation. This faithful teacher has informed us what Christ conferred on the world. Finally he tells us that at the future resurrection all His saints will rejoice in Him with joyful hymns of praise. Thus the psalmist has recounted the present with marvellous brevity and has promised us future rewards to rouse the greatest hope. Heavenly King, grant that we too may be rescued from the barrenness of sin and more abundantly watered by the river of Your mercy. May we deserve to grow fat, so that in the company of Your saints we can sing continually to You a hymn of praise.

COMMENTARY ON PSALM 65

1. *Unto the end, a psalm of David, a canticle of the resurrection.* Though these expressions in the heading appear to be very well known because of our earlier explanations, it will be quite appropriate to repeat these from time to time so that the purpose of the whole title can be more clearly acknowledged. As has been said, *unto the end* points to the Lord Saviour; in Paul's words: *For the end of the law is Christ, unto justice to everyone that believeth*[1] The word psalm denotes Him unambiguously, because the psalm sounds forth from the upper part, just as His deeds and words sounded forth.[2] We have said that David means "longed for" and "strong in hand,"[3] expressions pertaining especially to our King and Lord Christ. It now remains to explain the rest. This community-canticle, which as the preceding terms have taught us refers to the Lord Saviour, is proclaimed with reference to His glorious resurrection. Through it the Church advises the nations, which she knew beforehand would be believers through the Lord's grace, to rejoice together, for they were to be renewed in their Head. But since the Jewish nation imagined that it alone would attain the rewards of eternal life because the other nations were still devoted to and in thrall to idols, whereas the race of the Jews alone seemed to possess the law of the true Lord, though it was to sin through the vice of its infidelity, holy Church poured out this hymn in the spirit of prophecy. She maintains that not merely the faithful ones of the Jews but the whole community of all nations will have that hope of resurrection. As the prophet says: *I live, says the Lord, and the whole world shall*

be filled with my glory.[4] In short, as the opening words of the psalm have it: *Shout with joy to God, all the earth.*

Division of the Psalm

In contrast to the conviction of the Jews, who said that they alone before all men were to attain the life of the blessed, mother Church joyfully sings of the hope of a communal resurrection, interposing three diapsalms. In the first part she urges all to rejoice in the Lord's resurrection which will guarantee eternal rewards to all the faithful. In the second she invites all to join in meditation of God's works, so that a single attitude of belief may join together those whom a single reward appeared to await. Thirdly she again warns the nations to bless the Lord, for though He proves us by differing afflictions He will still bring us to the repose of His pity. In the fourth place she again invites all to take heed from the sign of their liberation and to put more trust in the Lord, blessing Him since He has deigned to hear her prayer.

Explanation of the Psalm

2. *Shout with joy to God, all the earth: sing ye a psalm to his name: give glory to his praise.* Holy Church, as we have said, says that the whole world must rejoice since it will come to believe in Christ the Lord. Jubilation[5] means exultation of heart such as cannot be expressed in words because of its boundless nature. So the psalm rightly took its beginning from such a word to demonstrate that the joy of so great a benefit cannot be grasped. When she says *all the earth,* she means not the soil but the faithful and devoted who could rejoice in such a wonder. This figure is called metonymy or change of name,[6] when what is contained is expressed by what contains it. By such preaching she refutes the Jews who thought that hope of blessed resurrection was promised only to them. Next comes: *Sing ye a psalm to his name.* After the inexpressible jubilation it was appropriate that she should encourage the peoples who were to believe to sing a psalm. She could thus unfold what she had conceived in mind by uttering praises; the first is known to God alone, but the second was to be heard by men. As Scripture has it: *With the heart we believe unto justice, but with the*

mouth confession is made unto salvation.[7] Her phrase, *to his name,* points to the Lord Saviour, by whose coming the world's wounds are known to have been healed. Let us note also the words, *give glory to his praise,* and drink in with thirsty hearts the heavenly remedy. The one who gives glory to His praise is he who joins in celebration of the Lord's praises in a crowded assembly of joy, so that he ascribes all to the Lord and considers that nothing is to be credited to human powers; for we must avoid and shun with all our might the attempts by human frailty to puff itself up with its own praises when it ought instead to incur blame by justified rebuke.

3. *Say unto God, How terrible are thy works! In the multitude of thy strength thy enemies shall lie to thee.* Let us hear what the Church teaches the nations to say in a single phrase and to encapsulate in short compass the great motivation of religion. *How terrible are thy works!* Though she says that the works of the Lord are terrible, she did not proclaim the degree of terror which they contain. My view is that the works of the Lord are to be feared on this count: we are to consider what can befall us if the Majesty which looked with pity on the world were to become hostile through the action of our sins. God deigned to become man for us; as Pope Leo the apostolic teacher writing to Flavian puts it: "The Creator of the angels alone endured to become one amongst mortal men. He was invisible amongst His own, but became visible amongst our fellow-men. He was beyond understanding, but sought to be understood. Abiding before time began, He began to exist in time. The Lord of all being took on the form of a slave and cloaked the boundlessness of His majesty. God is impassible, but He did not disdain to be a man exposed to suffering, and though immortal to endure the laws of death."[8] If we ponder this, the works of the Lord are terrible in our eyes when we cannot show to such high worth as this the course which heavenly love urges us to adopt for our salvation. Elsewhere we read: *Lord, I have heard thy hearing, and was afraid: I have considered thy works, and trembled.*[9] But this fear is loving and devoted, with the character of sweetness not bitterness. It begets hope rather than creates doubt. It intensifies desires and does not extinguish the flame of charity.

Next comes: *In the multitude of thy strength thy enemies shall lie to thee.* The multitude of strength was what cured men suffering from various illnesses. But His enemies lied in this multitude of strength when they said: *He performs these miracles by Beelzebub.*[10] They lied once more in the multitude of His strength when He said: *You will see the Son of man coming on the clouds of heaven,* and they said: *He has blasphemed: what need have we of further witnesses?*[11] Finally, they lied in the multitude of His strength when after the glory of the resurrection they gave money to the guards, and said to them: *Say that the disciples came by night and stole him away while we were asleep.*[12] In this way our revered mother in brief compass announced the mysteries of the holy incarnation.

4. *Let all the earth adore thee and sing to thee: let it sing a psalm to thy name, O One most high.* Because earlier she said that His enemies had lied, the world in general is now advised truly to adore the Lord Christ. She added: *Let it sing to thee,* and subsequently she repeated virtually the same words, but for those who scrutinise them carefully they are very different. In the first passage she wished us to interpret it as psalmody, but the second counselled works of holiness. When she says: *To thy name, O One most high,* she means, as was said earlier, the Lord Saviour who is rightly called the most High, for like Father and Spirit He is known to have nothing higher than Himself. The name is used particularly to confute the arrogance of the Jews, who believed that He was so abject that they did not fear to crucify Him. Arians too are found guilty under this head, for He who is the most High in His own Godhead cannot have one greater.

5. *Come and see the works of the Lord: how terrible he is in his counsels over the sons of men.* The bride of the eternal King invites the nations in this second section to enable themselves to behold the miracles of the Old Testament with devoted minds so that they may recognise in themselves the most true fulfilment of what happened in figure to the Jewish nation. The word *come* is appropriate, for it is addressed to people still afar off, since they were still lingering in the city of Babylon. *See* has the sense of "acknowledge with the mind's eye"; with their physical eyes they could not see things known to have happened earlier. By the works of the Lord she does not mean those which all men alike behold—sky, earth, sea and all that is within them—but she invites them to gaze in particular at the things which the people of greatest faith have spiritually acknowledged: the parting of the sea which lay open to the fleeing Jews, the people fed to satiety in the desert, the waters of the Jordan offering a crossing to their dry feet,

and the other experiences of the Jews which they experienced as a prefiguring. She added: *How terrible he is in his counsels over the sons of men*. He made the sons of men awesome and formidable when He manifested great miracles through them. But the following verses will make clear what these works are which she wishes nations as yet untaught to acknowledge.

6. *Who turneth the sea into dry land, and they will cross rivers on foot: there shall we rejoice at this happening*. These are the works of the Lord of which the previous verse advised us. He turned the sea into dry land when He afforded the Jewish people a land-route through the midst of the waves. That people *crossed rivers on foot* when the Jordan parted to right and left and He led the Jews' army into the promised land. But we must investigate why the plural *rivers* is set down here when we read that it happened only in the case of the Jordan. It is quite justified, for though it happened only at that river it is known to have taken place often there. Elias experienced such a crossing there, and at the return of his disciple the waters of that river opened for him likewise. Alternatively, it is characteristic of divine Scripture to speak of one for very many, and to speak repeatedly of several under a single one. Next comes: *There shall we rejoice at this happening*. She now hastens to reveal the mysteries of these works, because the Christian people subsequently took joy in the prefiguration of them. The crossing of the Jewish nation over the seas announced Christ's future baptism. The fact that they crossed rivers without hazard from the deep waters and with dry feet showed that they could traverse the billows of this world untroubled, and attain a most safe haven of repentance. So it was vital that the Church and her holy people should say that they would rejoice at this event, from which sprang the source of our joy and the origin of our eternal salvation. The expression, *there, at this happening*, is to be counted as one peculiar to divine Scripture.[13]

7. *Who by his power ruleth for ever: his eyes behold the nations*. She explained her previous words: *We shall rejoice at this happening*, with *by his power he ruleth for ever*. The princes of the earth can rule but not by their own power and not for ever. So these two phrases were added so that the power of the almighty King could be revealed. And so that the Gentiles who were still blind should not think that these promises were vain, she added: *His eyes behold the nations*, so that what they could not see of their own accord they could behold when inspired by

the sight of the true Light. The Lord illuminates those whom He looks upon; those whom He decides to attend He also sets free.

Let them who provoke him to anger not be exalted in themselves. The tendency of our frail nature is here described with apt brevity, for whilst we are doing deeds such as provoke the Lord to anger, we are puffed up within ourselves, eager to defend our sins all the more. But she forbids them to be exalted within themselves when they are to be found humble; the faithful should be exalted not in themselves but in Christ, for in Him their high position is secure and their rising will never fall.

8. *O bless our God, ye gentiles, and hear the voice of his praise.* She comes to the third section, in which she warns the nations to glorify the true God with harmonious proclamation. There follows: *And hear the voice of his praise,* in other words "Accept with trusting belief what the Father says of the Son." The voice of praise is: *This is my beloved Son in whom I am well pleased,*[14] and it must be listened to with unsullied and devoted minds, so that we may believe that the one and the same Lord Christ who was sprung from the Father before time began and is consubstantial with Him, was born of the virgin Mary and deigned to become like us when He took on human nature. Holy Church lives in this faith and advances in this faith, our belief that in the Lord Christ there is no humanity without true divinity, and no divinity without true humanity.

9. *Who hath set my soul to live: and hath not suffered my feet to be moved.* She now recounts the reasons why the mercy of the Lord is being proclaimed. These are the two mysteries of our liberation: first that He leads us through the gift of baptism to life (for we do not reach that goal through our own merits, but are drawn to it by the kindness of His mercy), and second that He does not allow us to be expelled from it though we are clearly burdened by grave faults. The One who sets us in life is He who said: *I am the way, the truth and the life.*[15] He who does not allow our steps to be moved is He who offered His hand to Peter so that he would not drown.[16] She next recounts these dangers from which she has been freed, so that you would not believe that they are mentioned without purpose.

10. *For thou, O God, hast proved us: thou hast tried us by fire as silver is tried by fire.* Up to now the Church seems to have prophesied in the singular, but now she speaks in the plural in the persons of her

members. Throughout these three verses she explains the severe afflictions with which the faithful are oppressed. God causes us to be proved when He permits the endurance of blessed suffering through different kinds of trials in the confession of His name; it is not by proving us but already by prior knowledge that He knows us. The various punishments of martyrs follow; the fire of charity tries that blessed conscience which is so inflamed by love of Christ the Lord that the tortures of blazing flames are overcome. But this is not a consuming but a cleansing fire; hence the citation of the analogy of silver, which is melted down by fire so that by this process it may become purer. The lump of silver would remain coated with dross if it did not lose its native dirt through the useful application of intense heat.

11. *Thou hast brought us into a net: thou hast laid afflictions on our back.* Thou hast brought us into a net means "You have made us bear the confining shackles which martyrs have deserved to endure." It was not a deceiving but a proving net such as would fetter the body but loose the chains of the soul, such as would not bring us to trial but would bestow absolution. She added: *Thou hast laid afflictions on our back,* that is, the scourgings which both Paul and the rest of the crowd of the faithful endured. They were humbled with whippings so that they would reject the pride which is devil-sent, together with delight in the world itself. When she says: *Thou hast laid afflictions on our back,* she means the physical pains which they endured from applications of the whip.

12. *Thou hast set men over our heads. We have passed through fire and water, and thou hast brought us into cool refreshment.* She says: *Thou hast set* in order to establish that all was done by His will. As the Lord says to Pilate: *Thou shouldst not have any power over me unless it were given thee from above.*[7] Next comes *men,* so that you may interpret this as sinners, for in savage persecutions they afflicted the holy martyrs with various tortures. *Over our heads* means "You gave them power to pass a capital sentence on us." She added: *We have passed through fire and water;* this took place when fire removed some martyrs and water devoured others, so that their deaths were seen to have been caused by these different elements. There follows the blessed promise of the world to come: *And thou hast brought us into cool refreshment,* so that

you might realise that all the Church's sufferings in her members have been imposed on her not as execrable punishment but to bring the blessedness of rest; for cool refreshment after burning troubles is that delightful and pleasant freedom from care which those who have deserved to suffer for the Lord's name obtain by that repayment.

13. *I will go into thy house with holocausts; I will pay thee my prayers.* At this point Christ's members revert to the singular; His body says that she will happily go into His house, that is, into the Jerusalem to come, in which are sought not holocausts of cattle but purity of souls. Note that just as in the three previous verses she spoke of the pains of martyrs, so now in the next four up to the end of the section she recounts the good fortunes of the blessed, so that she could strengthen in their grim tribulations the faithful to whom she promises these great rewards. *Holocaust* means "wholly burnt"; because earlier she had said that she was tried like silver by fire, here she justly says that she will offer a burnt offering, in other words her soul cleansed of its sins. Next comes: *I will pay thee my prayers,* which means "sing Your praises for ever, and always hymn Your mercy in the company of angels, powers, thrones and dominations." These are the prayers of the faithful, the longings of simple Christians, that those aligning themselves with the holiness of faith and good works may be received into that fellowship with Him.

14. *Which my lips have distinguished, and my mouth hath spoken when I was in tribulation.* She explains the prayers which she mentioned earlier, the ones *which my lips have distinguished;* even in tribulation the faithful like Job praise the Lord and always accuse themselves. So they are seen to distinguish their prayers with their lips, for there is no doubt that there is a distinction between the blame imputed to human nature and the praise always offered to the Godhead. Observe too the blessed holiness of her endurance; she says that after her resurrection she renders those prayers of praise which she sang when in tribulation, when we often sin through the flesh's frailty, and when the soul overcome by griefs is often not permitted to do the laudable deeds which it intended. But in this verse such abundance of love is shown by God's kindness that she is seen to have overcome all obstacles.

15. *I will offer up to thee holocausts full of marrow, with both incense and rams.* She is still expounding the prayers which she mentioned

earlier. *The holocausts full of marrow* are the sacrifices which we offer from the depths of pure hearts before God's sight. When we offer the heart's contrition in place of a holocaust, it should contain within it the most pure faith and the works of faith, which replace the marrow in the great richness of their offering, so that what we offer before God's sight may not be dry and empty. So she promises to offer such holocausts as contain the strength of marrow and the richness of saving faith. She added: *With incense and rams.* Incense denotes prayers offered like grains of incense in God's sight; elsewhere in Scripture we read: *Let my prayer be directed as incense in thy sight.*[18] *Rams* refer to the apostles who with their holy preaching emerged as leaders of the Christian people. Observe that she has joined the two together in the words, *with incense and rams.* Incense is truly most sweet to the Lord, for it is seen to be associated with the teaching of the apostles. But remember that this and the following verse are expressed in allegory. The offering by devoted people is expressed by signifying animals.

I will offer to thee bullocks with goats. We understand bullocks as the preachers who successfully ploughed men's hearts and stored the fruitful seeds of the heavenly word in men's thoughts. Goats are interpreted as those clad in shaggy vices in their zeal for Satanic wickedness; *hircus* (goat) is the same as *hirsutus* (shaggy).[19] But the Church offers them together with the bullocks, for when converted they confess to Christ the Lord. The thief who hung on a cross was a goat, but subsequently became a bullock when he attained before the Lord's eyes confession of the truth; for he said: *Remember me, Lord, when you enter your kingdom.*[20]

16. *Come and hear, and I will tell you, all of you that fear God, what great deeds he hath done for my soul.* She comes to the fourth part, in which she now calls not on novices but on the faithful and devoted. She now says nothing of her trials; she will speak only of the liberation of her soul. Let us hear what He has done for her soul, so that we too may learn to seek out what we know the Lord has bestowed on our mother.

17. *I cried to him with my mouth, and I extolled him beneath my tongue.* When these two requirements have been scrupulously ful-

filled, the Christian is made perfect. First he must cry to the Lord with his own mouth, that is, with an upright conscience rather than a perverted will. We say of people who are led astray in some way, "So-and-so is out of his mind; what he says is alien to him." So it is the one who makes unsullied entreaty to the Lord who cries with his own mouth, for what is clearly perverted belongs not to us but wholly to the devil. Secondly she says: *And I extolled him beneath my tongue. Beneath my tongue* means "in my conscience" for beneath our tongue lies our heart, in which with silent meditation we praise and from our viewpoint seem to extol Him known to be ever the most High. Note the order of topics: first she spoke of crying with the mouth, and then she passed to the heart's most pure feelings, from where we are usually heard though silent.

18. *If I have looked at iniquity in my heart, may God not hear me.* She carefully explains her words, *I have extolled him beneath my tongue.* He who praises God in his heart must not disturb his thoughts with mental pictures of another kind; he must not gaze on any iniquity but with the greatest diligence turn the whole of his mind on Him, so that the devil cannot find a place in him. Purity in one who prays depends on his having no foul thoughts to pollute him. What she is saying is: "If I have done this, may God not hear me," thus showing that people who do act in that way are mocked by empty apparitions.

19. *Therefore hath God heard me, and hath attended to the words of my prayer.* She says she has been heard because she has gazed in her heart at no iniquity. The cry which is unpolluted by human affairs rises to the Lord, for when we attend to Him we undergo such a change that He in turn pities and attends to us. Finally the words, *and hath attended to the words of my prayer,* follow. So let us pray that He bestows on us the purest of prayers, that when He has received our faithful entreaty He may hearken to us most attentively from the sanctuary of His paternal love.

20. *Blessed be the Lord, who hath not turned away my prayer nor his mercy from me.* The two things are interconnected; when God does not turn away a prayer, He undoubtedly grants His mercy, and when our prayer is rejected His mercy too is withdrawn. Let us also reflect on the beginning of the fourth section: *Come and hear what great deeds*

he hath done for my soul. The outcome of this most genuine promise
has followed at the end, for He is seen not to have turned away her
prayer, and shown not to have held back His mercy.

Conclusion Drawn From the Psalm

We have run through the psalm with accompanying explanation,
but now we must draw the composition together so that the power of
this canticle can be clearly acknowledged. First holy mother Church
addressed the nations for their salvation, with general instruction to
occupy themselves with the Lord's praises, so that our longing for
heaven may strip us of affection for this world. Next she invites us to
learn that the miracles of the Old Testament seemed to be accorded to
the Jews of those days as a prefiguration, so that the people who
succeeded them may be roused to the highest expectation, for what
was granted to the folk of old proclaimed the benefits of the regeneration to come. She further instructed us on the various disasters which
this Christian people endures, so that through the Lord's pity they
may be freed and through His generosity may attain that blessed native
land. This is a unique promise, an enviable guarantee, that we are
guarded in this world by His protection, and set in our eternal reward
by His generosity in the next. If we ever concentrate on this with
undeviating mind, we never fear the hazards of this world, but with
the utmost joy we shall sing the final words of this psalm: *Blessed be the
Lord, who hath not turned away my prayer nor his mercy from me.*

COMMENTARY ON PSALM 66

1. *Unto the end, in hymns, a psalm of a canticle.* The two terms,
hymn and canticle, appear to point to virtually the same hidden meaning unless they are carefully examined, for both are seen to denote
praise of the Lord. We have defined a hymn as a poem composed
according to the law of some metre;[1] all the psalms in Hebrew are
fashioned in this way. When they are defined merely as such in the
headings, they are known to have been played with pipes[2] and drums.

But the hymn which the prophet now sings has the words *unto the end* placed first, because the whole prayer is undoubtedly concentrated on the Lord Christ. A psalm of a canticle is one sung unaccompanied by the human voice. But through the terms here we realise that both could be combined, so that the psalm was sung to musical instruments by the human voice. So every song is also a hymn, but not every hymn is a song. This indicates the distinction for us: psalms without a canticle could be played on instruments alone.

Division of the Psalm

Following the resurrection-song of Psalm 65, the prophet has appended in marvellous sequence his prayer that we may be blessed and deserve to be led to knowledge of God, which our own merits cannot themselves attain. So in the first section he addresses the faithful, and prays that with them he may deserve to be blessed by the Lord, so that they may be enlightened in mind and come to realise that Christ the Lord must be proclaimed among all nations. Then he turns to the Lord, and with the spirit of prophecy he says that the peoples are to confess to Him because He judges the nations justly. Thirdly, he repeats the verse which he previously spoke, and adds that the earth has now yielded her fruit; so he asks that we may be blessed with the repetition of those words.

Explanation of the Psalm

2. *May God have mercy on us, and bless us: may he cause the light of his countenance to shine on us, and may he have mercy on us.* In directing his prayer, the prophet had hasty recourse to the necessary words; he did well to ask for mercy first, for he did not presume upon the effect of his own merits. First came the request to God to have mercy, and later that He should grant the gift of His blessing. The Lord's blessing always enlarges us. If we bless Him, we progress in a total sense; if He blesses us, He grants us gifts which will benefit our souls. But let us investigate what blessing the prophet asks for, because many are granted through the Lord's generosity. He blessed Adam before the sinning with the words: *Increase and multiply, and fill the world and*

subdue it.[3] He blessed Abraham when He said: *Blessing, I will bless thee, and multiplying, I will multiply thy seed as the stars of heaven, and as the sand that is by the sea shore.*[4] He also blessed the earth to produce various crops so as to remove the need caused by our frailty. But the psalmist sought the blessing which he expounds later, that God should remove the darkness from our minds, and enlighten us with the brightness of the Lord Saviour; for the next words are: *May he cause the light of his countenance to shine on us.* This was the blessing he asked for, that God should cause the light of His countenance to shine on them, for they could not behold Him since they did not have the benefit of light within their own resources. Human faculties cannot behold Him unless they are bathed in the brightness of His splendour. He repeats: *And may he have mercy on us;* It is a necessary repetition, for the mercy of the Lord is the starting-point for our spiritual progress, and we are maintained in goodly hope by His generosity. This figure is called *epembasis,*[5] in other words frequent repetition of an expression.

3. *That we may know thy way upon earth, thy salvation in all nations.* Here he has clearly stated the point of the previous words, *May he bless us and cause the light of his countenance to shine on us.* These blessings are helpful in this world in bringing us to a knowledge of that way of the truth which is the Lord Saviour, who leads us to life. None will be able to stray from that path except one who presumes to digress from the Lord's commands. And to save us from the necessity of proving by other examples who it is who is the Way, he next explained it with the words: *Thy salvation in all nations.* Thus we are saved from believing that this Way is in a single place, and the nature of the benefit to the world could be acknowledged by the witness of His name. This term salvation is clearly apt for the Lord Christ, because blessed Simeon when receiving Him in his arms said: *Now dismiss thy servant, O Lord, in peace, because my eyes have seen thy salvation, which thou hast prepared before the face of all peoples.*[6] Notice too that in the previous verse he speaks to the faithful people, and then suddenly turns to the Lord Christ; there is nothing wrong with this, for this is what the members must say to their Head. This figure is called *prosphōnēsis*[7] or exclamation, when in the midst of other remarks we suddenly direct words to the Lord.

4. *Let peoples confess to thee, O God, let all peoples confess to thee.* After the prophet has prayed that faith may grow among peoples, he

passes to the second section, in which he says to the Lord: *Let peoples confess to thee, O God. Confessing* is an ambivalent word, for it is known to denote both praises and lamentations for sins. Here both meanings must be inferred, so that people both confess their sins and never cease proclaiming the Lord's glory. In short, the word is seen to be used twice in the one verse so that you might realise that faithful people must make total confession. The addition of *all* shattered the foul activities of the Donatists, who believe that the Lord's Church is not spread throughout the world.[8]

5. *Let the nations be glad and rejoice: for thou judgest the peoples with justice, and will direct the nations upon earth.* We must investigate why he advises the nations to be glad and rejoice, even though he states that the Lord will pass judgment; for the guilty conscience can be afraid when it hears that the Lord of truth will judge us. But he is speaking of those who have now confessed their sins and cannot fear the future judgment. Christ is not their Judge but their Advocate, for they have condemned themselves by their confession. So the nations should rejoice and be glad, for by their confession they have deserved to anticipate His coming. The cause of their joy follows: they are known to have made confession to the merciful Judge who can cleanse the hearts of the humble and prostrate the necks of the proud. So that you should heed the confession we have mentioned, he says: *You will direct the nations upon earth,* that is, in this world, where You make them confess their faults so that they cannot be undermined by satanic error.

6. *Let the peoples, O God, confess to thee: let all the peoples confess to thee.* He passes to the third section, in which he repeats a verse of the second, but then appends something quite different. In the previous verse he stated: *Let the nations be glad and rejoice,* but now he says: *The earth hath yielded her fruit;* so that though the beginnings sound identical, the sense does not seem to advance similar reasons because of what follows. Some authorities have sought to interpret these peoples which he repeatedly mentions as the twelve tribes which will obtain the grace of a reward at the judgment to come.

7. *The earth hath yielded her fruit. May God, our God, bless us. The earth hath yielded her fruit,* namely the peoples' confessions, which with necessary repetition he earlier proclaimed were sounding forth. The word *her* is appropriate, for she received it through the Lord's

devoted generosity. She did not bring it forth from the devil's seed. The earth yielded her fruit also when the crowd of different nations accepted the Lord Saviour. They were full of thorns and thistles through Adam's sin, but bestowed life-giving fruit when they obeyed the Lord's commands. Then the faith of the apostles burst out into various tongues when the holy Spirit filled them; then the world acknowledged virtues beyond reckoning; then in truth did the earth bring forth its fruit, when it abandoned the thorns and thistles of the devil. And because the fruit was able to come forth, a blessing is rightly demanded, for He says: *May God, our God, bless us.* He had already named God once, but so that it might not be thought that He was the god of the Gentiles (for though enmeshed in futile errors they claim to worship God) he added: *Our God,* so that in truth we may believe that the only God to be worshipped is He whom the holy Catholic Church worships and confesses, the Father, Son and holy Spirit.

8. *May God bless us, and all the ends of the earth fear him.* He says again: *May he bless us,* which must often be repeated and clearly desired unceasingly. Because it is always necessary, it is obviously always profitable. This figure is called *tautology,* or repetition of the same expression.[9] Let us further observe how fear of God is requested among great gifts, when after the plea for a blessing the prayer is made that fear of Him be granted to the ends of the earth. This is amongst the chief gifts of God, that those who know fear of Him do not cease also to love Him. As Solomon puts it: *The fear of the Lord is the beginning of wisdom,*[10] and in another psalm we read: *Let all the earth fear the Lord.*[11] But this fear does not arise from human apprehension, but is afforded by divine inspiration. So the prophet with pity sought this fear for the ends of the earth, so that both might begin to believe and guard their beliefs with prudent anxiety.

Conclusion Drawn From the Psalm

How very broad are the fields of faith embraced by this psalm in its most pleasurable succinctness! The prophet begged the Lord Christ to deign to bless us with abundance of love by His coming, so that the salvation of the world awaited by the nations might become manifest to them, and they might experience the fruit of His mercy with the greatest depth of religious feeling. So this psalm should be both sweetest by its brevity, and preeminent through the worth of its prophecy, since all those generations earlier it foretold what the world now acknowledges as its salvation. Eternal King, grant that just as we recognise that You came in the lowliness of the flesh, so may we realise that You have been bestowed on us also as a merciful Judge by the power of Your Godhead.

COMMENTARY ON PSALM 67

1. *Unto the end, a psalm of a canticle of David.* We must appreciate the force of the initial expression from the fact that though it is termed *the end* it is always placed at the beginning, for it indicates the source and eternal beginning of things. As Christ Himself says in the gospel: *I am the beginning, which is why I speak to you.*[1] Next comes: *A psalm of a canticle,* which as has been said[2] is usually sung unaccompanied by the human voice. *David* denotes the Lord Himself, whom the expression, *the end,* also proclaims. This is a long psalm, and to relieve our weariness it is marked out with five diapsalms, by means of which we have appropriately signalled the divisions. In other psalms divisions are perceptible by human observation, in so far as the Lord inspires us; but these breaks which divine authority has imposed through diapsalms are to be followed without reservation. We must realise that throughout the psalm its composer speaks in mystical allegory; he is completely full of the gospel revelations, and shows himself especially concerned with a pious description of Christ's ascension.

Division of the Psalm

The prophet is filled with the spirit of foresight, and at the beginning of this psalm by expressing his desires he appropriately proclaims what is to befall the Lord's enemies, and what is to happen to the faithful at the judgment to come. Thus he can frighten the disloyal with the prospect of punishment, and delight the Lord's servants with the promise of their reward. In the second section he shows the virtues which the Lord has bestowed on the Jewish people, and then states how He has fashioned His Church out of them. In the third part he uses the figure of the mountain to denote the Lord Saviour, and emphasises the benefits which He accorded the Church when He raised her up by the gift of His resurrection. In the fourth section he proclaims that the pride of the Lord's enemies will be shattered, and says that conversions and martyrdoms of both sexes will emerge out of even the worst of them, when the advent of the salvific Lord has shone upon the world. In the fifth section he says that the Lord must be blessed in the churches where the apostles and Christ himself preached, and prays that He may deign to preserve the gifts He has given to His faithful. He also warns those who linger in this world as though in Egypt or Ethiopia to come in haste to the Lord. In the sixth part he gives an instruction to all to hymn the Lord Christ who has now made clear the miracles of His resurrection, and then ends the psalm with praise of the Lord.

Explanation of the Psalm

2. *Let God arise, and let his enemies be scattered: and let them that hate him flee before his face.* The prophet seems confidently to desire what he knows will come to pass. He is asking for Christ's resurrection, by which his opponents the Jews were to be scattered, for when they saw the power of His resurrection they trembled at their own wicked deeds. The vengeance exacted from them is expressed by the one word; for that people were not gathered into a single nation, but were scattered in small numbers[3] over the whole world. Next follows the punishment of that curse beyond reckoning, so that they flee before the face of Him who we know is everywhere. How grim a condition it is to be always fleeing yet unable to avoid the presence of the hostile Judge! He added: *That hate him* to indicate those who have remained obstinate. We attribute hatred to those situations in which we confess that we can get no rest.

3. *As smoke vanisheth, so let them vanish away: as wax melteth before the fire, so let sinners perish before the presence of God.* In these two verses the punishment of sinners is foretold by two images. Smoke is a

dark, thick mass which rises from the flames of this world that perish; the further it rises, the thinner it becomes through the empty air. Sinners are appropriately compared to it, for they bring forth from the fire of their wickedness smoke-bearing activities which through the action of pride rise to higher levels but inevitably like smoke vanish through their own self-exaltation. The second comparison which describes them follows. Wax is a soft, pliant substance gathered from honeycombs which melts under the fire's heat so that its substance is utterly dissipated. This image is appropriate for the wicked, for at God's judgment sinners disappear before His presence as the frail wax is consumed by the proximity of fire. Observe that the psalmist does not say that those to be tortured by enduring fire can be destroyed here and now in their substance. Rather he says that they will perish before the presence of God, because they will never attain His grace and benefits, though some misguided men have sought to claim that they will.[4] Note that in these verses the figure *parabole* appears,[5] a comparison between things differing in kind; for smoke and wax are seen to be compared to sinners.

4. *And let the just feast: let them rejoice in the sight of God: let them be delighted with gladness.* Just as earlier the punishment of sinners was pronounced, so now the future reward of the just is recounted. By feasts we mean choice and abundant supplies of foodstuffs with which the body is refreshed and the appetite often whetted. This is the image used for nourishment of the faithful and fattening the just, who are filled but still long for more, and are stuffed insatiably with the delights of heaven. Next is appended where these delights are found. *In the sight of God,* where happiness is always desirable and genuine. What exultation we experience under the gaze of the great Judge, when He whom we justly fear in this world is the object of our joy when He is present before us, and we have been set free by His kindness! The psalmist added: *Let them be delighted with gladness,* so that the fact that they are glad can delight them; they know that their gladness will not be ended, and they gain a sweeter delight in it because they do not feel that they will lose it. So the impending happiness of that blessedness is signified in what we may call glistening melodies.

5. *Sing ye to God: sing a psalm to his name: make a way for him who ascendeth upon the west. The Lord is his name. Rejoice in his sight.* After

recounting the punishment of the very wicked and the future rewards of the just, the prophet encourages the people to anticipate with faithful hearts what they had heard, and to join in singing praises to God with lyrical joy. That person sings to God who with a pure and faithful mind continually practises contemplation of Him. That person sings a psalm to His name who carries out the works which God prescribes. Next follows: *Make a way for him,* in other words, prepare and purify your hearts so that the holy Lord may deign to enter them. Alternatively, fill all men with blessed preaching; as the prophet Isaiah says: *Prepare ye the ways of the Lord, make straight his paths.*[6] The One for whom this path is made is now proclaimed: it is He *who ascendeth upon the west.* The Lord Christ and no other ascends upon the west by rising from the dead to lead our captivity captive,[7] and so that death, which held us subject to the sins that bound us, might forsake us now that we were free. It was inevitable that the darkness of the west should yield when the Sun of justice was seen to have risen over it. That none should doubt who ascends on the west, he says: *The Lord is his name.* So none should doubt that the Lord Saviour, whom the wicked Jews thought fit for slaughter as an ordinary man, is God. Next comes: *Rejoice in his sight;* not in the presence of men, where joy is transient, but in His sight in which purity of heart takes continuous delight, so that whatever the hardships suffered in this life it is always roused by thought of future reward.

6. *They shall be dislocated from his presence, who is the father of orphans and the judge of widows: God in his holy place.* After saying that the blessed are to rejoice in the sight of the Lord, he now says that the plunderers and the wicked, who with savage greed rend apart orphans and widows, are to be driven from his sight. Such men are troubled and exceedingly fearful; they are driven from His presence when they hear these words: *Go into everlasting fire, which was prepared for the devil and his angels.*[8] He explains whose presence it is from which they shall be dislocated: *The father of orphans and the judge of widows,* of whom elsewhere we read: *Thou wilt be a helper to the ward and the widow.*[9] What will be the extent of the sufferings of that plunderer who afflicted with evil mangling those under the protection of his Judge? The psalmist put *father* and *judge* in the genitive case so that by joining them together he could demonstrate what God is. He further added: *God in his holy place.* We must understand from this "He

who preserves His decree unchangeable and stable." As father Augustine said of Him: "You change the seasons, but You do not change Your designs."[10]

7. *God who maketh men of one mind to dwell in a house: who bringeth out them that were bound in strength.* In this and the following two verses comes a statement of who God is according to the twelfth type of definition which in Greek is called *kat'epainon* and in Latin *per laudem;*[11] God is He who makes men of one mind to dwell in a house. As the Acts of the Apostles has it: *The multitude of believers had but one heart and one soul.*[12] An alternative explanation is that prophets and evangelists were of one mind in the Lord's house, and spoke the word of truth in harmonious proclamation. Elsewhere the prophet himself is to say: *How good and how pleasant it is for brethren to dwell together in unity!*[13] For in this house dwell those who are joined with each other in reciprocated charity. *In a house* indicates the Church. Next comes: *Who bringeth out them that were bound in strength.* Here he points to the human race whom God freed by the power of His strength when they were bound by the law of sin; for He bound the devil, and brought out them that were bound whom the devil kept in captivity. *Brought out* expresses the idea well, for He freed them from hell and raised them to the joys of the heavenly kingdom.

In like manner them that provoke to anger, that dwell in sepulchres. He still speaks of them that were bound, whom He brings forth by His strength; they provoke the Lord to anger when they blaspheme and indulge in wicked associations. These are the ones who in their lives dwell in sepulchres, that is, they are buried in the malodorous activity of the flesh. There is mention of them in another place too: *Their throat is an open sepulchre.*[14] For though He roused the dead before men's eyes, He delivered the human race from sepulchres when He restored to them the joys for which they prayed because of their true faith.

8. *O God, when thou shalt go forth in the sight of thy people, when thou shalt cross through the desert.* We must add to this verse: "Thou shalt be recognised." The psalmist still continues with praise of God's activities. God went forth in the sight of the people of Israel when He appeared in a column of fire, and when in the desert He filled them with abundance of manna.[15] But this verse is better related to the Christian people: He goes forth in the sight of the people when by His

strength He brings out them that were bound, when He revives those that dwell in sepulchres. The person of fidelity beholds Him on recognising His devotion and power in His mighty works. Further, He crossed through the desert when He came to the Gentiles, whom no prophet approached and who like the desert were rendered desolate and strangers to the Lord's words.

9. *The earth was moved: for the heavens released their drops in the presence of God, mount Sinai in the presence of the God of Israel.* After the interposition of a diapsalm, he passes to a second beginning in which he recounts what the divine power granted to the people of Israel. *The earth was moved:* in other words, the men of earth by witnessing such great miracles believed. *The heavens released their drops in the presence of God,* when in place of raindrops manna came down in God's presence, because His presence was acknowledged through a column of fire and of cloud. Mount Sinai too smoked in the presence of God when Moses happily received the Law there on two tablets; for it is written in Exodus: *All mount Sinai smoked because the Lord had come down on it.*[16]

10. *Thou wert setting aside for thy inheritance a free rain, O God: for it was weakened, but thou hast made it perfect.* He explains his earlier words, *the heavens released their drops.* The free rain was that which the Jewish race deserved at that time in their eagerness to eat; the world experienced an unprecedented miracle to satisfy their desire. That rain was indeed free, and not the general rain which is sprinkled everywhere. Finally these words follow: *Setting it aside for thy inheritance, O God;* for God did not grant to other nations what He then pityingly bestowed on the Jewish people. His inheritance was the Jewish people; as we read: *The Lord's portion became his people, Jacob the lot of his inheritance.*[17] If this inheritance was temporarily weakened through utter disbelief in the Lord Saviour, He perfected it when He admitted the other nations to add to the ranks of believers.

11. *In it shall thy animals dwell: thou hast prepared the poor in thy sweetness.* Because he had earlier said of the Lord's inheritance *but thou hast made it perfect,* he now adds the means by which He made it perfect. The animals were the Gentiles who were empty of true religion, but when they came to the Lord they became His, for they now lack nothing and are filled with the full light of reason. They will

dwell in the Church when through the Lord's pity they have come to accept the worship of the true religion. He next explains once again what these animals are with the words: *Thou hast prepared the poor in thy sweetness. Thou hast prepared* suggests the predestined, who from the beginning of the world have been prepared through God's mercy. *In thy sweetness:* this is not the world's sweetness for here they suffer bitter things, but the sweetness to come in which God's poor are superior to the richest kings.

12. *The Lord shall bestow on those who preach the word many powers.* This verse is construed as: "The Lord shall bestow many powers on those who preach the word." He gave many powers to the apostles who preached His word with reverent praise, for they were permitted to heal crowds of invalids. It is certain that the gospel itself contains many powers; what has greater strength than the saving of souls who could perish through their guilty errors? As the apostle James says: *A man must know that he who causes a sinner to be converted from the error of his ways saves his soul and covers a multitude of sins.*[18]

13. *The king of virtues is of the beloved, and the beauty of the house resides in division of the spoils.* We must analyse this verse with greater care, for it is complex through the subtle meaning of the words. We must interpret *the beloved* here as the Son of the Father; as the Father says in the gospel: *This is my beloved son in whom I am well pleased.*[19] This figure is called *antonomasia*, meaning "set in place of the name," when a different expression is used but in such a way as to make the necessary clarification.[20] So the King of angels and powers, who commands the virtues, is the Father of the Beloved; and this is appropriately interpreted to refer to the Son as well, for another psalm says of Him: *The Lord of virtues, he is the king of glory.*[21] It is certain that this description fits the holy Trinity; but here he wishes it to be understood of the Father, because he wrote *of the beloved,* that is, Christ. Next comes: *And the beauty of the house resides in the division of the spoils.* The beauty of God's house is recognised when the spoils of the devil, in other words wicked men, are transferred to God's Church, for the spoils of the devil are those people whom the Lord delivered with strength when they were bound.[22] As He Himself says in the gospel: *No man enters into the house of a strong man and robs his goods unless he first binds the strong man; and then shall he plunder his house.*[23]

With these spoils He has adorned the house of His power, and has brought joy to holy Church, since He frustrated the desires of the fierce enemy.

14. *If you sleep amongst the midst of lots, the wings of a dove covered with silver, and the hinder parts of her back with the appearance of gold.* Here sleep does not connote the stupor of slumber or oblivion to the world such as we usually experience in sleep; by sleeping he means here resting in the commands of the Lord, and relaxing for that purpose. For with the authority of the Fathers we must interpret *lots* as the two Testaments, amongst which the psalmist warns Christians to seek restraint and rest. So the sense is that his advice to the faithful is: "If you sleep surrounded by the two Testaments, in other words if you lay your soul to final rest in the divine scriptures. . . ." The Lord attests that sleeping stands for death when in the gospel He says: *Lazarus our friend sleepeth, but let us go to wake him out of sleep.*[24] Next comes: *The wings of a dove covered with silver;* as we said earlier, throughout these passages we must understand "will bear you up." Wings signify the speed which leads us to that native land if we desire to obtain rest here through the Lord's law. The dove covered with silver denotes the Church, rightly called a silvered dove because she has the innocence of a dove and through her divine utterances she gleams with silvery brightness. Of her Scripture says: *One is my dove, one is my chosen one.*[25] The hinder parts, that is, the last days, of this dove gleam brightly with the appearance of gold because when she has left this world her grace will gleam more brightly than gold. Note that in this world she is compared to silver, but the psalmist says that at the resurrection she will be adorned with the appearance of gold. As was already said in Psalm 44: *The queen stood on thy right hand in golden clothing, surrounded by variety.*[26]

15. *When he appointeth heavenly rulers on the earth, she shall be whited with snow in Selmon.* After the silence of a diapsalm, he passes to the third limb of the psalm, in which he recounts the gifts which the Lord has bestowed on the Church by conferring on her the glory of resurrection. *Heavenly rulers* are the apostles and holy bishops or other faithful, who by heaven's gift have been able to rule their bodies in praiseworthy fashion. The ruler (*rex*) gets his name from ruling (*a regendo*); this title is rightly allotted to those who by the power of heaven have been able to discipline worldly desires. As Paul says in

rebuking certain persons: *You rule without us, and I would to God you did rule that we also might rule with you.*[27] So when the Lord harmoniously appoints and distributes these rulers over that dove which he mentioned earlier, they will be made whiter than the snow in Selmon; that is, those who are known faithfully to rule and govern the Church gleam whiter than snow. As for the phrase, *in Selmon,* the name of this mountain means "shadow," and here is appropriately interpreted as divine power.[28] It is this power which defends us from the surge of vices, refreshing us and granting us heavenly gifts. As the angel announced to the blessed Mary: *The holy Ghost shall come upon thee, and the power of the most High shall overshadow thee.*[29] Elsewhere we read: *Protect me under the shadow of thy wings.*[30] This is *shadow* in the good sense; then in the following verse he is to praise the mountain. The expression, *whited,* can bear also a bad sense, as we read in the Acts of the Apostles: *God shall strike thee, thou whited wall.*[31] The gospel too attests this sense: *You are like to whited sepulchres, which are full of dead men's bones.*[32]

16. *The mountain of God, a fruitful mountain, a curdled mountain, a fat mountain.* By the fifth type of definition, which in Greek is called *kata tēn lexin* and in Latin *ad verbum,*[33] the prophet explains what the mountain of Selmon earlier mentioned actually is; it is as if he said: "By mountain I mean the Lord Saviour Himself, of whom the prophet Isaiah prophesied: *In the last days the mountain of the Lord shall be prepared on the top of mountains, and it shall be exalted above the hills: and all nations shall go to it.*"[34] He added: *A fruitful mountain,* for from it unfailing sweet streams descend, containing waters which irrigate and are spiced with heavenly sweetness. He appends: *A curdled mountain,* because it nurtures infants which have to be fed not on solid food but on curdled milk; he further added: *A fat mountain,* because it is always most fruitful through its own fertility. What a mountain, so briefly praised but abundant in the nature of its heavenly attributes! From it waters of life run down; milk is provided for the salvation of babes; spiritual fatness is observable; all that is believed to be the highest good is implanted in the grace of this mountain.

17. *Why have you taken this to be the fruitful mountains? It is the mountain in which God is well pleased to dwell.* He said earlier that the mountain is to be interpreted as the Lord Saviour; and now the prophet censures any suggestion that these mountains are to be com-

pared to the lofty peaks of the apostles, though we know that they too through God's grace are fruitful. In adding: *It is the mountain in which God is well pleased to dwell,* he clearly indicates which mountain we should understand here. Christ is the only mountain who was pleasing to the Father as His dwelling-place; as He Himself attests: *This is my beloved Son in whom I am well pleased.*[35] The words, *to dwell in,* have a common reference to Father and Son; as Christ Himself says in the gospel: *I am in the Father, and the Father is in me.*[36] The expression, *in which God is well pleased to dwell in it,* is not appropriate to normal speech, so we are to say that it is a peculiarity of divine Scripture, just as in Psalm 65 the psalmist said: *There, in it.*[37]

For there the Lord shall dwell unto the end. After referring to those mountains which he had said were not to be understood, those comparable to the high peaks of the apostles (for he was speaking of the Lord Saviour, Mountain of mountains, holy One of holy ones, King of kings, Lord of lords), he returns to the Author of salvation, saying that the Lord Christ dwells in those mountains, that is, the apostles, until the end. This means to the most perfect limit of His majesty, the end without end, the perfect fullness of all good things.

18. *The chariot of God is a manifold mass of ten thousand, thousands of them that rejoice: the Lord is among them in Sina, in the holy place.* It is customary for divine Scripture to speak in allegory, so that when it says one thing it wishes to be understood differently, and you will find this often in this psalm. So here *chariot* indicates the harnessing of men, for charity binds holy people as animals are joined by straps and yokes. So the Lord says: *My yoke is sweet and my burden light.*[38] So the Lord's chariot is the common mind of the saints, which He bestrides like a charioteer and controls so that they perform His will by the law that wins salvation. But to show that the chariot is not entrusted to horses but assigned to the thoughts of men, he speaks of *A manifold mass of ten thousand,* which is well seen to refer to countless people, not to horses. He added: *Thousands of them that rejoice,* which must be understood as referring to the faithful particularly. To reveal the fullness of their joy he says: *The Lord is among them;* this is the climax of their great joy, the wondrous sweetness of all blessings. Next comes: *In Sina, in the holy place. Sina* is the mountain of the desert on which Moses received the Law, and its meaning is "command."[39] The Lord

truly takes his rest there, for His presence is usually observed in sacred commands.

19. *He has ascended on high, he has led captivity captive.* How beautifully this behaviour at His triumph is described through the figure of the *idea!*[40] The idea is that vision which arouses our emotions by setting the future before our eyes. Christ crucified descended into hell, and having freed souls from captivity led them to heaven. It was inevitable that death should perish when life penetrated its kingdom. These are the spoils mentioned earlier by which holy Church is adorned, and from which the kingdom of the Lord is to be filled. He ascended simply because He had descended to deliver us. *On high* means above the heavens, because He is known to transcend all heights and glories, and He sits at the right hand of the Father. Who could now have doubts about the freedom granted to the faithful, since death is destroyed and captivity led captive?

He has given gifts to men, yea, those who do not believe that you dwell therein, Lord God. He still continues with the image of the triumph, when a holiday is proclaimed to arouse boundless joy, and gifts are proffered. The gifts of the Lord consisted of the bestowal of the mighty works of the Spirit upon the apostles. Alternatively, there is the explanation of the teacher of the Gentiles: *To every one of us is given grace according to the measure of the giving of Christ.*[41] At this point we must supply the words "He converts them," so that the statement can make sense to us without tampering with the words. For *those who do not believe that you dwell therein,* in other words, those who do not bother to enter the innermost abode of the Lord seeking to dwell with the faithful in His house, are converted by the Lord God, who in pity bestows faith in Him on the human race. This is the grace which is granted freely, for His blessings go before us when His good will is also granted to us.

20. *Blessed be the Lord day by day: God our salvation will make our journey prosperous for us.* After that description of the triumph comes a short but mighty statement of praise: *Blessed be the Lord day by day,* that is, He must be blessed every day and at all times. He who has ascended on high, has led captivity captive, and has given gifts to men, will make our journey prosperous for us. That journey denotes the course of life which has already become prosperous because the world

recognises its Redeemer. He added: *God our salvation,* so that no-one should have doubts about the prosperity of his journey if his saving guide is the Lord Christ. Let those taking pleasure in man-made shows tell me: what do they observe in the stately exhibitions mounted by consuls which is comparable? Let them direct their minds and eyes, for their salvation let them mentally gaze on this scene from which they can be directed not to fleeting joy but to exultation without end.

21. *Our God is the God who saves us, the outcome of the Lord's death.* After the break of a diapsalm, he passes to a fourth new beginning, in which he states how the Lord saved us by His death. He said: *Our God, the God who saves us;* let us understand here: "has the power to save us." So He who saves us is our God Jesus Christ, who condescended to die for us, who has ascended on high and achieved what has been mentioned. Finally follows: *The outcome of the Lord's death.* The outcome of the Lord's death delivers us, causes us to quit enduring death; so I think this is a splendid addition, to prevent human weakness asking why I die, or why I fail. Our plaints are tended by a great healing, the outcome of the Lord's death. The Lord's death brings as outcome the resurrection for which the faithful long. It was truly a wonderful and unique outcome because He emerged from hell, and by His gift granted us our departure from there.

22. *But God has shattered the heads of his enemies, of those who traverse heads of hair in their sins.* To counter the belief that evil deeds of stubborn men would go unavenged, he says: *But God has shattered the heads of his enemies,* that you might be aware that vengeance is visited also on the unfaithful and stubborn. *The heads of his enemies* are the sponsors of the Jewish secession, but doubtless also the teachers of heretics. The Jews persecuted Christ in the flesh, but the teachers of heretics rage more cruelly against Him in His Godhead, if that is not a sacrilegious statement. Next comes: *Those who traverse heads of hair,* in other words, those who seek out petty detail of lying allegations, so that they seem to be traversing and scrutinising even men's very heads of hair. This indicates the sophistry of their foolish questions, which ignore what will be profitable and in execrable argumentation seek out what is inessential. Then to prove that their researches are empty, he added: *In their sins.* In their case the meditation which led to sinning was foolish; in their camp are Manichees, Priscillianists, Donatists,

Montanists and the rest who involved themselves in the foul odours of their muddy doctrines.[42]

23. *The Lord said: I will convert them from Basan: I will convert them from the depths of the sea.* In this verse we must follow totally the authority of the most learned Jerome, because his clear translation disposes of all our questions.[43] *The Lord said;* let us examine what He said, for it is some great promise which the Lord makes. Basan means "aridity";[44] it had gained possession of the human race through the aridity of sin, but the Lord converted them to His greenness when He poured streams of salvation over them, and made crops sprout in their lives, which previously bore destruction. He added: *I will convert them from the depths of the sea;* understand "those whom he has freed from the deep waters of this world." We have already seen from our repeated reading that *sea* must be interpreted as this world, bitter to the taste and rough with waves of vices.

24. *That thy foot be stained with blood: the tongue of thy dogs which were enemies, at his doing.* He now explains the destiny to which the people who he earlier stated are to be converted from the depths of the sea will be led. His *foot,* signifying their implementing a good mode of life, attains the blood of glorious martyrdom. The people who previously walked in the sea of pleasure He subsequently made to walk in blood, which is a hard road for the flesh but a blessed path for the soul; this is the path which we tread through His mercy, if we place our hope and hearts in Him. Next is added an obscure statement which we must none the less embrace eagerly: *The tongue of thy dogs which were enemies.* In Scripture, dogs are cited in both a bad sense (as when Paul says: *Beware of dogs, beware of evil workers*)[45] and a good sense as here. Of dogs in this good sense the Canaanite woman says in the gospel: *Yes, Lord, for the dogs too eat of the crumbs that fall from the table of their masters.*[46] In another psalm comes the statement: *They shall be converted at evening, and shall suffer hunger like dogs.*[47] These dogs never cease to bark for the Lord, and guard His house with the most prudent intelligence. So here the psalmist says: *The tongue of thy dogs which were enemies, at his doing.* These dogs earlier were enemies, but subsequently they have defended the Lord's Church with noisy barking. He added here the only possible source of this transformation, *At his doing.* He means the Lord, who changes bitter into sweet, sadness into joy, accursed illness into sound health.

25. *Thy goings have been observed, O God: the goings of my God the king, who is in his sanctuary.* The whole of this verse indicates the incarnation of the Lord Saviour. It says: *Thy goings have been observed, O God,* whether through the appearance of the body which He took on, or through the traces of His preaching, by which He walked with innocent and holy steps in this world. The additional words, *the goings of my God the king,* clearly indicate the Lord Saviour, for He walked in the world as King in a special sense, as Scripture records in the inscription of the Passion: *King of the Jews.*[48] The psalmist clearly described His body with the words: *Who is in his sanctuary,* for the body of the Lord Christ was a holy temple, in which lay the fullness of the Godhead which traitorous men could not see.

26. *Princes had precedence, joined with singers in the midst of young female timbrel-players. Princes* denotes the apostles, princes of the people who believed and also had precedence in the sanctity of their teaching; so they were made leaders because the people subsequently followed them. He added: *Joined with singers;* so that you would not believe that they were few in number, he aptly added a crowd of singers, who now sounded forth the Lord's praises not only in song but also in goodly deeds. Next comes: *In the midst of young female timbrel-players,* that is, young ladies in the flower of youth who exploited their timbrels, in other words, the tension of their bodies, for the praises and glory of the Lord, wasting themselves away by fasting and rejoicing the more in the affliction of the flesh. This is what God's power achieves even today with many maidens. But other spokesmen have suggested that by timbrel-players is meant the churches, whose halls in unison celebrate the Lord's praises amidst the people's rejoicing, which is in a sense comparable to timbrels. The psalmist is to speak of these churches in the next verse.

27. *In the churches bless ye God the Lord from the fountains of Israel.* After the break of a diapsalm, the psalmist has moved on to the fifth part of the psalm, in which he states where the Lord should be blessed. He says to the faithful: *In the churches bless ye the Lord,* for the Lord should be blessed not in various meeting-places of pagans nor in the grottoes of heretics, but in the Catholic Church where there is right faith and true confession of it. He is rightly praised where He is not cursed; how is He to accept praise from the person who defiles himself with unholy superstition? Next comes: *From the fountains of*

Israel, that is, from the Christian teaching which the apostles poured into the nations. A fountain of religion flowed out from them through the other nations. Fountain (*fons*) is derived from *fovere* (to warm)[49] because it revives our bodies when wearied with toil.

28. *There is Benjamin, more youthful in fear. The princes of Juda their leaders, the princes of Zabulon, the princes of Nephthali.* We have said that this manner of speaking is peculiar to the divine scriptures when it intersperses Hebrew names for some hidden meaning. There is no doubt that all the prophets longed for the blessed era of the gospel-preaching; and here the psalmist earnestly seeks this, and by the names of the tribes is shown to have pointed to the Lord Christ and to the apostles themselves. *There is Benjamin, more youthful in fear; There* means in the temple at Jerusalem, where Paul heard the Lord's words, as the text of the Acts of the Apostles clearly expounds;[50] or as some have it, *there* means in the Church, where the psalmist said they must hymn their praise. *Benjamin* points to the apostle Paul who was of the tribe of Benjamin, for he himself says: *For I am an Israelite of the seed of Abraham, of the tribe of Benjamin.*[51] *More youthful in fear* refers to the fact that he was youthful in years, as Luke states in the Acts of the Apostles in comment on the suffering of blessed Stephen: *And false witnesses laid down their garments at the feet of a young man whose name was Saul.*[52] Though youthful in years, he was still more youthful in fear when he collapsed at the words of the Lord who in pity thundered at him: *Saul, Saul, why persecutest thou me?*[53] The word youthful, *adolescens,* derives from *adolere,* to grow.[54] *The princes of Juda* indicate the Lord Saviour, who was descended from the tribe of Judah, as John says in *Revelations: The lion of the tribe of Juda, the root of David, hath prevailed.*[55] The psalmist added: *Their leaders,* meaning leaders of the people set in the Church; this must be referred not only to Paul or the Lord but also to those whom he mentioned next: *The princes of Zabulon, the princes of Nephthali.* Zabulon and Nephthali were tribes established by the Jewish people from which the rest of the apostles are said to derive their origin; all these are well termed princes, because the crowd of the faithful followed them as men most worthy of honour and primacy. The term princes includes also those who are not kings, as we read at the dedication of the tabernacle in Exodus when twelve princes, one from each of the tribes of Israel, offered gifts.[56] It is appropriate to explain too the meanings of the names themselves since

they are known to be apt for the Church. Judah means "confession," Zabulon "dwelling of strength," Nephthali "my enlargement."[57] If you examine these carefully, you will associate them appropriately with the Catholic Church.

29. *Entrust it to thy power, O God: confirm, O God, what thou hast wrought in us.* After that most blessed proclamation of the Lord's coming, the prophet, as if he has now received a gift beyond reckoning, turns to the Father and says: *Entrust it to thy power.* The power of the Father is the Lord Jesus Christ; as Paul says: *Christ, the power of God and the wisdom of God.*[58] *Entrust* refers to the distinction between Persons, for they have perennially the one wish and the one power. The psalmist describes the task: *Confirm, O God, what thou hast wrought in us.* It is a large request that God confirm in us that faith in Him which He has deigned to give us. It was the Lord's work that the blind Gentiles were inspired with the light of truth, and could recognise the true Lord Saviour. As Paul has it: *Blessed be the God and Father of our Lord Jesus Christ, who has blessed us with all spiritual blessings in heavenly places: he chose us in him before the foundation of the world, that we should be holy and unspotted in him.*[59]

30. *From thy temple, which is in Jerusalem, kings shall offer presents to thee.* Since gifts are usually offered in the temple, he says here that they must still be offered from the temple at Jerusalem. So who are the kings who offer presents from the temple at Jerusalem? They are those who dwell in God's Church living an upright life, who offer up the purity of their hearts, when the final reward is attained, when the wheat is separated from the chaff, and when Jerusalem undivided becomes mother of all who have lived under Christ's law. We can interpret *Kings* in two senses: the very emperors offer themselves to God, or the word represents the faithful granted the merit of ruling their bodies through Christ's grace. Observe that Jerusalem means nothing other than the Lord's temple, in which lies the vision of peace, unadulterated by the hostility of heretics sowing disharmony.

31. *Rebuke the wild beasts of the forests, the council of the bulls amidst the cattle of the people.* So that the sacred faith mentioned by him may be strengthened by the protection of confession, the prophet says: *Rebuke the wild beasts of the forests,* that is, "refute the proud and aggressive who remain unbending in debased belief, so that Your

attack on them may be reinforced protection for the faithful." He uses
the image of wild beasts for wicked men or for the devil as in the
words of another psalm: *The boar out of the wood hath laid it waste, and
a singular wild beast hath devoured it.*[60] He added *The council of the bulls
amidst the cattle of the people;* supply "must none the less be rebuked";
in other words, the fierce heretics who with heads held high seduce
innocent souls and draw to their herd those whom they deceive with
their unhappy beliefs. Then too *the cattle of the people* are the women
of the most fickle character whose inclinations are easily led, who
follow teachers of wickedness as cattle follow bulls. Of them Paul
says: *For of these sort are they who creep into houses and lead captive silly
women laden with sins, who are led away with divers desires, ever learn-
ing and never attaining to the knowledge of the truth.*[61] So the reason
why such people are rebuked is next appended.

*That those tried with silver may not be excluded: scatter thou the
nations that delight in wars.* The usefulness of that rebuke is revealed,
for whilst falsehood is refuted, truth is none the less approved. It is
necessary to rebuke the wild beasts of the forests, to reject the bulls, to
inveigh against the cattle of the people so that those who are tried—
that is, those whom spiritual love has continually guided towards purity of heart, as like the purest silver they shed by heat the dross of
their vices—may be strengthened and make progress. There is added
the decision to scatter heretics, for they are the nations that delight in
wars; in other words, those who strive by disputations not to make
spiritual progress but to enslave innocent souls by their perverted
persuasion.

32. *Let them swiftly make offerings from Egypt: let Ethiopia hasten to
offer her hands to God.* We are not reluctant to interpret this verse too
according to the translation of father Jerome, who is to be followed
because of the true sense of the Hebrew, and who frees us from the
grip of ambiguity.[62] Egypt and Ethiopia are always used in a bad sense
to express the murky blackness of their inhabitants; this is the figure
called *synecdoche,*[63] or the whole from the part. It points to the world
which was subject to the devil and oppressed by the thick darkness of
vices, but here is illumined by the Lord's light, and has deserved to
attain the gifts of eternal light. So the prophet advises the peoples of
the Gentiles swiftly to make gifts from Egypt to God, in other words,

their souls cleansed of the foulness of the world. Ethiopia too must hasten to offer her hands to God; this is a metaphor drawn from men at war, for to avoid a cruel death they offer their hands to the victors, and thus by laying down their arms they may escape the hazard of death. In this sense Ethiopia too is warned not to linger in entrusting herself to God so that she may prosper in defeat whereas she was bedraggled when at liberty.

33. *Sing to God, ye kingdoms of the earth, hymn ye the Lord.* He ended this section too with a fine exhortation. By saying *Ye kingdoms of the earth*, he sought to point to the whole human race, for though there are nations without kings, the term embraces all nations imaginable. The word *sing* here implies purity of soul, and the word *hymn* those holy works known to be acceptable to the Lord.

34. *Hymn God who mounteth above the heavens of heavens from the east: behold, he will give his voice, the voice of his power.* After the interval of a fifth diapsalm, the prophet passes to the sixth section, urging the faithful to hymn God who has risen from the dead. The God whom they were to hymn is described: it is He who *mounteth above the heavens of heavens*, none other than the Lord Jesus who came down from heaven to liberate the weakness of our nature. He mounts above the heavens of heavens too in sitting at the right hand of the Father. We must observe that you will often come across in divine Scripture heavens in the plural; though we read that *In the beginning God made heaven and earth,*[64] on occasion both are found in the plural forms *coeli* and *terrae.* This manner of speech is quite widespread, for we speak loosely of singular things in the plural, and of plural things in the singular. His phrase, *from the east* clearly denotes Jerusalem which lies in the region of the east. From there the Lord ascended to the heavens before the eyes of the apostles; the earth teems with many miracles in which the belief of the faithful is schooled more by what they see than by what they read. The apostolic father Leo has spoken beautifully and truly about this: "What elsewhere cannot but be believed, there cannot but be seen."[65] Why does the understanding strain when it is instructed by the sight? Why are words read and things heard doubted, when all the mysteries of human salvation accumulate before the sight and the touch? So I say that we should not pass over that

image of the tabernacle which the blessed apostle Paul so wonderfully applied to the triumphal ascension in his Letter to the Hebrews: *But Christ, being come a high priest of the good things to come, by a greater and more perfect tabernacle not made with hands, that is, not of this creation, neither by the blood of goats or of calves but by his own blood, entered once into the Holies, having obtained eternal redemption.*[66] And again: *For Jesus is not entered into the Holies made with hands, the patterns of the true, but into heaven itself that he may appear now in the presence of God for us.*[67] So this splendid deed which is here described with outstanding joy is shown to have been an appropriate prefiguration of that tabernacle. Next follows: *Behold, he will give his voice, the voice of his power.* This can be understood in many ways. He gave His voice when He said to the man with the palsy: *Get up and walk,*[68] when He raised Lazarus, when He bade the demons vacate the persons who were besieged. He will also give the voice of His power when He bids the human race rise again on the last day. What more powerful act could there be than to restore ashes into a living body and living substance, to escort that mortal nature to gain the gifts of eternal life? As we read in the gospel: *The hour will come when all that are in the graves shall hear his voice and shall come forth.*[69]

35. *Give ye honour to God over Israel: his magnificence and his power are in the clouds.* He still continues with the exhortations. When he says: *Give ye honour to God,* he urges them to win honour themselves, for he who gives praises to God makes himself praiseworthy, and likewise he who gives honour to Him undoubtedly seeks distinction for himself. The expression, *over Israel,* denotes the Catholic Church, in which God is truly beheld when we experience Him with upright faith. So He can be seen only where the people are known truly to confess to Him. Next comes: *His magnificence and his power are in the clouds. Magnificence* refers to His always performing great things, *power* to the fact that the outcome observes His command, for He does all that He pleases in heaven and on earth.[70] This magnificence and power of the Lord are said to lie in the clouds, but not the visible clouds which give rain and become thick and dense; he refers to certain powers abounding in superhuman reason which serve the Lord's commands by their intellectual state. Of them it is said: *I will*

command my clouds to rain no rain on it.[71] The word clouds abounds in many meanings; it refers also to apostles and prophets.

36. *God is wonderful in his saints, the God of Israel.* So that you may not interpret the clouds as those in the sky, he says: *God is wonderful in his saints,* whether they are angels or men who obey His orders. He repeats *The God of Israel* so that he may implant in men's hearts the place where the God of wonders appeared.

He will give power and strength to his people, blessed God. So that none may lose confidence because of human weakness, and believe that they are failing to attain such great rewards, it is affirmed by truthful promise that the Lord will give the power of patience and the strength of faith to His faithful so that they can attain eternal rewards. To indicate more clearly who can bestow the gifts he earlier mentioned, he added: *Blessed God,* in other words, He who must be blessed by the mouths of all and at all times so that just as He never ceased to bestow kindnesses, so He may always receive blessings. We must not believe that His praises will be briefly unfolded by these two words, for the person who ponders the Scriptures blesses the Lord, the person who fulfils His commands by holy action blesses the Lord, and the person who faithfully confesses to Him blesses the Lord. In this way that briefly defined praise is diligently discharged during the period of our whole life.

Conclusion Drawn From the Psalm

This spacious psalm has run on like those great rivers which bring more abundant fertility to the fields as they lay hold of more land. But this is a river to be absorbed not by the mouth but by the ear. It is a river to be drunk by the mind, not the body. It is a river which ever irrigates without watering; it inebriates pure minds, and brings back to mental sobriety those who are drunk on sins. It is the water which at once removes thirst and hunger, which does not ooze away after we digest it, and which once drunk perpetually increases. Let us pray that this stream may uninterruptedly possess us. We shall be no barren desert, but a fruitful field if through the Lord's kindness the course of this river keeps us for ever in its hold. Remember that this psalm has described the Lord's ascension with a vividness which is remarkable, and excels all the other psalms.[72]

COMMENTARY ON PSALM 68

1. *Unto the end, for them that shall be changed, by David.* All are aware that *unto the end* refers to the Lord Saviour, who in this psalm will recount His passion in such a way that the authority of the gospel witnesses to His words, and the apostle Paul is also instructed to follow its example. We read in the gospel: *They gave me gall for my food, and in my thirst they gave me vinegar to drink;*[1] and elsewhere: *The zeal of thy house hath eaten me up.*[2] Then too the apostle Paul says: *Let their table become as a snare before them, and a recompense, and a stumbling-block; let their eyes be darkened, that they see not, and their back bend thou down always.*[3] These verses, watchful reader, you will find written in this psalm. So who could doubt that this psalm squares with the Lord's passion, when it is lent such notable and great authority for the expression of this meaning? Next comes: *For them that shall be changed.* This change, then, points to the Christian people who have abandoned the wickedness of the old man, and have been changed by the gift of a new birth. The expression, *for them,* must be taken as meaning that the passion of the Lord is revealed to have been truly bestowed for all the faithful. The name David is also appended, so that both beginning and end of the heading may accord with the Lord Christ. As He says of Himself: *I am alpha and omega, beginning and end.*[4] Thus the power of the entire psalm is announced by the arrangement of this heading. Remember that this is the fourth of the psalms to discourse at greater breadth on the passion and resurrection of the Lord.

Division of the Psalm

Hitherto I have marked the divisions unhesitatingly with the help of diapsalms, realising that such separations are rightly made where heaven-sent silences emerge. But now we must pray to the Lord that just as He provides our path on earth He may likewise grant us careful journeys in the depths below. Throughout the whole psalm, as we have said, Christ speaks in the persona of a slave. In the first section He begs the Father to grant Him safety, since He has suffered many hardships and attacks undeservedly at the hands of the Jews. In the

second, He asks on behalf of His members that the hope of the faithful
residing in His resurrection may not be frustrated; He says that He has
borne with untroubled mind all that those wicked men were seen to be
heaping on Him. In the third part He begs that His prayer be heard so
that his stainless way of life may be freed from the foulness of this
world. He says that God knows the extent of the snares with which
His enemies oppress Him so that through the dangers which they have
contrived He may meet His passion and death. In the fourth part, by
virtue of His foreknowledge he proclaims the future fate which could
befall His enemies. In the fifth section, speaking as a slave He proclaims that He is poor; and accordingly He says that he will offer
praises to the merciful Father, and urge the faithful to trust in the
Lord, who has freed His Church from the confrontation of this world,
and has forseen for His saints a life in that abiding happiness to come.

Explanation of the Psalm

2. *Save me, O God, for the waters are come in even unto my soul.* All
that is sane in our minds proclaims that the Godhead of Christ is
impassible; but He took on our weakness, which could have been
subject to destruction. It is in keeping with that dispensation that He
now cries: *Save me, O God;* as He was obliged not to shrink from the
death which He had voluntarily undertaken, He asked for the aid of
resurrection so that His humanity could be more speedily saved. He
suffered because He sought to do so; those who witness to Him also
suffer, but unwillingly. This was how the Lord spoke to the apostle
Peter: *When thou shalt be old, another shall gird thee and lead thee
whither thou wouldst not.*[5] The reason is now given why He asked to be
saved: *For the waters are come in even unto my soul.* Quite often divine
Scripture attests that waters should be interpreted as the rebelliousness of the common folk and the uprisings of the people, as in the
passage: *Perhaps like the waters they had swallowed us up,* and immediately after: *Our soul hath passed through a torrent: perhaps our soul had
passed through water unsupportable.*[6] So the Jewish people entered even
the soul of the Lord Saviour, when with wicked hearts they presumed
to crucify Him.

3. *I stick fast in the mire of the deep, and there is no substance: I am

come into the depth of the sea, and a tempest hath overwhelmed me. First we must gain acquaintance with the figure called *characterismos,* which in Latin is termed *informatio* or *descriptio.*[7] The Lord is shown to be describing His future passion by certain allusions. But let us investigate this verse minutely, for it is seen to be of considerable profundity. God created man from the mire of the earth as it existed at that time, but not from the mire of the deep; men became the mire of the deep when they were held subject to original and daily sin. Through this mire of hell the Lord was stuck fast when the crowd of mad Jews cried out: *Crucify him, crucify him.*[8] Their flesh was the mire, for it had surrendered to original sin, but their wicked guile had lent it the additional title of mire of the deep. *Limus* (mire) is derived from *ligans humum,*[9] binding the earth. Next comes: *And there is no substance.* All evil has no substance, because that which has not been created by the Lord cannot be called substance, for it does not subsist but occurs, and it does not abide outwardly but only appears to exist on emerging.[10] So He truthfully says that our flawed nature was not a substance, since He knew that He had not created it. We read similarly in another psalm: *And my substance is as nothing before thee,*[11] specifically not the substance which God could create, but that which was flawed when it succumbed to the persuasion of the devil. Alternatively we must simply interpret thus: "I was crucified through the wickedness of the Jews, and the flesh has not the power to escape the deadly suffering." He added: *I am come into the depth of the sea, and a tempest hath submerged me.* How can He who walked over the sea with implanted steps, who stretched out His right hand to Peter so that he would not drown, say that He has been submerged by a tempest? Here the depth of the sea denotes the extensive madness of the people, and again the tempest is the roused rebelliousness of lunatics. It was this which submerged the Lord Saviour when it forced His progress to the cross.

4. *I have laboured with crying: my jaws are become hoarse: my eyes have failed, while I hope in my God.* We must ask how it is that He says here: *I have laboured with crying,* whereas we read in the gospel: *He answered them not a word.*[12] Isaiah too says this: *He was led as a sheep to the slaughter, and as a lamb before the shearer he did not open his mouth.*[13] Both statements are true, were fulfilled; for He was silent when betrayed so that the dispensation in His regard should attain the finality

which brought salvation to the world. But He certainly cried out when He said: *Just Father, the world hath not known thee,*[14] or again; *Father, if it be possible, let this chalice pass from me,*[15] and again; *Father, forgive them for they know not what they do.*[16] He also laboured with crying when He said: *Woe to you, scribes and Pharisees; woe to the world because of scandals,*[17] and such like. So He laboured with crying when faithless men did not listen to Him. The labouring suggests crying which goes unheard, for we do not speak of labouring when referring to people who we attest have gained their prayer. Later come the words: *My jaws are become hoarse.* When hoarseness seizes our jaws, our words reach the ears of others with distorted sound. So He rightly says that His jaws are become hoarse because that sacrilegious people wholly failed to listen to His words. He added: *My eyes have failed, while I hope in my God.* Let us believe that the eyes which failed in the Lord were His physical eyes closed in death, for He who never sinned by the law of the flesh kept the eyes of the heart ever alert in His divinity.

5. *They are multiplied above the hairs of my head who hate me without cause.* We know that our hair has been given us as adornment for the head. In the same way the apostles were given to the Church, so that as locks adorn the head so too all the faithful may be seen to beautify the Church. So to show that the number of the unfaithful is greater than that of the committed, He says that the faithless Jews were multiplied above the number of hairs, that is, above the number of true believers. But if you wish to interpret the phrase literally, it has been expressed by the figure of *auxesis,*[18] so that by this means he could indicate the size of the Jewish mob. Next comes: *Who hate me without cause;* obviously without cause, since they persecuted Him whom they ought to have begged to show kindness. We are said to hate a person without cause when we curse him without his having given any offence; thus already in Psalm 34 we find the words: *For without cause they have hidden their net for me unto destruction.*[19]

My enemies are grown strong, who wrongfully persecute me: then did I pay what I took not away. Earlier He described His enemies as *multiplied over the hairs of his head,* and so that you would not think them merely numerous and not harmful, He has added: *They are grown strong,* when they are shown as achieving what they were trying to perform. So that you might realise that it was their own guilt that roused them, He added: *Who wrongfully persecute me,* in other words, without cause, as He stated earlier. It was indeed wrongful that He who had come to save the Jewish people should instead have encountered them as enemies. He added: *Then did I pay what I took not away.* Adam when persuaded by the devil took away when he dared to lay hands on what had been forbidden by the command imposed on him. He was rightly condemned to death because he chose to spurn Him who enjoined life. But Christ did not take away anything sinful. He knew no wickedness, yet He accepted the cross as if He had committed some crime, and on our behalf He paid the penalty not justly deserved with His own person. So that He could discharge the bond of our death, He himself paid to the necessary extent for the entire guilt.

6. *O God, thou knowest my foolishness: and my offences are not hidden from thee.* He passes to the second section, where He now speaks in the person of His members; for the Christ whom Paul describes as *the power of God and the wisdom of God*[20] cannot be foolish, but He is said to be foolish as representing them who, as the psalm-heading states, are known to have been changed. From being foolish they became truly wise, because after their great sins they perceived the grace of true religion. Of them the same apostle says: *The foolish things of this world hath God chosen that he may confound the wise.*[21] In similar fashion Christ speaks of the Head when referring to His body when He says: *My offences are not hidden from thee,* for it is certain that all we do is wholly clear to God, whereas often the things which we perpetrate are unknown to ourselves, for sins whisk them away. Of human ignorance it has been well said: *Who can understand sins?*[22] So these offences are rightly to be attributed to those who are to be absolved from their debts. The Lord Christ had no sins; as He Himself says: *The prince of this world will come, and in me he will not find anything.*[23] Of Him Isaias too says: *He hath done no sin, neither was there deceit in his mouth.*[24] Rather, Paul describes him as: *Him who knew no sin, he hath made sin for us,*[25] in other words the Father set His Son as a Victim to be sacrificed for sins. Father Augustine in his *Enchiridion* has elegantly handled and discussed this topic.[26] So we must interpret *foolishness* and *offences* here as referring to His members. This figure is called *tapinosis* or depreciation,[27] when the greatness of something is diminished by the most demeaning words.

7. *Let them not be ashamed of me who look for thee, Lord God of hosts:*

let them have no fears for me who seek thee, O God of Israel. See how this verse has clarified the fact that His earlier words were spoken on the part of His members, for Jesus Christ prays that they who with splendid longing maintained hope of His resurrection when they could not behold it with bodily eyes should not be ashamed of Him. As the Lord Himself said: *Many prophets and just men have desired to see the things that you see, and to hear the things that you hear.*[28] So the weakness of the flesh prays that it may turn out in no way other than the holy Spirit had foretold through the prophets. When He speaks of *Lord God of hosts,* He is showing that nothing is impossible to God's omnipotence; for He who governs hosts must necessarily achieve all things at His will. Observe too how this is shifted to the mystery of the resurrection. He says: *Let them have no fears for me who seek thee, O God of Israel;* in other words, "Let them not endure the scoffing of men about My lying asleep when they are known to be seeking You." He did well to add *God of Israel,* so that they should not be diverted by the weakness of the flesh when they could observe His divinity.

8. *Because for thy sake I have borne reproach: shame hath covered my face.* He returns to His own identity for the next six verses almost up to the end of the section, recounting the various taunts which He endured from the Jews. This figure is called *synathroismos* or in Latin *congregatio,*[29] when we assemble many things in a single group to arouse odium. He bore reproach when the Jews said to Him: *You cast out devils by Beelzebub,*[30] and elsewhere: *Behold a man that is a glutton and a wine-drinker, a friend of publicans and sinners,*[31] and in another place: *Is not this the carpenter's son?*[32] and so on. There follows the usual reaction that befalls those who are abused when on a good errand; their chagrin momentarily becomes greater, the more they realise that unjust rebukes are fashioned against them.

9. *I am become a stranger to my brethren, and an alien to the sons of my mother.* He calls the Jews here brethren for they were joined to Him by proximity of blood; He became a stranger to them when they refused to show belief in Him. He was Himself descended from the seed of Abraham in the flesh, but they were disinherited by their evil deeds and divorced from their connexion with the patriarch. As Christ says in the gospel, *If you were the sons of Abraham, you would have done the works of Abraham.*[33] He added: *And an alien to the sons of my mother.* We term as alien any person dwelling temporarily in our

house who is received not through blood-relationship but as a foreigner. By His mother He means the synagogue, from which He was sprung when He deigned to be born of the Jewish race. He calls sons of His mother those whom He earlier described as His brethren; but these sons, if they had been truly sons, would not have regarded the Lord Christ as an alien, but would have received Him as a most dear brother.

10. *For the zeal of thy house hath eaten me up: and the reproaches of them that reproached thee are fallen on me.* This is the judgment which the evangelists relate.[34] Accordingly none should doubt that this psalm foretells the truth of the Lord's passion, since the incarnate Son of God spoke these very words. The zeal of God's house devoured Him when He fashioned a rope and overturned the chairs of the dove-sellers and the tables of the money-changers, to teach them that the holy temple was one thing and an office for business another. What followed this zeal is clearly appended: *And the reproaches of them that reproached thee are fallen on me.* For after those unworthy men were rebuked by salutary warnings, they directed reproaches at Him like a shower of weapons, so that in return for holy admonitions they offered the exchange of rebukes. They said: *Is not this the son of Mary and Joseph?*[35] and elsewhere: *We know not from whence he is,*[36] and such like which the mad crowd of Jews uttered. But as regards His words, *of them that reproached thee,* we must ask why He says that the Father was reproached when we do not read that any such thing was done by the Jews at the time of the Lord Christ's passion. Yet the Father was reproached by them as He is to state in Psalm 77: *And they spoke ill of God. They said: Can God furnish a table in the wilderness?*[37] Or when those madmen said of the calf which they had fashioned: *These are thy gods, O Israel, that have brought thee out of the land of Egypt.*[38] So Christ the Lord rightly says now that the reproaches are fallen on Him which they levelled in earlier times at God the Father, so that you may be aware that this was done from wicked habit rather than as an innovation. Next comes: *Are fallen upon me.* These words are to show the outcome of death which He undertook when He deigned to accept the cross. Evils fall upon us when we cannot avoid them.

11. *And I covered my soul in fasting, and it was made a reproach to me.* We speak of fasting when we abstain from bodily food and refrain from satisfying our hunger by eating anything. The Lord Christ uses

this metaphor and says He fasted because He could not find any faith at all in men when He greatly longed for it. We find the same expression in Psalm 34: *But as for me, when they were troublesome to me, I clothed myself with haircloth and I humbled my soul with fasting.*[39] Similarly He said He was thirsty when He approached the Samaritan woman and asked for water with the words: *I thirst; give me to drink,*[40] when He desired to acknowledge from her lips the faith which He sought. But because this fasting was derived from men's lack of devotion, He said: *I cover my soul,* meaning that He wrapped it, so to say, in a cloak of sadness. Next comes: *And it was made a reproach to me.* Good men are always a reproach to the wicked, because they are quite unwilling to countenance their crimes. They carefully withdraw from them, join in no compact with them. These reproaches bear witness to the slaps, scourgings and spitting which the Lord Saviour endured from the mad crowd.

12. *And I made haircloth my garment: and I became a parable to them.* Haircloth signifies the sadness and tears when the Lord was affected by the weakness of the human condition, and wept when He was about to raise Lazarus up;[41] for nowhere do we read that the Lord wore haircloth. Further, He became a parable to the Jews when He appeared to teach that people of the flesh by means of certain similitudes. As we read in the gospel: *The Lord spoke a parable to the crowd.*[42] In another psalm He says: *I will open my mouth in parables.*[43] A parable is a comparison made by some similitude between things differing by nature. This was the manner of His forethought, so that those who could not understand heavenly things were able to take in what they heard through earthly parallels.

13. *They that sat in the gate were exercised in my regard: and they that drank wine made me their song.* Those who sit at the gate are they who mingle with gatherings of men in unremitting curiosity. Just as a city-gate receives crowds of people departing and returning, so the various crossroads or streets are filled with large numbers; in fact *porta* (gate) gets its name because everything is conveyed (*portari*) from there.[44] He is saying that His passion was the gossip of the Jewish nation so that no-one was found to be a stranger to such conversation. This argument is attested by the gospel-passage in which Cleophas was questioned by the Lord before He revealed Himself, and Cleophas replied: *Art thou the only stranger in Jerusalem, and*

hast not known the things that have been done there in these days?[45] All the citizens are shown to have taken part in this gossip, since the Man thought to be unaware of the affair is called a stranger. Up to this point He has spoken of the rebukes and abuse of the Jews; next, in my opinion, He speaks of the faithful: *And they that drank wine made me their song.* Those who sing to God are people whose direction is decided by praiseworthy activity, and who perform by deeds the heavenly commands which they accept as advice. His words, *they that drank wine,* force us to relate this passage to the faithful; this is not the wine inducing drunkenness but the spiritual wine of which we read: *Thy cup which inebriateth me, how goodly it is!*[46] The ones who sang were they who through their heavenly understanding drank the nectar of salvation. Other commentators[47] apply this phrase to the faithless Jews, who thought that their designs had been achieved, and who in total intoxication chattered about the execution of the Lord.

14. *But as for me, my prayer is to thee, O Lord: the time of thy good pleasure, O God, in the multitude of thy mercy.* He passes to the third section, in which in answer to the abuse of the Jews the heavenly Teacher explained the holy nature of His prayer, thus suggesting that we should confront the taunts of men not with fiery brawling but with devoted prayers. Let us now examine what *the time of thy good pleasure* is. It is the time when He freed the world, which was in danger of imminent destruction, by the blessing of His incarnation. This is the time of His good pleasure, of which the apostle Paul says: *Behold, now is the acceptable time, behold, now is the day of salvation.*[48] It is the time which prevailed over all ages, the time which repaired the falling world, the time which bestowed eternity and salvation. He appropriately explains how this time emerged; He says it was *in the multitude of thy mercy.* If the multitude of His mercy had not existed, we could certainly not have been redeemed in our subjection. It was no slight mercy which overcame such massive sins. There was indeed a multitude of wickedness, but the mercy which prevailed was much more abundant. As Psalm 50 has it: *And according to the multitude of thy mercies, blot out my iniquity.*[49]

Hear me in the truth of thy salvation. Once He had mentioned the time of mercy, at which through His passion He afforded salvation to the world, the next step was to pray that His resurrection too might come to pass, which He had truthfully promised through the prophets.

So He prays to the Father not in His divine nature, in which He is always His equal, but in the weakness of His assumed humanity, in which He is lesser than the Father.

15. *Draw me out of the mire that I may not stick fast: deliver me from them that hate me, and out of the deep waters.* Through the weakness of the flesh which He had taken on, a powerful exposition is made here of the wretchedness in which the human race lies; we are instructed that we too should pray to God in the same words which we know our Head used in prayer. We must clearly investigate briefly here why He earlier said that He was stuck in the mire and here prays that He may not be bogged down in it. He was stuck in the mire precisely because He was confined by the frailty of the flesh which He had assumed, as a result of which He underwent the death of the cross. Here He appropriately begs that His soul should become a stranger to muddy desires, that is, to the longings of this world. This request is fittingly undertaken on behalf of His members, for He himself could not stick fast in the mire as He had no stain of sin. *Deliver me from them that hate me:* this clearly refers to the Jewish people, for when Christ rose again their hatreds were made vain and ineffective. His phrase, *out of the deep waters,* clearly signifies that people who were deep in the evil of their design, and rough in their uprisings against Him.

16. *Let not the tempest of water drown me, nor the deep swallow me up: and let not her pit shut her mouth on me.* This verse expresses a sentiment similar to a previous one. In verse 2 of the psalm He says: *I am come into the depth of the sea and a tempest hath overwhelmed me;* here too He asks that He be not drowned by the waves, that is, by the most fierce storm of this world, which like the sea overwhelms souls when it envelops them in the vice of wickedness. In short, He fittingly works in this theme throughout the whole discussion; He says: *Nor let the deep swallow me up.* The deep is precisely the deep of sins which greedily, so to say, gulps down the souls of the wicked, so that those who lose hope about their evil deeds cannot return to repentance. As Scripture has it: *The wicked man, when he is come into the depth of sins, contemneth.*[50] He reiterates His earlier message in different words but with the same sense: *And let not her pit shut her mouth on me.* A pit is a hole in the earth dug quite deep, into which sinners actually fall, metaphorically speaking, when they do not abandon a wicked intention, and it hastens to shut its mouth upon them when they persist in

their most wicked purpose up to the time of their death. So He begs that all this be removed from Him, because He had no contagion of sin, in order that His members might realise the enormity of the dangers overhanging them if they were not revived by the kindness of the most merciful Lord. This figure is called *metabole*[51] or repetition, when a single idea is repeated with a change of words. *Pit* is found here in the bad sense, as in Genesis: *Now the woodland vale had many pits of slime;*[52] into them are dispatched the sacrilegious and the wicked. There are also pits mentioned in the good sense, indicating that the divine Scriptures are based on depths most profound; for example, those of the patriarch Abraham, of Isaac, and of Jacob, or that from which Moses in the desert sated the Jewish people at the Lord's command.[53] Both kinds of pit have the same name, but their purpose is different; the first kind leads to hell, the second conveys us to the kingdom of heaven.

17. *Hear me, O Lord, for thy mercy is kind: look upon me according to the multitude of thy tender mercies.* Now that the dangers of human frailty have been expounded as was necessary, He returns to the prayer that wins salvation, speaking on behalf of His members: *Hear me, O Lord.* He adds the reason why He should be heard: not that human nature deserves it, but because the Lord's mercy is kind and always ready to do good when the prayer made to Him is holy, and the entreaty wholly untainted. The sacred Teacher sought to explain that kindness, so He added: *Look upon me according to the multitude of thy tender mercies.* He always returns to that mercy, which He knows is the advocate of the weak, and before which all sins give place, however numerous they are known to be. Observe that where the Father's love is sought, it is always the person who is said to be looked upon; for if the Lord regarded our sins He would undoubtedly condemn us.

18. *And turn not thy face away from thy boy, for I am in trouble. Hear me speedily.* The role of human person which He assumed is preserved. Just as He prayed that He might be looked upon, so now He begs that the Father should not turn His face away from His boy. We often find the Lord Christ described as a boy because of the purity of His innocence. The simplicity of youth bestows on a boy the blessing of aversion from vices and from the malice of the world. As Christ Himself attested: *Of such is the kingdom of heaven.*[54] *Boy* is used as in the text: *Behold my boy whom I have chosen, my beloved in which my soul*

delighteth,[55] and in another passage: *A boy is born to us, and a son bestowed on us.*[56] So He rightly asks for a speedy remedy, for He knows that He has been placed in affliction. Salvation is sought with all our strength when it is desired at a time of necessity.

19. *Attend to my soul and deliver it: save me because of my enemies.* He says: *Attend to my soul,* so that it may gain true deliverance when the Godhead is appeased and looks kindly on it. The reason too follows why it should be attended to: *Save me because of my enemies.* Because of His enemies He sought the most speedy aid of resurrection, so that those who had spurned Him when crucified would have to believe in Him when He rose on the third day. Thus when freed by such a blessing they could be rescued from eternal damnation.

20. *For thou knowest my reproach, my confusion, and my shame: in thy sight are all they that afflict me.* The Lord Saviour shouldered reproach, confusion and shame as He shouldered death; He did not bear them as one guilty, but endured them all though innocent, so that like a good Master He could in pity and by the example of His own patience school us when placed in a similar plight. He endured reproach when the Jews said: *He blasphemed: what further need have we of witnesses?*[57] He endured confusion when the mad throng of Jews cried: *He saved others, he cannot save himself.*[58] He endured shame when beaten by slaps and scourgings, and handed over to Pontius Pilate as one guilty, when he was a spotless Lamb. Next comes: *In thy sight are all they that afflict me,* that is, those who did such things were already set before the eyes of the Godhead, although as yet they had clearly not been brought to the moment of judgment. That they should commit a wicked crime in the presence of the Majesty is calculated to rouse odium.

21. *My heart hath expected reproach and misery. And I looked for one that would grieve together with me, but there was none: and for one to console me, and I found none.* His heart expected reproach and misery when of His own volition He endured the iniquities of the Jews and His various sufferings, and out of consideration for the peril of humankind He cheerfully accepted His passion. As we read in the gospel: *With desire I have desired to eat this pasch with you.*[59] That crucifixion could not have been profitable if the desire for it had not been there; in the face of His desire and willingness, the madness of the Jews could have no chance whatever of prevailing. Next comes: *And I*

looked for one that would grieve together with me, but there was none. If you investigate the Lord's passion, you will find that His disciples too grieved when He was consigned to Pilate, and so did many others of the faithful when He was led to the cross. But we must not interpret the psalm here as referring to the grief of the faithful when they showed it in all possible ways, and Peter because of it was told: *Get thee behind me, Satan.*[60] Here we must instead look for sadness in His persecutors, but they were as one in scorning it, showing no allegiance to Him when they joyfully carried out their crime. Even in the midst of His passion the Lord prayed for them, saying: *Father, forgive them, for they know not what they do.*[61] No grief of theirs revealed a comrade for Him, for He saw that they carried out their crime with obdurate minds. He added: *And for one to console me, and I found none.* Holy teachers find consolation in the people who benefit from the words of their preaching, but because the Jews' obstinacy resisted the Lord Saviour, He justly says that He has found no-one to console His heart.

22. *And they gave me gall for my food: and in my thirst they gave me vinegar to drink.* This verse brought to a climax that passion of the Lord which we must revere. Matthew recounts that when the Lord said: *I thirst,*[62] He was offered gall mixed with vinegar, so that the bitter and sour drink could truly reflect the Jews' deeds. Christ said: *I thirst,* because He could not find in them the faith for which He longed; they offered Him their most bitter manners which were amended by no remorse.

23. *Let their table become as a noose before them, and as retribution, and a stumbling-block.* In His prayer after He has explained the passion to come, He passes to the fourth motif. This is not a curse but a prediction of what is to befall; throughout the entire section He predicts that the Jews will experience a fate commensurate with their deeds. The Lord's table is a mental feasting on both Laws; on it those who hunger with mental greed for the Lord's delicacies feast as dinner guests, and are filled with the most health-giving drunkenness of the holy Spirit; that table is the one which the apostles' circle surrounded as they ate the feast served by the gift of heaven. *Table* is found in both good and bad senses. As Paul says: *You cannot be partakers of the table of the Lord and of the table of devils.*[63] The Jews occupied the sacred table when they observed the Lord's commands with integrity. But

once they began to abstain from the food of faith, their table which lay
before them was consigned to the Gentiles, so that the deprivation of
their blessedness might irk them the more since it lay before their
eyes. That is how the Lord rebukes them in the gospel, with the
words: *The kingdom of God shall be taken from you and shall be given to a
nation yielding the fruits thereof.*[64] In case anyone is troubled by His
phrase, *their table,* when it is known to be actually the Lord's table, the
Lord likewise says in the gospel: *In your law it is written;*[65] not that the
Law belonged to the Jews, but it is known to have been proclaimed to
them. Next comes: *As a noose,* implying that the Jews might be bound,
and might fall by that letter of the law which they tried to tighten on
others. The words, *and as retribution,* are added, because the deprivation of that table bestowed on the Gentiles was retribution for their
evil deeds. Since they were unwilling to feast at that table, they are
seen deservedly to be excluded from it. Also added are the words: *And
a stumbling-block,* for when they abandoned the Source of peace, they
awakened brawls and debased practices among themselves, It was a
severe punishment and a stern vengeance when no food passed their
lips, and they lost the means of refreshment for the human race.

24. *Let their eyes be darkened that they see not: and their back bend
thou down always.* It is clear that this was the penalty allotted to the
harsh Jews, that their eyes should be darkened and they should not see
the true Sun. Those unwilling to attend to Him have the punishment
of blindness imposed on them. He added: *And their back bend thou
down always.* Those weighed down by excessive weight of sins experience the fate of perpetually stooping and bending their necks to the
earth. They are given no chance of looking up to heaven, for they are
burdened with the weight of sins. *Dorsum* (down) connotes dropping.
His word, *always,* is applied to the wicked who were not converted
through rendering any satisfaction.

25. *Pour out thy indignation over them: and let thy indignant anger
take hold of them.* The use of *pour out* indicates the greatness of His
anger, which like a river flows down in spate. *Over them* likewise
denotes this; not only can it reach them, but is seen to overwhelm
them. Next comes: *And thy indignant anger.* Indignant anger occurs
when severe vengeance is awakened at the execution of the sinner,
and the feared penalty ensues. He added: *Let it take hold of them,* just as

though it were seizing with a pair of hands the condemned and terrified persons; they cannot evade the punishment allotted to their
crimes.

26. *Let their habitation be made desolate: and let there be none to
inhabit their tabernacles.* It is clear that both these fates befell the Jews,
for the city of Jerusalem was destroyed and numerous people captured.[66] Private houses were abandoned and the tabernacles, in other
words, the Lord's temple or the King's palace, remained without a
worshipper. Observe that he called their private houses a habitation,
but spoke of inhabiting the Lord's temple; in the first expression there
is a habitation for our bodies, but in the second we inhabit when we
throng with the attitudes of committed hearts.

27. *Because they themselves have persecuted him whom thou hast smitten: and they have added to the grief of my wounds.* In the midst of the
most just punishment of the unfaithful is explained the cause of the
Lord's passion, for they persecuted Him who was smitten, they executed with accursed savagery Him who had been consigned to them.
As He Himself says: *You would have no power over me unless it had been
given from above.*[67] We also read: *He that spared not his own Son, but
delivered him up for us all.*[68] Moreover, Scripture expresses more absolutely the fact that God often smites for our salvation, as in the passage
of Deuteronomy: *I will kill, and I will make to live. I will strike, and I
will heal.*[69] So the Lord Jesus Christ says that He was struck to achieve
the allotted order of things by which He suffered. But the Jews
emerged accursed because they were shown to have fulfilled by their
cruel aspiration what had to be done on behalf of the world. Next
comes: *And they have added to the grief of my wounds.* The loving
Lord's grief of His wounds lay in His not obtaining satisfaction of His
thirst and hunger for a faithless people; the Jews imposed the passion
glorious for Christ but most destructive for themselves. They imposed an abhorrent end on Him who had come for the salvation of all.

28. *Add thou iniquity upon their iniquity: let them not come into thy
justice.* The first iniquity of the Jewish nation was that they destroyed
the prophets who were sent to them. Iniquity was added on their
iniquity when they chose to crucify our Lord Jesus Christ Himself.
The parable of the husbandmen and the vineyard in the gospel attests
this: *A man planted a vineyard and made a hedge round about it,* continu-

ing up to: *They cast him out of the vineyard and killed him.*[70] *Add thou iniquity* is a metaphorical statement, just as elsewhere we read: *The Lord hardened Pharaoh's heart.*[71] It is not that the Lord imposed wickedness, but that He allowed to happen what He judged was advantageous for the salvation of many. The punishment for the sin is appended: *Let them not come into the justice* of the Lord, that is, let them not share with Christ in the kingdom of justice. Those who in this world observe justice with the clear sight of the mind attain that justice which is the Lord's kingdom. This cannot be attained by the faithless, who have been blinded by obduracy of heart. Alternatively, we may interpret: *Add thou iniquity upon their iniquity* as "They slew the prophets, and killed the Lord."

29. *Let them be blotted out of the book of the living, and with the just let them not be written.* It is quite well known that such words are frequently said in Scripture about God metaphorically. Erasure, writing, possession of a book are aids bestowed on man to assist his memory, so that what he could not retain through mental weakness he could acknowledge with the help of writing when something demanded it. Moses addressed the Lord in this way: *If thou do not spare this people, strike me out of the book that thou hast written.*[72] But this book is the Lord's imperishable knowledge and abiding judgment. So the statement about the Jews: *Let them be blotted out of the book of the living,* means not that their names were written down, but that they considered they were. What is written there is indelible, because it is wholly ordained by predestination. No outcome will be able to affect what heavenly providence has decreed. Next follows: *And with the just let them not be written;* this is the same mode of speech, stating that God writes down what He will carry out at the Judgment. As He says in the gospel; *But rejoice in this, that your names are written in heaven.*[73] He says that this cannot happen to those not changed by rendering devoted satisfaction, as the psalm-heading lays down.

30. *But I am poor and sorrowful, and the salvation of thy countenance, O God, hath embraced me.* After He has appropriately prayed with prophetic proclamation for what was to befall the Jews, He passes to the fifth section, in which He expounds in many ways the holiness of His purpose as it emerges from the economy of the incarnation. He says: *I am poor and sorrowful;* His poverty is described by Paul: *Being rich, he became poor for our sake, so that through his poverty we might be*

rich.[74] His sorrow is described by Isaiah: *He himself hath borne our iniquities, and hath sorrow for all.*[75] Why does He say: *I am,* when many poor persons are sorrowful? The reason why He appropriated sorrow to Himself was because no other shouldered it for the sin of the whole world. This is the use of *metriasmos* or moderate statement,[76] when we depreciate some important matter by a lowly prayer. It is frequently employed with reference to the person of the Lord Christ. Next comes: *And the salvation of thy countenance, O God, hath embraced me.* The almighty Word embraced humanity precisely when He deigned to reconcile the world to God; *The salvation of thy countenance* is the figure of the only-begotten Son, in which He is equal to the Father. This is rightly said to bring salvation, because through it medicine is bestowed on the faithful.[77] The phrase, *embraced me,* describes Him in a role lesser than that of the Father, so that He might be set at the Father's right hand, and cast off His poverty and sorrow.

31. *I will praise the name of God with a canticle: and I will magnify him with praise.* This can properly be understood as uttered on behalf of those who are changed, in other words, His members. Our Head praises the name of the Lord with a canticle in the Church when there is great unity of the faithful in their song of exultation. He both *praises* and *magnifies* in us, because He knows that we truly offer praise. If He hungers when we are hungry, and thirsts when we thirst, how does He not praise with us when we offer praise?

32. *And it shall please God better than a young calf that bringeth forth horns and hoofs.* Here the power of psalmody is explained. Praise poured out from a pure heart is much more acceptable to God than the slaughter of cattle can please Him. In earlier times the regular offering was a young calf sacrificed to atone for sins. This victim signified the gifts of the innocent and their new life to come, which would have a means of defence in its horns and protection for its feet in its hooves, by means of which they could tread underfoot the rough features of the world with their most holy manner of life. His expression, *bringing forth horns,* denotes that the Christian people ever increases every day through the Lord's power.

33. *Let the poor see and rejoice: seek ye God, and your soul shall live.* After He has said that sacrifices of praise are greater than the ritual slaughter of cattle, he turns to His poor, reminding them that they should rejoice, since the offering now is dependent not on resources

alone but on the feeling of the heart, in which even the poor person can be very rich. So do not boast, you wealthy ones, because you can possess calves bringing forth horns and hooves, for God spurns these things and looks for a most pure heart, which is possessed rather by those who do not with guilty mind seek your riches. Next comes: *Seek ye God, and your soul shall live.* He advises the poor to seek the food of the mind rather than that of the body, and to long for the bread of angels by which the soul is filled instead. Let us examine what He says: *Your soul shall live,* The souls of sinners also live, but we use the word *live* correctly of that which participates in the happy life of blessedness, whereas that which is burdened by enduring sadness and the heaviest griefs may indeed live, but we justly regard it as dead.

34. *For the Lord hath heard the poor: and hath not spurned his prisoners.* We are gratified to hear that the poor are heard; but let us investigate more carefully who these poor are. The poor of Christ, as we have often said, are those who despise the riches and pleasures of this world, and choose poverty in human affairs so that they can be filled with spiritual feasting. The Lord Christ says that they are heard who are filled with poverty in this world, and rejoice in the security of their poverty as if they possessed the world's entirety. As Paul's advice has it: *As having nothing, and possessing all things.*[78] As for His phrase, *and hath not spurned his prisoners,* we are all in common imprisoned by the law of sin, and enmeshed so to say in chains because we seek human desires. But the Lord does not spurn His prisoners, in other words those bound by His laws. Those whom He acknowledges as chained by His rules He frees from the noose of the flesh.

35. *Let the heavens and the earth praise him, the sea and all things in them.* We are offered here a brief, comprehensive statement. The mention of heaven means that all heavenly things must praise Him, the mention of earth all earthly things, the mention of the sea all things that swim. Then, so that the conclusion might embrace the totality, He added: *And all things in them.* So whatever creature is known to exist is invited to praise the Lord. In the same way Paul embraces all things with the words: *That in the name of Jesus every name should bow, of those that are in heaven, on earth, and under the earth; and that every tongue should confess that the Lord Jesus Christ is in the glory of God the Father.*[79]

36. *For God will save Sion, and the cities of Juda shall be built up. And they shall dwell there, and they acquire it as an inheritance.* What we powerfully grasp from the greatness of these praises is the nature of the Lord's work in the building up of His Church; for sky, earth, sea and all that are in them are urged to praise the Lord, for He will save Sion which is wearied with many persecutions and hardships. Sion is set next to the temple at Jerusalem; it is quite a small hillock, but great in the nature of its name, for it means 'observation'.[80] From it alone is God descried, and on it are directed tne hearts of the faithful and the one blessedness of all rational creatures, if they ponder on the Lord as Creator. The cities of Judah were built up when the Catholic Church through holy humility was spread through the whole world. The Lord takes joy not in buildings with walls, which will certainly crumble with age, but in the devotion of the faithful, the living stones from which the Jerusalem to come is built. The phrase, *cities of Juda,* is well formulated, for it means the cities of the Lord Saviour, who by physical descent is sprung from Judah. As we read of Him: *The lion of the tribe of Juda hath prevailed.*[81] But so that you would think not merely of cities but also of the dwellings of the future, He says: *And they shall dwell there.* The faithful alone dwell in the place where they abide with constancy in purity of mind. This is the Church, in which Christians dwell on earth. They acquire it as an inheritance when through the Lord's pity they attain the eternal Jerusalem; for the inheritance is that which will be granted not by death but by the Testator who lives for ever.

37. *And the seed of his servants shall possess it, and they that love his name shall dwell therein.* A blessed promise brings this psalm to a close, but we must match with the greatness of the reward an equal attempt to apply our understanding. We must interpret *seed* here as holy activity and not physical descent. It is clear that those who boasted descent from Abraham were rebuked, for the Lord said to them: *If you were the children of Abraham, you would have done the works of Abraham.*[82] But if we are willing to interpret *seed* as good actions, as has been done in many texts, we can uphold the statement without qualification. The persons who imitate those pleasing to God by the worth of their actions will possess the land to come, which will not change or end, but is the kingdom of the Lord which He faithfully promises to His

saints. So that you would not drag down the meaning of this seed to mere physical origin, in which the Jews make their greatest boast, He added the general instruction: *And they that love his name shall dwell therein.* His earlier phrase, *the seed of his servants,* is identical with *they that love his name* here. *Shall dwell therein* bears the sense of "They will attain enduring blessedness." This land does not bring forth thorns and thistles, nor does it feed men by toil, nor breed poisons, nor ever lose its inhabitants; for it will get its light not vicariously through sun and stars, but more blessedly and lastingly from its own Creator. Observe that the psalm is brought to a close in due sequence. First, it was uttered in the person of the Lord Christ; then it began with a prayer; thirdly, it related the events of the Lord's passion; fourthly, it agreed in harmonious truth with the words of the gospel; and fifth, it ended its message with hope for the faithful people. Thus this is the fourth psalm which through the earlier proclamation of the Law prophesied the Lord's passion.[83]

Conclusion Drawn From the Psalm

We have listened to a psalm wondrous in its heavenly arrangement, in which it is clear that the power in His divinity is matched by the humility in His humanity. The sacred Word took on the nature of our weakness—the psalm-heading says that it is: *For them that shall be changed*—so that He might free us from a truly deserved death by the death which was not His due. He entered the confines of Hell so that the lower regions could be opened up. Death was conquered by the arrival of the Saviour, and rightly forfeited its enduring darkness once it received the eternal light. He conquered the devil by means of the human nature which Satan held subject; in his strength Satan was overcome by the weakness of the flesh, when God raised above all creatures endowed with reason that which was feebler than all the spiritual powers. As the apostle remarked: *To which of the angels has he said, Sit at my right hand?*[84] No other nature has been made one with Christ except that of our flesh, which He took and which was glorified. Truly almighty, truly merciful is He who made blessed what was condemned, restored what was lost, freed what was subjugated, made our miseries strangers to us, and by His own death enabled man to live, when though He was created immortal the devil had caused Him to die. Almighty God, we pray that having deigned to suffer for us in the flesh, You may bestow on us the crown of which You deign us worthy.

COMMENTARY ON PSALM 69

1. *Unto the end, of David, to bring remembrance that the Lord saved me.* As has quite often been stated, *the end* and *David* indicate the Lord Saviour, towards whom these words of the faithful are directed, for the whole of this psalm is spoken in the name of the martyrs who toiled under various persecutions but never ceased to keep their hope planted in the Lord. The phrase, *to bring remembrance,* has been added. There are two ways in which we remember: first, when in recollection of sins we fear heavenly justice, and second, when with pure hearts we cling fast to the benefits granted us. So in Psalm 37 where these words occur' there is fear of future judgment and recollection of sins; but in the present passage hope of liberation and the promised trust in our future reward are maintained. To demonstrate that he remembered this, he added: *That the Lord saved me,* so that it could be shown that this recollection was born not of fear but of the kindness which had been received. It was fitting that, since in the previous psalm the Lord Christ had recounted His passion, and had added the hope of resurrection, so here His members should speak in similar vein after their Head, so that they might proclaim their faithful sufferings, and entertain hope of the resurrection for which they prayed.

Division of the Psalm

The crowd of martyrs and confessors toiling under manifold but blessed calamities pray to the Lord in the first section to be freed from dangers at the hands of persecutors, so that He may nullify their taunts. Thus when these enemies have been converted they may be ashamed of their former words and so find salvation. In the second section they pray that the crowd of the faithful may exult in glorifying the Lord, since He deigns to aid and deliver His poor and needy ones.

Explanation of the Psalm

2. *O God, give thought to my assistance: O Lord, make haste to help me.* The holy proclamation has its beginning in the Lord, for the psalmist knows that from Him comes protection to those in danger. So that the band of most blessed martyrs might reveal their hardships, they say: *Give thought to my assistance.* We ask for assistance when we are prostrate before dangers, so that once we are raised by some remedy we can overcome the calamities of different sufferings. *Give thought to* means "Look kindly on," for the Lord witnesses all things, even when He is not besought. But people in danger tend to believe that they are delivered if they know that they can be observed by the Lord. So that the blessing which they knew would come should not be postponed further, they added: *O Lord, make haste to help me. Make haste* is uttered as though the divine mercy were tarrying, and the tortures were becoming more grievous owing to its delayed arrival. So in their haste to be delivered from the calamity of this world, they say to the Lord: *Make haste.* In Him are combined both will and speedy completion, for all things serve the Creator because all things are slaves to His command. Thus many matters are enclosed in one short verse; this figure is called *epitrochasmos,* or whirling of speech,[2] when things to be understood in a broader sense are explained briefly. But the most eloquent Cassian, who is not to be followed in all things indiscriminately, in his Tenth Conference,[3] in which he discourses at length about the usefulness of this passage, attaches such glory to it that whenever his monks undertake a task, they do not begin without declaiming this little verse three times. By repeatedly reiterating it, he shows that memorising it is extremely useful.

3. *Let my enemies be confounded and ashamed that seek my soul: let them be turned backward and blush for shame that ponder evils for me.* The crowd of martyrs in imitation of their Head demands an improvement in their enemies with the words: *Let my enemies be confounded and ashamed.* Such confounding takes place when a wicked conscience in zeal for the truth acknowledges its desires and is troubled

because of the wickedness of its deed. Being ashamed occurs when we realise that justice has been damaged by our action, and we fear to incur punishment for these matters. Such shame comes upon people who condemn their wickedness and who in eagerness for conversion hasten to return to love of the Lord. The crowd of the faithful did well to speak of their soul in the singular, for as Scripture says they have one soul and one heart.[4] So their enemies sought the soul of the faithful not to show it reverence, but to give satisfaction to their gods by detaching it from its body. This occurred in the sufferings of martyrs, when the hostile persecutor slaughtered them. The expression *sought* we find also in the good sense, as in the passage: *Flight hath failed me, and there is no one that hath sought my soul;*[5] because the word is ambiguous, the additional words, "To deprive me of it," are appended here[6] to make you realise that *sought* is being used in the bad sense. The next words are: *Let them be turned backward and blush for shame that ponder evils for me.* The person who is turned backward is, as we have often said, the one who abandons debased intentions and follows the Lord's commands. So the meaning is this: "Let those who have evil intentions experience this retribution so that they do not continue in their iniquity." What devoted hostility of saintly persons this is, even when considered as hostility! They desired a better fate for their enemies than the enemies seemed to seek for themselves in time of prosperity.

4. *Let them be presently turned away blushing for shame that say to me: 'Tis well, 'tis well.* This is a refinement of the earlier sense, that those known to rebuke the most committed persons with false praises should in shame swiftly be compelled to abandon their intention. *'Tis well* is the expression of one who praises; but here we must interpret it as spoken ironically or jeeringly, since it is clearly spoken by enemies. Alternatively it rebukes those who praise the afflictions and pains of martyrs, but do not ascribe to the glory of the Creator what has been granted them through abundant love; jeering at disasters of others and praising men for their unassisted achievement are both sinful.

5. *Let all that seek thee, O Lord, rejoice and be glad in thee, and let such as love thy salvation say always: The Lord be magnified.* After this statement about the wickedness and the conversion of persecutors, the second section prays that all who love the Lord Christ should rejoice and be glad. For persecutors, confusion and shame are sought; for the

devoted, exultation and abiding joy. As the Lord says in the gospel: *And these shall go into everlasting punishment, but the just into life everlasting.*[7] But the psalmist inserts this mode of rejoicing appropriately, for by saying *in thee* he confesses that the joy which boasts in human presumption is transitory. Joined to this is: *All that seek thee, O Lord.* They do not seek You by their own powers, but are sought out by Your fatherly love. You gazed from heaven and sought that the human race might seek You; for the Lord came to us that we might deserve to return to Him. But those who seek the Lord are advised for their welfare on what they ought to say. They must say always: *The Lord be magnified. Always* indicates continuing time, because we must never cease praising the Lord. So that the meaning may become clearer to us, the order of words should be: "Let them who love your salvation always say: *The Lord be magnified.*" We should realise that the word *magnified* has been adopted from human practice, for it is he who is extolled with praises and grows in men's good opinions who is magnified. But God experiences no increase, for He is known to be Fullness in its unique and inexpressible totality. He cannot grow from any external source, for He continually gives growth to all created things. But we profit from magnifying Him, and our awareness ever increases when with pious hearts we offer praises to God.

6. *But I am needy and poor: God helps me: thou art my helper and my deliverer, O Lord: make no delay.* When the crowd of the faithful followed the example of the Lord's passion, they transferred His very words to their psalmody. For in another psalm the Lord says in His own person: *But I am needy and poor: the Lord is careful for me,*[8] just as here the words are spoken on the lips of the blessed. But when the faithful say here: *I am needy and poor,* they indicate that those men to whom they refer in: *Let my enemies be confounded and ashamed that seek my soul* are those rich in the world's goods. But let us examine why[9] splendid poverty declares herself everywhere needy and poor though she is most rich in heavenly treasure. It is precisely because she has no worldly resources, and because inwardly, where she is always rich, she is always soliciting, seeking and receiving. As Paul has it: *Brethren, I do not count myself to have apprehended,*[10] and again: *If any man think that he knoweth anything, he hath not yet known as he ought to know.*[11] You see that such men as continually long to obtain the grace of the Godhead are deservedly called needy and poor. We are needy

when we are continually in need, poor when with eager mind we always hasten to attain His blessings. Next comes: *God helps me*, that is, in the affliction of the world where we battle with the opposition of vices, where we endure unclean spirits as enemies, and are freed by the Lord's pity. To this was added the twofold prayer that the Lord should be both a Helper in need and a Deliverer from the disaster of this world. Notice that the psalm says: *You, Lord*, so that the whole of our hope must keep its gaze implanted on Him. The next words are: *Make no delay*. It is the tendency of those in danger to consider that help is slow in coming, though it is offered most speedily. The Lord performs everything appropriately and in due measure, but we think that what we seek with great longing is slow in coming.

Conclusion Drawn From the Psalm

The whole of this psalm gleams with the light of heavenly philosophy, for it is fashioned with moral honesty. It seeks a remedy in afflictions, and confusion for enemies which will be most salutary for them, so that being subject to evil actions they may in shame abandon their wicked deeds. It simultaneously holds out hope of happiness and eternal joys for the good, and begs the Lord, our Protection in the greatest affliction, to come with all speed so as to remove the burdensome troubles of this world by His attendance. Once He is sighted, the pride of the devil, which formerly reigned with wicked tyranny, comes crashing down. He who bound the world with bonds of sin was himself imprisoned; after ruling the human race for long with the most wicked sway, he has through the Lord's power been brought to the point of fearing holy men. So we must say frequently and with longing: *Thou art my helper and my deliverer, O Lord: make no delay.*

COMMENTARY ON PSALM 70

1. *A psalm of David, of the sons of Jonadab and the former captives.* The meaning of David and of psalm are now very well known through frequent repetition. But the mention of the sons of Jonadab and the

former captives suggests the power of the psalm by mention of the historical causes of it. It warns us at the threshold about the question posed deep within it. The prophet Jeremias recounts[1] that Jonadab was a priest of God who instructed his sons to spend their days in the temple and to comport themselves with praiseworthy sobriety. It is known that they did this, and they obtained great favour with God for their obedience. Here they represent the committed faithful. The name itself points to the meaning, for Jonadab means "the willing one of the Lord,"[2] that is, one who served the Lord with voluntary desire. In the words of Scripture: *I will freely sacrifice to thee.*[3] Next comes: *And the former captives.* The text recounts the history of the kings. When the people of Israel spurned God's instructions, they were condemned to undergo the first, second and third captivity.[4] But so that they would acknowledge their situation and return to the Lord's worship with minds converted, He announced through the prophet before the first captivity took place that this evil would befall them. But they remained obdurate with their customary wickedness. So the captives here represent defiant persons who though often warned were unwilling to reform. So we are advised by this heading to show the devotion of the sons of Jonadab, and not the defiance of the Jews who deserved to be enslaved. The whole psalm is ascribed to the faithful person who rejects hope in the world and trusts to the Lord with unsullied devotion. With the whole force of his mind he commends to us the favour of the Godhead, so that by it we can be freed from the entanglements of our sins.

Division of the Psalm

By the figure of *ethopoeia*[5] a representative person is introduced who was freed from the captivity of sins and clung to the divine commandments. He proclaims to us the egregious love of Christ the Lord, which is always bestowed gratuitously without being preceded by any merits. In the first part of the psalm he continually begs that he be delivered from the iniquities of men so that he may deserve to render thanks to the Lord. In the second part he prays that in his old age he may not be deprived of the blessings of Him whose aid protected him in his youth. In the third section he recounts the Lord's gifts, and promises to offer continual thanks.

Explanation of the Psalm

O God, I have hoped in thee: Lord, let me not be confounded for ever. Once again here the comely face of the hypothetical syllogism[6] smiles on us in this manner: "If, O God, I have hoped in thee, Lord, let me not be confounded for ever: but, O God, I have hoped in thee: therefore let me not be confounded for ever." Now with the Lord's help let us deal with what follows. One of the faithful is selected who from the earliest days has been, and now does not cease to be, and will always till the end of the world continue to be, a person of total integrity in the Lord. He places all his hope in the Lord, and recommends to us the signs of divine grace so that we may not be emptied of the good fortune of His gift through false presumption in our own powers. Let us understand the meaning of the prayer that he be not confounded for ever: it means when we are repaid at the Judgment, where the punishment consists of being wholly confounded. In this life we are often confounded to our benefit, when we are recalled from a most wicked intention, and our shift to good conduct induces praiseworthy shame in us after long rejoicing in our wickedness. So he stated first the reason why he should not be confounded for ever, namely because he has hoped in the Lord.

2. *Deliver me in thy justice, and rescue me. Incline thy ear unto me, and deliver me.* When he says: *In thy justice,* he seeks divine mercy, for it is the role of divine justice to spare the suppliant, since it has pleased His fairness to pardon the person known to condemn his own actions. He says "Deliver me from looming dangers, rescue me from the power of the devil"; this is so that he may not be condemned with the devil for eternity. When he says: *Incline,* he proclaims that he is lowly and prostrate. Unless God's grace inclines to deliver man, we cannot attain by our own merits the mercy for which we long. No man's merit touches the Lord unless in His mercy He bends low to reach sinners.

3. *Be thou unto me a God, a protector, and a place of strength: that thou mayst make me safe. For thou art my firmament and my refuge.* Unless the passage is carefully considered it can affront some, because it is seen to have added to God's protection a fortified place, as if a place could defend a person when heavenly power does not protect him. But the first statement begs that his soul be protected from spiritual enemies, and then he asks also for physical safety, which is defended from

the darts and swords of enemies by a well-fortified place. The meta-phor is drawn from fortresses, because we escape opponents when we are defended by well-fortified places. But the divine protection *is* this place; as the psalmist says in another psalm: *Protect me under the shadow of thy wings.*[7] When we are with Christ, we fear none of the devil's ambushes, for when divine protection is at hand, that most wicked of creatures is cheated of his aspiration. Observe how beauti-fully each term is accorded its proper description; firmament is asso-ciated with protector, refuge with place of strength. He rightly be-lieved that both come to him from the Lord, for he achieved nothing by his own powers. I reckon that there is a further distinction here; the Lord is said to be a firmament in this world, where patience too is sought, whereas He is a refuge in that eternal blessedness where by then no danger is feared.

4. *Deliver me, O my God, out of the hand of the sinner, and out of the hand of the transgressor of the law and of the unjust.* That man who represents us all—he had been enslaved by the law of sin, but was sure that he was being delivered by divine grace—cries out that he may be rescued from the harmful power of the sinner, who always aims to achieve what is undoubtedly at odds with the divine law and with justice. But because he had spoken of the sinner in general, he now subdivides him into two aspects with the words: *Out of the hand of the transgressor of the law and of the unjust.* The transgressor of the law is the person who accepts it but then acts contrary to the rules of its commandments; the Jews fall into this category, for as distinct from other nations they are known to have accepted the Law. The unjust are the pagans, but also Jews who are not restrained by any law of the Lord, but do whatever they please like beasts. So the psalmist is shown to have embraced all sinners in these two categories. Paul too speaks in this way about the two kinds of sinners: *Whosoever have sinned without the law shall perish without the law: and whoever have sinned in the law shall be judged by the law.*[8]

5. *For thou art my patience, O Lord: my hope from my youth.* He explains why he should be delivered from the hand of the sinner: it is because the Lord was his patience, so that by concentrating on Him and believing that his salvation depended on Him, he could endure all things with a glad spirit. Patience is the willing and lasting endurance of harsh and difficult things for some honourable or useful end.[9] Next

comes: *My hope from my youth.* He put patience first, and his hope appropriately followed. Paul too says the same: *Tribulation worketh patience, and patience trial, and trial hope.*[10] The first stage is that with God's grace we are tried through patience, and then through His gift we shall deserve to obtain the hope that bears fruit. As for the addition, *from my youth,* this indicates the age at which he believed in the Lord, for whatever the time of life we come to Him, it is appropriately called our youth since we gain the fullest strength and solidity at that stage. Alternatively, *from my youth* indicates the time at which he began to war on the devil's wiles, for youth is the time chosen for battle, and is ready for hard struggles with the vigour which is most appropriate.

6. *By thee have I been strengthened from the womb: from my mother's womb thou art my protector. Of thee shall I continually sing.* Let us scrutinise this verse a little more carefully, so that no sense of incongruity may impede us. He spoke of *my hope from my youth.* How could he put his strength in God when he quickened in his mother's womb without the resource of reason, especially as we read in Scripture: *For behold, I was conceived in iniquities, and in sins did my mother conceive me?*[11] But we must interpret womb here as the womb of holy mother Church, in which we are first conceived with the basic teaching of the faith, and then born of water and the holy Spirit. The Lord can be our strength when we come to Him with the gift of faith. He added: *Thou art my protector;* precisely so, since He protects and defends us against the wicked deeds of the devil, and in this world affords us escape from possible death under the weight of sins. Next follows our repayment of these rewards, so that just as the kindnesses are never-ending, so the singing of psalms ought to be unceasing; for if no time is empty of gifts, why should anyone interrupt praise of the Lord? *Continually* signifies both the present and the future age. In this world we sing to Him to win deliverance; in the next we give thanks for our eternal reward. So the Lord ought always to be praised, for all His gifts are unceasing.

7. *I am become unto many as a wonder: but thou art a strong helper.* The person of faith becomes a wonder in this world, where his aims differ from what the crowd of sinners holds dear. Sinners seek riches, the man of faith poverty; in short, sinners seek joys whilst he seeks sadness. So how can he not appear as a wonder when he is seen not to

accord with the agreed conduct of the many? This verse is what the
orators have termed the "low" type of pleading, which is thought to
be so contemptible as to be reckoned instead a monstrosity. But men's
allegations must be ignored when the divine powers are known to
support us; all opposition is transient when our Helper is shown to be
exceedingly strong. But when the psalmist uses the word *helper*, he is
warning us that with the support of God's grace we too must struggle
for the good, and strive not to be found hostile to the divine
kindnesses.

8. *Let my mouth be filled with thy praise, that I may be able to sing thy
glory, thy magnificence all day long.* Up to this point he has mentioned
how the Lord had bestowed various kindnesses on the human race;
now he further begs the Lord that he may be able to render Him fitting
thanks. If the Lord does not fill our mouths, the tongue is not moved,
and honourable longings are not aroused. If we ponder the matter, it is
a great blessing for us to ask for all that there is, and not always to
shrink from asking. Our Creator is more offended if we abandon the
devoted urgency of supplication. Next comes the reason why he desired his mouth to be filled with praise of Christ: namely, *that I may be
able to sing thy glory.* Glory is praise hymned by the mouths of many;
but to this goodly gift he added continuity, for when he says: *All day
long,* he is surely not saying that we must stop praising the Lord at
night, especially as the Catholic Church consoles itself at that time
with the Lord's praise. It is at that time that Vespers, Nocturns and
Matins are completed while the faithful throng keeps vigil.[12] When he
spoke of the day, he included night in it; as we read in Genesis: *And
evening and morning became one day.*[13] This figure is known as *synecdoche,* the whole from the part.[14] He speaks of the Lord's magnificence
because He has granted great favours; He has bent His ear to him in
his lowliness, protected him in danger, delivered him from the hand of
the sinner, strengthened him from the womb, and decreed to protect
him from leaving that mother's womb. So the entire praise of these
benefits mentioned is enclosed in the single word, magnificence.

9. *Cut me not off in the time of old age: when my strength shall fail, do
not thou forsake me.* He comes to the second section, in which with
greater urgency he begs that he should not be cut off by the Lord in the
time of old age, when the wearied powers of the body require greater
assistance. But old age here we must interpret not only as our final

years but also as the time when strength of soul ages through frequent afflictions and through bearing witness. This is the point of *when my strength shall fail,* in other words, when steadfastness of patience is undermined and grows soft, and cannot shoulder the burden of affliction laid on its resources. So he asks that he should not be forsaken at that time, for he will be able to endure it all in the company of the Lord.

10. *For my enemies have spoken against me, and they that watched my soul have consulted together.* The reason is given why the Lord's love is appealed to for help. It is because the zeal of those ambushing him has been fired by seizing on his weakness, for they think that one who cannot confront them through the failure of his strength can be easily taken by guile. So that these enemies of his soul should not be regarded as a minor threat, he directs his words against those who were watching him; they were not seeking to save him, but were eager to deceive him. Next comes: *They have consulted together.* Enemies in a united body are always harsher; burdens carried in an undivided bundle are heavier. He next explains the nature of this consultation with these words.

11. *Saying, God hath forsaken him, pursue and take him, for there is none to deliver him.* So this is what that most faithful man feared, whether in affliction or in old age. Enemies in the flesh whose observation is worldly rather than spiritual, on seeing a man wearied with crowding disasters, believe that he has been forsaken by God, for they think that divine grace resides solely in strength of the body. Pursue him, they said, because he could not flee; take him, because he could not fight back against their most violent attacks. They believed that the Lord had forsaken him because they felt that he had been consigned to their harsh hands. Some have thought that this verse is to be applied to the Lord Saviour as well; but a more fitting interpretation of the words is that we should not suddenly with incongruous variation change the identity of the person whom we have put at the centre of the psalm. Next comes: *For there is none to deliver him.* They were certainly out of their minds when they based their judgment on the evidence of their eyes—as if God were withholding rewards from those whom He exposes to injustices, and does not wish rather to crown those who He thinks should be put to the test. This is the judgment of the man who takes the eye as criterion; he said that the

Lord was absent because he did not believe that any visible aid came to His faithful. He thought that one who was not visible to human sight did not exist.

12. *O God, be not thou far from me: O my God, look to my help.* Human weakness believes that God is far away when help is slow to come to it. God does not advance by motion, and does not proceed from place to place. He fills all things in a manner beyond description, and administers all things by the powers of His will. So the psalmist asks that God's grace should not forsake him, abandoning him to the more oppressive traps of the wicked. He added: *O God, look to my help.* Because he knew that he would be afflicted, he prays that a fitting patience be accorded him through the help of the Lord. The person whom the Lord helps does not faint through grieving over evils; he is buoyed up by hope all the more when weighed down by the burden of afflictions.

13. *Let them be confounded and come to nothing that detract my soul: let them be buried with confusion and shame that seek my hurt.* He passes on to most salutary rebukes such as the Catholic Church is accustomed to utter. *Let them be confounded;* understand: "When they see that Your dispositions remain unchanged." *Let them come to nothing that detract my soul* refers to those who foolishly contradict us, who make a habit of growling against upright behaviour with snapping detraction. His advice is that such persons are overcome by the virtue of patience; he has recommended us to bear with them to the degree that they seem in their contradictions to fail more than we do, so that at any rate they are wearied by their excessive protestations and abandon them, even if they cannot be convinced by reason so as to cease to attack us. Next comes: *Let them be covered with confusion and shame.* The correction of the wicked which will ensue is depicted in the finest words. He said: *Let them be covered,* as though their faces were to be masked with a ruddy veil of shame, as often happens to those who turn to a better life and condemn their earlier deeds. He added: *That seek my hurt;* this recalls the woman who said to her husband Job when his life was at hazard: *Reproach God, and die.*[15] This is what wicked counsellors usually do; they pay compliments to bodily health, but are seen to assail our souls with hidden wounds.

14. *But I will always hope in thee, and will add to all thy praise.* Once he has detailed the improvement which he prayed would change sin-

ners, he turns to his own delight and advantage. Just as sinners saw no sign of divine power, so he says that he always hopes in the Lord. This figure is called *syncrisis* or comparison,[16] when someone shows that his case is better than his opponent's. Next comes: *And I will add to all thy praise*. This is quite obscure unless we ponder it more carefully. Though nothing can be added to God's praises, since His perfection at which we must marvel allows of no increase, yet it can be hymned with a fresh proclamation by men. When I say that the Father's Word created heaven and earth and all within them, I have praised the Lord with perfect devotion; but when I add that the Word became flesh for the salvation of all, I have increased the fullness of His praise. The words that follow attest that this addition to His praise is wholly concerned with the incarnation of the almighty Word.

15. *My mouth hath proclaimed thy justice, thy salvation all the day long, because I have not known worldly business*. The justice of the Father is the Lord Saviour; he promises that he will proclaim Him to the nations. So that you would not chance to think that some other justice was meant, he added: *Thy salvation*. What else could the man of faith proclaim other than the source of the Christian faith, of the fecund growth of churches throughout the world, of the emergence of the world's salvation through the glorious incarnation? *All the day long*, as we have often stated, indicates continuing time. Next comes: *Because I have not known worldly business*. This part of the verse clearly raises a problem unless it is carefully analysed: if every man of business is to be wholly condemned, those known to practise other occupations do not escape this punishment; for what is business except seeking to retail at a dearer price objects which can cost less? Then too we read in the Fathers' lives that the famous Paphnutius, a most holy man, was purchased by a business man who experienced a revelation;[17] and even today we find men in God's Church handling merchandise who are persons of the most committed faith. It is the very wicked action, and not honourable property, which is condemned. We read in Scripture that the rich man does not enter the kingdom of heaven,[18] yet the patriarchs Job, Abraham, Isaac and Joseph also had abundant wealth. So the business men who are reckoned as accursed are those who have no thought whatsoever for the Lord's justice, who are corrupted by an uncontrolled desire for money, and who load their wares with a dishonest rather than a just price. Such men as these the

Lord cast out of the temple with the words: *Make not the house of my Father a house of traffic, a den of thieves.*[19] So in my view the meaning to be embraced here is something like this: "My mouth has proclaimed thy justice, because I have not known the worldly business which is polluted by evil actions."

16. *I will enter into the power of the Lord: O Lord, I will be mindful of thy justice alone.* Men reckon to acquire power by business, and thus to become outstanding in this world. But this blessed man disregards such a plan, and says that he is entering into the power of the Lord, that is, into the heavenly kingdom, for it is true blessedness to have entered there. He uses the words, *I will enter,* to show that the heavenly Jerusalem is closed to the faithless but open to the faithful. He next recounts what he will do there: *O Lord, I will be mindful of thy justice alone.* This will be at the time when He separates the lambs from the goats, when in the justice of a moment He judges all the people of the nations, and dispatches the wicked to hell and the faithful to eternal rest. Then indeed he will be truly mindful of the Lord's justice alone, since he knows that it is wonderful and unique.

17. *Thou hast taught me, O God, from my youth: and till now I will declare thy wonderful works.* We have said that *youth* ought to be interpreted as the time at which a person has begun to attain divine grace, because he then starts to be strong and powerful in his soul's strength. *Thou hast taught me* has reference either to the divine books or to the faith infused from heaven. So that you would not believe that this knowledge was won only at the outset, he speaks of what is the regular experience of blessed hearts in the phrase, *and till now;* the teaching he has received seems to have accumulated through the extent of his days. Next comes: *I will declare thy wonderful works.* They were wonderful indeed; the ignorant one was instructed, the faithless one became committed, the sinner became the justest of men. So he proclaims that he will declare these things which God's mercy had performed in him.

18. *And unto seniority and senility, O God, forsake me not, until I show forth my arm to the generation. . . .* Among the Greeks these two terms, seniority and senility, are distinct; by seniority they mean solemn dignity, and by senility the final years.[20] But because Latin did not regard the two as distinct, the two stages are here named with the similar terms, *senecta* and *senium.* So the sense is like this: because he had said that he had been taught from his youth to proclaim the Lord's

justice and nothing else, he now begs that the Lord should not forsake him in his mature and senile years, so that strengthened by His power he may be able to unfold His praises until his death. But let us examine the periods to which these ages are to be assigned. The youth of the Church was when the Lord Christ was crucified, when the host of martyrs gave battle, when the power of the Church was manifest with the deaths of the faithful. We name as seniority the age now in progress, which is very close to the end, when the faith flourishes and the people of God increases through all the churches, and the fleeting seasons of the world are shrinking. By senility I think we must understand that sinking stage when the savage tyrant[21] shall come, and a host of martyrs will close this life with the end for which they long. Next comes: *Until I show forth thy arm to the generation.* The man of faith who has been introduced is speaking, and is asking the Lord that he may remain in the gathering of the Church till his seniority and senility, till he can proclaim the Father's arm, the Lord Saviour, to the next generation of men. As we read in Scripture: *And to whom is the arm of the Lord revealed?*[22] So the Christian religion may be extended through the devotion of the whole world, especially when at the end of time the predestined number of the saints is attained.

19. . . . *to all that is to come: thy power and thy justice, O God, even to the furthest heights.* To all that is to come is to be joined to the final word of the preceding verse, generation. So that you may not chance to think that the arm of the Lord, the Lord Christ, was to be proclaimed only to those living at the time when He became flesh for us, he added: *That which is to come,* so that you would know that this proclamation is to be made until the end of the world. Next comes: *Thy power and thy justice, O God;* understand with this, too, *until I show forth. Power* has reference to the grace of the incarnation, by which He deigned to deliver man, and *justice* to the judgment by which He is known to have imposed death on the disobedient Adam. The inverted order of the two need not trouble you, since you often find this in holy Scripture. *Even to the furthest heights* declares that both attributes are wonderful and splendid; man who before had been rightly condemned by justice has been renewed by grace. Let us direct our understanding also *even to the furthest heights,* for the God-man sits at the right hand of the Father, reigning with Him and the holy Spirit through the ages without end.

What great things thou hast done! O God, who is like to thee? After he has stated that the grace of the Creator and His justice have been advanced to the furthest heights, he passes to the third section, in which with lyrical joy he hymns the great justice which the Lord has shown to sinners, and in turn the great mercy of His love shown to the converted. For he deprived the disobedient Adam there and then of the pleasure of Paradise, but swiftly admitted the penitent thief to its joys. These are the great things which he attests that the Lord has done; for He shows Himself to be uniquely powerful in judgment, and like to no other in setting men free. When we read: *What!* we should do so with wonder, for none can understand or praise these things worthily. *Magnalia* (great things) is derived from *magnitudo* (greatness), for they seem to cast a spell on human minds because of their splendour. He also inserted here: *Who is like to thee?* for from His works He is known to be unique. The greatness of a deed attests the power of its author.

20. *What great troubles hast thou shown me, many and grievous! And turning, thou hast brought me to life.* The words, *what great*, are likewise to be pronounced with wonder, for they imply sufferings innumerable. Note also his expression, *hast thou shown*, for He shows harsh troubles to the faithful for the moment, but though they seem grievous and many they none the less redound to our good, conducing to our profit. *Many* points to their number; *grievous* to their nature. Next comes: *And turning, thou hast brought me to life.* If you ponder the nature of the Word, He is found to be always unchangeable and immovable. *Turning* is used metaphorically for "You have made me turn," since I had been misshapen through the regimen of sin. The affliction of the faithful leads to life; as the gospel has it: *Blessed are they that mourn, for they shall be comforted.*[23]

21. *And hast brought me back again from the abysses of the earth. Thou hast multiplied thy justice, and turning, thou hast counselled me.* We interpret *abysses* as the depths of the divine mind; as the psalmist says elsewhere: *Thy judgments are a great abyss.*[24] But here the words *of the earth* have been added, so that you must understand the deep immersions and chasms of sins, from which he proclaims he has often been recalled to life's joys. But let us note the purpose of his saying *again.* *Again* is put here for "repeatedly," for something repeated on many

occasions. On Psalm 6 we followed the authority of the Fathers in saying that the Lord grants us remission of sins in seven ways: by baptism, martyrdom, almsgiving, releasing our debtors from debts, conversion of our brothers, abundance of charity, and repentance.[25] Perhaps our frailty is assisted by other kinds of remission as well, but we must realise that the word *again* is used so that the means of healing it may be seen to be more frequently available. The words, *thou hast multiplied thy justice*, are set down as expounding the previous meaning; He multiplies His justice when He deigns to assist us in the various causes of affliction. The Lord's justice is often mentioned when He performs an act of mercy; likewise His justice is called mercy, for they are always joined to each other. As we read in Psalm 100: *Mercy and justice I will sing thee, O Lord.*[26] Next comes: *And turning, thou hast counselled me.* We ought to observe how fatherly this expression is; though He rebukes his servants with the affliction mentioned, He does not allow them to remain melancholy, but consoles them with the holy address of sacred Scripture. Counselling ought to be interpreted as consolation, for it composes our spirit, lightens our hardship, and heals our minds when they are wounded by various maladies.

22. *But I will confess to thee thy truth in the vessels of the psalms.* Since by kindly exhortations the Lord has promised eternal rewards to the faithful, at this point the just psalmist, representing the generality of the faithful, gladly proclaims that he hymns the truth—namely that the promises of the Lord will be fulfilled, since he cannot misrepresent the promise of the eternal Truth. The definition of the psalms as vessels of the truth is splendid; they are so to say the spiritual casks preserving the Lord's wine with its taste unpolluted.

I will sing to thee, O God, with the harp, thou holy one of Israel. We have often said that faithful Christians possess two very great strengths, a spiritual strength for sound belief and an actual strength for sound action; and by using a musical image he promises to offer both these to the Lord. So far as spiritual strength goes, he promised in the previous verse to sing a psalm; as for the actual, he says that he praises the Lord on the harp. As we have often said, the sound of the psalm comes from the upper parts, while the harp transmits a melody to the heavens from the lower parts.[27] He states to whom the psalm is sung or the harp played, namely, the holy One of Israel; not the mistaken deity of pagan belief, but Him whom true faith had revealed to our forefathers.

23. *My lips shall rejoice when I sing to you: and my soul which thou hast redeemed.* Lips means the mouth of the inner man, for the mind too has its voice with which it silently cries to the Lord. So that you would understand the words in a spiritual sense, he added: *My soul which thou hast redeemed;* the soul, then, rejoices with its inner lips, for it knows that it has been redeemed.

24. *Yea, and my tongue shall meditate on thy justice all the day: when they shall be confounded and put to shame that seek evils for me.* Just as earlier he said: "I will hymn thy truth in the vessels of the psalms and on the harp," wishing to denote the powers of soul and body, so he promised that the lips of his heart would sing, but now he has added that his tongue will meditate on the justice of God. By his tongue he means the substance of his body, which will meditate most fully on the praises of the Lord when it sets eyes on His kingdom at the resurrection. So that you would interpret this as at the end of the world, the next words are: *When they that seek evils for me are confounded and put to shame.* This will happen in its entirety when the just are placed on the right and the wicked on the left. Enemies are confounded and put to shame in two ways, either when they show repentance and realise that they have sinned, or at any rate at the coming of the Saviour, when with their own eyes they shall see clearly what they did not think could happen. So that is the time of carefree joy for holy men, when the wicked shall no longer have the chance of lording it, and the just will rejoice when the end of all ills comes, and the Lord grants His blessings without cease; in this joy the unwearying supplication of Christians abides.

Conclusion Drawn From the Psalm

The whole of this psalm lauds with the greatest concentration the Lord's grace freely given, but it also advises us that the incarnation of the Word, through which salvation has emerged for the human race, is to be proclaimed as blessedly close at hand. It is like the sun, which as it rises with the approach of daylight sends ahead the rosy dawn, so that the eye is prepared and can gaze upon the grace of that outstanding brightness. Our fathers believed that the aggregate of the psalms was to be apportioned between the mysteries of the Old and New Testaments. They allotted seven decades to the sabbath, which undoubtedly belongs to the prior mode of worship, and eight decades to our period, for we revere the Lord's Resurrection every week on the eighth day. Thus by this double reckoning the sacred total of the psalms is seen to contain both Old and New Testaments; for what can count as one hundred and fifty individually can indicate fifteen decades if considered in groups of ten. So this total of psalms is appropriately adapted to the New and Old Testaments. We must clearly recognise that in the first part, belonging to the Old Testament, the psalmist intermingles also the new signs of the mystery. He speaks of the Passion of the Lord Christ in the seven decades, and includes much concerning the Old Testament in the eight, so that both groups of seven and eight are seen to be appropriate in every way to our worship. But we must remember that the psalms often draw attention to arithmetic or to other disciplines, and we shall be careful to mention them later when the time is ripe; thus these topics though briefly treated will not seem to have been passed over. The sole exception is that we shall be most careful to eschew astrology, which is sacrilegious, and which the judgments of notable philosophers have also condemned.[28] So let us draw this present volume to a close, that this brief respite may rekindle the reader's enthusiasm, and the ensuing separate section of psalms on the significance of the New Testament may be fittingly commenced. Amen.

COMMENTARY ON THE EIGHT DECADES THAT RELATE TO THE NEW TESTAMENT

Preface

Now that we have explained the seven decades, which as we mentioned typify the Old Testament, let us now pass on to the remaining eight. Their number is acknowledged to signify most fully to us the mystery of the Lord's resurrection;[1] and so once we have scrutinised these sections carefully, the Book of Psalms may be seen to have truly embraced the treasure of the whole of divine Scripture. Though all the books of Scripture are full of spiritual riches and suffused with great illumination, in my view you will find none of them which is shown to be full of such significant heavenly topics. It should not trouble you that the part which we have said has reference to the mystery of the Old Testament begins with the blessed state of the Lord Saviour,[2] and likewise that in the psalms that follow this you will find events clearly enacted in the earliest times. These facts should not be interpreted as in any sense a refutation, for on the one hand the Old Testament is full of the New, and on the other the New frequently makes mention of the Old. Now let us turn to the heading which is seen to refer to the mystery of the New Testament by the interpretation of the name in it, for it is inscribed *On Solomon*.

COMMENTARY ON PSALM 71

1. *A psalm on Solomon.* Solomon is translated as "peacemaker."[1] Now who is truly a peacemaker except the Lord Christ? He it was who recalled man to the obedience of his Creator when he had been deceived by the devil's wiles, and who made him worship the Prince of salvation when he was most wretchedly following the originator of death. Christ the Mediator between God and men even today intervenes on our behalf. His own words truly attest that we rightly call Him peacemaker, when He says: *My peace I give to you, my peace I leave to you.*[2] But this is not the peace troubled by wars or shattered by any disturbance; it is the peace which remains for ever unshaken and eternal, which no enemy's hostility destroys. It is the peace of which the prophet says: *I will give you true consolation, peace on peace.*[3]

Division of the Psalm

The prophet speaks throughout the psalm, pointing to the coming of the Lord Saviour, and clearly manifesting alternately His humanity and His divinity in one and the same person. In the first section he addresses the Father, begging for His Son the role of judging the nations which is known to have been predestined before time began. In the second part he says that at the Lord's judgment the sons of the poor will be saved, and the pride of the devil undoubtedly brought low. He is also seen to indicate in marvellous fashion the birth from the Virgin, by means of certain parallels. In the third part he recounts what blessings have accrued from the holy Spirit and from the Lord Christ born of the virgin Mary. In the fourth section he says that He is to be adored by all kings because He has freed the human race from the power of the devil. In the fifth he proclaims that once seen by human eyes He was the mainstay of believers and an undoubted Source of progress for the just. In the sixth he relates that praises are to be delivered to the eternal Lord with the unanimity of the whole world. In the seventh he delivers with the sweetest devotion a hymn to the

Lord Christ. It is thus obvious that a clear and manifest beginning to the New Testament has been fashioned in the course of this psalm.

Explanation of the Psalm

2. *O God, give to the king thy judgment: and give to the king's son thy justice.* It does not appear that the word *God* has designated a particular Person, but since the words, *give to the king's son,* follow, it is quite clearly seen that the Father is invoked here; for Son is a related term, suggesting what it does not actually state, just as mention of a slave implies also the existence of a master. We must realise that these terms alone can be sufficient to distinguish and declare the Persons of the holy Trinity. These are the only distinguishing names in the holy Trinity; the other terms, "nature," "power," "eternity," "omnipotence" and the like, are known to be common to all three. So the most blessed prophet, fired by glorious longing, asks the Father that the judgment which he knew was to come would be entrusted to the Son. As we read in the gospel: *The Father does not judge anyone, but has consigned all judgment to the Son.*[4] Judgment (*iudicium*) is the statement of the law (*iuris dictum*) because the law is pronounced in it. So that the request should be shown to be most genuine, he repeated it in the following phrase, for the words, *give to the king's son thy justice,* are identical with the earlier ones, *give to the king thy judgment.* In divine Scripture you often find repetition when there is emphasis on a statement, as in: *He that dwelleth in heaven shall laugh at them, and the Lord shall deride them,*[5] and: *The heavens show forth the glory of God, and the firmament declareth the work of his hands.*[6] The following verse too is adduced in the same sense. This figure is called *epimone*[7] or frequent repetition of a statement, when the same thing is repeated in different words to drive home the point. We must remember, however, that whenever the Lord Christ asks for a concession to be granted Him, or some other urges it for Him, it is clearly His human nature which is being indicated; whereas the all-powerful Word, possessing all that the Father has, needs to be given nothing. As He Himself says in the gospel: *All that the Father has is mine.*[8]

To judge thy people with thy justice, and thy poor with judgment. He explains the reason why he asked that the judgment be entrusted to the

Son, namely that He may judge the world with the Father's justice, which is undoubtedly the Son's as well. He says to the Father: *With thy justice*, so that none may with sacrilegious effrontery consider that the holy Trinity is at odds with itself in any matter. Next comes: *And thy poor with judgment*. He says of the poor too that they are the Father's, though they are proclaimed to be the Lord Christ's as well, so that we may have this same realisation that there is no separation of power in the majesty of the Trinity. As Christ Himself says in the gospel: *All that the Father has is mine*.[9] So God's poor are those who have abandoned worldly arrogance and devoted themselves to humility in all things. If a poor man waxes proud, he is not God's poor, and equally if a rich man loves humility he is not rich in a worldly sense. It is the intentions and not the labels of such men which should be scrutinised.

3. *Let the mountains receive peace for thy people, and the hills justice.* We have often stated that *mountains* indicates the apostles and prophets, who are securely raised to the heights and draw near to the grace of heaven. So these men are to receive peace, in other words, Christ, so that He may be proclaimed to the faithful people; the Lord's people are those who believe in Him, and have embraced the life of the spirit. Next comes: *And the hills justice*. The hills stand for the rest of the blessed who are at a lower level; they are seen to proclaim the commands of the Lord in an upright way. The peace earlier mentioned indicates the Lord Saviour, and likewise *justice* undoubtedly points to Him. As we read elsewhere: *Justice and peace have kissed each other*.[10] Christ is rightly called peace because through Him man is reconciled to God, and He is rightly called justice because He will judge the world with equity, for He overcame even the devil with justice rather than with the force of strength.

4. *In his justice he shall judge the poor of the people, and he shall save the children of the poor, and he shall humble the calumniator.* Up to this point his utterance has been a prayer, but now he passes to the second part, and by the power of prophecy he relates with the most beautiful variation of different comparisons the gifts which are to be granted at the Lord's coming. Whereas earlier he said to the Father: *In thy justice*, he now speaks of the Son with the words: *In his justice*, so that you may firmly grasp that there is no disharmony or division there; the Father's justice is undoubtedly also the Son's. Otherwise it is possible

to put a different construction on the words. Christ's poor by the judgment of this world are shown to be contemptible, for people do not vouch for them, and they are dislodged from any seat of honour. But God will judge the poor not with human justice but with His own, for He prefers to choose those whom proud mortals have despised. He appended the phrase: *Of the people* to which we must supply the adjective "faithful"; the Lord has not chosen each and all of the poor, but those of whom He said: *Blessed are the poor in spirit, for theirs is the kingdom of heaven.*[11] Next comes: *And he shall save the children of the poor.* Christ's poor are the apostles or the prophets, who chose the Lord's poverty and spurned the wealth of this world; of that Lord it was written: *Though he was rich, he became poor for our sakes.*[12] Their children are the Christian people, who were begotten by their preaching and through their teaching gained the merit of believing. As the apostle puts it: *My little children, of whom I am in labour again until Christ be formed in you,*[13] and again; *In Christ Jesus, by the gospel, I have begotten you.*[14] So He will save those who He knows are the children of the apostles. The psalmist added: *And he shall humble the calumniator.* The calumniator denotes the devil, the proud, cruel, insatiable leader of all wicked men. Let us investigate why he was called the calumniator. Judges of old used to implant the letter K when their verdict was guilty,[15] and since a cruel prosecutor is eager for the condemnation of others, they sought to call the soldier branded with the letter K a calumniator. So a calumniator is one who strives by refined trickery to convert the innocence of another into guilt, and this seems quite appropriate for the devil, who is known to hunt the human race with his wiles for all these centuries. What calumny can there be greater than to be the originator of sins, and to wish to claim for oneself the worship of the world? The Lord will bring this tyrant low when he is condemned with the unfaithful, and the faithful see themselves reigning with Christ.

5. *And he shall continue with the sun and before the moon throughout all ages.* Here is expounded the honour paid to the holy incarnation which abides in union with the Word; for He sits at the right hand of the Father, reigning in everlasting glory. The sun here is interpreted as the Word of the Father, the Son of God, the God-man who abides as the one Christ from two and in two separate and perfect natures. Of him the wicked are to say: *The sun has not risen on us, and the light of*

justice has not shone on us.[16] Next comes: *And before the moon throughout all ages*—we must supply here the words previously used, *he shall continue.* Christ continues before the moon, that is, before the eyes of the Church which beholds Him with the eyes of the heart. The Church is rightly compared to the moon,[17] for it has no brightness of its own but receives its light in an unchanging manner from the sun, as astronomers carefully expound together with other teachings. It is certainly wonderful and quite profoundly remarkable that the courses of so many constellations, and the complex and delicate measurements of such mighty objects, could have passed into human knowledge. So this was the way that the Church obtained light in a measured way from the true Creator; at one point it seemed to be on the wane through persecutions, but now that it has obtained peace it is again at the full, enjoying the clearest light. The words, *throughout all ages,* signify utter eternity; as Scripture has it: *And of his kingdom there shall be no end.*[18]

6. *And he comes down like rain upon the fleece, and as showers falling gently upon the earth.* Here the very mystery of the glorious Nativity is expounded. That Lord of virtues before whose face the earth trembles and is shaken, and every creature is in disarray because He cannot in any sense be endured when He chooses to be recognised in His full power, sought to descend gently into the womb of a maiden with no din, like rain upon the fleece of a lamb. This was to demonstrate His moral strength all the more by restraining His indescribable power. As Paul has it: *Who being in the form of God, thought it not robbery to be equal with God; but emptied himself, taking the form of a servant, being made in the likeness of men, and in habit found as a man.*[19] But let us ponder the nature of the comparison attached to this great event. Fleeces are the wool of sheep; they take in water in such a way that they do not split or tear, and again they discharge the water without damage to themselves.[20] So if any of you remain sceptical, give ear to this verse; you should be ashamed to withhold that belief in the highest Godhead which His lowest creatures manifest. Next comes: *And as showers falling gently upon the earth,* that is, they fall most gently like dew. If you ponder this with mind unsullied, you will have no hesitation about the virgin birth. He has established by this twofold parallel that great miracle so that it can be believed without any hesitation. Hence the great Ambrose with wondrous brightness lit what we

might call the candles of the Church when he said: "Come, Redeemer of the nations,/Reveal the virgin birth./ Let every age marvel;/ Such a birth is fitting for God."[21] So too the utterance of the most blessed Pope Leo has flashed out like a lightning-shaft. He says: "He was conceived of the holy Spirit in the womb of the virgin Mary; and she brought Him forth with virginity unimpaired."[22] Worthy indeed are the Fathers and those who wax strong in the citadel of the papacy, when their sweetest teaching could proclaim so great a miracle.

7. *In his days shall justice spring up, and abundance of peace, till the moon be raised up.* He now passes to the third section, in which are described in due sequence the nature and extent of the Lord's gifts at His rising. We must grasp the meaning of the words, *justice shall spring up;* it sounds as if it did not exist before, whereas Justice always reigned with adorable majesty. In fact, *shall spring up* refers to the period from the holy incarnation, when He was to be brought forth in birth from a virgin. For *justice* is the Word of the Father; that Word made every creature and all times. Of Him we read: *Truth is sprung out of the earth, and justice hath looked down from heaven.*[23] He added *And abundance of peace, till the moon be raised up;* here too we must supply "shall spring up." So there is abundance of peace as long as the religion of the Christians extends through the whole world. *Till the moon be raised up,* in other words, for so long as the Church is extended and increased, so that the established total of those who are predestined is fulfilled.

8. *And he shall rule from sea to sea: and from the river unto the ends of the earth.* The sense of *he shall rule* is nothing other than that the Lord Christ, the subject of the prophecy in the earlier verses and of the words which follow, becomes more widely known through religious observance. This cannot possibly refer to Solomon, son of David, for he is known to have been king only in the Jewish nation, and we must interpret *sea* here as the ocean which encloses the area of the whole world, as some authorities state, surrounding it with its girdle. Should you seek to interpret this passage as referring merely to the seas in our vicinity, you will not be able to supply the sense of the circumference of the whole world which the verse indicates. Next comes: *And from the river unto the ends of the earth.* The brevity of the statement is splendid, but great are the mysteries it has showered on us. *From the river* means from the Jordan, from where the most salutary prescrip-

tion of holy baptism issued throughout the whole world. This is the use of the figure of *periphrasis* or circumlocution;[24] it indicates the circumference of the whole world by seas and river.

9. *Before him the Ethiopians shall fall down: and his enemies shall lick the ground.* We must interpret the Ethiopians as sinning people, for just as Ethiopians are covered in the foulest skins, so the souls of transgressors are enshrouded in the darkness of wicked deeds. So these Ethiopians, representing sinners, fall down before Him when they prostrate themselves in the humility of repentance. He further added: *And his enemies shall lick the ground.* The psalmist said that those whom the pity of the Lord will spare fall down before Him; the enemies named here are the obdurate Jews who will continue in their obstinancy, What then is their punishment? They lick the ground, that is, they taste the earth, for whatever an individual licks he tastes, and for them as for the snake the earth is the food of their chastisement. We say that this is rightly to be compared to the snake's lowly status, for those who were unwilling to believe that Christ is God are to be condemned by means of such vengeance.

10. *The kings of Tharsis and the islands shall offer presents: the kings of Arabia and Saba shall bring gifts.* As father Jerome recounts,[25] Tharsis means "contemplation." There is no doubt that this must be interpreted as the faithful absorbed in contemplation of God. So the kings of Tharsis, who are those who master their vices, offer presents to the Lord when they are shown to serve Him with devoted hearts. *The islands* are those who have repelled from their persons the vices that encompass the world; the sea of the world, which is known to have soaked into the hearts of the unfaithful, does not master them. An island (*insula*) is so called because it is set in the deep (*in salo*).[26] So their[27] gifts are those of a pure heart which are offered on God's altars, the offering of the sacrifice which the Lord sweetly accepts. Next comes: *The kings of Arabia and Saba shall bring gifts.* Arabia stands for people who indulge themselves in pleasurable earthly delights, for just as that land titillates the nostrils with different aromas, so these men are induced to the most degenerate pleasures by the enticements of the world. So the kings of Arabia are those who subject the allurements of bodies to stern discipline. Likewise though Saba, from which the Sabaeans get their name, is preeminent in physical pleasures and full of attractive odours, its people have been converted and offer up the

sweeter gifts of virtues. As for the expression, *shall bring,* it refers to their self-offering, for after the Lord's coming the sacrifices of cattle ceased.

11. *And all the kings of the earth shall adore him: all nations shall serve him.* He passes to the fourth section, where he says that the Lord will be adored by all nations, and he subsequently expounds His kindnesses. By *all kings* he wishes us to understand all nations, for there is no race which does not adore its Creator in some part of its people, So that you would not think that he was speaking solely of kings, he added: *All nations shall serve him,* that is, those separated by both tongues and lands throughout the world. So the faithlessness of Donatus[28] is seen to be rebuked here, for he thinks that the Church is localised, whereas it is clear that it extends throughout the entire world. Observe too that he said: *Kings shall adore,* and they are thought worthy of adoration; whereas nations are said to serve and they are known to have earthly masters.

12. *For he hath delivered the poor from the mighty, and the needy that had no helper.* He gives the reason why the Lord Christ is served by all nations; it is because He has freed the poor, in other words, the faithful ones, from the mighty devil whom he has earlier called the calumniator. In another place he calls him strong, as in the gospel passage: *No-one enters into the house of the strong to rifle his vessels unless he first binds the strong.*[29] These words, *strong* and *mighty,* indicate the devil's ill-will and not his distinction, his wicked craftiness rather than his praiseworthy leadership. Next comes: *And the needy that had no helper.* Here the words, *he hath delivered,* must be understood as shared with the previous statement. We have said that *needy* implies more than *poor,* for the needy man has no sustenance for life, and cannot exist on his own resources. So the Lord Christ delivered these people when He came into the world, and most justly repressed the guile of the devil, and granted gifts of spiritual wealth to the poverty of the human race without seeking anything in return. So the psalmist rightly added: *That had no helper,* because the human race had consigned itself with accursed superstition to the worship of idols; and what help could be gained from them when they did not possess even the feelings which cattle have?

13. *He shall spare the poor and needy: and he shall save the souls of the poor.* When he says: *He shall spare,* he is showing that all men in general are sinners; so He spares those who are bound by some guilt. So He will spare even His elect, who though exemplary in their holy manner of life need to have certain faults forgiven them. But so that we would not think that the Lord spares them only to the extent of freeing the poor from the tortures due to them, he added: *And he shall save the souls of the poor.* Thus He grants future rewards also to those whose sins He forgives. So this action, too, saving the souls of the poor, cannot apply to Solomon, for it is certain that this is appropriate to the Godhead alone.

14. *He has delivered their souls from usuries and iniquity: and their name shall be outstanding in his sight.* Usuries is derived from use, for such loans of money secure continual increase. Likewise those who live in sin get an increased return on their wicked deeds, when the evils they commit in this passing life accrue to them in eternal disaster. So faithful souls are delivered from these usuries, that is, from the obligations of sin, when through repentance they win forgiveness through God's gift. Next comes: *And their name shall be outstanding in his sight.* To be called Christians is indeed an outstanding name; the splendour is derived from their King, and they boast in the high title derived from His name. Isaiah is known to have prophesied this in rebuking the Jews when he said: *And the Lord God shall slay thee, and call his servants by another name,*[30] namely Christians. He added: *In his sight,* for they will live before Him and in His kingdom. How happy is that presence—to be always before God and no longer to fear offending Him! Further, this reward consists of seeing Him, whereas even our thoughts can in no way draw near Him at the present time. Thus in these few short words some indication, however abridged, is afforded us of that blessedness to come.

15. *And he shall live, and to him shall be given the gold of Arabia, and they shall take their prayer from him: they shall bless him all the day.* Here is the fifth aspect of the division we mentioned, in which he says that the presence of the Lord bestowed the aspiration of faith and lent support to the world. When he says: *And he shall live,* he is revealing the eternity of His majesty, just as in the Old Testament we often find

the words, *the Lord lives.* So He lives not with the life of any creature, which is all even the angels obtain, but in the unique blessedness which the holy Trinity alone enjoys. Next comes: *And to him shall be given the gold of Arabia.* The gold of Arabia is said to be purer than that of other lands, being precious for its outstanding brightness. It is an apt comparison for wisdom, for in Scripture we read: *Receive prudence as silver, and wisdom as tested gold.*[31] So from this wisdom, denoted by the gold of Arabia, a gift will be given to the Lord when devoted persons come to Him with hearts wholly purified. Or perhaps the phrase points to the gifts of the Magi which are rightly compared to the gold of Arabia, for they were offered with purity of heart. The ancients called the colour of gold most beautiful, and so they suggested that *aurum* (gold) was derived from *aura* (air)[32] because it shines with a most attractive colour. Even today we call something golden if we seek to regard it as beautiful. Next comes: *And they shall take their prayer from him.* It is clear that this is with reference to His humanity, when with His own lips He established how we should pray. The favour brought by the Lord's prayer and ever enjoyed by the Church is well known. The most holy father Cyprian, bishop of Carthage and martyr, first expounded it,[33] and with wondrous beauty of eloquence enlarged the deep profundity of its brevity. The psalmist added: *They shall bless him all the day. All the day* indicates the period of our entire life, which is appropriately called the day because the hearts of the faithful are not blacked out by any darkness.

16. *And there shall be a firmament on the earth on the tops of mountains: above Libanus shall the fruit thereof be exalted. The tops of mountains* denotes the outstanding status of the prophets; we have often said that mountains are to be interpreted thus. The firmament of these mountains is none other than the Lord Christ, for the prophecies made about Him through the prophets were clearly fulfilled at His coming. Next comes: *Above Libanus shall the fruit thereof be exalted.* Because earlier the psalmist compared God's saints with mountains, God Himself is the Mountain of mountains. He is the chosen Mountain, and so its fruit can be compared with the Lord Christ. For on Mount Libanus, as we have often stated, outstanding cedars grow to the loftiest height. But what can be imagined which is like the Lord's fruit, from which the saints sprout high? No matter how high tall trees

extend, even touching the clouds, there is nothing comparable to the ascent of the blessed to the joys of the heavenly kingdom.

And they of the city shall flourish like the grass of the earth: let his name be blessed for ever more. This seems to raise a problem, for he is now comparing the earth's grass to eternal life, whereas we read that it is often compared with wicked men. But this ought not to exercise us at all; in the same way Christ is called a lion because it is the powerful king of beasts, but on the other hand the devil is regarded as a lion because it is known to be fierce and savage. In the same way grass as the primary harvest of the earth is green and most acceptable, and so quite appropriately compared with the Lord's saints, yet it is rightly used also as a simile for sinners, since it is quickly parched and cropped. Thus the same object is most suitably used for comparison through consideration of its different qualities. But the just man of the city, that is of Christ's Church, will flourish like the grass of the earth, for the point of the comparison with the saints is its beautiful green-ness, not its transient life. We must note too that he says: *They of the city shall flourish*, and not *in* the city, because having left the city of this world they will flourish in that enduring blessedness; here they are afflicted with tribulations so that there they may be crowned with lasting joy. Next follows: *Let his name be blessed for evermore.* After describing the blessedness of the saints, the psalmist returns to praise the Lord, through whom they are blessed. It is as if he were saying: "Let God be glorified for ever, for we recognise that He will afford eternal glory."

17. *His name continueth before the sun. And in him shall all the tribes of the earth be blessed: all nations shall magnify him.* The gate to the sixth section is opened, where are disclosed both the eternity of the Lord and the general service accorded by all lands. So that none with blasphemous thought might imagine that the holy Son of God is bounded by time, the psalmist proclaimed that His name abides before all that is created. As the gospel has it: *In the beginning was the Word, and the Word was with God, and the Word was God. The same was in the beginning with God.* This, then, is His name which abides for ever. So that you may realise that it is the Word which was established before the sun, the next gospel words are: *Through him all things were made, and without him nothing was made.*[34] So you see that His name existed

before all created things, for He is the Creator of all things; *nomen* (name) is so called because it makes a thing known (*notum*). Here the psalmist cites the sun to represent all created things, because it is the most welcome object to shine on our eyes. This is the type of figure called synecdoche, connoting the whole from the part.[35] Next comes: In him *shall all the tribes of the earth be blessed. Him* is the Lord Christ; compare the words to Abraham: *In thy seed shall all the tribes of the earth be blessed.*[36] Because he has mentioned tribes, he wants to avoid your interpreting this as referring merely to a few nations which have their peoples split by this categorisation, so he has added: *All nations shall magnify him.* When he says: *Shall magnify,* he means simply: "shall praise," for who can make Him greater when all the Virtues and the highest creatures serve Him? But by proclaiming Him we are magnified, because we progress by praise of Him. No perverse judgment can deny that these words are directed towards praise of His divinity.

18. *Blessed be the Lord, the God of Israel, who alone doth great and wonderful things.* This is the beginning of the seventh and last part, in which after all the themes have been covered, the Lord Christ is praised with great joy. When we proclaim the Lord we are said to bless Him, not because He is sanctified or gains increase through us, but when He sanctifies us by His blessing, protection and growth ensue. The identity of this Lord he clearly suggests by the fifth type of definition:[37] *The God of Israel,* that is, the God of the whole earth. As another prophet says: *He who delivers thee will be called God of Israel, the God of all the earth.*[38] The psalmist added: *Who alone doth great and wonderful things,* for He needs no helper. For though both angels and many just men perform miracles, they do not achieve them by themselves, but with the help of the Lord.

19. *And blessed be the name of his majesty for ever and for all time: and the whole earth shall be filled with his majesty. So be it, so be it.*[39] In his previous verse he says that God is blessed; secondly he says here that the name of His majesty is blessed. This is because Christians get their name from Christ, and the word has filled the boundaries of the whole world with sacred worship. Just as Christ Himself is eternal, so praise of His name abides. What follows, *the whole earth shall be filled with his*

majesty, is a reference to His saints who were filled with His brightness. Here we must interpret earth as every faithful person such as the
Lord truly deigns to fill. He added: *So be it, so be it. So be it* denotes
desire, but repetition of the phrase deep longing. We must note that it
is set down to enhance the sacramental nature of certain psalms rather
than, as some have thought, to impose the unity of a book on the
several sections.[40] It is a magnificent psalm, attended by this redoubled
desire, because the Lord's coming necessarily induced heartfelt
longing.

Conclusion Drawn From the Psalm

Distinguished listeners, let us ponder the fact that weapons of
upright faith were long ago provided for us against the unholy warfare
of Eutyches and Nestorius,[41] so that we may believe that God, the Son
of God, the Lord Jesus Christ, exists and abides with two most true
and perfect natures in one Person. Since we are instructed by the
force of such great authority, we need not toil to subdue those heretics. Since we find both natures delineated in this psalm, the debased
teaching of Eutyches, who defends the one nature,[42] is ruled out of
court; and when the single Person of Christ the Lord is proclaimed,
the poisonous teachings of Nestorius[43] are being condemned, for
though this psalm speaks of two forms of activity, it is seen to proclaim the one Person of Christ the Lord. The psalmist did not make
reference to the plural because he wished us to believe that there is
one Son, He who was born of the Father before time began, who took
on the flesh of our mortality in the womb of the Virgin. He was of the
same nature as the Father in divinity, and of the same nature as ourselves in humanity. Invisible in divinity, He became visible in humanity. He deigned to suffer as a man for our sake, though as God He was
not in Himself subject to suffering. He did not lower the height of His
divinity, but exalted the lowliness of the flesh. This is what the holy
prophecy states, and what the words of the gospels often suggest. This
is what the blessed Church sings throughout the whole world, so that
the man who does not establish himself on this steady base is seen to

be outside the Catholic faith. Remember too that this is the fourth psalm of those which we initially said would discuss the two natures.[44]

COMMENTARY ON PSALM 72

1. *The praises of David, son of Jesse are ended. A psalm for Asaph.* Whereas in earlier headings David alone is seen to have been written, here the psalmist added: *Son of Jesse.* Doubtless this was so that we should realise that this David was the father of Solomon, so the phrase was appropriately appended to the prophet to explain his identity. This is the ninth type of definition, which the Greeks call *kath' hupotupōsin,* and the Latins *per quamdam imaginationem,*[1] when the name of the mother or father is given and our thoughts are thus led to a realisation of who the individual is. Many features are assembled for such general explanation of individuals. For example, "Socrates, son of Sophroniscus; his mother was Phaenarete; he was bald, pot-bellied, snub-nosed."[2] All these details are known to point to and to identify Socrates alone. In this procedure, however, such definitions are required as can separate the individual person sought from all the rest. So he says that the praises of this David are ended. Unless we examine this closely, it seems wholly contradictory, since he says in what is virtually the middle of the corpus that the praises of the prophet have come to an end. Let us examine from the beginning the reason for this statement. When the people of Israel were delivered from the land of Egypt by miracles visible to human eyes, they rendered praises to God by sacrifices of cattle and by the harmonious sound of musical instruments in return for benefits bestowed. This was performed symbolically until the fulfilment of the time when Christ the Lord came. So these transient praises offered in return for divine kindnesses were ended and transformed, for now the Catholic Church conducts the sacrifice of the body and blood of Christ, and the holy singing of psalms.

Next comes: *A psalm for Asaph.* The Hebrew tongue attests that Asaph signifies "synagogue,"[3] which worshipped the Lord. But through witnessing the prosperity of evil men, the synagogue had declined into most wicked thoughts. Asaph himself speaks in this psalm as spokesman of the synagogue, the meaning of which his name embodies. He will say a great deal about the Gentile nations and about those who accepted the law of the Lord. These comments are made usefully for our improvement, so that we may not be defiled by thoughts similar to those of the synagogue.

Division of the Psalm

As we have said, Asaph speaks throughout the psalm as the symbol of the synagogue. In the first section he says that he envied worldly happiness when he noted the peace possessed by sinners. He wonders why the enemies of God and the pagans attained such great prosperity that they seemed to raise their voices as high as heaven. In the second part he says that his people will return to a healthy attitude, being ashamed of the wickedness of their early thinking, until they deserve to understand and to behold the final fate of the wicked. In the third section he attests that evils are the lot of the unholy, because they were seen to scandalise holy men by their happiness, but he claims that he himself has been freed from these evils by the Lord's kindness. In the fourth part he explains how through the Lord's mercy he has obtained perfect understanding.

Explanation of the Psalm

How good is the God of Israel to them that are of right heart! Asaph recalled that he had been envious of the happiness of this world, and he has become extremely melancholy because the Lord allowed sinners to flourish in this life. So he condemned himself, and uttered sentiments both true and sweet, saying that God is good, but only to those that are of right heart, that is, to those who through their zeal for goodness understand His actions. So it is observed that God's dispositions are displeasing to the wicked and perverted by reason of their sacrilegious thoughts. Thus God shines as the brightest sun on eyes that are healthy, but He seems dark to those whose eyes are in the grip of disease.

2. *But my feet were almost moved, my steps had well-nigh slipped.* So that you may realise that the holy man had uttered the previous remark

in self-condemnation, a regular practice of just persons, he confesses his own error, saying that he had almost fallen when the Lord's dispensations irrationally displeased him. Scripture frequently uses the image of the foot for a mental judgment to which one stands firmly committed. He says that his foot was almost dislodged when his mind was at odds with true understanding. When he says *almost,* he is stating that he swiftly returned to the path of truth, so that he also condemned the mistake which hastily crept up on him. Next comes: *My steps had well-nigh slipped.* We have said that *steps* connotes the human actions by which we tread the paths of our lives. So these steps of goodly living had almost slipped into the opposite course when through the heart's ingratitude such weighty admissions were made to the wicked. Observe that he says that his steps had well-nigh slipped, and not actually fallen. This was to make you realise that our mental vigour can trickle away like water once it begins to be at odds with right thinking. From this we understand that frequently wicked thoughts creep into the hearts of holy men, but that such men return to their earlier wholeness when with the Lord's help they quickly gain correction over themselves.

3. *For I envied sinners, seeing the peace won by their sins.* The reason followed why his steps seemed to slip; it was because he envied sinners, to the point of resenting their untroubled life. What inappropriate jealousy, to envy persons doomed to destruction, and to consider as blessed those sure to be smitten by eternal damnation! Next comes: *Seeing the peace won by their sins.* The truth is that this peace is not experienced but is merely apparent, mocking our gaze but swelling to its own destruction. When sinners are seen to be wealthy, to lord it over many people, and to have no fears in this world, they are thought to have peace, but this peace is always at odds with their consciences, and there is a struggle within them. It has no external enemy, but wars upon itself.

4. *For there is no failing and cause of their death, and no strength in their stripes.* He says there is no failing to cause their death, that is, they do not more quietly sink into death, and they are not immediately oppressed by the final day; but though extended life is granted them for repentance, they are seen instead to intensify their crimes. Next comes: *And no strength in their stripes*—understand: "does not exist." Even if it should happen that they are oppressed by some adversity in

this world, their sadness does not appear to be long-lived. So they do not have recourse to a doctor, for they have not been long afflicted at all by worldly sicknesses.

5. *They are not in the labours of men, neither shall they be scourged with other men.* Let us understand here by other men the saints, who both endure toils in this world and suffer the scourges of different afflictions so that they may undergo correction and deserve to return to the Lord. This experience does not befall stubborn sinners, for it is granted only to those who are committed, so as to achieve their salvation. But if we account the statement as made against spiritual wickednesses, it can appropriately be applied to those who do not in this world experience punishments appropriate to their evil deeds. Those who are to be condemned by divine command with their adherents are not scourged in the company of others; for tribulation in this world is for the faithful that correction for which they pray. The wicked do not receive it because they will be excluded from future rewards.

6. *Therefore their pride hath held them fast: they are covered with their iniquity and their impiety.* Let us observe the goal attained by the unremitting composure of sinners, and let us stop envying their joys, for we see that they have tumbled into a pit. The freedom enjoyed by evil men invests them with total arrogance; their unpunished wantonness continually nurtures contempt, and they do not believe that they are subject to harm because they have no fear of anything which can confront them. His phrase, *hath held them fast,* implies "laid hands on them," so that they cannot wriggle clear as they are now held tightly bound. Their pride is in fact the devil's; for Satan was behind this sin, which condemned him to eternal torture. Next comes: *They are covered with their iniquity and their impiety.* If he had said: "They are clothed," perhaps their heads at any rate would have been exposed, but when he says "covered" we realise that they are totally submerged. *Iniquity* can take a less grave form, but he added: *Impiety,* which is known to be the worst of all evils. Realise too that this verse and those that follow describe the crimes and manners of wicked men.

7. *Their iniquity hath come forth as it were from fatness: they have strayed over into the disposition of the heart.* Malice is the outcome of emaciation, when a person ponders some crime through being bereft of worldly riches; but iniquity comes out of fatness, when those who through the Lord's gift are filled with the riches of this world perform

some wicked deed to offer insult to God. A sin is fat and strong when it is committed wilfully rather than under constraint. He says that they committed wrong when they had plenty, rather than that they pondered some crime with the excuse of poverty, so that their guilt should be intensified. He added: *They have strayed over into the disposition of the heart. They have strayed* implies that they wandered from straight paths. Even today we say that our thoughts have strayed when they have wandered from some true course. Sinners strayed or wandered *Into the disposition of the heart*, when though endowed with reason they became slaves to idols without feeling, which is the foulest of conditions.

8. *They have thought and spoken wickedness: they have spoken iniquity on high.* To think wickedness is a twofold evil when propounded openly as if it were a good, for when a person who ought to have been sorry for thinking of wrongdoing publicises the evil deeds which he devises, he redoubles the guilt; it is sacrilege to utter thoughts especially impious. Next comes: *They have spoken iniquity on high.* This is the outcome of a traitorous mind, to utter blasphemous words against its Creator, so that the abusive utterance rouses to anger Him whom none can praise with words sufficiently worthy.

9. *They have set their mouth in heaven, and their tongue hath passed above the earth.* That person sets his mouth in heaven who believes that Jupiter, Mercury and the rest—monsters rather than divine powers—are like to God. He too sets his mouth in heaven who with the will of a tyrant oversteps the human dimension, and thinks that there will be none to avenge his evil deeds. Instead he is guided by arrogant wickedness, and believes that God does not observe the deeds for which He is deferring the punishment. Next comes: *And their tongue hath passed above the earth.* Those whose words rise above their human status especially pass above the earth; while actually frail and weak, they reckon that they possess the privileges of immortals.

10. *Therefore my people will return here: and full days shall be found in them.* Once he has described the freedom of the wicked and the customs of the depraved, he now passes to the second section, and says that his people will return to the path of truth because they will be filled with the Lord's enlightenment. But because we use the word *return* of people who have left their native heath, it is appropriate to

interpret such people here as those who at one time accepted and abided by the law of the Lord, but who through diverse worldly desires have scattered but have been corrected and have returned to the Lord's commands. So Asaph says that the people who have returned to acknowledge the truth through the Lord's generosity have come back to their senses. Next comes: *And full days shall be found in them.* The days are full when Christ the Lord, whom the prophets foretold, deigned in the fullness of time to draw near. As Paul has it: *But when the fullness of time was come, God sent his son.*[4] So it was then that full days found the Jewish people emptied through their unfaithfulness, when some persons among them laid bare their hearts and deserved to behold the Lord Christ.

11. *And they said: How did God know, and is there knowledge in the most High?* He is now clearly explaining the mentality by which those who he earlier mentioned had returned, go astray; so that the Lord's mercy is made explicit, for He converts blasphemers into just men, and the fools among the people into men of wisdom and devotion. They were sceptical that God knew that those of great depravity had committed so many wrongs, when they saw that all the prosperity in the world accrued to them. They did not realise that they were incurring heavier punishments because they were long awaited yet were known to be stuck in their stubbornness. Psalm 93 says of such men: *And they have said: the Lord shall not see, neither shall the God of Jacob understand.*[5] Next comes: *And is there knowledge in the most High?* This is a blasphemous thought begotten of wilful stupidity, to have doubts that there is knowledge in Him who bestows wisdom on the human intelligence, who enriches the very angels and powers of heaven with the light of foreknowledge. The etymology of *scitus* (knowledgeable) is in fact *scire citus* (quick to know).[6] So the psalm earlier mentioned states: *He that planted the ear, shall he not hear? He that formed the eye, shall he not consider? He that chastises nations, shall he not rebuke?*[7]

12. *Behold, these are sinners, and yet abounding in the world they have obtained riches.* It is revealed that he was wearying the hearts of the foolish, whose reasoning is without reason, whose discussions lack counsel, whose thoughts have no savour; to the point that they did not believe that God knew the course of events, merely because sinners

possessed riches. As if He pledged such riches to the just and faithful, and did not wish those to whom He promised the kingdom of heaven to be poor in this world!

13. *And I said: Then have I without cause justified my heart, and washed my hands among the innocent?* Asaph confesses that he too has been deceived by foolish reflections. As he said earlier: *My feet were almost moved, my steps had well-nigh slipped.* So when he proclaims that he has rejected such ideas, he does not permit debased thoughts to enter at all into our minds. So the phrase, *then have I without cause justified my heart?* is to be uttered in a tone of rebuke, suggesting that a person thinks that he has been beguiled by empty hope if he considers that the reward of justice has not been bestowed on him in this world. The word cause (*causa*) derives from the word for chance (*casus*),[8] which is often favourable but often unfavourable. This kind of cause is called ambivalent by the orators;[9] it is frequently a feature in deliberations when the mind is uncertain of the outcome. He added: *And washed my hands among the innocent.* He is still developing the thought which he began, as if he were saying: "What advantage have I gained from my praiseworthy manner of life, if those who do not abandon vices possess riches?" The man who washes his hands among the innocent is he who performs devoted works according to a programme worthy of praise; Pilate did not wash his hands among the innocent when he consigned the Lord after scourging to be nailed to the cross.

14. *And I was scourged all the day: and my guide came in the early morning.* It is as if he were still relating his pains, which in his view he was enduring in vain, so that Asaph who was scourged was poor, while the impious person was untroubled and retained his riches. His reflections were most wicked, but correction was close at hand; his situation was like that of the sick who are freed from a long ailment when at the end of their sickness the flame of fever burns more fiercely in them. Next comes: *My guide came in the early morning.* See now how he who was burning with the heat of illness has now returned to a healthy temperature. He says that his guide is the Lord Christ, who revealed to us the way of truth by the proclamations of the gospel; by rising again in the early morning, He shifted our hope from this world and directed it to the kingdom of heaven.

15. *If I said: I will speak thus, behold there is the generation of thy*

children, for whom I have made dispositions. By now he is schooled in the truth close at hand. He ponders within himself, and as he is drawn towards this momentous issue, he wavers with a multitude of thoughts. He said: "If I tell the people that God does not trouble with mortal things. . ."; he then considers that his earlier proclamations made to the Israelites have come to their minds, that they should worship God, Creator of heaven and earth, who by His wisdom orders all things, and renders to good and evil persons according to the nature of their deeds. How then could he speak differently to them, when his earlier teaching was known to be to that effect?

16. *I believed that I should get to know: this is a labour before me.* It is the first step to knowledge when we begin to realise that we do not know at all what we previously thought we knew. Earlier he had persuaded himself that God does not care for mortal things, since he saw that sinners possessed riches. But now he considers that he should investigate, so as to deserve to ascertain the truth of the matter. So it is clear that the earlier notion has been rejected, when a search is made to discover another. Next comes: *This is a labour before me.* As he sweated, it was indeed toilsome for him to discover the clear truth about so great a matter, so that he could both despise the good fortunes of sinners, and by pondering the truth itself praise the Lord's long-suffering. His words, *before me,* reveal the force of the difficulty, for who can break through this mass of ignorance except by the grace of the Godhead? As we read in another psalm: *And through my God I shall go over a wall.*[10]

17. *Until I go into the sanctuary of God, and understand concerning their last ends.* At last Asaph grasped what he made haste to understand. He returns to the view that he could not discover the truth of the preceding question except by observing the divine law, which is the sanctuary of God, and by attaining understanding of the final fate of sinners; for at the future judgment the human prosperity seen to flourish momentarily here will be condemned. By this solution all hesitation is removed, for the devoted mind should not be affronted at feeling that it is better schooled by such experiences. This kind of speech is termed "deliberative" when arguments are propounded which make us uncertain, and the judgment is selected which is appropriate to both the useful and the honourable.[11] He said something which raised a doubt in their minds; *If I said, I will speak thus.* It was at

that moment that the grisly inconsistency struck him: *Behold, this is the generation of thy children, for whom I made dispositions.* Finally the judgment is chosen to bring salvation to all: *This is a labour before me, until I go into the sanctuary of God, and understand concerning their last ends.* Thus the deliberative type is achieved by observing the rule with its parts. We must in fact realise that all the arguments follow from the topics chosen; when cited as generalisations they are appropriate to logicians, but as expressed in specific, particular issues they are undoubtedly fitting for orators.

18. *But indeed because of deceits thou allotted harm to them: when they were lifted up, thou hast cast them down.* Asaph passes to the third section, in which he recounts the vengeance exacted from sinners, which he had earlier said would be a heavy burden on them in the future. So that we should not believe that they would be wholly immune from harm in this world, or that their crimes would go unpunished, he says: *Thou hast allotted harm to them.* So even though they attain worldly success, they bear within them the guilt which cannot utterly forsake wrongdoers. For even in this world such people often incur the destruction which they did not even suspect. Next comes: *When they were lifted up, thou hast cast them down.* When he said: *Thou hast cast down,* he meant that they were dashed to pieces from a height; and so that you would grasp this, he added: *When they were lifted up,* in other words, when they mounted to the heights of arrogance with ruinous glory. Reflect on the fact that he indicates that the moment of destruction is precisely when they rose high; he did not say "After being lifted up," but "when they were lifted up." Their being lifted brings their fall, their lifting up spells their plunging down, for they strive to attain that peak which collapses with a sudden landslide. As was already stated in another psalm: *I have seen the wicked highly exalted, and lifted up like the cedars of Lebanon: and I passed by, and lo, he was not,*[12] and the rest.

19. *How they are brought to desolation! They have suddenly ceased to be: they have perished by reason of their iniquity. How* is his exclamation of wonder that the person who flourished in such great prosperity suddenly seems desolated. *Desolated* means deserted by those possessions which engulfed him like a populous household; for there is no doubt that this can happen to wicked men when they meet the fearful death which is their due. Next comes: *They have suddenly ceased to be;*

he explains further how evil men are brought to desolation, whereas he previously marvelled[13] that prosperity was theirs. As for the phrase, *they have suddenly ceased to be,* it denotes the arrival of sudden death. And so that you would not believe that this is the death that comes to all, he added: *They have perished by reason of their iniquity;* for wicked men cease to be in this world so that they may die in calamity without end at the condemnation to come.

20. *As the dream of him that awakes. O Lord, in thy city thou shalt reduce their image to nothing.* This is a splendid comparison. He compares the prosperity of the wicked to a dream of those who come to consciousness. Often we are beguiled by illusory images, and dream that we attain things which we seek with excessive longing. The poor man suddenly becomes rich, the malefactor is found to be honourable, one man contracts a desirable marriage, and another attains a high post of his ambition. All these realised wishes suddenly vanish; when our eyes open, we no longer see what we beheld when they were closed. See, then, how that success of the wicked which prompted wonder attains the status of a dream; dead men cannot go on possessing riches, just as those who awaken lose their delights. Since this phrase is added to the previous words, we must put a full-stop after it. Next comes: *O Lord, in thy city thou shalt reduce their image to nothing.* He says at this point that in the heavenly Jerusalem the wicked cannot be visible to God's eyes, but just as in this world they disfigured the Lord's image in themselves, so in the native land of the future their image will not be visible, for they will be dispatched to isolation in hell. So their image will perish when Truth itself, which is at odds with them, withdraws itself from them, and they cannot preserve the likeness to that truth when they possess none of its blessedness, for an image is a fashioned likeness of some existing thing.

21. *For my heart has been delighted, and my reins loosed.* Earlier he prophesied that the wicked were to be detached from the Lord's kingdom, and now he explains that it was through them that his heart had looked enviously and with harmful delight on worldly blessings. So clearly it is a most serious sin when a person provides the occasion for the defilement of another's conscience; and likewise it is no small virtue to show example with the Lord's help to good persons. He added: *And my reins loosed.* We have often stated that *reins* is an expression denoting constancy of mind; just as the reins hold in the

body, so constancy maintains the soul's stability. So he said that his reins were loosed because with unguarded longing he had sought the happiness of worldly things.

22. *And I was brought to nothing, and I knew not: and I became as a beast before thee.* He had rightly been brought to nothing in clinging to such desires, so that by envying sinners he seemed to wrong his Maker. It is the man seen to be emptied of true understanding who comes to nothing. Further, he says that he did not know this. Ignorance of one's sinning is a boundless ignorance; so another psalm says: *Who understands sins?*[14] Next comes: *I became as a beast before thee.* He rightly calls himself a beast, for the envy of the flesh resided in him like an animal without reason. In God's eyes those who resist His instructions and aspire to sentiments other than those contained in His sacred commands are like cattle. As the words of another psalm have it: *Do not become like the horse and the mule who have no understanding.*[15]

23. *And I am always with thee: thou hast held my right hand.* When he says: *And I am always with thee,* he shows that with unsullied mind he believed in the Lord as Creator, and was a stranger to idols. But he erred in not being able to discern the Lord's judgments on the prosperity of sinners. So here the distinction has to be fully made, for his thinking is now fully stated. Next comes: *Thou hast held my right hand.* He said: *Thou hast held my hand,* and so that you would not think that it was the left hand, for that side of the body too has a hand, he added the word, *right.* The person whose right hand is held by the Lord is always forgiven and freed; when Peter was sinking, the Lord held his right hand,[16] and made him tread with steady step on the liquid element.

24. *By thy will thou hast conducted me: and with glory thou hast taken me up.* Here too is indicated the Lord's grace by which He redeemed sinners. He did not say: "By my merits," but: *By thy will thou hast conducted me;* supply "to the most healthy understanding," to which he returned after death-dealing thoughts as though from the tomb, when the Lord brought him to life. Next comes: *And with glory thou hast taken me up.* Here he proclaims the coming incarnation of the Lord, in which He devotedly deigned to assume the human condition. What is more remarkable than that through the incarnation of the Word mortal nature is set at the right hand of the Father, and will judge the living and dead, whereas after the sinning of the first man it

lay subject to the devil's temptations? Hence John, bishop of Constantinople, said in most praiseworthy and specific terms: "Let us be
aware what that nature is to which He said: 'Share my seat.' It is that
nature which heard the words: 'Thou art earth, and unto earth shalt
thou go.' "[17]

25. *For what remains for me in heaven? And besides thee what have I
desired upon earth?* After stating how by the Lord's will he has been
delivered from base thoughts, he comes to the start of the fourth
section, in which he is now free, and recounts the blessings of His
mercy. When he asks: *What remains in heaven?* we must understand:
"What further am I to seek other than what you are to bestow on
earth, the blessing of Your incarnation, so that the one Christ as
God-man is manifest with two and in two distinct and perfect natures,
and by the grace of redemption forgives me when I was condemned by
the law of sin?" The words that follow: *And besides thee what have I
desired on earth?* he utters as a rebuke against himself, as though he
were saying: "Ignorant of the truth, what did I hope for on earth,
desiring as I did blessings common to sinners, when You were preparing benefits which would abide for ever?" These are the riches
which we should preferably and healthily desire; this is the success in
which the Christian delightedly abounds, so that he is poor in this
world but rich in heaven.

26. *My flesh and my heart have shown a defect: thou art the God of my
heart and the God that is my portion for ever.* *Defect* is so termed
because it has no effect. The thoughts of the flesh had rightly indicated a defect, for they knew that they had sinned. But he makes
confession to Him to whom it is a remedy to expose one's guilt;
confession of sins brings an untroubled mind. Note that in the one
verse *heart* is used in both a good and a bad sense. The heart showed a
defect, its wicked thinking; but the God of the heart indicates good
understanding, when he now realised for his own good that he had
gone astray. We must also observe that divine Scripture often speaks
of intentions coming out of this part of the body; in the words of
Scripture: *From the heart of man come forth evil thoughts.*[18] Some say
that the seat of wisdom lies in the head, but we should rather believe
Him who speaks of our hearts, for He has fashioned them. Next
comes: *And the God that is my portion for ever.* God is the portion of
that person who associates himself in belief with His majesty, and

commends himself by his praiseworthy activity. By the addition, *for ever,* he promised that he would always keep close to Him. It is truly the mark of perfect men never to seek to depart from Him without whom it is our fate always to go astray.

27. *For behold, they that go far from thee shall perish: thou hast destroyed all them that are disloyal to thee.* He recalls those of whom he earlier said: *They have suddenly ceased to be, they have perished by reason of their iniquity.*[19] Those who went far from him were the slaves to idols, showing no reverence for the true God. For the spokesman who believed in God had withdrawn for a short time to return, as has often been said, once he had restrained his debased thoughts about the happy lot of sinners. Next comes: *Thou hast destroyed all them that are disloyal to thee.* We are disloyal to God when we move away from His chaste love with counterfeit thoughts, and when we put the world's soft living first, and do not accept the discipline of the heavenly commands. It is clear that those who seek the worship of idols and the empty superstitions of wickedness do this; in short, all that is believed which is contrary to the Catholic faith is a mark of disloyalty, and the outcome of defiled thoughts.

28. *But it is good for me to adhere to God, to put my hope in God, that I may declare all thy praises at the gates of the daughter of Sion.* See, the thought which we mentioned has been made clear; though he defiled himself with debased reflections, he did not abandon worship of the Lord. He says that it is good for him to adhere to the Lord; the one who cleaves close to the Godhead is he who attaches himself to Him with true faith and praiseworthy actions. Just as he declared that the wicked were far from the Lord, so he proclaims that he himself sticks fast to Him, so that by espousing the opposite course to theirs he may obtain a wholly different recompense. Next comes: *To put my hope in God.* He explains the word which he used earlier, for he who puts his hope in the Lord adheres to God, for nothing can be happier than to entrust all things to Him who can provide appropriately profitable means to those who worship Him. He added: *That I may declare all thy praises at the gates of the daughter of Sion.* We have often said that Sion is a mountain set in Jerusalem, which means in our language "contemplation."[20] It is clear, then, that the daughter of this contemplation is the Catholic Church, in which the believer of pure mind truly renders

praises to the Lord. *At the gates* demands to be interpreted as the very entrance into Christianity, when the people of fresh rebirth are brought to a realisation of the true faith.

Conclusion Drawn From the Psalm

How marvellously this Asaph, whose name means "synagogue," both rejected his past errors and laid hold of the blessings of the faith to come! He pondered wisely, his choice was outstanding; so that following the promise in the previous psalm of the Lord's coming which brings salvation, the number 72 seems appropriate to it, since he separated the two parts of his thoughts in just measure, and with impartial control made the whole attain equipoise.[21] The formation of the Christian is completed by this advice, so that he who hastens to commend himself to the Lord does not fail through debased thoughts. Grant, O Lord, that You do not make us envy the men whom You condemn by Your truth; but let us curse those whom You abhor, and be fond of those whom You love; for only those who follow Your wishes with a most devoted heart can have their portion with you.

COMMENTARY ON PSALM 73

1. *The understanding of Asaph. Understanding* signifies the divine insight which this psalm fully examines with eagerness to show devotion. Asaph, as has now often been remarked, means the gathering[1] which is now called the Church. With pitiful lamentation she bewails the future disasters of the city of Jerusalem. What wondrous devotion, what astonishing kindness of heart, to lament a future ill as though she were experiencing it, and to mourn coming events as if they were already known to be endured! This kind of utterance, so full of charity and prompted by love of one's neighbour, you will find sung in this psalm and in Psalms 78 and 136. We should however realise the distinction between those who repent and those who lament, for sad tears are common to both. Those who repent pray, because of their sins or transgressions in general, that the Lord may pardon their

wicked deeds and not punish their misdemeanours at the Judgment; but those who lament bewail with the eyes of love the destruction of the city and the death of their fellow-citizens which they have already endured or at any rate are soon to endure. This is the sense in which Paul urges love of our neighbour, exhorting us *to rejoice with them that rejoice, to weep with them that weep.*[2] Now let us look at the arrangement and setting of the psalms. Psalm 71 promised that the Lord's incarnation would come. In 72 Asaph put his transgressions behind him, and chose the course to follow. In this psalm there is lamentation for the destruction of the city, so that the Jews' extreme hardness of heart should at least feel fear at the disasters to their city. The good Physician has done all he could, if the sick man wished to recover his health. Let us remember, however, that the authority of the Church relates that Jerusalem was ravaged in the days when the most cruel people of the Jews crucified Christ the Lord, so that there can be no doubt what temporal evil that obstinate transgression sustained. Now let us turn to the rest of the psalm.

Division of the Psalm

The people of the Israelites, embracing in figure the most devoted synagogue, speaks throughout the psalm. In the first part she laments that she has been consigned to the Gentiles, so that the reckless behaviour of the enemy had polluted the Lord's sanctuary, and she mentions that the unrepentant hearts of certain Jews had provoked the judgment of the Lord; however, she prophesies that as the outcome of all this they will be converted at the end of the world. The second part states that at the coming of Christ human superstitions and acts of wickedness were destroyed, and recounts that He has done great and various deeds, incidentally asking that the erring Jews should be lent help. In the third section she asks that mindful of His promises He should rescue the seed of Israel from extinction, and that the arrogance of the Romans, who puffed themselves up insufferably, should mount to His sight. Let us listen to this psalm with attentive minds, for it is a wonderful lamentation for the destruction of Jerusalem.

Explanation of the Psalm

O God, why hast thou cast me off unto the end? Why is thy wrath enkindled against the sheep of thy flock? The Jewish people is ushered in, begging the Lord to divert imminent destruction from the Israelites. The word *Why* represents enquiry rather than censure, for Asaph is justly terrified, and asked why the Lord's sanctuary should endure such impious plundering. He was afraid that because the ravaging of the temple had been permitted, the Jewish people too would be utterly exstirpated. For when reverence is not accorded to holy places, who can be considered safe? *Cast off* means rejected, equivalent to: "You have excluded us from Your protection." *Unto the end* here points to the destruction and captivity which we read that Jerusalem endured from the Romans in the days of the emperors Vespasian and Titus.[3] Next comes: *Thy wrath is enkindled against the sheep of thy flock.* Sheep connotes the Jewish people, so that mention of the flock should rouse the pity of the devoted Shepherd. He added *thy* because we invariably temper our vengeance towards those who we recall once belonged to us.

2. *Remember thy congregation, which thou hast created from the beginning: thou hast delivered the sceptre of thy inheritance, Mount Sion in which thou hast dwelt.* Carefully observe the many ways in which he seeks the good will of the Judge, so that the good Judge's mind may be enticed to bestow the customary kindnesses. So he asks that God be willing to consider the blessings He bestowed on them, rather than their transgressions. The congregation of the Jews clearly gained the upper hand with His help, when He caused them to gain strength under the people of Egypt, and deigned to free them at the chosen time with notable miracles. Whereas He creates and orders all men, He is said to have created the Jews in a special sense, for He gave them the Law, bestowed prophets on them, and granted them great miracles. *From the beginning* means the beginning of that faith and developed cult which the Hebraic people received through Moses. Next comes: *Thou hast delivered the rod of thine inheritance.* The Lord's inheritance was the Jewish people, for as long as they served Him with untainted hearts. He called this inheritance a rod because of His

servant Moses, who was ordered to do great things with a rod, so that reinforced by divine strength the Jews could fearlessly emerge from the land of Egypt. It was through this rod that the obstinacy of the Pharaoh was shaken; through it the waters of the Red Sea were parted; through it streams flowed forth from the dry rock. So rightly this inheritance was called a rod, since it could achieve such great miracles. The rod was mentioned here to reveal the great gifts which God had granted through it. He also mentioned that notable peak of perfection, *Mount Sion in which thou hast dwelt,* for the earlier miracles led to the blessings of this mountain. There is no doubt that all the events of the Old Testament took place so that the promised truth of the New should ensue. The expression, *Mount Sion in which thou hast dwelt,* means nothing other than the city of Jerusalem, where the people of Israel settled. He declares that the Lord Christ's bodily presence resided there, so that God should not allow the region in which He deigned to appear to human eyes to endure the foulest of plundering. That land did indeed glow with miraculous events, and was worthy of reverence through the Lord's visitation, for there it was granted to behold with bodily eyes that to which it is the greatest joy even to accord belief. This argument is called "by praise of the thing harmed";[4] the odium towards the enemy grew to the degree that the holy places were to be ravaged by their obstinate behaviour.

3. *Lift up thy hand against their pride unto the end: what things the enemy hath done wickedly in thy holy places!* These are the words not of an angry man but rather of one who desires the remedy of correction. The prayer of the Israelite certainly prevailed, for where has the worship of the Christian religion flourished more than in the city of Rome, which before all other regions freed itself of pagan superstitions? So the power of the Lord was raised among them, when the grace of humility transformed their arrogance and led them *unto the end,* that is, to the Lord Saviour. How imposing are the most sacrilegious traces of the temples visible there! And how numerous the blessings of heavenly churches and holy martyrs which cast their glow! Once we have surveyed both groups, the power of the Lord Christ can be truly understood, for out of such superstitious crowds He created the most holy city. Next comes: *What things the enemy hath done wickedly in the holy places!* *Enemy* connotes the Roman people, who at that time, as has been stated, were regarded as notable

worshippers of idols. They acted wickedly in His holy places when the priests and the whole Jewish nation either lay prostrate beneath the sword or were enslaved and reduced to captivity. The history of Josephus, recounted in seven books, describes this most fierce war.[5]

4. *And they that hate thee have boasted in the midst of thy shrine: they have set up their ensigns for signs, and they knew not.* The consequence of the contempt which they showed for the most sacred temple was that a greater odium grew against those reckless men; it seems almost as if they despised the Godhead Itself when they were found guilty of plundering that holy religion. But though repentance should be the outcome of all sin, it is stated here that they boasted, so that they seemed not merely to have sinned but also to have arrogated that wickedness to their own glory. He further added: *They that hate thee,* so that what was patently committed by those enemies should not be patiently endured. Next comes: *In the midst of thy shrine.* The phrase underlines their boundless scorn; they are said to have committed sacrilege not in some remote place but in the midst of the shrine. As for the further phrase, *they set up their ensigns for signs, and they knew not,* this refers to the eagles, snakes and other symbols which the Roman army usually deployed in battle, or at any rate to the statues which commemorated victory, and which emperors set up over the arches of gates to redound to their praise. There follows the additional phrase, *as signs,* uttered with bitterness so that the very repetition would rouse the just Judge to speedy vengeance. This figure is known as *epembasis,*[6] when the same words are repeated in juxtaposition for additional effect, here showing that what had been granted by divine dispensation was set in place by human powers. So that you may understand that this was the thought which the psalmist conceived, he added: *And they knew not.* If they had known, they would have rendered sacrifices to You and to no other, nor would they have chosen to return to the worship of demons. The captivity or destruction occurred long after it is known to have been prophesied; for when the words were uttered, the temple had not as yet been established at Jerusalem, for we read that it was built by Solomon, the psalmist's son. So the great power of the heavenly prophecy was truly made plain, seeing that its destruction was foretold before its construction could have occurred.

5–6. *As they were placed on the high point of the road. As with axes in a wood of trees, they have cut down its gates in that very place: with axe and hatchet they have brought it down*. The more the contempt of those enemies is emphasised, the speedier the vengeance that is being demanded; for in these two short verses his bitterness of mind is fiercely indicated, to the point of his saying "They have set up their signs in Your temple, just as the statues of emperors are often raised on eminences in the streets, so that the recollection of travellers may be stimulated by such sights." What could be more detestable than that they should have the gall to set up in the inner sanctum of the temple what sacrilegious emperors presume to instal in the streets? There follows another pitiful complaint expressed by comparison: he says that the gates of the most revered temple were levelled by axes, just as forests offer woodcutters free access where no guard or opposition is met. The ancients derived *ianuae* (gates) from Janus, because in their view entry to the new year was through him. He further added: *In that very place*, that is, in the temple, so that the nature of the deed caused added resentment owing to the religious nature of the place. Next comes: *With axe and hatchet they have brought it down*. An axe is a two-headed iron tool fashioned for cutting wood, suitably adapted for slicing beams; it gets its name (*bipennis*) since it is doubly sharp, for the ancients used *pinnus* to mean sharp.[7] A hatchet (*ascia*) is an iron tool curved like a hooked nose; the craftsman's hand uses it to slice more carefully what he knows is a tinier section. To show that Jerusalem was totally ravaged, he says that both great and small things were brought down by these craftsman's tools, for all that an axe could hack or a hatchet sever was brought down with harsh hand. To express the prophet's grief here, the thought of Jeremiah should be set down: *See if there be sorrow like to the sorrow which is mine. The Lord hath delivered me into hands, and I shall not be able to stand.*[8]

7. *With fire they have burned thy sanctuary: they have defiled the dwelling-place of thy name on the earth*. His grief increases when the disaster of the destruction intensifies. The axe and hatchet could bring down only timber, but finally fire devours the whole building simultaneously. What then, I ask, could have happened to private dwellings, when the enemy's rage did not spare the Lord's sanctuary? His phrase, *with fire they have burned*, is the figure called pleonasm[9] in secular literature, where use of superfluous words is permissible; but in my view this figure is not suitable in divine Scripture, for there every-

thing is useful, vital and perfect. This mode of speaking we must regard as equivalent to our common expressions, such as "With my ears I heard," "With my eyes I saw"—though one cannot see with others' eyes or hear with others' ears. Next comes: *They have defiled the dwelling-place of thy name on earth.* The dwelling-place of His name was the temple which Solomon built as a wondrous structure; at its dedication he prayed: *I have built a house to his name,*[10] and the rest. This dwelling-place, then, which the power of heaven visited, was defiled by the hand of the plunderer, who levelled to the ground the towers known to have been erected for the Lord's praise. Observe that in these four verses the most notable figure of *auxesis* (In Latin called *augmentum*)[11] is employed. The harshness of the deed continuously intensifies, so that those who transgress so dreadfully must be confronted by the almighty Judge. This is usefully and aptly used in expressions of both praise and blame, as Paul did when he says: *Knowing that tribulation worketh patience, and patience trial, and trial hope; and hope confoundeth not,*[12] and the rest.

8. *They said in their hearts, the whole kindred of them together: Come, let us suppress all the feastdays of the Lord from the land.* The ills earlier recounted could have aroused the Lord's pity if the arrogance of the Jews had not remained unbending; for though they suffered such hardships, their minds did not abandon their blasphemies. For they spoke in their hearts, and so that such men might not seem to be a mere few, he added: *The whole kindred of them together;* so in view of their unrepentant hearts, their disaster was rightly not postponed. Next follows: *Come, let us suppress all the feastdays of the Lord from the land.* Here are recorded the words of the angry Jews, for they had seen their city overturned, and God's sanctuaries profaned; and so they cruelly and crazily said: "Let us abandon the Lord's law, for He has disdained to avenge us." Those who strove to crucify the Lord Christ did not reckon that they could merit a much more grievous fate. Asaph could not have uttered such words as from his own mouth, for in the psalm-heading his name was prefaced with the word: "Understanding."

9. *Our signs we have not seen: there is now no prophet: and he will know us no more.* They were the most demented of men, for they thought that after their guilt signs would be afforded them such as they appeared to merit before that most monstrous sin. What affected their

minds was the thought of the great nations which their ancestors had
laid low with the Lord's help, and the kingdoms which they had sub-
dued with a sudden concerted charge; and now that they had incurred
the greatest guilt, they said that they had been deprived of those signs
which they knew had been bestowed earlier on their devoted forefathers. Next comes: *There is now no prophet, and he will know us no
more.* These continue to be the words of the despairing Jews; for in
ancient times whenever the Israelites were oppressed by any disaster,
they approached prophets and were instructed by them at the command of the Lord on what they ought to have done; but their obstinacy
constrained them to disobey them. But now since they had no prophets since the coming of the Lord was fulfilled, they said that they had
been abandoned by the Lord when they did not set eyes on those to
whose advice they had become accustomed. Scripture says of such
men: *The sinner, when he is come into the depth of sins, contemneth.*[13] All
these words could be spoken only by the Jewish people, for they are
not appropriate to the Romans, who at that time were slaves to sacrilegious idols. So Asaph, showing true understanding and outstanding
in holiness, uttered this wonderful entreaty on the Jews' behalf. But so
that we should not think it merciless of the Godhead that his plea on
their behalf when heard was not approved, he made additional reference to the faults and loss of hope of the Jews, so that they rightly
incurred the vengeance owed them because there was no repentance
commensurate with their many sins.

10. *How long, O God, shall the enemy reproach? Is the adversary to
provoke thy name for ever?* His cry is that of a man seeking a helper, he
laments as one wounded who looks for a physician, when he says to
the Lord: "How long will You endure these reproaches which the
unbelieving Jew utters in Your face?" He says this not to cause their
destruction, for he judged them worthy of tears, but so that God might
improve them through the blessing of confession. Next comes: *Is the
adversary to provoke thy name for ever?* This explains his previous
words. The Lord endures the murmurings of the faithful till He takes
pity and induces His adversaries to confess His name; for He has the
power to correct those who depreciate Him in such a way that those
who earlier spoke words of self-destruction are later heard proclaiming words which bring salvation. The word "provoke" (*irritat*) is
taken from dogs' growling, in which the letter R is most conspicu-

ously audible. *For ever* here points to the evening of the world, when the greatest number of the Jews will come to believe.

11. *Why dost thou turn away thy face, and thy right hand out of the midst of thy bosom for ever?* He addresses the Lord as if He is affronted and angry, as One unwilling to gaze on a sinning people still apparently persisting in their wickedness. For by His wondrous dispensation the Lord when appeased corrects those on whom He directs His gaze, and chastises those on whom He looks with kindness. Next comes: *And thy right hand out of the midst of thy bosom for ever.* Here another mystery of the Old Testament is adduced. Just as Moses was allowed to perform miracles with a rod, so he was ordered to thrust his hand into his bosom, and when it was brought out again it was found to be leprous; then he was ordered to insert it again, and it was at once healed.[14] This indicates that the Jewish people was to become impure by abandoning the Lord Christ, but that it would recover its former health by returning to Him. The purpose of mentioning this was to foretell that the Jewish people was returning to its earlier sound health. This demonstration is called the *ab eventu* ("from the outcome")[15] when a speech proceeds towards the goal which the spokesman knows that the sequence of events attains. But so that we should not linger too long in recounting such things as this, he hastens to proceed to praises of the Lord, so that he may utter all he can to Him who is known to perform such great works.

12. *But God is our king before ages: he hath wrought salvation in the midst of the earth.* The understanding of Asaph proclaimed earlier in the heading passes on to the second part, with the spirit of prophecy foretelling that the Lord Saviour will come; by means of the demonstrative type of speech[16] he recounts all the miracles which the Lord performed in heaven and on earth. Because he intends to speak of His incarnation, he attests that the Lord was already King before the foundation of the world, so that no-one would believe that He was a mere lord in time. As He Himself says in the gospel: *I was born into this world.*[17] Ages (*saecula*) are so called because the seasons circle back on themselves (*in se*).[18] Next comes: *He hath wrought salvation in the midst of the earth.* Although this can be interpreted as relating to the miracles He performed, which He is known to have achieved before men's eyes, it would be better for us to understand it as referring to the salvation of souls which He achieved by His life-giving preaching.

In the midst of the earth means under the eyes of all peoples, a sense indicated by *earth*. This figure is known as metonymy,[19] when the content is indicated by the container.

13. *Thou by thy strength did make the sea firm: thou didst crush the heads of the dragons in the waters.* He wishes clearly to demonstrate his earlier statement that the Lord Saviour (who deigned to suffer for us, to destroy death by dying, to bestow freedom on captives and rewards on the condemned) was King before ages, so he recounts the miracles which He earlier performed amongst the Jewish race. He made the watery depths of the Red Sea firm when the waters on both sides became so motionless that they made a land-route out of the ship-bearing deep. Next comes: *Thou didst crush the heads of the dragons in the waters.* He appropriately expounds the mystery of that earlier miracle. That crossing of the Red Sea prefigured the waters of holy baptism, in which the heads of dragons—in other words, unclean spirits—are reduced to nothing when the water of salvation cleanses those souls which the spirits befouled with the filth of sins. Observe that in this and four further verses he assembles individual items of praise by the figure called *synathroismos;*[20] so that the very enumeration of His powers might soften the heart of the affronted and most powerful Judge.

14. *Thou hast broken the head of the dragon: thou hast given him to be meat for the people of the Ethiopians.* Whereas earlier he spoke of dragons' heads in the plural, he now mentions *dragon* in the singular, so that he seems to point to Satan himself, whose wickedness waxes with his strength. When he is cited in the singular, it is being emphatically denied that there is any equal to him among evil spirits. His head was broken when his pride was cast out of heaven; he did not deserve to preserve his native brightness, for by choosing darkness he blackened himself. The psalmist added: *Thou hast given him to be meat for the people of the Ethiopians.* We interpret Ethiopians appropriately as sinners who had previously been most foul because their minds were darkened, but on turning to the Lord they began to have the devil as meat, when they had their fill of disparaging him. Even today when we want someone to be considered as very wicked we call him a devil. We "blow him away" when any sin has been committed,[21] and he is called the author of all error; just as he attacks Christians, so he is torn to pieces by all with the repugnance of curses. So whereas he was

previously reverenced by pagans, he is now gnawed by the teeth of Christians' reproaches. Alternatively, the faithful now converted can have the devil as meat when they make progress through his ambushes and temptations, for through his persecution men become martyrs, and obtain their crowns by the gift of patience when he afflicts them. So he is rightly labelled the meat of those whom he directs towards the goal of their prayerful longing by frequently wearying them.

15. *Thou hast taken up the fountains and the torrents: thou hast dried up the rivers of Ethan.* The whole of this is spoken in allegory about sinners. He calls *fountains* those whose wicked deeds were continually flowing along, and *torrents* those suddenly roused and rushing along with swift sallies. The Lord will break up these two types of sinners when he cuts them away from the devil's retinue. Next comes: *Thou hast dried up the rivers of Ethan.* He refines the earlier sense; God not merely breaks up and sunders rivers or floods which have gathered through the devil's wickedness, but he also dries them up and removes them. When a river dries up, it is clearly reduced to nothing; and this is seen to happen when the overflowing designs of the devil, bringing a multitude of sins, have come to nought.[22] *Ethan* in Hebrew means "strong,"[23] and we have often said that this connotes the devil.

16. *Thine is the day, and thine is the night; thou hast made the sun and the moon.* The literal sense of this and the next verse is clear to all, for the Lord is Creator of all things, but it is more appropriate to seek out their spiritual sense. We may interpret *day* as the just on whom the light of wisdom ever shines, and *night* as the worldly who are darkened by the impact of sins. As another psalm has it: *Day to day uttereth speech, and night to night showeth knowledge.*[24] But when he says: *Thine is the day and thine is the night,* he shows that God performs great miracles in both, so that he enlightens the day with the gift of His fatherly love, and makes the night share His kingdom once it is cleansed of sins. He added: *Thou hast made the sun and the moon.* All these terms are more clearly explained by citation of examples: the sun indicates the wise person, and the moon the fool, as in the passage: *The wise man abides as the sun, but the fool changes like the moon.*[25] This is a splendid description; the astonishing achievements of the Almighty are marked by comparisons with the creation. But we are to realise that in all this the Lord Creator shows His customary and abundant fatherly love.

17. *Thou hast made all the borders of the earth: the summer and the spring, thou hast made them. Be mindful of this thy creature.* It is quite appropriate for us to call all the apostles and prophets *borders of the earth,* for just as borders mark out the limits of lands, so those who proclaim Christ maintain the laws of the true faith. Next comes: *The summer and the spring, thou hast made them.* By citing these seasons, he indicates the faithful whose strength lies in different forms of activity. Some are like the summer heat, fervent in the warmth of faith and drawn even to martyrdom; others are like the spring, gentle in manners and serving the Lord with placid devotion. The Lord has created all these and similar temperaments; by His grace is granted all that is manifest in men's good dispositions. He added: *Be mindful of this thy creature.* He offers the reason why the earlier catalogue was recounted, asking that He who regularly performs great deeds should also take pity on and show kindness to the sinning Jews. To elicit the benevolence of the kindly Lord he repeatedly recounts His benefits, so that He may deign to be mindful of those whom He deigned to create.

18. *The enemy hath reproached the Lord, and a foolish people hath provoked thy name.* He recalls the words uttered earlier: *Come, let us suppress all the feast-days of the Lord from the land,*[26] and the rest. The enemy was none other than the Jews, who uttered words against the Lord which seemed to rebuke Him, though no creature can sufficiently thank Him in any respect whatsoever. Next comes: *And a foolish people hath provoked thy name.* They were foolish especially in acting unworthily, for they listened without protest to what they ought totally to have rejected. Through this they provoked the Lord to anger, for they stated that such a fate had befallen them not through their sins but through the alleged injustice of the Lord which allowed them to be destroyed though they did not merit subjugation. So let us ponder this most salutary arrangement of the psalmist's prayer: he pleads for the guilty but continually confesses their transgressions. If the Jews had done this with devoted minds, they could have avoided as a community the punishment which was their due.

19. *Deliver not up to beasts the souls that confess to thee: forget not to the end the souls of thy poor.* Asaph passes to the third section; "understanding" rightly precedes citation of his name, for he confessed the sins of the people earlier, but with the presumption that those who

were devoted would be delivered by the Lord. In fact the holy man
begs for what he knew would be the outcome, that God might not
betray the souls of the faithful lest the devil attains his ends. For even
then among that people there were such vessels of mercy as Simeon,
Nicodemus, Nathaniel (to whom the Lord bore witness with the
words: *Behold an Israelite indeed, in whom there is no guile*)[27] and the
rest who were pleasing to the Lord through purity of heart. By *beasts*
he meant the devil and his agents, whose heads, as he said earlier, God
crushed on the waters.[28] Next comes: *And forget not to the end the souls
of thy poor.* He speaks of those who have rejected the arrogance of the
world and sought the most holy humility, asking that the benefits of
the Lord Saviour be not denied them, but rather that they be enriched
by His generosity because they have become His poor.

20. *Have regard to thy covenant: for they that are in the darkness of
the dwellings of iniquity on the earth have been filled.* "Have regard," he
says, "so that You may deign to fulfil what You are known to have
promised earlier." As Scripture says: *Behold the days will come, says the
Lord, when I will bring to pass for the house of Israel and the house of Juda
a new covenant, not according to the covenant which I arranged for their
fathers.*[29] In the former covenant the promises were bounded by time,
such as the land of promise and subjection of enemies. He had to grant
such things to an unschooled people so that they would subsequently
hasten without fear to the world of the spirit. But the promise in the
new covenant is of a life free from anxiety, a kingdom of which there
will be no end, but enduring blessedness and the glorious contemplation of the Lord. This is the covenant, then, for which he says the
Lord must have regard, so that He must swiftly proffer to an erring
people the benefits which will be profitable to them. Asaph has truly
become understanding when he asks for the means by which the
whole world would gain forgiveness. And note with what wisdom he
runs through this entire request; because there were no virtues which
he could have ascribed to the sinning people, he remembered the
Lord's promise which is always fulfilled. Another argument for showing pity follows, termed the absolute nature:[30] *For they that are in
darkness have been filled,* in other words sinners plunged in the darkness of ignorance. This is like Christ's own prayer for them from the
cross, when He said: *Father, forgive them, for they know not what they
do.*[31] But let us repeat this verse so that the interrelation of the words

can appear more easily. He said: *Have regard, for those that were in darkness have been filled.* They were filled with iniquities, and it was inevitable that darkness should overcome them; they are rightly likened to darkness, for they have lost the light of wisdom. He added: *Of the dwellings of iniquities on the earth.* These Jews belong to the dwellings of iniquities on the earth, in other words, they are worldly men from the house of iniquities. So that you should not interpret *the earth* in a good sense here, there is a splendid definition of the body of the unfaithful, that is, *the dwellings of iniquities,* for men corrupted by evil deeds admit all vices like a lodging house.

21. *Let not the humble be confounded: the poor and needy shall praise thy name.* In place of those seen to cause offence he sets those accustomed to possess the Lord's grace, so that love for the devoted might limit hatred for the insolent. This technique of argument is quite suitable when a pleasing person replaces one who is loathed. It is not the humble but the arrogant man who is confounded, for he does not acknowledge God's glory, but attributes to human merits whatever blessing he has received by the Lord's gift. Contrariwise the humble continually praise God and always accuse themselves; they realise that their wisdom is the gift of the Godhead, but their sinning issues from themselves. He begs that the humble be not confounded, for they are aware that whatever blessings they have received must be ascribed to the gifts of the Lord. Next comes: *The poor and needy shall praise thy name.* Let us see how glorious this poverty is, how blessed this need is proved to be which praises the Lord without recourse to words, and in harmony hymns the virtue of His patience. The proud man is dumb even if he sings; the poor and needy praise the Lord even when they are seen to keep silence. This is a blessing beyond reckoning if pondered inwardly. The poor man is called God's, the rich man is allotted to the world; the poor man belongs to the eternal King, the rich man to the fleeting hour. He who is outwardly rich possesses nothing for himself; it is the poor man who should rather be called self-sufficient, for he is known to have stored outstanding virtues in the treasure-house of his soul.

22. *Arise, O Lord, judge thy own cause: remember thy reproaches with which the foolish man hath reproached thee all the day.* After all that he has uttered he now pleads the cause of the Judge so as to move Him more effectively by making known to Him the nature of His concern.

Now he directs his words to the Lord Himself, asking that He adjudi-
cate His own cause against those who never cease to sound against
Him with their wicked whispers. He judges His own cause when He
makes sinners aware of the palpable facts, so that they may be converted and proclaim what in their stupid thoughts they had denied.
Next comes: *Remember thy reproaches;* he means those earlier mentioned: *There is now no prophet, and he will know us no more.*[32] He added:
With which the foolish man hath reproached thee, all the day—words
appended to what precedes, for these rebukes were mouthed by foolish men. So that they would not be thought to have been uttered
momentarily, he added: *All the day,* so that their continued repetition
riled the gentleness of the most patient Judge.

23. *Forget not the voices of them that seek thee: let the pride of them
that hate thee ascend continuously to thee.* In the first sentence he again
interspersed the prayers of the faithful, so that God would not reject
the petitions of those who are known to cry to Him with all their
hearts' devotion, begging that they may find Him whom they seek,
and deserve to behold Him for whom they search. Next comes: *Let the
pride of them that hate thee ascend continuously to thee.* We note that
this is fittingly applied to the Romans, of whom he previously said: *In
the midst of thy shrine they have set up their ensigns;*[33] he sought to rouse
the all-powerful Judge most emphatically against the foes of Jerusalem. Pride is the vice which the Lord particularly abominates. It was
through pride that both the angel fell and the blessedness of the first
man was lost. Notice how prudently this most cutting vice is set at the
end; he intended to conclude with what could be stored in the confines of the memory. This is the simple and prudent lament of those
who are devoted to the Lord in purity of heart; those who show
obedience by holy rules of life cannot be seduced in their grief, however severe it is.

Conclusion Drawn From the Psalm

Worthy listeners, you have heard how sweet are the duties of religious love to those who are most committed. You have heard how
they are unwilling that their descendants should bear the melancholy
of enduring with countless tears the prospect of their future calami-

ties. This indeed is the holy perfection of charity, to expound to them the future dangers which they fear will descend on their successors. What could the psalmist do about this vision of disaster, the coming of which he so clearly lamented with afflicted heart? So let us observe the consistency of truth afforded by the holy Scriptures, how Asaph earlier grieved for a Jerusalem still flourishing, for which many years later Jeremiah shed tears at the end of the captivity. Both laments show love, both are splendid; but in some sense the psalmist is seen to have been the more pitying, for we appreciate that he is shattered by most bitter grief at a time when he still enjoys prosperity. So it is right for us to reflect that the whole texture of the psalter is adorned with sparkling variation; now there is the joy of those who rejoice, now the groaning of those who repent; now there is wholesome instruction, now the grief of those who lament; now the foretelling of the incarnation that brings salvation, now the promise of rewards, now the fear of punishments, now praises of the Lord. Just as a garland interwoven with the sweetest flowers gives off an attractive fragrance, so we observe how the book smells sweetly with the different scents of the virtues.

COMMENTARY ON PSALM 74

1. *Unto the end corrupt not: a psalm of a canticle of Asaph.* The words of the heading are obscure unless considered in their due order. As we have often said, Asaph connotes the synagogue, but the believing assembly rather than that which continued obstinate. We read that after the Lord's Resurrection many thousands of Jews made confession; amongst other evidence Acts of the Apostles attests this.[1] So this Asaph now warns the Jews not to corrupt their faith *unto the end,* that is, their faith in the Lord Saviour, whose merit deserved their belief and who devised the reward of salvation. As long as these gifts are not squandered, we remain unharmed; but when they are cheapened, we are exiled from the Lord's sight. We have said that a psalm of a canticle lies in distinguishing practical activity from spiritual contemplation. The careful reader will elicit all this from this psalm.

Division of the Psalm

At the outset the faithful Jews proclaim that they will tell of all His miracles. In the second part King Jesus Christ Himself speaks, promising to judge justly when the time of universal resurrection comes. He also warns us against daring to do anything against God's commands, so that eternal punishment may not rack us.

Explanation of the Psalm

2. *We will confess to thee, O God, we will confess to thee, and we will call on thy name: I will relate all thy wondrous works.* In this single verse the rule of sacred devotion is explained in due sequence. The Jewish people who were to believe in the Lord Christ, and who the heading warns not to *corrupt unto the end,* bursts out and with great devotion pledges its praise. As we have often said, confession means the proclamation of something by the combined voices of many; for even if a single person is said to have confessed, it is acknowledged that he is joined to others who preceded him in the faith, or to those who follow him. The phrase, *we will confess to thee,* is repeated; this repetition attests the firm nature of the promise, for repetition is never employed casually but is used to denote firm decision, as in the phrase, *my heart is ready, O God, my heart is ready,*[2] *and similar statements. To thee* was inserted so that the cult of others should be excluded; true devotion is that which most justly reveres the Creator and no other. Let us ponder also that if we confess even once to a crime before an earthly judge, it often entails death; but frequent confession to God results not in hazard of death but in salvation. The run of words is really splendid. First the spokesman says that he is confessing, that is, lamenting his sins, and later that he is calling on the Lord's name; it is apt that we should first through His gift cleanse our hearts by confession, and thus call on the Lord's name to obtain help. To whom will He be able to come except to those who He knows are His own? If one not committed to Him calls on Him, he appears to be demanding judgment rather than pardon for himself. So we must preface our requests in this way so that we can call on God's clemency with confidence. He added: *I will relate all thy wondrous works.* Whereas earlier he said: *We*

will confess in the plural, here he says in the singular: *I will relate*. It is
appropriate for the people of God both to speak in the singular and to
bear the sense of the plural. This is the voice of the faithful which is
introduced here, for only those who knowingly serve God with unsullied devotion deserve to rehearse His wondrous works. As we read
in another psalm: *But to the sinner God hath said: Why dost thou declare
my justices?*[3] and the rest. But who could relate all those wondrous
works of heaven save him who proclaims in brief the holy Trinity as
Creator of all things, and ascribes to its undivided will all that is done
in heaven and on earth with a dispensation beyond telling?

3. *When I shall choose a time, I will judge justice.* The change of
speaker has presented us with the reply. This allows us to grasp how
Asaph in the previous verse understands the rule of perfect religion,
and so deserves to be heard so quickly. For now the Lord Christ says:
When I shall choose a time—He means the time at which He became
man. As it says in the gospel: *He hath given him power to do judgment,
since he is the Son of man.*[4] Listen to what He says in His divine nature:
*All things whatsoever the Father hath are mine, and mine are the Fa-
ther's.*[5] The nature which receives and that which bestows are the one
Lord Christ; as Paul puts it: *And one Lord Jesus Christ, by whom are all
things, and we by him.*[6] Next comes: *I will judge justice;* this is so that
men's hearts may be pricked before the time of the Judgment, and may
pray more eagerly in this world to be forgiven, so that when they pass
to the Judgment to come they may not undergo a decision of the Judge
contrary to their expectation.

4. *The earth is melted, and all that dwell therein: I have strengthened
the pillars thereof.* The Lord says that before His coming the earth
comprised a human race dissolved from the solidity of truth into the
ruin of sin, for it had abandoned its Creator and was enslaved to
sacrilegious idols. But He then explains how He came to the aid of the
melted earth with the salvific incarnation: *I have strengthened the pillars thereof.* We must interpret pillars as the apostles, who were
strengthened at the resurrection after becoming unsteady at the Lord's
passion. The Lord Himself steadied them when He said to the apostle
Peter: *Peter, how often hath Satan desired to have you to sift as wheat!
But I have prayed for you, that your faith fail not; and you being once
converted, confirm your brethren.*[7] Notice the most appropriate verbal
contrast; after the earth was melted, the strengthened pillars were able

to come to its aid. The apostles are aptly compared to pillars, for they repress the vices below, and raise up heavenly virtues to the grace of the divine kingdom.

5. *I said to the wicked: Do not act wickedly; and to the sinners, Lift not up the horn.* These words mean the same as *I have strengthened the pillars* earlier. Through the prophets and apostles He transmitted the warnings of the Old and New Testaments, that evil men should not do wicked deeds but should turn quickly to God and make humble satisfaction. The truly devoted Physician laid down the rule for health so that human weakness should not contract harmful diseases. Next comes *And to the sinners, Lift not up the horn.* Here too supply "said"; but previously He told the wicked to put an end to all sinning, whereas now he turns to that most heinous fault of making excuses, with which mankind is sorely afflicted. When a person cannot bear to say he is guilty, and in his guilt thinks up some external causes to find excuses for his sins, now accusing the devil and now assailing the words of one who prompted him, he appears to be lifting up his horn, because he strives to blame his sin on others. So such people cannot be restored to pardon, because they have abandoned the remedies of confession.

6. *Lift not up your horn on high: speak not iniquity against God.* The repetition of this witness shows the fear of heavy vengeance, for an injunction expressed by repeated command is always the occasion of sterner punishment. When He says: *Lift not up your horn on high,* He is urging men to abandon blasphemous thoughts, for it is the person who ponders evil and murmurs back against God who lifts up his horn on high. Observe the words that follow: *Speak not iniquity against God;* he still continues to impugn excuses so as to remedy the vice. A person speaks iniquity against God when he reckons that things are ordained so that he cannot avoid sins at all. He says that he has done some wicked deed not through his own fault but by the compulsion of the stars, and thus he prefers to ascribe to the Creator the sin which he committed of his own volition. How much more tactful and useful it would be to confess his crime! But when he performed some wicked deed, he neglected to call on the Redeemer of all so as to be freed of his sin.

7. *For neither in the east, nor in the west, nor in the desert hills.* This verse requires something to be supplied so that its meaning can become clear to us. He says: *For neither in the east, nor in the west, nor in*

the desert hills, and we must add: "Is the Lord absent for the purpose of recognising you," for it is clear that He is wholly present everywhere. As we read in another place: *The spirit of the Lord filled the world.*[8] In secular literature this figure is called *eclipsis* or deficiency, when some words are omitted from the full sense.[9] But here it was employed not for lack of words but to encourage more eager investigation of what was suppressed by necessary silence. So blasphemers must stop thinking sacrilegious thoughts when the Judge proclaims His presence, for knowledge of all things in the sphere of truth is available to Him. So that none should be surprised that in this survey of the world only two quarters are mentioned, we must expound the passage better by offering the spiritual sense if we can. Let us interpret the east as those persons notable for heavenly brightness, and the west as sinners from whom the light of truth is as yet hidden. Perhaps we should regard the desert hills as false preachers who claim for themselves a place on the hilltops as a preaching platform, but are deserted by the truth like all heretics and pagans. So since God is known to attend on and have knowledge of all races, no-one should evince any such presumption as may condemn him at the final judgment.

8. *For God is the judge: one he putteth down, and another he lifteth up.* See how the whole unholy matter is settled, *For God is the judge.* Since He is judge, there is no doubt that He is just, for when He is called the judge He is undoubtedly regarded as most just. And so that the word, *Judge,* may be shown to embrace this, a straightforward account of the Judgment is given: *One he putteth down, and another he lifteth up.* He puts down the proud in particular and lifts up the humble, for the proud man has trust in himself, but the humble man trusts in the Lord. Similarly we read in the gospel: *Every man who exalts himself shall be humbled, and he who humbles himself shall be exalted.*[10] So you see that the just Judge delivers a sentence appropriate to the parties.

9. *For in the hand of the Lord there is a chalice of pure wine full of mixture: and he hath poured it out from this to that.* We have frequently said that a chalice (*calix*) is a drinking measure by which bodies fainting from thirst are restored; it gets its name from the hot (*calidus*)[11] drink which we often take when we are feasting. So the Lord's law is splendidly called a chalice, for when it is circulated, drunk and stored inside, it provides souls with the sweetest nourishment. Next comes: *Of pure wine, full of mixture.* In the divine Scriptures wine connotes

the heavenly mystery such as occurred in the water jars which the Lord ordered to be filled with water;[12] the liquid from the streams changed its nature and took on a red colour which it did not naturally have. This is why blessed Ambrose in his hymn for the holy Epiphany[13] showed wondrous eloquence with the most vivid brightness of words. The word *pure* indicates what is unadulterated, what is ever genuine and clear. It brings persons renewed to the glory of virtue, not to the vice of drunkenness, and in the words of another psalm: *And thy chalice which inebriateth, how goodly it is!*[14] The Lord's chalice is *full of mixture*, so that though continually drunk it is never emptied. *Mixture* points to the New and Old Testaments; the mixture of the two effects the most health-giving drink for souls. The Jews indeed had wine to drink, but it was not mixed because they were unwilling to admit the nourishment of the New Testament. Likewise Manichees did not drink mixed wine, because they accepted the New Testament in part but rashly rejected the mysteries of the Old Law.[15] He added: *And he hath poured it out from this to that.* Here he points unambiguously to the two communities of Jews and Gentiles, for He took from the mouths of unbelieving Jews that which he poured out for the converted peoples of the Gentiles as their drink. It was a blessed and untroubled refreshment to obtain the chalice of salvation from Him who always knows how to provide what will be beneficial. This manner of speaking is peculiar to sacred literature, for one can hardly ever find it, I think, in secular writing.

But the dregs thereof are not emptied: all the sinners of the earth shall drink of them. The word dregs is used for the remains of wine which settle into a concentrated thickness once the liquid above it is seen to be consumed. Since he earlier said that the chalice was full, he here stated that the dregs were not emptied because they could not be reached, for its fullness never diminishes though all men drink from it. Dregs is not to be interpreted here as lees, but as the last and lowest part of the wine; for how could the wine which he earlier described as pure and unadulterated contain lees? So that you might realise that the cup was by no means emptied as far as the dregs, he resumes the theme of the full chalice with the words: *All the sinners of the earth shall drink of them.* This points to an event which we have often mentioned, that the Jews at the end of time will drink of this chalice with other sinners, when they shall deserve to show belief and shall join the

Catholic Church in unity of faith, for they all belong to that group which will through the Lord's kindness deserve to obtain belief, whereas many sinners will remain unbending in their ways.

10. *But I will rejoice for ever: I will sing to the God of Jacob.* When Christ says: *I will rejoice,* and: *I will sing,* He refers to His members, for He rejoices when they rejoice, and He sings to the God of Jacob when the Church sounds forth its psalmody. Whatever the limbs perform well, as has often been said, is reasonably ascribed to their Head.

11. *And I will break all the horns of sinners: and the horns of the just shall be exalted.* See how the voice of the Judge, the voice of the Almighty, has sounded forth. He who has just sung psalms in His members now breaks all the horns of sinners. In that adjudication all the powers of the wicked will be humbled, and the horns which are here raised to lofty heights will be broken and scattered. So the proud should note how base it is to imitate hornless cattle in this world, and they should blush to advertise themselves by means of those attributes which are soon to be the mark of their disfigurement. Next comes: *And the horns of the just will be exalted.* This figure is known as *catachresis* or bold metaphor,[16] when foreign terms of things are lent to those which do not have them. The horns of the just are in fact gifts bestowed at the Judgment to come; they are indeed strongly lifted up because they will endure in perennial beauty. In this world we see the horns of sinners which will not exist in the next; in this world we do not see the horns of the just which are bestowed as an undying gift in the next. That humility which in this life is seen as neglected will later be outstandingly adorned; what greater reward will its glory be able to possess than the espousal of it in this world by Him who will be the source of all blessedness without end?

Conclusion Drawn From the Psalm

We have heard the words of the Lord uttered not from the heights of heaven but from the sacred writings of the Psalter. We must obey Him all the more readily as He has deigned to offer advice to us all together. When the Lord spoke to Moses, the lightning flashed, the thunder crashed, the whole of Mount Sinai smoked, and fear of death penetrated all men; the command which brings life reached mankind in a manner which made them believe that they would perish through great hazard. So see how we must continually marvel at the kindnesses of the Lord Saviour if only we can understand them, for we carry His words every day in our hands. The Lord's wishes are revealed to us enclosed in the divine writings; He makes them available by His bodily appearance, so that the inner eye of the heart may be schooled for our welfare. He is never silent if we have recourse to Him in His writings. He is always ready to offer a vital response, and He is never at any time found to be absent if we seek Him with pure hearts. So let us, as the psalm urges us, renounce the pride which secludes the wicked from Him, and let us love the humility which joins the saints to Him in heavenly love.

COMMENTARY ON PSALM 75

1. *Unto the end, in praises, a psalm of Asaph: a canticle to the Assyrians.* All the terms of this heading ought to be thoroughly familiar from our previous explanations, and it only remains to expound the one new phrase, *to the Assyrians.* Assyrians means "those who proceed directly";[1] they are always learned in the rules of the faith, and hasten to tread right paths. Asaph addresses them, singing the praises of the Lord with marvellous variation.

Division of the Psalm

Asaph, whose name we have said means "the synagogue,"[2] addresses "those who proceed directly," that is, the faithful Jews, in the first section; he points to where the name of the Lord has become widely known through the declaration of His powers. In the second section he speaks of the Lord's wonderful deeds. In the third, he counsels the committed ones never to cease offering gifts to the God who inspires fear, and who purifies the hearts of princes with salutary improvement. These sections are separated by the intervention of diapsalms.[3]

Explanation of the Psalm

2. *In Judaea God is known: his name is great in Israel.* This verse can raise a query: why is it stated that in Judaea God is known, when we are certain that the Lord Christ was crucified there? We must investigate what Judaea is, so that the truth of the statement can be clear to us. Though the Jewish people was divided into twelve tribes, it is known that they got their name from Judah, son of Jacob. From his line they appointed kings to rule them by God's dispensation, so that the royal line passed down from its physical origin to the coming of the heavenly Prince. So it is clear that the true Judaea is Christ's Church. Judaea means "confessing"[4] or believing in that King who came from the tribe of Judah through the virgin Mary. Those who have alienated themselves from Christ, that is, from the stock of Judah which is agreed to be the origin of their name, are not strictly Jews, for when they betrayed the Lord they said: *We have no king except Caesar.*[5] So how can they properly be called Jews when they proclaimed that their king was Caesar and not Christ? Next comes: *His name is great in Israel.* We have said that Israel means "one who sees God."[6] How can they reasonably claim this name when they did not acknowledge God, and decided to crucify Him as if He were a man? As Paul remarks: *If they had known it, they would never have crucified the Lord of glory.*[7] So this name too they have lost, since they were wholly unwilling to believe in His majesty. Poor creatures! They have lost their titles as well as their holy privileges. This psalm then, as we have said, speaks to those who were illumined by the true Light, and set apart from the wickedness of the unfaithful. The name of the Lord is indeed great among them, since with pure hearts they confess Him as *King of kings and Lord of lords.*[8]

3. *And his place is established in peace: and his abode in Sion.* This proclamation that the Lord's place is peace is a marvellous and pithy statement, for He cannot take rest anywhere except in the person who can live an untroubled life. As Scripture has it: *Upon whom does my spirit rest, save on him that is humble and quiet, and who trembles at my words?*[9] That person is known to be at peace with the Lord who does not dispute His commands with opposing desires, who follows the command of the Master, and who bends his own will to every heavenly precept. True peace resides in possessing harmony with worthy

manners, and in disputation with vices. We must also note that the psalmist allotted a place to the Lord who is not bounded by place; but although He is everywhere and is not restricted to any region, He is said to dwell locally in those whom He deigns in kindness to visit. Next comes: *And his abode in Sion*. Sion, as we have often stated, is a mountain situated at Jerusalem, and the meaning of its name is "contemplation," by which God is perceived by the hearts of the faithful. Though the venerable Godhead does not reveal himself to bodily eyes, the highest divinity does not refuse His presence to the most unsullied thought, for it is in that where we apparently bear our image of Him. The person who has deserved to gaze on Him with a pure heart becomes Mount Sion. So He dwells in the one who is seen to apprehend Him, and He who embraces every place in spacious extent is said in wondrous fashion to take rest only in holy minds.

4. *There hath he broken the horn-shaped bows, the shield, the sword, and the battle. There* means in that peace and contemplation of the Godhead which he mentioned earlier; for where the Lord of peace deigns to dwell, these weapons are broken, and such things cannot prevail except when purely human strife is seen to be aroused. *Horn-shaped bows* connote the malice of the proud from whom come wounds and impious dangers upon innocent persons. The shield is here to be interpreted as that assumed for the most wicked struggles undertaken by the devil's deceits, and the sword is for inflicting dangerous and visible wounds. Lastly he introduced battle, which is seen to be wholly opposed to peace. We know that all these are broken and shattered when the Author of peace is clearly present. This figure is called *enargeia* or imagination, when it presents an action before the inner eye.[10]

5. *Thou enlightenest wonderfully from the everlasting hills*. He passes to the second section, in which he proceeds to expound the various miracles of the Lord. So that we should not ask the source of this enlightenment, he added: *From the everlasting hills*, that is, from the preachers who are indeed everlasting hills, for they continue in their enduring and unchangeable loftiness. Earthly mountains are transient and lifeless, but through the Lord's gift the preachers are ever wise, and know that they are enduring. The psalmist preserved the order of the truth splendidly: he said that the Lord enlightens through the everlasting hills because he bestowed on the prophets and apostles

what was spread throughout the whole world by holy preaching. Store in your memory the fact that by the epithet *everlasting* he distinguished true preachers from false heretics who cannot be called everlasting, for once they teach perverse doctrines soon to fade they will be wiped out together with their beliefs.

6. *All the foolish of heart were troubled. They have slept their sleep: and all the men of riches have found nothing in their hands.* He earlier said that the faithful were enlightened by the Lord through the hills, and now he has stated that the foolish of heart are troubled and confounded; and rightly so, for the holy preaching which enlightened the just caused the foolish to be troubled. So they retreated from the true light, and followed the clouded desires of the world. They slept in their waking hours, for they were asleep to good deeds since they were always confounded by the tumult of errors. The psalmist did well to call the life of the unfaithful a sleep, for neglect of what will be profitable and the pursuit of the transient is not wakefulness. He was right to emphasise *their* sleep so that he could distinguish this from the repose of the blessed. *Their* sleep is seductive and deceptive, so that at one time they rejoice that they have acquired riches, at another that they have contracted a well-connected marriage, and at another that they have been elevated to high distinctions. But note the confounding that attends them: *And the men of riches have found nothing in their hands.* Alone of men they lose what they never truly possessed; in that demented experience of loss they grieve, although they never had the pleasure of enjoyment. Observe how he denotes and defines the greedy. He speaks of the men of riches, that is, those who are slaves to their money with captive minds. Next follows a splendid example of *emphasis;*[1] they continue to search in their hands though they are aware that they have held nothing. For *emphasis* embraces two forms of exaggeration; on the one hand it suggests more than it says, and on the other it also establishes what it does not say. Here it is the type which suggests what it does not say. The phrase, *men of riches,* indicates that they possessed what the whole world longs for, and like those who dream in sleep, they were mocked when they vainly sought to grasp what they desired.

7. *At thy rebuke, O God of Jacob, they have all slumbered that mounted on horseback.* Whereas a rebuke usually makes active people alert and watchful, the psalmist says that at the rebuke of the Lord, the God of

Jacob, the unbelievers slumbered; precisely so, since they heard the holy warnings with inattentive and sluggish hearts. He next explains the identity of those who slumbered; they were those that mounted on horseback, in other words, grew in arrogance and roamed through the allurements of this world as though on galloping horses. If you seek the cause of their headlong hurry, it was because their enthusiasm slumbered, their eagerness snored, and their speeding course proceeded in the tomb of sleep. An example of this was the Pharaoh, who mounted his chariots and his horses, despised the rebukes of the Lord with stubborn mind, and through his slumbering passed into the eternal sleep where no rest is found.

8. *Thou art terrible, and who shall resist thee then, because of thy wrath?* Let us examine a little more carefully the message of this verse. The psalmist earlier said that the Lord rebukes those who mount on horseback, in other words, leap into arrogance; he now says that at the Judgment He is terrible to all, when He comes in the glory of His majesty to condemn the proud and to bestow enduring honour on the humble of heart. On this earth many resist His commands when they prefer to seek the things which are forbidden by His warnings; but at the Judgment *who will resist thee?* This is to be understood in the negative sense, because no wicked men can show resistance there where they know that the Lord condemns all villainous deeds. *Then* refers to the time of the Judgment, also called the day of anger and rage,[12] because there will be no further restraint in God's longanimity when punishment is now inflicted on the wicked.

9. *He has hurled his judgment from heaven: the earth trembled, and was still.* Here the very force of the adjudication is described; the Judgment comes down from that peak of power like a javelin hurled by the strongest and most unerring hand. But whereas an earthly spear inflicts a temporal blow, the Judgment will wound the wicked eternally. Next comes: *The earth trembled, and was still.* The earth, as has often been remarked, here denotes the most heavy and bloated sinners who will be condemned by the authority of God's judgment. They will tremble when they hear: *Go into eternal fire.*[13] They will be still when they are admitted to eternal damnation. But this stillness is without rest; they desist from their evil deeds but they are not at rest in their pains, for they will be tortured in eternal flames.

10. *When God rose in judgment, to save all the meek of the earth.* This

verse is to be joined to the previous one. The psalmist says: *The earth trembled and was still when God rose in judgment.* The phrase "rising in judgment" is splendid, for on earth when Christ was judged, He bore everything in silence, though at the Judgment too He will pronounce on all things without anger. The word *rise* is adopted from the practice of judges on earth, who on passing harsh sentence are said to rise because they appear wrathful when punishing crimes which have been committed. So that you would not think that the Judgment was to be held solely to condemn the wicked, he added: *To save all the meek of the earth.* The meek of the earth are those who are not carried away with flaming desire by any worldly vices, but deport themselves with untroubled self-control, as has been said earlier, and are shown to have placid peace of mind. They are saved when through the Lord's gift they obtain the promised rewards.

11. *For the thought of man shall confess to thee: and the remainders of thoughts shall celebrate holiday before thee.* He passes to the third section, advising us that as the Lord is the only One to whom the highest celebration is owed, they should offer their vows to the God who inspires fear, who can transform the arrogance of princes to the most humble sanctity. Our thoughts confess to God only when they condemn our past sins by offering humble satisfaction. But because human frailty must always bewail its sinning, he added: *And the remainders of thoughts shall celebrate holiday before thee.* The remainders of thoughts are the recollection of the wickedness of our past sins, after shedding of tears and sustained contrition of heart. This is what celebrates holiday before the Lord, when we feel that we have been delivered from the death imposed by sins. Hence the Jews when cleansed of the foulness of sins are bidden to offer to the Lord the service of joy; this is what in my view Psalm 50 touches upon. For when the psalmist says: *Wash me yet more from my iniquity, and cleanse me from my sin,*[14] the wickedness of the past is confessing to the Lord through fear of the judgment to come. Do you wish also to hear the prophet celebrating holiday in spirit? After many intervening verses this is what follows: *Then shalt thou accept the sacrifice of justice, oblations and whole burnt-offerings; then shall they lay calves upon thy altar.*[15] In this way the blessed brotherhood of the psalms shows consistency in their shared truth.

12. *Make vows and offer them to the Lord your God: all you that are*

round about him offer presents to the terrible one. Since it is fitting that
we should fulfil all the precepts of the Lord, and it is necessary for us
to listen to the words of His command, Asaph too here warns us that
we should first make vows and later offer them to the Lord. This is
quite appropriate advice, for there are many things which we must
discharge even if we have not promised them; for example: *Thou shalt
not kill, thou shalt not commit adultery, thou shalt not steal,*[16] and the
other sins which we are forbidden to commit. There are other things
which we are not compelled by any law to fulfil, such as maintaining
virginity, retiring to the desert, and disciplining ourselves with daily
emaciation by fasting. So the psalmist invites us to promise such
works; if we do not promise them, we are not in any sense bound to
perform them. It is legitimate to seek marriage, to remain within the
holy community of the Church, and to take joy in suitable refreshment. But when the actions which are better than these have been
pledged, the psalmist bids that they be rendered. As Paul puts it: *He
that giveth his virgin in matrimony doth well, and he that giveth her not
doth better.*[17] The psalmist added: *To your God,* to indicate the faithful
who exult in the worship of the holy Spirit. Next comes: *All you that
are round about him offer presents.* By *all* he means those whom he bade
to make and offer vows—not the pagans and heretics, but those who
hasten to offer gifts at His altar according to Catholic custom. The
task is performed round about Him when the gifts of the faithful are
offered on the most sacred altars. As for his expression, *to the most
terrible one,* he is thinking particularly of those who are devoted to
Him; He is known to be also kindly to them. As Scripture has it: *Serve
the Lord in fear, and rejoice unto him with trembling.*[18] He is not terrible
to the wicked and to those who despise Him, for if they feared the
Lord they would comport themselves honourably in life.

13. *Even to him who takes away the spirit of princes, to the one who is
terrible before the kings of earth.* The faithful preacher is still proclaiming the mighty deeds of the Lord. He says we must make vows to the
terrible One who takes away the spirit of princes, meaning the spirit
of pride or arrogance. So that you would note that they have been
converted, he added: *Before the kings of the earth,* meaning those found
worthy to rule and govern their bodies through the Lord's kindness.
For here we are to understand *kings* as those emptied of the spirit of
pride, and not swollen with power; so far as these are concerned, it is a

greater miracle that they were not punished when puffed up with pride, but rather granted conversion and set free.

Conclusion Drawn From the Psalm

See how Asaph, who was said in the psalm-heading to be advising those on course, has proceeded as far as the mysteries of the Lord Christ. He states that He whom the madness of the Jews loudly claimed for crucifixion is terrible before kings. So understand, you stubborn people, that you are not on course but are gone astray, since you refused to listen to this adviser whose prompting is so wholesome in all matters. This is why you live dispersed in alien kingdoms and do not conduct your sacrifices, for you preferred to love the Roman sceptre rather than that of your own land. Since those who make confession are called *Judaei* (Jews) in the Latin language, how can you claim this name when you are so oppressively stubborn? So why do you not heed this great punishment, when you have lost your very title after all else?

The text of the psalms has here reached the half-way mark. Through the Lord's generosity we have completed the same number as that which we know still remains for us to complete. Let us pray that He who granted us grace in the psalms that lie behind us may grant us effective help in those yet to come.

COMMENTARY ON PSALM 76

1. *Unto the end, for Idithun, a psalm of Asaph. Unto the end,* as we know, points to the Lord Saviour. We have stated also in earlier psalm-headings what the name Idithun is to mean: "leaping over them."' It is clear that Asaph is the name for the assembly. So now that we have offered an explanation of these terms, we are to understand here the gathering which has leapt over the vices of this world with triumphant progress, and has attained that end which has no rival that can be ascertained. So the whole of this psalm will be sung by the faithful gathering subsumed under the name Asaph.

Division of the Psalm

This Asaph, who we have said leaps over vices, attests in the first section of the psalm that he cries to the Lord, and hints that he has been further schooled by his afflictions, a fate which often befalls the faithful. In the second section he outlines the thoughts which are wont to assault the hearts of those who toil in this world. In the third part he maintains that through the kindness of the Godhead he was converted to better sentiments, so that with resolute mind he pondered the work and power of God, through which by diligent practice he is seen to have made progress. In the fourth part he continues with an explanation of how through the Lord Saviour divine miracles have been enacted through the nations.

Explanation of the Psalm

2. *I cried to the Lord with my voice: my voice to God, and he gave ear to me.* This Asaph, who excels at leaping over worldly desires, cries to the Lord not for bodily health or acquisition of wealth or winning high position, but for love of the Lord which is already infused in those made perfect, so that contemplation of the Godhead may bring him spiritual consolation in this training ground where he practises confession. The phrase *with my voice* represents the type of utterance already defined in Psalm 73, where he says: *With fire they have burned my sanctuary,*[2] and the like. In secular literature this figure is called pleonasm; we can explain it without embarrassment even though father Augustine is known to have mentioned it very often amongst other types of expression.[3] We must note that only he who seeks the things which the Lord promises to bestow on the faithful cries to the Lord; we know that the person who asks Him for transient things does not cry to the Lord, even though he seems to beseech Him. He repeats the words, *my voice to God;* we must supply "reached." But he does not specify what he sought—and rightly, for it is not necessary to tell Him what to grant us, for He alone has the knowledge to bestow what is fitting. So they are truly wise who entrust themselves to the power and dispensation of the Godhead; Him alone they seek, and the outcome is all that is good for them. This is the message of the prophet

Isaiah: *Lord our God, give us thy peace; for thou hast bestowed all things on us.*[4] Next comes: *And he gave ear to me.* Note that this utterance to the Lord, so short but magnificent in its devotion, sought that He should deign to give ear; what is there that He has failed to give us when out of pity He has granted such a request? For His gaze on us spells deliverance, and a bestowal of gifts so great that even the greedy suppliant ceases to beg for them.

3. *In the day of my trouble I sought God with my hands lifted up before him in the night: and I was not deceived. I refused to comfort my soul.* Those obsessed with worldly desires in times of affliction usually pray to be freed from the enforced condition which they bear. For example, a sick person asks for good health, a traveller for his native land, a poor man for money for his needs. But Asaph, seeking to include in a short petition all that would benefit him, did not make loud mention of his straits or impatiently obtrude his afflictions; as though at peace and unaware of his evils, he sought with his whole heart the contemplation of the Lord in the day of his trouble. His next words are: *With my hands lifted up before him in the night, and I was not deceived.* Here he includes an account of how he sought the Lord as a man should, and the reward which followed his action. *With my hands* means "by good works," which are known to accord with God's commands. *In the night* refers to life in this world, which is obscured by the darkness of sins though appearing to have light. *Before him* means not before men's eyes but in secret; as Christ Himself says: *Do not do your justice before men,*[5] and so on. Things occur in His presence when not directed at human eyes to obtain the swollen pride of empty praises, as when a man publicises some good deed of his. Next comes: *And I was not deceived.* Truly that person is not deceived who obtains fulfilment of promises. But we must investigate more carefully why he says: *I refused to comfort my soul,* when he was already rejoicing in contemplation of the Lord. The holy man rightly refuses to comfort his soul with gifts sought by human desires; for example, by seeking restful relaxation when wearied by vigils, or by refreshing the body with suitable cheer when exhausted by fasting, or by dispelling melancholy by gossiping with friends. For Asaph there was only one consolation, to fix his concentration always on the Lord.

4. *I was mindful of God, and was delighted, and was exercised, and my spirit for a moment swooned away.* See how he was utterly restored

when he refused to have his soul consoled by worldly things. When we are mindful of God, we are suffused with a gift of unalloyed sweetness; nothing can equal the experience of beginning to be filled with divine grace. Next comes: *I was exercised, and my spirit for a moment swooned away.* He says he was exercised by that contemplation of God, when he pondered the wisdom with which He orders all things, the power with which He controls everything as He simultaneously performs all events and arranges so many things with a marvellous dispensation. It was inevitable that his understanding should swoon when things so countless and so huge gathered in a single recollection. As we read elsewhere: *I considered thy works, and was afraid.*[6] The expression *for a moment* is well said; even though he seemed to swoon momentarily, we realise that he could be restored a little later.

5. *My eyes anticipated the vigils: I was troubled, and I spoke not.* He passes to the second section, in which he recounts his fevered thoughts. He says that his eyes anticipated the vigils which he customarily observed in his praises of God. Our practice normally terms these "nocturnal"; those who always concentrate on spiritual meditation must have recourse to these, for preoccupation makes our thoughts wakeful; only those wholly free of concern find sleep. Next comes: *I was troubled, and I spoke not.* He shows that it was indeed at night when in recollection he sought the secrets of his heart; for he was troubled by calling sinners to mind, for the human race was rushing headlong down the steep slope of wicked deeds. Though he himself had now risen above worldly vices, he was tortured with devoted sorrow for others. So he was silent, for in the depths of night he had no consolation from human conversation; at that hour those who deliberate ponder more carefully.

6. *I thought upon the days of old, and the eternal years.* He embarks on the "deliberative" mode of utterance, which we shall demonstrate at the end of this section,[7] for it carefully unfolds in its separate parts. He explains why he was troubled: it was because he thought upon the days of old, that is, the days of Adam, because of which the human race was kept in subjection to sins. Of that time the psalmist says elsewhere: *Behold, thou hast made my days old.*[8] But these days are brief, transient and fleeting in their variety as they slip by; in contrast with these days of old he cites *the eternal years.* Whereas the former perish

in a moment, those which are to come endure perennially. In these days of ours death is lord, but in those to come continuing life reigns. Our days are gnawed by devouring sadness, but in the future days the just will rejoice in untroubled blessedness. Finally, in these days all that comes flees away, whereas in the days to come whatever is bestowed will remain. But why does the person already dedicated to God set the eternal years against the days of old? He was pondering why the human race longs for and seeks so eagerly the days which slip away and which none can retain, and why we neglect and despise and disbelieve in the eternal years, which alone we ought especially to desire, just because we cannot visualise them at the present time. So he was right to be troubled, for he realised that sinners are subject to such debased convictions.

7. *I had them in mind: and I meditated in the night with my own heart: I was exercised, and I fanned my spirit within me.* The beginning of this verse is to be appended to the previous one. It runs like this: *And the eternal years I had in mind,* not like foolish people, who do not believe or store in their memory what they hear, but consign to forgetfulness what they have too carelessly taken in. Asaph has in mind the eternal years, for he believed that they would come. It is the person who makes his soul consider something in the light of reason who *meditates with his own heart.* We speak with our souls in silence, we are exercised with our souls without speech; we are not alone when we struggle with them in disputations on which we embark. Next comes: *I was exercised, and I fanned my spirit within me.* This process of deliberation is appropriately expressed; we are exercised when we sweat over countless reconsiderations, and as if we were on the wrestling ground of the soul we are wearied with the grappling of the spirit. The spirit is fanned when like a wind it rushes from one point to another with the swiftest reflexion, for the spirit is the soul's strength which strives to fulfil its aims.

8. *And I said: Will God then cast off for ever, or will he not so order things as to be pleased still?* When our Asaph who leaps over the vices of the whole world was pondering his hardships, and his spirit was exercised by protracted reflexions, he said: "Will God then cast off for ever the human race, so as not to take prior thought for us by the merciful nature of His coming?" Asaph already apprehended the future kindnesses of the Lord, for he was discussing the fatherly affec-

tion of that heavenly mercy which had been promised. Next comes: *Or will he not so order things as to be pleased still?* The "not" here is affirmation rather than denial; He will indeed order things, in other words, ensure that the human race is pleasing to Him when He shall deign to reveal the mysteries of the incarnation. His word *still* expresses his expectancy rather than grief; for though he believed that it would come to pass, he was sure that the development would occur at a later time.

9. *Or will he cut off his mercy until the end from the world and his generation?* The mercy of the Lord lies in His having deigned to be born in the flesh of the virgin Mary to support our weakness. The Lord did not cut this off, for He promised through the prophets that it would come for the salvation of men. When bishop Stephen wrote on this passage in his encyclicals to the emperor Leo, he framed these remarkable words: "The Son donned the tunic of the body, that is, the whole man, from the holy Virgin. The holy Spirit wove it in a manner beyond description. His entry cannot be described, but His departure can be understood. His coming was unseen, but His departure was visible. He entered as God the Word; He departed also as Man."[9] *Until the end* points to the fullness of time when He deigned to come; of this time the apostle John said: *Little children, it is the last hour.*[10] He added: *From the world and his generation.* From the world, that is, into which it had been decreed that He would come; from His generation, that is, from the Jews whom He deigned even to call brothers because of the blood-relationship. What a splendid promise, what a saving intimation, if only they had deserved to acknowledge what was granted them by this unique gift!

10. *Will God forget to show mercy, or will he in anger restrain his mercy?* We ourselves can forget what occurs to our minds and then escapes us; but how can God, in whom mercy is substantially present, forget what is demonstrably not removed from Him? So Asaph foretold God's mercy because He foresaw His coming. What more powerful mercy can there be than that by which the world's calamity is known to have been removed? Next comes: *Or will he in anger restrain his mercy?* Observe the remarkable order in which this coming is described: mercy is adduced everywhere because this important gift is accorded to the wretched. It is easier for the Lord to restrain His anger, which we know is remote from His tranquillity; but we should

believe that He is more inclined to mercy, which is never detached from His majesty. As He says through Isaiah: *I shall not take vengeance on you for ever, nor will I be angry with you for all time.*[11] So He will not restrain His mercy in anger, but rather He will refrain from anger in mercy, as long as devoted conversion is forthcoming in this world. Remember too that in the case of the Lord anger is mentioned in a loose rather than a precise sense.

The deliberative type of utterance is now completed. Let us now present the constituent parts which are suitably embodied in their verses. His reflexions sought to compare the days of old with the eternal years according to their natures and achievements. These he stored in his mind, and he gave his spirit free rein to roam between them with prolonged vacillation. But then in the third limb he adopted a fixed and unwavering sentiment, as often happens in the course of deliberations, for he said: *Will God then cast off for ever, or will he not so order things as to be pleased still?* and the two further verses which are seen and established to be in harmony with that judgment.

11. *And I said: Now I have begun: this is the change of the right hand of the most High.* With the intervention of a second diapsalm he now passes to the third section, in which after adopting a most wholesome frame of mind upon contemplation of things that are good, he maintains that he is appropriately transformed. He says first: *Now I have begun*—begun, that is, to be wise, to understand, to attain the brightest light, for he was intending to rejoice in the works of the Lord. But the purport of *now I have begun* is made clear in the next statement. This figure is called *epexegesis* or explanation of a previous statement;[12] he says: *This is the change of the right hand of the most High.* Change is an ambivalent term, for we are said to be changed when we fall into the worst situation on the impulse of some error. But so that no such interpretation should be made here, he says that the change regularly induced by the Lord's right hand has occurred in him. The right hand of the most High is Christ the Lord, through whom we are so changed that after our status as slaves we merit even the title of sons. He felt taking place in him the change which he rejoiced was to be granted at some time to the Christian people.

12. *I remembered the works of the Lord: for I will be mindful of thy wonders from the beginning.* He says that the change wrought in him sticks in his memory; he deserves to undertake better things now that

it is clear that the blessings bestowed on him are not absent from his heart. But so that he should not appear to be ecstatic about himself alone, there follows: *For I will be mindful of thy wonders from the beginning,* the wonders which the devoted God of mercy bestowed on the human race. First, the creation of Adam in His own image and likeness; second, the acceptance of the offering of the just Abel; next, His preservation of diverse living creatures in the ark of Noah as a sacred sign of the Church when the flood-waters rose; fourth, the foreshadowing of His coming with heavenly devotion when Abraham was sacrificing his son; and finally His deigning to come in person to free mankind. These, I think, were *the wonders from the beginning* which soothed the holy man when he recalled them.

13. *And I will meditate on all thy works, and I will be exercised in thine observances.* Let us appreciate the point which this outstanding man who leaps over the world has reached. He promises with the help of the Lord's mercy to meditate with diligent reflexion on His works, that is, on the divine Scriptures, in which there is no tedium and no satiety, for the more one drinks of them the more fully one seeks their sweet meanings. On this Psalm 118 will have much to say. But because it is not sufficient for the faithful merely to read without also showing with diligent devotion the fruits of good works, he says: *I will be exercised in thine observances,* in other words, "I will engage myself in Your saving precepts with humble application." To speak of being exercised when we perform the Lord's commands through His merciful agency is well said.

14. *Thy way, O God, is in the holy one: who is a great god like our God?* He passes to praises of the Lord, in which He relates His power and His mildness, so that the repetition of such praises may win the good will of the most devoted Judge. It is clear that the holy man had made cast-iron promises, for he is undoubtedly schooled in both books and works when he bursts forth with devoted exultation in praise of the Father. He says: *Thy way, O God, is in the holy one.* The holy One is Christ the Lord; as He Himself says: *Preserve my soul, for I am holy.*[13] He also calls Himself the Way, as in the words: *I am the way, the truth, and the life.*[14] But since He revealed to men the faith by which the Father could be perfectly known, He is justly called the Way of the Father, because through Him we have heard how the Trinity was to be worshipped; He said: *Go, baptise all nations, in the name of the Father,*

and of the Son, and of the holy Spirit.[15] Next comes: *Who is a great god like our God?* Now as one schooled he joyfully exults in the holy Spirit, preferring the power of the Lord to all idols which were worshipped on earth with false belief. They were most tawdry, weak and contemptible, but our Lord is great, strong and awe-inspiring, doing all that He wills in heaven and on earth; hence this verse is uttered against those who were to be rebuked because they were still blinded by errors of superstition, so that those unhappy persons may acknowledge Him whom they shun, and recognise what they are following. This figure is named *syndyasmos*, rendered in Latin as *collatio* or *coniunctio;*[16] it occurs by comparison of opposites, persons or cases being compared for contrast or similarity.

15. *Thou art the God that alone does wonders: thou hast made thy power known amongst the nations.* When he says: *Thou art the God,* he reveals the essence of the divine majesty. As He Himself says: *I am who am.*[17] Being properly belongs to Him whose existence is confined by the help of none, but who continues ever great, ever lofty, ever unchangeable, by the power of His nature. So it is He who alone does great wonders, for though He has often allowed His saints as well to perform them, He alone harnesses the wonderful processes to achieve His will. But let us examine why He said *alone,* when both Son and holy Spirit cooperate in all things; he said *alone* because we truthfully confess the holy Trinity as one Lord, one God. As He Himself said: *Hear, O Israel: thy Lord God is one God.*[18] Next comes: *Thou hast made thy power known amongst the nations,* that is, when He sent to this world the Lord Saviour, who as Paul says is: *The power of God and the wisdom of God.*[19] He made Him known both when those familiar with His looks came to know Him, and when those who with faithful hearts believed that He was the Son of the Father pondered on Him more deeply. So He became known to the unfaithful ones only in body, but to the faithful in His Godhead as well. As He says in the gospel: *Blessed are the pure of heart, for they shall see God.*[20]

16. *With thy arm thou hast freed thy people, the children of Israel and Joseph.* He refines on his previous thought: he explains what the Father's clemency has bestowed on the human race, for with His arm, in other words, the Lord Saviour, He has freed His people. As Scripture has it: *And to whom is the arm of the Lord revealed?*[21] So that you would not be in doubt about which people He freed, there follows: *The*

children of Israel and Joseph. We have often said that the word people, though apparently stated in the singular, embraces in meaning the plural number; so we must interpret *the children of Israel* as the crowd of Jews who came to believe, and the children of Joseph as the other crowd composed of Gentiles. But whether they were the crowd of believing Jews, or the crowd that assembled when the Gentiles were called, they are the one people of God, though at the time when they show their belief they appear to be separate. As Christ says in the gospel, *But sheep there are who are not of this fold: them also must I bring, that there may be one fold and one shepherd.*[22] We note that the faith of the Gentiles is not inappropriately called by the name Joseph; for this Joseph, though the son of Jacob who was first called Israel, was betrayed by his brothers and made his way to the Gentiles where he was accorded honour and power, so that the land of the Egyptians was ruled by his control. Hence it is reasonable that by his name are signified the Gentiles who believed with devoted hearts in the Lord Saviour. The name Joseph itself means 'the growing one',[23] and this is fitly applied to the Gentiles, amongst whom the Church of Christ is ever increasing. So the meaning is this: from the people of Israel and the gathering of the Gentiles He freed with His arm, the Lord Saviour, those who chose to believe in Him with purity of heart.

17. *The waters saw thee, O God, the waters saw thee and were afraid, and the depths were troubled.* He passes to the fourth section, where he is now exultant, and relates the powers which the majesty of the Lord Christ evinced. Earlier he had said of Him: *Thou hast made known thy power among the nations;* now he says of Him: *The waters saw thee, O God.* Divine Scripture often attests that *waters* denote people since it relates that they both see and fear; for these are waters which were able to know and fear the Lord by rational feeling. Observe what he appends here: *The waters saw thee and were afraid,* for it could not happen that the waters, a brute element, observed and feared so mighty a manifestation of miracles. Next comes: *And the depths were troubled.* This expression too we must interpret as meaning people in great numbers, who like that liquid element are affected by hurricanes of vices; but they were happily troubled, for they attained eagerness for conversion. Observe that all that follows to the end of the psalm is spoken in the language of metaphor, by which things differing in kind are compared with each other.

18. *Great was the noise of the waters: the clouds sent out a sound: for thy arrows have passed over.* The noise of the waters is great when sweet psalmody is offered, when guilt is removed by groans and tears, when thanks are rendered for a gift received. The different prayers of people resound in sacred churches like the crashing of the sea. He beautifully appends why the noise of the waters is great: it was because the clouds sent forth a sound. We have often said that clouds signify preachers, of whom Scripture says: *I will command my clouds not to pour rain on that rain.*[24] They uttered that great sound when they made known the precepts of the Lord throughout the whole world; as another psalm earlier proclaimed: *Their sound hath gone forth unto all the earth, and their words unto the ends of the earth.*[25] This is the cause of the noise of the waters, this is why the depths were troubled, because these words of proclamation bestowed the zeal of devotion on erring people. Next comes: *For thy arrows have passed over.* We appropriately interpret these as the evangelists, who like physicians pierced devoted people to their hearts' depth by their proclamations, inflicting not wounds but salvation.

19. *The voice of thy thunder is a wheel. Thy lightnings enlightened the world: the earth shook and trembled.* This too is expressed by comparison, for the voice of thunder rolls round as if it were heard emanating from sounding wheels. As the din pours out from the heights, it passes through the regions of heaven with whirling rumbling, so that we hear a circling, winding sound. Or preferably we are to understand the wheel as the world, because the world is fashioned like a wheel with perfect roundness. So in the wheel which is the universe the voice of thundering came forth when those who proclaimed Christ filled the orb of the whole world with words of thunder. There follows the effect of those clouds and that thunder: *Thy lightning enlightened the world.* The divine benefactions are recounted by worthy metaphors, so that heavenly matters may be expounded by parallels from above. The lightnings which enlightened are the divine precepts shining with the light of truth, which with their wholesome illumination put to flight men's darkness throughout the whole world. He explains the effect of these thunderings and lightnings; the earth, that is our bodies, shook and trembled when they heard this great miracle. He says that

they are shaken and trembling who heard the word of God with faith, and by Christ's gift attained the zeal of conversion.

20. *Thy ways are in the sea, and thy paths in many waters: and thy footsteps shall not be known.* If you wish to interpret this literally, His way was in the sea when He walked before men's eyes on the surface of the water, and summoned the apostle Peter to come to Him.[26] Or preferably we are to understand *thy ways in the sea* as "in the thoughts of men," which vacillate like the deceptive sea; but in that sea He has His ways, for with abundant love He subjected them to Himself. The *many waters* are the identical crowd of converted Gentiles, in whom are the Lord's paths which are His ways when He deigns to come to them. Next comes: *And thy footsteps shall not be known.* We must read this as an accusation that when He came openly and revealed Himself by such great miracles, He went none the less unrecognised by the faithless Jews. So Asaph reasonably rebukes them, for they refused to believe in such great majesty and such immediate benefits. For *footsteps* reveal bodily presence, a footstep being the mark of the sole which we make when we walk.

21. *Thou hast conducted thy people like sheep, by the hand of Moses and Aaron.* This miracle can be attributed to no other; so undoubtedly the previous accusation that they did not know His footsteps is levelled at the Jewish people. They were led by the hand of Moses and Aaron, that is, by the works which they performed in strange and various miracles. He did well to say *like sheep,* for they were not sheep, since by disbelieving they became goats. Here the word *like* denotes not actuality but appearance. Moses means "taken up," because he was taken from the river by the daughter of Pharaoh;[27] Aaron, "mountain of strength."[28] The names are seen to expound the powers which they manifested, for Moses amongst other deeds by the Lord's command worked on the waters, when in the Red Sea he gave the Hebrews a path on dry land, indicating that by the gift of baptism the faithful people were to be freed. Aaron had an image of the Church which he well compared to a solidly fortified mountain, for the Church is outstanding in holy honour and rests on solidity of faith. We read that under these leaders the people of the Israelites gained their freedom by divine power.

Conclusion Drawn From the Psalm

Idithun, you are truly one who outstandingly leapt over human concerns. You have sung this psalm with wonderful instruction. When troubled by afflictions, you said that you gained no consolation. But then your reflexions are seen to have attained perfection of expressed judgment. Thirdly, you became aware of being now blessedly transformed, but you do not relax your attitude in your happy state. Since you proclaim that you are always intent on the great works of the Lord, you are seen to have made continual progress in an accession of wisdom. Fourth, you hymn Christ's miracles with great rejoicing, and as you enumerate them in their diversity, you reveal to the Christian people the instruction by which they may be saved. Grant us, Lord, Your command that with customary devotion we may be cleansed, so that we who are so different from You in the nature of our actions may through Your mercy share in partnership with You.

COMMENTARY ON PSALM 77

1. *The understanding of Asaph.* Whenever *understanding* is found in headings, the significance of some outstanding matter is being revealed to us. Though we use *understanding* in general of what makes us heed good and evil, in the psalms it is found when our thoughts advance to the Lord with perfect discernment. We have said that Asaph in Hebrew means "synagogue," or in Latin *collectio,* a gathering. But because the psalmist prefaced the name with *understanding,* he made it clear that the faithful synagogue can give voice here; for only the hearts of the faithful can rebuke the wicked.

Division of the Psalm

This psalm is seen to be very long, and accordingly it ought to be more carefully explained in its numerous divisions, so that its meaning can shine out more clearly by such separation, and may efface the weariness of its length by being broken up into sections. In the first part of the psalm, two short verses are seen to be ascribed to the Lord's person; the purpose of this is that respect for the ensuing words may be enhanced when the King himself was seen to speak the exordium. In the second part Asaph speaks more expansively, rebuking the Jews because they have shown themselves ungrateful for the Lord's great benefits. They were deformed by wickedness, and utterly refused to submit their hearts to the Lord's commands. In the third part are enumerated all the gifts which God's power bestowed on the people of Israel, yet they did not cease grumbling. The fourth section states the nature of the vengeance which rose up among them, and tells how that sentence was softened by the Lord's pity. In the fifth part they were punished for their murmurings, but they returned to entreat the Lord in recognition of His great works. In the sixth section they again spoke with guile and pursued their customary errors, but the Lord's mercy did not permit them to be scattered, though this penalty could have been justly imposed on their evil deeds. The seventh part describes how they roused the Lord in the desert, when on their account the Egyptians were sorely afflicted by ten plagues. In the eighth the kindnesses of the Lord are recounted, and again the guilt of Jewish obduracy is appended. In the ninth the most stern vengeance follows, resulting in His consigning the people to captivity and abandoning the tabernacle of Silo, in which He was seen to dwell among men; and subsequently He chose Mount Sion, and David His servant, so that from his seed Christ the Lord should be born to come as saving Physician to the world. Thus in the psalm there is the description from the beginning of the choice of the Jewish race right up to the coming of the Lord Saviour.

Explanation of the Psalm

Attend, O my people, to my law: incline your ear to the words of my mouth. God speaks here at the beginning, for He gave the law to the Jews through Moses. And when He says: *Attend to my law,* He does not wish what is said to be taken in with the ears so much as that we should observe the truth of His words with the eyes of the heart. It is the person who with committed mind observes the things being said who attends to what he hears. When He says: *My people,* He certainly means those who were obedient to His commands. Neither prophets nor other just men could be called strangers to our faith, since they accepted in spirit those acts of the early days. As Paul says: *For I would not have you ignorant, brethren, that our fathers were all under the cloud,* and a little later: *And did all eat the same spiritual food, and all drank the same spiritual drink.*[1] Next comes: *Incline your ear to the words of my mouth.* Here he lays down the disposition of listening, for the person who wishes to grasp wholeheartedly what he has heard is seen to incline his ear so that he may humbly and readily hear what wells forth from the mouth of the holy Power. Observe that he to whom is assigned the important role of listening is already accepted as one of the faithful.

2. *I will open my mouth in parables: I will utter propositions from the beginning.* He has made the listener attentive to Him when He says that He will speak in parables; He cannot be heard negligently since He promised to speak out so imposingly. Parable in Greek means a parallel, by which we indicate what we wish to be grasped by certain comparisons. We call someone a man of iron when we wish it understood that he is hard and strong; when we wish to convey that he is swift, we compare him to winds or birds. Observe that God says that Asaph is His mouth, for Asaph is to speak later. So it was right that *understanding* should precede his name, since so great a favour of bearing witness was to be entrusted to him. There follows: *I will utter propositions from the beginning.* He who causes another to speak is himself speaking. Though the speech is activated through the agency of another, the holy Spirit whose precepts are proclaimed is actually speaking. As the apostle Peter says: *For prophecy was not brought about by the will of man at any time, but the holy men of God spoke inspired by the holy Ghost.*[2] Propositions means obscure and hidden questions to be solved by the process of debate; we offer advice more appropriately on these in their due place. *From the beginning,* that is, of the Old Testament, as Asaph will say below.

3. *How many things we have heard and come to know, and our fathers have told us.* Having thus assigned the exordium with its place of honour to the person of the Lord, he passes to the second section, in which Asaph is introduced as spokesman; we must accept his bidding as heavenly not human instruction. *How many* reveals the multitude of things. *We have heard* refers to the words of the prophets, *and come to*

know is applied to the new Testament. Things were heard when they were prophesied and when they were fulfilled through the Lord Christ. Next comes: *And our fathers have told us.* His fathers are Moses and the other prophets of the Old Testament, who spoke at length about the coming of the Lord. They were enlightened, and they preached what Asaph too foresaw as coming to pass. They would not have been just men if they had not seemed to believe what they said.

4. *They have not been hidden from their children, in another generation.* He states that these great tidings which he says their fathers proclaimed about the coming of the Lord were not hidden from their children, that is, from the spiritual children who imitated them. His words, *in another generation,* now signify the gathering not of the Jews but of the Gentiles, for by the blessing of the undivided Trinity they are reborn of water and the holy Spirit; so these children too are filled with the true light of understanding.

Declaring the praises of the Lord and his powers, and his wonders which he hath done. The order of the words is like this: Our fathers have announced to us, declaring the praises of the Lord. To declare the Lord's deeds is to praise Him, for when His works are recounted, His glory is ever increased. His *powers* indicate the occasions on which He freed the Jewish people, when He delivered them from the wicked dominion of the Pharaoh; His *wonders* indicate His feeding of them in the desert by mighty miracles, and His bringing to subjection before them of the most powerful nations with only the slightest effort. He added: *Which he hath done,* so that they should be seen to be not only promised but also fulfilled. All these events are recounted from the history of the Old Testament; history is the trustworthy account of past events, far removed from the recollection of our age.

5. *And he awoke a testimony in Jacob, and made a law in Israel.* He passes to what he mentioned earlier, *I will utter propositions from the beginning,* for the beginning is the Old Testament from the pages of which He is to speak later. The statement that He awoke a testimony in Jacob perhaps recounts the occasion when Jacob struggled with the angel, and as a foreshadowing of the future he was touched on one thigh, and he limped;[3] this pointed forward to the division of the people of Israel, some of whom held fast in firmness of faith, while others preferred to abandon their salvation. This was a testimony of the people later to err or to believe, which that struggle of Jacob

foretold. By *awoke* the psalmist meant bringing to light what seemed to be buried in the sleep of ignorance. This is what he promised in the earlier words: *I will open my mouth in parables;*[4] He intended to speak of such things, beginning at this point. Next comes: *And made a law in Israel,* that is, to urge them to be devoted to their Lord so that they should not slip into wayward errors through indulging themselves in vacillating desires. The particular point of *made a law* is that it was a yoke for sinners, a burden imposed on the fickle, a model testimony for those about to stray; so elsewhere Scripture says: *For the law is not made for the just man.*[5] This is what he meant earlier with: *I will utter propositions from the beginning.* But the conscientious reader will apply these words to the appropriate passages, for it would be tedious to state them at every point.

What great things he commanded our fathers, that they should make the same known to their children, that another generation might know them! 6. The children to be born will rise up and declare them to their children. These verses indicate that the instructions of the Lord were transmitted from generation to generation, so that none might think that what is known to have been assigned to all was given to one only; for the Jews received what undoubtedly passed over to Christians. This is why there is the addition, *that another generation might know them*—not Jewish but clearly that chosen from the Gentiles, for *another* here points to outsiders rather than kinsfolk. As for the words following: *The children to be born will rise up and declare them to their children,* the psalmist undoubtedly wishes them to be understood as the Christians, for they handed on the holy proclamation to their successors in order to confer on them the salvation of souls.

7. *That they may put their hope in God, and may not forget the works of their God, and may seek his commandments.* The usefulness of the Father's proclamation is clearly demonstrated here, that their successors may place their hope not in the law which punishes but in the gift of grace which redeems. Next comes: *And may not forget the works of their God* as the faithless Jews did, for they were forgetful of their Creator and turned to the worship of demons. He added: *And may seek his commandments;* true recollection of the highest God lies in fulfilling His commands with devoted hearts.

8. *That they may not become like their fathers, a perverse and exceedingly bitter generation; a generation which set not their heart aright, and*

whose spirit was not faithful to God. In these two sentences the faithlessness of the Jews is rebuked in these fine definitive statements. He says: *That they may not become like their fathers,* who were *a perverse and exceedingly bitter generation; perverse,* because they refused to accept the truth, for those who do not follow a straight guideline inevitably remain twisted, and *exceedingly bitter,* that is, harsh beyond all bitterness, since they armed themselves to destroy Him who had come to save them. Next follows: *A generation which set not their heart aright,* or, as he said earlier, were perverse, for if they had set their hearts aright they would not have become perverse or been made strangers to God. It is the person who corrects himself in accordance with God's commands who sets his heart aright; he ponders no course of action with the pride of human presumption, but knows that all is governed by the economy of the Godhead. The repetition of *generation* has reference only to those who have stuck fast in their obstinacy, but there were those amongst the Jews who served the Lord with pure hearts. He added: *And whose spirit was not faithful to God.* It is the person who does not realise that the works of God lying before his eyes are to be attributed to spiritual mysteries, but seeks to refer them solely to what he sees, whose spirit is not faithful to God. This was the case with the Jews, who concentrated solely on the wonders before them, failing to submit them in a wholesome manner to the spirit's understanding.

9. *The sons of Ephraim who bend the bow and shoot their arrows have turned back in the day of battle. Ephraim* is translated as "fruit-bearing" or abundance. He was the younger son of Joseph; we read in the Old Testament that Jacob his grandfather blessed him and accorded him the first place by reversing the order of his hands. Ephraim's sons, who overflowed with divine gifts and flourished because of the blessing given their father, perished through their lack of faith, for they bent the bow and shot arrows when on the admonition of Moses they said: *All that the Lord hath said, we will do and listen to;*[6] but they *turned back in the day of battle* when they said to Aaron: *Make us gods that we may adore them.*[7] You observe that all this is unfolded by means of parallels and propositions, for the meaning here is applicable to those who promise anything with headlong haste, but are not eager to persevere in the same conviction, as happened to the apostle Peter, who three times denied Christ after promising that he would die with him.[8]

10. *They kept not the covenant of God, and in his law they would not walk.*

11. *And they forgot his benefits, and his wonders that he had shown them.* The reason is given why the sons of Ephraim turned back in the day of battle: it was because they did not keep the covenant of God, and would not walk in His law, and they forgot His benefits and wonders that He had shown them. This is so clear as to require no explanation.

12. *Wonderful things did he do in the sight of their fathers: in the land of Egypt, in the field of Tanis.* He comes to the third section, in which he describes the blessings bestowed after the crossing of the Red Sea. The people concerned are those mentioned earlier, *the perverse and exceedingly bitter generation.*[9] He tells of the miracles performed in the sight of their fathers Moses, Aaron and other elders, so that by reason of these clear events they should have believed more firmly, because their fathers' account is so sweet and unwavering. To remove every particle of doubt, he mentioned both the region and the site where the events recounted are known to have taken place. The expression, *in the field of Tanis,* is not idle, for Tanis means a humble instruction, which Christ when on earth is known to have taught when he said: *Learn of me, for I am meek and humble of heart, and you will find rest for your souls.*[10] This too He did in the sight of their fathers, when He proclaimed the commands of the New Testament.

13. *He prised apart the sea, and brought them through: and made the waters stand as in a vessel.* Though the sea is a liquid element, he preferred to speak of breaking rather than dividing it; it was indeed prised apart, for it continued to exhibit an unnatural solidity on both sides, so that it was not so much the sea as a rock-face that seemed to have been hewn out. *Brought them through,* that is, to the safety of the land which had been promised them; they seemed to advance to it sharing the same fortune, without fear of the sea. The following phrase, *he made the waters stand as in a vessel,* has application to his statement, *he prised apart the sea,* so that the water stood motionless as though enclosed in vessels. Note how the parallels promised are unfolded.

14. *And he led them out in the cloud of the day, and all night with brightness of fire.* He explains his previous words. He led them out in the cloud of day, for the day signifies the Lord Christ; though He was

the true Light of day, He was hidden from faithless people by the cloud of His flesh. So a wondrous type of utterance has shone forth here, the recounting of ancient events in such a way that it seems to express what is still to come. We must listen to the words in one sense but none the less understand them in another; neither is open to doubt, for both are wholly true. These are the promised parallels arranged with heavenly integrity, these are the most indubitable signs of the truth. Next comes: *And all night with the brightness of fire.* Here more clearly still he is pointing to the Christians, whom the Lord guards with the brightness of His light in the darkness of the world. Paul attests that all this happened to the Jews as a foreshadowing, when he says: *For I would not have you ignorant, brethren, that our fathers were all under the cloud, and all passed through the sea. And all in Moses were baptised, in the cloud and in the sea.*" So we must always give abundant thanks because with great miracles of this kind He foretold the rewards which He was to bestow on our undeserving selves.

15. *He broke apart the rock in the wilderness: and gave them to drink as though in the great deep.* Let us ponder how the miracles revealed contrasted with each other. He first caused the waters of the sea to dangle like a rocky cliff, and now he says that the rock welled forth with flowing water. This was to show that all created things obey His commands, though they appear by nature to be diametrically opposite to each other. When the psalmist spoke of the wilderness, he intensified the favour of the gift bestowed; God performed such a miracle in the place where there was no other resource at a time of need. He used the expression, *gave them to drink*, to appear to be suggesting packhorses rather than men, for they did not know how to render thanks for such great kindnesses. The words, *as though in the great deep*, made clear the abundance of the torrent of water which poured out as though from the boundless depths of the sea. Observe that everywhere he makes the noun *abyssus* ("the deep") feminine, as the Greeks do.

16. *He brought forth water out of the rock, and brought forth waters like rivers.* He repeated the point to hammer home the marvellous favour by which water came out of the substance which had grown hard through its natural dryness. So that you would not think that only a trickle flowed out, he added: *Like rivers*, which flow abundantly down from the breasts of the mountains. He was pointing out that

water comes forth to us from the Rock that is Christ; this is the water which does not fail or suffer reduction. As Christ Himself says in the gospel: *He that shall drink of the water that I will give him shall not thirst for ever, but it shall become in him a fountain of water springing up into life everlasting.*[12] Paul says that the rock indicates Christ: *And they drank of the spiritual rock that followed them: and the rock was Christ.*[13]

17. *And they added yet more sin against him: they provoked the most High to wrath in that parched place.* Added means "increased," for when confronted with such great miracles they failed to believe, though the change in the natural order of the elements cried out to them. By "sin" he meant their unbelief; it is clearly a most wicked fault to seek benefits from God and not to offer due thanks when they have been experienced. Next comes: *They provoked the most High to wrath in that parched place.* We have often stated that such utterances, which assign to the Lord descriptions of human weakness, are metaphorical, and are used to clarify the explanation of matters difficult and hard for us to comprehend. They provoked Him to wrath when they did not believe that He was causing difficulties for them, though they saw that He could achieve such mighty deeds. It is obvious that it is the greatest sin against God to say that anything is impossible for Him, for He can perform most effectively what He decides to fulfil. *In that parched place* is well said; it applies not so much to the land as to their minds. Though drenched by many miracles, they became parched by the barrenness of their infidelity, for they applied themselves wholly to the desires of the flesh, and were sated merely in belly and not in their affections.

18. *And they tested God in their hearts by asking meat for their desires.* It is one thing to ask by testing, but another to ask by confessing. The Jews made their request by testing, and once they had obtained it they spoke unworthy words. We use the expression *test* for demanding something in crafty language, so that the words seem ingenuous but there is malice deep down. So these people were not spiritual in soul, but craftily demanded meat for the flesh. We say that meat is given to sick people to keep their souls in their bodies, not because it is food for the soul, but because physical strength seems to be maintained in this life by means of it.

19. *And they spoke ill of God, and said: Can God furnish a table in the wilderness? Numquid* (can God?) here must be taken as expressing an

accusation; it stands for "No, God cannot. . . ." What a wicked sin, not to believe that the Almighty can achieve what He is known to perform every day! For, as Scripture says: *He giveth food to all flesh.*[14] So what is so hostile to Him as not to believe that He carries out what He has bidden? Hence this is a harsh sin, for such lack of faith does wrong to heaven. *Table* points to the food by which we are restored when hungry. And when he speaks of furnishing it in the wilderness, the suggestion is being made that what is often found in a place of abundance could not have been provided in a desert empty of provisions. How very foolish and ridiculous a madness to have ascribed human resourcelessness to the power of God!

20. *Because he struck the rock, and the waters gushed out, and the streams overflowed, can he also give bread, or provide a table for his people?* It is a most foolish reflexion after citing an example of a mighty miracle to think it possible that the Author of it can be found wanting in other respects. How could He who ordered waters to flow from the rock not cause the heavens to provide food for His needy people? Could a just Father provide the first but be unable to achieve the second alone? However, a most just punishment attended this mad sin a little later; this was to prevent anyone presuming to have such thoughts subsequently.

21. *Therefore the Lord heard, and delayed and postponed action; and a fire was kindled in Jacob, and wrath arose in Israel.* He passes to the fourth section, in which the sins of the Jews are assembled by the figure of *synathroismos,* which in Latin is termed *congregatio.*[15] God knows the thoughts of those who grumble, even if their tongues are silent, for He alone can hear the inner, silent discourse as though it were the shout of a loud voice. But notice what he said first, *He delayed,* and now he adds: *He postponed action;* He did not wish to be thought unable to give the grumblers their fill by taking vengeance there and then. Instead He delayed the punishment to show His patience, and He imposed delays to reveal His power; only then did He take fitting vengeance on their sins, when He had exposed the guilt of their unbelieving hearts by carrying out those miracles. Next comes: *And a fire was kindled in Jacob.* The meaning of Jacob is "supplanter";[16] the name is often the symbol for the Gentiles, who by coming to Christ are seen to have supplanted the people of Israel, for when the Gentiles entered the Jews are known to have been driven out. So

among the Gentiles, who we have said are indicated by the name
Jacob, the fire of love was kindled; the Jews' loss of sanctity through
their murmuring was commensurate with the progress of the Gentiles
attained through the zeal of their confession. He added: *And wrath
arose in Israel.* Just as he says that love was kindled in Jacob, so he
proclaims that wrath arose in Israel, so that the Gentiles were fired to
gain grace, but the Jews were impelled towards sin.

22. *Because they believed not in their God, and trusted not in his
salvation.* Earlier he said: *Wrath arose in Israel,* to show that they were
obstinate; now the cause of their obduracy is revealed. He says that
they did not believe in their God. So that you would not think that
there was another God, there follows: *And trusted not in his salvation,*
that is, in the Lord Saviour, so that not only did that grumbling bring
them odium, but it also caused the condemnation of the mental obstinacy which followed it.

23. *And he commanded the clouds from above, and opened the doors of
heaven.* He attested at the outset that these events were described in
parables and propositions. So although they seem to have occurred in
the course of history, we must nonetheless relate them to the Lord
Saviour so that the earlier statement becomes clear to us. The clouds,
that is, the preachers, were commanded so that by means of the doors
of heaven, in other words the holy scriptures, their glorious proclamation could announce the coming of the Lord's salvation, which is truly
eaten as manna when it is tasted in that revered revelation.

24. *And he rained down manna on them to eat; he gave them the bread
of heaven.* 25. *Man ate the bread of angels: he sent them supplies of corn
in abundance.* The beginning of the first verse here follows on from
what precedes. He said: *He opened the doors of heaven,* and he continues: *He rained down manna on them to eat.* He used the expression
rained down to show the huge abundance of food which descended
from heaven like rain. So that you would be in no doubt what that rain
was, the next words are *manna to eat.* The meaning of manna is,
"What is this?" We appropriately associate it with holy communion,
for whilst this food is sought with wonder, the gift of the Lord's body
is revealed. He added: *He gave them the bread of heaven.* What is this
second bread of heaven but the Lord Christ, from whom things heavenly obtain their spiritual food and enjoy delight beyond reckoning?
Finally follow the words: *Man ate the bread of angels.* Christ is well

called the bread of angels, since they truly feast on His praise; for we must not believe that angels eat physical bread, but feast on that contemplation of the Lord by which the creation in heaven is renewed. In fact this heavenly bread fills the angels and feeds us on earth; it delights them through contemplation, and renews us by its holy attendance on us. He added: *He sent them supplies of corn in abundance.* He is still pursuing his previous theme, calling the manna "supplies of corn" rather than merely "corn," to express the abundance which could outstrip the people's greed. Finally follow the words *in abundance;* we call something abundant when it cannot be devoured by a greed however rapacious.

26, 27. *He removed the Auster (south wind) from heaven; and by his power brought in the Afric (south-west wind). And he rained upon them flesh as dust: and feathered fowls like as the sand of the sea.* So far as the historical sense is concerned, he states that these winds were commissioned as conveyances to take the abundance which had been prescribed to the allotted camp. But because they must be explained also in the spiritual sense, let us now explain their figurative application. We know that the Auster and the Afric are winds from the south, coming from the brighter and hotter quarter. When they blow, the sluggish cold is driven out, and mild weather introduced. So in the same way the Lord's words, hot with the fire of love, were like the Auster and the Afric, bringing a healthy warmth to the world, and they rained food upon the people so that the souls of the faithful might obtain most abundant satiety. For *dust* here means the refinement of understanding which is roused and ever rises to thoughts of heaven: the *sand* is the immeasurable abundance of wisdom, seasoned with the savour of the salt sea: the *feathered fowls* are longings for heaven, with which the devoted soul grows fat, as though stuffed with flesh meat. Appropriately added to the sand are the words *of the sea*, for sand can appear also in rivers and does not then have the savour.

28. *And they fell in the midst of their camp, round about their tents.* He says that in order to deprive the grumblers even of the labour of gathering what they sought with great longing, the food fell not only round their tents but also in the midst of their camp. The word *castra* (camp) is derived from *castitas* (chastity),[17] because an army occupied with wars had no time for base luxury. For us, however, the point being made is that within the fold of holy Church we can obtain all the

heavenly blessings if we ask that our worthy desires be fulfilled by God's gift. So the words have a power beyond reckoning, both authenticating the historical reliability and bestowing the possibility of understanding in the spiritual dimension.

29. *So they did eat, and were filled exceedingly: and he gave them their desire.* See how those who believed that any task was difficult for God were refuted. They gained their longing of the flesh, but their reason was starved; their bellies were filled, but their minds empty. This figure is called *synchōrēsis*,[18] or concession, when things are granted to those who violently desire them, though they cannot be profitable to them.

30. *They were not defrauded of that which they craved. As yet their meat was in their mouth: and the wrath of God came upon them. 31. And he slew very many of them: and brought down the chosen men of Israel.* He comes to the fifth section. This follows from his previous statement:[19] *The Lord delayed and postponed action, so that they should not be defrauded of that which they craved.* This was to prevent the possible demonstration of the idea lodged in their sacrilegious hearts, that God was powerless because of the difficulty of what they craved. The word *fraudati* (defrauded) comes from *fraus*, which means "broken faith." So they were filled for their own destruction, not that they might live in consequence, but rather die. Observe what follows: *As yet their meat was in their mouth*, that is, when they feasted on manna and the flesh of quails. The word *esca* (meat) derives from *edere* (to eat).[20] He added: *And the wrath of God came upon them. And he slew very many of them: and he hindered the chosen men of Israel.* Here he touches upon the famous account of Exodus. In the absence of Moses who was receiving the Law of the Lord on the mountain, the people in madness rose against Aaron, asking that gods should be accorded them, as all the Gentiles seemed to have. Then it was that the sacrilegious calf made its appearance, in the worship of which they themselves were to low in an unprecedented way. Then God in anger said to Moses that the people of the Jews had sinned gravely; and when Moses went down he held an assembly, and twenty-three thousand of them are said to have been wiped out; and Aaron, the chosen one of the Lord, fell into sin, for Scripture says: *The people was struck because of the sin of the calf which Aaron made.*[21] Their most wicked grumbling

was a stumbling block to Moses as well when he said: *Can we bring you forth water out of this rock?*[22] It was because of these words that he was prevented from entering the promised land. This was how the wantonness of those who sinned hindered the chosen ones of Israel.

32. *In all these things they sinned still: and they believed not in his wondrous works. 33. And their days were consumed in vanity, and their years in haste.* Those sins which are ever growing and heavily increasing arouse God the more; and since they did not wish to believe in His wondrous works, he says that their days were consumed, devoured, so to say, by wasting enervation. The days of sinners speed by in haste; as Scripture has it elsewhere: *Bloody and deceitful men shall not live out half their days.*[23]

34. *When he slew them, then they sought him, and they turned to him before dawn, and came to him. 35. And they remembered that God was their helper, and the most high God, their liberator.* It was not those who he says were slain that sought God, but the rest of the crowd entreated Him when an example was made of such men. It is the habit of just people, whether before they suffer evils or while they suffer them, to seek God with fidelity; but wicked men rush to Him with vacillating longing when they are confounded by some necessity. So the Jewish people feared God's anger when they saw their comrades destroyed at the time when fire came down from heaven, as we read in Numbers, and killed 14,700 people because they stirred up the most unjustified rebellions against Moses and Aaron because of the death of Core and his comrades. The following sentences: *And they turned to him before dawn, and came to him. They remembered that God was their helper and the most high God their liberator,* are a reference to the time when the Lord was angry, and the furthest points of the camp of the Jewish people were consumed with heavenly fire; when this happened, they begged Moses to entreat for them to the Lord. So the holy man entreats in daylight, the unholy man before daylight. As Scripture has it: *It is vain for you to rise before the dawn.*[24] But they seem to have done this out of fear of danger rather than from the fear of heaven, since he is going to go on speaking later of their infidelity. Observe that here the Father is called liberator; the Son is also a liberator, for we read in the gospel: *If the Son shall make you free, then you will be free indeed.*[25] The holy Spirit also liberates; as Paul says: *The spirit of life in Christ*

Jesus hath delivered me from the law of sin and of death.[26] So there is no doubt that the holy Trinity has equal powers, and each Person fulfils equally whatever He wishes.

36. *And they loved him with their mouth: and with their tongue they lied unto him.* 37. *But their heart is not right with him, nor was faith accounted to them in his covenant.* He passes to the sixth section, in which he relates that the Jews went back to their sinning ways, but he declares that the Lord showed mercy to them. He says: *And they loved him with their mouth, and with their tongue they lied unto him.* This is the fate of those who regard their belief as moved solely by fear. For if love is not mingled with the fear of God, He is not sought in the heart's entirety. It is certain that it is the keenest of sins for a man to say that he confesses to Him with his tongue, whilst his heart deep down is at odds with Him; does God not know all that goes on within us when He is in Scripture's words: *The searcher of heart and reins?*[27] He does not hear merely what the tongue proclaims, as a human person does. It is the person who faithfully believes His testimonies who truly loves Him. *Fides* (faith) gets its name from words uttered (*quod fiant dicta*).[28] The Lord Himself offers a testimony like this verse when He says: *This people glorifies me with their lips, but their heart is far from me.*[29] The prophet Isaiah rightly offers evidence of them with the words: *Thy neck is as an iron sinew, and thy forehead as brass.*[30]

38. *But he will be merciful and forgive their sins: and will not destroy them. And many a time did he turn away his anger from them, and did not kindle all his wrath.* Here he quite appropriately appends the exemplary occasion when Moses in entreaty for his sinning people said to the Lord: *I beseech thee, forgive the sin of this people, or if not, strike me out of the book which thy hand hath written.*[31] The Lord Christ likewise prayed for them as He hung on the cross: *Father, forgive them, for they know not what they do.*[32] The result of these entreaties was that the Lord's anger was appeased in their case. He forgave their sins, for admittedly not all but many of them deserved to draw clear of them to make satisfaction to Him.

39. *And he remembered that they are flesh: a spirit that goeth and returneth not.* When He pondered the frailty of those sinners, it affected the kindly Judge, because their physical blindness did not behold the light of heavenly wisdom; accordingly he says that they must

be awaited, for if their spirits had been immediately banished, they would have lost the opportunity for repentance. *Caro* (flesh) gets its name because it is dear (*cara*) to the soul.[33] Man's death is described with marvellous brevity as *a spirit that goeth and returneth not;* we must mentally add "to this world," for it will obviously return to its body at the resurrection.

40. *How often did they provoke him in the desert: and moved him to wrath in a waterless land.* 41. *And they turned back and tempted God: and grieved the holy one of Israel.* He comes to the seventh section, in which once again he briefly points to their obduracy and bitterness. For in what follows he recounts the many blessings accorded them by divine power in the desert or amongst the Egyptians, thus revealing that while he always makes provision for them in their wickedness, they are unmindful of his kindnesses and do not cease to sin.

42. *They remembered not his hand in the day that he delivered them from the hand of the oppressor.* Affliction usually implants clear recollection, but those unfaithful people could not even retain the memory which grief always stamps most strongly on our minds; remembering means recalling to mind. The expressions, *the hand of the Lord* and *the hand of the oppressor,* are well applied; for the action of both is indicated by this noun, but how very different they are, though they appear to share the same word! The one succeeded in delivering the people, whereas the other sought to go on controlling them for their own destruction.

43. *How he wrought his signs in Egypt, and his wonders in the field of Tanis.* He marked the one event under the two names. In Egypt He wrought the signs which the psalmist will mention later, but He also revealed His wonders in the same land, in the field of Tanis. Tanis is a city of Egypt in which the wonders of which we read were performed. The signs implanted in Egypt on their obstinate hearts were so to say the marks of a branding iron, whereas the *prodigia* (wonders), being derived from *porro dicere* (forward statement), were a prefiguring of what was to come,[34] for all those blows which they suffered in the early times had some significance. So what is shown to have taken place in Egypt were rightly called signs and wonders. We have said that Tanis is translated as "lowly instruction";[35] this is acknowledged as necessary and salutary for us in this world, where we must be

humble and bent low as we continually beg for pardon. But the just will be raised up when at the resurrection they receive gifts which will abide for ever.

44. *He turned their rivers into blood, and their rain-showers too that they might not drink.* At this point the first plague of the Egyptians begins.[36] Just as we read in the gospel that water was turned into wine,[37] which denoted that people were changed for the better, so here its transformation into blood announces that sinners interpret the causes of spiritual things in a bodily sense. Blood is introduced here to denote the flesh, and undoubtedly the Jewish people took this materialistic view. He further says that both their rivers and their rain-showers were turned into blood, so that in their preoccupation with the thoughts of the flesh they did not understand the heavenly preaching in a spiritual sense. The literal sense of this and of what follows is clear, for the words of the divine history show that these events occurred in Egypt.

45. *He sent among them the dog-fly which devoured them, and the frog which destroyed them.* 46. *And he gave up their fruits to the blast, and their labours to the locust.* The dog-fly is the sting inflicted to take vengeance on wanton villains; the frog is the most loquacious vanity of heretics, which is detained by foul thoughts and never stops prattling with persistent croaking. The blast is base love, which devours what is honourable by imperceptibly diminishing it. The locust is malicious and persistent detraction, which gnaws at the deeds of others by envious opposition.

47. *And he destroyed their vineyards with hail: and their mulberries with hoar-frost.* 48. *And he gave up their beasts to the hail, and their possessions to the fire.* The hail represents the Lord's threats which pummel the stiff-necked, and strip them of the foliage of their joy. The frost is the preliminary and purposeful ill-will which does not allow the toil of others to come to fruition. Next comes: *And he gave up their beasts to the hail.* By the death of cattle is signified the downfall of foolish people who are cut down by countless evils and routed like lowly beasts. He added: *And their possessions to the fire.* Fire is found in both a good and a bad sense; here, however, it is clearly inflicted in anger, and we must interpret it as the base cupidity which ravages our possessions, in other words our mental state, with accursed ambition. There remains the tenth of these early plagues, and we shall mention it

in its due place,[38] for two verses are clearly interposed to accentuate the evil which follows. But it is worth noting that three of the plagues —blast, frost and fire—which he mentioned here do not appear at all in Exodus. It says there that fire came down mixed with hail to blight the crops, not to set fire effectively to their possessions. In fact, in place of these three, there are recounted three others, sciniphs, boils, and darkness.[39] You often find such variation in Scripture to achieve apposite understanding of events; for example, the heading of Psalm 33 reads: *A psalm of David when he changed his countenance before Abimelech, who dismissed him and sent him away,* whereas in the book of Kings we do not read that Abimelech was king of Palestine, but Achis.[40] These names, as we have said, have been changed in accordance with the nature of the typology, and we must recognise a similar procedure here as well. It is clear that Augustine gathered similar examples in his book on the harmony between the gospels.[41]

49. *And he sent upon them the wrath of their own indignation: indignation and wrath and trouble: sallies prompted by wicked angels.* The stages of vengeance are recounted in a most realistic description. First the Lord is angry at our sins when we are not converted by any remorse. Then He abandons men's wickedness to their own indignation, wrath and trouble, so that those who disdain obedience of the divine commands are afflicted by their own perversities. As Scripture has it: *Therefore God gave them up to the desires of their heart, unto uncleanness, to perform what is not right,*[42] and the rest. The indignation of a wicked person relates to his swollen arrogance, wrath to his wicked recklessness, tribulation to his disordered despair. Then through the agency of wicked angels they rush headlong into unlawful sallies; they are stripped of divine protection, and become the booty of the most harmful beasts. We must also observe that he says that the sallies were made by evil angels, which implies that it was not through good angels that God destroyed sinners. Yet it was through the good angels to whom Abraham and Lot were found worthy to dispense hospitality that He destroyed Sodom and Gomorrha.[43] It was also through a wicked angel that the transgressor was tempted in the account of the book of Kings, where it says *The evil spirit from God came upon Saul.*[44] Just men, too, like Job and the apostle Paul and others of that kind were tried by the devil. It is clear that all created things are subject to the discretion or command of the Creator.

50. *He made a way for a path to his anger, and he spared not their souls from death: and their cattle he shut up in death.* When he says that the Lord made a way by which he could take vengeance on those hapless men, he shows that they could not be reached unless they were deprived of the Lord's protection. The expression, "the anger of the Lord," is a metaphor; it consists of what he describes earlier, sallies by evil angels. The devil is not allowed to make these except through God's will. He next explains what this anger achieved. *And he spared not their souls from death.* The expression, *their souls,* must be interpreted as meaning the men whom He is known to have slain in that calamity. The words of Exodus attest that the soul stands for the whole man, as we have said: *So all the souls that came out of Jacob's thigh were seventy.*[45] This expression is the result of the figure of *synecdoche,* which signifies the whole from the part.[46] Next comes: *Their cattle he shut up in death.* Note how he says that all things relating to human sustenance or consolation were ravaged, so that we may judge that the wicked and obstinate were visited by worthy punishment.

51. *And he killed all the first-born in the land of Egypt: the first-fruits of their labour in the tents of Cham.* Here, then, is the tenth plague of the first-born, which God's anger threatened through wicked angels. It was of such a nature and extent that without prompting the Egyptians forced the Israelites to depart, though previously they refused to let them go. The things which are first-born are those which first occur to our thoughts with reverence, like the greatest commandment to love God with our whole heart and to show charity to our neighbour too in all ways. When these thoughts perish, we are afflicted by the loss of our first-born, and are deprived of the offspring of reason. Let us clearly reflect that God afflicted the Egyptian people with ten plagues, and adorned the Hebrew people with the gift of the ten commandments, so that you may realise that vengeance was inflicted and grace bestowed by this mystery of the number ten. Next comes: *The first fruits of their labour.* These are identical with the preceding phrase, *all the first-born;* for the first-fruits of labours are relevant to all that the human potential can embrace. Just as earlier he said: *In the land of Egypt,* so he repeats here: *In the tents of Cham;* for Cham was the father of Canaan, whose descendants are known to have gained possession of the land.

52. *And he took away his own people as sheep: and guided them in the*

wilderness like a flock. 53. And he brought them out in hope, and they feared not: and the sea overwhelmed their enemies. 54. And he brought them to the mountain of sanctification, this mountain which his right hand purchased. He comes to the eighth section, in which the kindnesses of the Lord are recounted, and the sin of Jewish obduracy is appended. Though these kindnesses seem to be associated with the previous verses, in this verse the outcome of the tenth plague is revealed, namely, that the people of the Lord was delivered from unholy slavery and reached the promised land in safety. But a problem can be raised at this point, for those whom He took from the land of Egypt He did not lead to the mountain of sanctification, which refers to Mount Sion where we know Jerusalem stands. But since the discussion is about the Jews, it is clear that those who succeeded their forbears and are acknowledged to have carried on the Hebraic name and race, are known to have been led to this city. He is pointing out, however, that many of them through the blessing of conversion came to the Catholic Church, which he wishes us to understand here, and this has indeed happened; for this is the Church which our Christ, the right Hand of the Father, sought out. It is also clear that we are to understand the previous verses in a figurative sense. The expressions *sheep* and *flock* signify the Christian people, who feed in this world as though in the wilderness, as long as they do not pursue longings for worldly things. We have been brought out in hope from the land of Egypt, that is, from the darkness of sins, for we have obtained the light of faith. *And the sea overwhelmed our enemies,* the devil and his agents, when the bath of sacred rebirth cleansed us. As Paul says, what happened to them in figure announced the tidings of our salvation.[47]

And he cast out the Gentiles before them: and by lot divided land among them by the rope of distribution. 55. And he made the tribes of Israel to dwell in their tents. He cast out the Gentiles before us when barbaric and boorish errors are banished from us. He divides the land of promise among us when He gives to each a blessed portion according to our worth. The phrase, *the rope of distribution,* is adopted from those who used to divide land by stretching across a rope. Next comes: *And he made the tribes of Israel to dwell in their tents.* The divine Scriptures have revealed to us that the people of the elect will be gathered in the place or retinue from where the arrogant angels are known to have been driven out; so He will bestow the tents, which the angels in their innocence still possessed before their pride brought them to ruin, upon the tribes of Israel, that is, those who see God.[48]

56. *And they tempted and provoked the most high God: and they kept not his testimonies.* 57. *And they turned away, and did not make observance as their fathers did, and they were turned into a bent bow.* He now speaks of the perversity of the Jews, and then explains what happened to them when God was angry, in order that disobedient persons may fear examples such as this. The bent bow is the malice of sinners, which does not inflict wounds from afar, but rather directs the darts unerringly at themselves. This clearly is the experience of the crafty, who in trying to inflict wounds on others are seen to turn their cunning plots upon themselves.

58. *They provoked him to anger on their hills, and sought to vie with him with their graven things.* The hills denote the arrogant, swollen thoughts of men, to which the Lord is always found to be opposed when with wicked presumption they eagerly espouse the worship of demons. They vied with him when they bestowed on accursed images the honour due to the Lord. This sort of vying is to be understood in the bad sense rather than the good sense, for note what follows.

59. *The Lord heard and despised them, and he reduced Israel totally to nothing.* The ninth and remaining part is begun, in which the species of vengeance are recounted, and then the coming of the Lord Saviour is announced. Several people usually raise the question why God is said to have taken vengeance on all, when only some of them sinned. This ought not to be a stumbling block to devoted minds. Though He consigned the race to captivity, He nonetheless preserved those who through purity of conscience were pleasing to Him; but those whom He deemed worthy of the crown of eternal glory He tried all the more by afflictions. If we probe the innermost truth, those who were free in mind did not suffer captivity, and they were not abandoned to the enemy within because their awareness could not be drawn away from the Godhead.

60. *And he rejected the tent of Silo, his tent where he dwelt amongst men.* Silo was the city where we read that the Lord's ark was set.[49] From there the Jews obtained divine responses through the entreaties of their priests before the temple was built at Jerusalem. So this was the tent which he says the Lord rejected, in which He had deigned to dwell among men. As we read in another prophet: *See what I have done*

to Silo, where my tent was.[50] But we must fear that in indignation He may abandon the tents of our bodies, in which the holy Spirit dwells when we comport ourselves properly through God's kindness. As Paul puts it: *The temple of God which you are is holy.*[51]

61. *And he delivered their strength into captivity, and their beauty into the hands of the enemy.* He is recounting the occasion when the Jews were conquered by foreigners and exposed to their slaughter and plundering.[52] So strength and beauty are a reference to the ark of the covenant, through which they regarded themselves as unconquerable and outstanding in the highest renown of splendour.

62. *And he enclosed his people with the sword, and despised his inheritance.* The result was that the people fell ignobly into destruction beneath the sword, for the distinction of the ark was seen to have been removed from them. Those whom He despises He destroys, and none can assist the man who is seen to be abandoned by divine consolations. He despised His inheritance when because of the monstrous nature of their crimes He banished the people whom He had chosen from amongst many nations. *Hereditas* (inheritance) is derived from *herus* (master), for a lord is known to possess it by lawful right.

63. *Fire consumed their young men: and their maidens were not lamented.* We must interpret fire here as the anger of warring men which devoured those consigned to it like a consuming flame. Next comes: *And their maidens were not lamented.* Lamentation is an activity of man at leisure; and since all stood in fear of overhanging dangers, none of them could perform the just rites at another's funeral. *Lamenta* (laments) owes its derivation to memorials within the house (*intra lares monumenta*),[53] this being the burial-custom of the ancients.

64. *Their priests fell by the sword: and their widows were not mourned.* We read that during the captivity the sons of the priest Heli were put to the sword by the foreigners. The wife of one of them thus widowed suddenly gave birth and prematurely died.[54] So it happened that his widow went wholly unmourned, since they were all preoccupied by the widespread deaths. We must believe that this fate befell many widows among the people, since divine authority has cited a plurality of widows, and we know that no detail recorded is otiose.

65. *And the Lord was awakened as one out of sleep, like a mighty man surfeited with wine.* We have stated that human habits like these are

often attributed to the Lord to make situations clear. In saying these words the psalmist plays the role of madman, who when the Lord does not assist those in danger regards Him as one surfeited with wine. But He is asleep only to the indifferent and unfaithful who do not rouse Christ by any psalmody or good works. He rightly becomes a stranger to those who in their madness consider that He is asleep so far as they are concerned. He whose patience was believed to have slumbered is also awakened to vengeance when provoked by evil deeds. We recognise that this should be our reaction all the more in this case; the foreigners awakened Him when they set the ark of His covenant amongst the idols, and now their fate as the outcome of such a deed follows. We must however investigate the phrase *like a mighty man*, for men are quick to anger and powerful in strength when after excess of wine they often arise from sleep. Finally the blessed Jerome, one of our truthful interpreters, substituted "strong" for *mighty*.[55]

66. *And he smote the enemies on the hinder parts: he put them to an everlasting reproach.* We read in the first book of Kings[56] that because of the damage done to the consecrated ark the foreigners were smitten on their hinder parts, so that they even suffered the dreadful fate of being gnawed alive by mice. This remains a perennial reproach on them, because no other was punished in this way. Similarly He afflicts sinners in the afterlife, for He does not leave them their due, and they are so to say devoured by mice when the devil's hostile troop surrounds them.

67. *And he rejected the tent of Joseph, and chose not the tribe of Ephraim.*

68. *But he chose the tribe of Judah, mount Sion which he loved.* The judgments of the Lord are made clear by the harmony of the names themselves. Joseph signifies "increase,"[57] and is found in both a good and a bad sense, but here it must be interpreted in the bad sense, for he is clearly rejected. Ephraim is rendered as "fruitbearing" or "abundance,"[58] Judah as "confessing" or "glorifying."[59] We must also commit to memory the fact that holy Scripture by means of Hebraic names quite often announces hidden secrets to us. There is no doubt that this type of utterance is peculiar to sacred literature, for such clues are wholly absent from secular writing. *He rejected the tent of Joseph*, then, because though Joseph himself had been a just man, his directly physical descendants are known to have desired worldly prosperity and

success in the flesh. Likewise He did not choose the tribe of Ephraim, because they became presumptuous through their material abundance in the harvest of this world. He rightly chose the tribe of Judah, so humble in its confession and praiseworthy in its manner of life, and so from this physical stock the Lord Saviour came to us. Next follows: *Mount Sion which he loved;* he points to the Catholic Church, of which the Lord says in the Song of Songs: *She alone is my dove, she alone my beloved.*[60]

69. *And he built his sanctuary as of unicorns: on the earth he founded it for ever.* Unicorns signifies those who possess a single hope in the most holy Trinity, towards which the consecrated hearts of the faithful are humbly raised, and they rely on the constancy of faith as the strongest of horns. Next comes: *On the earth he founded it for ever.* Though the Jerusalem which is predestined lies in the age to come, it is known to be founded on earth, that is, in the hope of eternity entertained by holy persons. As Peter was told in the gospel: *Thou art Peter, and on this rock I will build my Church and the gates of hell shall not prevail against it.*[61] See then how it is known to be founded on earth in the dimension of eternity; for elsewhere too we read of the Church: *God founded it for ever.*[62]

70. *And he chose his servant David, and took him from the flocks of sheep: he brought him from following the pregnant ewes.* 71. *To feed Jacob his servant and Israel his inheritance.* A most appropriate and beautiful description is introduced here. Because he had said He chose Judah, he now says He chose David, for David was closely related to Christ the Lord in the humanity which He assumed. But we do better to understand this of the Lord Saviour Himself, for in the gospel the blind cry out: *Son of David, have mercy on us.*[63] And because they had spoken the truth so trustingly, they were swiftly healed. Next comes: *And took him from the flocks of sheep: he brought him from following the pregnant ewes.* By this parallel with David, son of Jesse, here as elsewhere the mysteries of the Lord Saviour are revealed. David was removed from the sheep, and attained the kingship; our Lord performed the role of shepherd, and sits at the right hand of the Father, and is truly *King of kings and lord of lords.*[64] The statement that the ewes were pregnant is not idle, for the Lord's flock is fertile in spiritual grace, and is known to have numerous children. As we read of the Church in the Song of Songs: *Thy teeth are like a flock of shorn ewes*

which come up from the washing, all with twins, and there is none barren among them.[65] He added: *To feed Jacob his servant, and Israel his inheritance.* We see more clearly that this is said of the Lord Saviour, who alone was able to fill His flock with the bread of heaven, and to rescue His inheritance above all from all the dangers which confront our souls. We can interpret *Jacob* as the Christian people dwelling here on earth, and *Israel his inheritance* as the future assembly which will feast on contemplation of the Lord; this cannot on any account have reference to any temporal king.

72. *And he fed them without malice in his heart, and conducted them with the feeling of his hands.* The whole of this relates generally to the Lord Saviour, for He alone was without sin; by the phrase *without malice* he shows that sins are to be expressed by this word. The Purity, the Sanctity, the Majesty that came from heaven was shown to have taught what He himself carried out, and undoubtedly He did what He taught. The outstanding Teacher fed those whom He deigned to teach; as He Himself attests: *Not in bread alone doth man live, but in every word of God.*[66] *Without malice in his heart;* as Scripture says elsewhere: *There is no guile in his mouth.*[67] *The feeling of hands* points to the practical sanctity to which He guided His faithful by their glorious emulation of Him. This too can hardly be appropriate in any way to the temporal King David, but the whole passage becomes harmonious and beautifully consistent when applied to the Lord Christ.

Conclusion Drawn From the Psalm

In a number of psalms it is our custom to seek out the advice which divine authority offers us. In this case the psalmist made a beginning in such a way that it seems to be an explanation rather than an exordium. He said that he would speak in parallels and propositions, so that every reader could quickly gain acquaintance with the appearance of the psalm, once the shape of the diction had been explained. So he maintains that the Jews were driven out because of their sins, and the Christians were admitted, and he expresses this in such a way as to make the purpose of both Old and New Laws hang as it were on the one beautiful cluster. So let us love its extended account, for while the history is being recounted, the grace of the New Testament is being made clear. It is like the tossing ocean, which offers shafts of light commensurate with the shaking it induces. At one moment its brightness shines out, and at another its shadowy appearance engulfs us; in that same element variety appears, though there is no addition to or diminution of its colour. Similarly the marvellous variety of this psalm both recounts the history and hints at a quite different spiritual sense. Psalm 104 resembles it in this respect. Just as the coming mysteries of the Lord are foretold in the deeds of David, so the sacred signs of the Christian people are revealed through the miracles granted to the Jews.

COMMENTARY ON PSALM 78

1. *A psalm of Asaph.* As we have often mentioned, the meaning of the name is suited to those actions accommodated to the Lord's commands and grace. *Asaph* means "synagogue,"[1] a title appropriate for the Catholic Church, because those who have shone out with the brightness of God's grace are not to be reckoned foreigners by Christians. Add to its number the prophets, patriarchs and people already devoted to Christ before the Christian era began. So this psalm, like Psalm 73, is wholly a psalm of lamentation which bewails future times as though they were past, and with the eagerness of devoted love implores Christ the Lord to help the nation which will be sorely afflicted through the hardness of its heart.

Division of the Psalm

Before we discuss the division, we must briefly insert an indication of the events, so that the text of the psalm may be heard with fuller understanding through prior exposition of the circumstances. The first book of Maccabees informs us that when King Antiochus came to Jerusalem, the city was savagely stripped of its wealth. He placed idols in God's temple, and by forcing the Jews to sacrifice to his gods created many martyrs.[2] So Asaph, who as we have said plays the role of the faithful people, speaks throughout the psalm. In the first section he recounts all that Jerusalem and the Jewish people have endured in the days of King Antiochus. In the second part he asks the Lord to pour out the spleen of His anger on these powerful enemies, and to deign to be merciful to the sins of His servants. In the third place, in the spirit of prophecy he begs for vengeance not by praying for destruction, but with eagerness for correction.

Explanation of the Psalm

O God, the nations have come into thy inheritance. Though David lived long before King Antiochus, the psalmist was filled with the holy Spirit, and as usual recounted all that he foresaw would occur as though it had already happened. So Asaph wept and suddenly cried to the Lord: *The nations have come,* as though they were now bursting into the walls and the dreaded captivity was commencing. *Gens* (nation) is so called because it is sprung from one stock (*genus*). *Into thy inheritance* denotes Jerusalem, where the inheritance of God was implanted among holy men like Mathathias, Eleazar, the seven brothers with their holy mother; like the thousand who so as not to violate the sabbath allowed themselves all to be killed by the enemy without resistance;[3] like the others of whom men's knowledge remains wholly unaware. The psalmist added: *Thy,* to rouse the anger of the Judge against the harsh foes; they had come, he said, to harm the property belonging to the Judge. Ancient orators in seeking to arouse odium and resentment against their opponents used such expressions at greater length.

They have besmirched thy holy temple, they have made Jerusalem like a storehouse for fruit. Most appropriately the harm to the consecrated temple is the first thought of the holy man, so that he should lament at the outset what he knew was an insult to God. *Besmirched* means defiled; on that occasion the sanctuary of the Lord was not overturned, but the wicked heathens set up statues in the holiest places with sacrilegious presumption, so that an impure spirit could be adored where the true God was worshipped. This is what we read in the book of Maccabees about Antiochus: *He commanded the holy places to be profaned, and the holy people of Israel. He ordered altars to be built, and temples and idols, and swine's flesh to be immolated,*[4] and the rest. Next comes the most grievous and insulting simile: *They have made*

Jerusalem like a storehouse for fruit. This figure is called *parabole,* when things dissimilar in kind are compared.[5] Fruit-storehouses is the term for the huts which market-gardeners build for themselves to fend off the sun's harmful rays and to keep the unscrupulous hands of thieves off the greens and the vegetables; they abandon them as useless once the harvest-season is over. So the nations which ravaged Jerusalem regarded the uniquely beautiful temple as cheaply as a hovel for produce which is abandoned as worthless and paltry once the summer is over. So Isaiah too says: *The daughter of Sion shall be left as a covert in a vineyard, and as a hut in a cucumber-plot.*[6]

2. *They have given the mortal remains of thy servants to be meat for the fowls of the air: the flesh of thy saints for the beasts of the earth.* After his complaint about the affront to God's temple, he passes to the killing of human beings to prove the enemy guilty of homicide in addition to the guilt of sacrilege. A greater charge is superimposed on these; after slaughtering them with monstrous cruelty, the enemy cast out the corpses unburied to the wild beasts. Contempt for dead bodies is more than a little odious, for if burial is a duty of devotion, to cast out bodies to the fowls of the air is certainly a mark of great cruelty. By speaking of *thy servants* he is referring to the martyrs who flourished because of the widespread persecution in that period of captivity. As we read in Maccabees: *Many of the people of Israel held fast and were strong in determination not to eat unclean things: and they chose rather to die than be defiled with food forbidden by the Lord.*[7] Next comes: *The flesh of thy saints for the beasts of the earth.* The one event is described with twofold variation, so that this diverse description of a cruel deed could oppress the ears of the most devoted Judge. It was not enough to consign the dead to the birds; they also allowed the beasts to lacerate the bodies.

3. *They have poured out their blood as water, round about Jerusalem; and there was none to bury them.* He still dwells on the hyperbole. He does not wish speedily to abandon his anger, because their action set a harsh precedent. By his phrase, *as water,* he increases the odium attached to those cruel deeds, since the enemy believed that they were permitted to shed human blood like the water which runs down, without blame attaching to anyone. The additional phrase, *round about Jerusalem, and there was none to bury them,* reveals the most wicked extent of that criminal slaughter, for the massacre had developed not

only within the city but also around its walls, to such a degree that none could conduct the office of burial since all were affected by a like fate. As we read in the previous psalm; *Fire consumed their young men, and their maidens were not lamented.*[8]

4. *We are become a reproach to our neighbours: a scorn and a derision to them that are around us.* He says that the splendid fame of the people of Jerusalem, notable through the whole world, has been transformed into the reproach of their neighbours, so that their former shining nobility is matched by their subsequent sordid detestation. As Jeremiah puts it in his Lamentations: *How doth the city sit solitary that was full of people! How is the mistress of the Gentiles become a widow! The princes of provinces made tributary!*[9] And a little later: *This is the city which was called the crown of glory, the joy of all the earth.*[10] Next comes: *A scorn and a derision to them that are round us.* He redoubles the same lament with verbal variation, so that the reproach which he had mentioned may be exposed more clearly. He says that the Jews were a scorn, though previously they had been venerated through their devotion to the Lord. They were truly held in derision when men saw consigned to captivity the nation to which they had long witnessed so many kingdoms yielding. The additional phrase, *them that are around us,* is not otiose, for the reproaches witnessed by neighbours are always more grievous; for we have constantly to bear the reflexions which the benefit of great distance allows us to forgo. So the whole text mounts to a crescendo from the beginning, and forms that most notable figure called *auxesis,* in Latin *augmentum.*[11] Where are the orators who have adapted such service of the truth to the rhetorical art approximating to it? Observe the arguments wielded by talented simplicity rather than malicious craftiness.

5. *How long, O Lord, wilt thou be angry for ever? Shall thy zeal be kindled like a fire?* He passes to the second section, in which he begs the devoted Judge not to be angry with the Jewish people for ever, for He has indicated His future coming by the holy proclamations of the prophets. Though those holy men were suffering evils, they knew that the Lord would certainly not abandon them. As another psalm has it: *The Lord chastising has chastised me, but he has not delivered me over to death.*[12] Moreover, with the spirit of prophecy he announces that what he foresaw would come was taking place; for at the time of the captivity Mathathias, one of the Jews, was fired with enthusiasm for

the tradition of his fathers; and because he saw his fellow-citizens being dragged to the worship of idols, he assembled the rest of the faithful, and in the company of his sons leapt on the army of King Antiochus with such great anger that he freed himself from the yoke of slavery, and most splendidly spurned the sacrifices enjoined on him.[13] He went so far in the love of his holy devotion as to kill a certain Jew on the very altars as he was sacrificing to the idols.[14]

6. *Pour out thy wrath upon the nations that have not known thee: and upon the kingdoms that have not called upon thy name.* After he has recounted the most grievous disasters of the Jewish race, he now supplicates the just Judge that those who ravaged them should endure afflictions, for they were wholly ignorant of His name. He says: *Pour out thy wrath,* meaning, "Discharge your indignation in abundance over your enemy, so that they may be overwhelmed by Your powers as they now oppress us." He realised that men's triumph can last only so long as the divine power permits. And when he says: *That have not known thee,* he is palliating the faults of the Jews; for though many of them had sinned, there were none the less those among them who attended to the Lord's commands. He says that those wholly ignorant of the Lord's name are rightly to be attacked, and thus their own inexcusable guilt is lightened by comparison with the greater sin. The juxtaposition of *upon the nations* and *upon the kingdoms* is not idle; first his prayers were directed against the people, and then against the kingdoms for cruelly authorising such deeds.

7. *Because they have devoured Jacob, and have laid waste his place.* He put forward the name of the most acceptable patriarch to represent the sinning nation, so that the recollection of that most holy man could lessen the sins of the people. This figure is called *antiprosopon,*[15] when a most acceptable person takes the place of one who is unwelcome. The expression, *they have devoured,* signifies "They have caused to be devoured"; he is revealing the savagery of the wicked nation for having exposed the corpses of the dead to be eaten by wild beasts. Alternatively, those who are devoured are denoted as those who have abandoned the Lord's law and are glutted with wicked superstition. Next comes: *And have laid waste his place.* He laments the destruction and desolation of the most beautiful city, for by the wicked tyranny and pressure of the heathens it was stripped of the dwellings of its citizens.

8. *Remember not our long-standing iniquities of old. Let thy mercy speedily come before us, for we are become exceedingly poor.* By confession of their sins he makes the Judge kindly disposed to them; his aim was to win forgiveness by necessary entreaties, since he could not clear himself in justice. But since Asaph knew that in Antiochus' time a number of Jews would be led astray to abandon worship of the Lord, and to cultivate sacrilegious idols, he could not make entreaty merely on account of their established iniquities, since he knew that they were going to commit great crimes in times to come. But I think we must regard *long-standing iniquities* here as analogous to those faults of old by which men sinned for countless years through the impious wickedness of the world. As another psalm has it: *Behold, thou hast made my days old.*[6] Next follows: *Let thy mercy speedily come before us.* He who fears the judgment of the Lord rightly longs for the Lord's mercy to come before him, for unless clemency precedes the sinner it will not absolve the guilty one at the Judgment. He added: *For we are become exceedingly poor.* Poverty is lack of good works in us, and we have no justice to offer if rigorous equity makes a scrutiny of us. To *poor* he appends the word *exceedingly,* so that none might think that he should presume upon the worthiness of his actions once he realised that he was exceedingly poor in deserving merit.

9. *Help us, O God our saviour, for the honour of thy name.* When he says: *Help us,* he is perhaps alluding to the struggle which Mathathias was to take up to free the Jews from the calamity of superstitions; he was praying to be aided by the Lord's power, since all hope was lost in human strength. He well understood his own weakness, for he called with all his power on the saving Physician, so that once the Jews were rescued they could render honour to His name. It is helpful to suggest that he should be aided for the Lord's honour rather than for his own merits.

O Lord deliver us, and forgive us our sins for thy name's sake. He who loses hope in his own strength hastens of necessity to the help of the almighty Judge, so that what cannot be granted through his own deeds may be bestowed through devotion to the holy name. This is why He is called Saviour, because He saves those who hope in Him, transforming the punishment which looms over sinners into rewards.

10. *Lest at some time the Gentiles say: Where is their God?, and it becomes known amongst the nations before our eyes.* He gives the reason

why he begged that the Lord's people be delivered, namely, so that those faithless men should not make the familiar taunt: *Where is their God?* Though men of faith endure various scourgings, they cannot endure it when the Maker of all creatures is insulted. Their remark, *where is he?* implies either that He is not there or that He cannot defend them. Observe how essential it was that he report this reproach at the time of their disasters, for it suggested an insult to God. Next comes: *And it becomes known amongst the nations before their eyes;* we must understand here the vengeance which the Lord is wont to exact from the unfaithful, when He compels them to condemn their wicked desires. When he says: *Before our eyes,* he is demanding speedy vengeance, so that he may see occurring what he knew could eventually be granted.

Avenge the blood of thy servants which has been shed. He now deals with the third and last part, begging that the Lord avenge the blood of the faithful, who endured martyrdom for His name. Vengeance is the means by which force and injustice are repelled by just retribution. But here the prayer seems to be directed towards the conversion of the enemy. For when temporal vengeance is exacted from them in this world, they escape the destruction of eternal damnation; it is in this sense that we read in Revelations[17] that the souls of martyrs under God's altar demand to be avenged by divine decree. This vengeance is to be interpreted as we have defined it, for saintly men do not seek a cruel vengeance since they accept the precept: *Pray for your enemies, do good to those that hate you,*[18] and the like. Finally the Lord Himself, who executes most powerfully His own commands, spoke these words on the cross: *Father, forgive them, for they know not what they do.*[19]

11. *Let the groans of the prisoners come in before thee. According to the greatness of thy arm, take possession of the children of them that were punished by death.* He speaks of those whom the impious heathen had imprisoned for the sake of the Lord's name. With frequent groans they begged the almighty Lord that His Church should not perish among their brothers, even if the punishment which threatened destroyed themselves. Saintly persons always pray for what leads to the spread of the faith. Next comes: *According to the greatness of thy arm, take possession of the children of them that were punished by death.* This most devoted and heartfelt prayer rises, that the Lord should not

remove from His own possession the children of those who were punished by death because of the religion that is His; for at that time there was a crowd of martyrs beyond counting, whose descendants long to be the possession of the Lord so that they may not be contaminated by any error. For when He possesses us, the rights of the devil over us are not maintained.

12. *Render to our neighbours sevenfold in their bosom: the reproach wherewith they have reproached thee, O Lord. Render* means much the same as *avenge* earlier;[20] even if it brings physical affliction, it none the less ensures the salvation of souls. *Neighbours* refers to those on their boundaries of whom he said earlier: *We are become a reproach to our neighbours.*[21] *Sevenfold* indicates the perfection of the heavenly gift when we are filled with the enlightenment of the holy Spirit; of this another passage has it: *As silver tried by the fire, purged from the earth seven times.*[22] There is no doubt that this refers to their conversion, for they receive the gift that they may be transformed for the better. *In their bosom* we must interpret precisely as "in the depth of their souls," where the splendour of conversion always takes place. Next comes: *The reproach wherewith they have reproached thee, O Lord.* They have committed injuries; let them speak forth praises. They were unbelieving; let them be devoted. They were blatantly proud; let them become humble. It is when the Lord is praised in the mouths of those who reviled Him that He is seen to be gloriously avenged.

13. *But we, thy people and the sheep of thy flock, will confess to thee for ever.* In my opinion he is speaking of the remnants gathered together by the enthusiasm of Mathathias, whose merits enabled them to maintain the Law of the Lord. They are truly the Lord's sheep, for they proclaimed His glory and remained steadfast in faith. But this verse can be interpreted also in a general sense, so that the Christian people too is intermingled with them, for, as we have often said, from the two peoples a single gathering of saints was formed. We must note how sweetly he has ended his lamentation, by saying that it is the Lord's flock for whom he was making such devoted entreaty, so that He would no longer be angry with those whom He remembered as his own.

And until the world's end we shall recount thy praise. He adverts here to the most blessed psalmody of the age to come, which the saints' chorus will unceasingly utter—not to instruct others, for no person there will be unschooled, but to offer due honour, and to feast on the sweetness of the praises themselves.

Conclusion Drawn From the Psalm

This is the second psalm which has bewailed the glory of Jerusalem with devoted lamentation. But we must realise that Psalm 73 embraces the captivity which the city endured under the Romans, whereas this psalm laments the sacrilegious and most savage plundering by King Antiochus. We must also ponder and store deep in our minds that we are being advised to rejoice with zealous charity at the blessings on God's Church, and again to feel sore grief at her disasters. As Scripture has it: *Happy are they who rejoice in your peace, and happy all who will be saddened at your several scourgings.*[23] So it is fitting that with the eagerness of a neighbour we join to our own sorrows whatever befalls any of the faithful. As Paul puts it: *If one member suffer anything, all the members suffer with it; or if one member glory, all the members rejoice with it.*[24] These are the means by which that lofty charity is sought, the means by which that proclaimed unity is achieved.[25] If you examine the cause of this blessing more deeply, it is the source from which is born the divine affection which is known to enrich the Lord's Church.

COMMENTARY ON PSALM 79

1. *Unto the end, for them that shall be changed, the testimony of Asaph, a psalm.* If one seeks to repeat hackneyed observations to men who are learned and schooled for salvation in Christ's lecture-room, it causes annoyance; since all the terms in this heading are now known, it remains merely to investigate the one new expression, *the testimony of Asaph.* This Asaph, who earlier was fearful and anxious, and was seen in earlier psalms to be offering entreaties for the sins of the synagogue, is now filled with such presumption that he seems to be offering a testimony of conversion on behalf of those who are transformed for the better. He is speaking of the first coming of the Lord Saviour,

who led man towards the gifts of a holy life when he was vitiated by the law of sin, and by the rooting of His power made steady the vineyards which had been brought out of Egypt. This is the meaning of *the testimony for them that shall be changed.* So this is a hymn sung about the coming of the Husbandman and about the Lord's vineyard, so that His coming may now be demanded in clear rather than shrouded prayers. This is seen to be the second psalm with this theme.[1]

Division of the Psalm

Asaph, whom the heading proclaimed at the outset to be changed, prays in the first section for the coming of the Lord. The second part attests how the vineyard which is the Church has spread through the whole world. In the third part, deploying the image of the vineyard, he prays that the Church may be visited by the blessing of the incarnation, and he begs that he himself may cling close to the Lord.

Explanation of the Psalm

2. *Give ear, O thou that rulest Israel: thou that leadest Joseph like sheep: thou that sittest upon the Cherubim, show forth.* By the second type of definition which in Greek is called *ennoematike,* and in Latin *notio,*[2] the coming of Christ the Lord is demanded with great longing, so that He may appear to be most clearly signified by what He does. This type of definition is known to depict each and every person not by his essence but by his actions. So the address is rightly made to the king of heaven and earth *who rules Israel,* under whose control all things were created and are administered. But though all things lie in His power, He is said to rule those who know how to deport themselves with manners approved by heaven. This is why *Israel* is appended, because He governs with mercy those who look to Him in purity of heart; for Israel, as has often been said, means "he who mentally sees God."[3] *Give ear* has the implication of "Pour the light of Your fatherly love on us, so that we who are in ourselves shrouded in darkness may become visible by the brightness of Your face." Next follows: *Thou that leadest Joseph like sheep.* We must interpret *Joseph* as

the faithful people, who are led into the Lord's pens like sheep gathering to pasture. The very name Joseph means "without reproach,"[4] which is certainly apt for the devoted people. Observe that particular verbs have been allotted to each person; Israel is ruled, and Joseph led. He added: *Thou that sittest upon the Cherubim, show forth.* The meaning of Cherubim is "fullness of knowledge,"[5] on which Christ the Lord clearly sits. But since the Lord still remained within the cloak of His majesty, the psalmist asks that He should appear in the blessing of the holy incarnation, so that He may strengthen His faithful with the most unswerving belief. Observe that the texture of this verse contains a triple invocation to show that the holy Trinity performs together all things.

3. *Before Ephraim, Benjamin and Manasses: stir up thy might, and come to save us.* Obviously these are names of the Jewish race. The psalmist begs that the Lord appear before them with spiritual might, in other words, that as had been promised through the prophets He should be born of the Jewish nation. But since these names in the usual fashion of divine Scripture are clearly not idly inserted, we must investigate most eagerly their meanings. Ephraim means "fruitfulness," Benjamin "son of the right hand," and Manasses "forgetful."[6] Clearly these attributes lie within the Lord Saviour. He was fruitful when after His body had lain slaughtered for a time He rose to the everlasting kingdom of heaven. He is the "Son of the right hand," that is, Son of the almighty Father. "Forgetful" points to when He was oblivious of the injuries done to Him, when set on the cross He prayed for the Jewish people. So the psalmist entreated that the Lord come with these powers, and he was in no doubt that He would manifest them. Next comes: *Stir up thy might, and come to save us.* His knowledge of the profit which we were to gain through the Lord's incarnation is matched by the enthusiasm of his prayer that the Lord should stir up His might and come to wash away the sins of the human race. What longing or prayers or vows would be sufficient to beg for what could save the world from its own impiety?

4. *God of powers, convert us and show us thy face, and we shall be saved.* Since he believed that miracles were to be performed within him, he rightly called on the God of powers, who alone has the strength to deliver us from the death of disbelief. Because he knew that he was crooked, he vehemently demanded that he be converted.

Who but the Lord of powers is the right Person to do this? He alone
has the power to fulfil all that He wishes. After the blessing of conver-
sion, the appropriate phrase following is: *Show us thy face,* for the
Godhead is wont to look kindly on men whose hearts are converted.
The additional words, *and we shall be saved,* clearly point to the Lord
Saviour, by whose incarnation we were truly saved.

5. *O Lord God of hosts, how long wilt thou be angry against the prayer
of thy servant?* We must take this as referring to the time of the Lord's
coming demanded by Asaph. Because in accordance with the divine
dispensation it had to be postponed for a time, he asks: "*How long wilt
thou be angry against the prayer of thy servant,* so that You are failing to
bring to realisation what You are known to have promised?" Observe
the devotion and longing of the suppliant; he believed that the Lord
was angry with him, since He was slow to lend aid to the human race.

6. *Wilt thou feed us with the bread of tears, and give us for our drink
tears in measure?* After this prior realisation that he could be kept
waiting, he recounts the ills which the Jewish people were to endure.
He says: *Wilt thou feed us with the bread of tears?* thus showing that
they would live under affliction. The bread of tears is a life full of
griefs; but in that life we are fed through the Lord's pity, for we are
not snuffed out by those disasters and hardships, but rather schooled
by them. Next comes: *And give us tears for our drink?* First he mentioned bread, and now he speaks of drink as well. These are the two
things by which all human beings live; all food is designated by bread,
all liquids by drink. What moment could they have free of tears when
their very lamentation was seen to refresh them? *In measure* means
distribution within limits. As Paul says: *God is faithful; he will not
suffer you to be tempted above that which you are able, but will make also
with temptation issue, that you may be able to bear it.*[7]

7. *Thou hast made us to be a contradiction to our neighbours: and our
enemies have jeered at us.* This *contradiction* we must regard as that
heathen opposition aroused in debased controversies against those
who proclaimed Christ; these opponents believed that they could defend the deities which the Gentiles were seen to adore in their temples. Or better, the verse appears to recall the period mentioned in the
verses of the previous psalm; when under King Antiochus certain
Jews were sacrificing to idols, they were contradicting those seen to
maintain the law of the Lord;[8] and so we must interpret *neighbours* as

parents close to them as next of kin. Next comes: *And our enemies have jeered at us.* Those enemies were justified in jeering, for they witnessed so wicked a struggle between them, with one section abiding by the old religion, and the other under compulsion becoming slaves to idols.

8. *Lord God of hosts, convert us and show thy face: and we shall be saved.* He repeats the verse which he is seen to have set down four verses above; for when a person longs for something, he often tends to repeat what with intense prayers he begs may come. So it is the face or presence of Christ by which we have been saved and have escaped the nooses of death, and which bestows the kingdom of heaven on the unworthy and the trusting alike.

9. *Thou hast brought a vineyard out of Egypt: thou hast cast out the Gentiles and planted it.* He passes to the second section, in which he recounts the historical events by means of allegorical utterances. This figure is called *metabole,*[9] the frequent repetition of the one thing with a variety of words. The vineyard is described throughout these six verses up to the third division. The vineyard stands for the Jewish race, clearly denoting a type of the Church; from it was sprung the gathering of the faithful. Vineyard (*vinea*) gets its name from vines (*vites*).[10] This vineyard He led out of Egypt by means of great and notable miracles, and then, having driven out the Gentiles (that is, the Hethites, Jebusites, and their other neighbours),[11] the wonder-working Husbandman planted it there. This is the testimony offered, as mentioned in the heading, of the transformation of the Jews, for here too the vineyard is being most splendidly compared with the Church. Just as the vineyard bears vital fruit amidst the foliage doomed to fall, so the Church is adorned with the fruit of the saints amongst the overhanging crowd of sinners. The saints are squeezed by the affliction of this world as by winepresses, but they can produce the sweetest juice. Alternatively the vineyard when implanted is more productive, and when pruned it multiplies; and this is properly applied only to the Church, which regularly grows under the pruning-knife of suffering, and ever spreads amongst her holy people under the blows of persecutions. The passages which follow announce how this vineyard has spread throughout the whole world.

10. *Thou hast made a path in its sight, and didst plant its roots, and the land was filled.* The Lord made a path for this fruitful vine which

embraces the extent of the world, when He deigned to appear before
its sight. The cause of its growth was its beholding its Husbandman,
and its receiving from Him the rain of preaching, so that it could
produce the sweetest fruit. Next comes: *And didst plant its roots, and
the land was filled.* Its roots are the prophets who were planted by the
labour of the heavenly King. From those roots the vineyard stretched
forth fruitful sprouts, and occupied the whole world with the pleasant
shade of the faith.

11. *The shadow of it covered the hills: and the branches thereof the
cedars of God.* The breadth and height of this vineyard are fittingly
explained. It can cover those whom it nourishes, since its shadow
fructifies and fosters greater growth of what it is seen to cover more
completely. But what sort of vineyard is it which covers the hills?
Surely a heavenly one, since every part of the earth however high is
beneath the sky. Next comes: *And the branches thereof the cedars of
God.* He did well to speak of branches, since he made mention of
cedars; for when vines mount trees they are termed branches. Though
at Psalm 36 we said that cedars connote pride,[12] the addition here *of
God* makes us interpret them as martyrs, who are set on the highest
peaks of Christ's Church; and the Church protects them, for they are
known to lie in her bosom.

12. *Thou hast stretched forth its branches unto the sea: and its boughs
unto the river. Branches* indicates the Lord's disciples, to whom He
says in the gospel: *I am the true Vine, and you are the branches.*[13] *The sea*
is to be understood as the most holy belief of all nations. He says: *Thou
hast stretched forth* since this vineyard through the apostles' preaching
spread to all parts of the world. We cannot regard it as bounded by
place, for the psalmist has already said of it: *Thou didst plant its roots,
and the land was filled.*[14] By its boughs he means the children of rebirth,
for they flowed forth from the river Jordan, where the Lord deigned
to be baptised to provide the pattern for our salvation.

13. *Why hast thou dismantled the wall thereof, so that all they who pass
by the way strip it?* He wonders why this vineyard, which derives its
origin from the Jewish people, has had its fence destroyed, in other
words, why the Lord's protection has been removed. The wall is the
defence made of nothing but stones; this is the usual circumvallation
for vineyards, and the psalmist rightly continued with his earlier metaphor by exploiting such a word. Next comes: *And all strip it.* We must

take *strip* here in the bad sense; compare the words of Jeremiah; *Behold, O Lord, and consider that thou hast stripped us: priest and prophet are missing from thy sanctuary.*[15] So *strip* here means "seize and tread underfoot," as passers-by often do when in their desire for plunder they seek to nullify the hard work of others. *Stripping* refers to the plucking of the grape from the vine, with which God through the prophet Isaiah threatens even this vineyard of ours: *I will take away the hedge thereof, and it shall be wasted: I will break down the wall thereof, and it shall be trodden down.*[16] He added: *Who pass by the way.* He means the Gentiles, who passed by the Way which is Christ the Lord and continued with sacrifices to idols.

14. *The boar out of the wood has exterminated it, and a singular wild beast has devoured it. Exterminated,* that is, scattered it everywhere beyond the boundaries of its native land, as happened to the Jews; the sense is identical to the earlier phrase, *they strip it.* Perhaps we should interpret the boar as Vespasian, who showed himself tough and savage to the Jews.[17] This label of boar shows him as a foe of the Jews, for they were known to consider this beast as unclean among the rest. *Out of the wood* means from the Gentiles, who are rightly compared to rough woodland, for as yet they were not implanted with fruitful seed. The boar (*aper*) is so called because it dwells in rough (*asper*) regions.[18] The *singular wild beast* denotes Titus, son of Vespasian, who conducted the closing stages of the war with such grinding ravaging that he destroyed nation and city;[19] he devoured them in fearful fashion like hay—an inevitable end to the vineyard once the wall was seen to be down. The boar because of its aggression and excessive strength can be interpreted in a spiritual sense as the devil; *out of the wood* implies that the devil's intentions are always rough and devious. Observe that in these six verses the vineyard is described by the fourth kind of definition called *hypographike* in Greek and *descriptionalis* in Latin;[20] it clarifies with the appropriate meaning the object of enquiry by encircling it with words and facts.

15. *Turn again, O God of hosts: look down from heaven and see, and visit the vineyard.* 16. *And perfect the same which thy right hand hath planted: and upon the son of man whom thou hast confirmed for thyself.* Having expounded all the preceding detail, Asaph passes to the third section, in which he begs the almighty Farmer to visit the scattered vineyard which He deigned to plant, and to look down on the Son of

man whom He has confirmed for Himself. Now that he is changed for the better, he makes the sole remedy for everything entreaty to Christ the Lord. When he says: *Turn again, O God of hosts,* he is begging Him to look brightly on His suppliants and aid them in their danger. Next comes: *Look down from heaven and see;* understand "in what stormy waters the human race is toiling, by what sins it is being dragged to hell, and in what vices it takes pleasure," the result of which is undoubtedly to be snuffed out in eternal death. But when he says: *Visit this vineyard, and perfect the same which thy right hand hath planted,* he demands the coming of the holy incarnation, so that the vineyard which has been planted may prosper in the presence of its Cultivator, for without Him it could not contribute fruit nor experience profitable cultivation. He added: *And upon the son of man whom thou hast confirmed for thyself.* The earlier word *visit* has been fully clarified; for the Son of man is Christ the Lord, begotten of the virgin Mary, born of the Father before all ages. He was confirmed precisely when the truth of the Father's voice sounded forth with reference to Him in the words: *This is my beloved Son in whom I am well pleased: hear ye him.*[21]

17. *Things set on fire and dug out by hand shall perish at the rebuke of thy countenance.* We must interpret *things set on fire and dug out by hand* as referring to human vices. For a person is ignited by the fire of greed or by the heat of pride when he has perpetrated wicked crimes. They are dug out by hand when we lay an ambush for others by sinful action and seek to deceive them, all unaware that we are falling into the pit ourselves. So these sins will perish at the rebuke of the Lord's countenance, when sinners are to hear the words: *Depart into everlasting fire, which was prepared for the devil and his angels.*[22] They will behold no longer Him whom they have lost through their own wicked deeds.

18. *Let thy hand be upon the man of thy right hand: and upon the son of man whom thou hast confirmed for thyself.* The great mystery, the great gift of the Godhead is being expounded. There could perhaps be some doubt about the salvation of Israel, but only until the coming of the saving Lord. When He came, the promise was fulfilled in its entirety; the Church no longer separates from Him, for she is joined in spiritual love for her Bridegroom. When Asaph says: *Let thy hand be upon the man of thy right hand,* he asks that the holy incarnation should accomplish its work, for He is the right hand of the Father. Of Him else-

where the psalmist says: *For I will not trust in my bow, neither shall my sword save me. But thy right hand and thy arm, and the light of thy countenance.*[23] Then after his fashion by way of explanation he repeats what he has already said: *And upon the son of man;* the phrase, *Let thy hand be,* must be attached to this and to the previous phrase, with the sense of "Let your holy action bring your promises to fulfilment." The Son of man is the Lord Christ Himself, who is also the right Hand of the Father. Next comes: *Whom thou hast confirmed for thyself.* He was indeed confirmed before men, as we have already stated, when the voice of the Father's truth sounded forth with reference to Him, saying: *This is my beloved Son, in whom I am well pleased: hear ye him.*[24] I am not reluctant to repeat this passage to make the point clear, for obviously the words are repeated with the same authority.[25]

19. *And we depart not from thee. Thou shalt quicken us, and we will call upon thy name.* This short verse is connected with what precedes. He says: *Let thy hand be upon the man of thy right hand,* that is, "Deign to send Your Son to free the guilty world from the crime of sinning"; then: *And we depart not from thee,* in other words, "Once we have mentally laid hold of You, we continually gaze on You with the eyes of the heart, and we cannot divert our devotion from You, since we are seen to have vehemently sought the coming of Your Son." The advantage of not departing from Him is next explained: *Thou shalt quicken us, and we will call upon thy name. Thou shalt quicken us* when we lay aside the death of sinners and are reborn of water and the holy Spirit. *We will call upon his name* is a pointer to the fact that following the saving instruction of the Lord Christ we constantly call on the Father's name in our daily prayer.

20. *O Lord God of hosts, convert us; and show thy face, and we shall be saved.* The sweetness and usefulness of this short verse can be inferred from the fact that he repeated it three times in this psalm, so that the charm of its rosy hue could adorn, so to say, the plain of this flower-bearing meadow which extends in fixed rows. For in this short compass Asaph expounds the ordered course of the whole of religious life. First the Lord must convert us; second, He must show His face; third, He must save us. He does not show His face before converting us, and He does not save us unless He has gazed on us with the light of His love. So this verse is to be stored in the mind, for through its brief formulation we seek what is seen to aid us.

Conclusion Drawn From the Psalm

It is abundantly clear that Asaph here is changed for the better. He beheld Christ's vineyard[26] extended over the whole world, and its vine-leaves overshadowing mountains and cedars. It is a truly blessed vision, and reflexion on its beauty renews us. One vineyard casts the shade of its leaves over the whole world, so that not one of the faithful is made swarthy by the sun. Scripture says of them: *The sun shall not burn thee by day, nor the moon by night.*[27] The vineyard bears as its juicy grapes holy fruits; it bears martyrs, rears prophets, begets apostles, brings forth innumerable faithful. All the splendid achievements in holy Church are appropriately incorporated in this imagery.

COMMENTARY ON PSALM 80

1. *Unto the end, for the presses. For Asaph, on the fifth day of the sabbath.* It was pointed out that in earlier psalm-headings *for the presses* made allusion to the Church; but since we said earlier that this prefiguration lay in the treading of grapes, let us now explain it by the harvesting of olives. When a heap of olives is pounded and subjected to weights applied by the skill of farmers, and begins to be squeezed under considerable pressure, both foul dregs[1] and oil of the richest purity ooze out. There is no doubt that this can occur in persecutions of the Church, when she both manifests pure hearts before God, and clearly thrusts foul consciences before Him. *The fifth day of the sabbath* means the fifth day after the sabbath, when in that state of the world the Lord created animals out of the waters, as consultation of the reading of Genesis attests: *God said, Let the waters bring forth creeping creatures having life.*[2] This makes a connexion with the grace of baptism by means of a beautiful parallel, for baptism does indeed bring forth living creatures by its fruitfulness, for the sanctified waters receive persons defiled by their wicked deeds and make them spotless. Let us however assemble in one sequence the statements expressed severally. The drift of the heading is of this order: *Unto the end* denotes the Lord Christ, *for the presses* the Church, *Asaph* the gathering, *on the fifth of the sabbath* the baptised. From this we infer

that the psalm will address the gathering reborn in the Lord's Church. Asaph here does indeed in an historical sense address the Jews, but the psalm is better understood in the spiritual sense as referring to the Christian people.

Division of the Psalm

In the first part of the psalm Asaph speaks to the faithful, bidding them sound forth praises to the Lord on various musical instruments, for He has deigned to grant His people many blessings. In the second part come the words of the Lord, threatening them against worshipping idols, and bidding that He alone be adored who is wont to bestow beneficial gifts. In the third part Asaph, again speaking in his own person, makes a further observation, rebuking the unfaithful for their deceitful behaviour after the gifts of the Lord have been bestowed with abundant generosity.

Explanation of the Psalm

Rejoice to God our helper: sing aloud to the God of Jacob. This Asaph, who we have often said denotes the synagogue, warns the faithful people not to cease praising God with the greater joy, for He has deigned to rescue them from the most savage dangers. He uses the word *Helper* to denote the true God, for the counterfeit god is no helper but a strangler, no healer but one who inflicts wounds, not one who lifts up but one who fiercely forces us down. His word *our* attests that he is offering advice to the committed. *Iubilate* (rejoice) is derived from *iuvare* (to delight);[3] when people could not be content with verbal rejoicing, their most copious joy, failing to find words, took physical form; this teaches us that we must give thanks to the Lord with glad hearts rather than be troubled by any care as we sing. If we despise earthly things, we always take joy from the One whom an uncertain and wavering mind cannot reach. *Jacob* denotes the Christian people,[4] with whom the earlier synagogue harmonises; what is known to have been taken from the synagogue was transferred by grace to the Christians, and the phrase, *on the fifth of the sabbath,* refers to them, for they experience a new and holy rebirth.

3. *Take a psalm, and offer the timbrel: the pleasant psaltery with the harp.* Both of these are musical instruments, but are seen to convey important messages. He is saying: "Take a psalm, and offer good works." The psalm's purpose is to communicate the divine words, for as we have often said it is shaped in such a way that its tuneful belly is at the top;[5] this shape is appropriate for the psalm, which always sounds forth heavenly mysteries. The timbrel has skin stretched over its two conical sections which are joined at the pointed end, and it resounds when struck; in the same way the human body when beaten by tribulation for the Lord's sake is more sweetly attuned to heaven's commands. So this passage warns us to receive God's words and to offer earthly things to the Lord; for we properly offer the timbrel to God when we give alms, when we discipline our bodies with fasting, when we despise equally the vices of this world and their author. He added: *The pleasant psaltery with the harp.* He advises us that these too are combined most pleasantly, so that the words of God contained in the psaltery and the harp which is known to denote human actions should join together in a single unity, for their combined melody is seen to be acceptable to the Lord. The psaltery denotes the same as the psalm, the harp the same as the timbrel; the psalmist has briefly enclosed the same message with variation of terms. It has often been explained how the harp is fashioned in contrast to the psaltery.[6] In this and the following verse an "enthymematic" or rhetorical syllogism[7] shines out similarly; it was enjoined on Israel to sing also of the judgment before the God of Jacob, so they must sound forth on the trumpet at the beginning of the month, on that special day of their celebration. Now let us examine the rest.

4. *Blow up the trumpet at the beginning of the month, on the day of your noted solemnity.* Amongst other obligations observed by the Jews was the injunction to sound forth with the trumpet for seven days from the first day of the seventh month.[8] Even today they go through the motions of doing this, without realising that the reason for the command was that the seven-formed grace of the holy Spirit was to be proclaimed to those who were to be baptised throughout the whole world. So now Asaph advises faithful Christians to sing the praises of the Lord in tones of proclamation, once they have attained the joys of new rebirth. When mention is made of a trumpet, it indicates a proclamation with grandiloquent cries. Another prophet similarly says: *Cry,*

and lift up thy voice like a trumpet![9] It should also be observed that we are enjoined to hymn the Lord and celebrate the solemn day with instruments for musical performance; just as those instruments sweetly combine to produce pleasant melody and a single harmony, so all our actions can be directed to the Lord, and offered to His ears with the most pleasant intonation. The discipline of music incorporates great power and knowledge which brings delight; teachers of secular literature, through the generosity of God who grants all that is useful, have made it possible through theoretical texts to ascertain what was earlier regarded as hidden from view in the nature of the world.[10] The first division of this discipline, then, is into harmonics, rhythmics, and metrics. The second division, that of musical instruments, is between percussion, strings and wind. The third division is into six harmonies, the fourth into fifteen tones. In this way the virtue of this most beautiful discipline is unfolded by such distinctions drawn by men of old. We read in secular works that many miracles were brought forth by these measures. But we need say nothing of this fabulous material; we read that by means of David's tuneful harp the demon was expelled from Saul.[11] The divine reading attests that the walls of Jericho at once collapsed at the din of trumpets.[12] So there is no doubt that the sounds of music, at the Lord's command or with His permission, have unleashed great forces.

5. *For it is a commandment in Israel, and a judgment to the God of Jacob.* He explains the reason why they must sound forth with the trumpet; it is because the law was given through Moses amongst the people of Israel, and once it was made known, no-one ought to have sinned. *A judgment to the God of Jacob* means to the God of the Christians; for He will judge[13] creatures endowed with reason according to heavenly truth. As it says in the gospel: *The Father does not judge any man, but has given all judgment to the Son.*[14] So it is clear from this wonderful arrangement that the Lord must be praised, for He both gave the law and made known the Judgment to come before His majesty. We have said that Jacob signifies the people who follow, who were adopted by Christ's grace and thus overcame the injunctions imposed by the original punishment.

6. *He ordained it for a testimony in Joseph, when he came out of the land of Egypt: he heard a tongue which he knew not.* Joseph means "increase";[15] the interpretation of this name is testimony to the He-

brew people who came out of the land of Egypt in increased numbers.[16] But the event provides an apposite parallel for our generation. Just as the Jews were saved and extricated through the waters of the Red Sea, so we are delivered from the land of Egypt, that is, from the sins of the flesh, and reborn through regeneration by the sacred water. The very name of the Red Sea is not otiose; just as it is known as Red, so the baptismal water can be labelled red, for it came forth mixed with blood from the Lord Saviour's side. Next comes: *He heard a tongue which he knew not.* We must interpret tongue here as the precepts of the New Testament, for if you understand it as "language," how did the Jewish people hear a tongue which they did not know, when we are sure that the Lord Christ spoke in Hebrew? So the passage means that in the gospel they heard a tongue or precepts which their earlier knowledge did not embrace; alternatively it refers to the time when the apostles were filled with the holy Spirit, and spoke in unknown and varied tongues.[17]

7. *He removed his back from the burdens: his hands had served in baskets.* Though this too seems to be addressed to the historical occasion when the Jewish people in Egypt lived under various constraints, being compelled now to make bricks and now to haul earth in baskets, we can with further application make it relevant to the role of Christians, from whose backs God removes the burdens of sins when they prostrate themselves in holy humility. As Christ Himself says: *Come to me, all ye who labour and are burdened, and I will refresh you.*[18] We use the word baskets for the receptacles used in throwing away scourings of dirt, to enable the cleanliness of a place to shine out. So it is those who are involved in the impurities of sins who keep their hands in those baskets, but we are freed from this slavery by the Lord when we are cleansed of the foulness of our crimes.

8. *Thou calledst upon me in affliction, and I delivered thee: I heard thee in the secret place of tempest: I proved thee at the waters of contradiction.* At this point the words of the Lord Saviour are cited, and this could be a division of the psalm if a diapsalm did not follow this verse, and where we think it more appropriately marked. But since the speaker is changed here, it is the figure known as *ethopoeia,*[19] when we bring in someone to make a speech. Kindnesses are attributed to Him so that their sin may be reckoned the more serious. For He frees us from affliction, He hearkens to the hardships in the secret place of our

tempest; but He proves us when heretics contradict us, at the time when we are roused by verbal challenges as though by blasts of winds. But if you refer the phrase to the historical context, it was when the people of Israel with sceptical minds demanded water in the desert.[20]

9–10. *Hear, O my people, and I will speak, Israel, and testify to thee: O Israel, if thou wilt hearken to me, there shall be no new god in thee: neither shalt thou adore a strange god.* After the interposition of a diapsalm, a feature which we must carefully observe in psalm-divisions, he passes to the second section. Though speaking comes before hearing, at this point *hear* comes first, so that you may realise that the word is directed to our understanding, and not to any passing sound in our ears. He further says: *O my people,* to exclude the dregs which are thrown away as lees by the presses of the Church. God's people are they who cannot be confused with the wicked through any intermingling of behaviour, but who continue to be most chaste in Christ's grace with the richness and purity of oil. Next comes: *Israel, and I will testify to thee.* Whereas in this world witnesses are usually brought before the judge, the Lord of the judgment himself says that He is the witness of the truth. This is to ensure that no-one would doubt that his deeds would be duly weighed in the presence of such an Assessor, but He explains this subsequently; for the Lord testifies when at the Judgment, over which He presides in His majesty, He shall pass sentence on each according to the nature of his deeds. There will be no need of witnesses for that judgment; the judgment itself will offer testimony of our actions. He will say to the just: *I was hungry, and you gave me to eat: I was thirsty, and you gave me to drink,*[21] and the rest. He will set against the wicked the fact that they did not do such things, and thus His judgment is seen not to lack evidence.

He added: *O Israel, if thou wilt hearken to me, there shall be no new god in thee.* He repeats the address Israel, so that Israel may realise that they are His servants, and may direct their vows obediently to the Lord's commands. A great mystery is enclosed in a single word, so that already at that date a future heresy could be overcome by a declaration of truth. He said: *There shall be no new god in thee,* so that none would think that the Word of the Father existed within time. One who is new has someone who is older; so if He cannot be termed new, men of sound mind must proclaim Him as coeternal. And so that none can call the God-Christ new out of the knowledge that He was born of the virgin Mary and that His humanity demonstrably came to pass in time, He says: *There shall be no new god in thee;* for He was begotten of the substance of the Father before all beginning, and He abides with Him in equal coeternity, reigning for all ages without end. So our forbears with wondrous and holy brevity established as the formula of belief that the two natures abide united and perfect in the one Lord Christ, and so by this health-dealing remedy the diseased and foul-smelling utterances of all heretics were sealed off like some noxious aperture. His phrase *in thee* means "in thy heart," where truth and not falsehood should be found. He added: *Neither shalt thou adore a strange god.* Whereas earlier He forbade the worship of a new god, here He prohibited the adoration of a strange god, so that believing in a new god and ministering to idols with sacrilegious devotion should be considered virtually identical sins. So Arians should realise with whom they are linked when they sunder themselves from the sound Catholic base.

11. *For I am the Lord thy God, who brought thee out of the land of Egypt: distend thy mouth wide, and I will fill it.* Just reasons are given why a strange god should not be adored. First, because our God is unchangeable and eternal; as He said of Himself: *I am who am.*[22] Then, so that we should understand that all eventualities which will profit us come from Him, He says: *Who brought thee out of the land of Egypt.* This second type of definition is termed in Greek *ennoematike* and in Latin *notio.*[23] It is always achieved by judging an individual on his deeds, which are seen to be relevant to him and not to others. This passage, historically speaking, is addressed to the Jews, but it is an admonition to Christians generally, for He leads us out of the land of Egypt when through the grace of rebirth He frees us from the foulest sins to which we were held in subjection when our hands, as the psalm says earlier, served in baskets. Next comes: *Distend thy mouth wide, and I will fill it. Distend* means spread or scatter abroad by confession in particular or by admonition, so that you seek to utter what seems worthy to be heard. Our thoughts are filled with spiritual grace when our mouths are seen to be distended for praise of the Lord, so that we embark on it through His grace and fulfil it by His gift. As Paul puts it: *Be ye also distended. Bear not the yoke with unbelievers.*[24]

12. *But my people heard not my voice: and Israel hearkened not to me.*
13. *So I let them go according to the desire of their heart, and they shall walk in their own wishes.* Though the Lord filled the distended mouths of the prophets, He says that they were not heard by the people of Israel, since they utterly failed to fulfil His commands. He addressed His people as the oil, but the lees could not listen and were to be spat out as useless. He added: *So I let them go according to the desire of their heart, and they shall walk in their own wishes.* Vengeance commensurate with their sin follows, for the person abandoned by the Lord's protection does not get away scot-free. Those whom He abandons He afflicts, for the retribution exacted from all evil men is to be deprived of that great good. The sinner thinks it a form of benefit if he is allowed to be sated with his own desires, but Paul says: *God gave them up to the desires of their heart, unto uncleanness,*[25] and the rest.

14-15. *If my people had heard me, if Israel had walked in my ways, I should have reduced their enemies to nothing, and laid my hand on them that troubled them.* We must ask why He called them His people when they would not listen to Him. He called them His own because He gave them the law and revealed to them great miracles, so that their guilt was greater when His chosen people sinned with regard to Him. And note how in the first of these verses the later words clarify the message. *My people* is denoted by *Israel. Had heard me* bears the sense of *had walked in my ways,* for the man who is found not to oppose the Lord's commands hears Him and walks in His ways. Notice that the proper order is preserved. First instruction is given to us, and then fulfilment of what was heard; next comes the reward which the uncommitted could not deserve: *I should have reduced their enemies to nothing, and laid my hand on them that troubled them.* The words are to be taken in a general sense: He opposes our enemies when we dedicate ourselves to Him with humble satisfaction. If we oppose God by evil action, He in turn refrains from refuting our enemies, and He does not lay a protecting hand on those who have drawn away from Him with proud struggling. So we must realise that when He turns away from us, it is not absence of fatherly love but the sting of severe vengeance. From time to time the protection of holy men is also suspended when they are tried by tribulations and affliction. But He allows the just to be tried in such a way as not to desert them, whereas He allows the wicked to be afflicted in such a way as to make Himself a stranger to them.

16. *The enemies of the Lord have lied to him: and their time shall be for ever.* After these words of the Lord, Asaph turns to the third section, rebuking His enemies with an appropriate imprecation. The liars are those who bind themselves with honourable promises, but slip back again into the most heinous errors. This could not have been said of pagans, for they had not been bound by any promise to the Lord. And so that on seeing these men flourishing in this world you should not believe that they had been left untouched, he added: *And their time shall be for ever.* He means the time of punishment, when they will be told: *Depart into everlasting fire.*[26] Of them we also read: *Their worm shall not die, and their fire shall not be quenched.*[27] This figure is called *eclipsis* in Greek and *defectus* in Latin;[28] it is not an omission through ignorance, but a deliberate concealment to elicit detection.

17. *He fed them with the fat of wheat; and filled them with honey out of the rock.* Here the dutiful love of the Creator is expounded; He filled his enemies, that is, those who were ungrateful for His kindnesses and who earlier were said to have lied. *With the fat of wheat* means either manna or the body of Christ the Lord. We use the word *adeps* for the bodily fat of animals, and it is improperly applied to wheat to denote that it contains some goodness within. *With honey out of the rock* means from the wisdom of Christ, for He is the Rock from which the honey of heavenly teaching flowed. *He filled them,* that is, with His holy preaching, but the traitors fasted from the food of faith and listened with deaf ears.[29]

Conclusion Drawn From the Psalm

Let us now return to that earlier statement, and like bees settling on the sweetest flowers gather the sweet honey by repeated visits, for whenever we go back to the means of salvation we always draw the essentials from it. So let us most zealously ascertain why the statement was made that *there shall be no new god in thee,* if we wish to be truly Israel. In this statement the most sacred power of the whole faith is contained; in these words the nature of His indescribable majesty is made plain. If no new god is accepted, then beyond doubt the holy Trinity is seen as coeternal; there is no younger Person where none is shown to be older. So the Father is eternal, the Son is eternal, the holy Spirit is eternal. We recognise a distinction in Persons but a unity in nature. The Father is almighty, the Son is almighty, the holy Spirit is almighty. There is a threefold name, but one strength and one power. The Son was begotten of the Father in a manner beyond understanding. The holy Spirit proceeds from the Father and Son in a manner beyond telling. Their power is not accidental, but undivided and abiding. They share the supremacy, Their kingdom is without end, Their glory is eternal. The Trinity alone creates, forgives sins, grants the kingdom of heaven. Next comes: *Neither shalt thou adore a strange god.* A strange god is one who through the debased behaviour of madmen becomes part of their sacrilegious cults. He does not possess the essence of divinity, but welcomes the glory of false majesty. He did not create men but was fashioned by them. He is truly strange, for he is found to have a mind estranged. If we shun both new and strange gods, the grace of the true God is gained; for He can cast out those with unworthy ideas of Him, and can afford worthy blessings to those of upright belief.

COMMENTARY ON PSALM 81

1. *A psalm of Asaph.* It was stated in the Preface that all the psalms are by David, but that those which bear a different title in the heading have been so designated because of the meaning of the names in them. Here Asaph is mentioned to denote the synagogue, which deserved to behold the Lord Saviour in His bodily presence when the Word deigned to become flesh, and to be executed to bring the grace which gave us life. In short, the psalm itself begins: *God hath stood in the congregation of gods.* My judgment is that we must not leave unmentioned the reason why the ancients called "synagogue" what we now in Christian times call the Church. The general meaning of synagogue is "congregation," which does not sufficiently denote a concourse of people, whereas *ecclesia* (Church) means "convocation," the assemblage of different nations. Convocation is an appropriate term for

those who excel in reason, and so we realise that God's Church has always increased by reason both of its name and of its merits.

Division of the Psalm

Asaph, whose name is set in the heading because of its meaning, speaks against the Jews throughout the whole psalm about Christ's coming, in the first section advising them that God has stood in their midst, and that therefore they should not associate with sinners. In the second part he warns them to grasp that He is the Christ, though He seemed to be poor and needy when He took on the flesh. In the third section he says that they were given the distinction of becoming sons of God, but that through their own fault they have fallen into the snares of death.

Explanation of the Psalm

God hath stood in the congregation of gods: in the midst of them he distinguishes gods. In a single word Jesus Christ is revealed to us with marvellous brevity; for that God stood in the congregation who also sits at the Father's right hand. These are physical locations; for if you allude to His majesty, He is wholly and fully everywhere, and cannot be said to stand or sit in His nature as God, for He is not circumscribed by any spatial limit. But Asaph, enlightened by the divine gaze, cries out that Jesus Christ as God has stood in the synagogue, and a crowd of impious men strove to resist Him; He sought to correct with fatherly love those who He knew were madly acting against themselves. John the Baptist too speaks of Him in this way: *There stands in the midst of you one whom you know not.*[1] Asaph added: *Of gods*, so that you might more clearly realise that this was said of the men amongst whom Christ is known to have dwelt. As Jeremiah the prophet foretold: *Afterwards he was seen on earth, and conversed with men.*[2] We quite often find men referred to as gods; so the Lord says to Moses: *Behold, I have appointed thee the god of Pharaoh.*[3] And further on this very psalm is to say: *I have said: You are gods, and all of you the sons of the most High.*[4] In the same way too we call men sons of God; should you relate this expression to the nature of the Godhead, there is only the one Word which should truly and strictly be so named. Sometimes we also call the heavenly powers gods by abuse of language; for example, Paul says: *For though there be they that are called gods, either in heaven or on earth, yet to us there is but one God, the Father.*[5] Next comes: *In the midst of them he distinguishes gods.* See how His incarnation is still being announced with its physical location: when he speaks of their midst he is pointing to a place surrounded by engulfing crowds. *He distinguishes gods,* in other words the apostles and the just who followed the advice of and faith in His majesty. This distinguishing has reference to that foreknowledge and divine understanding which rescues us from the weight of sin and guides us to the kingdom of heaven. So Paul too says: *For who distinguishes thee?*[6]

2. *How long will you judge unjustly, and accept the faces of sinners?* His expression, *how long?* indicted their long-standing habit, for they most obdurately resisted the Law which they had received; they inflicted the most terrible deaths on candid prophets; they preferred to crucify rather than to honour the Son of God who came to them. So the expression, *how long?* was justified, since they voted even to execute their very Creator, in so far as their wishes permitted it. *Accept the faces of sinners* refers to those unwilling to recognise Him in that rebellion which led to the crucifixion; instead, they acted crazily with the crazy, they clamoured with the lunatics, and with scowling faces they adopted the posture of sinners. If they had remained distinct in their appearance, they could likewise have separated themselves by their actions.

3. *Judge for the fatherless and the needy: do justice to the humble and the poor.* After the intervention of a diapsalm, he passes to the second section. In this he more strenuously urges the Jews to identify Him whom they looked upon, and to realise that He whom the Powers and Dominations of heaven serve became humble for their sakes, that He who is the Ruler of all became fatherless, that He who cannot spend himself in giving became needy, that He who possesses all created things in heaven and earth became poor. So he warns that He whom the wanton Jews sought to have exstirpated should be justified. It was splendid to call Him fatherless, for no father in the flesh afforded Him human consolations; just as before the world was formed the Word was motherless, so at the time of the incarnation the Lord Christ lived with no earthly father.

4. *Rescue the poor, and deliver the needy out of the hand of the sinner.*
These words are seen to refer to those who refrained from soiling
their hands with the murder of the Lord, but were unwilling to confront those wicked deeds of rashness so as to free Him from physical
harm, and themselves from collusion with depravity. Of them Scripture says elsewhere: *The dumb dogs were not able to bark.*[7] So these men,
who were to sin through a wicked crime, are being warned not to
desist from rescuing Him when He is unjustly betrayed; for when you
can confront depraved men, you share the sin if you cease to oppose
them. It has been explained many times that *poor* and *needy* can be used
with reference to the Lord Saviour, for when He became man, He
simultaneously shouldered the need of our poverty. As He says elsewhere: *I am poor and sorrowful.*[8]

5. *They have not known nor understood: they walk on in darkness: all
the foundations of the earth shall be moved.* A valid inference and a pithy
statement, that those who walked in darkness did not understand. Paul
says of them: *If they had known, they would never have crucified the Lord
of glory.*[9] Next comes: *All the foundations of the earth shall be moved,* so
that you can truly realise to whom the previous verses referred. He
tells of the sign which is known to have occurred at the Lord's crucifixion, as the gospel-teaching witnesses: *The earth quaked, the rocks
were rent,*[10] and the rest. If this passage of the psalm is given other
explanations, as the unfaithful Jews will have it, it can in no sense be
apposite. The earthquake can be interpreted also in the spiritual sense:
at that time many sinners, in other words men of earth, saw this great
miracle and believed. One of them, the centurion, cried out *Indeed this
was the Son of God!*[11]

6. *I have said: You are gods, and all of you the sons of the most High.*
He passes to the third section, applying his words to the apostles and
to the rest of the just. For that distinguished title is applied solely to
the faithful, of whom he said earlier: *God hath stood in the congregation
of gods.* So the promises they had received were such that if they had
observed the Lord's commands, they would have been called sons of
the most High, but assuredly by grace and not by nature, for only the
Word is substantially and specifically called God's Son, as in the
passage: *The Lord hath said to me: Thou art my son.*[12] However, all who
accept His sacred commands are called His sons, as we read in the
gospel: *As many as received him, he gave them power to be made the sons*

of God.[13] So observe that through the thirteenth type of definition which the Greeks call *kat'analogian* and the Latins *iuxta rationem*,[14] men are called gods and sons of God; the figure makes its appearance when a lesser object is defined by the name of a greater. This definition by comparison is also called "from the lesser to the greater," for men are less than gods.

7. *But you like men shall die: and shall fall like one of the princes.* He addressed the previous verse to the just, but now slants his words towards the wicked. He rebukes unbelievers, who preferred to die through pride rather than to live by obedience. By the phrase, *like men,* he points precisely to sinners who were redeemed by no payment and were not freed from subjection. He added: *And shall fall like one of the princes. One of the princes* denotes the devil, who fell headlong from heaven and incurred the punishment of his rebelliousness.

8. *Arise, O God, judge thou the earth: for thou shalt inherit among all the nations.* Whom does he bid arise but Him whose execution was foreseen? *Judge the earth* is addressed to Him of whom it was written: *When the Son of man shall come in his majesty, and all the angels with him, then shall he sit upon the seat of his majesty, and all nations shall be gathered together before him.*[15] *Thou shalt inherit among the nations,* that is, the earth just mentioned which the blessed shall possess and shall obtain the eternal joy of great happiness.

Conclusion Drawn From the Psalm

Listen, you Jews; understand, you obstinate people, the great tidings which Asaph has spoken concerning the Lord's coming. If you do not know the utterances of your prophets, why do you revere them? Approach the Catholic priests; let your ears be opened, so that by the Lord's gift you can escape from your prolonged deafness. And you who bubble with the baneful heat of Nestorius and Eutyches[16] must be tended by the first verse of this psalm. Of whom is it said *God hath stood in the congregation of gods?* And then: *In the midst of them he distinguishes gods?* He stood there precisely in His humanity; He alone, the same Lord Jesus, distinguished them by His divinity. Both natures are true and perfect. To maintain that there are two divided natures corresponding to two persons in Christ is an error of the same order as believing that there is one intermingled nature, though in the unity of one Person. To you the verse of Sedulius is to be addressed: "Both are equal in error, though they follow different paths."[17] For if He did not raise men to heaven, tell me, whom did He redeem? He took on the role of servant, but did not relinquish that of king.[18] It was not the lot of anyone to perish, once he embraced the means by which he could never perish. If, followers of Eutyches, there is only one nature as your confused beliefs maintain, how can it be foretold that the Son of man is still to come in judgment? Or how will the wicked look on Him whom they have pierced?[19] Finally, so that this belief may be wholly eradicated, after the Resurrection Christ Himself replied to doubting Thomas: *Put in your hand, and see, for a spirit hath not flesh and bones, as you see me to have.*[20] Consider also what foolishness attends you; when you say that one nature was made out of two, you either believe that the result was a mingling, or you shamelessly affirm that one or other perished. Why do you shrink from confessing what our fathers decreed after the revelation of the holy Spirit? At any rate, if you do not wish to proclaim that there are two natures, unmingled, unchangeable, undivided and unseparated, say that there are two substances and two forms. As Paul has it: *Being in the form of God, he thought it not robbery to be equal with God; but emptied himself, taking the form of a servant, and in habit found as a man.*[21] It only remains for you not to lay up eternal destruction by shunning the treatment which brings salvation.

We must realise that this is the fifth of the psalms which we earlier mentioned were written about the two natures of the Lord Christ.[22]

COMMENTARY ON PSALM 82

1. *A canticle of a psalm of Asaph.* We have often explained the meaning of a canticle of a psalm, both in the Preface and in the psalm-headings where the context demanded it: namely that the power of these terms impels us to realise that we must continually direct our minds in the course of active pursuits to the contemplation of God. There is no doubt that Asaph conveys the sense in Latin of *congregatio* (assembly). But whenever this Asaph comes into prominence, as we have already

remarked, he is not the author of the poem, but appears to be appositely inserted into headings because of the meaning of his name and the powers of the psalms.

Division of the Psalm

Asaph, who has already made many prophecies in earlier psalms about the Lord's incarnation, is now in the first section to speak of His second coming. He asks that since at the end of the world the Lord's enemies will be exalted to the heights through Antichrist, His judgment may quickly take place, so that the lengthy licence of the most oppressive enemy may not be able to ravage the entire Church. In the second section, he prays that vengeance may be exacted from them by citing the names of persons similarly hostile, and he prays for their correction rather than seeks to curse them.

Explanation of the Psalm

2. *O God, who shall be like to thee? Do not be silent, nor restrain thyself, O God.* This figure is known as *epanalepsis*, the repetition of the same word at the beginning and end of a verse.[1] We must ponder the import of this beginning, for it encloses in its conspicuous brevity hidden truths of momentous matters: who shall be like to Him who in the speed of a second made heaven and earth and all that is in them? Though the Lord Jesus Christ, who lived among the Jews, was considered by those faithless ones to be most like only to men (for they went so far as to cut Him with scourges and to condemn Him with a vicious sentence), this outstanding man beholding Christ in the greatness of His power rightly proclaims that there is none like Him; for though He was clothed genuinely in the flesh, He did not lessen the powers of His divinity. He deigned to dwell with us, but remained perpetually with the Father. So *who shall be like to thee?* is a truthful utterance. Next comes: *Do not be silent, nor restrain thyself, O God.* Here the power of His future coming is already being declared, for He who judges is not silent, and He who is revealed by the manifestation of His power does not restrain himself. Clearly at His first coming these attributes were not in evidence, when *he was led as a sheep to the*

slaughter, and as a lamb before his shearer, and he did not open his mouth.[2] He also restrained His power when He allowed Himself to be arrested as one accused, and to be brought before Pontius Pilate without a struggle. These characteristics will cease at the future judgment, when the power of divinity will shine out.

3. *For lo, thy enemies have made a noise: and they that hate thee have lifted up the head.* He makes the phrases correspond to the previous ones. To *Do not be silent* he appends: *Lo, thy enemies have made a noise;* for *Nor restrain thyself* he offers as reason: *They that hate thee have lifted up the head.* The whole of this is more appropriately suited to the days of Antichrist, when the Lord's enemies will sound forth in noisy rebellions. He did well not to say "have spoken" rather than *have made a noise,* so that he rightly denies to them the words of human beings, since they did not make rational utterances. Note too that he spoke of them in the plural: *They that hate;* but he then said: *They have lifted up the head,* though he could have said "heads." But all madmen have Antichrist as their one head. He says that their head is lifted up because he will glory in great power to the point of promising to say that he is a god on high.

4. *They have cunningly plotted against thy people, and have consulted against thy saints.* This is a laughable rather than a grievous complaint, that these enemies doomed to perish laid plans against the Lord's people, and strove to deceive them with cunning falsehood, that is with crafty will; for the Lord's people are seen to be protected by zeal for the truth. But so that their fickleness might be expounded at greater length, he added: *Against thy saints,* so that they were trying not only to practise guile on ordinary people, but to inflict destruction in a sense on men of heaven.

5. *They have said: Come, let us destroy them so that they be not a nation: and let the name of Israel be remembered no more.* He recounts the empty words of those madmen which he rightly said earlier were sounded forth rather than spoken. That most savage persecution of Antichrist is to be carried out with the intention of utterly abolishing the Christian name from the earth as though it were some evil; they do not know that when they seek to kill Christ's servants they will augment the number of saints with their constant persecution. His men-

tion of a nation in the singular indicates the Christian people; for though we are instructed that they are gathered from many nations, they are rightly called a single nation, for they are known to be sprung from the one origin of baptism. Alternatively, that persecutor could have called them a single nation because he knew that they were joined together for one purpose; or the phrase can be interpreted by the figure of *exallage* or exchange,[3] when the singular is used instead of the plural.

6. *For they have contrived with one consent: they have made a testament against thee.* In the divine Scriptures a testament is not merely associated with the dead but is also a treaty made between living persons, for Scripture dissects and attests the intentions of those who make an agreement; for example, we read that Laban and Jacob made a testament when during their lives they were instructed to make certain agreements between them.[4] Even wicked men are said in a sense to have made a testament when with united eagerness they persecute those who dissent from their error. Observe that by his words, *against thee*, he aroused odium against his enemies. This type of argument orators have appropriated to their own causes, and have grown accustomed to rousing the sympathy of judges thereby in every possible way.

7. *The tabernacles of the Edomites and the Ismahelites. 8. Moab and the Agarens, Gebal and Ammon and Amalec: and foreigners with the inhabitants of Tyre. Yea, and the Assyrian also is joined with them: they are come to the support of the sons of Lot.* The catalogue of the names embraced in these three verses recounts the enemies of Christ. Let us reveal the meanings of them so that all may be seen to be appropriate to the era of Antichrist. Edomites means "bloody" or "earthly"; Ismahelites "obedient to the world" and not to the Lord; Moab "from the father," signifying the sinner, in the sense that disobedience is ascribed to his father Adam; Agarens "aliens"; Gebal "empty valley"; Ammon "rebellious people"; Amalec "licking people," that is deceitfully fawning; Tyre "shortage"; Assyrian stands for the devil himself, who came with the Assyrians to attack the faithful; Lot means "declining,"[5] so that this name is rightly placed at the end, as if he were saying: *They are all gone aside, they are become unprofitable together;*

there is none that doth good, no, not one.[6] The mob of abandoned men which is to gather under Antichrist was clearly denoted by alluding to such names as these, so that you might realise that all these names of wicked people were rightly concentrated in that crowd. We must remember that these verses have been run together by means of the figure of *polysyndeton;*[7] if you review them carefully, you will find that they are linked by several conjunctions.

10. *Do to them as thou didst to Madian and to Sisara: as to Jabin at the brook of Cison.* 11. *Who perished at Endor, and became as dung for the earth.* He passes to the second section, in which with the spirit of prophecy he prays that retribution may come on them, as the sequence of later events brought to pass. Because he had earlier described their behaviour by the assemblage of names, now too his prayer that retribution may befall them takes the form of citation of those similar nations which the people of Israel overcame with the Lord's help. Madian means "errant judgment"; Sisara "exclusion of joy"; Jabin "the worldly-wise,"[8] of whom Paul says: *Where is the wise? Where is the scribe?*[9] All these men perished at the brook of Cison and the stream of Endor, and they became as dung for the earth when their corpses rotted and decomposed. As we read in Scripture: *Thou art dust, and unto dust wilt thou go.*[10] So this sort of end is sought for those who shall continue in their obstinacy, for just as those men fought against the people of Israel, so the forces of Antichrist will fight against the most faithful persons of that future time, namely the Christians.

12. *Make their princes like Oreb and Zeb and Zebee and Salmana, all their princes.* He continues with the same kind of catalogue, in which merely an explanation of the names is necessary; we recall that we have just stated the purposes for which they are cited. Oreb means "dryness," Zeb "wolf," Zebee "victim," and Salmana "shadow of disturbance."[11] He is praying that all these things may befall Antichrist's army, which will not be saved by any conversion; in these gloomy titles which they bear, their accursed death is already visible. We claim that this type of utterance is peculiar to the divine Scriptures; we can experience the power of the utterances by the meanings of the names.

13. *Who have said: Let us possess for ourselves the sanctuary of God for an inheritance.* The sentiment is the same as that earlier: *Come, and let us destroy them so that they be not a nation: and the name of Israel will be remembered no more.* Here he alludes to the chief sponsors of evil counsels. *Let us possess for an inheritance* is set against what is called the Lord's inheritance; they preferred to strain to attack the inheritance which the Lord rightly claimed for Himself. He next explains what this inheritance is: it is *the sanctuary of God,* the Christian people, of whom Paul says: *For the temple of God is holy, which you are.*[12]

14. *O my God, make them like a wheel: and as stubble before the face of the wind.* 15. *As a fire which burns forests, as a flame burning mountains.* We have combined these two verses because of the similarity of content, in which manifold disasters are foretold to unbelievers. When wicked men involve themselves in evil thoughts, they become like wheels which are seen to rear their back section and shift their front to the rear; they make no progress, but wear themselves out with continuous gyration. Next comes a second comparison: the fickleness of sinners is entrusted to the motion of the wind, and flits here and there, being continually stirred in uncertain movement. *The face of the wind* denotes the presence of that wind, for the wind is not visible to our eyes by any shape. We feel its physical presence only because we are whipped by its onset and its passage through us. The fire and the flame represent the time of the Judgment, when the thickest forest of sinners and the mountains of pride will be burnt up.

16. *So shalt thou pursue them with thy tempest: and shalt confound them with thy wrath.* The phrase, *so shalt thou pursue them,* takes up his earlier statement; they are to be destroyed as the previous similes relate. Further parallels are appended: *With thy tempest, and with thy wrath thou shalt confound them. With thy tempest,* that is, at the time of the Judgment, which is rightly compared with a tempest first because it is unforseen, second because it confounds us with sudden din, and the swift scope of the danger removes the opportunity for making plans. A rainstorm is a roused rebellion of the atmosphere by which we are utterly terrified and oppressed by a deluge of water. Next comes: *And thou shalt confound them with thy wrath.* We have often said already that anger cannot be appropriate to the deity; the descrip-

tion is drawn from the behaviour of men, who in judging wicked men are stirred by mental heat. Men are not disposed to find others guilty unless they are roused by the wicked deeds which they have committed.

17. *Fill their faces with shame: and they shall seek thy name, O Lord.* Up to this point he has prophesied the punishment awaiting those who remained obstinate in their wicked deeds; now he turns to those who are to believe through the Lord's gift. When they have found none to praise their sins, their faces are filled with shame; they prefer to ponder at the present time the evil deeds they have done. A rebuke often sets them right when they see that they incur general blame.

18. *Let them be confounded and troubled for ever and ever: and let them be apprehensive, and perish.* He turns back to the obstinate who will not possess God's gifts. Some persons can be confounded and ashamed for their salvation in this world, when they accept the gifts of conversion; but those who will be condemned to eternal vengeance *are confounded and troubled for ever and ever.* Next comes: *Let them be apprehensive, and perish.* The meaning is identical with what he said before. It avails them nothing to be apprehensive in the next world, for those destined for eternal punishment perish.

19. *And let them know that the Lord is thy name: thou alone art the most High over all the earth. Let them know* refers to both types of sinners, both those who are to perish through their obduracy, and those who make satisfaction and are freed. All of them know the omnipotence of the Lord, for He alone is the most High; for they realise that He both spares the converted and condemns the obstinate to eternal vengeance.

Conclusion Drawn From the Psalm

Let us remember that this Asaph has been purposefully introduced into eleven psalms earlier, so that the adamantine hearts of the Jews might be beaten and softened by frequent mentions of the synagogue, and that they might make progress at any rate towards that title to which they were seen to be devoted. So the healing of those who proclaim the faith is available to them, if the obstinacy of those wicked men does not impede them. All that concerns the Lord's incarnation is brought to pass, all that attests the belief of the Gentiles is made clear.

There remains the time of the Judgment which we all undergo in common. But before that we must believe, so that at the Judgment the vengeance which is prophesied cannot condemn us in our wickedness.

COMMENTARY ON PSALM 83

1. *Unto the end, for the presses, for the sons of Core, a psalm.* The meaning of *unto the end* has often been explained. Though in previous psalm-headings we have explained that *for the presses* has reference to the Church, it is none the less appropriate carefully to investigate why the Church has apparently received such a title. A hanging grape untouched by hand and an olive-berry on a tree give no hint of the high quality of their most succulent juice, but when they reach the press and are subjected to a heavy weight, they are squashed and a harvest of the sweetest liquid wells out which was not obvious when the grape or olive was hidden in its foliage. In the same way when God's Church is crushed by afflictions and persecutions, the merits of her saints, hitherto unrealised in tranquil times, become clear. So the crushing of the press sanctifies, the pounding ameliorates. Its work brings a heavenly reward, and punishment in the present spells eternal rest. It is not otiose that the phrase, *for the presses,* occurs only in Psalms 8 and 80 as well as here; this shows that this symbol of the Church is connected with the holy Trinity, for it is consecrated by repetition of the number three. We have said already earlier that Core means *calvum* (bald);[1] the meaning of this name indicates to us the place of Calvary, where we know that the Lord Christ was crucified. So *the sons of Core* points in every sense to Christians, and this psalm is sung in their person. Observe that this is the second psalm concerned with the most precious love of the Lord,[2] which above all else associates us with divine grace.

Division of the Psalm

Introduced here is the single shared persona of the sons of Core; through the meaning of Calvary which we have mentioned they are associated with Christ the Lord. In the first part of the psalm he reveals the Church's love which is beyond his reckoning. In the second section he proclaims that blessed is the person to whom the Lord lends help and to whom He grants the grace of confession. In the third part he says that it is far better for the outcast to dwell in the house of the Lord than to enter the tents of sinners with worldly distinctions of any kind.

Explanation of the Psalm

2. *How lovable are thy dwellings, O Lord of hosts!* The son of Core, who is reborn in spiritual fecundity and is appropriately squeezed out from the presses of the Church, longs to attain the future Jerusalem, in which there are to be no longer any heavy afflictions, and in which he is to enjoy untroubled blessedness and tranquil happiness. His word, *how*, showed that he could not express the degree of the experience, but he penned it to give the impression of its being without limit; for who could grasp the vehemence with which that afflicted man demands rest, or with which the mortal condition seeks eternity? As for his phrase, *O Lord of hosts*, he felt that there was some great power inherent there, so that though he could not express in words the nature of the benefit, he sought to show that it was a great blessing. This figure is called *emphasis;*[3] it leaves more to be understood than is expressly said.

3. *My soul longeth and fainteth for the courts of the Lord. My heart and my flesh have rejoiced in the living God.* Whatever is attempted which is beyond human powers, produces a fainting proportionate to the scale of the enterprise. It is inevitable that the mind should faint when directed towards what it cannot attain in the here and now. This most holy man pondered the Lord's powers and rewards, those heavenly blessings and joys and that Jerusalem formed of mortal peoples but now rejoicing for ever. It was inevitable that in his joys his thoughts should give up the attempt, for they could not there and then attain what they longed for. But he next explains how manly this fainting is, and how strong this weariness, when he says: *My heart and my flesh have rejoiced in the living God.* Though both these parts seem to make reference to the flesh, there is no doubt that the heart can be

regarded as the understanding, for when we wish to proclaim a person's wisdom we unhesitatingly praise his heart. He is saying that both elements of which human beings consist, body and soul, have erupted into heavenly joy. What we must observe here is the degree of holiness for which this man is famed, for not only his soul but also his flesh which is known to be more subject to wilful transgression has through its happy lot burst into exultation for the Lord, for it forsees the blessings of the future age which it believed it was gaining through His generosity.

4. *For the sparrow hath found herself a house: and the turtle a nest for herself where she may lay her young ones.* Whereas earlier he said that soul and body were rejoicing in exultation at the Lord, here we find that he has set down these two species of birds to recommend to us a type of simile. A sparrow flies exceedingly swiftly, and cannot bear to dwell in forests, but longs to seek for itself a home in holes in walls. When it has found such a home, it is delighted and glories with great joy, for it believes that it is no longer in danger of ambush from various enemies. The soul finds joy in a similar way, when it realises that a lodging is prepared for it in the kingdom of heaven. The turtle is most chaste in his controlled abstemiousness, for he is content with a single mating, and is known to build a nest for his fledglings; he does not seek a home readymade as the sparrow does, but hastens to fashion a new one for himself from odds and ends. It is not otiose to compare our flesh with him, for our flesh rejoices to set its works to the Lord's command. It is through the flesh that offerings of fasting are sweetly made, that we give food to the poor, bury the dead, tend the sick, visit the imprisoned, and perform the other tasks of devotion known to be exhibited through the services of the body. Others have identified the turtle with holy Church, since she can share wedlock only with Christ the Lord.[4]

Thy altars, O Lord of hosts, my king and my God. This verse is matched with the earlier ones. To the phrase, *Thy altars, O God of hosts,* is to be attached the words of the first verse of the psalm, *how lovable they are!* This figure is known as *apo koinou* or "in common,"[5] when an earlier phrase is matched with a later one. Since he had earlier spoken of the house of the sparrow and the nest of the turtle, he now shows what meaning we should have taken from them. On these altars the faithful soul chirrups as though giving thanks for a most pleasing house; on these altars such works of the flesh as are holy are placed. On that altar is established the most constant hope; on it the souls of the blessed enjoy heavenly feasting at a banquet unending. There gaining our fill makes us eager for more, and a blessed hunger never leaves us. He added: *My king and my God.* Rex (king) is derived from *regere* (to rule); *Deus* (God) is from *creare* (to create),[6] though the title is seen to suggest fear as well.

5. *Blessed are they that dwell in thy house, O Lord: they shall praise thee for ever.* He foretold here what blessing those altars bestow; for if a person is accounted blessed here, when universal success attends him for a time and he is shattered by no adversity, what are we to think of the happiness in the next world, to which nothing parallel in quality nor in continuity can be found? This blessing cannot be explained in human words, but he does not maintain silence about its source. He says: *They shall praise thee.* That is the source of this blessed happiness, and he added: *For ever,* so that you might realise that it is unending. I ask you: what is the nature of the happiness to come in that age, when we shall be allowed to be glad in great measure, and never be able to renounce that gladness?

6. *Blessed is the man whose help is from thee, Lord: the ascent is in his heart.* Having completed this contemplation of future happiness, he passes to the second point, in which he shows that God's servant is blessed even in this world; this is to prevent us believing that rewards even in this life are wholly denied to the faithful. His phrase, *whose help is from you, Lord,* revealed the toils and difficult struggles endured here. He added: *The ascent is in his heart;* the ascent is indeed in the heart of the blessed man whose help is from the Lord, for he always makes progress, he always ascends, and he is raised all the higher towards heaven to the degree that the Lord offers help. Such, for example, is the meaning of our expression "He has mounted the first step," when a person with the Lord's help has prevailed over lust. When he gains ascendancy over pride, he climbs a second; when he overcomes greed, he mounts a third. He climbs up as many steps as the vices from which he is delivered. Thus this definition of the blessed man is achieved by the fifth type of definition which in Greek is called *kata tēn lexin* and in Latin *ad verbum,*[7] for it embraces what the blessed man is. It is he *whose help is from thee, O Lord.*

7. *He has made dispositions in the vale of tears, to the place which he*

has arranged: for he who gave the law shall give a blessing. The vale of tears is the humility of the penitent, from which a person rises to higher things as far as he had plunged down to make that satisfaction. In case you should ask to where he was taken up, he added: *To the place which he has arranged.* This place which is arranged denotes nothing other than the future kingdom of the Lord, which we shall have the blessed fortune to attain if we seek to reach it by observing the rules which the Lord laid down; for He who established the place also arranged the steps to it. The person who wishes to obtain the reward must listen to what is prescribed. Next comes: *For he who gave the law shall give a blessing.* Since the time for prophecy established by the Lord's law had come but the gift of grace had not yet arrived, the psalmist says that He who earlier gave the law of justice[8] would give a blessing, in other words His grace. This teaches us that the Lord Christ is clearly the Author of both Old and New Testaments, since the verse says that He who gave the Law shall give a blessing.

8. *They shall walk from virtue: the God of gods shall be seen in Sion.* Initially virtue lay in the Law, and now there is virtue in grace; but the virtue which redeems is more joyful than the virtue which judges. May He who gave both grant that, since we sinners do not deserve to obtain blessings through the Law, He may deign to bestow forgiveness on us through grace. But the Christian must realise that he must walk from virtue to virtue, so that he does not relax into idleness. Next comes: *The God of gods shall be seen in Sion.* See how he says that the two forms of virtue merge in the one Person of Christ, for He who gave the Law and grace was seen at Jerusalem on Mount Sion. It has just been explained in Psalm 81 how we are to interpret: *God of gods;*[9] divine Scripture never stops calling holy men gods. The phrase God of gods is like King of kings and Lord of lords. He said: *He shall be seen,* not "He is known"; the second is a universal experience, but the first was the privilege of a few.

9. *O Lord God of virtues, hear my prayer: give ear, O God of Jacob.* So that you may realise that there is truly one God of those virtues of which he said: *They shall walk from virtue to virtue,* he himself confessed this with an exclamation: *O Lord God of virtues.* Who is this God of virtues? He is the God of Jacob, the Lord Christ, known to be the most merciful Supplanter[10] of his enemies, since He causes their debased wickedness to attain the straight path of the virtues. Alterna-

tively the psalmist wishes us to interpret like this: just as God caused Jacob to be called Israel because he had seen God, so He should allow this most faithful man who speaks here to behold the eternal glory of His majesty.

10. *Behold, O God our protector: and look on the face of thy Christ.* He passes to the third manner of address, in which he prays that the Lord Saviour may become known to the world. This most holy man does not long for this in a spirit of doubt, but rather demands that what he knew would come might come quickly. Because he knew that the world was to be saved through our Redeemer, he asks that the Father should gaze on the human race in such a way that He looks on the face of His Christ—not that He fails to look on Him at any time, but so that the coming of the incarnation should make known to the nations Him who was clearly unknown to them in appearance. This figure is called *hypallage* or in Latin *permutatio*," when He who gazes is said to be gazed upon, or some similar inversion is found such as is often applied in the divine Scriptures. For example: *The Lord looked down from heaven on the children of men to see if there were any that did understand or did seek God.*¹² Here *to see* means "to cause them to see." Likewise in *understand my cry*, the prayer is not that He who knows all things as they are should understand, but that He should induce understanding in those known to be ignorant.

11. *For better is one day in thy courts above thousands. I have chosen to be an abject in the house of God rather than to dwell in the tents of sinners.* These courts are the courts of the Lord for which earlier he witnessed that he was longing and fainting, and in which he rightly aspires to dwell for a single day; for that day is never-ending, as it does not begin with sunrise or end with sunset. There is no tomorrow and no yesterday; it remains unchangeable in abiding singleness. *Above thousands* refers to life in this world, where thousands of days suffer an end, and where the entire total when multiplied is less than one day in heaven. So since we experience nothing of its kind, such longings for it are quite appropriate. This figure is known as *parison*,¹³ the balancing of a statement in which two contrasting positions are set down with one preferred, as the psalmist has done here earlier and will do later. Next comes: *I have chosen to be an abject in the house of God*

rather than to dwell in the tents of sinners. The wise man made his decision not with the eyes of the body but by the appearance of truth itself, preferring to be an abject in the Lord's house rather than to dwell in the sinful glory of the world. What splendid abjectness is the first, and how exceedingly foul is the distinction of the second! That abjectness is what is earlier called the vale of tears, and it is undoubtedly superior to all palaces, for even if we lament there for a time it is the source of endless joy. An abject person is so called if he is considered to be the lowest in the estimation of men; but in God's eyes he is esteemed as more honourable, because it is because of God's name that he is seen to be despised among men.

12. *For the Lord God loves mercy and truth: grace and glory the Lord will give.* The reason is given why the Lord's house must be loved more than the tents of sinners: it is because in His Church there is first mercy, because He makes just men out of sinners, and because He has not denied them the truth of the reward which was promised. As Paul has it: *Who before was a blasphemer, and a persecutor, and contumelious. But I obtained the mercy of God.*[14] And a little later: *I have fought a good fight: I have finished my course: I have kept the faith. There is laid up for me a crown of justice which the Lord, the just judge, will render to me on that day.*[15] See how he has included both the mercy and the truth of the Lord. He further adds: *Grace and glory the Lord will give.* So that you would not think that grace alone was bestowed on holy men in this world, the words, *And glory the Lord will give,* follow. Here on earth He first offers grace so that the sinner may be converted to life; and in the future He will give glory, so that when justified by the divine gift, we may deserve to be consorts of the angels. Grace (*gratia*) means "freely given" (*gratis data*); as Paul has it: *If by grace, it is not by works; otherwise grace is no more grace.*[16] It is in fact the Lord Christ's grace which prepares, assists, strengthens and crowns us.

13. *He will not deprive of good things them that walk in innocence.* The punishment of being excluded from the gift of the Godhead is confined to the wicked. Now it is certain that innocence abounds in God's gifts, but this kind of innocence must be recognised as lying within the limits of the meaning of the word. The innocent person is he who harms no-one. So such a person cannot be deprived of God's

benefits, for he has already obtained the gifts of blessed conversion. The innocent person in fact is he who is set in the vale of tears, *who chose to be abject in the house of God rather than to dwell in the tents of sinners,* and the similar descriptions made earlier by the psalmist.

O Lord God of hosts, blessed is the man that trusteth in thee. He could not describe all the blessings apprehended by his holy spirit, and so we must interpret these as words of wonder: "O Lord God of hosts, you perform such mighty blessings that man cannot recount them!" In these final words he made an addition to his initial phrase: *Blessed is the man that trusteth in thee.* This figure is called *para prosdokian,* or in Latin *inopinatus exitus;*[17] this occurs when some point is made but then another is appended, So let us understand, so far as we can, how this heavenly meaning gleams with manifold beauty; he brought to a close with a few words what he could not explain in many. That person is blessed who has placed his hope in eternal happiness; he is blessed whose possessions do not fade; but finally he is perfectly blessed whose hope in the Lord continues unbroken.

Conclusion Drawn From the Psalm

This is a wonderful psalm, more pleasant than any worldly delight; for it has made the presses of the Church so wholly sweet that we regard it as more desirable to be oppressed by this burden than to be supported by the world's blessings. So we now rightly say: *My soul longeth and fainteth for the courts of the Lord.* But we beg the holy Trinity that just as the sweetness of this psalm which we have read has made its impact on our minds, so may the grace which God in His pity has poured into us remain continually within us.

COMMENTARY ON PSALM 84

1. *Unto the end, for the sons of Core, a psalm.* It is certain that the psalm-headings indicate the Lord Christ. As Paul says: *For the end of the law is Christ: unto justice to everyone that believeth.*[1] *For the sons of Core, a psalm.* We have already often explained the meaning of Core.[2]

Let this brief intimation suffice: this psalm concerns those who have already put their belief with pure minds in the Lord Saviour. This is known to be the third psalm concerning the first coming.[3]

Division of the Psalm

In the first part of the psalm, the prophet briefly thanks the Lord because the people sprung from the ancient stock of the Jewish nation has come to the worship of the Lord Saviour. In the second part he recounts how the Lord deigned to soften His anger towards the Jewish people; he seeks the coming of Christ, at which human blindness obtained the clearest light of belief. In the third part he directs his words towards himself, and with the spirit of prophecy proclaims the coming of the incarnate Word.

Explanation of the Psalm

2. *Lord, thou hast blessed thy land: thou hast turned away the captivity of Jacob.* The psalmist foresees the wonders to come, and joyfully exults in them as though they have come to pass. He proclaims that the land is blessed by the Lord's coming, the land being nothing other than the flesh which He deigned to take on. We have often stated that the patriarch Jacob signifies the faithful people who were freed from captivity by the devil when they deserved to be saved by the pitying Lord.[4] His words, *Thou hast turned away captivity,* show that the captivity had been intensified through human wickedness, but removed by God's pity.

3. *Thou hast remitted the iniquity of thy people: thou hast covered all their sins.* To remit means to cancel a debt not because of an intervening circumstance but from considerations of devoted love. Thus the Lord remitted the guilt and caused the guilty to gain pardon. This is what the earlier words mean: *Thou hast turned away the captivity of Jacob;* for it was captivity to sin, when the world was subject and in thrall to idols. But when the Lord Saviour came, those idols were undoubtedly lost to view, that is, obliterated. At His coming our freedom raised its head, and the devil's arrogance was shattered and lay prostrate. Next comes: *Thou hast covered all their sins.* The Lord's

kindness is clearly acknowledged when our sins are seen to be covered. When we loathe them, we gain forgiveness, and then we become untroubled since those sins are not called to account. Clearly this kindness was bestowed on the human race when the Lord who brings salvation deigned to come to us. Observe that throughout these two verses the figure of *homoioteleuton*[5] is found, for several words end with identical letters. He said *benedixisti, avertisti, remisisti, operuisti* (Thou hast blessed, turned away, remitted, covered).

4. *Thou hast mitigated all thy anger: thou hast turned away from the wrath of thy indignation.* After the interval of a diapsalm, he passes to the second section, recounting how the Lord deigned to mitigate His anger, and how salvation emerged for those over whom despair loomed because of the character of their misdeeds. As Christ attests in the gospel: *I was sent only to the sheep that were lost of the house of Israel.*[6] But observe the expression, *thou hast mitigated,* and the degree to which it operates; he is again attacking the sins which the sacrilegious wantonness of the Jews committed against the Lord Saviour, in their zeal for rebelliousness. With the phrase, *from the wrath of thy indignation,* we must understand "for He averted the death of the Jews when He came as Physician to the sick, and as Author of salvation to those overrun with plague." This must be regarded as applicable not merely to the one nation but to the benefit of the entire world.

5. *Convert us, O God our Saviour: and turn off thy anger from us.* Earlier he stated: *Thou hast covered all their sins;* but now he asks afresh: *Turn off thy anger from us.* But both are appropriate if we consider the occasions of sins. With regard to the wicked deeds which the Jewish people had previously committed, he earlier gave thanks because all were shown to have been mitigated by the coming of the Lord; but here again he makes entreaty because of the sins to come, for he foresaw that they would again commit cruel crimes at the passion of the Lord. In short, he says: *Convert us,* so that instead of persecutors they may become defenders; instead of blasphemers, preachers; instead of disputants, disciples. His expression, *Us* embodies the people of whom he speaks. We must similarly interpret *Turn off thy anger from us,* as an entreaty that the punishment which is owed should not smite the Jewish people.

6. *Do not be angry with us for ever, and do not extend thy wrath from*

generation to generation. He knew that the Lord's patience bears with men's sins, and so he asks that He should not smite them with eternal damnation, but should soften them with enticements, bring improvement to them by supporting them, and correct them by admonition—all of which he knew that He would do. But we must analyse His mention of two generations. As some maintain, the first stretches from Adam to Christ, and the second is that which through the grace of baptism reaches its close at the end of the world. So his prayer is that the Lord should not seek to be angry with the second generation because He was justly wrathful with the first through the nature of their stubbornness; even if the second cannot be free from sin, he asks that through the grace of baptism and the satisfaction sought by confession they may be purged of the foulness of their guilty deeds.

7. *Thou wilt convert us, O God, and bring us to life: and thy people shall rejoice in thee.* With wonderful piety he begs the Lord, attesting that we do not win our conversion by merits, but that it emerges through His gift when our spirit manifests a salutary desire for something on its own behalf. He says: *Thou wilt convert us, O God, and bring us to life;* in other words: "You set before us a longing for conversion, so that we can attain entry to life". When You bestow this, then Your people will successfully rejoice in You after unhappily rejoicing in themselves. This is what happens to the converted once they begin to obtain the blessing of the Saviour.

8. *Show us, O Lord, thy mercy: and grant us thy salvation.* He was well aware that the Lord would come, but he asks to behold these blessings not just with his physical eyes in company with the rest who are non-believers, but also with the most pure gaze of the heart. The mercy of the Father is the Lord Saviour; that blessed troop asked that He be made manifest to them in the bright light of the true faith, not merely covered with the veil of the flesh but also conspicuous in the clear light of His power. He added the identical phrase, *grant us,* when He spoke of Christ; what He meant was: "Grant Your salvation so that we may embrace and possess and enjoy Him with the gift of eternal glory." To the unfaithful He merely appeared, but was not also granted; the psalmist says: *Grant,* then, so that when He is received in our hearts through heaven's gift, He can be removed by no trials.

9. *I will hear what the Lord God will speak to me: for he will speak*

peace to his people and to his saints. He passes to the third section, in which he proclaims the coming of the Lord Saviour with a most beautiful figure. For after praying that the Lord would appear to him, he is filled with sudden enlightenment, as though he has obtained his request, and he says: *I will hear,* that is, I shall not hinder myself by speaking, for I now realise that I have heard what I am to believe. We recognise that this type of utterance is peculiar to divine Scripture, for in my opinion nothing like it is found in secular books. You see the power of prophecy made manifest by these words. The Lord, that is the holy Spirit, speaks within so that the psalmist may appear to be able to speak without. He listens inwardly so that he may be listened to outwardly. The prophet silently learns what the people can hear when it strikes their ears.[7] Next comes: *For he will speak peace to his people and to his saints.* God's Peace is the Lord Christ; he says that the holy Spirit will speak of this Peace, for He is to tell of His Incarnation. When the psalmist spoke of the people, he said *his* people, not the uncommitted. He referred to the holy men who pleased the Lord by their edifying manner of life. The Lord Christ is their Peace, but He is a stumbling block and a foolishness to the unfaithful; they endure war in their sacrilegious hearts, for they do not follow the Author of peace along upright paths. But let us scrutinise this verse a little more attentively, for he refutes sinful minds by witnessing to the truth itself. Here the nature of the holy Spirit is clearly stated: He is the Lord God. Where are they who say that the holy Spirit is inferior to Father and Son, and is so lowly that He is thought not to have discretion over His own will? Let us listen to the holy Spirit who of His own accord said through His prophet that He was the Lord God. We read in the Acts of the Apostles too that the holy Spirit said openly that He was God, when Peter said to Ananias: *Why has Satan tempted your heart that you should lie to the holy Spirit?* And a little later when he wishes to reveal who the holy Spirit is, he says: *Thou hast not lied to man, but to God.*[8] This same Peter says in his letter: *The holy Spirit sent down from heaven, on whom the angels desire to look.*[9] If He were not equal to the Father and the Son He would not be accorded the most venerable honour and equality with them at baptism in the name of the Godhead; in the words of the Truth Itself: *Go, baptise all nations, in the name of the Father and of the Son and of the holy Spirit.*[10] This testimony alone should be quite enough for the human race, for where the single name of the Godhead is uttered, no diversity of nature or power is found."

10. *And to them that are converted to him. Surely they were close to fearing him as their salvation, so that his glory may dwell in our land.* Those converted to him signify the penitents who abandon the baleful freedom of the world and choose to shoulder blessed slavery to Him. When the whole world burned with the foulest devotion to idols, only the Jews were thought to be close to fearing the Lord, for they had received the Law through Moses, and were seen to be committed to the one God. The phrase, *close to fearing,* is used because all their actions were according to the flesh, and they wantonly vexed Him with various sins. People who accepted the Law in the physical but not the spiritual sense were said not to fear but to be close to fearing. So that you may realise that this was said of them, Paul similarly says: *And coming, he preached peace to you that were afar off, and peace to them that were near.*[12] But though they were like this, the Lord Saviour none the less chose to be born in the flesh from their race. For the virgin Mary who brought forth Christ had that origin; the Lord dwelt amongst them; the miracles which we read and to which we give assent were enacted there.

11. *Mercy and truth have met each other: justice and peace have embraced.* This figure is called *somatopoeia,*[13] or "according bodily existence," when things without bodies are lent a bodily presence; for though mercy and truth, peace and justice are abstractions, he allotted footsteps to two and embraces to the other two, both being bodily attributes. After he has stated from what nation the Lord was to be born, he now explains what benefits the coming of the holy incarnation has imparted. Through the Lord's gift, the two Testaments have been united in an interlinked chain. In the New Testament comes mercy, by which the human race is freed through grace; in the Old stands truth, in which the Law and the proclamation of the prophets are contained, as was already said at Psalm 70.[14] These two have met each other not to maintain their opposition, but to fulfil the grace of promised perfection; for it is clear that what was seen to be divided by eras has become one. So as to emphasise clearly the nature of the alliance, he restated with varied repetition of terms the fact that the two states, justice and peace, had lastingly entered into reciprocal

harmony by a kind of loving embrace. Such an embrace tends to occur when people see each other after a long time; in loving enthusiasm they hug each other with arms entwined.

12. *Truth is sprung out of the earth: and justice hath looked down from heaven.* Truth sprang out of the earth when the Word was made flesh from the virgin Mary. As Christ Himself says: *I am the way, the truth and the life.*[15] Justice looked down from heaven when God's Son by a wondrous dispensation came to the rescue of the imperilled human race. The meaning can be interpreted in another way: Truth springs from the earth when the confession of a sinner is offered, and Justice looks down from heaven when there is forgiveness of sins. This was the outcome of the tax-collector's prayer: Truth sprang from the earth when he cast his eyes down and prayed to God with confession of his sins, and justice looked down from heaven when the tax-collector went away justified rather than the Pharisee.[16]

13. *For the Lord will give goodness: and our earth shall yield her fruit.* This verse too is fittingly applied to the humility of the penitent, for the Lord by His kindness provides the disposition for confession, that most profitable rain of tears, so that our flesh is watered by devoted weeping, and can win abundant rewards.

14. *Justice shall walk before him: and shall set his steps in the way.* Our view is that this verse likewise is to be applied to those who obtain correction by devoted entreaties to the Lord. Justice will walk before them when they acknowledge the reality of their evil deeds, and humbly pray that their wicked and brazen acts be pardoned them; through the graces won by devoted lamentation, they atone for the chain of evil deeds gleefully committed. Then indeed do the men who earlier wandered on execrable paths set their steps in the way which is Christ.

Conclusion Drawn From the Psalm

Blessed David, we have heard what the Lord spoke inwardly to you. May the peace which reigned in your heart come upon us too. Behold, a true king ruled by such virtue; he is the temple of justice, the palace of devotion, the treasure-house of mercy. It was right that earthly things were subject to you when your Commander was such a Lord.

Observe what can transcend every command and every proclamation: from your seed the almighty Word took flesh, and through that Word the human race obtained the gift of redemption.

COMMENTARY ON PSALM 85

1. *A prayer of David. Oratio* (prayer) is a general term deriving from *oris ratio* (the way of the mouth).[1] When uttered in a human court, it is composed with extreme skill and sophistication; when poured out to God it emerges in simple and humble entreaty. But this humility and simplicity in prayer is appropriate to the sacred word, if as mother Church teaches we proclaim in Christ the Lord the two perfect and most true natures of God and of man; for in so doing we shall be confounded by no contradiction of truthful statements if we apply appropriate terms to holy qualities. If you wish to know the power of His Godhead, listen to the gospel: *In the beginning was the Word, and the Word was with God, and the Word was God. The same was in the beginning with God. All things were made by him, and without him was made nothing.*[2] If you wish to acknowledge His weakness as man, listen to the teaching of the apostle Paul: *Being made in the likeness of men, and in habit found as a man. He humbled himself, becoming obedient unto death, even to the death of the cross.*[3] So when He speaks in His human capacity, this must not be regarded as frailty in His divinity, for He raised up things human in such a way as in no sense to diminish the divine. So the one and same Lord Christ is addressed in prayer because He is the Son of the Father, and prays because He is the Son of man. On the one hand He is Creator and on the other created; Lord yet also servant; sharer in our mortality yet also destroyer of death itself. It follows from this that throughout the divine books in the most appropriate places He always manifests His two forms of activity. If you, the committed reader, hold fast to this fact with faithful mind, you will realise that everything can be truthfully established in your eyes. We must moreover recognise and maintain with firm mind that when the Lord Christ pours out a prayer, it is holy instruction to the faithful, a pattern for the good, an example of pure humility; when uttered by inferiors, it is satisfaction for sins, confes-

sion of crimes, atonement for faults. In the first case we have the role of the Teacher, in the second erasure of error is being sought. He prayed though innocent, just as He endured the cross though blameless. He wept for Lazarus to demonstrate to us love of one's neighbour. He fled from persecutors to discourage in us the boldness of impetuous rashness. Our far-sighted Teacher did this and similar things to reveal to us the truth of the holy incarnation, and to confront the Manicheans and others such in the future. The mention of *David* points to the Lord Saviour, either because the meaning of the name, as has often been stated, is "brave of hand" and "longed for,"[4] or because Christ is descended from his stock; for in His humanity He is David's son, and in His divinity the Lord Creator. If you behave like a careless sailor and abandon this rudder, you will undoubtedly shatter the ship of your faith on the most jagged rocks. Observe that the psalm is the second to bear the heading of Prayer.[5]

Division of the Psalm

The Lord Christ makes the prayer throughout the whole psalm, saying in the first section things clearly attributable only to Him. In the second part He prays in humbler vein for His members, whose Head He is. In the third part, reverting to His own person He says what we realise is relevant to Him in particular. But one and the same Christ, God and man, utters the entire psalm.

Explanation of the Psalm

Incline thy ear to me, O Lord, and hear me, for I am needy and poor. As we have earlier explained, Christ in the role of servant entreats the almighty Father to hear His prayer. His expression, *incline*, shows that the human condition could not reach the Father if in His supreme devotion He did not incline His majesty to us. *Ear* denotes here not our physical ear but the spiritual hearing by which He recognises the prayers of those who make entreaty; we have already often explained that such statements are made of God metaphorically. *Hear me* implies "So that my desires may be fulfilled," "so that by rising again I too may be saved, for through My death the world is to be saved." His

statement that He is needy and poor describes the condition of humanity which He had assumed; in itself that condition can possess only
what it has received as a gift from the Godhead. The needy and poor
should hearken and console their spirits with this honour; for the
Lord of creation applies to Himself what the faint of spirit often think
to be the description of wretchedness. But Christ does not exclude
those who though rich serve the Lord with pure minds; God's needy
and poor are all who possess the merit of emptying themselves of the
evil attitudes of this world.

2. *Preserve my soul, for I am holy: save thy servant, O my God, that
trusteth in thee.* He emphatically explains who is needy and poor: it is
the Lord Christ, who with truth calls Himself holy, for He has trodden underfoot the enticements of the world by the manners of His
heavenly life. Let the followers of Apollinarius[6] hear that the Lord
Christ has the soul and assumed nature of the perfect man, for He
could not avoid having what He is known to have come especially to
save. No-one frees what he does not deliver from the power of the
invader; and if a protector has nothing to claim as his own, the condition of incurred captivity continues. Note how salutary for us is the
formulation here proposed. He who had truthfully called Himself
holy and a stranger to the enticements of the world prays that He may
be saved by the Godhead, so as to instruct us that salvation does not lie
within the powers of men. As the prophet Jeremiah says: *Cursed be the
man that trusteth in man, and whose heart departeth from the Lord,*[7] and
so on.

3. *Have mercy on me, O Lord, for I have cried to thee all the day.* The
one and the same Christ Jesus, who is God and man, asks for mercy
though He bestows mercy; He is teaching us that the Lord's kindness
can be wholly obtained by constancy in prayer. As He Himself says in
the gospel: *It is good to pray and not to faint.*[8] Those persons should
listen to this verse who with perverse will despair of repenting at the
close of their lives, and have resort to making excuses with unholy
intent, although they realise that in the gospel-account help was
granted in the twinkling of an eye to the thief already impaled on the
cross; likewise in the other cases which the text of divine Scripture
with wondrous kindness affords us to nurture the hope of mortal men.
It is right that we should always make supplication, since we are often
guilty of going astray. It is an evil beyond reckoning that men should

deprive themselves of the most wholesome hope, since the divine clemency bids us make entreaty to Him without ceasing. Let us aim at this in the flower of manhood, when we are still young, and let us seek it when advanced to frail old age. He who has sinned with wickedness deserving punishment must never cease to pray. The danger is that while we seek an occasion for entreaty, we may alienate the Lord's mercy from us by such a pretence. The phrase, *all the day,* expresses one's entire life, so what is indicated is an unending cry through many seasons and courses of years as if they were a single day. The person whose tongue is silent but who continues to cry out with good works is making loud utterance to the Lord.

4. *Give joy to the soul of thy servant, for to thee, O Lord, I have lifted up my soul.* Our Source of cheerfulness and Fount of joy asks that His soul be gladdened. He speaks in his role of servant, for He rightly called Himself such, since He was born of the virgin Mary who proclaims herself a handmaid. When the angel told her that Christ the Lord would be born of her, she replied: *Behold, the handmaid of the Lord; let it be done unto me according to thy word.*[9] In another psalm too we read: *I am thy servant and the son of thy handmaid.*[10] So He asks that His soul be gladdened, for He did not lower it to the ground but ever raised it to the Lord, where reside true joy and unending tranquillity. In this way the Church's Head gave examples to His other members by recounting His own actions.

5. *For thou, O Lord, art sweet and mild, and plenteous in mercy to all that call upon thee.* This does not refer to Him in his essence, for no creature can grasp that, but by the fifth type of definition, which in Greek is called *kata tēn lexin,*[11] we have most beautifully revealed to us the nature of God. He is sweet, because after the bitterness of this world He is sweet to those who hasten back to Him; He is mild because he bears with sinners for a long time. He is plenteous in mercy, because though our sins are numerous His devoted love is much more abundant, for it forgives so many offences. It remains for us to entreat Him continually, since we hear that He does not refuse His protection to all that call on Him.

6. *Take in with your ears, O Lord, my prayer: and attend to the voice of my petition.* Let us examine how appropriately the sequence of this prayer develops. First came the request that words of entreaty should rise, and then that God should listen when asked. But the words, *take*

in, do not demand momentary acceptance, but ask that the prayer be stored in the inner being of His majesty, just as we know that a man takes in things through his ears and implants them in the memory. The additional words are: *Attend to the voice of my petition,* so that God may lend a hearing with concentrated mind. The whole statement is allegorical, aimed at intimating the power of the Godhead by describing human tendencies.

7. *I have called upon thee in the day of my trouble, because thou hast heard me.* Whereas earlier He said: *I have cried to thee all the day,* here He seems to intensify His great petition with the words: *I have called upon thee in the day of my trouble.* Though holy men continually make entreaty of the Lord, in time of affliction their prayers are more strenuous since they are under pressure to demand help. We must ponder this manner of speaking found very often in the divine Scriptures, by which He says that He has called because He was heard, though the cry precedes the possibility of God's hearing it. This figure is called *anastrophe* or inversion,[12] occurring whenever sense or words are inverted for some fine effect.

8. *There is none among the gods like to thee, O Lord: and there is none according to thy works.* Great praise is enclosed in a brief statement. His phrase, *none among the gods is like to thee,* points to the idols of the pagans which were still being worshipped in the world with perverted devotion. As we read elsewhere similarly: *For all the gods of the Gentiles are devils.*[13] The word *gods* can also be applied to men who were called gods. But observe that this is not a statement of what God is, but that there is none like Him; this type of definition is termed in Greek *kat' aphairesin tou enantiou,* and in Latin *per privationem contrarii*[14] of the thing being defined. He further added: *And there is none according to thy works;* understand "like to Thee." This phrase too He enclosed under that definition earlier mentioned; for who in the speed of a second could create sky and earth and all that is in them, or keep them in perpetual existence?

9. *All the nations thou hast made shall come and adore before thee, O Lord: and they shall honour thy name.* Whereas previously the Jewish nation was the only one known to worship the one God, He foretells that all nations kept in thrall to idols would come to worship Him; for anyone who honours the Lord Christ truly worships the Father, and obliterates the mistaken notion of those who think that adhesion to

the Lord is not spread through the whole world. His statement, *All the nations thou hast made,* is proof of this total universality, for no race exists which He has not created. As Scripture says elsewhere: *Who made heaven and earth, the sea and all things that are in them.*[15] He added: *And they shall honour thy name.* When God is told: *They shall honour thy name,* it is a figurative statement for "The faithful will be honoured by reason of Your name," for men's worship does not make God worthy of honour, since we know that He undoubtedly bestows all honours.

10. *For thou art great, and dost wonderful things: thou art God alone.* With the close of this verse He completed the hymn to the Godhead which He began earlier. The devil regarded himself as great when he said: *I will set my throne at the north, and I will be like the most High.*[16] Even today proud men count themselves greater than all others. But no-one can be truly called great except God alone, for nothing can be remotely compared to His power; He is subject to no change, but continues always in the glory of His nature. He added: *And dost wonderful things: thou art God alone.* Though we read that Pharaoh's magicians performed various miracles, here it is said that God alone can do miracles—a true statement, if we weigh the nature of the deed according to the truth of the word miracle. Those actions cannot truly be termed miracles which are counterfeit and serve no useful purpose, merely charming our beguiled eyes. The word *alone* was used because the holy Trinity is one God, distinct solely in Persons, and not separated by any difference of nature. As Scripture states elsewhere: *Hear, O Israel, the Lord your God is one Lord.*[17] And Isaiah likewise says: *For thou art just, and there is no God except thee.*[18]

11. *Conduct me, O Lord, in thy way, and I will walk in thy truth: let my heart rejoice, that I may fear thy name.* Now that He has ended the prayer and fittingly completed praise of the Godhead, He passes to the second part, in which He prays on behalf of His members that the Lord may grant them what will avail them. By His words, *conduct me, O Lord, in thy way,* He indicates that He has not been there hitherto; this cannot be appropriate to the Lord Christ, for He Himself says: *I am the way, the truth and the life.*[19] The statement is more appropriately interpreted as spoken for the faithful whose Head is the Lord. Unless they are conducted on to the way, that is, to Christ, they cannot surely walk in the truth. Next comes: *Let my heart rejoice, that I*

may fear thy name. What the fear of the Lord is we find stated in a wonderful sequence. In the fear which we encounter in this world, a cause of danger or of some hardship precedes; but in fear of the Lord, the heart's joy precedes, so that one may deserve to draw near to the sweetness of that fear. It is indeed fitting to have the kind of approach which the human race feels is granted for their salvation. The person who dreads our Judge is condemned, but he who stands in awe of Him is holy. Both emotions are to be mingled; we must be fearful in hope and glad in fear. As another psalm has it: *Serve the Lord with fear, and rejoice unto him with trembling.*[20]

12. *I will praise thee, O Lord my God, with my whole heart: and I will honour thy name for ever.* This is appropriately referred to every Christian, for true confession is that which comes forth from the mind's entire depths. As the Law teaches: *Thou shalt love the Lord thy God with thy whole heart and thy whole soul.*[21] But the person who puts his entire hope in the Lord also praises with his whole heart. He does not put his trust in the transient consolations of the world, once he has trained himself on the Lord with total purity of mind. His final words, *for ever,* indicate that He will take His place among the saints and make the Lord's praises resound continually when He has received the promised rewards in that state of blessedness.

13. *For thy mercy is great towards me: and thou hast delivered my soul out of the lower hell.* A confession of praise is offered up, and an explanation of *mercy* is appended. When He says: *For thy mercy is great toward me,* He proclaims an unspoken kindness, but by adding: *Thou hast delivered my soul out of the lower hell,* the nature of the kindness is clarified. But let us ponder the fact that since He speaks of the lower hell He reveals the existence of an upper hell. In the *Topics*[22] such expressions are said to be etymologically related when they develop from the same term and are transformed in various ways, as in the expression, *the lower hell,* here. We perhaps not irrationally think of hell as being below the earth, since we read in the old Testament of Dathan and Abiron: *The earth opened up and devoured them, and they went down alive into hell.*[23] But we are uncertain by what route souls are transported there, for it is not stated there on divine authority. However, the fact that hell has a lower part is attested by the passage of the gospel which says that when the avenging flame tortured the wicked Dives, he raised his eyes and saw Lazarus in the bosom of Abraham.[24]

It is accordingly clear that both were in the world of the dead so that they could see each other, and that Dives raised his eyes from the lower region to the higher. But though both seemed to be in hell, our teacher Augustine[25] reckons that in accordance with the difference between their merits, a higher place is to be assigned to holy men, and a lower place to sinners. So in the present passage the faithful people in giving thanks says that their soul has been delivered from the lower hell, which is the region of punishment.

14. *O God, the unjust are risen up against me, and the assembly of the mighty have sought my soul: they have not set thee before their eyes.* He passes to the third section, in which He expounds the mystery of His passion and the glory of the Resurrection. The God-man speaks in His role as servant, arising from His birth from the virgin Mary. When He speaks of the unjust, He means the Jews, who rendered Him evil for good. The words, *against me,* point to their declaring Him guilty though He was innocent, and to the slaughter of their King by the mad mob. *The assembly of the mighty* is the gathering of the arrogant, who with bestial din and crafty dealing abandoned just counsels, and sought to take His life. He mentioned too the common tendency of wicked minds: they did not set God before their eyes, Any person committing a wicked deed totally fails to set God before His eyes, for if He thought of Him as present he would at once be deterred from the sin which he had planned.

15. *And thou, O Lord, a God of compassion, and merciful, patient, and of much mercy, and true.* The Father's majesty is delineated by these individual expressions of praise. This is the twelfth type of definition which the Greeks call *kat' epainon* and the Latins *per laudem.*[26] He is compassionate because He shows mercy in individual matters; He is merciful because the very nature of the Godhead is always devoted. He is patient because He bears with sinners and invites them to pray for conversion. Next comes: *And of much mercy.* He added this word again because our weakness always obtains more of it by frequent forgiveness. He added: *And true,* because God cannot withdraw His promises through any weakness. These statements are made of the Father in such a way that we realise that their whole content lies also in the Son and the holy Spirit.

16. *O look upon me, and have mercy on me: give power to thy boy, and save the son of thy handmaid.* The Son, as having endured the passion,

begs the merciful, patient and true Father to look upon Him and aid Him by a most speedy resurrection. The Father had mercy on Him to the extent of raising His mortal nature to the glory of resurrection and eternity; and the request for this is couched in such terms that He declares that He has already performed it. Indeed, in the gospel He speaks in this way: *Destroy this temple, and in three days I shall raise it up.* So that this could not be interpreted in any other way, the evangelist adds: *But he spoke of the temple of His body.*[27] Next comes: *Give power to thy boy.* This is the power to which He Himself witnesses: *The Father doth not judge any man: he hath given all judgment to the Son.*[28] In the holy Scriptures Christ is often called a boy because of His innocence of mind. As Isaiah says: *For a boy has been born to us, and a son has been given to us.*[29] And again: *Behold my boy: I will uphold him. My elect: my soul delighteth in him.*[30] He added: *And save the son of thy handmaid:* precisely a handmaid, because He was to be born truly and uniquely of Mary ever a virgin, and she proclaimed herself the handmaid of the Lord, as we said earlier, when the angel announced to her the coming birth.

17. *Show me, O Lord, a sign for good, that they who hate me may see and be confounded: because thou, O Lord, hast helped me and hast comforted me.* A sign gets its name because it signifies what is to come,[31] and warns us to change our attitude in accordance with what is seen. Here we can perhaps advert to the famous incident of Jonah, who spent three days in the whale's belly and was disgorged safe and sound on the shore as a type of the Lord's resurrection.[32] As the gospel words have it: *An evil and adulterous generation seeketh a sign, and a sign shall not be given it but the sign of Jonas the prophet.*[33] So you see that any other sign was refused, and this one only was promised. We can also fittingly refer this sign, whose appearance He demanded, to the Lord's resurrection, especially since the words, *for good,* follow. What is more outstanding than the good by which the divine power was declared and the hope of believers strengthened by a truthful promise? Next comes: *That they who hate me may see and be confounded.* It is the Jews who hate Christ, and he asks that they may see His resurrection so that their hardness may be transformed. The phrase, *may be confounded,* anticipates a good outcome, for the person who is confounded because of his wickedness is undoubtedly changed for the better. If we are confounded in this world, we gain improvement; but

those not confounded will be condemned at that adjudication. He added: *Because thou, O Lord, hast helped me and hast comforted me.* The sequence of the words here is like this: *So that they who hate me may see, because thou, O Lord, hast helped and comforted me. And they may be confounded,* that is, "when they see Me, whom they thought contemptible, in glory." *Thou hast helped me,* that is, in contradicting the argumentative and in confronting the unjust grappling of the Jews, in which they will always be overcome[34] by the testimony of the truth. *Thou hast comforted me* in the face of the most savage persecutions of the madmen, which He most patiently endured like the onset of a storm.

Conclusion Drawn From the Psalm

Let us ponder the humility of the prayer poured out to the Father by the Lord Saviour in His passion. He was wholly without sin, but in representing our weakness He asked to be delivered from the dangers of this world. So men's rashness should blush to be arrogant, for they have no doubt of their guilt. Christ prayed for His enemies, and patiently accepted death, whereas we wish to avenge our injuries if attacked by the comments of detractors. May He who afforded an example grant the gift of patience, so that by following His footsteps we may be able to avoid the errors which bring death.

COMMENTARY ON PSALM 86

1. *For the sons of Core, a psalm of a canticle.* To refresh our memories let us briefly remind ourselves what has already often been stated; there seems little point in reciting what has been effaced from our minds. *The sons of Core* signify faithful Christians to whom the prophet proclaims the city of God, so that their longing for this great glory may be enhanced. Next comes: *A psalm of a canticle,* to raise us from the tents of this world to an understanding of the heavenly city. For the psalm sounds forth from the upper parts,[1] and reminds us to ponder heavenly things and to rejoice in them with songs of salvation.

Division of the Psalm

This is a short psalm, but it is clearly divided by two diapsalms. Mindful of our stated purpose, we explain the divisions by indicating the limits of each section. In the first part, the prophet speaks to the faithful, proclaiming the heavenly city. In the second, the Lord Saviour by citation of different names announces that this city will come to believe, and in tones of rebuke asks the synagogue why she has not known God when the devoted faith of the Gentiles believed in Him. In the third part, the prophet in a single verse touches on the blessedness of the age to come. Thus the clear change of spokesman removes from us all the darkness of confusion.

Explanation of the Psalm

The foundations of it are in the holy mountains. It is a feature of human reflection that on coming to full consciousness after considerable thought, we burst out with some part of our meditations. The beginning of this psalm seems to be of this kind. Though the prophet has previously said nothing of the city of God, he seems to discuss the foundations of it as if he has already said something about its summit. A new order of outstanding praise is developed; the prophet seemed to make a beginning with the foundations of the heavenly city, so that the great solidity of the whole superstructure would be evident when its foundations were praised first. This is as it should be, for its foundation is the Lord Christ, who holds fast His Church in such a way that it cannot totter through any agitation. As Paul has it: *For other foundation no man can lay but that which is laid, which is Christ Jesus.*[2] So he rightly began with Him who is known to be the beginning of all things. Josephus, too, whom a certain writer has called "the buffoon of the Jews," in Book 8, Chapter 3, of the *Antiquities* had a great deal to say about the structure of the Temple, which is known to have been built by Solomon. We ourselves had the Tabernacle, which was the representation of the Temple in earlier times, and the Temple itself painted and inserted in the body of our larger Pandect,[3] so that what the text of divine Scripture says of them might be put before our eyes and revealed more clearly. *In the holy mountains* refers to apostles and

prophets, who are called mountains because of their solidity of faith
and outstanding sanctity. So they are rightly accorded this label, for
the true Church of God was established on them.

2. *The Lord loveth the gates of Sion above all the tabernacles of Jacob.*
See how he now speaks of the city whose foundations he has already
praised. This figure is called *anastrophe* or inversion,[4] when what
ought to have been expressed first is placed second. He says: *The Lord
loveth the gates of Sion;* as we have repeatedly said, Sion is a mountain at
Jerusalem. The meaning of the name is "watch-tower,"[5] for the Jerusalem to come is fittingly observed by means of it. The Lord loves its
gates which are faith, charity, baptism, repentance and all that admits
into that city the people it has gained. Alternatively, as some have it,
the gates signify the twelve apostles, whose holy proclamation opened
the grand abodes of the eternal King to the faithful. But we must
zealously investigate his additional phrase: *Above all the tabernacles of
Jacob.* The tabernacles of Jacob denote the Catholic Church which is
now being built up; she is always at war with the opposition of the
world, keeping herself fit with route-marches. And since she bears the
representation of the Jerusalem to come, in which there is blessed life
and unending happiness, that spiritual city is rightly said to be loved
more than is the Church, for in the life to come there is said to be no
confusion or anxiety. Observe that he proclaims[6] that the future city is
loved more, but with the implication that the Church too is undoubtedly held in affection.

3. *Glorious things are said of thee, O city of God.* After his fashion he
describes the future as if it were the past. This city will in fact be
praised by the Lord's witness in the second section. Glorious things
are rightly said of the city known to be worthy of praise from the
Creator's lips.

4. *I will be mindful of Rahab and Babylon, if men know me: behold the
foreigners, and Tyre, and the people of the Ethiopians, these were in it.*
The second part of this psalm opens like a cloud from which the Lord
thunders, indicating by the names that they will be assembled from
diverse nations. Rahab was a harlot who secretly admitted the spies of
Joshua when they visited Jericho, and let them out by another exit so
that they should not be captured.[7] Her name means "pride."[8] She was
converted by God's generosity, and deserved to obtain mercy. She is a
type of the Church, which takes in souls endangered by the vice of

pride, and lets them out into life by another route, the way of humility and patience. Babylon is the city of the world, and means "confusion";[9] it indicates the people of this world, who with minds blinded were slaves to wicked idols, but who through the Lord's mercy were enlightened and became Christians. So in this verse He says that He is mindful of Rahab and Babylon, that is, the people of this world, as many as have humbly turned to His worship. Similarly in the gospel Christ replied to the arrogant Pharisees: *Amen I say to you, the publicans and harlots shall go into the kingdom of God before you.*[10] Next comes: *Behold the foreigners, and Tyre, and the people of the Ethiopians, they were in it.* He continues in the same vein: foreigners are outsiders to the Jewish people, but whereas the Jews refused to believe, the foreigners were received into the inner sanctum of the Church. In the words of the Acts of the Apostles: *To you it behoved us first to speak of the kingdom of God, but because you reject it and judge yourselves unworthy of eternal life, behold, we turn to the gentiles.*[11] Tyre signifies the hardship resultant upon the affliction of penitents;[12] the people of the Ethiopians had been most foul owing to the blackness of their sins, but they were brought together in this city of the Lord so that the quota of shining saints might be attained from their number in the fatherland. This is the prophecy foretold in the previous verse: *Glorious things are said of thee, city of God;* for what is more glorious than that the disgusting foulness of once errant peoples should assemble into the single beauty of the holy city? Remember that this type of utterance, by which the intention of a passage can be understood by interpretation of names, is peculiar to holy Scripture.

5. *The mother of Sion will say: This is a man. And he was born a man in her, and the Highest himself hath founded her.* Perhaps it is not inappropriate here to interpret the mother of the Catholic Church as the synagogue, since she alone of the greatest part of the world's population said that the Lord Saviour was a man; she did not deserve to believe or understand that He is God. At this point we must split up the sentence, because what follows clearly introduces a different meaning. The next words are: *And he was born a man in her,* which are to be read as an affirmation. He does not say that a man was born in the sense that the synagogue said it earlier. She in her error thought He was a mere man, but now the Lord in an explicit statement maintains of Himself: *And he was born a man in her;* for God did in truth become

man when He took on the flesh. As the evangelist says: *The Word became flesh*,[13] that is, the Son of God became man, not to detract at all from His divinity but to advance worthily the nature of humanity, which He had determined to free. Then so that you would not chance to believe that the Lord Christ was a transient being, He added: *And the Highest himself hath founded her*. In other words, Jesus Christ, who was considered to be only a man, Himself founded the synagogue by His own dispensation. He not merely bestowed the Law through Moses, but is known to have been the Beginning before the commencement of the world. As He witnesses in the gospel: *I am the beginning, which is why I speak to you*.[14] So He was rightly termed the Highest, so that no heresy could call the Father greater.

6. *The Lord has told of the writings of peoples and of princes, of them that have been in her.* The Lord prophesies what He will say at the time of the Incarnation about the declaration of the ancient Scriptures. Often in the gospel He reminds us what Moses and the prophets foretold of Him, with the double purpose of instructing unbelievers and of showing that He was the Author of those Scriptures. The princes are Moses and the prophets in the synagogue, whose witness He was to recount; so that you would not perhaps interpret this as other princes, He speaks of *them that have been in her*, that is, in the synagogue.

7. *The dwelling of all of us who as it were rejoice in thee.* He comes to the third section, in which it is the prophet's turn to speak once more. He begins and ends in the one verse, briefly embracing what could not be included in discussion however lengthy. This figure is called brachylogy[15] or abbreviated speech, when we enclose several matters in a few words. Would you like to hear how far beyond understanding that joy is? Paul says of it: *Eye hath not seen, nor ear heard, neither hath it entered into the heart of man, what things God has prepared for them that love him*.[16] Accordingly the phrase, *who as it were rejoice*, is splendid, because the joy will not be such as is experienced here when at one moment we rejoice in acknowledging our sons, or at another we are pleased at the bestowal of riches and honours, or when we have other transient experiences which bring fierce delight after great effort. But how much greater is the joy of heaven, when the fullest delight in this world is said to be scarcely a reflection or likeness of the world to come! He added: *The dwelling of all of us is in thee. All of us*

refers to the faithful, who have believed that the Lord Christ will come or has come. *The dwelling is in thee* is addressed to Jerusalem, to which he earlier said: *Glorious things are said of thee, city of God.* In this dwelling the affliction of the just has ceased. Prayer is past, and praise succeeds it. Enduring tranquillity abides because no subversion enters. Eternal joy continues, for it is certain not to be broken by any dissension.

Conclusion Drawn From the Psalm

That city of the faithful has been praised in the demonstrative genre.[17] That city is wonderful not in temporal blessings but in eternal happiness. Though the things said of it seem few, the minds of all are seen to be rooted in astonishment at it; for this praise is not extended by verbal argumentation, and it does not swell through human effort, but rather is compressed by such great brevity that it scarcely seems possible to take anything from it. How blessed is he who with the Lord's guidance reaches that city, where every thought is overwhelmed, and each and every desire transcended! As is the nature of that most sweet and untroubled state, such happiness is obtained there as is destroyed by no opposition. Grant, Lord, that what we cannot explain here in words we may behold there by Your gift.

The Jerusalem which is still on earth and bears the stamp of that secret abode in heaven was praised in the second section; and rightly, for it is the visible home of such great virtues.[18] In it the angel came down and stirred the pool to heal the sick and prefigure holy baptism.[19] In it Silo at the Lord's command washed away the darkness of the blind man, and restored the gift of light to his condemned eyes.[20] In it Christ's table, filled with heavenly delights, gave spiritual plenty to the apostles, and so that we should not be left unfed after that meal, the sacred chalice bestowed on us both communion and salvation. In it the hardest of stones revealed the footsteps of the holy Redeemer where He stood to be heard before Pilate His judge;[21] in it the pillar witnesses the scourging of the Lord who was bound to it;[22] in it is seen the crown of thorns which we know was set on the Lord of salvation so that the spikes driven into the entire world could be nullified. In it is preserved the reed which struck the Lord's head to announce to all

lands that He was the Beginning of creation.[23] In it the cross of salvation and of glory hallowed that venerable place. In it remains the lance
which pierced the Lord's side so that the healing which flowed from it
might aid us.[24] In it His tomb even today gives life to believers; in it
the site of the resurrection raises the hearts of the faithful to heaven.
There stands Sion, outstanding among mountains; there, as the disciples reclined in the dining-chamber with doors closed, the Saviour
miraculously entered.[25] There are too the other glories which that rich
homeland won through the Lord's passion. Since Jerusalem gleams
handsomely with so many miracles, and like the constellations possesses a second heaven, who would presume to call it tiny when it is
known to have filled the territories of the world with most holy faith?
For it is there that the beliefs of the blessed feed the eyes of men.[26]

COMMENTARY ON PSALM 87

1. *A canticle of a psalm for the sons of Core: unto the end: for Meleth to
make answer: understanding of Eman the Israelite.* Since I have no
doubt, most diligent reader, that your memory, strengthened by regular explanations, recalls the meaning of *canticle of a psalm,* and *unto the
end,* it remains for us to examine the new and later entries of this
heading. *Meleth* means a chorus singing the divine words.[1] The addition *to make answer* indicates that instrumental music preceded, and
that the chorus made solemn reply. Next comes: *Understanding of
Eman the Israelite.* Eman means "his brother,"[2] the word with which
Christ the Lord calls those devoted to His precepts and works. As He
says in the gospel: *Go, tell it to my brothers.*[3] Israelites means "seeing
God";[4] it is clear that this is the experience of those illuminated by the
holy light of the Lord through the mystery of obedience. But since this
psalm is to tell of the passion of Christ the King, and to draw most
faithful Christians to the model for imitation, the chorus was put first
to make answer, so that just as they made a single harmony from many
voices, so the united gathering of the faithful may make one reply to
Christ the Lord. They are Israelites too, deserving to be called His
brothers through the kindness of heaven.

Division of the Psalm

Throughout the whole psalm the Lord Saviour speaks from His experience of the dispensation by which He suffered. In the first narration He begs the Father's help, recounting by means of various similes the contempt which the Jewish people was to manifest to Him. The second part recounts His future sufferings, maintaining that the dead cannot be roused by physicians so as to be able to confess to the Lord. In the third narration He states that those who are buried do not proclaim God's mercy, and that the abandoned do not sound forth the Lord's praises. So He prays that the resurrection will come with all speed. As He continues on this course of His prayer, He is the Spokesman of His members, recounting the various sufferings which He endured commensurately with the devoted people.

Explanation of the Psalm

2. *O Lord, the God of my salvation: I have cried in the day and in the night before thee.* At Psalm 85⁵ we stated that Christ prayed in His status as Son of the virgin Mary, depicting the lowliness of the human weakness which He deigned to assume. Similarly here when He prays to the Father He shows us how we should make entreaty; in proclaiming God as the Author of His salvation, He very fully but briefly expounded all that need be said. In this way the Best of teachers never ceases to give the advice which He knows will be of service to the human race. *In the day* denotes joy, *in the night* announces affliction; since human life comprises both times, He was declaring that He cried to the Lord continually.

3. *Let my prayer come in before thy sight: incline thy ear to my petition, O Lord.* The great power of prayer at its purest is shown here; truthful words are not scattered on the unsubstantial breezes, but they seem to come before the Lord's presence like a spokesman, and to discharge their appointed task in the place which our physical persons cannot reach. The Lord inclines His ear when He mercifully deigns to listen not in any physical sense (we have often said that He has no body) but by the wondrous application of His power.

4. *For my soul is filled with evils, and my life has drawn nigh to hell.*

We must observe that His request to be heard takes a new form, for He says that His soul is filled with evils; they are not His own, for He had no sins, but the wicked deeds of the world under which humanity toiled. In His devoted pity for us He had burdened His soul with these evils, sharing the grief of all men. As He said in Psalm 34: *They repaid me evil for good, making my soul barren.*[6] Not that He was barren, but He stated that He hungered through their unbelief. This verse can be referred to His own melancholy, if you relate the word *evils* to those iniquities which the Jewish people inflicted on Him. Next comes: *And my life has drawn nigh to hell.* This is connected with the time of His glorious passion. As He says in the gospel: *My soul is sorrowful even unto death;*[7] for He grieved for our sake, and shouldered our death for us.

5. *I am counted among them that go down to the pit: I am become as a man without help.* He is chiding those who believed that He had died as one of the crowd. This figure is called *parabole*, or comparison of things unlike by nature;[8] for it was quite anomalous to compare the unique and wondrous passion to the deaths of the rest of mankind. This figure embraces many of the subsequent verses. By *pit* He meant either a burial place or the deepest depths of hell. Next comes: *I am become as a man without help. I am become:* that is, amongst those who with lunatic minds failed to believe in His divinity, and who thought that He had perished with the rest of mankind.

6. *Free among the dead. Like the wounded who are cast out and sleep in their tombs, whom thou rememberest no more: and they are cast out from thy hand.* Here He indicates particularly His own person. He alone was free among the dead, for He also sundered the bars of death. His death alone was free, for it was voluntary; *He had the power to lay down His life and to take it up again.*[9] But though He was free among the dead, He was regarded by those madmen as one of the wounded who sleep. The Lord was truly called free, for He deigned to free the human race. He still has in mind those foolish persons who thought that once the Lord had been wounded by the lance, and was both slain and buried, He had passed on like any criminal in the common lot of mankind. But to separate Himself from them He added: *Whom thou rememberest no more,* in other words, "Those whom You disregard, for through the action of their sins they are estranged from You." He says the same thing of the wicked in another psalm: *Their memory hath*

perished with a noise.[10] He added: *And they are cast out from thy hand.* Just punishment is meted out to their wantonness; they had believed that the Lord Christ was without the resource of divinity, and were seen to be cast out from the Lord's hand, since through the action of their sins they were excluded from His guidance.

7. *They have laid me in the lower pit: in darkness and in the shadow of death.* He is still passing judgment on the lunatic Jews. The word *pit* is used for both hell and a burial place; it also bears the sense of profoundest disaster in this world, which is the meaning He intended here, for His persecutors consigned Him to the abject condition of death. They unjustifiably satisfied themselves that He was dead, and did not believe that He would be avenged. *In darkness* suggests that He was abandoned and ignored in blind oblivion, so that none sought Him or rescued Him. *In the shadow of death* indicates the place of sinners, for death confronts the shadowy and dark spirits of wicked men. Joy does not illumine them, and they are plunged in the enduring darkness of their melancholy. *Shadow* is sometimes found in the good sense, as in: *Beneath the shadow of thy wings,*[11] and elsewhere: *We shall live in his shadow.*[12] So the word has varied senses according to the nature of the passages.

8. *Thy anger is strong against me, and all thy passions thou hast brought against me.* This was the belief of those permitted to prevail for their own destruction, that through God's anger Jesus Christ had confronted the hazards of the passion. The evangelist recounts the words of the faithless people: *Let him deliver him, if he desires it.*[13] Next comes: *And all thy passions thou hast brought against me.* These words are still quoted as characteristic of the wicked thoughts of the Jews: God was believed to have brought His passions, in other words, His most explosive rage, against Christ, when He caused Him to be crucified. They thought that this death was a punishment, for they did not visualise the glory of His dispensation.

9. *Thou hast removed my acquaintances far from me: they have set me as an abomination to themselves: I was delivered up, and came not forth.* He passes to the second section, in which He relates the course of the passion by ascending stages of hardships. Whereas earlier He spoke of the most wicked contempt of His persecutors, He now speaks of that of His acquaintances, meaning the apostles; for He labels as acquaintances those who gained the merit of observing Him with clear

gaze. By virtue of His divinity, He knew all persons as acquaintances, but was Himself known by only a few. These acquaintances were removed far from Him when they were scattered at His passion. As Scripture has it: *I shall strike the shepherd, and the sheep shall be scattered.*[14] He was set as an abomination when the passing scribes and Pharisees jeered at Him on the cross with the words: *Vah, he that destroyeth the temple of God and in three days doth rebuild it,*[15] and the rest. Next comes: *I was delivered up, and came not forth.* This is a marvellously subtle statement. He was delivered up by Judas to the gangs of madmen, but He permitted His own arrest. The most powerful Lord lent support to their feeble hands. He who cannot be confined by place was bound with chains; He whom the angels praise with trembling listened to loathsome words of offence. But *He came not forth* from the cloak of His body; He was unwilling to demonstrate His power, and He endured all that the cruelty of Jewish wickedness inflicted on Him. *He came not forth* in wholly refusing to demonstrate His superior strength. Alternatively, the phrase refers to the confinement into which Pontius Pilate thrust Him as though He were a weakling.

10. *My eyes were weakened through poverty: all the day I cried to thee, O Lord: I stretched out my hands to thee.* Nowhere do we read that the bodily eyes of the Lord Christ were weakened; much more should we refuse to believe that His inward eyes were enfeebled, for they always shone forth with holiness. It remains for us to interpret the eyes of Christ as the apostles, for they always waxed strong with heavenly light in His body which is the Church. But they were *weakened through poverty* because they had not yet received the holy Spirit; once they were strengthened by the Spirit, they subsequently had no fears whatsoever of human tortures. The word *inopia* (poverty) is formed as an antonym to express *nulla copia* (no abundance).[16] *All the day I cried out to thee, O Lord,* comes next. We must distinguish the sense of *cried out* here; this continuation through the whole day must be referred to that crying which is prayer and the performance of good works. *I stretched out my hands to thee;* as usual He wishes this to be interpreted as the works which He ever extended to the Lord by goodly actions. If, as some believe, we imagine that the phrase must refer to the cross, all that follows will be at odds with this interpretation.

11. *Wilt thou do wonders for the dead, or shall physicians raise to life*

and confess to thee? This must be read as a negative statement. But we must analyse His words: *Thou wilt not do wonders for the dead,* since clearly countless people have been brought to life again. But He certainly did not do wonders for the dead in the sense of nonbelievers, for their lack of faith could not induce them to conversion; for wonders befall only those who behold the great deeds of the Lord with the eyes of belief. Next comes: *Or shall physicians raise to life and confess to thee?* This too is a negative statement, because physicians, who people believe bring health to the sick by the successful application of their skill, cannot revive the dead. So they should confess to the Lord, for without the Lord's services they cannot even impart bodily health to the sick. Alternatively a subtler interpretation is possible; they cannot revive souls which are dead through sins, so those whom the wounds of their unfaithfulness have shattered must be brought to life by a truly genuine confession.

12. *Shall anyone in the sepulchre declare thy mercy, or thy truth in destruction?* He passes to the third narration; in this and the following verse He employs the figure of *emphasis,*[17] in which we must grasp the words which draw attention to what He does not say. These words, *shall anyone in the sepulchre declare thy mercy?* must be read in the negative sense so that we can realise that the persons accustomed to declare His mercy are the living and the faithful. *Sepulchre* here indicates the minds of the unfaithful, of whom it was said earlier: *Their throat is an open sepulchre.*[18] Sepulchre is the right word, for in it is contained the soul which has died through sins; in other words, He wishes us to understand here those who will not come to believe in the Lord. No-one, it seems, has told them of the Lord's mercy, for they were unwilling to accept it with devoted hearts. We say that a speech has succeeded when the listener registers the effect; this is the point of what follows: *Or thy truth in destruction?* for no-one is thought to have spoken the truth when the indifferent listener seems to disregard it. Destruction is the appropriate description for when the truth is not accepted, and stubbornness alone is maintained.

13. *Shall thy wonders be known in the dark, or thy justice in the land of forgetfulness?* All this develops in a similar pattern but with different language; by rejection of what is not the case we realise the opposite actuality. The wonders of the Lord are not witnessed by minds enfolded in darkness, for by ignoring God they have lost the light of

wisdom. His justice too cannot be ascertained in earthly forgetfulness, in other words in the total darkness of the body which abandons spiritual warnings because its desires are dominated by the vices of the flesh. Remember that all these things are said so that His soul may not be abandoned in hell, and that He may obtain a most speedy resurrection. In this way the Lord's praise could be acknowledged through His kindnesses.

14. *I too, O Lord, have cried to thee: and in the morning my prayer shall come before thee.* In opposition to what has been said earlier, the Lord Christ, together with His faithful, says that He cries to the Lord because of His coming resurrection. He recounts the most splendid nature of His varied afflictions so that Christian peoples may be schooled by such instruction, and especially strengthened. By saying *I too,* He shows that He has cried out together with His members, of which Christ is Himself the Head; when He cries out and instructs the Church, when He prays with His faithful, He shows that they are one body. So remember that to the end of the psalm He recounts the various disasters which He Himself endured in the persons of His martyrs. I think that the figure of *synathroismos,*[19] by which many circumstances and many hazards are gathered together, must be noted here. Next comes: *And in the morning my prayer shall come before thee.* These words are to be handled with care so that there may be no contradiction to that rule of the highest truth which says that the Lord's grace comes before all things. The body of the Church which is brightened by the morning, that is, by good works, says that its prayer comes before the second coming of the Lord, which is Judgment Day; now this prayer was bestowed through the Lord's gift. So it is rightly stated that their prayer came before Him, for that future event which we still await was eagerly sought many generations before. He will come at the appropriate time, but our longing must be demonstrated by fervent requests. He does not distinguish us as His if He is not sought with the greatest prayers by us when He comes. Since the statement is quite clearly made about Him, He cannot here be speaking in His own person; rather we must interpret it as spoken on behalf of His members in the Church.

15. *Lord, why casteth thou off my prayer? Why turnest thou thy face away from me?* Here is expressed the longing of that most holy mind,

because He bore with impatience the delay before the world could be truly saved. The Lord is believed to cast off our entreaty and to turn away His face when He postpones our aspirations; and though He does what will benefit us, we are grievously upset when our requests are delayed. This verse He appropriately utters as Spokesman of martyrs who become wearied in this world through such unattained longings. Their requests are postponed to enrich them, and are delayed to gain them glory. Assent to their prayers is not so advantageous as is the postponement which increases their benefit. In the same way fire is checked by wind-bellows in order that it may be ignited to greater life.

16. *I am needy, and in labours from my youth: and being exalted have been humbled and troubled.* The Church appropriately speaks these words, for from her youth she has been wearied through needs and labours in the world. As we read in another psalm: *Often have they stormed me from my youth.*[20] But she grows through persecutions, she is enhanced by the oppression of the times, she is always exalted by her lowliness. The longer period of her life consists not of feeble weariness but of mature perfection. Next comes: *And being exalted I have been humbled and troubled.* This is clearly specifically appropriate to the members and not to the Head. *Exalted* refers to the earlier time when each individual among the faithful pondered human affairs with arrogant heart. *I have been humbled* describes when through the compassion of divine grace they embraced the healing gift of confession; *troubled* refers to when they condemned their evil deeds with a proclamation of repentance. What blessed trouble is this which effaces eternal disgrace! All that contributes to the guilt of those who repent is forgiven in the eternity to come.

17. *Thy wrath has passed over me, and thy terrors have troubled me.* *Passed over* is well phrased, implying that it did not remain too long, for when one of the faithful disciplines himself he escapes the anger of the Lord with a rebuke. By specifying *me*, the Church in her usual way bears witness that the affliction of the faithful has been directed against her. Next comes: *And thy terrors have troubled me;* these are the terrors of the judgment to come, which as we know all sinning flesh fears. It is clear that this too is applicable only to the Lord's members.

18. *They have surrounded me like water all the day: they have compassed me about together.* Those sins which are condemned by the

punishment of the law surround men like water, for they are known to gush out from all sides. From what quarter are we to believe that sins do not come, seeing that they are strangers to us at no moment of the day? So they are rightly compared with waters which hem us in with their most abundant flood. The whole verse is appropriately interpreted as expressing the view of the members.

19. *Friend and relation thou hast put far from me: and my acquaintances, because of my misery.* This has been the frequent experience of holy martyrs, from whom men's support has been withdrawn because of fear of death. *Friend* refers to those joined in honourable pursuits through similarity of character; *relation,* to those joined to us by kinship; *acquaintances,* those who are neither friends nor relations, but have learned of our existence by hearsay or sight. The feared misery of suffering often causes these classes of people to distance themselves from faithful servants.

Conclusion Drawn From the Psalm

This is Christ's chorus which the prefatory heading proclaimed, in accordance with the meaning of the name Meleth; for the faithful people, following His most holy passion, gave answer with a most splendid imitation. On one side the prison held confessors in confinement; from another the blood of martyrs welled forth, more precious than purple garments and fine linen; from another the words of the apostles thundered through the whole world; from another the sacred faith came forth like the brightest sun; from another, even today people hasten to embrace deaths which are transient in search of the rewards of eternal life. So let no person fear the wretchedness which makes men blessed. Let none tremble at the tortures which bring lasting security; let none fear the sadness which bestows eternal joy. How slight a thing is momentary death when its purpose is to win enduring life! How slight an imposition is the judgment of men, enabling us to obtain divine forgiveness! Who would be ashamed of the pains which the Lord Christ deigned to bear? Who would regard as dishonour what our Creator chose to endure for all? So let us shoulder for Him disaster in this world if we wish to possess with Him our enduring portion.

COMMENTARY ON PSALM 88

1. *The understanding of Ethan the Israelite.* We are to explain the words which the psalmist set down, not so much to observe the nature of the heading as to advance our understanding, so that the truth of the matter may shine out more clearly for us. Ethan means "solid,"[1] Israelite "seeing God." Because the purpose of this psalm was to recount the praises and promises of the Lord, it is clear that Ethan's name was added to it to indicate the unchangeable steadfastness of faithful words. *Understanding,* as we have often said, is to be referred to heavenly matters, to which the person of right understanding truly directs his mental insight. The psalm will have much to say about the hope of Christians and the magnificence of the Lord. No-one is misled in these matters if, as he prays, his mind finds strength in the most steadfast will of Ethan.

Division of the Psalm

This Ethan, whose name we have said means "solid," is filled with such great mental illumination that he is quite rightly called an Israelite. At the outset of the psalm he says that he will sing of the Lord's mercies, for He has promised many future benefits to His faithful people. In the second part he enumerates the praises and power of the Lord in different ways. The third section recounts the Father's promises to the Lord Christ. In the fourth, the Lord Christ is said to have been consigned to enemies to undergo the passion which He bore. In the fifth, he begs for support for human frailty, for the sons of men have not been fashioned by Him for no purpose. The sixth begs the Lord to fulfil His promises, which He is said to have made to His servant David, and to be mindful of the reproaches which His servants were enduring from wicked men.

Explanation of the Psalm

2. *Thy mercies, O Lord, I will sing for ever. I will show forth thy truth in my mouth in generation after generation.* A man who is to speak so steadfastly is rightly termed "solid." Ethan is to tell of the Lord's mercies, which ever abide eternally unwavering, and are to be hymned with never-ending praises; for the Lord showed wonderful devotion to the human race in order to seek back what was lost and to save what was wounded. The additional phrase, *in generation after generation,* denotes the two peoples, Jews and Gentiles, to whom he attests he will pronounce the truth which he states later. Next comes: *Thy truth in my mouth,* so that what he had grasped in thought he could truly utter on his lips. *In my mouth* is well phrased, for what comes out of the mouth quickly slips away, but what is in the mouth is hymned with lasting devotion.

3. *For thou hast said: Mercy shall be built up for ever: in the heavens thy truth shall be prepared.* This is the truth which the holy man had announced that he would proclaim. He was right to proclaim it with confidence, since the Lord had promised it unconditionally. He who follows the words of truth cannot be deceived. But let us examine the meaning of: *Mercy shall be built up for ever.* There are certain groups which cannot come into being without the prospect of destruction, such as worshippers of idols and those who pursue wicked practices. These men cannot be built up for good unless they have been brought down by their vices; as Jeremiah was told: *Behold, I have set thee to build up and to destroy.*[2] But the Lord's mercy is not destroyed, but ever flourishes and increases. Next comes: *In the heavens thy truth shall be prepared.* The heavens, as we have often said, denote the apostles, whose proclamations ensured that the Christian religion was instilled into the nations. The whole of this section up to the diapsalm is to be structured with the insertion of intervening colons, for it all follows on from: *Thou hast said.* This figure is called *apo koinou,* or in common,[3] when earlier words are attached to what comes later.

4. *I have made a covenant with my elect: I have sworn to David my servant.* He now recounts the Lord's words which he earlier mentioned as the Lord's utterance. Though the Lord seems to have made proclamation to all, this covenant He made only with the elect who chose to put faith in His gift, so that those who boasted physical

descent from the seed of David would not bind Him to such a promise. He added: *I have sworn to David my servant;* God's oath is seen to
lie in the certainty of His promise, for only He who has the power to
fulfil what He has pledged gives a just and definitive promise. Human
frailty is prevented from binding itself with promises on oath, because
it does not lie in its power to carry out what it pledges. So God most
fully swears when He promises all things in His own right. The word
itself makes the point; our expression, *iuravit* (he swore), is for *iure
oravit* (he uttered by right),[4] in other words, spoke justly.

5. *Thy seed will I prepare for ever: and I will build up thy abode for ever
and ever.* We have reached the promises made by the Father to His
servant David. The Lord Christ, who was to come by physical origin
from David's seed, was *prepared for ever* as King of kings and Lord of
lords. The phrase, *I will prepare,* has reference to His humanity, not
His divinity, by which He is consubstantial, almighty and coeternal
with the Father. Next comes: *And I will build up thy abode for ever and
ever.* This promise refers wholly to the Lord Saviour. At that time He
was promised the throne which was later to be installed in the hearts
of the saints; for every saint is the abode of the Lord, in which he sits
in the dignity of His majesty as though it were the most splendid
throne. As we read of the holy Spirit as well: *And there appeared to
them parted tongues, as it were of fire, and it sat upon every one of them,
and they were all filled with the holy Spirit.*[5]

6. *The heavens shall confess thy wonders, O Lord, and thy truth in the
church of the saints.* He passes to the second section, where he is to
sing of the mysteries of the divine power. The heavens, which are the
authentic preachers, will confess the mighty miracles with which the
Lord orders the world according to His wish; they tell how every
creature obeys His commands, and they proclaim that changes in creation do not occur by chance, as certain most foolish persons have
believed,[6] but that the world is kept in being by His power which
defies explanation. He added: *And thy truth in the church of the saints.*
He said that the wonders were to be proclaimed everywhere, but the
truth was to be confessed in the church of the saints. There we believe
that *the Word was made flesh;*[7] there the holy Trinity is accepted in
such a way that the one Lord is praised as God by the mouths of all.

7. *For who in the clouds will be comparable to the Lord, or who among
the sons of God will be like to God?* We have often said that the clouds

are those who preach God's word, and who rained divine grace on the nations through the holy Spirit; none the less they were subject to the law of sin. They were powerful in performing miracles, and awe-inspiring in their preaching; but which of them could be like Christ, even though He clothed Himself in the garb of the flesh? It is one thing to have power in one's own right, but another to gain fame vicariously. Likewise He could contain no evil *among the sons of God*, for He is the Son by nature, but they are saints through grace. He was without sin, but they are known to have been stripped of sin by Him. This verse is uttered in case anyone with sacrilegious effrontery considered Him only a man.

8. *God who is glorified in the assembly of the saints: great and terrible above all that are about him.* He explains his earlier statement: He who held all things in being could have none like Him. The Lord Christ who is proclaimed by the saints is called *great* because He is God, and *terrible* because of His wondrous power; *above all that are about him*, in other words, the saints whom he earlier called *sons of God*, and who are kept close to Him by the gift of His grace. But he is rightly acknowledged to rise high above them, for all are known to gain glory through Him. Realise that in running through the next verses up to the diapsalm he deploys the twelfth type of definition, which in Greek is called *kat' epainon*, and in Latin *per laudem*;[8] by different proclamations of praise the identity of this Lord is revealed.

9. *O Lord God of virtues, who is like to thee? Thou art mighty, O Lord, and the truth is round about thee.* Following upon his earlier words comes the most appropriate judgment: "*Who is like to thee?* for You are the Lord of virtues." Saints are enriched by virtues but do not dispense them; whereas You govern those things by which they excel through Your gift. The phrase, *who is like to thee?* is rightly repeated. You are powerful in Your own right; they get their power from You. They are enlightened by Your truth; but Your truth always resides inseparably with You.

10. *Thou rulest the power of the sea: and appeasest the motion of the waves thereof.* He now states the various counts on which he clearly shows the unique power of the Lord. *The power of the sea* is the worldly distinction which has often swiftly swollen up and risen against Christ's martyrs. But so that you should not think that such purposes take their rise from their own power, he further says: "You rule over

them, for You realign their fierce movements for the advantage of the saints." As Christ Himself says in the gospel: *You would have no power over me unless it were given to you from above.*[9] Because He had said: *Thou rulest,* there follows a worthy demonstration of this, for He appeases the waves of that sea. Observe that he says *appeases* and not "removes," for if He were to remove wholly the movement[10] of those waves, martyrs would not obtain a crown. But if you prefer to interpret in a historical sense the idea that the Lord appeases the waves of the sea, a noted passage of the gospel attests this; for when His disciples were in danger, He ordered the wind to fall and the sea to be calm.[11]

11. *Thou hast humbled the proud one, as one that is wounded: and with the strength of thy arm thou hast scattered thy enemies.* There are some who are humbled to their destruction, and others who bend low to seek grace. So that you would interpret the phrase here in the pejorative sense, he wrote: *The proud one, as one that is wounded.* He means the devil, who raised himself higher than his potential and was humbled by his vice to a condition foreign to his nature, afflicted in mind rather than in body. Thus that most wicked creature fell from heaven as one wounded into the impenetrable density of the lower air.[12] As the Lord says in the gospel: *I saw Satan like lightning falling from heaven.*[13] *Enemies* refers to the unfaithful Jews, who have been scattered through countless nations by the power of the Lord Christ; divine authority attests that He is the Arm of the Father, as we have often stated.

12. *Thine are the heavens and thine is the earth: the world and the fullness thereof thou hast founded.* Because he had earlier spoken of twin miracles,[14] he now confirms them by the proof advanced in this short verse. The reason why He triumphed over the proud devil in heaven, and on earth over the faithless Jews, was precisely because heaven and earth belong to Him. Why should the devil or the Jew wax proud in regions not belonging to them, when both heaven and earth were seen to have their Creator? Next comes: *The world and the fullness thereof thou hast founded.* This rebuke is still addressed to the Jews, so the sense is: "Why did those foolish men seek to savage You in this world when You, O Christ, are its Founder?" With boundless madness they seem to aspire to what is clearly beyond human powers. *The world* refers to the extent of the entire universe, *the fullness thereof*

to all creatures known to exist in it. By such enumerations he briefly encompassed all things.

13. *The north and the sea thou hast created: Thabor and Hermon shall rejoice in thy name.* The north continues the reference to the devil, who said: *I will place my seat in the north, I will be like the most High.*[15] We appropriately interpret the sea as the puffed up, wicked powers of the men of this world, which are with sacrilegious purposes mounted against the Lord's commandments, not for their own profit but for their heavy fall. He rebukes both, saying that they should not place confidence in themselves when it is certain that they were created by their Lord. Creatures ought not to wax arrogant against their Creator, for they received the possibility of life from Him. Next comes: *Thabor and Hermon shall rejoice in thy name.* Thabor and Hermon are mountains in the province of Syria; their names contain great mysteries. Thabor means "the coming light," referring especially to the coming of the Lord Saviour, of whom it was said: *He was the true light which enlightens all men coming into this world.*[16] Hermon means "a curse on him," that is, upon the devil, who endured this from Christians after the Lord's coming.[17] It was appropriate that the devil of darkness should be overcome by the presence of light. So these mountains will rejoice in the name of the Lord, just as elsewhere His faithful say: *Not to us, O Lord, not to us, but to thy name give glory.*[18]

14. *Thy arm is with might. Let thy hand be strengthened, and thy right hand exalted.* We often read that the arm indicates human power; as the prophet says: *Cursed be the man who maketh flesh his arm, and whose heart departeth from the Lord.*[19] But the only power man can have is that granted him for the moment. But the passage here, *thy arm is with might,* is intended to denote the Lord Saviour, and the sense is that all power is His. His power never weakens, for He continually does all that He wishes in heaven and on earth. He added: *Let thy hand be strengthened, and thy right hand exalted. Hand* and *right hand,* if we ponder them carefully, are very different. He is asking that His hand, in other words, His action, may be strengthened against the proud, so that when they are humbled by afflictions they may be led most swiftly to zeal for conversion. In *let thy right hand be exalted,* perhaps the sense is: "Let the number of the predestined be glorified, for they will be set at Thy right hand."

15. *Justice and judgment are the preparation of thy throne: mercy and*

truth shall go before thy face. The Lord's throne is ever eternal, but it will appear to us to have been prepared when we see Him administering justice, for at that time His holy equity will become clear, and He will be revealed as the true Judge; then the mysteries of the angels will be seen. The preparation of His throne comes to pass when these things are beheld by men at the general resurrection. Next comes: *Mercy and truth shall go before thy face.* This is quite appropriately applied to the era of this world. Mercy and truth will go before His face, that is, before the declaration of the Judgment. *Mercy,* because He spares the converted; *truth,* because He renders what He promised. So both present and future eras are clearly indicated by these words.

16. *Blessed is the people that realises jubilation. They shall walk, O Lord, in the light of thy countenance.* The most holy man Ethan announced by the heading has been seen to proclaim God's mysteries; now he embarks on varied praises of the blessed people by what the rhetoricians call the demonstrative type of speech.[20] He exclaims: *Blessed is the people that realises jubilation,* in other words, the people who are known to have placed their boundless joy not in their own powers but in God's strength. Jubilation is an abundant and indescribable joy of mind. To ponder this in the hidden depths of the heart is characteristic of a blessed people, and we successfully attain it if we confess its Author with a pure mind. The statement is also a most profitable one if it is understood in this additional sense: that people is blessed who not only sing the praises of God with their lips, but also understand them with the mind's light. This understanding depends on examining holy Scripture according to Catholic guidelines; one must grasp the words of our forbears according to the teaching which brings salvation, and align them all with the devotion of upright faith, rather than consent to the debased view of heretics. He added the reward which attends such men: *They shall walk, O Lord, in the light of thy countenance.* That blessed people, which he says realises jubilation, walks in the light of His countenance when they continue unceasingly to contemplate the holy Trinity. *Walks* means "lives," because this period of our lives is spent in a kind of journeying to and fro.

17. *And in thy name they shall rejoice all the day: and in thy justice they shall be exalted.* He still continues with the reward granted to the people who realise jubilation; for when he says to the Lord: *They shall*

rejoice in thy name, he is forbidding them to exult in personal pride, so that mortal men may not be deceived and set their joy where all things are transient. Next comes: *All the day,* which indicates the span of our whole life, for we must never abandon the source of enduring and abundant joys. Once they have rejoiced in this way, the result is that they are exalted in the Lord's justice, when at the resurrection they are placed at His right hand. So this is the nature of the gifts which he says are prepared for those who realise jubilation. So let us abandon that harmful neglect, and rouse ourselves to the blessed pursuit of understanding, so that both in this world through the generosity of the Lord we may engage in sweet feasting from it, and in the next we may enjoy the gift of enduring joy.

18. *For thou art the glory of their strength: and in thy good pleasure shall our horn be exalted.* It is fitting that their horn, that is, their power, shall be exalted, for they have set their strength and glory in the Lord Saviour, of whom the Father says: *This is my beloved Son, in whom I am well pleased;*[21] for when all that is bestowed is attributed to Him, he becomes our praise and our perfect joy. Observe that here *horn* is used in a good sense, but elsewhere in a bad sense, as in: *Save my lowliness from the horns of the unicorns;*[22] the double sense is reasonable, for the conferment of power makes for both good and evil results.

19. *For the taking up is of the Lord: and of our king the holy one of Israel.* He has explained why the horn of those who believe in Him is exalted: it is because the taking up, in other words the glory of the incarnation, is shown to have been fulfilled by the holy One of Israel. All who have hope in that incarnation are raised aloft from the depths of sin, when we are placed into eternal joys through the support of His mercy. See, then, the explanation of the gifts promised to the people which realises jubilation. The remarkable praise of the demonstrative genre is now completed, so that in each individual instance His power is related, and we may the more clearly demonstrate who the Lord is. Now let us ascertain something of the third section.

20. *Then thou spokest in appearance to thy sons, and saidst: I have laid help on one that is mighty, and have exalted one chosen out of my people.* So far Ethan has spoken in his own person. Now he passes to the third section and proclaims the words of the Father spoken about the Lord

Saviour, so that the earlier praise might be taught without hesitation now that the Father's authority has also maintained it. We have often remarked that the saints are called God's sons not by nature but by grace; so to these sons, prophets and preachers of the Word, the Lord spoke in appearance when He made them behold the tidings which they told. So this phrase reveals that the prophets did not speak their words in ignorance; they based themselves on the certainty of contemplation, and beheld in mind what they proclaimed with their tongues. This is why prophets got the further name of seers. Next comes: *I have laid help on one that is mighty.* Let us investigate the intended sense of help laid on one that is mighty, for the one who seeks help is not mighty, and he who is mighty does not need help. But this phrase we can appropriately interpret as referring to the general body of the Church, which as we all know is mighty and specially chosen. He is saying that the Lord Christ has been given to her as a help; as Christ says of himself in Psalm 2: *But I am appointed king by him over Sion his holy mountain.*[23] Or at any rate if we wish to interpret the words: *I have laid help on one that is mighty* as referring to the Lord Christ Himself, we must understand the statement as if he were saying: "The Father gave witness to the mighty, that is, to the Son; as when in the gospel these words were spoken to Him as witness: *I have both glorified your name, and will glorify it again.*"[24] This then is perhaps the meaning of help laid on one that is mighty. He added: *I have exalted one chosen from my people.* The prophet Isaiah relates that the Lord Christ was called the chosen One when he says: *Behold my servant, I will uphold him: my chosen one, my soul delighteth in him.*[25] He was exalted, as Paul says: *For which cause God also hath exalted him, and hath given him a name which is above all names, that in the name of Jesus every knee should bow, of those that are in heaven, on earth, and under the earth.*[26] *Out of my people* refers to the Jewish nation, from which it is established that the Lord Christ was born.

21. *I have found David my servant: with my holy oil I have anointed him.* The words, *I have found David,* clearly denote Christ Jesus whom he earlier called mighty. It is established that the name David is often ascribed to Him, for it means "strong of hand" and "longed for."[27] The ascription here is especially likely since the words that follow cannot in any way be apt for David or for any just man other

than the Lord Saviour. Of Christ it has already been said in another psalm: *Therefore God, my God, hath anointed thee with the oil of gladness above thy fellows.*[28]

22. *For my hand shall help him: and my arm shall strengthen him.* These words apply to Him in His role as servant which He adopted in the virgin's womb. God's hand helped Him in His sufferings, and the Lord's might strengthened Him, to enable the devoted Redeemer to endure the passion which was put before Him for the salvation of the world. This figure is called *characterismos,* and in Latin *informatio* or *descriptio,*[29] when we present a picture of an absent person by certain indications which bring him before us. This figure in fact embraces the whole of this section with beautiful variety.

23. *The enemy shall have no advantage over him, and the son of iniquity shall not harm him.* How could this verse at any rate refer to David, who endured enemies stronger than himself, and who sinned at the devil's prompting? This must be taken as a true reference to Christ; for though the devil, the wanton foe of the human race, raged against Him, and though Judas the son of iniquity presumed to harm Him, neither of them found any sin which they could justly lay against Him. As Christ Himself says: *Behold, the prince of this world shall come, and shall not find anything in me.*[30]

24. *And I will cut down his enemies before his face: and them that hate him I will put to flight.* Christ's enemies are cut down before His face when through His presence they are sundered from their sins and faults by the benefit of conversion; for when His countenance deigns to gaze on sinners, they are cut away from their debased ways and cannot lend assent to their shady sins any longer, for through the Lord's pity they attain the presence of the true light. They that hate Him are put to flight when they abandon their wicked life and begin hastily to seek cures for it; for mindful of their sin they shun their evil deeds and with the most salutary haste align themselves with the Lord's kindnesses. So it is a blessed flight from sins to have sought the refuge of the Lord. As has already been said in another psalm: *Thou art my refuge from the trouble which hath encompassed me.*[31]

25. *And my truth and my mercy shall be with him: and in my name shall his horn be exalted.* The Father says of the Son: *My truth and my mercy are with him,* so that we may realise that nothing is possessed separately, but that the virtues possessed by the Father are owned also

by the Son. As Christ Himself witnesses: *All that the Father has is mine, and all that is mine is the Father's.*[32] His *truth* refers to the Judgment, and with it He will judge the world; His *mercy,* to the devotion by which He forgives sins and imparts with gratuitous generosity all that He grants us. Next comes: *And in my name shall his horn be exalted. Horn* here indicates the most invincible power, of which Christ Himself says in the gospel: *All power has been given to me in heaven and on earth.*[33]

26. *And I will set his hand in the sea: and his right hand in the rivers.* The sea indicates all nations, over which our Saviour received the glory of dominion when with devoted minds they humbly gave credence to His name. *In the rivers* perhaps denotes the running water by which people born for new life are won for the Lord Saviour. Alternatively by rivers he means the river Jordan, in which the Lord made holy the example of His own baptism. In the same way we speak of "heavens" for heaven and "lands" for land and "seas" for sea; if you wish to look for further examples, we have Athens, Thebes, Mycenae and the like.[34]

27. *He shall cry out to me: Thou art my father, my God, and the support of my salvation.* 28. *And I will make him my first-born, high above the kings of the earth.* In these two verses the wickedness of the Jews is wholly vanquished. What could be clearer or plainer than that we should believe that it is the Son who cries to the Father, and in turn to believe that it is the Father who addresses the Son? Though the two terms are related to each other, and it is sufficient that one be mentioned so that the power of both can be grasped, he sought to exclude all obstacles of ambiguity, and set down and affirmed both. Yet even today the mad wilfulness of the Jews continues its errant ways, though the cause of the error has been removed. This is the fourteenth type of definition, which the Greeks call *kata to pros ti* and the Latins *ad aliquid,*[35] when one term is expressed in such a way that it seems possible for another to be understood from it. Next comes: *And I will make him my first-born, high above the kings of the earth.* We must examine why he has spoken of the first-born, as though the Father has begotten a Son in substance so that a second may follow. But it is clear that this manner of speaking is peculiar to divine Scripture, as in the gospel-passage concerning Joseph and Mary, where it says: *And he knew her not till she brought forth her first-born son.*[36] It surely does not

follow that Mary ever a virgin is believed to have brought forth a second son after the Lord Jesus Christ? The word *first-born* is in fact appropriate, though He alone is shown to have been born of the substance of the Father; for He Himself says: *I am Alpha and Omega, the beginning and the end, the first and the last, the leader and the source of David,*[37] so that there is no justification for challenging *first-born,* since it is clear that He is both beginning and end. *I will make him* means "I will appoint him"; as He says in Psalm 2: *But I am appointed king by him.*[38] The expression, *high above the kings of the earth,* is similar to the words of Psalm 71: *And all the kings of the earth shall adore him.*[39]

29. *I will keep my mercy for him for ever: and my covenant faithful to him.* These words refer to Him in His role as servant, for He undoubtedly wielded the mercy of the Father in eternal glory, for enduring power was given to Him in heaven and on earth. The covenant was faithful to Him when all that the prophets foretold about Him was fulfilled with truth unimpaired.

30. *And I will make his seed to endure for evermore: and his throne as the day of heaven. For evermore* denotes eternity. The seed of David is Christ the Lord, who is set in eternal glory, and reigns with the Father and Spirit for ever and ever. *His throne* is the power of the Judgment to come, which must be conducted with such integrity that it gleams with heavenly light before all the saints. We must realise that days here on earth, which succeed each other in their round, are quite different from that future day which is never-ending with enduring light. Of that day Psalm 83 says: *For better is one day in thy courts above thousands.*[40] So it is rightly called *the day of heaven,* for it can know no darkness of night through the interposing of the earth.

31. *If his children forsake my law, and walk not in my judgments.* 32. *If they profane my justices, and keep not my commandments.* He utters these two verses about the Christian people, who are truly called sons of the Bridegroom, for they are reborn of mother Church by water and the holy Spirit. If they forsake the Lord's law and walk not in His judgments, if they profane His justices and keep not His commandments, the following verses threaten that appropriate vengeance is the outcome.

33. *I will visit their iniquities with a rod: and their sins with stripes.* He passes to the sentence threatened by the previous words. He visits with a rod when He imposes stern punishment. In the same spirit Paul

when writing to the Corinthians says: *What will you? Shall I come to you with a rod? Or in charity and in the spirit of meekness?*[41] He also visits us with stripes, when He takes lighter vengeance on us; for a rod strikes us in one way, but whips flick us in another. Clearly each of these befalls Christian people according to the nature of their sin, enabling them to make progress towards salvation. As Solomon puts it: *For whom the Lord loves, he chastises; he whips every son whom he accepts.*[42] See now what follows.

34. *But my mercy I will not take away from him: nor will I do harm to my truth.* Whereas He spoke earlier of the members, He now returns to the Head. The Father says that He does not take away His mercy from Christ, but bestows it in all its fullness. As Paul says: *In him dwelleth all the fullness of divinity corporeally,*[43] that is, substantially and clearly. An alternative explanation is that the fullness of divinity is known to reside in the Lord's person; hence the comment in Psalm 30.[44] Next comes: *Nor will I do harm to my truth.* Earlier in the psalm the Father had promised: *For my hand will help him: and my arm shall strengthen him.*[45] How could He harm Him when He was seen to make such promises to Him? Note the words: *I will not do harm to my truth;* even if enemies were permitted to do harm, the Son was unharmed in the Father's truth, for His passion glorified and brought to fulfilment the whole world.

35. *Neither will I profane my covenant: and the words that proceed from my lips I will not make void.* This is repetition of His earlier words: *Nor will I do harm to my truth,* for it is clear that everything was fulfilled according to the dispensation of the truth. He did not profane His covenant by lying, but did what was honourable by trust-worthiness in deeds, for all that came forth from His lips (that is, all that He proclaimed through the holy prophets) was not made null and void by any falsehood. It was fitting for the prophets to be called the Lord's lips, for He deigned to speak through them.

36. *I have sworn once about my holy one: to David I will not lie.* It is customary for men often to swear so that a person may believe them; God swears only once, for no variation of time affects Him. We have said that His swearing consists of promising what is to come, for since none is stronger than He, by whose awful person could He bind Himself? He also says: *About my holy one,* that is, Christ, who said: *Preserve my soul, for I am holy.*[46] He added: *To David I will not lie,* in

which the Latin *si* bears the negative sense found also in common usage.[47]

37. *His seed shall continue for ever: and his throne as the sun in my sight.* The seed of Christ consists of all who put faith in Him with believing minds; in them the future kingdom was sown, so that the harvest to come may make this manifest. As Christ likewise says in Psalm 21: *My seed shall serve him.*[48] So the saints will endure for ever, continuing in a life both splendid and blessed; hence we do not properly use the expression *continue* with reference to those rejected from the Lord's kingdom. God's throne is to be interpreted here as the faithful soul in which He truly dwells, once he has filled it with the light of His majesty, for as Scripture has it: *The soul of the just man is the seat of wisdom.*[49] He added: *As the sun in my sight;* understand "shall be the soul of the just man," which we have said is the seat of the Lord Saviour. By the phrase, *as the sun,* He makes a comparison with things visible; if brightness in a created thing is great, how much better is the light which refers to the Creator.

38. *And as the moon perfect for ever, and a faithful witness in heaven.* He earlier spoke of the sun, which we said referred to the soul of the just man. Now He speaks of the moon, which is here appropriately an image of the human body, for it waxes and wanes at different ages. But He added *perfect* so that you would not imagine that there was now any mortal element in the spiritual body, but instead concentrate on its boundless eternity alone. Our bodies will be eternally filled with brightness, like a full moon; the moon, the frame of our bodies, will be the faithful witness, for in this and in nothing else God's promises are fulfilled. Observe, however, the words, *in heaven,* that is, in the holy man; those whose souls gleam with divine brightness will have bodies resplendent. As Solomon says: *The just shall shine, and shall run to and fro like sparks among the reeds.*[50] The moon is in fact often compared with the Church.[51]

39. *But thou hast rejected and despised and put off thy Christ.* Up to now Christ has been praised in the Father's words. Here Ethan passes to the fourth section, in which he utters in his own person words apparently contradictory to what goes before. Earlier the Father maintains that Christ will be avenged over His enemies, and He confirms this with a promise on oath; but here Christ is said to be spurned and betrayed. This must be understood in a double sense. We are to

see the earlier part as referring to the glory of the resurrection; or better, as father Augustine elicited,[52] we are to say that the earlier section refers to the Lord Saviour and this later part to the servant David, who was known to have been oppressed by many disasters; for the name Christ, which comes from being anointed, is certainly appropriate to both. *Thou hast rejected* refers, I think, to the comparison which the prophet Nathan uttered to David, by which David was ousted from his kingly dignity and compared to an unjust man who devoured a poor man's sheep. So the word *rejected* was well-chosen, for he was clearly condemned by his own judgment.[53] The sense of *despised* is "made contemptible," referring to when he was dislodged from the kingship, and in fleeing from his son Absalom walked with bare feet and endured the rebukes of the son of Jemini delivered with the most caustic insults.[54] *Thou hast put off* does not refer to that expression of pardon when the prophet once answered him *The Lord also hath taken away thy sin;*[55] he was put off in the course of his afflictions, when he was refurbishing his invaded kingdom. *Thy Christ* means "the anointed one," for at that time the leaders of the Jews were anointed on entering the kingship.

40. *Thou hast diverted the covenant of thy servant: thou hast profaned his holiness on the earth.* This is a reference to the race of the Jews, which continues to the end of the section. He uses a phrase characteristic of human utterance, *Thou hast diverted,* in other words, "Thou hast directed elsewhere"; what had been promised to the Jews passed to the benefit of none other but the Gentiles. No priest, no temple (for we know that it was destroyed) remained to the Jews, whereas the Christians obtained everything to the fullest degree. So the words, *thou hast diverted,* were appropriate, for what was taken from the unfaithful is known to have been granted to the faithful. *The covenant of thy servant* does not mean that David bequeathed it, but rather that the distinction had been promised him through the bequest of the Lord's birth. Next comes: *Thou hast profaned his holiness on the earth.* Profane means "irreligious," or that driven far from the shrine (*porro a fano*),[56] in other words, far from the reverence of the temple; for the sacrifice of cattle and observance of the sabbath, which were earlier carried out as a foreshadowing, were displaced upon the arrival of the truth. *On the earth* we must interpret as "throughout the whole world," where the Catholic Church is established.

41. *Thou hast broken down all his enclosures: thou hast turned his defences into fear.* An enclosure is what fortifies for defensive purposes an area prepared for some practical use; it is not built with a variety of materials, but solely by fitting stones together like a wall. This is the parallel which he uses to describe God's uncompounded and invincible protection, which had to be dismantled before the Jewish nation could be ravaged by enemy attack. The phrase, *thou hast turned his defences into fear,* is most impressive; through the action of their sins they came to fear the Lord Himself, though they were accustomed to be shielded by His protection. Observe that throughout these three verses different verbs emerge with similar sounds: *repulisti, sprevisti, distulisti, avertisti, profanasti, destruxisti, posuisti.* This figure is called *homoioteleuton,*[57] by which several words end with similar letters.

42. *All that pass by the way have robbed him: he is become a reproach to his neighbours.* We know that the Jewish kingdom was plundered of both its faith and its wealth. Those who passed through it removed its powers, and with the greatest force transferred to themselves the resources of its religion; they had the greater belief, though the Lord had not visited them in person to advise them. As He Himself said: *A people which I knew not hath served me: at the hearing of the ear they have obeyed me.*[58] So the Jews rightly became a reproach to their neighbours, for they refused to believe in the Lord of glory.

43. *Thou hast exalted the right hand of his enemies: thou hast made all his enemies to rejoice.* These events undoubtedly occurred when the Jews were consigned to their enemies, and endured plundering and slaughter on a huge scale. It is then that enemies rejoice, when one opposed to their wishes is humiliated.

44. *Thou hast turned away the help of his sword: and hast not assisted him in battle.* It was just that the sword did not afford him help, for he forfeited the power of the Godhead. Though the steel seems to offer a human means of defence, it does not prevail unless the right hand of heaven lends him strength. As a previous psalm has already stated; *for I will not trust in my bow: neither shall my sword save me.*[59] So the result was that the armed nation was disarmed, and when the few defeated the many, the many were unable to resist the few.

45. *Thou hast sundered him from cleansing, and cast his throne down to the ground.* The Godhead often cleanses those whom He whips, so

that He may welcome the person when cleansed whom He rejected when befouled with sins. Those whom He sundered or removed from cleansing He now determined to condemn. So the psalmist here indicates the Jews, who through mental obduracy chose to reject Christ. Their throne too was cast down on the ground, when after despising the Saviour Lord and King they no longer deserved to obtain a leader from their own race. For throne here stands for kingdom, which is rightly said to be cast on the ground, for the people were divided, shattered and dispersed in small sections through the whole world.

46. *Thou hast shortened the days of his times: thou hast covered him with confusion.* The existence of the Jewish kingdom which we mentioned, and which was promised eternity if they served the Lord, was indeed shortened by days of hardship, for they did not deserve to obtain the promise given to Abraham. That kingdom was deservedly restricted to a brief life, though they vainly promised themselves a long chain of years. He further added: *Thou hast covered him with confusion,* for they bear the foulness of their unbelief on their faces; even today, mingled in loathsome repugnance among all nations, they carry the reproach on their countenances. This is what Ethan with all his strength recounted with marvellous variation; but throughout he acknowledged that the Lord did not lie, for what He promised to David, His anointed, He bestowed on all Christians. The Jews have no just cause for complaint, for they chose to isolate themselves from that most genuine promise.

47. *How long, O Lord, wilt thou turn away unto the end? Does thy anger burn like fire?* Ethan passes to the fifth section, in which with a few words he asks the Lord to show pity and kindness to the Jewish people, for no man can deliver his own soul from hell. *Unto the end* we must here interpret as the end of the world, when as we have repeatedly said we await the conversion of Jews in boundless numbers. On this account Paul says: *Blindness in part has happened in Israel until the fullness of the Gentiles should come in. And so all Israel should be saved.*[60] So Ethan asks that He should not turn away until the very end, the time at which the faithful confession of the Jews is awaited. He added: *Does thy anger burn like fire?* We are moderately angry when we address a person with verbal rebukes, but we burn with anger when we plan vengeance. He has appended the words *like fire,* for fire consumes all it meets.

48. *Remember, O Lord, what my substance is: for thou hast not made the sons of men in vain.* Ethan, strengthened with constancy of mind, begs the Lord to deign to free by the glory of His coming this flesh of ours which is subject to sins, for it was not created so that He might allow it to perish like some useless thing; for in His recollection of our substance He both delivered the sons of men from death and gave them hope of great blessedness.

49. *Who is the man that liveth and shall not see death? Or who shall deliver his soul from the hand of hell? Who is?* must be read with a note of interrogation. This figure is called *erotema* or interrogation;[61] and we must supply the answer, "no-one." All men, whether just or sinners, will see death, which was first imposed on men by the law of sin. As Paul says: *Wherefore as by one man sin entered into this world, and by sin death, so death passed upon all men, in whom all have sinned.*[62] He mentions this here so that the human condition may deserve to obtain the Creator's pity in its calamities. So those who with evil presumption refuse to believe in original sin are fettered by a fate more wretched the more they proclaim they are free from this condition.[63] Next comes: *Or who shall deliver his soul from the hand of hell?* Here too we must understand "no-one." *From the hand* means "from the power" of hell. Since death comes to all men, it is inevitable that they do not remove their souls from the power of hell save through Him who delivered us from the dominion of the devil, and by dying subjugated death.

50. *Lord, where are thy ancient mercies, according to what thou didst swear to David in thy truth?* He passes to the sixth section, in which he begs the Lord to help a nation afflicted and frail in its human condition, and to fulfil the promises which he knew He had made to David. *Where are they?* is not an expression of resentment, but a query suggesting that the Lord is procrastinating. How could he be expressing doubts in Him when he says to Him: *In thy truth?* He is asking that the Lord speedily bring to pass what he knew that He would do. The ancient mercies of which he speaks are those which he recalled the Lord having rendered to the patriarch Abraham; he would not have called them ancient if he had not known that they came to pass before David's day.

51. *Be mindful of the reproach of thy servants, which I have held in my bosom, of many nations.* The order of words is as follows: "Be mindful

of the reproach of thy servants, comprising many nations, which I have held in my bosom." *Be mindful* is addressed to Him for whom things past and future are all present; but it is a mode of utterance frequent in humans to adjudge the Lord forgetful when He postpones His giving. The servants of God experienced reproach when the Gentiles were seduced by love of idols; for the title Christians was regarded as a crime, and the pagans judged worthy of persecution those who they knew were enthusiasts of the new cult. This reproach lay in the bosom (that is, in the secret feelings) of Christians because they were afraid to speak openly of what was known to be the cause of their destruction.

52. *The reproach which thy enemies have uttered, O Lord; with which they have reproached the change wrought by Christ.* He is explaining his earlier words, *the reproach of many nations.* We must interpret *they have reproached* as an accusation; in other words, they uttered as a charge what they ought to have believed and proclaimed. So that you would not be uncertain who uttered these words, he added: *Thy enemies, O Lord.* These are the worshippers of idols, who hastened by every means to oppose the sacred preachings. He repeats: *With which they have reproached* to intensify their sin; for they accused the faithful of conversion to Christ, whereas they ought to have regarded that conversion with the greatest reverence. It is a *change wrought by Christ* because He has summoned the old man to the new grace of rebirth, and has led him out of the darkness of sins into the light of true faith. He has also prepared for mortal man the joys of enduring life; and other such things as our Lord Christ deigned to bestow on sinners. This change wrought by Christ evaded the obstinate of heart, and adopted the faithful through the gift of His devotion.

53. *Blessed be the Lord for evermore. So be it, so be it.* After that most blessed and most holy change, it was right that praise of the Lord be appended, for He is known to have bestowed it on undeserving men. A splendid phrase was coined to counter the transient curses of the Gentiles: *Blessed be the Lord for ever more.* Their words are short-lasting, whereas praise of the Lord endures for ever, for He can bestow things such as are not confined by any end. Next comes: *So be it, so be it,* so that none might have doubts about those great promises when this repeated affirmation followed, and was appended as a postscript to the sacred commands of this good leader. We must regard this

verse as relevant to the praise of the psalms in general, rather than, as some have thought,[64] to some section of the book.

Conclusion Drawn From the Psalm

This Ethan is truly strong, not in bodily health but in constancy and strength of mind, for as a most faithful steward of the human race he has explained to us that inscribed instruction for life taken from the holy altars. Now let us pray that we may store in our minds what we take in with our ears. Our victory is achieved if after such sacred rites we dispute not against outsiders but against our own vices, and if we spurn earthly things and unhesitatingly seek the things of heaven. The meaning of the name Ethan warns faithful and patient Christians not to be broken by any adversity; as Paul, the greatest model of this virtue, says of himself: *In many more labours, in prisons more frequently, in stripes above measure, in deaths often. Of the Jews five times did I receive forty stripes save one. Thrice was I beaten with rods, once I was stoned; thrice I suffered shipwreck; a night and a day I was in the depth of the sea.*[65] There follow the other sufferings which crowded in on this second Ethan in fact rather than in word. To you, blessed apostle, is assigned this exchange of glory; just as you strengthened your holy preaching by the witness of the psalms, so may the psalms be explained by reference to your actions.

COMMENTARY ON PSALM 89

1. *A prayer of Moses, man of God.* As we have often remarked, expressions such as this are undoubtedly inserted in the headings because their meaning is seen to cast light on the text of the psalms. First is placed: *A prayer,* by which the Lord's anger is deferred, pardon gained, punishment avoided, and generous rewards obtained when he speaks to the Lord, gossips with the Judge, and pictures before his eyes Him whom he cannot see. By his prayer he placates Him whom he eagerly exalts by his actions. Prayer in some sense affords cloistered converse with the Lord, and offers an opportunity for intima-

tions; the sinner is granted access to the Judge's inner sanctum, and the only person rejected is he who is found lukewarm in his prayer. He seeks what he desires, he acquires more than he deserves. He approaches his prayer with melancholy, but departs from it in gladness. Prayer which is holy saves the committed and makes them blessed; it also welcomes the wicked. There are countless examples of this blessing, but it must suffice that the Lord Himself in giving us precepts for living deigned to pray. So it is appropriate that *a prayer* was placed before this noble and great man, who often softened the angry Lord with a marvellous mode of entreaty for us to follow. This is the third psalm which we acknowledge as containing *A prayer* in its heading.[1] As for *Moses*, that most famous man through whom the Lord gave the Law to the Israelites, it is clear that he was a minister of the Old Testament and a prophet of the New. Christ says of him in the gospel: *For if you did believe Moses, you would believe me too, for he wrote of me*.[2] Because this psalm joins both Testaments together, it was right that there was attached to it the name which by its force revealed the two mysteries, for Moses means "taken up,"[3] because he was lifted from the waters by the Pharaoh's daughter. The name denotes the Israelites through the connection with the Red Sea, and has reference to the Christian people through the grace of baptism. The words *man of God* are also appended so that no other might perhaps occur to you than the Moses honoured by converse with God and meriting the title of leader, so that he then acquired the name not of slave of God, but of man of God; for we use the word *man* not of servants but of free men and friends. As we read in Deuteronomy: *The Lord spoke to Moses face to face, as a man is wont to speak to his friend*.[4]

Division of the Psalm

Moses, a most holy man remarkable for his achievements, and venerable because of his converse with God, begins in the first section with praise of the Judge, briefly recounting His kindnesses and His power. Next he asks for support for our weakness, which he demonstrates with many instances. Thirdly, he begs that the coming of the Lord Saviour may become known more quickly, for he knew that it would afford benefits for the human race.

Explanation of the Psalm

Lord, thou hast become our refuge in our beginning and in our descent. The revered Moses, as the type of holy Church which he foreshadowed, gives thanks to the Lord by pouring out a prayer, saying that in the salt sea of this world He has become his notable refuge. To begin with, because he was cast out among the sons of the Jews to die; next he endured the wicked struggles with the king of the Egyptians; thirdly, the unprecedented miracles at the Red Sea; and finally the fearsome obstinacy of his grumbling people. But in all this the Lord became his refuge, for it is known that he was delivered from all dangers. So it is because he recalls his dangers that he is seen to have begun as he does. But to ensure that we interpret this as referring not to one man but to the universal Church, he spoke of *our* and not "my" refuge, for the Lord is ever the safest refuge for the whole Church storm-tossed in this world. Observe what follows: *In our beginning and in our descent. In our beginning* denotes ever since the human race began; *in our descent* means the period up to the end of the world, as the progeny of the human race is renewed and continues through each age; the phrase is equivalent to "always."

2. *Before the mountains were made, and the world was formed: from the beginning to the end of time thou art.* In the first verse he had stated: *Thou hast become our refuge,* and so that you would not assume that the Godhead was transient, he next described His eternal nature. So that we may appreciate this continuing existence most clearly, we must regard *mountains* here not as anything on earth but as the outstanding Powers of heaven, for the next words bring in the whole earth. With this interpretation the address to the Lord is truly fitting, for *thou art* means: "Before You fashioned the things of heaven and earth." *Before* here has no starting-point; it is declared to be unmeasured and beyond our understanding, for it is recognised to be earlier by those very beginnings. Next comes: *From the beginning to the end of time thou art;* this appears to suggest that before the beginning or after the end of time God is not. But here we must interpret *a saeculo et usque in saeculum* as "eternity," for the Greek manuscripts have "eternity," which our fathers have rendered *From the beginning to the end of time.* The words, *thou art,* are apposite to God for He has no past nor future. So Moses was told: *Thou wilt say to the children of Israel, I am*

who am, and he who is has sent me to you.[5] So the holy man did well to write: *Thou art,* because he remembered that he had heard these words from Him. Undoubtedly they refer to Father, Son and holy Spirit, for the essence of the undivided Trinity, which is truly and properly from That which is, always possesses as present the things which among ourselves we call past or future.

3. *Turn not man away to lowliness: and thou hast said, Be converted, O ye sons of men.* He passes to the second section, in which the holy man seeks from the Lord those things which he knew the Lord had commanded. He says: *Turn not man away to lowliness,* that is, "do not abandon him to the longing and ambition of this world." Here we must interpret *lowliness* as the earthly longing which in God's eyes is cheap and contemptible; it is not the glorious humility by which we confess our sins to the Lord. The holy man accordingly prays for what the Godhead commands, that men's wishes may not be cast down from the heights of heaven and be allowed to love the most lowly things of the world, those lowly things which grow foul through their own tawdriness. Next comes: *And thou hast said, Be converted, O ye sons of men.* Here *and* stands for "because" so that the sentence is unified and reveals to us the cohesive sense. You observe how praiseworthy the earlier request is, for because the Lord has ordered the sons of men to be converted, they are to be saved by reason of His pity. Who else can free us from the ambition of the world save Him who taught the faithful to seek the kingdom of heaven? So he rightly begs that men should not be abandoned when they fall on the slippery slopes, for they have been told: *Be converted.*

4. *For a thousand years before thy eyes are as yesterday which is past, and as a watch in the night. . . .* The reason is given why worldly ambition must be avoided: a thousand years in God's sight are not merely few but are considered to have wholly passed like yesterday. This figure is called *tapeinōsis* or depreciation,[6] when the size of something is reduced to insignificance; that extended chain of generations is compared not even to a single day in the present, but to a day past. He used the finite number thousand to express an indefinite number, perhaps indicating the age of those men of old who lived to an extreme age. Next comes: *And as a watch in the night.* To make you realise that the thousand years mentioned earlier were circumscribed, they are now compared not to a single day past but to a brief period of night.

The night guard which regularly imposes wakefulness on men is reckoned in periods of three hours' watches; since groups of sentinels relieve each other, the period of duty is not long nor wearisome. The comparison of human life to watches in the night was splendid, for all is done in darkness and fear, because men's minds are encompassed and assailed by sins of the flesh. We must place a comma after this verse, for the statement is now extended.

5. . . . *Which are accounted as nothing, so shall their years be: let him fade like grass in the morning.* These words go with the previous verse. Just like the two earlier expressions, *yesterday* and *a watch in the night,* which are reckoned as nothing, he added: *So shall their years be;* so as he said a little earlier, we must pray: *Turn not man away to lowliness.* He added: *Let him fade like grass in the morning.* Those fleeting and transient events are still being compared with human life. Grass often vanishes in a moment, whether devoured by animals or worn away; likewise the years of men which are accounted as nothing. *In the morning* means in the course of the life which they enjoy, traverse and complete; they can gain no satisfaction from their length of life, for they experience its close with swift speed.

6. *Let him flourish in the morning, and pass on: let him fall, grow dry, and wither in the evening.* The weakness of the flesh is well compared to the fleeting life of plants. *In the morning* indicates the whole of a man's life, in which he is known both to flourish and to pass on; *in the evening,* which denotes the sunset, states the time at which he passes from the world. As soon as he falls in death, he dries up into a corpse and then withers to dust, a fate known to be shared by both plants and human bodies. But we must not regard morning and evening here as the one day, in my opinion. They are not to be joined as component parts, for each of them is set down to enable us to grasp the notion of a brief period. These points are being elaborated with greater care so that no-one may delude himself that the life of man is very long.

7. *For in thy wrath we have fainted away and are troubled in thy indignation.* The holy man is mindful of their previous deeds, and recalls God's indignation which he endured because of the Jews' grumbling when the Lord said to him: *I see that this people is stiff-necked: let me alone that my wrath may be kindled against them, and that I may destroy them: and I will make of thee a great nation.*[7] So he was disturbed by this fearful recollection when he made entreaties for a

people like that. *We have fainted away* expresses the weariness of human weakness; *we are troubled* sprang from contemplation of terror of death, which they feared because of the vengeance which was their due.

8. *Thou hast set our iniquities before thy eyes: our life in the light of thy countenance.* He speaks of the past era when the Jewish people was visited by both miracles and punishments. Through not believing what they saw, they suffered the eye of the avenging Judge. In another passage Scripture says: *Blessed are they whose iniquities are forgiven, and whose sins are covered.*[8] The sins which obtained forgiveness were covered, whereas those which endured immediate vengeance were exposed.

9. *For all our days are spent: and in thy wrath we have fainted away. Our years laid plans like a spider.* He states that the shortness of human existence was the outcome of the Lord's anger, for men sinned through counting on a longer life. Later he will remark that they encountered this short span after the longevity of the previous era. When he says: *All our days are spent,* this is a reference to their abbreviated years. The next words: *And in thy wrath we have fainted away,* refer to the afflictions and hardships which we bear in this short life, for our wantonness could be corrected only by the clear evidence of being hounded by the Lord's whip. There follows a most appropriate comparison, *our years laid plans like a spider,* a parallel which makes clear the barrenness of our lives; for a spider is a feeble and scraggy creature which craftily weaves webs for passing flies so as to obtain its food. Likewise the years of those bent on wicked activities are spent on empty and cunning stratagems. *Aranea* (spider) gets its name because it is dried up (*arida*)[9] and very crafty. Observe how the verb here denotes the activities themselves; he states that *they laid plans,* not "they carried them out," to show that the years passed without any profit, for their life was one of hesitant reflection rather than of fruitful blessings.

10. *The days of our years in them are seventy years: but if among the powerful, they are eighty years, and the greatest number of them are labour and sorrow.* If we seek to interpret these years literally, you will find that many people even in their nineties are in good health, whereas others not yet seventy are wholly enfeebled, so that the statement here seems impossible to stand. But we more appropriately apply

the number seventy to the Law, which prescribed observance of the sabbath as the seventh day, and we most fittingly associate the number eighty with the Christian people, who reverence the eighth day as the Lord's resurrection-day with holy joy.[10] Thus by this numeration he seems to have pointed to the two Testaments, as we have already remarked at Psalm 70, the point at which we divided our work.[11] These are the precepts by which faithful souls are governed with most wholesome health of mind. To the number eighty he added: *Among the powerful,* because it was when the Lord Saviour appeared to us that we truly began to have power. So these are *the days of our years,* which bestow on us the brightness of a praiseworthy life, and so they are appropriately called *days,* for during them we behold the Lord in His words with enlightened mind. Observe what follows: *And the greatest number of them are labour and sorrow.* In other words, the person who goes beyond these two Testaments is engulfed in the greatest toils and griefs; whereas ordered differentiation between the two preserves the rule of heaven, this does not involve any greater or lesser regard for either, such as is manifested by heretics.[12]

11. *For mildness will come upon us, and we shall be corrected. Who knoweth the power of thy anger, or can number thy wrath for fear?* He now elaborates on his earlier statement: *The greatest number of them are labour and sorrow.* He says that we must not go beyond the precepts of the Law, for Jesus Christ, who is Mildness perfected, comes upon us and corrects and improves us if we wantonly ignore His Testaments. Since he used the word *corrected,* he prefaced it with *mildness,* so that we may realise that all the changes wrought by God in the faithful result from the application of devoted love. Next comes: *Who knoweth the power of thy anger, or can number thy wrath for fear?* Moses, who had experienced the severity of the Lord's response to His errant people when they roused Him with incessant grumbling, rightly exclaims that no man's reckoning can measure His vengeance, and that the potentialities of angry action open to Him cannot be numbered. Observe in both instances that His boundless power is proclaimed, for just as the Lord's rewards cannot be understood in their fullness, likewise the measure of His vengeance cannot be grasped. He did well to add *for fear;* as another prophet remarks: *I have pondered thy works, and was afraid.*[13]

12. *Make thy right hand known to us, O Lord, and men learned in*

heart, in wisdom. The most holy man, whose understanding of both Testaments is outstanding, passes to the third section, in which he begs the Father that Jesus Christ may make His salutary appearance to the Jewish people and the Gentiles. To embrace both peoples He used the plural, *to us,* as he had already done also in the first verse. By *right hand* he means the Lord Saviour, of whom it was written elsewhere: *Thy right hand, O Lord, hath slain the enemy.*[14] He asks that Christ may be made known to them, for through Him is learned all that will profit us. Next comes: *And men learned in heart, in wisdom.* In his longing it is not enough for him to demand the coming of the Lord, for many who saw Him in the flesh were far from believing that He was God. So he added: *Men learned in heart, in wisdom,* in other words, those who showed understanding of the Lord Christ. The word *eruditus* (learned) means "delivered from all that is unschooled." He is the power and wisdom of the Father, and Moses asks to make His acquaintance not with his physical eyes but in his learned heart, for it was a boon truly to behold Him for those who deserved to see Him with enlightened minds.

13. *Change thy ways, O Lord, a little, and be entreated in favour of thy servants.* The holy man follows his usual practice, for in Exodus he says: *Be appeased upon the wickedness of thy people.*[15] By his very love and charm he begs the Lord to temper His justice with a little gentleness, so that He can be prevailed upon by those sinners with whom He was known to be justly angry. But we must notice that he did not say: "Change thy ways wholly," but *Change thy ways a little,* for this is more profitable to us when some lash of tribulation afflicts us. Often when admonished we can gain pardon for our sins by a most wholesome conversion.

14. *We are filled in the morning with thy mercy: we have exulted, and take delight all our days.* No-one is unaware of the fact that the Lord Saviour is given the name of Mercy, for He was bestowed on the wretched so that those known to have perished in every possible way through their own efforts might live through Him. So he says that they are filled with this Mercy *in the morning,* that is, through clear contemplation, for the holy man foresaw the coming of the Lord Christ. It was inevitable that his heart should exult in praise and take delight in contemplation all the days of his life, for his soul was filled with that gift, and rejoiced in heavenly exultation. This figure is called

idea,[16] when we present a future event to our eyes, so to say, and rouse the soul's emotion in a lively way.

15. *We have delighted for the days in which thou hast humbled us: for the years in which we have seen evils.* With how authentic a reckoning had he assessed the tribulations which divine Providence bestows on men! He said that he took delight in those through which he knew his people would experience wholesome humiliation. He knew that pride was harmful to the faithful, and he thanks the Lord for the means by which, as he realised, believers made progress. So he confesses that he took delight in those years in which he had seen evils, evils which he considered oppressive when endured by the human condition; but for the holy man who contemplated the truth, they were not merely not oppressive but according to his statement even sweet in his eyes.

16. *Look upon thy servants and upon thy works, O Lord: and direct their children.* His sacred awareness does not cease to perform in the interests of others what he achieved on his own behalf. It is perfectly well-known with what prayers he entreated the Lord on behalf of the Israelites; he now ends this psalm with a similar conclusion, asking that He spare the sinning Jews and set right their children by the gift of sacred belief. Thus if through their own wickedness they were scattered, their children at any rate might be converted at the end of the world and deserve to obtain forgiveness. As we have often said, he knew through the spirit of prophecy that this would be done. Ponder the words with which he enticed the devoted love of the good Judge. First he said: *Upon thy servants,* and then: *Upon thy works,* so that even if they did not deserve to obtain pardon by their deeds, the Creator's action deserving of the highest praise would gain it. This argument is termed by the rhetoricians "praise of the judge."

17. *And let the brightness of the Lord our God be upon us, and direct thou the works of our hands over us.* The brightness of the Lord is upon us when we are adorned by the stamp of His cross, and we bear the banner of His triumph on our foreheads. As Paul says: *But God forbid that I should glory save in the cross of our Lord Jesus Christ, by whom the world is crucified to me, and I to the world.*[17] So another psalm says: *The light of thy countenance, O Lord, is signed upon us.*[18] Next comes: *And direct thou the works of our hands over us.* He directs the works of our

hands over us when He grants us pardon for sins, so that when we have become crooked we may by His correction become most upright.

Conclusion Drawn From the Psalm

Let us ponder, men of the greatest wisdom, how many mysteries of the sacred law are revealed to us by the various numbers. Moses here by computation of the numbers seventy and eighty draws the lives of men together. The entire sequence of psalms is embraced by that number; the secret number encloses all the divine books.[19] Other mysteries of the divine law are contained in various numbers. We read that the grains of sand of the sea, the drops of rain, the hairs of men's heads are counted. So that we may in brief grasp the praise and power of the discipline of number, Solomon says that God has ordered all things in measure and number and weight.[20] Thus it becomes clear and indubitable to all that the discipline of arithmetic is pervasive everywhere. The authors of secular literature have examined number with greater care, and divided it into many sections; into even and uneven, perfect and imperfect, excess and deficiency, and the other categories most clearly contained in those authorities. Our own ancestors too have allowed persons of studious bent to read and to handle these categories with intelligence.[21] Let us ask God to open our understanding to all things, and by His enlightenment to lead us to true wisdom; for whatever you read, whatever you think through, will succeed in tasting sweet to you only if you season it with the spice of heaven's gift.

COMMENTARY ON PSALM 90

1. *The praise of a canticle of David.* When the expression, *praise of a canticle,* is used, we must not regard it as a commonplace. Praise can be understood also as a human pronouncement, but the praise of a canti-

cle can be interpreted only as divine praise. We must regard David here as the prophet himself; he will speak the first section of this psalm in sweet tones. It is a most pleasant psalm, as sweet as can be in the variety of its promises. Verses 11 and 12 are directed at the Lord Saviour Himself by the devil after he has tempted Him. We always confront demons with this psalm in devoted trust, so that they may be overcome by us by the same means by which they sought craftily to make observations against their Creator.

Division of the Psalm

In the first part David claims that every person of high fidelity is enclosed by divine protection. The second part hymns praise to the Lord Saviour. The third consists of words spoken by the Father to all faithful individuals, who as He knows hope in Him with the greatest devotion. He promises them protection in this world and rewards in the next.

Explanation of the Psalm

He that dwelleth in the aid of the most High shall abide under the protection of the God of heaven. Once again here a categorical syllogism[1] raises its head, in this way: The just man dwells in the aid of the most High. Now all who dwell in the aid of the most High will abide under the protection of the God of heaven. Therefore the just man will abide under the protection of the God of heaven. Now let us deal with the words of the psalm. Holy David was sunk in heavenly contemplation; suddenly there was revealed to him a person who through the devotion of total purity of mind continually rejoiced in heavenly protection. David asserts that many benefits have been bestowed by God on this person, so that our hearts may be more earnestly fired to devote themselves to the Lord, seeing that the faithful are promised great hope. This figure is known as *diatyposis* or description of appearance, when we describe the shapes and appearances of things or persons before our eyes.[2] *He that dwelleth* is to be taken in the positive sense of one who lodges continually, for dwelling (*habitare*) expresses the sense of remaining rather than departing. The person who puts all his hope not in his own strength but in the will of the most High, attains an absolute promise, for such a person is protected by the Lord in every way. And we must note that he says: *In the aid*, to denote that the really committed Christian intends to serve the Lord with laborious effort. Observe too how important tidings are revealed word by word. He says that he that *dwelleth* here shall *abide* there; in other words, he that does not forsake God in this world will remain with Him always in the eternity to come.

2. *He shall say to the Lord: Thou art my protector and my refuge, my God, and I will trust in him.* The spokesman is one who renounces harmful trust in his own resources, and believes that the only thing of benefit to him is what heaven's devotion deigns to grant him. One who says: *Thou art my protector* maintains that he has thrown himself entirely on God's kindnesses, so that he boasts of what we may call a blessed intimacy. Again, one who says: *And my refuge, my God* proclaims that he has no other help; when shaken by the storms of this world, he attests that he wishes to flee to the harbour of divine mercy. So that you would not think that following this blessed protection and refuge nothing remained to be sought, there follows: *And I will trust in him*, so that no-one may at any time put trust in his own most feeble self, but rather always in Him who is known to embrace all things. If Adam had adopted this attitude, he would not have engineered his own guilt, nor transmitted death to his successors.

3. *For he hath delivered me from the snare of the hunters: and from the sharp word.* He explains the nature of God's gift, for He can free us from the wiles of our enemies, spiritual and physical. He compares them with hunters who set snares consisting of nets to catch wild beasts, so that they can entangle them all unknowing in crafty ambushes. Next comes: *And from the sharp word.* The sharp word is every statement uttered against the divine commands and served like a lethal drink. It is true that we are diverted from goodly purposes by sustaining injuries or derision, but it is the word which is especially sharp and wholly harsh in its bitterness. Then again if we hear fawning words seasoned with honey but mixed with bile, we must regard them with hostility for they are known to be against the divine commands. Often statements uttered in the softest words are more deceitful. So the Lord delivers us from this most grievous sharpness and bitter sweetness when we advance along His path without branching off to left or

right, where we know that the devil has laid snares; he has not dared to
set them on the path, that is, in Christ Himself, for he cannot wound
the faithful there.

4. *He will overshadow thee with his shoulders, and under his wings
thou shalt trust. His truth shall compass thee with a shield.* In this and the
next two verses what most beautiful images the prophet uses to praise
the Lord's kindness to the most holy person introduced earlier![3] He
recounts the appropriate rewards for him whose character he earlier
approved. We must investigate these rewards with care, to see if by
the aid of the Lord's grace we can elicit some worthy meaning. The
Lord's shoulders are enactments of miracles, by means of which the
divine power is demonstrated as though by the shoulders. His wings
are the prophets' warnings, which if accepted with pure minds lead
faithful souls ever to heaven. Perhaps you will ask what this overshadowing will bestow, so that the sun does not scorch you by day nor
the moon at night; or again, what the Lord's wings confer. The answer
is the Lord's protection, which you should realise you possess like a
mother's devotion amongst the hazards of the world. As Scripture says
elsewhere: *Jerusalem, Jerusalem, how often have I sought to gather together thy children as the hen doth gather her chickens under her wings,
and thou wouldst not?*[4] Next: *His truth shall compass thee with a shield.*
The shield that men wield covers only the part of the body against
which it is placed, but God's shield encompasses and defends us on all
sides like a wall. We must interpret *truth* as the Lord Christ's incarnation; as we read in Scripture: *Truth is sprung out of the earth;*[5] it
overshadows us with its shoulders, and makes us trust beneath its
wings, and guards us with the protection of its shield.

5. *Thou shalt not be afraid of the terror of the night.* 6. *Of the arrow
that flieth by day, of the business that walketh about in the dark: of
destruction, and the noonday devil.* Just as earlier he listed the types of
defence, so now in these two verses he reports the kinds of hazard, for
salvation is much more welcome when we realise the horde of dangers
which we have avoided. *The terror of the night,* then, is the cloudy
persuasion of heretics. *The arrow that flieth by day* is open persecution
by tyrants. *The business in the dark* is the debased study by which the
mental eye of right believers is blinded. *The noonday devil* is the massive danger ignited by the heat of persecution, in which destruction is
often feared and human weakness overcome; the word for destruc-

tion, *ruina*, stands for *repetens ima*, seeking the lowest level.[6]
Throughout all these allusions and definitions what is made clear is
that we can fear none of them, since we are saved by the Lord's
protection.

7. *A thousand shall fall from thy side, and ten thousand from thy right
hand: but one shall not come nigh thee.* In the first section he spoke of
the most faithful man, and since the limbs are joined to their head, he
passes in the second part to the Lord Christ, to show that those who
he said had lain in ambush for God's servants would experience retribution for their sins. But let us investigate these verses a little more
carefully. Those already known to be predestined for the ranks of the
blessed cannot fall at His side or at His right hand; this verse refers to
those whose presumption leads them to believe that they will obtain
what they are far from deserving. He said that they will fall, suggesting that they will topple from that lofty blessedness which their rash
and faithless souls promised them. The *side* of the Lord Saviour is the
circle of just persons who as He promised the apostles will pass judgment with him at the resurrection. Even today when as judges we
make a request of the emperor or the king, we say to him: "Set us at
your right hand"; the phrase suggests: "We offer you counsel with the
most faithful devotion." *Latus* (side) is so named because it lurks
(*lateat*)[7] beneath the arm. Men's hopes often vainly promise them high
status; this is why he says that those who promise themselves such
things beyond their deserts will tumble down from that glory. Because
those known to attain a hope of such magnitude are few, he maintains
that a thousand will fall from His side, that is, from the lofty dais of the
adjudication. He attests that ten thousand will fall from His right hand
(for many believe that they will be set at His right hand) because they
too had entertained a false expectation unjustified by their merits.
This decree castigates especially those puffed up by some blessing of
prosperity, who consider themselves holy though they are not. He
uses the finite figures of a thousand and ten thousand for indefinite
numbers. Next comes: *But one shall not come nigh thee,* in other words,
none of those who in self-deception promise themselves God's kingdom, but who in fact will be far distant from the Lord, for while they
put hope in their own merits they do not have recourse to the remedies of offering satisfaction.

8. *But thou shalt consider with thy eyes: and shalt see the reward of the*

wicked. With thy eyes expresses the clear and perceptive sight of God, by which men's merits are judged; men are weighed by the divine justice, and will be set on His left or His right. Next comes: *And shalt see the reward of the wicked,* a concept identical with the earlier: *Thou shalt consider with thy eyes,* for that consideration will be the reward of merits. *Thou shalt see* means: "You shall make it seen," as in: *The Lord hath looked down from heaven upon the children of men, to see if there be any that understand and seek God.*[8]

9. *Because thou, O Lord, art my hope: thou hast made the most High thy refuge.* After earlier speaking of the retribution against sinners, he suddenly added: *Because thou, O God, art my hope,* a statement alien to the previous sense. This figure is known as paradox, when an extraordinary or unexpected close is appended.[9] But let us examine more carefully what the prophet means by: *Because thou, O Lord, art my hope.* When the Lord rose again, the other members which lay in the death of sin gained the hope of resurrection. What the rest of the body needed to hope for was anticipated by the Head. But the holy man conceived this hope of resurrection because the Lord Saviour Himself by His death is seen to have set His refuge in the most High. As Psalm 30 has already stated: *Be thou unto me a God, a protector, and a house of refuge to save me.*[10] So he rightly follows the example of Him through whom he knew he would live for ever.

10. *There shall no evil come to thee: nor shall the scourge come near thy dwelling.* Here is powerfully recounted the blessed state of the humanity He assumed; for he says that though the Lord endured both taunts and scourges from the Jews in this world, no evil could approach His dwelling, that is, His holy body. He spoke rightly, for *the scourge* is divine vengeance, which is wont to restrain human crimes. As we read elsewhere: *Many are the scourges of sinners.*[11] So the scourge is said with the greatest truth not to have visited Him, for He was known to live a spotless life; the scourge mentioned here is that which punishes sins and exacts vengeance for wicked deeds, so by mention of the scourge, there is a denial that sin drew near to the Lord Christ. This type of utterance is the figure called *hypallage,*[12] often found in both secular and sacred works.

11. *For his angels have been given charge over thee, to guard thee in all thy ways.* 12. *In their hands they shall bear thee up, lest thou dash thy foot against a stone.* The words in these two verses are cast in the Lord's

face by the devil,[13] who was sceptical of His divinity, and presumed to tempt Him. But where Satan fell we must walk with care, for when the leader slips, the next in line is cautious. We have often said that there are two natures in the Lord Saviour, the united natures of God and man abiding with perfection in one and the same Person, so that He is proclaimed and believed by all to be the one Son of God, as our fathers taught when enlightened by Truth Itself. They said that the Son alone of the Trinity took the form of a servant, a form joined to Him to make His person one, so that the Son of God and the Son of man are the one almighty Christ Jesus, and this precludes proclamation not of the Trinity but of a Quaternity, which God forbid! The result is that when lowly features are ascribed to Him they are undoubtedly to be put down to His humanity, whereas when the thunder of greater power rolls, it is appropriate to ascribe it to His divine strengths. Both senses are preserved here and later. The expression, *Angels have been given charge over Him,* is a reference to human weakness, as the gospel similarly attests with: *And there appeared to him an angel from heaven, strengthening him.*[14] Then, to make totally clear His human nature, the psalmist added: *Lest thou dash thy foot against a stone,* in other words, lest He transgress against the Law, which was known to be inscribed on tablets of stone. He has come to teach this Law to the nations, and to maintain it in its fullness without diminution, so that it would bring salvation.

13. *Thou shalt walk upon the asp and the basilisk: and thou shalt trample underfoot the lion and the dragon.* At this point God's power which governed such savage elements is being emphasised. All these labels are fittingly applied to the devil. He is the asp when he strikes covertly; the basilisk when he openly spreads poison; the lion when he attacks the innocent; the dragon when he devours with wicked greed those who are off their guard. But at the Lord's glorious coming all these lay prostrate at His feet. Subjugation of such fierce creatures was possible only for Him who is known to be in His divinity coeternal and consubstantial with the Father. If we handle these matters carefully according to the proclamation of the holy Fathers, and we are not discomfited by any heretical perversion of madmen, we shall find that everything squares with the account given in total truth.

14. *Because he hoped in me, I will deliver him: I will protect him, because he hath known my name.* He passes to the third section, in

which the Lord Father replied with kindly condescension to that most just of men who we saw was introduced in the first part. With this promise He sought to strengthen the hearts of the faithful. So He promises to free from the evils of this world this blessed man who dwells in the aid of the most High, because he has put his hope in the Lord's power. Next comes: *I will protect him, because he hath known my name.* He explains the nature of His promise to deliver him: protected from the devil's every ambush, he is to become a stranger to Satan. He further added the reason for this devoted deliverance; *Because he hath known my name.* He knows the Father's name, and he considers the Son to be no less than the Father, not regarding Him as a created Being, as some wholly deranged persons do,[15] but rather with sound mind proclaiming Him Creator.

15. *He called to me, and I will hear him: I am with him in tribulation: I will deliver him, and I will glorify him.* The Lord promises this blessed man who trusts in His protection the unique reward of hearing him when called upon, and of granting him benefits in two ways. He says: *I am with him in tribulation,* with reference to this world where devoted hearts are afflicted with more searing hardships; so Christ Himself says in the gospel: *Behold, I am with you even to the consummation of the world.*[16] Secondly, note what follows: *I will deliver him, and I will glorify him.* The just man is accordingly to be delivered from this world and glorified when he is set in blessedness where affliction will no longer have a place.

16. *I will fill him with length of days: and I will show him my salvation.* He is still enumerating the rewards which He promises to the blessed man. *Length of days* is eternal life brought to no end but continuing self-supporting with constant strength. Next comes the climax of the entire reward which has no end: *And I will show him my salvation.* This is the promise made to the faithful as their highest recompense: they behold the Lord Christ, Author of salvation. When He appears and is beheld with the heart's enlightenment, He will satisfy the entire hopes and desires of the just. This is the sense in which in the gospel too He promises Himself to those who rightly believe in Him: *I will manifest myself to them.*[17] These words of the psalm could not be referred to Christ, as some claim, for He is both the Lord of salvation and the eagerly sought Hope of believers. It

would be better to interpret this, as we have often suggested, as referring to His members.

Conclusion Drawn From the Psalm

This psalm has marvellous power, and routs impure spirits. The devil retires vanquished from us through the very means by which he sought to tempt us, for that wicked spirit is mindful of his own presumption and of God's victory. Christ by His own power overcame the devil in His own regard, and likewise conquers him in ours. So this psalm should be recited by us when night sets in after all the actions of the day; the devil must realise that we belong to Him to whom he remembers that he himself yielded. I reckon that it is not without significance that such a glorious psalm takes the ninetieth place, for we acknowledge that by this recurrence of thrice three tens it stretches out towards the almighty and indivisible Trinity.

COMMENTARY ON PSALM 91

1. *A psalm of a canticle, on the sabbath day. A psalm of a canticle* reminds us that we must give thanks to the Godhead in all our actions; for *psalm,* as has often been stated, denotes spiritual works which rise upwards to the Lord Christ. In them we should sing and ever offer thanks, for by His kindness we are freed, whereas by our own efforts we were bound with the chains of sins. The person who devotes all his life to giving thanks is singing a psalm. *The sabbath day* denotes rest, by which we are schooled to desist from all vicious action, and by the holiness of heavenly deeds to give our minds a holiday from vices. The Jews do not observe the day properly, for they have put a literal sense on observance of it; rest on the sabbath truly comes to those who apply the Lord's commands to the New Testament meaning, and really understand what they know has been stated as a prefiguration. So in this psalm we must accept the words of the Church, which we know informs us that the sabbath day means the rest to come.

Division of the Psalm

At the outset the Church speaks, stating that it is good to sound forth praises to the Lord. She proclaims that the foolish and irreligious person is wholly unaware of this. Secondly, she maintains that sinners will speedily perish like grass. Thirdly, she says that the just flourish like the palm tree, and grow like the cedars of Libanus, so that she may correct wanton fears, and the committed may rejoice in the blessed promise extended to them.

Explanation of the Psalm

2. *It is good to confess to the Lord, and to hymn thy name, O most High.* Holy mother Church says that it is good to confess to the Lord; she wished at the very outset to issue briefly a profitable proclamation. As has often been said, we confess in two ways: when in condemnation of our sins we continually beg the Lord's mercy, and also when we always attribute benefits received to His kindnesses, and we do not claim as meritorious what is granted by His compassion. So whichever of the two occurs, *it is good to confess to the Lord.* Then she turns and says to the Lord: *And to hymn thy name, O most High;* the phrase, *it is good,* must be understood as earlier. Hymning means performing the Lord's commands by devoted deeds, so that just as the psaltery sounds forth from its upper parts, so our action may mount to the ears of the Godhead. So one short verse must embrace the accomplishment of holy and manifold actions.

3. *To proclaim thy mercy in the morning, and thy truth through the night.* Our lives are marvellously embraced by two words. The *morning* denotes joy, but *night* is known to signify sadness. So when we are happy through His kindness, we ought to proclaim His mercy, for He vouches for the unworthy and is good to the wicked. Likewise we should proclaim His truth through the night, that is, in affliction, when certain hardships are seen to oppress us, for we deservedly suffer what we endure through the burden of sins. Thus at both times we should most justly declare the Lord's praises.

4. *Upon the ten-stringed psaltery, with canticle and harp.* Clearly the ten-stringed psaltery denotes the ten commandments of the Law, for

they are strings which if we strum with the character of goodly deeds will play the tune of salvation and lead to the kingdom of heaven. But we should be aware why this number is seen to be attached to so important a theme; it is the number which the Pythagoreans call the Tetractys[1] or the divine group of four, for it embraces in brief what is capable of infinite extension. One, two, three and four make ten; when continually reproduced and repeated, this number extends into protracted and boundless calculations. In no sum is anything new beyond this sequence found; it is seen to be so assembled as always to be calculable, since it is not changed by any new elements. So such a number rightly embraces the shape of the whole of our redemption, for with its slanting lines it imitates by its impress the figure of the holy cross, and its constituent numbers end with the roundness of a beautiful circle.[2] He added: *With canticle and harp;* these represent the joy of good works, in other words, the pleasure shown in distributing alms. As Paul says: *God loves a cheerful giver.*[3] *Harp* indicates active deeds which though achieved with toil and tension will bear the greatest fruit if fulfilled with the addition of joy. The man who performs good works without harsh melancholy is singing with the harp.

5. *For thou hast given me, O Lord, a delight in thy doings, and in the works of thy hands I shall rejoice.* Observe that the canon of the truth is maintained everywhere, so that we may not attribute to human powers what God's generosity has bestowed. Harmful pride is the outcome, and arrogance hostile to God swells up when our human weakness shows presumption about its own potential. So mother Church says that she takes delight in the Lord's doings, for whatever blessing she received she attributed without reserve to His holy design. So that the wholesome nature of this rule we have mentioned might be maintained, she proclaims that she exults not in her own blessedness but in His works. As Paul has it: *We are his workmanship, created in good works.*[4]

6. *O Lord, how great are thy works! Thy thoughts are become exceeding deep.* All God's works are indeed seen to be deep to human reflection; whichever of them you seek, you know it undoubtedly extends very far. But it is better to acknowledge these works through her own words, so that we may not seem to introduce some extraneous element. After saying that His mercy must be proclaimed in the morning and His truth in the night upon the ten-stringed psaltery with canticle

and harp, she stands more fervently amazed at the works of the Lord themselves, and at the wonders of His dispensation. She observes His magnificence with the greatest admiration, so that we may be moulded by imitation of Him, and succeed in escaping the dangers of this world for our salvation. In this matter His *thoughts are become exceeding deep;* just as the devil fell through pride, so the human race can be pardoned through the gift of humility. By the description *exceeding deep,* she shows that this assessment goes deeper the more one ponders it carefully and with greater intensity. This, then, is a form of perfect knowledge, to realise that God bestows things of such quality and dimensions as human thought cannot appreciate. As we read in the prophet Habacuc: *I have pondered thy works, and was afraid.*[5]

7. *The senseless man shall not know: nor will the fool understand these things.* Appropriate comment is made on the differing circumstances. Just as she said of herself: *For thou hast given me, O Lord, a delight in thy doings, and in the works of thy hands I shall rejoice,* and the rest, so she proclaims that unbelievers cannot recognise the Lord's kindnesses. This figure is called *parison,*[6] or balancing of statements which often consist of like observations but more usually of dissimilar ones. The senseless man is he who is emptied of heavenly wisdom and known to be teeming with human guile. He will not know God's works precisely because he believes that things happen by chance, as certain philosophers have said.[7] She added: *Nor will the fool understand these things.* The fool is he who fails to know things divine, and does not understand the worldly affairs which we colloquially call mindless. So naturally they do not understand what was said earlier, because they are not fired by any rationale of heavenly contemplation.

8. *When sinners shall spring up as grass, and all the workers of iniquity shall appear, that they may perish for ever and ever.* She passes to the start of the second section, in which she says that sinners flourish like grass for a brief period in this world; but at the Judgment, when they obtain a worthy recompense for their deeds, she maintains that they swiftly perish. As the prophet Jeremiah says: *Every man is grass, and all man's glory is like the bloom of grass.*[8] Her statement, *and all the workers of iniquity shall appear,* points to the coming time of the Judgment, for even though men guilty of many crimes are apprehended in this life, not all those who work iniquity can be evident to us, especially as we cannot here detect the impure of spirit; whereas when

they come to judgment they will be visible to human eyes. The reason why they will appear comes next: it is to gain not glory but ruin, in other words, to perish for ever and ever. The punishment of the damned is splendidly explained; they do not perish in such a way that they cease to exist, but they perish for ever and ever, never being freed from their tribulations.

9. *But thou, O Lord, most high for evermore.* We must understand "will endure," not as the Jews imagined, being a mere man ripe for slaughter like the mass of mankind. It is appropriate to have this vision of the Lord Saviour so that by contrast the sacrilegious faithlessness of the Jews may be overcome.

10. *For behold, thy enemies, O Lord, shall perish: and all the workers of iniquity shall be scattered.* God's enemies are the worshippers of demons, or any seen to oppose His commandments. This is called hostility to God, but is demonstrably more harmful to the individual who opposes Him, for the person who does not follow the Lord's commands persecutes himself. The devoted Creator can be angry only when we are seen to be hostile to ourselves. Finally she appends the identity of these enemies; they are the workers of iniquity. They will be scattered when they are separated from the Lord's flock, when they do not deserve to enter His kingdom, for only those who have pleased the Lord with most devoted purpose can assemble there.

11. *And my horn shall be exalted like that of the unicorn: and my old age in plentiful mercy.* The unicorn sometimes denotes pride, as has already been stated in another psalm: *Save my lowness from the horns of the unicorns.*[9] But here it indicates exaltation of the unity which the Church rightly says will be glorified at the end of the world, when the faithful are seen to obtain worthy rewards. That unity is an exalted strength. Just as in this world horns are an adornment for beasts, so in the next the glory of the saints adorns the Church. She said: *Shall be exalted,* because her high status will appear loftier to sinners plunged into the hell of humiliation. Next comes: *And my old age in plentiful mercy.* Old age has a white head of hair, and my opinion is that this comparison is apposite to the Church, for all the merits of the saints will gleam as if with the clearest glow of a white head. *My* was not an otiose addition, for old age in humans is the victim of oppressive illnesses, and moves towards its close. Its laments make it burdensome, and it has an ugly colour. By contrast the old age of the Church

leads to enduring life, to wondrous blessedness, to unique beauty, so that those who have deserved to be numbered in that assembly gleam like God's angels. She further added: *In plentiful mercy,* so that you would be aware of the many gifts and the blessings which are beyond doubt unending. The whole description is contrasted with the old age of this life, which is burdened by oppressive ills.

12. *And my eye has gazed on my enemies: and my ear has heard the malignant that rise up against me.* These are the enemies of the Church who she earlier said work wickedness. They will be exposed at the Judgment, when those who are under cover in the world will be brought into the open there, together with their works. Her angry eye gazes on them then, when she sees them shepherded to the left side. Next comes: *And my ear has heard of the malignant that rise up against me.* The malignant insurgents are the rich people of this world, who with unholy arrogance despise the poverty of the Church on earth. The ears of all the faithful will hear them when they condemn their own desires and deeds with their rebukes. As Solomon puts it, they will say: *What hath pride profited us? Or what advantage hath the boasting of riches brought us?*[10] There they are heard condemning their own aspirations, whereas in this world they account themselves most blessed.

13. *The just shall flourish like the palm-tree: he shall multiply like the cedar of Libanus.* Holy Church begins the third section, in which she recounts the rewards of the blessed by means of comparisons, just as earlier she used them in saying that the deeds of sinners were condemned. Sinners were compared to grass which springs up beautifully green but quickly dries up and dies; the just man she most appropriately compares to the palm tree. The palm tree (*palma*) is so called because it fosters peace (*pacis alma*);[11] it is the reward for victors in the contest. As Paul says: *Now I press towards the palm of the heavenly vocation.*[12] At the lower level the trunk is rough and uneven, but when it grows high it is filled with the sweetest fruit and is adorned with projecting branches like the sun's rays. Likewise the life of the just in this world is full of hard toils, but is known to be most beautiful in heaven. There follows a second comparison with the cedar, which is known to be much taller than palm trees. Its wood is smooth and most sturdy for bearing weights. Though it grows high everywhere, it rises higher on Mount Libanus. In the same way the just man is famed with

diverse praises, and is said to have the loftiness of the cedar and the beauty of palm trees. This figure is known as *ison*[13] or equality, when certain things which are comparable are associated with each other in praise or blame.

14. *They that are planted in the house of the Lord shall flourish in the courtyards of the house of our God.* Since she has compared just men to select trees, she now with the briefest mention points out the pleasant prospect and beauty of the Catholic Church. Its description as a plantation points to the Lord's predestination, for only those planted in it will have a most abundant growth. Consider too what is made clear by *they that are planted in the house of the Lord shall flourish*, namely, that those planted in the Church through the Lord's grace here will flourish in every way when they gain entry to Jerusalem. The courtyard is the name for the entry to the dwelling, whereas the house denotes the inner parts; both cannot at the same time aptly designate the one thing. The just man is said to be well planted here, for he is firmly established by the roots of the virtues in the bowels of the earth; he will justly flourish in the courtyard when at the commencement of the resurrection he will rejoice in the happiness of the gift which he shall hear: *Come ye, blessed of my Father, possess you the kingdom prepared for you from the foundation of the world.*[14]

15. *They shall still increase in a fruitful old age, and they shall suffer well.* Old age in men is dry and barren, but the Church begins to be most fertile when through the Lord's mercy she is brought to the end of the world. What a green old age, maturing like the blossoms! It is clear that this house is roofed by the sky, for men are planted in it to flower; for at the end of the world the number of saints swells under the impetus of frequent persecutions, so that the number of the predestined may be swiftly attained. Earlier she said similarly: *And my old age in plentiful mercy.*[15] She added: *And they shall suffer well*, because the sufferings of the blessed seek the kingdom of heaven.

16. *That they may declare that the Lord our God is just, and there is no iniquity in him.* As the saints, of whom she earlier said: *They shall suffer well*, begin to accept their divine rewards, they will declare that the Lord is just, for He has presented the gifts promised to His servants. *And there is no iniquity in him*; all whom He permitted to hazard their lives on His behalf in this world He will adorn with the crown of martyrdom in the next.

Conclusion Drawn From the Psalm

Holy mother Church has instructed us how sinners perish like grass, and how the just flourish like the palm tree; she also described how those oppressed in this life with numerous afflictions rejoice in the change of their lot. This is the sabbath day announced by the psalm-heading, on which the just will gladly celebrate the Lord's praises, and in their freedom from the persecutions of this world will rejoice in untroubled relaxation. She promised blessings to save us from despair, and uttered weighty threats to save us from sinning. All the advice which she deigns to offer is given on our behalf.

COMMENTARY ON PSALM 92

1. *The praise of a canticle for David himself, on the day before the sabbath, when the earth was founded.* We have repeatedly said that *canticle* relates to praise of the Godhead. As for the addition: *For David himself,* this is clearly directed to the Lord Christ, who is truly said to be strong of hand and longed for,[1] since He alone can provide what He wishes, and is sought with unique affection by those who worship Him. Next comes: *On the day before the sabbath, when the earth was founded.* The day before the sabbath denotes the sixth day of the week, which clearly precedes the sabbath; but as we read in Genesis that dry land appeared on the third day,[2] we must enquire why he says that the earth was founded on the sixth day. Here we must interpret it as man, for he is appropriately denoted by the earth, as in the words *Earth thou art, and unto earth thou shalt return.*[3] We read that as part of the creation the Creator made man on the sixth day. Just as He created him when the sixth light dawned, so at His coming He renewed him in the sixth age. We read that according to the authority of the Fathers, the first age runs from Adam to Noah, the second from Noah to Abraham, the third from Abraham to David, the fourth from David to the migration to Babylon, the fifth from the Babylonian migration to the preaching of John the Baptist, and the sixth from the preaching of John to the close of the age when it is clear that the Lord

Saviour came and mercifully bestowed the foundations of His faith upon man when he was storm-tossed by diverse disasters. Then it was that the earth was founded, when the belief of the human race was founded on Him. So praise of His holy incarnation is sung within the texture of this psalm.

Division of the Psalm

The first topic describes His beauty, the second His strength, the third His deeds, the fourth His power, the fifth praises of the whole creation, the sixth the truth of His words, and the last praise of His house which fittingly basks in eternal joy. So the praise of the demonstrative genre[4] is fashioned on these seven arguments as bases. Our procedure in other psalms has been to signal the divisions by the numbers, and this will suffice here, since the numbers themselves are seen to be suitably placed to separate the interconnected subject-matter.

Explanation of the Psalm

The Lord hath reigned, he has clothed himself with beauty. This is the first statement of the thesis, which we have labelled "beauty." The prophet observes what is to come, and with great exultation hymns the Lord who is to reign; not that His dominion began in time, but because the eternal King became known to the human race through the manifestation of the sacred incarnation. Next comes: *He has clothed himself with beauty,* in other words, He has shown the beauty of His majesty, as we read in the gospel when He was transfigured on Mount Tabor in the presence of His disciples: *And his face did shine as the sun, and his garments became white as snow,[5]* as white as no laundryman can make them on the earth.

The Lord has clothed himself with strength, and hath girded himself. This is the second motif, which we called "strength." Notice that the earlier sentence ended with the same word with which the second began.[6] This is the figure called *epembasis,[7]* when some expression is repeated to enhance the beauty of the diction, as in: *Hymn our God, hymn him: hymn our king, hymn him,[8]* and similar passages. He clothed

Himself with strength when at His passion He replied to the Jews as they sought to arrest Him: *I am he;* they retreated, and seized with great terror fell to the ground, though they had come to take Him by force.[9] If we interpret these two statements in the spiritual sense, they are wholly harmonious. He clothed Himself with beauty for those to whom He appeared in the truth of faith as God's Son; and He clothed Himself with strength in the face of those who refused to believe in Him, and by threatening judgment He foretold to them that the wicked would suffer due punishment. *He hath girded himself* perhaps indicates when he girded Himself with a towel and washed the disciples' feet.[10] That gesture of humility also showed beauty, because the Lord of heaven deigned to show the most humble submission to His servants. He also showed strength by bringing down malice and pride when He humbled the devil.

For he hath established the world which will not be moved. The third topic of the thesis appears; we earlier called it "His works." He established the world, in other words, the Church, when He said in the gospel: *Thou art Peter, and upon this rock I will build my church, and the gates of hell shall not prevail against it.*[11] This is true praise and a wondrous proclamation, that the earth which denotes the Church scattered through the world is not moved at all, though it is battered by frequent shaking.

2. *Thy throne, O God, is prepared from of old: thou art from everlasting.* This is the fourth motif, which we earlier called His power. The prophet wishes us to understand the throne as that on which Christ sits on the Father's right, or alternatively the throne which He occupies is the minds of the faithful; so we read: *On whom does my spirit rest save him that is humble and silent, and that trembles at my words?*[12] *Prepared* denotes predestination, for all that happens to occur in the dispensation of the world lies in that truth. *From of old* points to Christ's incarnation from the virgin Mary, when He instructed the apostles and the rest of the faithful with the fullness of His majesty. *From everlasting* is directed to His divinity, by which He reigns co-eternally with the Father and knows no confinement in time. By these words are denoted one Person but the two natures of the Lord Christ, so it is vital quite frequently to remind ourselves of this canon by

means of appropriate passages, as the authority of the Fathers maintains. I only wish that the impudence of crazed heretics would subside,
so that our repetition of it would appear indecorous rather than
necessary.

3. *The rivers have lifted up, O Lord, the rivers have lifted up their
voices, with the voices of many waters.* 4. *Wonderful are the surges of the
sea: wonderful the Lord on high.* This is the fifth citation of the thesis,
the praises of the whole creation. Here the prophet, elated by his
vision of God's love, says that the rivers well forth the praises of the
Lord. This figure is called *prosōpopoeia,*[13] when words are attributed to
inanimate things; it is found very frequently in the divine scriptures.
But it is good for us to seek out the nature of these rivers which lift up
their voices and cry out. They are surely the apostles, who have drunk
of the holy Spirit. The Lord Himself, the Source of the rivers and the
Fount of the waters, bears witness in the gospel: *He that believeth in
me, out of his belly shall flow rivers of living water.*[14] So the very rivers
welled forth watering words, and lifted up their most holy voices in
their preachings. They are rightly said to be lifted up, since these
rivers offered their saving praises to the Creator, whereas earthly
rivers do not direct their courses upward but rather flow downhill.
After speaking of the preaching of the apostles, he now explains how
the Church makes progress through the Lord's bounty; *the voices of
many waters* denotes the nations which assemble to proclaim the
Catholic faith in praise of the Lord. So *wonderful surges of the sea*
develop from these voices; in other words, the saving ascent of souls
springs out of the salt waters of this world. The sea is the abundant
gathering of salt waters, and in the same way the Church embraces her
wise people in Catholic unity, and their *wonderful surges* come to pass
when they abide in the Lord's commands with steadfast minds. He
wishes to ascribe all this to the Lord Himself, through whom all
existing blessings flow—the apostle James says: *Every best gift and
every perfect gift is from above, coming down from the Father of lights*[15]—
so he says: *Wonderful is the Lord on high,* for the life of mortals is not
worthy of praise except in the case of those whom He raises on high.

5. *Thy testimonies are become exceedingly credible.* The prophet
spoke of the Lord's coming, an event which he most truly foresaw.

Now he expounds the nature of the praise, for *the testimonies of the prophet* were *become exceedingly credible*, when the saving incarnation of the Word which had been foretold to the world made its appearance. At His glorious coming was revealed all that was kept hidden in the sacred books. Which of the wise could have doubts about the promise of the gifts when the very Fullness which was promised arrived?

6. *Holiness becometh thy house, O Lord, unto length of days.* The seventh and last remaining topic is appended, which we said ought to be labelled "praise of His house." The house of the Lord, then, is the universal Church, which we know is established round the circumference of the world. Holiness, in other words "the abundant blessing of Thy coming," becomes it. This is the beauty which can transcend all adornments, for it beautifies without ever forsaking it, and unifies so that it is wholly unfragmented. But this holiness, a beauty most outstanding, is not imparted for a moment, but is granted eternally; for *length of days* denotes an eternity which cannot be ended. As someone has said, a thing is not long if it has an end-point. So the perfection of the Lord's coming is praised by these seven components of the demonstrative genre.[16]

Conclusion Drawn From the Psalm

See how the sixth day of the week is revealed in the Lord's incarnation, which the psalm-heading foretold. The foolish people who believe that the glorious advent of the Lord is to be darkened by depreciatory comment should pay attention to this psalm. Through that coming the power of the most holy Trinity was announced to men; through it sprang the washing of holy baptism; through it were bestowed the gifts of holy communion; through it the gifts of different charisms flourished; through it death lay prostrate and life rose up; through it the devil was conquered; through it man is known to have been freed. The angels rejoice and the heavens glory, yet—what sacrilege!—man is still found ungrateful, though the Lord's unique help afforded to him is made evident.

COMMENTARY ON PSALM 93

1. *A psalm for David himself, on the fourth day of the week.* The first words are familiar, but we must examine with greater attention the meaning of: *On the fourth day of the week.* This is the fourth weekday from the sabbath, the day on which the Lord at the beginning of the world established the stars of heaven with wondrous arrangement. This is to be referred to the holy men of whom this psalm is to speak. They are deservedly compared to the stars of heaven, for on earth they gleam with their heavenly style of life. The prophet distinguished this and the two previous psalms by mention of such days, investing them with great mystery, so that he would be seen to show the power of the psalms by the meaning of their content.

Division of the Psalm

The prophet observed that the human race was confounded by the heinous belief that God had no care for men, since they saw that by a reversal of fortunes the just were oppressed by opposition, and the wicked exalted in prosperity. So in the first section he asks God to penalise the proud, because on this analysis he saw that the world was besmirched by them. In the second section he attacks those who were blaspheming with their stupid grumbling, believing that God had no care for human affairs, though He is seen to have granted understanding to His creatures. He counts as blessed the person who despises success in this world, and is constant in reverence towards God. In the third part he seeks to win their allegiance, and so he says that God is his refuge, and will take vengeance on sinners.

Explanation of the Psalm

God is the Lord of vengeance: the God of vengeance hath acted freely. The prophet observes that wicked acts of blasphemers have mounted by leaps and bounds to unrestrained licence, so he threatens them with the Lord's punishment which is as heavy as fearful thunderbolts, so that they may be terrified by fear of such great majesty, and become strangers to their debased deeds. He speaks of God as an awe-inspiring name deriving from the word for fear.[1] So that you may realise that this is the Lord Saviour, next comes: *The Lord of vengeance,* in other words, He who will judge the world and will come to oppress the stubborn with just vengeance. So who would not be terrified when he heard this? What person with the wit to realise that he is a sinner would not tremble before the Avenger? He says again: *The God of vengeance hath acted freely,* in other words, has passed judgment without hindrance, as He did when He charged the Pharisees and those in power with their wicked deeds.[2] He acted freely also when He taught the people in the temple as One with authority.[3] Similarly in another passage the Father says of Him: *I will set him over my salvation, I will have confidence in him.*[4] So clearly He acted freely, for His truth could not be rebuked and His power could obviously not be withstood. What was within Him was a voluntary humility, not the necessity of patience.

2. *Lift up thyself, thou that judgest the earth: render a reward to the proud. Lift up thyself* is addressed to Him in His lowliness, when as we know He was seized by wicked men and crucified. But though He endured this for our redemption, He was then lifted up in His majesty in the presence of His disciples, when as men know He rose to enduring glory. So this most holy man prays for what he knows will come to pass. These are not words of command, but words by which the judgment of an undoubting spirit and the devotion of a longing heart are revealed. Next comes: *Thou that judgest the earth;* he sought to identify openly the Lord Christ, who will judge the earth, in other words, worldly men, with the power of His majesty. Then, so that you should note the reference to the wicked, he added: *Render a reward to the proud.* The proud are they who are lost in their ill-will, and seem unable to attain the Lord's mercy by any act of satisfaction. *Proud* is the label attaching itself both to the devil and to those who follow his debased deeds. So the reward which will be rendered to them is to hear the words: *Go into eternal fire, which was prepared for the devil and his angels.*[5]

3. *How long shall sinners, O Lord, how long shall sinners glory?* He still continues with the earlier line of thought, and speaks of those

sinners who stick fast to their unbending wishes. By asking: *How long shall sinners glory?* he is pointing to this world in which their acts of arrogance are boundless; for on Judgment-day they cannot glory, since they obtain the punishment due to them. The repetition here exposes the pain of the long period of waiting, for the obtrusive boasting of wicked people is always oppressive to the innocent.

4. *They shall declare and speak iniquity: all who work injustice shall speak it.* A declaration means some announcement in a loud voice in the presence of others; he speaks of those who not merely plan evil deeds in their hearts but also freely noise them abroad, with the result that they both destroy themselves and infect others who are deceived. Next comes: *And shall speak iniquity.* Since declaring means speaking, the sense seems to me that we are to take the declarations as public acts of persuasion, whereas we can interpret speaking as private conversations, so that there may be no moment which is a stranger to the sins of the wicked. *Iniquity* is undoubtedly common to both verbs, for it is ascribed to those puffed up with depraved fluency of speech. But so that you would not regard their behaviour as the mere speaking of words, he added: *Who work injustice,* so that they might continually appear as abhorrent in word and deed. Notice carefully how he ceaselessly builds up the increase in sinning up to the end of the section; this figure is called *climax*[6] or gradation. It is an attractive ascent for speakers to swell higher by amplification. Paul did this too in his account of the virtues: *Who shall separate us from the love of Christ? Shall tribulation, or distress, or famine, or the sword, or nakedness, or persecution?*[7] and what follows.

5. *Thy people, O Lord, they have brought low: and they have afflicted thy inheritance. Thy people* means the faithful folk who he says are brought low, because they heard insults addressed to God. A dedicated servant is inevitably pained when he happens to hear something of the utmost irreverence said about his master. *Inheritance* denotes the Christian people who he says are afflicted because arrogant persecutors have tried to wear them down with countless calamities. Notice the restrained word *afflicted* rather than "destroyed"; for the faithful always make progress when tested, and the more human violence is mounted against them, the greater the heavenly protection afforded them. As Solomon says: *Fire tests silver, and the trial of tribulation acceptable men.*[8]

6. *They have slain the widow and the stranger, and they have mur-
dered the fatherless.* We also read: *Be to the fatherless as a father, and as
a husband to their mother.*⁹ We are further instructed in the Pentateuch
about the stranger: *Thou shalt not harm the foreigner and the stranger,
because you also were strangers in the land of Egypt.*¹⁰ So here to emphasise the crime, he speaks of slain widows, strangers and fatherless;
those whom the Lord commanded us to protect and help were not
spared by that criminal band. Notice the motif which the orators call
*praise of what is harmed;*¹¹ already then the truth impressively expressed
what human cleverness now directs to appropriate uses.

7. *And they have said: The Lord shall not see, neither shall the God of
Jacob understand.* The proud heaped up their wicked deeds. They
increased their wickedness by adding blasphemous words to the
slaughter and affliction of the innocent. This figure is called *sarcasmos*
or hostile derision, which so to say pierces the flesh.¹² They stated that
the Lord did not see what wicked actions they were known to commit; they reckoned that their evil deeds were not observed, for they
noted that they were not swiftly struck down. What fools they were
to coerce the Lord's patience towards the wrongs inflicted by their
weakness! They said that He did not observe their deeds, and they
believed that He could not apprehend them, whereas the kindly Ruler
cries out: *It is not my will that the sinner should die, but that he be
converted and live.*¹³ It is the God of Jacob who speaks, the God of the
Christian people. Divine Scripture habitually repeats this title *God of
Jacob,* for the Catholic Church which comes later is denoted by Jacob's name.¹⁴

8. *Understand now, ye senseless among the people: and you fools, be
wise at last.* Having explained the nature of the malevolent, he passes
to the second section, in which he warns them finally to abandon their
wicked opinion. He labels as senseless those established in the Church
who are bitten by worldly success. He appended: *Among the people,*
because they proclaim their debased understanding loudly in their
gatherings, and are seen teaching what they have most wilfully learnt.
He calls *fools* those ignorant of true religion who blaspheme in open
contradiction to it, saying that God does not see what men do, and
does not apprehend their sins. Next follows: *And, you fools, be wise at*

last; in other words, "You madmen, heed the Lord's devotion, you who assume that He disregards the deeds which He is known to check by His commandments."

9. *He that planted the ear, shall he not hear? Or he that formed the eye, doth he not consider?* 10. *He that chastiseth nations, shall he not rebuke, he that teacheth men knowledge?* In these two verses the most splendid and compelling argument runs through the individual aphorisms; it must be interpreted as rebuke. What he is saying is: Has He who bestowed ears on His various creatures denied Himself the power of hearing? Will He who fashioned the eye be without sight? Will He who rebuked the nations in the prophets' proclamations refrain from judging them? Will He that taught men knowledge be continuously without reason? On the contrary, the Craftsman of the world who dispensed a limited amount to each individual has assigned to none as much as He knows is in Himself. So empty presumption should cease to aspire to utterly false fantasies. Only the Godhead can know all things truly and perfectly. Let us further examine how splendidly the order of words develops. He says: *He that planted the ear,* but the next words are not: "Has He no ear?" but: *Shall he not hear?* A similar kind of expression follows: *Or he that formed the eye;* he did not say: "Has he no eye?" but *Doth he not consider?* This was to demonstrate that in God reside the powers of hearing and seeing, rather than physical faculties. The dialecticians decided to call these brief and exceedingly clear modes of argument *enthymemata* or mental conceptions,[15] which orators often exploited for their brevity to make appropriate distinctions. Here there is clearly a syllogism consisting of proposition and conclusion contrary to each other. The proposition was: *He that planted the ear,* and the opposing conclusion: *Shall he not hear?* and the further examples of the kind which follow in this verse.

11. *The Lord knoweth the thoughts of men, that they are vain.* After his earlier statements comes a true observation, that the thoughts of such men are wholly and utterly vain. It was well said that *the Lord knoweth,* for those seized by debased thoughts cannot know it of their own accord. We call *vain* whatever departs from the truth, whatever does not bear profitable fruit.

12. *Blessed is the man whom thou shalt instruct, O Lord: and thou shalt*

teach him out of thy law. The blessed man effectively contrasts with those who are vain, for just as the vain are mocked by fleeting thoughts, so the blessed are strengthened by the truth of heavenly teaching. So he passes to those whom in the psalm-heading he compared with the stars of heaven. He next explains how this kind of blessedness develops, with the words, *and thou shalt teach him out of thy law*. The blessed are not deceived by vanities, but are filled with the true kind of teaching, and become truly blessed since they have savoured the gifts of heavenly wisdom.

13. *That thou mayst relieve him from the evil days, till a pit be dug for the wicked*. Clearly the benefit of the sacred law is that the Christian learns patience amidst the afflictions of this world, for they are always softened by patience. As we read in Scripture: *With expectation I have waited for the Lord, and he regarded me*,[16] and the like. Days are evil when unjust men are seen to abuse us, when worldly success attends our persecutors. But see what follows. We are to wait *till a pit be dug for the wicked*, in other words, till the time when the burial day dawns for the wicked, when the unholy ones no longer show arrogance and cease to rejoice in their prosperity. On that day they obtain the correction which they put off in this life.

14. *For the Lord will not cast off his people: neither will he forsake his own inheritance*. As he had earlier said: *That thou mayst relieve him*, so now he maintains that he will not be cast off, and states that his weariness in seeking the reward of a crown lasts only a short time. By his people he means faithful Christians who hasten to the Lord with unsullied purpose of mind. Next comes: *Neither will he forsake his own inheritance*. Human inheritance is that which passes to a successor on the departure of the previous owner; but Christ's inheritance, though sought at the cost of His blood, never parts from its Source, but is possessed in company with Him notwithstanding.

15. *Until justice be turned into judgment: and who possess it? All that are upright in heart*. Men's justice is turned into judgment when the apostles or those who approximate to their merits will, as was promised them in the gospel, *sit on twelve seats to judge*[17] in the company of Christ. This justice of the faithful, which in this world was subject to the scrutiny of the wicked, will then judge all the wanton and the

arrogant. As Paul puts it: *Know you not that we shall judge angels? How much more things of this world.*[18] To remove any possible doubt of their identity, the question is asked: *Who possess it?* meaning "that justice," and his reply is: *All that are upright in heart.* The upright in heart are all the saints, who are conversant with the divine rule and do not pursue errors by diverging from the way.

16. *Who shall rise up for me against the evil-doers? Or who shall stand with me against the workers of iniquity?* He passes to the third section, in which he maintains that God is his only helper against hostile spirits. Because there is no man strong enough to grapple with them by his own strength, we must take this as a question: *Who shall rise up for me?* In other words, no-one stands with me to fight against demons, for men prefer to follow demons by wickedly imitating them. An enemy, not a follower, is an opponent. He added: *Or who shall stand with me against the workers of iniquity?* It is as if he were about to fight in the battle-line and be wounded by diverse javelins; and he does not conquer by hand-to-hand conflict, but rather obtains victory by suffering. This is the kind of conflict in which he who endures is victorious, and he who wounds loses. This is the sense which Paul expresses: *Our wrestling is not against flesh and blood, but against the principalities and powers of this darkness, against the spirits of wickedness in high places.*[19]

17. *Unless the Lord had been my helper, my soul had almost dwelt in hell.* With an eye first on human weakness, he nowhere finds one to help him. But when he turns to the Lord he at once finds a possible source of aid. He says: "Unless the Lord had been my helper, I would have fallen at once into that pit in which sinners can certainly be plunged." This is the sense of *my soul had almost dwelt in hell.* He could have been deceived by empty persuasion if he had not deserved to be freed by the Lord.

18. *If I said, My foot is moved, thy mercy, O Lord, assisted me.* Here is shown the benefit of a most speedy confession, for once he said he had slipped, he at once experienced God's gifts; he was delivered with a happy outcome, and was able to escape from his guilt because he did not deny his sin before the Judge. So it was that when Peter was summoned and walked on the sea-waves, he trembled with fear, but he

deserved rapid deliverance because he immediately cried out that in his weakness he was drowning; divine mercy at once attended him, and the extended hand rescued him when a lack of faith, against which we must beware, was causing him to drown.[20] Such is the power exercised by speedy confession at the outset. Mercy brings aid before punishment strikes.

19. *After the multitude of my sorrows in my heart, thy comforts have given joy to my soul.* His wounds indeed are many, but the medicine is wholly adequate, for he says that after the harsh pains have come consoling remedies. His phrase, *in my heart,* refers to his most salutary reflections, for when he pondered in his mind retribution in eternity, he undoubtedly scorned temporal evils. He was thus strengthened, obtaining the remedy by the means which he decided led him to Christ. These are the comforts which give joy to souls though bodies are seen to bear affliction.

20. *Doth the seat of iniquity stick to thee who dost fashion grief in thy commandment?* This must be spoken in the negative sense, implying: "Surely the place of ambush has no part in You?." For only what is known to be in harmony with His rules can draw close to the just Lord. The nature of Christ the Lord is thus explained by rejecting what He is not, which is the eighth type of definition, called in Greek *kat'aphairesin tou enantiou,* and in Latin *per privantiam contrarii.*[21] *The seat of iniquity* is the pleasurable possession of this world which cannot attach itself to the Lord, for He has warned His servants not to be enticed by such things. His own precept contains this: *Blessed are they that mourn, for they shall be comforted;* and again: *Blessed are they that suffer persecution for justice's sake, for theirs is the kingdom of heaven.*[22] By fashioning (*fingere*) we mean "moulding"; so we often call a potter a fashioner (*figulus*). Then again a liar regards himself as one who can fashion something. So the word is applied to many things, but properly understood when aptly associated with motives or persons.

21. *They will hunt after the soul of the just, and will condemn innocent blood.* We read that this has often occurred in the case of martyrs; harsh persecutors strive to trap innocent souls by some trick. *They will hunt* (*captabunt*) stands for "They will treat craftily" (*captiose tractabunt*) because they cannot find true cause for charging such people.

The words that follow, *and will condemn innocent blood,* are to be read as an abomination; the wickedness of men does not refuse to depict criminal actions as virtuous. The blood of holy men is grievously sought, though praise and obeisance ought to be offered them. The verse can also be applied to the Lord Saviour who was truly innocent and spotless, and who accepted the sentence of unjust condemnation for our redemption.

22. *And the Lord has become my refuge, and my God the help of my hope.* To demonstrate that the persecutions of men are powerless, he says that the divine refuge became more readily available to him when the arrogance of human persecution was at its height. It is through this persecution that the holy palms of martyrs take seed; through it the blessedness of their crown is prepared; through it the marriage-garment is granted; through it the kingdom of heaven is unbarred; and all that is sought with great longing is granted more readily when persecution rages. Next comes: *And my God the help of my hope.* The word *help* shows that he is still to suffer; for this reason he finally added: *Of my hope,* for in this world we still have hope, but do not possess the actuality, whereas when the time of revelation dawns, we shall leave the hope behind because by then we shall possess our desire. As Paul says: *For what a man seeth, why doth he hope for? But if we hope for that which we see not, we wait for it with patience.*[23] So just as earlier the prophet enunciated the cry of the saints with the words: *How long shall sinners, O Lord, how long shall sinners glory?*[24] so now he removed the reason for all hesitation with the words: *The Lord has become my refuge, and my God the help of my hope.*

23. *And he will render them their iniquity, and in their malice the Lord our God will destroy them.* See how all doubt has been dispelled by this most wholesome conclusion. At the appropriate time the Lord will repay their deeds to those whom He allegedly did not see or apprehend. But let us understand the meaning of the words: *He will render them their iniquity;* in other words, His repayment to wicked men will accord with their aspirations to evil conduct and not with the good which they are seen to perform all unknowing. Those who persecute persons who are very holy despatch them to the kingdom of heaven, but they believe that they are destroying them after deciding with evil

intention to slaughter them. Such men as these will be judged on the malice which they are known to have entertained. Observe that the term *malice* is said to be capable of all sins. Just as charity contains many kinds of virtues, so malice embraces different evil deeds. *He will destroy them*, that is, make them strangers to His kingdom; when they are excluded from this great gift, the wicked will then endure a punishment beyond understanding.

Conclusion Drawn From the Psalm

Let us observe the beauty with which this psalm shines forth, and how it is fittingly opposed to the grumbling under which the human race grievously toiled. Let no-one envy those who are to perish; let no-one reckon as happy those who will be condemned eternally. Instead, let us love the afflictions which make us blessed for ever. If we refrain from spitting out the physician's bitter potion so that we may be able to obtain temporal health, what person of sound mind would not seek the tribulation which he knew he could endure to obtain eternal joys, especially as the right hand of the Creator aids us more copiously when we are in wretchedness? So we ought not to be troubled, for he who assaults us is not as powerful as He who defends us.

COMMENTARY ON PSALM 94

1. *Praise of a canticle, for David himself.* The force of this psalm is not foretold by any obscure interpretation of names, nor by the parallel of any historical account. We read openly and briefly on the outside what is ascertained deep within. *Praise* denotes the voice's devotion, *canticle*, mental delight; both should be united in the act of psalm-singing so that our tongue's task may be fulfilled with the addition of joy. *For David himself* denotes the Lord Saviour, to whom this praise is sung. The first part of the psalm sings of Him, the second is uttered by the Lord Himself. Note that the praises of men are sung with exaggeration and exaltation, but God's praise must be uttered with a certain perfection, but when reconsidered is always found to rise higher.

Division of the Psalm

The prophet foresees that the crowd of Jews can show resistance to the Lord Christ, so at the outset he invites the Hebrew people to sing a psalm as he details the Lord's praises with the sweetest truth. Secondly, the Lord Christ Himself speaks, so that the Jewish people may not harden their hearts and may not undergo the experience of their fathers, who did not deserve to enter the promised land. So the marvellous economy of the psalm ensured first that the prophet encouraged the people with friendly enticements, and then the Lord Himself warned the most obdurate of them to soften their stony hearts by pondering the majesty of their Lord.

Explanation of the Psalm

Come, let us exult before the Lord: let us show jubilation before God our saviour. Like a judge's herald, the Church's cock which arouses the people invites those who pray to wake from the sleep of this world and sing praises to the Lord with happy exultation. *Come* is said to those who he feels are stationed afar off, who have not yet attached themselves with purity of faith. Though we never withdraw ourselves from the Lord since He is wholly everywhere, we none the less become distant when we are displaced through the nature of our deeds. As the Lord says through His prophet: *The people glorify me with their lips, but their heart is far from me.*[1] Next he reveals the feast to which he invites them: he says: *Let us exult.* But since there is also worldly exultation, which considerably dominates the minds of unfaithful people, he added: *Before the Lord.* One can truly presume with joy on Him when exultation elicits instruction rather than destruction. Next follows: *Let us show jubilation before God our saviour.* We have often said that jubilation is a great feeling of joy which cannot be put into words, but is uttered at the top of one's voice; it reveals the inner joy which language cannot express. When he says: *Before God our saviour,* he means the Lord Saviour, who brought salvation to us by dying, afforded us an example by suffering, and bestowed saving gifts by rising again. So the word *saviour* was more than enough to show to whom this praise was addressed.

2. *Let us anticipate his appearance with confession, and show jubilation to him with psalms.* Anticipation means performing some action before a person thought to be approaching can be sighted. *Appearance* means His presence at the time of His judgment, when He will be seen as fearsome by all. We have said that confession must be interpreted in two senses: we confess when we discharge the Lord's praises with pious devotion, and also when we condemn our sins in making the satisfaction of repentance. He warns us that we must do this in this world so as to confess our evil deeds before the coming of the Judge; otherwise He may come and search out the cause of our inevitable condemnation. Next comes: *And show jubilation to him with psalms.* Observe the control with which he orders the entire thought. He assigned tribulation to our confession and joy to our jubilation, so that once the devoted minds of the faithful were purified by this twin change in our affairs, they could be offered up. His repetition of *let us show jubilation* is not idle; it is to ensure that by the repetition you acknowledge what is absolutely necessary.

3. *For the Lord is a great God, and a great king above all gods.* For the next three verses reasons are given why we must show jubilation before the Lord. This figure is called *aetiologia,*[2] or explanation of the cause. By saying *for the Lord is a great God,* he shows that none other is to be preferred, for the word *great* is used only to denote Him who holds the citadel of highest power. Next comes: *And a great king above all gods.* We read that gods were often invented by men, for example Jupiter, Mars, Saturn and the other idols. As the psalmist is to say in the next psalm: *For all the gods of the Gentiles are devils: but the Lord made the heavens.*[3] We also read that holy men were established by the Lord as gods, as in the passage: *God hath stood in the congregation of gods: in the midst of them he judgeth gods.*[4] Over those gods, whether fashioned by men or appointed by Himself, the almighty Christ is a great King, for He excels them more than royal power can outshine private individuals. Truly indeed is He called King, for He both creates and rules all things.

4. *For the Lord does not reject His people. For in his hand are all the ends of the earth: and the heights of the mountains are his.* After speaking of the Lord's greatness, he passes to His wonderful and boundless clemency. He says that the Lord does not reject the Jewish people which he is known to have chosen for himself. From that people come

the prophets, from that people the apostles and many faithful persons who believed in the Lord with pure hearts. As Paul has it: *What shall we say, brothers? Hath God cast away His people which he foreknew? God forbid. For I am an Israelite from the seed of Abraham, of the tribe of Benjamin.*[5] Next comes: *For in his hand are all the ends of the earth.* This has reference to all nations subject with faithful devotion to Christ the Lord. One wall was the Jewish people, the other the summoning of the Gentiles, who at their coming with inseparable love pressed their lips, so to say, to the corner-stone which is Christ the Lord. Of Him it was written: *The stone which the builders rejected has become the head of the corner.*[6] He added: *And the heights of the mountains are his.* The heights of the mountains are earthly honours and worldly powers, which he says belong to the Lord so that we may not be dislocated through being puffed up by them. Though the sea runs high through fierce winds, it has the shore as its boundary; in the same way though worldly powers are not circumspect in boasting of their strength, they accept a limitation on their sway.

5. *For the sea is his, and he made it: and his hands formed the dry.* The sea denotes the nations, which are disturbed in this world by various blasts of vices. He says that they were made by the Lord so that you may realise that all things are subject to His will. Everyone who performs some actions has those acts under His control; as another psalm has it: *All the nations thou hast made shall come and adore before thee, O Lord.*[7] Next comes: *And his hands formed the dry.* Earlier he spoke of the sea and here of the dry, which is reasonably interpreted as the earth, for it is always intrinsically dry unless watered by river-floods or showers. In the same way our hearts are barren and dry, failing to bear good crops unless they are watered by the Lord's mercy and unless He deigns to steady our vacillating and tottering persons with the gift of His mercy. So, as was said earlier, we must append to all these verses: *Let us show jubilation to him.*

6. *Come, let us adore and fall down before him: let us weep before the Lord that made us.* At the beginning of the psalm he invites the people to show jubilation; now he urges them to seek the safety of repentance —and rightly, because earlier the people he invited to exult were novices, and he did not seek to impose on them a possible source of fear when they were still apprehensive. But after the glory and power of the Lord has been recounted, he appropriately imposed tearful

confession, for the spirit when instructed could not reject that most wholesome medicine. Note here that the posture for holy prayer is laid down. *Let us adore* means "let us bend and incline our bodies"; *let us fall down* means "let us prostrate ourselves before Him, and stretch ourselves out by wholly relaxing our limbs"; this tends to happen when the spirit is fired with deep compunction, and humbles itself in lowly prayers. He added: *Let us weep before the Lord that made us.* It is a gesture of great confidence to weep before Him who deigned in His devotion to fashion us. He speedily recognises His workmanship if He sees our hearts turned to Him. So weeping before the Lord means pouring out devoted tears and condemning our most wicked deeds, so that we may deserve to obtain forgiveness for the things which we abandon from fear of the Lord. If we pray with total purity of heart, He who made us will readily restore us. In this way the picture of persons praying is described by the figure called *characterismos*.[8]

7. *For he is the Lord our God, and we are his people and the sheep of his pasture, if today you shall hear his voice.* A threefold reason is given why the Lord is to be adored. First, because He is the Lord our God, so that the duty of adoration seems rightly to be offered Him. Secondly, because we are His people. And next comes: *And the sheep of his pasture;* this is the third clearly bestowed promise. The status of the people is again being defined; they are *the sheep of the Lord's pasture.* *Pasture* denotes the heavenly gifts on which the soul grows fat with sweet feasting. The definition of the Christian people as the sheep of the pasture is excellent, for they have the blessed lot of being filled with eternal delights. *Sheep* signifies simplicity of heart, a clear attribute of the people in harmony with their shepherd through their gentle devotion. But a single condition is imposed on all this, *if today you shall hear his voice,* that is, hear the words which He is to speak next. The flock which does not hear the shepherd's voice is not called his, and is not set in the pasture; as we read in the gospel: *My sheep hear my voice, and they follow me; and I know them, and no man plucks them out of my hand,*[9] and the rest. *Today* signifies always, for He who offers saving advice must be listened to continually. The apostle powerfully expressed the force of these words: *But exhort one another every day, while it is called Today.*[10] Up to now the prophet has spoken; now let us examine what follows.

8. *Harden not your hearts as in bitterness, according to the day of*

temptation in the wilderness. We have reached the second beginning, in which the Lord Saviour addresses the Jews to prevent their imitating the obstinacy of their parents and thus becoming exiled from the Lord's rest. He says: *Harden not your hearts,* for the hearts of unbelievers are quite stony, and truly comparable to rocks which do not admit fertilising rain because they are hard with the aridity of their barrenness. He further cites most famous examples, so that He may deter by mention of a most celebrated calamity those who He knew were headstrong. We read in Exodus[11] of the Jewish temptation, when they rose against Moses with grievous grumbling, saying that no food was being provided for them in the desert, and that no drinkable water was available from God's bounty. They were asking for necessities, but their intention was accursed because they had no belief in the power of the Godhead. So the sin of their parents has to be repeated to them so that they may fear the punishment which it deserves.

9. *Where your fathers tempted me, they proved me and saw my works.* *Where* denotes the wilderness, as he said earlier, where human frailty made trial of God. But at once the power of the Godhead was manifest, when food came from the lower air, and drink from the rock. The rock brought forth streams of water, but the hearts of the faithless hardened into a stony aridity. But what madness is it to continue to pursue the vices of those who we know were so severely punished? When He says: *Your fathers,* He is pointing as well to those obdurate people themselves, for each of them has that notorious father whom they are known to imitate. As the Lord Himself says to the Jews in the gospel: *You are of your father the devil.*[12] Next comes: *They proved me, and saw my works.* They tested Him especially when manna rained on them in their hunger, when a crowd of quails was bestowed on them, when a flood of water flowed out of dry rocks.[13] As for the addition: *And saw my works,* here their infidelity is being rebuked, for they beheld with physical eyes what they refused to believe with the heart's gaze. So He said: *They saw,* not "They believed."

10. *For forty years I was close to this generation, and I said: They always err in heart, and they have not known my ways.* This length of time is found to have been stated to indicate a great mystery. Whereas the Lord fasted for forty days to achieve this mystical number, and He completed forty days with the apostles after the resurrection so that the whole world might believe, the Jews were found to be resistant,

being unwilling to give assent to the benefits received over forty years. A greater fall is in store for them because a lasting arrogance swells in them.

11. *I swore to them in my wrath: they shall not enter my rest.* God is said to swear in two ways. He swears in a peaceful and gentle way, as we read in another psalm: *Once have I sworn about my holy one: to David I will not lie.*[14] But here He is said to swear in anger, because we find Him threatening vengeance. Clearly, however, this oath is relevant to the strength of the promise. If men swear to abide by their promises, how much more is God said to swear, so that what has been foretold may come to pass with the requisite consistency! But God swears by Himself, for He has no better; as He says to Abraham: *By my own self have I sworn, saith the Lord: I shall bless you with a blessing.*[15] But human persons call on God because they know He avenges infidelity. This is why men are forbidden to swear, because they cannot fulfil their promises by their own efforts. What then does the Lord swear? That the obdurate will not enter into His rest, but instead eternal death will embrace those who have not deserved to attain the blessings of making satisfaction to Him. It is right that they cannot enter into rest, for they offend Christ Himself who is the Gate to peacefulness. We must however investigate what His words *they shall not enter into my rest* mean. The teacher of the Gentiles explains the passage in this way, with the words: *And God rested the seventh day from all his works.*[16] So the person who has entered into His rest obtains rest also from his own works, as God did from His. He is pointing to the blessed time when the just, after the struggle of this world, enjoy eternal rest. This will be withheld from the unholy who have grown hard in their wickedness.

Conclusion Drawn From the Psalm

Listen, you Jews who remain obdurate with sacrilegious minds, so that if you do not recall your blessings, you may at least fear the punishments which are your due. What does failure to enter into the Lord's rest mean other than enduring undying torments? We beg you not to let the error of others involve you. Convert what your fathers sought into a nobler demand. If you ask for water in the desert, assemble at the Lord's font. If you long for manna, receive the body of the Lord Saviour. Those earlier gifts brought punishment to your fathers, but these bring eternal rest to you. You can do more. Overcome your predecessors in faith, spurn their unbelieving hearts. Listen, and with God's enlightenment believe what your forbears refused to accept when they beheld it, for their will was blinded. Do not dissemble, while there is still time. If you refuse to acknowledge God's warning now, you will later have to endure His judgment.

COMMENTARY ON PSALM 95

1. *A canticle of David, when the house was built after the captivity.* So far as the literal sense is concerned, the heading points to the time when the temple at Jerusalem is known to have been refurbished by Torobabel son of Salathiel,[1] after it had been levelled to the ground by a hostile band of Chaldeans. But since he says nothing of this kind in what follows, and since the headings of psalms are never at variance with their content, it remains for us to investigate it in the spiritual sense. A destroyed house is built up when a soul following the captivity of sin begins to return to an understanding of the truth through the generosity of the Lord. This house, which is the universal Church in which Christ dwells, is always raised up on living stones, because every day it gains increase in building from its confessors, and does not cease to be built up until the number of the predestined is attained at the end of the world. We must store this psalm in our minds as the second of those proclaiming the first and second coming of the Lord.[2]

Division of the Psalm

In the first section of the psalm the prophet warns all and sundry to sing to the Lord and to announce through the whole world the coming of the Lord's incarnation, for He is the true Lord over all gods. In the second section he advises the different races first to offer themselves and then to perform the tasks of proclamation by recounting both comings of the Lord, the first when He was judged by man and the second when He will come to judge the world.

Explanation of the Psalm

Sing ye to the Lord a new canticle: sing to the Lord, all the earth. In the previous psalm the prophet advised the Jews to abandon their hardness of heart, and come to believe in the Lord Christ. But because their obdurate malevolence was to remain in them, he now appropriately warns the Gentiles that they should address Him with a new canticle. It is the person who shrugs off the old man and is blessedly renewed by the grace of baptism who sings a new canticle to the Lord; and then the Lord's house is built up from him, when after the devil's dominion he is gained to join the number of the most blessed gathering. This is the song that consoles the purest of minds, this is the tune which brings pleasure deep within, when the soul which reckons that God's grace will free it from sins truly bursts into song. Next comes: *Sing to the Lord, all the earth.* The repetition is itself pleasant. There can be no tedium in such words when no person's emotions can be sated. By saying: *All the earth,* he denoted the Catholic Church, which we know extends through the whole world. Within brief compass he both refuted the Jews because he gave access to the Gentiles, and disposed of Donatus[3] because he did not refuse the grace of confession to all and sundry. So that you would interpret the command as addressed to men, he said: *Sing,* for men can truly sound forth the Lord's praises; and again, he joined the plural of *sing* to the earth, which would be quite inappropriate if he had wished to interpret it as the soil.

2. *Sing ye to the Lord, and bless his name: announce clearly his salvation from day to day.* It is not accidental that the repetition is built up with three-fold beauty, for Christ's praise is honour to the whole Trinity. We bless His name when we confess our salvation in every way. This figure is called *epimone*[4] or frequent repetition of a statement, which whether appropriately used in praise or in blame imparts great power of emphasis. Next comes: *Announce clearly his salvation from day to day.* The phrase, "one day after another," distinctly denotes two days. We reckon that this is a reference to the Old and New Testaments, for both shine with the brightness of the eternal Sun. The saving Lord is clearly heralded by them, for through the Testaments His future coming and His arrival were revealed. The prophets prom-

ised His coming, the evangelists declared that He had come. Thus the two heavenly days are shown to have declared His glory.

3. *Declare his glory among the Gentiles: among all the peoples his wonders.* Whereas earlier he said: *Announce his salvation,* here he says: *Declare his glory;* both expressions are most apt. The Lord was to be announced as Saviour, and His glory was to be declared through the Gentiles, because it proclaimed the Author of this great miracle. The Jew must listen, and realise that he was spurned through his wicked stubbornness; for he says: "Declare it not to the Jews, but to the Gentiles." To prevent your interpreting it otherwise, he added: *Among all the peoples;* by this phrase he embraced all nations wholly. Next follows: *His wonders,* in other words, the mystery of His incarnation: though He is the highest, He became the lowliest to deliver us. Let us appreciate the great blessing imparted by the building of the holy house, which as we know has embraced the whole earth.

4. *For the Lord is exceedingly great and praiseworthy: he is to be feared above all gods.* Here he explains why His wonders and His glory are to be proclaimed, *For the Lord is great.* This figure is called *aetiologia,* or explanation of the reason.[5] *Great* is a reference to His power, for He is more powerful than all things; *praiseworthy* to His devotion, for when we were captives He redeemed us with His precious blood. *Exceedingly* is appropriate to both, for the extent of His greatness and His praiseworthiness was beyond description, and because his mind could not assess them he neatly added: *exceedingly.* So his failure to explain his meaning was a most eloquent indication, and he expressed what he meant by his inability to grasp it. Next follows: *He is to be feared above all gods.* Here we must interpret *gods* as those invented in unholy belief by the Gentiles. He identifies them in the next verse; though they seem worthy of adoration and fear to foolish minds, the Lord is much more fearsome, for the multitude of His wonders is beyond understanding, and the fullness of His majesty beyond our grasp.

5. *For all the gods of the Gentiles are demons: but the Lord made the heavens.* By the fifth type of definition, called in Greek *kata tēn lexin* and in Latin *ad verbum,*[6] the identity of the gods of the Gentiles is wonderfully grasped; they are demons. Demons are of service to none. They believe in themselves, and always deceive, always mock. Though in Latin *daemones* are called 'knowing ones' as being divine

spirits (*di manes*),[7] in human conversation the term demons is a rebuke, for we use it for those whom we consider worthy of curses, and
reasonably so, for the knowledge which they have is not true knowledge as it does not conform to the control of their Creator. In similar
fashion we call philosophers wise men, but the definitive judgment of
Paul attends them: *The wisdom of this world is foolishness before God.*[8] So
it is vital that we regard these "knowing ones" as ignoramuses. A
demon, then, is a substance created by God which like that of the good
angels is superior to men, but which because of the effect of its pride
has reached the stage of abandoning its natural dignity, and is always
engaged in evil activities. Such are the demons which destroy other
men and deceive themselves. These are precisely the gods of the
Gentiles, which by fruitless prophecies and empty delusions about the
future hasten to deceive the souls of those who consult them. Next
follows: *But the Lord made the heavens;* observe what is indeed worthy
praise of the Lord, for when the psalmist says that He made the
heavens, he adequately indicates all the creatures formed within them.
Similarly we include the lesser in the greater when we speak of the
building of a city or the construction of a house; the remaining parts
are included in the general description. Observe what the implication
is of: *He made the heavens.* The gods were brought to view by the false
imagination of men, but God made the heavens, where those gods
deserve neither to approach nor to dwell. Alternatively, *heavens* denotes the apostles and holy men who habitually control the demons
through the Lord's gift. The demonstrative genre of eloquence[9] is
briefly encompassed here. He earlier poured abuse on the gods of the
Gentiles and later appended praises of the Lord, for the brightness of
day is more welcome when a dark night has preceded it.

6. *Confession and beauty are in his sight: holiness and magnificence in
his sanctification.* He shows that the usefulness of the Catholic religion lies in its advice to the whole community which it establishes. He
explains how people become beautiful and magnificent, for they have
deserved to obtain pardon for their sins. Beauty does indeed rightly
follow confession, for none can be beautiful unless cleansed by the
Lord's pity. Our sins make us foul, but the bath of repentance makes
us handsome. This is why he says that the most spotless beauty stands
before the Lord's sight, for it has been cleansed by faithful confession.
Next comes: *Holiness and magnificence in his sanctification.* He elabo-

rates on what he said earlier: holiness and magnificence, in other words, glory and enduring blessedness, are the beauty conferred on the faithful. *In his sanctification* denotes the words which the elect will hear: *Come ye, blessed of my father, possess ye the kingdom prepared for you from the foundation of the world.*[10] Observe the beauty which the sun does not make swarthy, which age does not diminish, which is always gleaming and new. It ensures no reverse, for it has no fault in its lasting nature. As for his word magnificence, it signifies that those who have deserved to be honoured by His sanctification are always great and always lofty.

7. *Bring ye to the Lord, ye native lands of the Gentiles, bring ye to the Lord glory and honour.* After proclaiming the great deeds of the Lord and the gifts to the blessed, in the second section he more earnestly counsels the Gentiles to renounce all delay and to bring glory and honour to the Lord. When he speaks of lands of the Gentiles, he means more than if he were merely to say "Gentiles." A race can embrace some foreigners; when we speak of a nation, we do not include outsiders, but denote a race consisting of only one blood. In this passage the wording is: *Ye native lands of the Gentiles,* so that no stranger, no foreigner would be excluded. *Patria* (native land) is derived from *patris atria* (the father's courts).[11] Next follows: *Bring ye to the Lord glory and honour;* he is urging one and all to bring glory and honour to the Lord. It is glory to the Lord when any individual lives a praiseworthy life, for the Lord is glorified in such people because He gains praise from the way in which the faithful live. As He says to His disciples in the gospel: *So let your light shine before men that they may see your good works, and glorify your Father who is in heaven.*[12] It is honour to the Lord when we thank Him for His gifts, and if we obtain any blessing we proclaim that it is bestowed by Him. As we read in the gospel: *Were not ten made clean? There is no-one found to give honour to God except this Samaritan.*[13]

8. *Bring to the Lord glory to His name. Bring up sacrifices, and enter into his courts.* Just as earlier he used *sing* in triple repetition, so here he uses *bring* a third time, so that you may acknowledge that the mystery of the holy Trinity always resides in Christian teaching. People bring glory to His name, then, when they change for the better in zeal for devotion, and in all things proclaim to themselves the consubstantial and almighty Trinity, separated only by Persons and not by

difference of nature. Next comes: *Bring up sacrifices and enter into his courts.* By sacrifices he does not mean cattle as victims, but the pure offerings of our conscience, from which no blood runs but devoted tears well forth. These are the sacrifices which he mentioned in Psalm 50: *A contrite and humble heart God does not despise.*[14] But realise that he first wrote *bring up,* and then *enter,* for those who do not bear such sacrifices are not judged worthy to enter the courts of the Lord. We must not regard it as idle that he used the plural courts, for the Lord's courts are the apostles or prophets, through whom the faithful gain entry to the Lord.

9. *Adore ye the Lord in his holy court: and let all the earth be moved from his presence.* The Lord is truly adored when the sacrifices indicated earlier are borne in, so that the entreaty of the confessor may deserve to reach the Creator's ears. It is not without significance that in the previous verse he wrote courts, but here speaks in the singular of court; from those courts—patriarchs, apostles, prophets—we attain this court, which is nothing other than the Catholic Church, in which the power of the Lord's majesty is adored. Next comes: *Let all the earth be moved from his presence.* Since he had told the faithful to take up their good works and enter, he now says that lovers of the world must be removed from His presence. He has not said: "Let the whole earth be moved into His presence," but *from his presence,* a phrase which we use also today to those whom we banish from our sight. They are well called *the earth,* because they do not abandon earthly vices. Yet others have stated that this verse must be interpreted in a good sense, suggesting that the earth is moved when the sinner is led to repentance by God's pity. Thus the unfathomable depths of divine scripture are both understood in various ways and seen to be established in the one truth.

10. *Say among the nations: The Lord hath reigned from the wood. For he hath corrected the world which shall not be moved. He will judge the people with justice, and the races with his anger.* Those whom he commanded to adore the Lord in His holy court he now urges to proclaim to the nations the venerable mysteries. They must say among the nations that the Lord will reign from the wood of the cross; not from the wood of the tree in Paradise, by which the devil was seen to hold the human race captive, but from the wood from which freedom raised its head, and life arose. On that wood in Paradise hung the death

caused by transgression, but on this wood shone forth the faith of confession. The first led to hell, but the second directs us to heaven. *Hath reigned;* let us understand this as "His reign became known," when the Lord Saviour appeared to the world; for when did He not reign, since He ever continues with Father and holy Spirit in the power of His omnipotence? Other translators do not render *from the wood,* but it is enough for us that it is maintained by the authority of the seventy interpreters.[15] The Lord's cross corrected the debased and twisted world when it converted the hearts of pagans by the rule of faith. We must interpret *world* here in the good sense; you often get a variation of meaning in the divine Scriptures, according to the nature of the passages. He says that this world shall not be moved at all, for it perseveres in the steadfastness of faith; it is not like that mentioned earlier: *Let all the earth be moved from his presence.* The earth there is moved to be converted from evil actions; the earth here is not moved, for it sticks in the steadfastness of true faith. Next comes: *He will judge the people with justice. People* is here better understood as the faithful who will be judged in the calm of heavenly mercy, when the Lord will present them with their promised rewards. As for the additional words, *and the races with his anger,* he is pointing to the proud and the wicked, who obtain their portion with the devil. Note how he indicates with two words the secret truths of weighty matters. Justice applies to the blessed, anger to the undying punishment of the impious. And observe that: *Say among the nations,* is to be prefixed to all the clauses in this verse.

11. *Let the heavens rejoice, and let the earth be glad: let the sea be moved, and the fullness thereof.* He earlier said: *He will judge the people with justice, and the races with anger,* words which reveal the time of the judgment to come; so now we have a most beautiful and pleasing digression. He says that at that time the heavens rejoice, and the earth is glad, and the sea is moved. *The heavens,* as has often been said, denotes apostles, prophets and other faithful on whom the divine Majesty is known to rest as though they were the heavens. *The earth* denotes sinners, but sinners who by the blessing of satisfaction have deserved to return to the Lord's grace. The earth itself can rejoice at the coming of its Judge, for it realises that it is absolved from its sins. Next comes: *Let the sea be moved, and the fullness thereof.* He makes the sea here represent the people set in the salt surge of the world and

tossed by various storms. They are moved to joy since they have obtained the gift of conversion. He spoke of the fullness thereof so that you would interpret it as the totality of the nations.

12. *The plains and all the things that are in them shall be joyful. Then shall all the trunks of the woods rejoice.* We must likewise interpret *plains* here in the good sense, because what extends with the most beautiful evenness we call level. So plains here means persons who thrive with fame for justice, who are not swollen with arrogance or crabbed with ill-temper, but well-balanced with mild gentleness. Next follows: *Then shall all the trunks of the woods rejoice. Then* denotes the second coming when He will judge the world. The trunks of the woods by themselves bear bitter and barren fruit, but when they are implanted they become rich with the sweetest fecundity; in the same way the nations, which had earlier been like the trunks of the woods, are brought into fruitful cultivation and will exult before the Lord's face with the great gift of joy. But when he says *all the trunks,* he wishes this to be interpreted as the part which could be implanted by goodly precepts and transformed.

13. *Before the face of the Lord, because he cometh: because he cometh to judge the earth.* Because he had stated that the believers will rejoice, he says that this will happen not in corners or remote places, but before the face of the Judge, for it will be a joy abundant and beyond reckoning when rewards are allotted and unending tranquillity is bestowed. So that you would not regard this as the first coming at the Lord's incarnation, he says: *Because he cometh,* and there follows: *Because he cometh to judge the earth.* If he had ended the statement after the first phrase, you could perhaps have interpreted it as the coming which is now past. But when he added: *Because he cometh to judge the earth,* he wished us to understand only the coming which we know we are still to endure. The prophet Ezechiel also attests it: *Thus saith the Lord God to these bones: Behold, I send spirit into you, and you shall live. And I will lay sinews upon you and will cause flesh to grow over you, and will cover you with skin: and I will give you spirit, and you shall live. And you shall know that I am the Lord.*[16] Daniel too says: *And many of those that sleep in the earth will come forth through clefts, some into life everlasting and others into reproach and confusion.*[17] The earth here means all the people of the world, so that He bestows rewards on the good, but eternal punishments on the wicked.

He shall judge the orb of the world with justice, and the people with his truth. First comes the comprehensive statement that the divine justice will judge the world, that is, all mankind; then follows the nature of the judgment with the phrase, *the people with his truth.* In the separation between right and left there will be two peoples to whom He will give the judgment of His truth. So those who have faithfully believed in Him can enjoy the blessedness of His kingdom, but those who have clung doggedly to the vices of the world endure the punishment which is their due in company with its originator the devil. We must certainly investigate the fact that here he speaks of the circle of the earth, and again in the next psalm he writes: *His lightnings have shone forth to the circle of the earth,*[18] and in numerous other places he relates that the earth is bounded by this circular shape; but then Psalm 106 encloses the area of the earth with four poles in the words: *From the rising and from the setting of the sun, from the north and from the sea.*[19] There is the clearest of examples too in the gospel of this standpoint, where it says: *He shall send his angels with a trumpet and a great voice, and they shall gather the elect from the four corners of the earth.*[20] So I think it justifiable to enquire how the earth can be both a square and a circle when these shapes are different as the geometricians state. Scripture calls the shape of the earth circular because it always seems round to those who examine its extremity; the Greeks call the circular form the horizon. But Scripture says that it is fashioned with four points, because they denote the four angles of the square contained within the earth's circle already mentioned. If you draw a straight line from the eastern point to both south and north, and likewise from the western point to south and north, you make a square within the earth's circle which we have mentioned. (Euclid in the fourth book of his *Elements* clearly explains how this square must be shown to be drawn within the circle.)[21] So holy Scripture rightly calls the face of the earth a circle, but also says that it is bounded by four cardinal points.

Conclusion Drawn From the Psalm

Let us listen to what the prophet advises us to sing to the Lord. Bring before Him living sacrifices. Let us have no truck with the devil, and our lot will be undoubtedly with Christ. Then, as the psalm-heading says, after our captivity to sins the Lord's house can be

built on us if we deserve to be accounted living stones. Let us suppli-
cate Him continually and beseech Him unceasingly. He will acknowledge the humble person when He comes to condemn the insolent. He
will not punish the sinner once He establishes that he constantly
confesses his sins.

COMMENTARY ON PSALM 96

1. *A psalm for David himself, when his land was restored again to him.*
Clearly *a psalm for David himself* is to be referred to Christ the Lord.
Next comes: *When his land was restored again to him,* in other words,
when sinners who had diverged in wicked wandering returned to Him
with the help of His grace in cleansed purity of heart. This happened
in the case of the Jews who after the impiety of the crucifixion attained the grace of conversion. The phrase can be interpreted also in
another sense, with the restored land appearing to denote the mysteries of His resurrection; for His body died according to the law of
mankind, but was restored by a unique gift of glory. So let us remember that this is the fourth psalm about His first coming,[1] by which
we know that the world was delivered.

Division of the Psalm

In the first section of the psalm the prophet describes the Lord's
powers after His resurrection in a varied proclamation, and condemns
with appropriate rebuke those who worship idols. In the second, he
turns his words to the Lord, rejoicing that the Catholic Church has
rightly put belief in its Maker. He also urges the faithful to rejoice in
the Lord, for it is His way to deliver those who are seen to be prostrate
under the attacks of cruel men.

Explanation of the Psalm

The Lord hath reigned, let the earth rejoice: let many islands be glad.
When the prophet surveys the world's confusion caused by men's
accursed superstition, he depicts the Lord's praises with wonderful

variation, so that the unfaithful may recognise the true God and cease to have faith in the emptiest of things. A start was made to embrace everything in short compass, and to remove all ravings: *The Lord hath reigned.* So who else is to be worshipped save Him who alone is known to command? Next follows: *Let the earth rejoice.* What would be left for idols, if the whole earth revered the name of the Creator? The thinking earth ought not to worship the most stolid stone, for he who seeks aid from inanimate objects denies himself any result. But there is one Stone which must be spiritually worshipped and feared; it is the Cornerstone. He added: *Let many islands be glad.* Since the Lord reigns through the whole world, the scattered Churches must be glad; they are well compared to islands because they are surrounded by the waves of the world, and are battered by countless persecutions barking all round them. But just as islands experience no damage from raging waves, so the holy Churches are visibly unaffected by the disturbances of their enemies. On the contrary, they break up on their rocks those who rush against them in mountainous waves. Note that he says *Many* and not "all"; this is because of the wicked ways of heretics, which impugn the fame of their Churches by their errors.

2. *Clouds and darkness are round about him: justice and judgment are the correction of his abode.* In this verse the wicked and the religious are told of the Lord's nature. He is seen as cloudy and dark to the uncommitted, for He does not gleam with any brightness on a darkened heart, just as the sun appears shadowy to the bleary-eyed. It is not the source of light but a contracted physical ailment which is responsible for the shadows. As the Lord says in the gospel: *I am come into the world that they who see not may see, and they who see may become blind.*[2] By contrast there follows: *Justice and judgment.* This is how the Lord appears to them who are most clean and pure of heart. He did well to call them *correction,* for they are stripped of the error of wickedness, and are the abode of the Lord Saviour. He now occupies them in His majesty; as Scripture has it: *The soul of the just man is the seat of wisdom.*[3] The logical order of words is this: "Of His abode they are the correction." This indeed is the case, because justice cannot reside in twisted minds. Observe that throughout this and the next four verses the first coming of the Lord is denoted by various allusions. This figure is called *characterismos,* and in Latin is termed *informatio* or *descriptio.*[4]

3. *A fire shall go before him, and shall burn his enemies round about.* A fire went before the Lord's coming when the hearts of the unfaithful seethed at the preaching of the prophets so that they were fired with the heat of anger, and they debated the murder of those preachers. So this is the fire which shall go before Him, but it devoured instead those who stirred it. As the prophet Isaiah says: *And now fire will devour thy enemies.*[5] Next comes: *And shall burn his enemies round about.* *Shall burn,* as we have stated, refers to the indignation and sudden mental heat which the enemies of holy Church experienced at that time. *Round about* we must interpret as "on all sides," for as the preachers were few, a countless crowd of enemies hemmed them in.

4. *His lightnings have shone forth on the orb of the world: the earth saw, and trembled.* This is a very fine and appropriate image. Just as clouds when they rumble and clash (so the physicists tell us) send forth darts of lightning, so the words of the prophets shone out as signs of truth. In fact you often find the prophets in the divine Scriptures compared to clouds; for example: *And I will command the clouds not to rain upon it.*[6] Let us further observe that here again the shape of the earth is described as an orb, as was done already in the previous psalm. The orb is also termed a circle. A circle, as the geometricians have defined it,[7] is flat and enclosed with a single circumference; all the straight lines which extend from the central point of the circle are equal to each other. Once we recognise this lay-out, the shape of the earth becomes quite clear to us. The whole world is also denoted by a straight line through the sky, called by the astronomers the diameter, as in the passage: *From the rising of the sun unto its setting, praise the name of the Lord.*[8] An intelligible line is length without breadth,[9] beginning and ending with a point. A point is that which is divisible into no part. But we must remember that all these—point, line, circle, triangle, quadrilateral and other concepts of this kind—when they come before our eyes are embraced by physical or sensible definitions, but when visualised solely by the mind are undoubtedly only intelligible. (You will find a fuller account of these, sedulous reader, in books on the discipline of geometry.)[10] Next comes: *The earth saw, and trembled.* *The earth saw* means that men recognised the word of the Lord with the heart's eye; *trembled* means that they were terrified by the newness of this great preaching, which made them realise that they

were worshipping mindless idols when they had a Lord worthy of adoration as their highest Creator.

5. *The mountains melted like wax before the face of the Lord: before the face of the Lord all the earth trembled.* Here the mountains denote men who seek high positions in this world, and harden with mindless superstition. They are splendidly compared with liquid wax, for they melt into repentance with an ease commensurate with the unbending immobility which they believed they possessed. When he says: *Before the face of the Lord,* he shows what made the mountains melt like wax. We read of this in another psalm too: *There is no-one that can hide himself from his heat.*[11] But when he says again: *Before the face of the Lord all the earth trembled,* he points to those who have been sighted by His pity and have attained the remedies of satisfaction. Even today we have proof of this happening, when worldly magnates, whether dubbed as pagans or heretics, condemn their superstitious aspirations, and choose instead to enter the Lord's service.

6. *The heavens declared his justice: and all people saw his glory.* After the earlier mention of the clouds, which we stated are interpreted as the prophets, he passes to the heavens, which we must understand as the apostles through whose preaching the Lord's saving justice became known to the world. Then comes: *And all the people saw his glory.* We must interpret *saw* here as "witnessed not with physical eyes but with the heart's eye"; for *glory* tends to be heard, not seen. Elsewhere we read words to be taken in the same sense: *And we saw his glory, as it were of the only-begotten Son.*[12] Alternatively, as some maintain, the coming of the Lord previously visible is being denoted. He spoke of fire, lightning, mountains, heavens; through all these his one aspiration is to announce the Lord Saviour. This figure is called *enigma*[13] or obscure statement, when he says one thing and wishes us to understand another.

7. *Let them all be confounded who adore idols, who glory in their statues. Adore him, all you his angels.* Now that he has prophesied the coming of the Lord, he rebukes those who adore idols, who are not ashamed after this great revelation has been made known to go on worshipping some unidentified rubbish. *Idolum,* an idol, is so called because it is *ipsum dolum,* guile itself, that is, devised by men's falsehood. The word for statue, *simulacrum,* is coined from *simulatio sa-*

cra,[14] because the honour belonging to another is accorded them. So both are clearly to be avoided on the evidence of the names themselves. Since impure spirits are eager to be adored when they claim for themselves false distinctions which their wickedness does not deserve to obtain, note what follows: *Adore him, all you his angels.* The good angel adores the Lord because with upright heart he recognises the Creator and does not allow himself to be worshipped by men. As the angel in Revelations says to John when he falls at his feet: *See thou do it not: I am thy fellow-servant and of thy brethren.*[15] But wicked angels command that they be adored, as in the gospel Satan said to the Lord Christ when he had taken Him up the mountain and shown Him the kingdoms of the world: *All these will I give thee if kneeling down thou wilt adore me.*[16]

8. *Sion heard, and was glad: and the daughters of Juda rejoiced because of thy judgments, O Lord.* The prophet passes to the second section, in which he turns to the Lord and exults joyfully because Sion, in other words the Catholic Church, took in the Lord's judgments with a pure heart. The person who hears the word and intends to believe rejoices that he has heard it; but he who takes it in with deceitful mind goes away saddened, for he has unwittingly heard what he refuses to believe. Sion, as we have often stated, is a mountain at Jerusalem, the meaning of which is "observation"; this is aptly applied to holy Church, for she always gazes on the Lord in His presence by the power of contemplation. Next comes: *And the daughters of Juda rejoiced. Daughters of Juda* denotes religious minds and proved individuals; they are called daughters of Juda because being known to have descent from Judah (hence their other title of *Judaei*) they chose to believe in Christ. He next explains why Sion was glad; it was: *Because of thy judgments, O Lord,* in other words, "Because You turn the sadness of Your servants into joy, and You lay low the proud devil with the virtue of humility."

9. *For thou art the most high Lord over all the earth: thou art exalted exceedingly above all gods.* We do well to interpret *over all the earth* as sinners, and *above all gods* we aptly understand as the just, who we have frequently shown are rightly called gods. Alternatively, by these two phrases he indicates that the Lord rules both earthly and heavenly creatures. As another psalm has it: *For all things serve thee.*[17]

10. *You that love the Lord, hate the evil one. The Lord preserveth the souls of his saints, and he will deliver them out of the hand of sinners.* It seems that here too a categorical syllogism[18] can be fashioned. The saints love the Lord because the Lord guards their souls and delivers them from the hand of sinners: all who love the Lord, because the Lord guards their souls and delivers them from the hand of sinners, hate the evil one: therefore the saints hate the evil one. Now let us discuss the words of the psalm. Here he addresses the good and the faithful, urging them to distance themselves from the devil's malice; he is rightly called the evil one, for all sin comes through him. Why then does loving the Lord entail hating the devil? Because, as Scripture says: *No-one can serve two masters.*[19] This figure is called *parison* or balance of statements consisting of dissimilar phrases.[20] So that no-one should fear to offend the devil, next comes: *The Lord preserveth the souls of his saints, and will deliver them out of the hand of sinners.* So now let none hesitate to hate the evil one, since the Lord is known to preserve the souls of saints. But observe that he speaks of souls, so that you would not confine yourself to bodies, which in many places He abandons to punishment so that He may bestow crowns on martyrs. He delivers souls from the hand of sinners when He does not permit them to be undermined by any wickedness, but delivers them unharmed in so far as He knows that they are pleasing to Him.

11. *Light is risen to the just man, and joy to the right of heart.* He says that to the just man light, that is the most true faith, is risen so that being enlightened he has the beliefs which guide him to the kingdom of heaven. The light on this earth, which men and beasts behold without distinction, is likewise the property of holy men, but that afforded by the Sun which is Christ is said to be peculiar to them. Of this light the wicked will say: *We have erred from the way of truth, and the light of justice hath not shone on us, and the sun hath not risen on us.*[21] Joy is undoubtedly risen to the right of heart when with God's gift they perform actions which they know will be of service to them. There is likewise a suggestion in this passage that lovers of the world enjoy neither assured joy nor true light.

12. *Rejoice, ye just, in the Lord, and give praise to the remembrance of his holiness.* Though earlier He spoke of the blessings which the just receive from the Lord's generosity, he now again reminds them that

they are to rejoice in the Lord and not in human aspirations or in the disastrous self-esteem of this world. As the prophet Isaiah says: *There is no joy to the wicked, says the Lord.*[22] But the just *give praise to the remembrance of his holiness* when they are set in the perennial kingdom, and recall from what depths of disaster in this world they have been removed through the Lord's pity.

Conclusion Drawn From the Psalm

Let us ponder how wholesome is the teaching by which this psalm orders us. It forbids the worship of idols from which we could have incurred eternal death. It aptly inserts praise of the Lord from which our life may undoubtedly benefit. It teaches us not to tremble at afflictions, nor to fear the ills of this world. We can escape all hazards, all mortal dangers with great profit if we love the Author of our salvation. As Paul says: *In all things we suffer tribulation, but are not distressed. We are straitened, but we perish not. Always bearing about in our body the mortification of Jesus, that the life also of Jesus may be made manifest in our mortal bodies,*[23] and the rest, which that outstanding teacher is known to have uttered for the instruction of the human race.

COMMENTARY ON PSALM 97

1. *A psalm for David himself.* These unadorned headings smile on us with the clearest verbal arrangement. They are related to the Lord Saviour. This psalm will tell of the glory of His incarnation and second coming. These topics are described with such varied grace that though they have been mentioned earlier quite often, they shine out before our human intelligence as ever new and marvellous. This is certainly the third psalm[1] on these topics; but these psalms which have embraced both comings of the Lord in a single narrative declare great mysteries to us. In telling of the first, they warn us to seek out the merciful Lord; and in telling the second, they bid us fear the Judge who is to come. This salutary and precious combination affords us reasons for both hope and fear.

Division of the Psalm

The prophet speaks throughout the psalm. In the first section he urges the Christian people to rejoice with the exultation of a new canticle, since the wondrous coming of the Lord Christ has been granted. In the second part he states more copiously in different ways that they must rejoice because the Judgment awaited by the just is known to be at hand, from which through the Lord's mercy they will obtain worthy rewards.

Explanation of the Psalm

Sing ye to the Lord a new canticle. The prophet urges faithful Christians to receive the sacrament of fresh birth, and to hymn together a new canticle about the Lord's incarnation. It is the new man who must sing a new canticle, not the old man who has not yet relinquished Adam's sins but continues with the transgression of the old man. The canticle is new precisely because the world has heard nothing like it. It is new because it is not grimy with age, but ever continues in the grace of its distinction. The source of this new canticle is later revealed.

For the Lord hath done wonderful things. His right hand and his holy arm have saved him. The reason is given for the new canticle: it is because the Lord has done wonderful things, when He made the blind see, the lame walk, the deaf hear, and performed similarly supernatural acts which the text of the gospel intimates. His saints also performed these deeds. Hear what follows, so that you may truly understand the unique dispensation bestowed in this new canticle. The prophet says: *Have saved him,* Him being Christ the Lord when He was a stranger to the sins of this world, and when He rose from the dead speedily within three days. *His right hand,* that is, the almighty Word, is what will save Him. Not that Christ and the almighty Word are two distinct beings, as the madness of Nestorius[2] falsely claims. Rather, he wants you to realise that He saved himself. As He said: *I have the power to lay down my life, and I have power to take it up again.*[3] So far as the addition of the arm is concerned, Isaiah likewise says of the Son: *And to whom is the arm of the Lord revealed?*[4] The right hand signifies marvellous deeds, the arm unique strength.

2. *The Lord hath made known his salvation before the sight of the Gentiles: he hath revealed his justice.* The Lord has made known His salvation, that is, the Lord Saviour, for He is the saving One of whom Simeon said in the temple as he took Him in his hands: *Now thou dost dismiss thy servant, O Lord, in peace, because my eyes have seen thy salvation.*[5] To express the truth of the matter in the clearest terms there follows: *Before the sight of the Gentiles.* As Jeremiah also says: *Afterwards he was seen upon earth, and conversed with men.*[6] The psalmist added: *He hath revealed his justice.* Earlier He had been proclaimed through the prophets beneath a veil, so to say, and when this was removed the appearance of truth emerged at His coming. Note that He is called the right hand, the arm, the salvation, the justice of the Father, so that you may realise that there is a single substance, a single power in both. At what point can He be separated, when it is established that His are not similar attributes but all that is the Father's? As Christ Himself says in the gospel: *All that the Father has is mine, and all that is mine is the Father's.*[7]

3. *He was mindful of his mercy to Jacob, and of his truth toward the house of Israel. All the ends of the earth have seen the salvation of our God.* The words *He was mindful* are used because He fulfilled His promises; this is the promise prophesied by Isaiah, *All flesh shall see the salvation of God.*[8] An appropriate description is pinned to this promise: *His mercy.* The Creator of heaven and earth deigned to become man, and by the blessing of His coming freed the human race which was bound by the chains of sins. Jacob, as we have often said, we may not inappropriately interpret as the people of the New Testament, for just as Jacob was preferred to his brother for the paternal blessing though he was the younger, so the Christian people gained preference over their predecessors of the synagogue in their progress to the faith. The variation in names must not trouble our understanding here, so let us examine why the words, *and of his truth toward the house of Israel,* have been added. This was so that we would realise that it was bestowed not only on the people who after the Lord's coming were called Christians, but also on those who believed that He would be born of a virgin. By *Israel* is denoted every faithful person who beheld God with a pure heart.[9] He showed mercy to Jacob and truth to Israel. Mercy was manifested when He came to deliver men; truth will be

seen when the saints behold face to face Him whom they have beheld (in Paul's words) *through a glass darkly*.[10] He added: *All the ends of the earth have seen the salvation of our God*. These words rule out all the distortions of the heretics who believe that the worship of the Lord Saviour has been granted to particular lands.[11] *They have seen* means "mentally beheld," a result evident through the whole world; for how many were able to see him with bodily eyes among the Jews? His words here, *all the ends of the earth have seen*, are undoubtedly to be understood of their faith, so that the truth of the words can be clearly established for us.

4. *Sing joyfully to God, all the earth: sing, rejoice, and hymn*. He comes to the second section, in which he urges different modes of rejoicing by those who are committed. But these words are aptly applied to the judgment of the Lord with which this psalm is seen to close. *Jubilate* (sing joyfully) means "break into expressions of joy with great delight," so that what cannot be articulated in the utterance of confused words can be made clear by the devoted outburst of the exultant speaker. *All the earth* means the whole Church, which placed its hope with unimpaired devotion in the Lord's coming. Next comes: *Sing, rejoice and hymn*. Though these words seem similar, there is some distinction between them. Sing (*cantare*) means to sound praises to the Lord, offering the service of the Christian voice at its most earnest; rejoice (*exultare*), to declare one's desires with great emotional intensity; hymn (*psallere*), to fulfil the Lord's commands by good works. He urges that this action be performed in many ways because we must rejoice in them with a variety of virtues. This figure is called *homoioptōton*,[12] for the different words, *iubilate, cantate, exultate, psallite*, end with similar sounds.

5. *Hymn the Lord on the harp: on the harp and with the words of a psalm*. These words are linked in most beautiful association, so that of themselves they seem to make a harmony. The instruments of the art of music are called into use to perform the heavenly task. This is essential to the words, so that the perfection may be indicated by certain analogies. That person hymns the Lord on the harp who by physical action performs the injunctions of the Godhead, who breaks bread for the hungry, clothes the naked, consoles the destitute, and performs the other works applicable to the heavenly commands. Next

comes: *On the harp and with the words of a psalm;* he has appended the same instructions in reverse order, so that whichever of them you do first, you realise that they are linked to God's grace in their entirety.

6. *With hammered trumpets and sound of horn make a joyful noise in the sight of the Lord our king.* Let us examine all these words which teem with divine mysteries. The book of Numbers[13] informs us that there were two types of trumpet among the Jews, with symbolic implications. The first was fashioned from hammered silver and is aptly associated with the holy Spirit who spoke through the prophets. The Spirit is called silvery from the purity and brightness of His words; as He Himself says elsewhere: *The words of the Lord are pure words, as silver tried by the fire, purged from the earth, refined seven times.*[14] *Hammered* denotes that the faithful make progress through the Lord's kindness when beaten by different sufferings; the more they are struck by repeated blows of the hard hammer, the more they increase. The hammer is the devil, of whom the prophet says: *The hammer of the whole world is broken.*[15] *The sound of horn* is the constant endurance of patience, which in the faithful lasts like the substance of horn. So on these trumpets the Lord is hymned by the person who in his devotion rejoices in twin virtues: he proclaims the Lord with pure heart, and he endures His mercy with the virtue of patience. Next comes: *Make a joyful noise in the sight of the Lord our king.* In this sentence the statement which in earlier verses was seen to be unfinished is completed; for here he states where we must sing, exult, hymn; where the harp must accompany the psalm, where the psalm must be sung to the harp, where we must sound joyfully on hammered trumpets and horns— that is, in the sight of the Lord our King, when at the Judgment the just will receive their promised rewards. In these diverse ways we are shown that we must rejoice in the Lord's sight by different deeds of holiness, and by our different gifts. Alternatively, he says that these things must be done on this earth, so that our minds may be ever concentrated on Him.

7. *Let the sea be stirred up, and the fullness thereof: the world and all who dwell therein.* Here terror of the future judgment and the fear of the wicked are described, when the sea which lies in the hearts of evil men and in the recollection of their sins is stirred up. He rightly speaks of the fullness thereof, because the numerous sins rouse great waves, and it is stirred up to the fullest extent when the guilty man

knows that he will be condemned. Next follows: *The world;* that too will be stirred up, for a new face was prophesied for it, as we read: *There will be a new heaven and a new earth.*[16] He added: *And all who dwell therein,* so that you would realise that it was actually spoken of men when he earlier said in figure: *Let the sea be stirred up.*

8. *The rivers shall clap their hands to that same purpose: the mountains shall exult before the face of the Lord because he cometh to judge the earth.* We have often remarked that divine Scripture uses diverse images so that the meaning of the words may be hidden from the unholy, and also so that the faithful may be more earnestly fired to seek out that meaning. So here too he states by manifold allegories that we must sing to the Lord. Allegory means saying one thing while meaning another.[17] Earlier he compared sinners to the sea, and now rivers denote holy men who have made good works well forth with heavenly fecundity. *To that same purpose* means "to the Lord Saviour," to whom, as has been shown, they made manifest the actions mentioned. But observe that all this is spoken allusively, for when do rivers have hands except when compared with holy men? Of them it was said: *He that believeth in me, out of his belly shall flow rivers of living water.*[18] Next comes: *The mountains shall exult before the face of the Lord.* Clearly mountains are often cited in both a good and a bad sense. Unholy men swell up with proud effort, attaining the hardness of crags with obstinacy of heart; but the gentle are most enduring in solidity of mind, and though bent low with devoted humility, they rise to the firmest of heights in the hope of future blessedness. These are the persons who will rejoice at the Lord's coming, since at the future judgment they will receive the gifts promised by Him. He added: *Because he cometh to judge the earth.* Here we fittingly interpret the earth as every sinner, for sinners always desire earthly vices. You observe that the whole tenour is directed to the time of the Judgment, so that you can see that all that has been said accords with it.

9. *He shall judge the world with justice, and the people with equity.* Here the world is to be interpreted as the unholy, who are often give the label of earthly. They are to be judged with justice, for they are not to be delivered from their wantonness by any remission. *The people* denotes those of the Jews of proven fidelity and the Gentiles who have become devoted, of whom Christ says: *And other sheep I have that are not of this fold: them also must I bring, that there may be one flock and*

one shepherd.[19] So this people is to be judged with equity, for those who here endured the harshest dangers for the Lord's name will receive their rewards there. As Paul says: *For we shall all stand before the judgment-seat of Christ, that everyone may receive the proper things of the body, according as he has done, whether it be good or evil.*[20] It is clearly stated where the judgment is to take place. As the prophet Joel states: *I will gather together all nations, and will lead them out into the valley of Josaphat: and I will plead with them there for my people and for my inheritance Israel.*[21]

Conclusion Drawn From the Psalm

Why is it that we often find mention in the psalms of musical instruments which do not seem so much to charm our ears as to challenge the hearing of the heart? Since the sounds mentioned here, together with the melody of flutes, are no longer part of the sacred mysteries of our day, it remains for us to seek out the spiritual sense of this matter. Music is the discipline which examines the differences and the harmonies of things in accord with each other, that is, their sounds. This discipline is rightly utilised to express images of things spiritual, for through its power concord exists in discordancy. Whether we are singing a psalm or actively discharging the Lord's commands, we are governed by the grace of the sweetest harmony. If you weigh the reasons for this with deep thought, you will find that every creature with reason, if living under the dominion of its Creator, is not excepted from this harmony. So we are rightly commanded to hymn the Lord unceasingly, to accompany a psalm on the harp, to sing a psalm to the harp, to make a joyful sound with hammered trumpets and horns, so that there is no doubt that these sweet-sounding instruments denote to us the harmony of praiseworthy actions.

COMMENTARY ON PSALM 98

1. *A psalm for David.* I cannot admire sufficiently the worth of this name, which is always attached to psalm-headings and directs our

mental vision to the Lord Christ. It is His honour and power which are hymned in this psalm. How great is the praise of this most holy man, that by his outstanding name the secret of this great majesty may be revealed! The citation of David enables us to identify the spokesman, and to think of Christ as strong of hand and longed for.[1] So now that we have identified the outstanding herald, let us await the coming of the great King.

Division of the Psalm

In the first section the prophet warns the entire people to make confession to the Lord Christ, because He is said to have administered judgment and justice in the case of Jacob. In the second, he urges the people to adore the Lord Saviour, who is seen to have been kind to Moses, Aaron and Samuel because they are shown to have kept His commands. So he says that the Lord must be exalted and adored, for He has deigned to listen to His faithful.

Explanation of the Psalm

The Lord hath reigned, let the people be angry: thou that sittest on the Cherubim, let the earth be moved. When he says: *The Lord hath reigned,* he explains that he is revealing the glory of His resurrection. It is not, as was previously thought, that He could not reign since He was apparently snuffed out by the Jews; here is being revealed the occasion when He said after His resurrection: *All power is given to me in heaven and on earth.*[2] Next comes: *Let the people be angry,* as being unable to cause any further harm. They are the object of heavy and stern derision when their wiles and tricks are shown to have inflicted not the slightest damage. The prophet's words: *Let them be angry,* is not a command to the people to bestir themselves to some crime; rather, he is telling them to be angry with themselves for having been seen to perform a wicked act. In this way they may come quickly to the salvation of conversion, since they have begun to condemn their actions of their own free will. If you wish to interpret it literally, there is a certain elegance about it, just as in the Acts of the Apostles we read that Paul was struck by the High Priest and said: *May God strike thee, thou whited wall;* and a little later when he was rebuked, he added: *I knew not, brethren, that he is the high priest. For it is written, Do not speak evil of the prince of thy people.*[3] Not that Paul was unaware who he was, but by a form of witticism he denied that he was a prince of the people. Likewise here it says: *The Lord hath reigned, let the people be angry,* understanding "since they will do no further harm." The words are clearly not an encouragement, but rather mockery. This figure is known as *astismos,* in Latin *urbana dictio,*[4] aiming at elegance and wit. Next comes: *Thou that sittest on the Cherubim, let the earth be moved. Thou that sittest* is the indicative mood, second person; he ends this statement by addressing the Lord Himself. *Cherubim* is a Hebrew word denoting fullness of knowledge;[5] the prophet shows that the Lord sits there as though on His throne. He also sits on men who are filled with the most abundant faith and virtuous deeds. He added: *Let the earth be moved;* this denotes what he said earlier: *Let the people be angry,* or preferably he is asking that sinners be moved to conversion, for as has often been said those who lust after earthly vices are rightly called *the earth.*

2. *The Lord great in Sion, and high above all people.* So that you might clearly identify the God that sits on the Cherubim as Christ, he called Him who deigned to appear in the region of Jerusalem: *The Lord great in Sion.* Notice his words, *the great Lord,* so that none would consider Him worthy of contempt because of the lowly suffering of the passion. He added: *And high above all people,* for He whom they had despised with irreligious minds stood out as King, high above all people. *Sion* means "observation";[6] this is the Church, in which the Lord is seen through reverent contemplation to be always spiritually present.

3. *Let them confess to thy great and terrible name, for it is holy.* The prophet says that after the Lord Saviour's appearance in the flesh which took place in Sion, the people of whom it was earlier said: *Let them be angry,* must confess Him. Thus it is that every day in the Catholic Church we see people who were earlier blasphemers reforming themselves a little later with the Lord's help. His name is called *great* because it has extended everywhere; *terrible,* because He will come to judge the living and the dead; *holy,* because His way of life continued spotless and heavenly. As He says of Himself elsewhere: *For the Lord has made His holy one great,*[7] and as Mary was told by the

angel: *Therefore the holy one that shall be born of thee shall be called the Son of God.*[8]

4. *And the king's honour loveth judgment: thou hast prepared equity.* Earlier he had said: *Let the people confess to thy name.* Now he clearly explains how they are to confess. *The king's honour* is the proclamation of praise which we always offer to Him by confession. *Loveth judgment,* in other words, we must love the Creator by pondering and discussing Him. He is not to be worshipped as a passing whim or in momentary thought, but rather with the consistent, clearly observed, considered judgment which is always a feature of pure hearts. Next comes: *Thou hast prepared equity,* so that men may realise that the faculty by which they can grasp or consistently impose equity is granted them by Him. This meaning is finally made clearer by the following verse. Or, as some have it, *the king's honour* is the just condemnation of the guilty, for a king's glory is always enhanced by the punishment of wickedness.

Thou hast done judgment and justice in Jacob. He set judgment among the faithful people when He enabled them to distinguish good and evil; and justice, when by abandoning idols they deserved to serve their Creator with humble devotion. *In Jacob* means in each faithful individual, because the devoted people is revealed by mention of this name.[9] *Thou hast done,* because no other except Him established and strengthened the Church. As Paul says: *For other foundation no man can lay, but that which is laid, which is Christ Jesus.*[10]

5. *Exalt ye the Lord our God, and adore the stool of his feet: for he is holy.* The prophet passes to the second section, in which he urges devoted people not to cease glorifying the Lord's name, so that by proclaiming Him they themselves may be seen to gain the chance of being exalted. But as we have often said, the Lord does not need the aid of human resources, for He is the highest power and the adorable perfection of all majesty. Next comes: *And adore the stool of his feet, for he is holy.* Blessed Augustine, that most sedulous researcher, maintained that we should regard the Lord's body which he took from the virgin Mary as the stool of His divinity, because of the nature of the humanity which He deigned to take up.[11] That body, subject to and joined with that power, is clearly higher than all creatures; as Paul says: *The foolishness of God is stronger than men.*[12] Elsewhere the apostle says of the Man Christ Jesus, Mediator between God and men: *For*

which cause God hath exalted him, and hath given him a name which is above all names, that in the name of Jesus every knee should bow, of those that are in heaven, on earth, and under the earth.[13] So now we must state what His feet appear to represent in this verse. They represent the steadiness of divinity which ever continues in the almighty glory of His nature like the unfailing steadiness of feet. So we appropriately regard the assumed body of the Word, though it is glorious, great and adorable, as *the stool of His feet* because of the lowliness of humanity. For when the Lord says: *Heaven is my throne, and the earth my footstool,*[14] it is clear I think that by the same appropriate parallel His footstool is being interpreted as the earthly body which He took from the virgin Mary. Observe that the psalmist did not say: "For it is holy," but *For he is holy;* this was so that by mental contemplation you could distinguish the body from the Godhead, assigning it to the one Person, the Word which *was made flesh and dwelt amongst us.*[15] He spoke of the feet of the Godhead, just as he spoke of the stool, by a metaphor. Thus we must perhaps further assume that he is denoting the final stage when the Lord deigned to assume flesh. So the evangelist John says: *Little children, it is the last hour,*[16] and the apostle Paul says: *When the fulness of time was come, God sent his Son, made of a woman, made under the law.*[17]

6. *Moses and Aaron among his priests, and Samuel among them that call upon his name. They called upon the Lord, and he heard them.* He mentioned the great men of ancient authority, and asserted that the Lord's grace was granted them so as to rouse the faithful to similar devotion. Note that here he speaks of Moses as priest, though we do not find the title accorded him in the Heptateuch; but though he did not offer victims as his brother Aaron did, he always expressed the prayers of the people before the Lord, an office recognisably the priest's. So he is rightly called priest here, for he made great supplication for the people when the Lord was angry. Samuel spent his life in the Lord's temple with praiseworthy sanctity, and anointed David king; but because he did not obtain the office of priest, being of the tribe of Ephraim[18] from which priests could not be appointed, the psalmist additionally said of him: *Among them that call upon his name.* He could not run through them all by name, for there was a huge list of them. He added: *They called upon the Lord, and he heard them.* The

effectiveness of their chaste prayers was briefly stated; He effectively heard their faithful entreaties.

7. *He spoke to them in the pillar of the cloud, because they kept his testimonies, and the commands which he gave them.* The words, *in the pillar of the cloud,* are not without point, for a pillar is always set in house-building to add strength and beauty. So the Lord spoke to them in this shape, which announced the future fabric of the Church. But whereas at that time He spoke to them through the cloud, He has deigned to speak and to appear to us more clearly by means of the sacred footstool, that is, through the incarnation. This footstool is loftier than all temples, much more preeminent than all spiritual creatures. As the apostle puts it: *But to which of the angels did he say, Sit on my right hand?*[19] Why is it surprising that He is called a stool, when He compared Himself to a worm, to the fuller's herb, and to a cornerstone,[20] not in lowly appearance but in humility of demeanour? By taking on such lowliness He made it as lofty as it had earlier been insignificant in this world. Next comes: *Because they kept his testimonies, and his commands which he gave them.* He adduces the reasons why the Lord deigned to listen to them; the person who keeps His commands truly loves Him. As Christ says to His disciples: *If you love me, keep my commandments.*[21] A testimony is the meaning of a preceding event established by certain signs. As the Lord says in the Heptateuch: *This shall be a testimony unto you.*[22] The commands refer to the Law, which they were seen to have received through Moses. So this shows that the most effective way of pleasing God is by our fulfilling His command.

8. *Lord our God, thou didst hear them. God, thou wast merciful to them, and vengeful against all their eager desires.* By saying: *Thou didst hear them,* and: *Thou wast merciful to them,* he shows that the longings of the saints are attained by goodly entreaties, and that they obtained the kindnesses clearly sought through necessity. But he added: *And vengeful against all their eager desires.* This was stated so that we should not seek invariably to be heard, for in their case both outcomes are seen to have been fulfilled; we know that sometimes they were heard when they prayed for successes, but that vengeance was also exacted on their aspirations so that human arrogance should not creep up on them. Though some are faithful and deserving of veneration for

their great devotion, they must be temporarily punished so that their hearts may not appear amenable to potential pride. As Paul says: *And lest the greatness of the revelations should exalt me, there was given me a sting of my flesh, an angel of Satan, to buffet me. For which thing thrice I besought the Lord that it might depart from me. And he said to me: My grace is sufficient for thee, for power is made perfect in infirmity.*[23] So we have heard that they were listened to, but we must also understand that punishment was exacted in their case; thus we may realise that the merciful Christ has acted with kindness on both counts.

9. *Exalt ye the Lord our God, and adore at his holy mountain: for the Lord our God is holy.* We find a part of this verse cited earlier as well, at the division of the psalm,[24] but the addition there is: *And adore the stool of his feet,* but here the prophet's injunction was not to adore the mountain, but to adore the Lord at His holy mountain. Undoubtedly this can be identified with mount Sion, which is the Church. She is the mountain of mountains, the holy one of holy ones, and Christ is her Inhabitant. So the prophet says that both actions are to take place in the holy Church. But we should observe that he laid down that the holy Lord was to be adored at the holy mountain. Just as praise of the Lord does not befit a foul mouth, so a mean place is not appropriate for His worship.

Conclusion Drawn From the Psalm

Let us observe that the countenance of this psalm shines so to say with the light of two most beautiful eyes. It frightens unbelievers so that they may be guided towards most pious entreaty, and it enjoins the faithful to adore the Lord Christ, for He can listen to those whom He loves. Blessed is the people which rejoices in such a command, for to acknowledge and love the Creator is a longing which breathes life. So when we hear the Lord Christ, it should rouse our exultation; it is the mark of the faithful servant to love a master. He who does not hold his helmsman in the highest affection proclaims that he himself is to be abominated. It is the rule of nature to believe it wholly impossible to be loved by one whom you do not seek with an affectionate heart. So let us show affection that we may be loved, let us seek that we may find, let us knock that we may enter to Him. To be lukewarm in seeking Him who you know can afford you eternal blessings is a mark of total madness.

COMMENTARY ON PSALM 99

1. *A psalm of confession.* Though *confession* appears at apposite points in the psalms, we find it here set uniquely in the heading; and rightly, because this whole psalm is concerned with the two forms of confession. The first is when we lament over sins, proclaim ourselves blameworthy and guilty, and with devoted tears beg that the Lord's mercy may be granted to us. The second is when we praise the blessings bestowed on us, or with great joy revere those imparted to others. *Confessio* is the same as *confatio,*[1] in the sense of repentance or the vocal praise of many, used to indicate that numerous people partake in it.

Division of the Psalm

In the first part of the psalm the prophet warns the world that they should praise the Lord with great joy because sad service to so great a Lord is unbecoming. So that the Christian should not imagine that he should invariably employ this kind of confession, in the second part he says that by repenting of the sins of our evil deeds, we may deserve to enter the gates of His clemency, for His mercy endures for ever.

Explanation of the Psalm

2. *Sing ye with jubilation to God, all the earth.* The prophet was troubled for the faithful people in case they believe that they are to serve the Lord with gloomy anxiety, so he began at once with jubilation, for ministering to the Lord with happiness of mind constitutes the perfect devotion of the just man. As Paul warns us: *Always rejoice: pray without ceasing: in all things give thanks.*[2] So that no person should think that he was last to be summoned, he added: *All the earth,* so that

it would be apparent that no man alive may decline to listen to these words. Jubilation, as we have often said, means being stirred by great mental joy without breaking into clearly expressed words. As for his statement, *sing ye with jubilation*, and the addition: *All the earth*, he often denotes great thoughts by use of different cases; though the earth is declaimed in the singular, he says: *Sing ye with jubilation*, which clearly expresses the plural. So you are to assume that *earth* here is intended to denote man rather than soil. Clearly the meaning is allegorical, allegory being a figure which says one thing and means another.[3]

Serve ye the Lord with gladness. Come in before his presence with exultation. Though service to the Lord is seen to be discharged by the various functions of ecclesiastical orders, monasteries of the faithful, solitary hermits and devoted laity, all are appropriately associated with these five words, *serve the Lord with gladness*, and not with murmuring or mental bitterness, as happened in the desert when the Jewish people murmured against the Lord. This gladness is nothing other than the charity which, in Paul's words, *is not puffed up, dealeth not perversely, is not ambitious*,[4] and the other statements which retail this outstanding virtue in wondrous description. So those who serve the Lord with gladness are they who love Him above all else and show brotherly charity to each other. What free servitude this is! What service, excelling all forms of dominance! Such servants are accorded a gladness such as is not enjoyed by the glory of kingships. Now observe the reward attendant on this gladness which is enjoined on us in this world; he says: *Come in before his presence with exultation*. It is much more difficult, much more glorious to rejoice before the presence of the great Judge, where we are warned to gather with moral awareness of the need to manifest the joys of humility, for He is known to be awesome to all men of pride.

3. *Know ye that the Lord is the very God: he made us, and not we ourselves. We are his people, and the sheep of his pasture.* At the beginning of this verse he speaks against the faithlessness of the Jews, who did not believe that the Lord Saviour was God, and so presumed to lay hands on their Creator. *Know* means "Understand that this Lord who you refused to believe was God's Son is the very God who made heaven and earth, who fashioned us as well to His image and likeness." Then, so that they would not think that man's creation was to

be attributed to their fathers' seed, he added: *And not we ourselves.*
Though the working of the flesh offers assistance to our birth, it is the
Lord who is known to bring us into this world, for He makes all
things come into being. Next follows: *We are his people, and the sheep of
his pasture.* He passes to the faithful people, revealing their identity
with most beautiful comparisons. They are sheep because they are
simple, and He is their true Shepherd. His pasture is the abundant and
sweet feast provided by the holy Scriptures; these are the pasture by
which the faithful soul is filled and led to the beautiful haunts of future
blessedness. So in these three verses he embraced the necessary action
and belief and understanding of the Christian.

4. *Enter his gates to confess him, his courts with confessional hymns.
Praise ye his name.* He passes to the second section. Previously he had
said that we must exult with the Lord's praises, so now he tells us how
each person must confess to Him. The Lord's gates are humble repentance, sacred baptism, holy charity, almsgiving, mercy and the other
commands by which we can attain His presence. So the prophet urges
us first to enter the gates of the Lord's mercy by means of this humble
confession, so that the plundering of the savage wolf may not come
upon us outside the sheepfold. He added: *His courts with confessional
hymns.* Understand here too with *his courts* the word "Enter"; he is
denoting prophets, evangelists, and all who have taught with the
Lord's inspiration. Clearly their words are the palaces of the Lord, for
He is found in them if He is sought with devotion of mind. But so as to
separate this confession from the earlier one, he said: *With hymns,* like
the Lord Saviour's when He said: *Father, Lord of heaven and earth.*[5] He
did not make confession for his sins, but discharged praises to the
Lord with unblemished love. An appropriate order is preserved: first
he offers confession, and his love now untroubled follows. He added:
Praise ye his name; a lighter punctuation-mark should be added here,
for clearly this is to be joined to the next verse.

5. *For the Lord is sweet: his mercy endureth for ever, and his truth to
age upon age.* So that no-one would consider himself wearied with
praise or enervated with grinding toil, he offered his reason why the
Lord's name is to be praised: *For the Lord is sweet.* When did faintness
blossom in sweetness, or how can the mind be sated when the appetite
is ever increasing? This delight cannot experience surfeit when the
mind gains consolation and is refreshed in such a way that its longings

are never laid aside. So that you would not regard the sweetness of which he speaks as transient, he says that His mercy endures for ever, for once He has bestowed the blessings to come, they are preserved by Him for ever undiminished. He added: *And his truth to age upon age. Age upon age* denotes both that which now exists and that which we believe is to come; for the Lord's truth is both here—as we read in Scripture: *Truth is sprung out of the earth*[6]—and in the age to come, when the gifts of His promises are fulfilled, and He will reign with His saints in an eternity of glory.

Conclusion Drawn From the Psalm

This psalm has offered wonderful instruction on both forms of confession, teaching us both to sing eagerly with jubilation to the Lord, and to lament the wounds of our sins without interruption. Both are necessary in this world, so that the person who is God's servant should neither despair through melancholy nor become puffed up in mind through prosperity. Just as man's health depends on the serenity of the humours, so the perfect Christian is he who remains immovably steady amongst the changing affairs of this world. So let us accept with eager mind what has been said. We are given understanding of the nature of the lamentation mentioned here by the instruction that the Lord is to be praised by it; and rightly, because spiritual growth and not guilt, rewards and not punishment, comely freedom not ugly slavery are the outcome of it.

COMMENTARY ON PSALM 100

1. *A psalm for David himself.* Though psalm-headings drawn from historical accounts are seen to show the thrust of the psalms, the simple headings too are known to contain the same power. The text of this psalm is indeed marvellous. It is enclosed within a pattern of perfect holiness, for it is to anticipate a hundredfold harvest of rewards.[1] But the heading contains what we know are most familiar words, so that its simple and clear strength can indicate the most lucid

and exceedingly noble meanings. *Psalm* signifies holy activity. Where *for David* is included, it is applied wholly to Christ's powers; you are to interpret nothing as referring to this earthly king, but realise that all is relevant to the heavenly King.

Division of the Psalm

The gathering of holy persons[2] which the Catholic Church ever begets and multiplies throughout the entire world states in the first part of the psalm that they are singing to the Lord of mercy and judgment, and are avoiding association with most evil men. In the second part the gathering asserts that she loves the faithful, with whom she lodges in a most pleasant dwelling, but that she drives from her heart demons and their approaches, for she knows that they have no portion whatever with God's servants. So moulded by such instruction we must both seek blessings and reject evils.

Explanation of the Psalm

Mercy and judgment will I sing: thee, O Lord, will I hymn. The heavenly crowd of the blessed on earth uttered the proem to embrace everything in brief compass, for the Lord's power is always either pitying or judging. But His mercy is never found without judgment, nor His judgment without mercy. Both are joined in an interlinked association; no act of His ever comes to light which is not seen to be full of all the virtues. Just as the psalmist speaks here of mercy and justice, so elsewhere instead of these two he has *Justice and peace,*[3] or again *Mercy and truth,*[4] or *Justice and judgment the preparation of thy throne,*[5] so that everywhere he shows God as devoted and just. Undoubtedly this manner of speaking can be counted among the peculiarities of divine Scripture. For on the glorious occasion too of His coming He first mentions mercy when He says: *Come ye, blessed of my Father,*[6] and the rest; but this is not without equity, for He renders His promises to the faithful. But next follows judgment, when He said to the wicked: *Depart from me, ye cursed, into everlasting fire,*[7] though this action is not unloving, for He is known to show vengeance only after much long-suffering. So you see that the two concepts are reconcilable with each other and shine forth in their due places. Sinners who wickedly despair of their salvation must accordingly listen to the Lord of mercy, whereas the proud who think that their wickedness will not be punished must visualise Him as Judge. So here the totality is sung briefly but fully, for in these two words all the Lord's works and the building up of the entire Church are clearly told. The gathering added: *Thee, O Lord, will I hymn.* He who strives to appease the Lord with his good deeds is hymning Him, for it is the sweetest virtue of harmony when our voices are seen to be at one with our actions. If the two are discordant and irreconcilably at odds, they cannot in any way achieve the measured song of psalmody, and the confusion of reciprocal contradiction fails to reach the Lord's ears.

2. *And I will understand on the unspotted way when thou shalt come to me.* This verse follows from the previous words. If controlled psalm-singing is properly directed to the Lord, see what it achieves: it makes them *understand on the unspotted way,* when the Lord deigns to come to them whom He so strongly supported. The gathering says: *I will understand,* in other words, "I shall believe with chaste feelings of the heart," so that what she did not behold with physical eyes she vividly discerned by the impulse of a longing soul. Since this was the desire of one who had now spiritual vision, she states how she orders that coming: it is *on the unspotted way,* for the Lord Christ was without sin, and walked through this world with unspotted tread. This is the sense of his words: *And I will understand on the unspotted way, when thou shalt come to me.*

I walked in the innocence of my heart, in the midst of thy house. Again a hypothetical syllogism[8] is unfolded. If the just man[9] walks in innocence of heart in the midst of the Lord's house, he does not set before his eyes any evil thing; but the just man does walk in innocence of heart in the midst of the Lord's house; therefore he does not set before his eyes any evil thing. Now let us observe what follows. By his words: *I walked,* he shows that he did not seek out most eagerly the life of this world, but that it was traversed as a passage. Then we find explained in a few words the implication of innocence. By it he deserved to dwell in the midst of the Lord's house so that he both gives a good example to the rest and shines forth with that worthy manner of life. We are given to understand the force of innocence by the fact that the holy Spirit appeared in the form of a dove because of its most acceptable simplicity, and the Son chose to call Himself the lamb of God because of its blessed gentleness. This shows that heavenly, true wisdom finds its rest in peaceful and humble hearts.

3. *I did not set before my eyes any evil thing: I hated those who committed transgressions. There did not cleave to me. . . .* Earlier he stated that he walked in the innocence of his heart in the midst of the Church; so now by the figure of *aetiologia,* which in Latin is called *causae redditio,*[10] he explains this in two ways. First, as far as the diapsalm he says that he has not associated with wicked men, and then up to the end of the psalm he maintains that he has none the less set his portion with the faithful, and has routed from his heart the wiles of the devil. So this figure is seen to have embraced the greatest part of the psalm. Now let us return to an explanation of the words. The person who believes that God avenges does not set before the eyes of his heart any evil thing, for one who is seen to ponder things heavenly must necessarily despise things of earth. But how could one who was in the world not have before his eyes any evil thing, unless such things were displeasing to him, and he refused to be seduced by sinful delight in them? So the holy gathering justly said that they had not set before the eyes of their hearts those wicked things which they had excluded from the inner recesses of their minds; we are rightly said not to see the things which we observe without pleasure. They explained how evils could not reach their inner eyes; it was because they continually hated those who committed transgressions. Each and every individual is said to keep an eye on the things which men judge that he can love; but the things which we avoid with accursed loathing do not come before our mental sight, though they are present before our faces. He added: *There did not cleave to me. . . .* The phrase is quite incomplete; it needs the start of the next verse, *The perverse heart.* We often find this in the Hebrew version of verses of the Psalter. A perverse heart can cleave only to those twisted by the wickedness of sins. Matching aspirations cleave to each other, and those which are opposed go their separate ways. The perverse does not merge with the upright, for it differs in variation of behaviour. We find here an example of the conjectural status,[11] by which enquiry is made of associates or manner of life.

4. *. . . The perverse heart. The malignant ones that turned aside from me I did not acknowledge.* We have said that *The perverse heart* is to be joined to the previous words to form a complete sentence. In *The*

malignant ones that turned aside from me I did not acknowledge, the malignant ones turning aside from me denote the heretics who in their debased teachings disagree with Catholic preaching, and cause themselves and their listeners to turn aside from straight paths on to most wicked ways. *I did not acknowledge* stated that those known to blaspheme against the Lord, though claiming that they are baptised and confirmed, are not acknowledged as loving God. Christians are truly recognisable when they do not pollute themselves by wickedness of belief.

5. *The one who in private slandered his neighbour, him did I persecute.* The heretic slanders the Catholic when he rends him in his absence with some jibe, but does not dare to grapple with him openly, for he knows that his claims are without substance. The speaker says that such men are to be persecuted so as to be stirred to eagerness for truth, for they are deceived and misled on sundry questions. We call our neighbour that person united to us in blood-alliance, or joined to us in close legal relationship. Though some heretics seem to accept with us the Old and New Testaments, they despise with accursed wantonness a right understanding of the holy Scriptures.

6. *My eyes were on the faithful of the earth that they might sit with me: the man that walked in the perfect way, he served me.* The holy gathering passes to the second section. Just as earlier they regarded the unfaithful as loathsome to them, so now they desire to associate with believers. Those eyes of the heart which they deflected from very wicked men they direct upon holy people. *The faithful of the earth* means Christians dwelling through the whole world. *That they might sit with me:* in other words, remain in the unity of the faith. Such a posture denotes both restfulness and mental stability. Some would like to attribute this verse clearly to the Lord Christ as well, because of the splendid words, but a sudden change should not be made when the character already introduced can alone suffice for the role. Next comes: *The man that walked in the perfect way, he served me.* This is indeed clear proof of faithful Christians, that they shine out in their own lives and gleam in association with those who serve them. As was already said in Psalm 17: *With the holy, thou wilt be holy, and with the innocent man thou wilt be innocent. And with the elect, thou wilt be elect: and with the perverse thou wilt be perverted.*[12] Though the laity are

clearly not exempted from this, it is obviously imposed in a special way on priests; the laity must have ministers who do not rebut the divine rules.

7. *He that worketh pride shall not dwell in the midst of thy house.* The gathering still continues with its earlier sentiments, saying that they have had no connection with proud men, so that they would not be thought to have approved of them by appearing to be friendly with them. The words, *in the midst of my house,* are to be understood as meaning that they have entrusted nothing to such men. The proud man has been given no outstanding distinction, has rejoiced in no power such as seemed to set him in the middle of the house as the cynosure of the Father of the household's contented gaze. From this we are made aware that in our undertakings we ought to form judgments in such a way as to show no favour whatever to most wicked men; those who are to be avoided because of their debased manners should not appear acceptable to us.

He that speaketh wicked things did not advance before my eyes. This verse too matches the previous ones. The gathering says that the person known to indulge in wicked slanders or foul converse is displeasing to them, for what is wicked incorporates all that heavenly devotion abominates. *Did not advance* means "failed to profit"; we may say that people advance when they profit by making progress, or improve their lot by some success. This does not usually happen to those especially who are eager to walk on crooked paths.

8. *In the early mornings I put to death all the sinners of the land.* After saying that they avoided association with evil men, from which sins often emerge, the assembly now turns to the inner sentiments of their minds, and fittingly explains how they have driven the tyrannical bane which ravages the human race—in other words, the foul temptation of demons—out of their innermost being. *In the early mornings* means at the very outset, when devilish temptations have begun to appear in us like the uncertain twilight. They must then be thrust out by prayer, dislodged by imprecations of loathing, so that they may not gradually swell up harmfully and lay hold of us like a mist-laden day. *The sinners of the land* are demons which by wicked onslaughts cause all flesh to sin. They are justly called sinners for they breed sinners. So when they are slain together with their works, the souls of men are undoubt-

edly saved. Clearly this takes place when tearful remorse is bestowed on us with the pity of God's dew.[13] It is not when we seek to offer this remorse that we prevail, but it is offered when it is bestowed by His generosity.

That I may cut off from the city of the Lord all who work iniquity. The Fathers have called a devoted soul the Lord's city, from which the devil is cut off when he is debarred from his purpose. What wickedness lies in his cruel and tyrannical will! It is not enough for him that he caused men to die, but he continues to press strongly so that they cannot revive and live. Do You, Lord, who behold this most shameless foe, afford Your strong defence so that he may not attain his aspiration, for he hastens with insatiable cunning to make You hateful to us. We beg You with Your own words, Your own admonitions: *Judge thou, O Lord, them that harm me: overthrow them that fight against me. Take hold of arms and shield: and rise up to help me.*[14]

Conclusion Drawn From the Psalm

We are aware of the character of this most holy man[15] who with pure mind sang of the Lord's mercy and judgment in the middle of God's house. We know how he shunned evil men totally, and was joined with the good in most welcome association, how with the most wholesome deliberation he expelled the base desires of his heart, so that he seems deservedly to have obtained this number, which denotes the appearance of the crown which we desire by bending the fingers of the right hand.[16] This is the reward of martyrs, the gift of virgins, and all that is outstanding in the Church is shown to attain the prize by such fruits. As Paul says: *As for the rest, there is laid up for me a crown of justice, which the Lord the just judge will render to me in that day.*[17] The world itself is said to be embraced in this figure. We read in countless authors that the sky is vaulted; we see the stars gleaming in spherical shape, and the sun shining with circular beauty; the moon too undoubtedly attains this shape when it is seen to reach perfection. So let us ponder the merit of this spokesman, and the elegance which he is shown to display. He seems to have been allotted to the number of this psalm because it contains the glory of great rewards and bears the likeness of heavenly creatures. I would feel shame to claim that I who am subject to sins have advanced in the fruitfulness of the number of one hundred, and that what we have said is applied to the merits of the saints has been bestowed on my unworthy person. But may God's power grant that at the Judgment we may undoubtedly rejoice at the forgiveness of our sins, and that He may not condemn us as we deserve. He alone can free us if we confess to Him.

NOTES

LIST OF ABBREVIATIONS

ACW	Ancient Christian Writers
CCL	Corpus christianorum, series latina
CSEL	Corpus scriptorum ecclesiasticorum latinorum
DACL	Dictionnaire d'archéologie chrétienne et de liturgie (Paris 1907–53)
DTC	Dictionnaire de théologie catholique (Paris 1903–50)
LSJ	Liddell-Scott-Jones-McKenzie, *Greek-English Lexicon* (Oxford 1940)
Martin	J. Martin, *Antike Rhetorik* (München 1974)
MG	*Patrologia graeca*, ed. J. P. Migne (Paris 1857–66)
ML	*Patrologia latina*, ed. J. P. Migne (Paris 1844–55)
OCD	The Oxford Classical Dictionary² (Oxford 1970)
ODCC	The Oxford Dictionary of the Christian Church² (Oxford 1974)
PSt	Patristic Studies
Rogerson-McKay	J. W. Rogerson and J. W. McKay, *Psalms 1–150* (3 vols., CUP 1977)
ZKT	Zeitschrift fur katholische Theologie

PSALM 51 [Ps. 52(51)]

1. For the history of Doech/Doeg, see 1 Sam. (1 Kings) 22.9 ff.
2. Jerome, *Hebrew Names* (CCL 72.103, 139); Augustine, *En. Ps.* 51.4 (CCL 39.625).
3. The emphasis on Antichrist is not found in Augustine's commentary; Cassiodorus' account is close to that of Cyril of Jerusalem (*Cat. lect.* 15.11 ff.), which prophesies that Antichrist will be a magician who will dominate the empire, persecute Christians, and be slain by Christ at His second coming.
4. 1 Cor. 1.31, cited also by Augustine, *En. Ps.* 51.7 (n. 2 above).
5. "Vivid narration"; see earlier, Pss. 34(33).4 and 37(36).35.
6. Eccli. 21.29.
7. Not in Martin, but see the references in LSJ.
8. Dan. 12.7.
9. 2 Cor. 12.21.
10. Dan. 11.43.
11. Col. 2.18 f.
12. Cf. Acts 10.38.
13. See Cicero, *Inv.* 1.49, and Pss. 63(62).13, 77(76).14 below.
14. "Omission"; Martin, 290, and Pss. 75(74).7, 81(80).16 below.
15. For the *genus demonstrativum*, above, Pss. 29(28).1, 33(32).4, 36(35).6.
16. See §9 above.
17. For the first, see Ps. 9.20 ff.

PSALM 52 [Ps. 53(52)]

1. This is Augustine's rendering of Meleth, not Amalech (*En. Ps.* 52.1 = CCL 39.638).

2. Gal. 4.19, cited also by Augustine (n. 1 above).

3. Above, Ps. 1.2.

4. Gen. 18.21.

5. Above, Ps. 27(26).3.

6. Gen. 22.1. Cassiodorus interprets, "Now I make you see that you love."

7. See Pss. 14(13).2, 30(29).2, 51(50).12.

8. *Nonne* actually combines *non* and affirmative particle *-ne* ("Is it not the case, then . . . ?").

9. Above, Ps. 24(23).5.

10. He means the distinction between evildoers and the faithful.

11. Cf. Matt. 8.12.

12. Reading *iustis* for CCL *iustus*.

13. Ps. 11(10).6.

14. For the senses of Sion, see Pss. 9.12, 20(19).3.

15. See Pss. 22(21).4, 25(24).22, etc.

16. Mal. 1.23.

17. See n. 15 above.

18. Jerome, *Ep.* 22.8 (= ACW 33.141).

19. See above, Ps. 14(13).

20. For such sentiments about the future salvation of Jews, see Candidus of Fulda, *Opusc. de passione Domini* (ML 106.96); cum enim intraverit plenitudo gentium, quae per Joannem designatur, tunc salvus fiet omnis Israel. Also Bede, ML 91.934 f., 1136 C-D; Lanfranc, ML 150.142.

PSALM 53 [Ps. 54(53)]

1. Cf. 1 Sam. (1 Kings) 23.19.

2. So Jerome, *Hebrew Names* (CCL 72.98); Augustine, *En. Ps.* 53.2 (CCL 39.646).

3. Not found in the handbooks, but see LSJ, s.v. *eirmos.*

4. Cf. Acts 9.1 ff.

5. Rom. 8.26.

PSALM 54 [PS. 55(54)]

1. Heb. 1.1 f.

2. Exod. 12.6.

3. Luke 18.39.

4. Ps. 110(109).1.

5. Ps. 13(12).4.

6. Luke 19.41.

7. The Vulgate takes the phrase with *conturbatus sum* in 3 ("I was grieved by the voice of the enemy"); Cassiodorus follows Jerome's later Hebrew version.

8. Matt. 27.42.

9. 1 Cor. 15.54.

10. The suggested connection of *pennae* with *pendere* is dubious, and the etymology of *columba* offered here is wild; Varro, *L.L.* 5.75, states that it is derived from the sound which it utters, a likely suggestion for the Greek form of the word.

11. Mark 1.35.

12. Isa. 35.1.

13. The words are not connected.

14. For the tower of Babel, cf. Gen. 11.4 ff.

15. Ps. 15(14).5 (sc. 'shall dwell in thy tabernacle').

16. Ps. 34(33).14.

17. For synecdoche, see Pss. 9.2, 22(21).1, 45(44).13, etc.

18. Cf. Ps. 22(21).7.

19. Above, Pss. 31(30).13, 35(34).13.

20. John 6.71.

21. See Pss. 25(24).7, 27(26).3, etc.

22. Ps. 34(33).9.

23. Martin, 207, and Pss. 59(58).17, 67(66).3 below.

24. Cf. Matt. 26.20 ff., 27.2, 27.45.

25. The etymology is correct.

26. John 18.33.

27. John 19.30.

28. See Intro. VI (in ACW 51).

29. 1 Cor. 15.51.

30. Matt. 22.16.

31. Matt. 26.66.

32. Prov. 25.20.

33. Ps. 69(68).16.

34. The phrase *viri sanguinum*, "men of bloods," is stated to be an idiosyncrasy of scriptural Latin.

35. Cassiodorus thinks of an O.T. exemplar like David (1 Sam. [1 Kings] 17.47).

36. See the Conclusion to the psalm.

37. Leo, *Ep.* 165.5 (ML 54.1161–3).

38. See Pss. 22(21) and 35(34).

Psalm 55 [Ps. 56(55)]

1. Cassiodorus reproduces Augustine's explanation of the significance of the heading; see *En. Ps.* 55.2 (CCL 39.677).

2. Cf. 1 Sam. (1 Kings) 27.2 f.

3. See Jerome, *Hebrew Names* (CCL 72.94). Augustine, *En. Ps.* 55.3 (CCL 39.679) is the immediate source of this and of the interpretation which follows.

4. Matt. 13.39.

5. Eph. 6.12.

6. The figure of *antiphrasis* (opposite sense) is often exemplified by ancient authorities with *lucus qui non lucet*; so Varro, *Reliquorum de grammatica librorum* (edd. Goetz-Schoell, p. 240); also Diomedes and Charisius (citations in Lewis and Short).

7. Eccli. 2.11 f.

8. The words are connected.

9. Gen. 3.15.

10. Cf. Luke 18.13.

11. 1 Tim. 1.13.
12. Ps. 32(31).5.
13. Ps. 50(49).15.
14. Mark 8.23.
15. Ezech. 18.23.
16. John 14.10 f.
17. *De Trin.* 15.17 (ML 42.1080).
18. See ML 35.2029.
19. John 1.14.
20. Ps. 110(109).1.
21. See Ps. 16(15).9 and Martin, 285.
22. Matt. 5.5.
23. Prov. 24.6.
24. Prov. 15.13.

Psalm 56 [Ps. 57(56)]

1. Cf. John 19.19 ff.; Augustine, *En. Ps.* 56.3 (CCL 39.695 f.) has already made this point.
2. Cf. 1 Sam. (1 Kings) 24.4.
3. See Pss. 3, 16(15), 28(27), 31(30).
4. Matt. 23.37.
5. Cf. Pss. 1.3, 5.11, etc., and Quintilian 8.3.77.
6. Phil. 2.9.
7. John 10.18.
8. Matt. 15.24.
9. Acts 9.4.
10. "Word for word"; see above, Pss. 17(16).13, 33(32).4, 46(45).2, etc., and *Inst.* 2.3.14.
11. Luke 23.21.
12. Prov. 18.21.
13. Actually Num. 14.21.
14. John 8.4 ff.
15. Matt. 26.66.
16. Eccle. 10.8.

17. Rom. 5.3.
18. Ps. 12(11).6.
19. See Pss. 3.3, 22(21).6, 47(46).7.
20. Luke 24.1.

PSALM 57 [Ps. 58(57)]

1. See Pss. 2.1, 26(25).1, etc.
2. Matt. 22.16.
3. John 19.6 f.
4. Reading *sic* for *si* of CCL.
5. At *Inst.* 2.3.15, topics are defined as *loci ex quibus argumenta dicuntur;* the *ex contrario* is the sixth type listed there. See earlier Pss. 26(25).4, 30(29).6.
6. Luke 6.37.
7. 2.18 (= ACW 5.147–150).
8. Pliny's account of the asp (*N.H.* 29.65) does not include these picturesque details, which Cassiodorus has obtained from Augustine's sermon at *En. Ps.* 57.7 (CCL 39.715).
9. The etymology is fanciful.
10. 1 Cor. 1.20.
11. Matt. 22.21.
12. Matt. 22.17.
13. Luke 23.31.
14. See Pss. 12(11).2, 23(22).1, 31(30).21, etc.
15. Wisd. 5.6.
16. Ps. 55(54).24.
17. 1 Tim. 5.6.
18. Wisd. 12.18.
19. On *auxesis* (climax) see above, Ps. 3.4.
20. The same point is central to the argument of Boethius in his *Consolation of Philosophy.*
21. Cf. Prov. 21.11 (LXX).

22. "From what follows," the ninth of the *argumenta* at *Inst.* 2.3.15.

PSALM 58 [Ps. 59(58)]

1. Cf. 1 Sam. (1 Kings) 19.11.
2. For Nestorius' belief that there were two separate persons in the incarnate Christ, see Intro. VI and bibliography in ODCC.
3. Cf. *Conc. chalc. act.* 2.5.34 (*Acta conc. oec.*, ed. Schwartz, 2.1.2).
4. John 14.30.
5. Luke 23.21.
6. Matt. 27.25.
7. See Pss. 3.3, 22(21).6, 47(46).7, etc.
8. Mark 3.27.
9. Cf. Luke 4.6 ff.
10. Ps. 19(18).6 f.
11. John 4.18.
12. Matt. 28.20.
13. John 14.10 f.
14. Gen. 22.12.
15. Ps. 2.8.
16. Rom. 11.25 f.
17. The fanciful etymology stems from Varro, *L.L.* 5.99.
18. Amos 9.11.
19. Mark 7.28.
20. Quintilian 8.6.52: "More obscure allegory is called *aenigma* (riddle)".
21. Cf. Apoc. 21.16.
22. Eph. 6.17.
23. Mich. 7.18.
24. Ps. 14(13).7.
25. Prov. 1.25 f.
26. Cf. Matt. 25.1 ff.
27. Luke 18.8.
28. Matt. 25.34.

29. In §4 above.

30. "Transfer of a preposition" (reading *prepositio* for *propositio* in CCL).

31. I Cor. 4.7.

32. See Intro. VI.

33. Cf. Acts 9.4.

34. Matt. 26.66.

35. Matt. 21.23.

36. Heb. 12.6.

37. Pss. 6.2, 38(37).2.

38. This strange interpretation of *consummatio* implies a connection with *consumere*, like the Douay version's "When they are consumed by thy wrath."

39. See at Ps. 93(92).1.

40. Exod. 12.5 f.

41. Acts 10.13.

42. Ps. 35(34).12.

43. A curious identification; prosphōnēsis (address) is used usually of a formal greeting to an emperor; the normal Greek equivalent of *exclamatio* is *ekphōnēsis*. The same identification is found earlier at p. 25.

44. Matt. 25.40.

45. Matt. 25.34.

Psalm 59 [Ps. 60(59)]

1. Eph. 5.8.

2. Cf. 2 Sam. (2 Kings) 8–10.

3. See Ps. 2.1.

4. See Pss. 25(24).7, 27(26).3, 38(37).20, etc.

5. Ps. 97(96).4.

6. Ps. 2.12.

7. Ps. 51(50).19.

8. 2 Tim. 2.5.

9. Ps. 23(22).5.

10. Matt. 10.17 f., 22.

11. 1 Peter 4.17.

12. See the reference in Ps. 42(41).8.

13. See Jerome, *Hebrew Names* (CCL 72.113); Augustine, *En. Ps.* 59.8 (CCL 39.759).

14. Matt. 11.30.

15. Cf. Gen. 31.17 ff.

16. For the false etymology, cf. Varro, *L.L.* 5.19 (excised from the text in the Goetz-Schell edition).

17. Cf. Jerome, *Hebrew Names* (CCL 72.67); Augustine, *En. Ps.* 59.9 (CCL 39.760).

18. So Jerome, *Hebrew Names* (CCL 72.82); Augustine, *En. Ps.* 59.9 (CCL 39.761).

19. Gen. 41.51.

20. So Jerome, *Hebrew Names* (CCL 72.65); Augustine, *En. Ps.* 59.9 (CCL 39.761).

21. John 12.24.

22. So Augustine (CCL 39.762: *in gentibus*); Jerome's rendering (CCL 72.76) is *de patre*.

23. Rom. 5.3 ff.

24. Jer. 1.13.

25. Isa. 14.13.

26. Cf. Jerome, *Hebrew Names* (CCL 72.65): *rufus vel terrenus;* Augustine (CC 39.763): *terrena.*

27. Isa. 52.7.

28. Eph. 6.15.

29. 2 Cor. 4.17.

30. Matt. 5.10.

31. Jer. 17.5.

Psalm 60 [Ps. 61(60)]

1. Ps. 19(18).5.

2. 1 Cor. 10.4.

3. Ps. 22(21).17 f.

4. See Pss. 20(19).2, 22(21).13, 28(27).6.

5. Rom. 5.3 ff.

6. Above, Pss. 1.2, 31(30).8, etc.

7. Reading *gens* for *mens* in CCL.

8. "The adducing of reasons"; cf. Pss. 16(15).9, 56(55).13.

9. Ps. 84(83).11.

10. An unacceptable suggestion.

11. John 16.22 f.

12. Ps. 116(115).18 f.

13. When the Donatists refused to accept Caecilius as bishop of Carthage because his consecrator Felix had been a *traditor* (311), they passed into schism, claiming that they alone constituted the true Church. The passage here suggests the continuing existence of the schism in the sixth century.

14. The conclusion of the parable of the sower at Matt. 13.8 was interpreted by the Fathers to suggest that martyrs and virgins bring forth fruit a hundredfold, and widows and those who live a celibate life sixtyfold.

PSALM 61 [PS. 62(61)]

1. See at Ps. 39(38).1.

2. Above, Ps. 24(23).5; for *nonne/ne non*, see 52 n. 8.

3. Augustine, *De Trin.* 15.3 (ML 42.1060).

4. "Correction of the previous statement"; see Martin, 280, quoting the identical Latin translation from Ps.-Iul. Ruf., *Schem. Dian.* 3.

5. John 19.28.

6. John 4.7.

7. Ps. 71(70).5.

8. Ps. 11(10).2.

9. Ps. 42(41).5.

10. Ps. 39(38).6.

11. Eccle. 1.2.

12. Jerome, *Ep.* 49.5.

13. Ps. 11(10).6.

14. 1 Tim. 6.17 f.

15. Ps. 2.7.

16. John 10.18.

17. John 5.22.

PSALM 62 [Ps. 63(62)]

1. 1 Cor. 12.26.
2. See at Ps. 60(59).10.
3. John 4.10.
4. Rom. 8.18.
5. Luke 17.17 f.
6. Cf. Exod. 17.11 ff.
7. Ps. 143(142).6.
8. 1 Tim. 2.8.
9. Ps. 50(49).16.
10. See at 7.6.
11. 1 Thess. 5.5.
12. 1 Cor. 6.17.
13. Mark 8.33.
14. Vespasian (69–79 AD) and his son Titus (79–81) crushed the great Jewish rebellion and destroyed Jerusalem, including the Temple, in 70.
15. Luke 13.32 f.
16. Cant. 2.15.
17. John 18.37.
18. John 14.10 f.
19. Matt. 5.34 f.
20. Ps. 132(131).11.
21. See at Ps. 52(51).10.

PSALM 63 [Ps. 64(63)]

1. See Pss. 3, 16(15), 28(27), 31(30), 57(56).
2. Matt. 16.22.
3. John 10.18.
4. Luke 23.21.
5. Ps. 51(50).9.
6. Matt. 20.18.
7. Matt. 26.66.

8. Matt. 27.25.

9. John 11.48.

10. Matt. 9.2.

11. Matt. 9.4.

12. Ps. 107(106).12.

13. See at 21.9. Cassiodorus uses the term to accentuate the contrast between the words and the failure of the designs of the Jews.

14. See *Hexapla* at MG 16.909 f., presumably known to Cassiodorus through Jerome's writings on the O.T. books. See H. D. F. Sparks, *Cambridge History of the Bible*, 1.514 f.

15. Matt. 27.40.

16. Matt. 27.42.

17. Acts 2.37.

18. Cf. Luke 24.30 f.

19. Matt. 25.34.

PSALM 64 [PS. 65(64)]

1. See Concl. to Ps. 15(14).

2. Cassiodorus, then, is suggesting that David (in the tenth century BC) prophesies the prophecies of Jeremiah and Ezechiel (in the seventh/sixth centuries BC) about the return to Jerusalem of the exiles in the years after 538 BC, when Babylon was captured by Cyrus.

3. So "they" in the title refers to the Jews of the captivity, and not to the two prophets.

4. Above at Ps. 9.12.

5. 2 Cor. 5.10.

6. Gen. 46.27.

7. Above, Pss. 9.2, 22(21).1, 45(44).13, etc.

8. 2 Cor. 5.19.

9. John 15.16.

10. Ps. 84(83).3.

11. 1 Cor. 2.9.

12. Cf. Matt. 13.23.

13. 1 Cor. 12.8 ff.

14. Eph. 4.7.
15. John 2.19.
16. John 2.21.
17. Ps. 104(103).25.
18. Matt. 4.19.
19. Ps. 45(44).4.
20. Ps. 30(29).12.
21. Like Boethius, Cassiodorus here as elsewhere defends the orthodoxy of Chalcedon against Nestorius and Eutyches, and more generally against Arianism.
22. Diana/Artemis and Apollo were twins; this is perhaps why Diana is associated with Delphi here, though the uncharitable suspicion lurks that Cassiodorus has confused Delphi with Delos, birthplace of the twins. Cythera, the island off the Greek Peloponnese, was a celebrated cult-centre of Aphrodite.
23. Ps. 23(22).5.
24. The word is actually derived from *locus* and *pleo/plenus*.
25. Isa. 65.17.
26. Ps. 46(45).5.
27. John 4.13 f.
28. Ps. 78(77).24 f.
29. Luke 12.6.
30. 1 Cor. 3.1 f.
31. See Matt. 13.23.
32. Isa. 54.1.
33. Cf. Luke 18.13.

PSALM 65 [Ps. 66(65)]

1. Rom. 10.4.
2. See *Pref.*, Volume I, pp. 28 f.
3. See at Ps. 2.1.
4. Num. 14.21.
5. The psalm begins *Jubilate Deo*.
6. Above, Ps. 2.5.

7. Rom. 10.10.
8. Leo, *Ep.* 28.4 (ML 54.195A).
9. Heb. 3.2.
10. Cf. Matt. 12.24.
11. Matt. 26.64 f.
12. Matt. 28.13.
13. With reference to the pecularitics of scriptural Latin.
14. Matt. 3.17.
15. John 14.6.
16. Cf. Matt. 14.31.
17. John 19.11.
18. Ps. 141(140).2.
19. The words are etymologically connected.
20. Luke 23.42.

PSALM 66 [PS. 67(66)]

1. Above, Ps. 40(39).4.

2. The Latin is *organis. Organum* means an organ at Ps. 150.4, 'quasi turris quaedam diversis fibulis fabricata'; but it must mean pipe here, since Cassiodorus believes that the psalms were all composed by David.

3. Gen. 1.28.

4. Gen. 22.17.

5. See Pss. 3.3, 22(21).6, 47(46).7, 57(56).9, etc.

6. Luke 2.29 ff.

7. *prosphōnēsis* is normally used of an honorific address to an emperor (Martin, 203), but see Pss. 55(54).17, 59(58).17.

8. Since the Donatists considered that those baptized or ordained by the *traditores* had not received the sacraments licitly, they found themselves at odds with the rest of the Church, believing that only they themselves formed the true Church. See also at Ps. 8.2.

9. The term is more generally used for the repetition of the same notion in different words. See at 21(20).3.

10. Eccli. 1.16.

11. Ps. 33(32).8.

Psalm 67 [Ps. 68(67)]

1. John 8.25.

2. Cf. above, p. 117.

3. Reading *raritate* (cod. Germ.) for *caritate* (CC).

4. Cassiodorus probably has in mind the view of Origen that fallen angels and men condemned at the Judgment (cf. *Princ.* 1.6 = ML 11.169; *Hom. 8 on Joshua* = MG 21.334) will ultimately be saved.

5. See at Pss. 1.3, 5.11, 17(16).8, etc.

6. Isa. 40.3.

7. Cf. Ps. 68(67).19; Eph. 4.8.

8. Matt. 25.41.

9. Ps. 9.35, where Cassiodorus reads merely *pupillo tu eris auditor*.

10. Augustine, *Conf.* 1.4.4.

11. See at Ps. 18(17).1.

12. Acts 4.32.

13. Ps. 133(132).1.

14. Ps. 5.11.

15. Cf. Exod. 13.21, 16.35.

16. Exod. 19.18.

17. Deut. 32.9.

18. James 5.20.

19. Matt. 3.17.

20. See Quintilian 8.6.29 for examples.

21. Ps. 24(23).10.

22. Reading *alligatos* for CCL *alligato*.

23. Mark 3.27.

24. John 11.11.

25. Cant. 6.8.

26. Ps. 45(44).10.

27. 1 Cor. 4.8.

28. See Jerome, *Hebrew Names* (CCL 72.119); Augustine, *En. Ps.* 67.21 (CCL 39.884).

29. Luke 1.35.

30. Ps. 17(16).8.

31. Acts 23.3.

32. Matt. 23.3.

33. See Pss. 17(16).13, 33(32).4, etc., for this "verbal definition."

34. Isa. 2.2.

35. Matt. 3.17.

36. John 14.10 f.

37. Ps. 66(65).6. The tautology in the Latin (*in quo . . . in eo*) is not reproduced in the Douai English version cited here.

38. Matt. 11.30.

39. So Jerome, *Hebrew Names* (CCL 72.77); Augustine, *En. Ps.* 67.24 (CCL 39.888).

40. On *idea*, see Ps. 9.5, 18(17).8, 33(32).13, etc.

41. Eph. 4.7.

42. See Intro. VI in ACW 51.

43. See Jerome, *Ps. iuxta Hebr.* 68.23, where the reading *de profundis* is found.

44. So Jerome, *Hebrew Names* (CCL 72.114); Augustine, *En. Ps.* 67.31 (CCL 39.891).

45. Phil. 3.2.

46. Matt. 15.27.

47. Ps. 59(58).7.

48. Mark 15.26.

49. The words are not connected; *fons* is cognate with *fundere*.

50. Cf. Acts 9.26 ff.

51. Phil. 3.5.

52. Acts 7.57.

53. Acts 9.4.

54. *adolere* actually means "to burn ritually," though it may in origin mean "to pile up" on an altar for burning.

55. Apoc. 5.5.

56. Cf. Exod. 35.27.

57. So Jerome, *Hebrew Names* (CCL 72.67, 73, 70); Augustine, *En. Ps.* 67.36–8 (CC 39.895).

58. 1 Cor. 1.24.

59. Eph. 1.3 f.

60. Ps. 80(79).14.

61. 2 Tim. 3.16.

62. Cf. Jerome, *Ps. iuxta Hebr.* 68.32. I read *offerant* for *offerent* of CCL.

63. See at Pss. 9.2, 22(21).1, etc.

64. Gen. 1.1.

65. Leo, *Ep.* 82.1 (ML 54.1103).

66. Heb. 9.11 f.

67. Heb. 9.24.

68. Matt. 9.5 f.

69. John 5.28.

70. Cf. Ps. 135(134).6.

71. Isa. 5.6.

72. For the theme of the Ascension, see §19.

PSALM 68 [Ps. 69(68)]

1. At §22 below; cf. Matt. 27.48.

2. At §10 below; John 2.17.

3. At §§23–4 below; Rom. 11.9 f.

4. Apoc. 1.8.

5. John 21.18.

6. Ps. 124(123).4 f.

7. "Characterisation"; see at Ps. 9.26, and Isidore, *Orig.* 2.21.40.

8. John 19.6.

9. This is fanciful.

10. The Neoplatonist doctrine of evil as the privation of good is taken over by the Fathers. Augustine, *Conf.* is a likely inspiration here, though Boethius espouses the same doctrine.

11. Ps. 37(36).6.

12. Matt. 27.12.

13. Isa. 53.7.

14. John 17.25.

15. Matt. 26.39.

16. Luke 23.34.

17. Matt. 23.13, 18.7.

18. See at Ps. 3.4 above.

19. Ps. 35(34).7.

20. 1 Cor. 1.24.

21. 1 Cor. 1.27.

22. Ps. 19(18).13.

23. John 14.30.

24. Isa. 53.9.

25. 2 Cor. 5.21.

26. Augustine, *Enchiridion* 41 (= ΛCW 3.49 f)

27. Above, Ps. 22(21).7.

28. Matt. 13.17.

29. "Gathering together"; above, Ps. 12(11).2, etc.

30. Matt. 12.24.

31. Matt. 11.19.

32. Matt. 13.55.

33. John 8.39.

34. Cf. John 2.17.

35. Luke 4.22.

36. John 9.29.

37. Ps. 78(77).19.

38. Exod. 32.4.

39. Ps. 35(34).13.

40. John 4.7.

41. Cf. John 11.35.

42. Cf. Matt. 13.24.

43. Ps. 78(77).2.

44. The etymology proposed by Varro, *L.L.* 5.142, and Servius, *Ad Aen.* 1.83.

45. Luke 24.18.

46. Ps. 23(22).5.

47. See Augustine, *ad loc.*

48. 2 Cor. 6.2.

49. Ps. 51(50).3.

50. Prov. 18.3.

51. Cf. Ps. 5.3 above; Quintilian 9.4.50 says that *metabole* is used of change of rhythm in verse rather than of change of sense.

52. Gen. 14.10.

53. Cf. Gen. 26.15 ff., 29.2 ff.; Exod. 17.6.

54. Matt. 19.14 (of little children).

55. Isa. 42.1.

56. Isa. 9.6.
57. Matt. 26.65.
58. Matt. 27.42.
59. Luke 22.15.
60. Mark 8.33.
61. Luke 23.34.
62. Cf. Matt. 27.34.
63. 1 Cor. 10.21.
64. Matt. 21.43.
65. John 8.17.
66. The city was razed by Titus after a long siege in 70 AD.
67. John 19.11.
68. Rom. 8.32.
69. Deut. 32.39.
70. Matt. 21.33 ff.
71. Exod. 10.20.
72. Exod. 32.32.
73. Luke 10.20.
74. 2 Cor. 8.9.
75. Isa. 53.4.
76. Above, Ps. 31(30).13.
77. "To bring salvation" renders *salutaris,* which has the double sense of "salvation-bringing" and "health-bringing."
78. 2 Cor. 6.10.
79. Phil. 2.10 f.
80. Above, Ps. 2.7.
81. Apoc. 5.5.
82. John 8.39.
83. See earlier Psalms 22(21), 35(34), 55(54).
84. Heb. 1.13.

PSALM 69 [PS. 70(69)]

1. In the psalm-heading.
2. See at Ps. 23(22).6, above.
3. John Cassian, *Conl.* 10 (= CSEL 13.297 ff.). The warning that "he

is not to be followed in all things" has reference to his espousal of a semi-Pelagian stance, which had been strongly rebutted by Augustine, but which reared its head again in the fifth and sixth centuries.

4. Cf. Acts 4.32.

5. Ps. 142(141).5.

6. Cassiodorus means us to supply mentally these words, *ut auferant eam;* they do not appear in verse 3.

7. Matt. 25.46.

8. Ps. 40(39).18.

9. I read ⟨*cur*⟩ *cum* for CCL *cum.*

10. Phil. 3.13.

11. 1 Cor. 8.2.

PSALM 70 [PS. 71(70)]

1. Jer. 35.6.

2. Jerome, *Hebrew Names* (CCL 72.107); Augustine, *En. Ps.* 70.2 (CCL 39.942).

3. Ps. 54(53).8.

4. 2 Kings (4 Kings) 17.6, 24.1f., 24.14 ff.

5. "Characterisation"; see at 16(15).1 above.

6. Above, Ps. 7.6.

7. Ps. 17(16).8.

8. Rom. 2.12.

9. The definition is taken verbatim from Cicero, *Inv.* 2.16.3.

10. Rom. 5.3 f.

11. Ps. 51(50).7.

12. At this date, Vespers formed the first part of the Night Office. Matins was performed at midnight, followed by Nocturns. See J. A. Jungmann, *ZKT* 72 (1956) 66 ff.

13. Gen. 1.5.

14. Above, Ps. 9.2.

15. Job 2.9.

16. Above, 20(19).8.

17. See *Historia Monachorum* 16 (ML 21.438 ff.). Paphnutius was an Egyptian monk, a disciple of Antony. At the Council of Nicaea he

excited wonder at the physical mutilation which he had suffered in the persecutions of 305–13.

18. Cf. Luke 16.19 ff.

19. John 2.16, Mark 11.17, Matt. 21.13.

20. Cassiodorus appears to be distinguishing between *presbeia* and *presbutēs*.

21. The savage tyrant is Antichrist, who in the formulation that goes back to Cyril of Jerusalem will inaugurate an era of persecution before being routed by Christ. See further at Ps. 9.20 ff.

22. Isa. 53.1.

23. Matt. 5.5.

24. Ps. 36(35).7.

25. See on Ps. 6.1.

26. Ps. 101(100).1.

27. See the *Preface*, p. 28 in Vol. I. The "sound of the psalm" refers to the psaltery described there.

28. It seems likely that Cassiodorus here recalls Augustine's comments at *De civ. Dei* 5.8, where Seneca and earlier Stoics are cited as ascribing fate or destiny to the will of the Godhead.

COMMENTARY ON THE EIGHT DECADES
THAT RELATE TO THE NEW TESTAMENT

1. See the Conclusion to Ps. 8.

2. See above on Ps. 1.

PSALM 71 [PS. 72(71)]

1. Jerome, *Hebrew Names* (CCL 72.138); Augustine, *En. Ps.* 71.1 (CCL 39.971).

2. John 14.27.

3. Isa. 57.18 f.

4. John 5.22.

5. Ps. 2.4.

6. Ps. 19(18).2.

7. "Dwelling on"; see at Ps. 13(12).1, 19(18).2.

8. John 16.15.

9. See the previous note.

10. Ps. 85(84).11.

11. Matt. 5.3.

12. 2 Cor. 8.9.

13. Gal. 4.19.

14. 1 Cor. 4.15.

15. The K was branded on the forehead of the person condemned to denote "calumniator"; see Cicero, *Sex. Rosc.* 57. The passage implies that soldiers on service were similarly branded.

16. Wisd. 5.6.

17. The symbolism of the sun as Christ and the moon as the Church is pervasive in the Fathers; see H. Rahner, *Greek Myths and Christian Mystery* (London 1962) ch. 4.

18. Cf. Isa. 9.7.

19. Phil. 2.6 f.

20. Cassiodorus here applies the image to the Virgin Birth.

21. This is the second stanza of Ambrose's hymn, *Intends qui regis Israel;* see A. Walpole, *Early Latin Hymns* (Cambridge 1922) 52.

22. *Ep.* 28.2 (ML 54.759).

23. Ps. 85(84).12.

24. See Quintilian 12.10.26, and Martin, 262.

25. So Jerome, *Comm. in Isaiam* 23.1 (ML 24.284B).

26. The etymology is spurious.

27. Reading *ipsis* for *ipsi* in CCL.

28. See Intro. VI at Vol. I and at Ps. 67(66).11.

29. Matt. 12.29.

30. Isa. 65.15.

31. Cf. Prov. 16.16.

32. The etymology is spurious.

33. Cf. Cyprian, *De dominica oratione* (CSEL 3.1.265 ff.).

34. John 1.1 f.

35. See above at Ps. 9.2.

36. Gen. 22.18.

37. The fifth type of definition is *kata tēn lexin;* see above at 16.13.

38. Isa. 54.5.

39. In the Vulgate, additional words inserted by an ancient redactor, *Defecerunt laudes David filii Jesse* ('the praises of David, son of Jesse, are ended') indicate that this concluded an independent collection of 'Davidic' psalms; see Rogerson-McKay, ad loc. Cassiodorus places them at the beginning of Psalm 72.

40. *Fiat, fiat* ends Psalms 41(40), 89(88), 106(105), thus indicating the close of Books 1, 3 and 4.

41. The heresies against which Cassiodorus deploys Psalm 72(71) here were of topical interest in his day, for Boethius takes them up in his fifth tract, *Against Eutyches and Nestorius*. In this work (date about 512) Boethius seeks to clarify the doctrine of Christ's two natures by recourse to philosophical analysis. See H. Chadwick, *Boethius* (Oxford 1981) 180 ff.

42. Eutyches is often regarded as the true founder of Monophytism. He was condemned at Chalcedon in 451 for denying that Christ shares our human nature. See M. Jugie, DTC 5 (1913) 1582 ff.

43. Nestorius succeeded to the see of Constantinople in 428; accused by Cyril of Alexandria and others of positing two persons in Christ, he was condemned at Ephesus in 431.

44. The first three are Psalms 2, 8 and 21(20).

PSALM 72 [Ps. 73(72)]

1. "Lively illustration," the ninth type of definition listed at *Inst.* 2.3.14; cf. Quintilian 9.2.14.

2. Compare Jerome's description of Socrates in *Adv. Jov.* 1.48 (ML 23.291): *simis naribus, recalva fronte, pilosis humeris et repandis cruribus.*

3. So Jerome, *Hebrew Names* (CCL 72.118); Augustine, *En Ps.* 72.4 (CCL 39.988).

4. Gal. 4.4.

5. Ps. 94(93).7.

6. A fanciful suggestion.

7. Ps. 94(93).9 f.

8. Again a fanciful derivation.

9. For the fivefold division of *causae*, including the *anceps* mentioned here, see *Inst.* 2.2.8 deriving from Cicero, *Inv.* 1.20.

10. Ps. 18(17).30.

11. For the deliberative speech, and its motifs of *utile* and *honestum*, see at Ps. 2.11.

12. Ps. 37(36).35 f.

13. Reading *mirabatur* (CCL *mirabantur*).

14. Ps. 19(18).13.

15. Ps. 32(31).8.

16. Matt. 14.31, but without mention of the right hand.

17. John Chrysostom, *Homily on the Lord's Ascension*, 3 (MG 50.446), incorporating Matt. 22.44, Gen. 3.19.

18. Matt. 15.19.

19. 19 above.

20. See at Ps. 2.3 above.

21. This seems to suggest that Ps. 73(72) follows appropriately after Ps. 72(71).

Psalm 73 [Ps. 74(73)]

1. See above at Ps. 73(72).1.

2. Rom. 12.15.

3. On Vespasian and Titus see Ps. 80(79) nn. 17, 19 below. Modern scholars regard this psalm as a lament for the destruction of Jerusalem by the Babylonians in 587 BC, or alternatively that by Antiochus in 168 BC.

4. Not listed under the commonplace arguments at *Inst.* 2.3.15, but see at Ps. 94(93).6 below.

5. A Greek translation of the seven books of the *Bell. Jud.* (date 75–79 AD) has survived; see the Loeb edition.

6. "Additional emphasis"; see at Pss. 3.3, 57(56).9, etc.

7. Quintilian 1.4.12 is the source, deriving the word from *bis* and *pinnus* (sharp).

8. Lam. 1.12, 14.

9. Quintilian 8.3.53 cites as here the example "I saw it with my eyes."

10. 1 Kings (3 Kings) 8.20.

11. See earlier at Ps. 3.4, 69(68).5; the figure *auxesis* refers more normally to heightened language at the conclusion of a speech, but Cassiodorus cites it as the equivalent of *climax*.

12. Rom. 5.35.

13. Prov. 18.3.

14. Cf. Exod. 4.5 ff.

15. *Ab eventu*, the phrase used here, is equivalent to *a consequentibus* at Ps. 10.2.

16. Above at Ps. 29(28).1.

17. John 18.37.

18. A fanciful derivation.

19. On metonymy, see at Ps. 2.5, 67(66).2, etc.

20. "Gathering together"; see earlier at Ps. 12(11).2, 58(57).8, 69(68).8, etc.

21. It was an old custom to "blow the devil out" of a child; see Augustine, *Ep.* 105, *ad fin.*

22. The text of CCL is awry, but the sense is clear.

23. So Jerome, *Hebrew Names* (CCL 72.81); Augustine, *En. Ps.* 73.18 (CCL 39.1016).

24. Ps. 19(18).3.

25. Eccli. 27.12.

26. See §8 above.

27. John 1.47.

28. See §13 above.

29. Cf. Jer. 23.5 f.

30. The *qualitas absoluta* and its subdivisions are mentioned by Fortunatianus (ed. Montefusco, Bologna 1979) 2.6.

31. Luke 23.34.

32. §9 above.

33. §4 above.

PSALM 74 [Ps. 75(74)]

1. Cf. Acts 2.41.

2. Ps. 57(56).8.

3. Ps. 50(49).16.
4. John 5.27.
5. John 16.15.
6. 1 Cor. 8.6.
7. Luke 22.31 f.
8. Wisd. 1.7.
9. See at Ps. 52(51).11 above.
10. Luke 14.11.
11. See at Ps. 11(10).7, 16(15).5 above.
12. Cf. John 2.6 ff.
13. The reference is to the hymn *Inluminans altissimus;* see A. Walpole, *Early Latin Hymns,* 62 ff. The ascription to Ambrose has been challenged on grounds of content, but Walpole rebuts the arguments, and the testimony of Cassiodorus supports him. For recent discussion, see J. Szöverffy, *Die Annalen der lateinischen Hymnendichtung* I (Berlin 1964) 53 ff.
14. Ps. 23(22).5.
15. Criticism of the ethical standards of leading Old Testament figures formed an important strand in Manichean criticism of orthodox Christianity. See e.g. J. J. O'Meara, *The Young Augustine* (London 1954) 65 ff.
16. See at Ps. 44(43).23 above, and Quintilian 8.2.5.

PSALM 75 [Ps. 76(75)]

1. So Jerome, *Hebrew Names* (CCL 72,60, *dirigentium*); Augustine, *En. Ps.* 79.1 (CCL 39.1111).
2. See above at Ps. 73(72).1.
3. See *Pref.* p. 31 f. in ACW 51.
4. So Jerome, *Hebrew Names* (CC 72.154).
5. John 19.15.
6. See above, at Ps. 22(21).4.
7. 1 Cor. 2.7.
8. Apoc. 19.16.
9. Isa. 66.2.
10. On *enargeia,* see at Ps. 34(33).4.

11. On *emphasis*, see at Ps. 25(24).7.

12. Cf. Soph. 1.15.

13. Matt. 25.41.

14. Ps. 51(50).4.

15. Ps. 51(50).21.

16. Exod. 20.13 ff.

17. 1 Cor. 7.38.

18. Ps. 2.11.

Psalm 76 [Ps. 77(76)]

1. See at Psalms 39(38) and 62(61) above.

2. Ps. 74(73).7.

3. Augustine's *Locutiones in Heptat.* (CC 33.379 ff.) exemplifies such features.

4. Isa. 26.12.

5. Matt. 6.1.

6. Cf. Hab. 3.1.

7. For the deliberative mode, see above, at Ps. 2.11. At the end of §10 below he summarises the sequence of thought.

8. Ps. 39(38).6.

9. This letter of Stephen, bishop of Jerusalem, to the emperor Leo (457–474) is missing from the *Codex Encyclicus* of Epiphanius. Cf. E. Honigmann, PS (1953) 169 ff.

10. 1 John 2.18.

11. Isa. 57.16.

12. See above, 7.4.

13. Ps. 86(85).2.

14. John 14.6.

15. Matt. 28.19.

16. "Coupling"; *collatio* is more normally regarded as the Latin rendering of *parabole* (Quintilian 5.11.23), which Cassiodorus mentions at the end of §17.

17. Exod. 3.14.

18. Deut. 6.4.

19. 1 Cor. 1.24.

20. Matt. 5.8.

21. Isa. 53.1.

22. John 10.16.

23. See Jerome, *Hebrew Names* (CCL 72.67); Augustine, *En. Ps.* 80.8 (CCL 39.1124).

24. Isa. 5.6.

25. Ps. 19(18).5.

26. Cf. Matt. 14.22 ff.

27. Cf. Exod. 2.10.

28. For these interpretations, see Jerome, *Hebrew Names* (CCL 72.141, 73).

Psalm 77 [Ps. 78(77)]

1. 1 Cor. 10.1, 3 f.

2. 2 Peter 1.21.

3. Cf. Gen. 32.25 and 31.

4. Cf. §2 above.

5. 1 Tim. 1.9.

6. Exod. 19.8.

7. Exod. 32.1.

8. Cf. Matt. 26.35 and 69 ff.

9. See §8 above.

10. Matt. 11.29; for the interpretation of Tanis, n. 35 below.

11. 1 Cor. 10.1 f.

12. John 4.13 f.

13. 1 Cor. 10.4.

14. Ps. 136(135).25.

15. "Assembling"; see at 11.2 above.

16. See Jerome, *Hebrew Names* (CCL 72.67).

17. The bogus etymology enjoys a long life; a similar formulation appears in the late twelfth century in William of Newburgh's *History of English Affairs* 1.20.

18. Cassiodorus appears to be applying this figure (on which, see Quintilian 9.2.51) not to literature but to conduct.

19. See §21 above.

20. The etymology is correct.

21. Exod. 32.35.

22. Num. 20.10.

23. Ps. 55(54).24.

24. Ps. 127(126).2.

25. John 8.36.

26. Rom. 8.2.

27. Ps. 7.10.

28. Another fanciful derivation.

29. Isa. 29.13.

30. Isa. 48.4.

31. Exod. 32.31 f.

32. Luke 23.34.

33. The etymology is fanciful.

34. *Signa* (signs) also means 'seals' or 'stamps.' *Prodigium* is actually derived from *prodicere* rather than *porro dicere*.

35. Cf. Jerome, *Hebrew Names* (CCL 72.132); Augustine, *En. Ps.* 77.12 (CCL 39.1078).

36. Cf. Exod. 7.20 ff.

37. Cf. John 2.9.

38. See §51 below.

39. See Exod. 8.17, 9.10, 10.22.

40. Cf. 1 Sam. (1 Kings) 21.13.

41. The work mentioned is *De consensu evangelistarum* (CSEL 43).

42. Rom. 1.24.

43. Cf. Gen. 19.1 ff.

44. Cf. 1 Sam. (1 Kings) 18.10.

45. Exod. 1.5.

46. See above, 9.2.

47. Cf. Heb. 9.9, 24, etc.

48. As Cassiodorus repeatedly states, the interpretation of Israel is "seeing God."

49. Silo (Shiloh), the city of Ephraim, kept the ark of the covenant at the time of the Judges (see Jos. 18.1 ff.).

50. Jer. 7.12.

51. 1 Cor. 3.17.

52. I.e., by the Philistines (Judges 13 ff.).

53. Another fanciful etymology.

54. Cf. 1 Sam. (1 Kings) 4.11.
55. Jerome, *Psalt. iuxta Hebr.* 78.65 (ed. de Sainte Marie, 114).
56. 1 Sam. (1 Kings) 5.1 ff.
57. See n. 23 to Ps. 77(76).
58. So Jerome, *Hebrew Names* (CCL 72.65).
59. So Jerome, *Hebrew Names* (CCL 72.152).
60. Cant. 6.8.
61. Matt. 16.18.
62. Ps. 48(47).9.
63. Matt. 20.30.
64. Apoc. 19.16.
65. Cant. 4.2.
66. Matt. 4.4.
67. Isa. 53.9.

PSALM 78 [PS. 79(78)]

1. Cf. Ps. 73(72).1, etc.
2. 1 Macc. 1.21 ff. Josephus, *Ant. Jud.* 12.6.226 ff., also records this sequence of events.
3. 1 Macc. 2.38.
4. 1 Macc. 1.49 f.
5. "Comparison"; above, Ps. 1.3.
6. Isa. 1.8.
7. 1 Macc. 1.65.
8. Ps. 78(77).63.
9. Lam. 1.1.
10. Lam. 2.15.
11. "Climax"; see Ps. 69(68).5 above.
12. Ps. 118(117).18.
13. 1 Macc. 2.15 ff.
14. 1 Macc. 2.23 f.
15. "With the opposite face"; the figure is not mentioned in the handbooks or in LSJ.
16. Ps. 39(38).6.
17. Cf. Apoc. 6.10.

18. Matt. 5.44.

19. Luke 23.34.

20. In §10 above.

21. In §4 above.

22. Ps. 12(11).7.

23. Unidentified.

24. 1 Cor. 12.26.

25. He refers to the motifs in 1 Cor. 11–13.

PSALM 79 [PS. 80(79)]

1. He refers to Ps. 19(18); see Ps. 19(18).1.

2. "Notion" or "idea"; see Ps. 1.1.

3. See above at Ps. 22(21).4.

4. Cf. Gen. 30.23 f.; this interpretation is at odds with that cited from Jerome at 77(76).16, 78(77).68 above.

5. So Jerome, *Hebrew Names* (CCL 72.63); Augustine, *En. Ps.* 79.2 (CCL 39.1112).

6. So Jerome, *Hebrew Names* (CCL 72.65, 62, 82); Augustine, *En. Ps.* 79.3 (CCL 39.1112).

7. 1 Cor. 10.13.

8. See Psalm 79(78) above.

9. "Change"; see Ps. 69(68).16 above, and Quintilian 9.3.38.

10. So Varro, *L.L.* 5.37.

11. See Exod. 3.8. CCL has Cethaei for Hethaei.

12. See on Ps. 37(36).35.

13. John 15.5.

14. See §10 above.

15. Lam. 2.20.

16. Isa. 5.5.

17. The emperor Vespasian (AD 69–79) had been appointed in Nero's reign to put down the Jewish rebellion (AD 66–70), but he left for Rome before the city fell.

18. The suggested etymology is fanciful.

19. Titus (emperor AD 79–81), elder son of Vespasian, succeeded to

the Jewish command on the accession of his father, and stormed Jerusalem in August 70.

20. "Delineating"; see *Inst.* 2.3.14.

21. Matt. 3.17.

22. Matt. 25.41.

23. Ps. 44(43).7 and 4.

24. Matt. 3.17.

25. See §16 above, *ad fin.*

26. Reading *vineam* for *veniam* in CCL.

27. Ps. 121(120).6.

PSALM 80 [Ps. 81(80)]

1. Reading *amurca caenosa* for *amurcam caenosam* of CCL.

2. Gen. 1.20.

3. *Iubilare* is in fact a loan-word from Hebrew.

4. See at Ps. 46(45).12.

5. See *Pref.* p. 28 in ACW 51.

6. See *Pref.* p. 27. Cassiodorus as elsewhere identifies psalm with psaltery here. Strictly speaking, psalm is the sound emanating from psaltery.

7. Above at Ps. 21(20).8.

8. The passage refers to the Feast of Tabernacles held from the 15th to the 22nd of Tishri, the seventh month of the ecclesiastical year. But Tishri was also the first month of the civil year, and celebration of the New Year led up to the Feast of Tabernacles, itself a commemoration of the Exodus and of the period when the Israelites dwelt in tents (*tabernacula*) in the wilderness.

9. Isa. 58.1.

10. It is impossible to annotate in detail the summary of musical theory which is presented here. There is an admirable summary of ancient doctrine in Winnington-Ingram's revised article ("Music") in the OCD. Cassiodorus included an extended section on music in his *Institutes* (2.5), which closely follows the order of topics treated here. There was at Vivarium a translation by Mutianus of a musical treatise by Gaudentius (see *Inst.* 2.5.10), and this was presumably his immedi-

ate source here, but Augustine's *De musica* and a treatise by Albinus which our author read in a library at Rome, may also be germane. It is uncertain whether Cassiodorus knew Boethius' *De institutione musica,* which goes unmentioned in the *Institutes.*

11. Cf. 1 Sam. (1 Kings) 16.23.
12. Cf. Jos. 6.20.
13. Reading *iudicabit* for *iudicavit* of CCL.
14. John 5.22.
15. See at n. 23 to Ps. 77(76).
16. Cf. Exod. 1.12.
17. Cf. Acts 2.4.
18. Matt. 11.28.
19. "Expression of character"; see at Ps. 16(15).1 above.
20. Cf. Exod. 17.1 ff.
21. Matt. 25.35.
22. Exod. 3.14.
23. "Idea" or "conception"; see at Pss. 1.1, 80(79).2, etc.
24. 2 Cor. 6.13 f.
25. Rom. 1.24.
26. Matt. 25.41.
27. Isa. 66.24.
28. "A leaving out"; see above at Ps. 52(51).11.
29. Reading *auribus obseratis* for *auribus assati eas* of CCL.

PSALM 81 [Ps. 82(81)]

1. John 1.26.
2. Bar. 3.38 (Baruch acted as secretary to Jeremiah, and his prophecy is often ascribed by the Fathers to Jeremiah himself).
3. Exod. 7.1.
4. §6 below.
5. 1 Cor. 8.5 f.
6. 1 Cor. 4.7.
7. Isa. 56.10.
8. Ps. 69(68).30.
9. 1 Cor. 2.8.

10. Matt. 27.51.

11. Matt. 27.54.

12. Ps. 2.7 (2.8 in this Commentary).

13. John 1.12.

14. "By analogy"; see Cassiodorus, *Inst.* 2.3.14.

15. Matt. 25.31 f.

16. See above, Intro. VI in ACW 51, and Ps. 21(20) Concl.

17. Sedulius, *Carmen Paschale* 1.325 (CSEL 10.39).

18. Reading *regis* for *legis* in CCL.

19. Cf. Zach. 12.10.

20. Luke 24.39.

21. Phil. 2.6 f.

22. See above, Psalms 2, 8, 21(20), 72(71).

PSALM 82 [PS. 83(82)]

1. See Martin, 302.

2. Isa. 53.7.

3. On *exallage*, see at Pss. 2.7, 19(18).5, etc.

4. Gen. 31.44.

5. The interpretation of these names is identical with that offered by Augustine at *En. Ps.* 82.7 ff. (CCL 39.1142 ff.). Though most meanings have been taken over from Jerome's *Hebrew Names,* it is interesting that for Ismahel Jerome offers *auditio Dei* (CCL 72.67) for Augustine's *auditio sibi,* and that Jerome offers for Gebal *vallis vetus,* and for Ammon *populus maeroris* (CCL 72.67 and 78).

6. Ps. 14(13).3.

7. See at Ps. 41(40).3 above.

8. See Jerome, *Hebrew Names* (CCL 72.82, 101, 94); Augustine, *En. Ps.* 82.9 ff. (CCL 39.1143).

9. 1 Cor. 1.20.

10. Gen. 3.19.

11. So Jerome, *Hebrew Names* (CCL 72.77, 101, 120, 101); Augustine (n. 8 above).

12. 1 Cor. 3.17.

PSALM 83 [PS. 84(83)]

1. See above, Ps. 42(41).1.
2. See Ps. 42(41).
3. See at Pss. 25(24).7, 55(54).15, etc.
4. See the discussion of Augustine, who first identifies the sparrow with the soul and the turtle with the flesh, but then compares the turtle with the Church.
5. See at Ps. 32(31).11.
6. A baffling suggestion if the text is sound. For the suggested link with Greek *deos* (fear), see at Ps. 22(21).2.
7. See at Ps. 17(16).13.
8. I read *iustitiae* for *iustitiam* of CCL.
9. See at Ps. 82(81).6.
10. Jacob is interpreted as "supplanter"; he supplanted his brother Esau in obtaining his father's blessing at Gen. 27.1 ff.
11. "Exchange"; see at Ps. 14(13).2.
12. Ps. 53(52).3.
13. *Parison* is more usually applied to syllabic balance of phrases; see Quintilian 9.3.76.
14. 1 Tim. 1.13.
15. 2 Tim. 4.7 f.
16. Rom. 11.6.
17. "Contrary to expectation," "unexpected outcome"; see LSJ s.v. *prosdokia*.

PSALM 84 [PS. 85(84)]

1. Rom. 10.4.
2. Above at Ps. 42(41).1, etc.
3. The earlier psalms are 19(18) and 80(79).
4. For Jacob = Church of the faithful, see Pss. 20(19).2, 53(52).7, 81(80).2, etc.
5. 'Identical ending'; see e.g. Quintilian 9.3.77.
6. Matt. 15.24.

7. Reading *verberata aure* for *verberato aere* of CCL.

8. Acts 5.3 f.

9. 1 Peter 1.12.

10. Matt. 28.19.

11. In this section Cassiodorus attacks the theology of the "Macedonians," who maintained the divinity of the Son but not that of the Spirit. The doctrine was repudiated at the Council of Constantinople in 381.

12. Eph. 2.17.

13. See LSJ *ad loc.*; the figure does not appear in the handbooks.

14. There is no discussion of the precise issue at Ps. 70. Cassiodorus is presumably referring to the final comments there on the interrelation between the Old and New Testaments.

15. John 14.6.

16. Cf. Luke 18.13 f.

PSALM 85 [Ps. 86(85)]

1. The connection with *os* (mouth) is clear, but there is none with *ratio*.

2. John 1.1 ff.

3. Phil. 2.7 f.

4. See above at Ps. 2.1.

5. The previous example is Ps. 17(16).

6. The heresy of Apollinarius (c. 310–90) was the first major Christological heresy, maintaining that Christ is human in body but not in spirit, so that He is not fully Man. See the bibliography in ODCC.

7. Jer. 17.5.

8. Luke 18.1.

9. Luke 1.38.

10. Ps. 116(115).16.

11. See above, Ps. 17(16).13.

12. See Martin, 305.

13. Ps. 96(95).5.

14. "Removal of the opposite"; see on Ps. 32(31).1.

15. Ps. 146(145).6.

16. Isa. 14.13 f.
17. Deut. 6.4.
18. Isa. 45.21.
19. John 14.6.
20. Ps. 2.11.
21. Deut. 6.5.
22. Cicero, *Topica* 3.12.
23. Num. 16.32 f.
24. Cf. Luke 16.23.
25. See Augustine, *En. Ps.* 85.1 ff. (CCL 39.1190).
26. 'By praise'; see above, Ps. 18(17).2.
27. John 2.19, 21.
28. John 5.22.
29. Isa. 9.6.
30. Isa. 42.1.
31. Cf. Varro, *L.L.* 7.14.
32. Cf. Jon. 2.1.
33. Matt. 12.39.
34. Reading *superabuntur* against *superabantur* of CCL.

PSALM 86 [PS. 87(86)]

1. For the identification of psalm with psaltery, see n. 6 to Ps. 81(80).
2. 1 Cor. 3.11.
3. This was Cassiodorus' collected edition of the books of the bible. The painting of the Tabernacle has already been mentioned at Ps. 16(15).1; see the n. there.
4. See above, Pss. 24(23).5, 53(52).5, etc.
5. Above, Ps. 2.7.
6. Reading *praedicatur* against *praedicitur* of CCL.
7. Cf. Jos. 2.1 ff.
8. Jerome, *Tract. in Ps.* 86 (CCL 78.113).
9. Jerome, *Hebrew Names* (CCL 72.62); Augustine, *En. Ps.* 136.1 (CCL 40.1964).
10. Matt. 21.31.

11. Acts 13.46.
12. See Ps. 83(82).7 above, and Luke 6.17.
13. John 1.14.
14. John 8.25.
15. See above at Ps. 50(49).9, and Quintilian 8.3.82.
16. 1 Cor. 2.9.
17. See above at Ps. 29(28).1.
18. Excising *rerum* from the CCL text.
19. Cf. John 5.2 ff.
20. Cf. John 9.7.
21. Cf. Matt. 27.11.
22. Cf. Mark 15.15.
23. Cf Mark 15.19.
24. Cf. John 19.34.
25. Cf. John 20.19.
26. From the fourth century onwards, Jerusalem had been a place of pilgrimage, and descriptive accounts of holy places and relics proliferated (see H. Leclercq, DACL 14.65 ff.). It seems none the less probable from the details assembled here that Cassiodorus himself visited the holy city in the course of his travels to Constantinople.

PSALM 87 [PS. 88(87)]

1. See Augustine, *En. Ps.* 87.1 (CCL 39.1201).
2. See Augustine (CC 39.1208).
3. Matt. 28.10.
4. Above at Ps. 22(21).4.
5. Cf. Ps. 86(85).20.
6. Ps. 35(34).12.
7. Matt. 26.38.
8. Above, 1.3, 5.11, 17(16).8, etc.
9. John 10.18.
10. Ps. 9.7.
11. Ps. 17(16).8.
12. Lam. 4.20.
13. Matt. 27.43.

14. Zach. 13.7.

15. Matt. 27.40.

16. Both *inopia* and *copia* may have their root in *ops*.

17. Above at Pss. 25(24).7, 27(26).3, etc.

18. Ps. 5.11.

19. "Assemblage"; above at Pss. 12(11).2, 23(22).1.

20. Ps. 129(128).1.

PSALM 88 [PS. 89(88)]

1. See above at Ps. 74(73).15.

2. Jer. 1.10.

3. See above at Ps. 32(31).11.

4. The etymology is unfounded.

5. Acts 2.3 f.

6. He refers to the Epicureans and their doctrine of *clinamen*, or swerve of the atoms, causing fortuitous conjunctions and changing the course of nature.

7. John 1.14.

8. "By praise"; above at Ps. 18(17).2.

9. John 19.11.

10. Reading *eum* for *eam* of CCL.

11. Cf. Matt. 15.32.

12. Like Augustine, Cassiodorus regards Satan and the fallen angels in the same way as the Middle Platonists regarded malevolent demons. Plutarch, *De genio Socratis*, and Apuleius, *De deo Socratis*, are enlightening in this regard.

13. Luke 10.18.

14. I.e. in verse 11.

15. Isa. 14.13 f.

16. John 1.9.

17. Tabor or Thabor lies a few miles east of Nazareth. Fourth-century writers, including Jerome, regarded it as the site of the Transfiguration. Hermon rises to 10,000 feet in NE Palestine. For the interpretation of the names, see Jerome, *Hebrew Names* (CCL 72.98 and 119), taken over by Augustine *En. Ps.* 88.13 (CC 39.1228).

18. Ps. 114(113).9.

19. Jer. 17.5.

20. Above, Ps. 29(28).1.

21. Matt. 3.17.

22. Ps. 22(21).22.

23. Ps. 2.6.

24. John 12.28.

25. Isa. 42.1.

26. Phil. 2.9 f.

27. See above, Pss. 9.26, 21(20).4, etc.

28. Ps. 45(44).8.

29. "Characterisation"; Isidore, *Orig.* 2.21.40.

30. John 14.30.

31. Ps. 32(31).7.

32. John 17.10.

33. Matt. 28.18.

34. The names of these towns are all plural in Latin.

35. 'With reference to something'; see Cassiodorus, *Inst.* 2.3.14. I emend the CCL reading *kata tou* to *kata to.*

36. Matt. 1.25.

37. Apoc. 1.8, 1.17, 21.6, 22.13, 22.16.

38. Ps. 2.6.

39. Ps. 72(71).11.

40. Ps. 84(83).11.

41. 1 Cor. 4.21.

42. Prov. 3.11 f.; cf. Heb. 12.6.

43. Col. 2.9.

44. Cf. Ps. 31(30).22.

45. In §22 above.

46. Ps. 86(85).2.

47. He refers to the elliptical construction by which *si David mentiar* means "If I lie to David (may I be struck down)," and hence "I will not lie."

48. Ps. 22(21).31.

49. This is often cited as Scriptural and referred to Wisd. 7, but no sentence is found there exactly like that, though Augustine, Gregory, Bernard, Julian of Norwich all cite it. See ACW 30.377 n. 5.

50. Wisd. 3.7.

51. See H. Rahner, *Greek Myths and Christian Mystery* (London 1962), ch. 4, "The Christian Mystery of Sun and Moon," where texts of Ambrose, Augustine and others equating the moon with the Church are discussed.

52. Augustine, *En. Ps.* 88, *serm.* 2.6 (CCL 39.1237).

53. Cf. 2 Sam. (2 Kings) 12.1 ff., esp. 5 f.

54. 2 Sam. (2 Kings) 15.30, 16.5–11.

55. 2 Sam. (2 Kings) 12.13.

56. The derivation from *pro fano* is correct.

57. Above, Ps. 85(84).3.

58. Ps. 18(17).45.

59. Ps. 44(43).7.

60. Rom. 11.25 f.

61. Above, Pss. 2.2, 15(14).1, etc.

62. Rom. 5.12.

63. Cassiodorus as a student of Augustine doubtless thinks of Pelagian doctrines. In his *De Orthographia* 144, he mentions the *Commentary on Romans*, "from which I excised the stains of Pelagian heresy."

64. Cf. Jerome, *Comm. in Ps. 40* (ed. Morin, 46).

65. 2 Cor. 11.23 f.

PSALM 89 [PS. 90(89)]

1. See Pss. 17(16), 86(85).

2. John 5.46.

3. Jerome, *Hebrew Names*, (CCL 72.141).

4. Exod. 33.11.

5. Exod. 3.14.

6. Above, Pss. 22(21).7, 38(37).6, etc.

7. Exod. 32.9 f.

8. Ps. 32(31).1.

9. The two words are unconnected etymologically.

10. Above, 8 Concl.

11. See Ps. 71(70) Concl.

12. Cassiodorus' cryptic comment presumably refers to the Manicheans' criticism of the Old and New Testaments, as reported by

Augustine in his *Confessions*; see J. J. O'Meara, *The Young Augustine* (London 1954) 65 ff.

13. Hab. 3.2.

14. Exod. 15.6.

15. Exod. 32.12.

16. Above Pss. 9.5, 18(17).8, etc.

17. Gal. 6.14.

18. Ps. 4.7.

19. According to the computation of the Septuagint, there are seventy biblical books; see Cassiodorus, *Inst.* 1.14.

20. Cf. Wisd. 11.21.

21. Cassiodorus discusses these subdivisions of arithmetic in his *Inst.* 2.4, with comments on the relevance of the discipline to Scripture made in the Preface to that book. On the general question of the study of arithmetic and the Greek authorities known in sixth-century Italy, see Alison White's chapter in *Boethius, His Life, Thought and Influence* (ed. M. Gibson, Oxford 1981) 162 ff. and H. Chadwick, *Boethius* (Oxford 1981) 71 ff.

PSALM 90 [PS. 91(92)]

1. See above, Ps. 1.2.

2. The clear source here is Martianus Capella 5.524: *diatuposis est descriptio . . . cum rebus personisque subiectis et formas ipsas et habitus exprimimus. . . .*

3. In §1 above.

4. Matt. 23.37, Luke 13.34.

5. Ps. 85(84).12.

6. A fanciful etymology.

7. Again a fanciful derivation.

8. Ps. 14(13).2; also Ps. 53(52).3.

9. See Martin, 288.

10. Ps. 31(30).3.

11. Ps. 32(31).10.

12. "Exchange"; see above, Pss. 14(13).2, 30(29).2, etc.

13. Cf. Matt. 4.6, Luke 4.10 f.

14. Luke 22.43.
15. The Arians.
16. Matt. 28.20.
17. John 14.21.

PSALM 91 [PS. 92(91)]

1. The Greek form *tetradaxetes* in the CCL text is not found in LSJ, but the reference is clearly to the *tetractys*. This is the representation of the number ten by the figure ⸪⸪ . Ten was the perfect number for the Pythagoreans, since it comprises 1 + 2 + 3 + 4. See the passages of Aetius and Aristotle, *Metaphysics* 985b23 quoted in Kirk and Raven, *The Presocratic Philosophers*, 230, 234.

2. The description is of the figures 1 and 0 which form the number ten.

3. 2 Cor. 9.7.
4. Eph. 2.10.
5. Hab. 3.2.
6. Above, at Ps. 84(83).11.
7. I.e., the Epicureans.
8. Actually Isa. 40.6.
9. Ps. 22(21).22.
10. Wisd. 5.8.
11. This is fantasy.
12. Phil. 3.14.
13. Cf. Martin, 271.
14. Matt. 25.34.
15. In §11 above.

PSALM 92 [PS. 93(92)]

1. For these interpretations of David, see above at Ps. 2.1.
2. Cf. Gen. 1.9.

3. Gen. 3.19.

4. Above, Ps. 29(28).1.

5. Matt. 17.2.

6. *Induit* ('he has clothed himself'). It is impossible to reproduce the word-order effectively in English.

7. See above at Ps. 3.3.

8. Ps. 47(46).7.

9. Cf. John 18.5 f.

10. Cf. John 13.4 f.

11. Matt. 16.18.

12. Isa. 66.2.

13. See Quintilian 9.2.31 f.

14. John 7.38.

15. James 1.17.

16. See n. 4 above.

PSALM 93 [Ps. 94(93)]

1. As often earlier, Cassiodorus connects Greek *deos* (fear) with Latin *deus*.

2. Cf. Matt. 23.1 ff.

3. Cf. Luke 2.46 ff.

4. Ps. 12(11).6.

5. Matt. 25.41.

6. See at Pss. 3.4, 58(57).10, etc.

7. Rom. 8.35.

8. Eccli. 2.5, 27.6.

9. Eccli. 4.10.

10. Deut. 10.18 f.

11. See above at Ps. 74(73).2.

12. See Quintilian 8.6.57; the word is derived from *sarx* (flesh), and means "flesh-tearing."

13. Ezech. 18.23.

14. See above at Ps. 20(19).2.

15. See Quintilian 5.10.1.

16. Ps. 40(39).2.

17. Matt. 12.28.
18. 1 Cor. 6.3.
19. Eph. 6.12.
20. Cf. Matt. 14.29 f.
21. See at Ps. 32(31).1.
22. Matt. 5.5, 5.10.
23. Rom. 8.24 f.
24. See §3 above.

PSALM 94 [PS. 95(94)]

1. Isa. 29.13.
2. See at Pss. 16(15).9, 56(55).13, etc.
3. Ps. 96(95).5.
4. Ps. 82(81).1.
5. Rom. 11.1 f.
6. Ps. 118(117).22; Matt. 21.42.
7. Ps. 86(85).9.
8. See at Pss. 9.26, 21(20).4, etc.
9. John 10.27 f.
10. Heb. 3.13.
11. Cf. Exod. 16.3.
12. John 8.44.
13. Cf. Exod. 16 f.
14. Ps. 89(88).36.
15. Gen. 22.16 f.
16. Heb. 4.4.

PSALM 95 [PS. 96(95)]

1. See Ezra (1 Esdra) 2 ff. These forms of the names and this geneal-
ogy are found in the gospels (Matt. 1.12, Luke 3.27).
2. For the first, see Ps. 50(49).

3. For the belief of the Donatists that they alone were the true followers of Christ, see Intro. VI, Ps. 8.2, etc.

4. "Dwelling upon"; see at Ps. 17(16).13.

5. See above at Pss. 16(15).9, 56(55).13, etc.

6. 'Word for word'; see at Ps. 17(16).13.

7. The suggested etymology is fanciful.

8. 1 Cor. 1.20.

9. See above at Ps. 29(28).1.

10. Matt. 25.34.

11. Again the suggested etymology is baseless.

12. Matt. 5.16.

13. Luke 17.17 ff.

14. Ps. 51(50).19.

15. *A ligno* is not in the Vulgate, but it is in the earlier Roman psalter which had been corrected with the aid of the Septuagint. Justin Martyr (*Tryph.* 7.3) accuses the Jews of having omitted these words.

16. Ezech. 37.5.

17. Dan. 12.2.

18. Ps. 98(97).4.

19. Ps. 107(106).3.

20. Matt. 24.31.

21. Euclid, *Elements* 4.6. This sentence is probably one of the additions inserted into the second recension made at Vivarium. See Adriaen I.12 f.

Psalm 96 [Ps. 97(96)]

1. See earlier Psalms 19(18), 80(79), 85(84).

2. John 9.39.

3. See n. 49 to Ps. 89(88).37.

4. "Sketch" or "description"; see at Pss. 9.26, 21(20).4, etc.

5. Isa. 26.11.

6. Isa. 5.6.

7. Cf. Ps-Cassiodorus, *Principia geometricae disciplinae* (Appendix to the *Inst.* in the Mynors edition, p. 169).

8. Ps. 113(112).3.

9. Cf. Varro ap. Gell. 1.20.7: *longitudo sine latitudine et altitudine.*

10. This appears to be a further addition in the second recension, as at 95.13; it seems clear that Cassiodorus was reviewing geometrical works at the time of this revision. Boethius' translation of Euclid (now lost) was known to him, for he mentions it in a letter to Boethius (*Variae* 1.45.4) written about 507.

11. Ps. 19(18).7.

12. John 1.14.

13. Above, Ps. 59(58).7.

14. The derivations are false.

15. Apoc. 19.10.

16. Matt. 4.9.

17. Ps. 119(118).91.

18. Above, Ps. 1.2.

19. Matt. 6.24.

20. Above, Ps. 84(83).11.

21. Wisd. 5.6.

22. Isa. 18.22.

23. 2 Cor. 4.8–10.

Psalm 97 [Ps. 98(97)]

1. See Psalms 50(49) and 96(95) above.

2. On Nestorius, see Intro. VI, Ps. 21(20) Concl.

3. John 10.18.

4. Isa. 53.1.

5. Luke 2.29 f.

6. Bar. 3.38.

7. John 17.10.

8. Isa. 52.10.

9. As we have often noted, the regular patristic interpretation of Israel is "seeing God."

10. 1 Cor. 13.12.

11. With reference to the Donatist schism; see at Ps. 8.2.

12. Reading *homoioptōton* ("similar ending") for *homoptōton* on the strength of Quintilian 9.3.78 ff.

13. Num. 10.2.
14. Ps. 12(11).7.
15. Jer. 50.23.
16. Isa. 65.17.
17. For the definition, see Quintilian 8.6.44.
18. John 7.38.
19. John 10.16.
20. 2 Cor. 5.10.
21. Joel 3.2.

PSALM 98 [Ps. 99(98)]

1. These two interpretations of David are now familiar; see at Ps. 2.1, etc.
2. Matt. 28.18.
3. Acts 23.3 and 5.
4. "Urbane saying"; *astismos* does not appear in the handbooks, but for *urbanitas* see Martin, 138 ff.
5. See above at Ps. 18(17).11.
6. See above at Ps. 2.7.
7. Ps. 4.4.
8. Luke 1.35.
9. For Jacob as the type of faithful Christians, see at Ps. 46(45).12, etc.
10. 1 Cor. 3.11.
11. See Augustine, *En. Ps.* 98.9 (CCL 39.1385).
12. 1 Cor. 1.25.
13. Phil. 2.9 f.
14. Isa. 66.1.
15. John 1.14.
16. John 2.18.
17. Gal. 4.4.
18. He was actually of the tribe of Levi, but came from Mt. Ephraim (1 Sam. [1 Kings] 1.1). Though of the priestly tribe, he is depicted as prophet and judge rather than as priest.
19. Heb. 1.13.

20. Ps. 22.6, Mal. 3.2, Ps. 118.22.
21. John 14.15.
22. Jos. 24.27.
23. 2 Cor. 12.7 ff.
24. See §5 above.

Psalm 99 [Ps. 100(99)]

1. Varro, *L.L.* 6.55, rightly connects *confiteor* with *fari.*
2. 1 Thess. 5.16 ff.
3. See above at Ps. 7.1.
4. 1 Cor. 13.4 f.
5. Matt. 11.25.
6. Ps. 85(84).12.

Psalm 100 [Ps. 101(100)]

1. Cassiodorus connects the number of the psalm with the parable of the sower at Matt. 13.8.
2. Later in the commentary Cassiodorus appears to forget that he has allotted the psalm to the congregation of the faithful; or at any rate he visualises the spokesman as the just man (see nn. 9 and 15) who may be the collective persona of the gathering.
3. Ps. 85(84).11.
4. Ps. 85(84).11.
5. Ps. 89(88).15.
6. Matt. 25.34.
7. Matt. 25.41.
8. Above Ps. 7.6.
9. See n. 2 above.
10. "A rendering of the reason"; see at Ps. 16(15).19 above.
11. On the conjectural status or basis (*status coniecturalis*) in rhetorical theory, see Quintilian 3.6.29 ff.

12. Ps. 18(17).26 f.

13. The imagery of the early morning is sustained in this expression.

14. Ps. 35(34).1 f.

15. See n. 2 above.

16. The curious statement appears to describe the disposition of the fingers expressing the number 100, the number of the psalm.

17. 2 Tim. 4.8.

INDEXES

1. Old and New Testaments

Genesis

1.1	138
1.5	170
1.9	394
1.20	292
1.28	117 f.
3.15	33
3.19	207, 310, 394
11.42 ff.	22
14.10	151
18.21	9
19.1 ff.	267
22.1	10
22.12	54
22.16 f.	414
22.17	118
22.18	194
26.15 ff.	151
29.2 ff.	151
31.17 ff.	66
31.44	309
32.25	253
32.31	253
41.51	67
46.27	98

Exodus

1.5	268
1.12	295 f.

2.10	249
3.8	287
3.14	246, 298, 372 f.
4.5 ff.	217
7.1	302
7.20 ff.	266
8.17	267
9.10	267
10.20	156
10.22	267
12.5	60
12.6	18
13.21	125
15.6	377
16 f.	413
16.3	413
16.35	125
17.1 ff.	297
17.6	151
17.11	86
19.8	255
19.18	126
20.13 ff.	237
32.1	255
32.4	147
32.9 f.	374
32.12	377
32.31 f.	264
32.32	156
32.35	262

33.11	371	1 *Kings*	
35.27	135	8.20	215
Numbers		2 *Kings*	
10.2	434	17.6	166
14.21	42, 106 f.	24.1 ff.	166
16.32 f.	333	24.14 ff.	166
20.10	263		
		Ezra	
Deuteronomy		2 ff.	415
6.4	246, 332		
6.5	333	*Job*	
10.18 f	402	2.9	172
32.9	126		
32.39	155	*Psalms*	
		2.4	184
Josue		2.6	359, 362
2.1 ff.	338	2.7	82, 304
6.20	295	2.8	55
18.1	270	2.11	237, 333
24.27	441	2.12	64
		4.4	438
Judges		4.7	378
13 ff.	271	5.11	125, 347
		6.1	177
1 *Samuel*		6.2	59
4.11	271	7.10	264
5.1 ff.	272	9.7	345
16.23	295	9.35	124
18.10	267	11(10).2	79
19.11	51	11(10).6	11, 81
21.13	267	12(11).6	43, 400
22.9 ff.	1	12(11).7	282, 434
23.19	13	13(12).4	19
24.4	38	14(13).2	384
27.2 ff.	30	14(13).3	309f.
		14(13).7	56
2 *Samuel*		15(14).5	23
8 ff.	62	17(16).8	129, 168, 345
12.1 ff.	365	18(17).26 f.	450
12.13	365	18(17).30	203
15.30	365		

18(17).45	366	46(45).5	103
19(18).2	184	47(46).7	395
19(18).3	219	48(47).9	273
19(18).5	71, 248	50(49).15	35
19(18).6	54	50(49).16	86, 226
19(18).7	427	51(50).3	149
19(18).13	145, 206	51(50).4	236
22(21).7	23	51(50).7	169
22(21).17 f.	72	51(50).9	92
22(21).22	358, 391	51(50).19	64, 420
22(21).31	364	51(50).21	236
23(22).5	65, 102, 149, 229	53(52).3	318, 384
23(22).6	441	54(53).8	166
24(23).10	127	55(54).24	49, 263
30(29).12	101	57(56).8	225
31(30).3	384	59(58).7	133
31(30).22	363	66(65).6	130
32(31).1	375	68(67).19	124
32(31).5	34	69(68).16	28
32(31).7	360	69(68).30	304
32(31).8	206	71(70).5	79
32(31).10	384	72(71).11	362
34(33).9	24	74(73).7	239
34(33).14	23	78(77).2	148
35(34).1 f.	452	78(77).19	147
35(34).7	144	78(77).24 f.	103
35(34).12	60, 344	80(79).14	137
35(34).13	148	82(81).1	410
36(35).7	176	84(83).3	99
37(36).6	143	84(83).11	73, 362
37(36).35 f.	204	85(84).11	185, 447
38(37).2	59	85(84).12	188, 382, 446
39(38).6	80, 241, 280	86(85).2	245, 363
40(39).2	404	86(85).9	411
40(39).18	164	86(85).20	343
42(41).5	80	89(88).15	447
44(43).4	291	89(88).36	414
44(43).7	291, 366	94(93).7	201
45(44).4	101	94(93).9 f.	201
45(44).8	360	96(95).5	331, 410
45(44).10	128	97(96).4	64, 423

101(100).1	177
104(103).25	100
107(106).3	423
107(106).12	93
110(109).1	18, 36
113(112).3	426
114(113).9	356
116(115).16	330
116(115).18 f.	74
118(117).18	278
118(117).22	411
119(118).22	441
119(118).91	428
121(120).6	292
124(123).4 f.	142
127(126).2	263
129(128).1	349
132(131).11	89
133(132).1	125
135(134).6	139
136(135).25	259
141(140).2	114
142(141).5	163
143(142).6	86
146(145).6	332

Proverbs

1.25 f.	56
3.11 f.	363
15.13	37
16.16	192
18.3	150, 216
18.21	42
21.11	50
24.6	37
25.20	27

Ecclesiastes

1.2	80
10.8	43

Canticle of Canticles

2.15	88
4.2	273 f.
6.8	128, 273

Wisdom

1.7	228
3.7	364
5.6	49, 186 f., 429
5.8	392
11.21	379
12.18	49

Ecclesiasticus

1.16	120
2.5	401
2.11	32
4.10	402
21.29	3
27.6	401
27.12	219

Isaias

1.8	277
2.2	129
5.5	289
5.6	140, 248, 426
9.6	152, 335
9.7	187
14.13	67, 332, 356
18.22	430
26.11	426
26.12	240
29.13	264, 409
35.1	21
40.3	124
40.6	390
42.1	151 f., 335, 359
45.21	332
48.4	264
52.7	68

52.10	432
53.1	175, 246, 431
53.4	157
53.7	143, 307 f.
53.9	145, 274
54.1	105
54.5	194
56.10	204
57.16	244
57.18 f.	183
58.1	294 f.
65.15	191
65.17	102, 435
66.1	440
66.2	232, 396
66.24	300

Jeremias

1.10	352
1.13	67
7.12	270 f.
17.5	69, 329, 356
23.5 f.	221
35.6	166
50.23	434

Lamentations

1.1	278
1.12	214
1.14	214
2.15	278
2.20	289
4.20	345

Baruch

3.38	302, 432

Ezechiel

18.23	35, 402
37.5	422

Daniel

11.43	5
12.2	422
12.7	4

Joel

3.2	436

Amos

9.11	56

Jonas

2.1	335

Micheas

7.18	56

Habacuc

3.1	241
3.2	376, 390

Sophonias

1.15	235

Zacharias

12.10	306
13.7	346

Malachias

1.23	12
3.2	441

1 Maccabees

1.21 ff.	275
1.49 f.	276
1.65	277
2.15 ff.	279
2.23 ff.	279
2.38	276

Matthew

1.12	415
1.25	361
3.17	III, 127, 130, 290, 291, 358
4.4	274
4.6	384 f.
4.9	428
4.19	100
5.3	186
5.5	37, 176, 406
5.8	246
5.10	69, 406
5.16	419
5.34	89
5.44	281
6.1	240
6.24	429
8.12	II
9.2	93
9.4	93
9.5 f.	139
10.17 f.	65
10.22	65
11.19	146
11.28	296
11.29	256
11.30	66, 130
12.24	109, 146
12.28	404
12.29	190
12.39	335
13.8	75
13.17	146
13.23	99, 104
13.24	148
13.39	31
13.55	146
14.22 ff.	249
14.29 f.	406
14.31	III, 206
15.19	207

15.24	41, 322
15.27	133
15.32	355
16.18	273, 396
16.22	90 f.
17.2	395
18.7	144
19.14	151
20.18	92
20.30	273
21.23	58 f.
21.31	339
21.33 f.	156
21.42	411
21.43	154
22.16	27, 46
22.17	48
22.44	207
23.1 ff.	400
23.3	129
23.13	144
23.37	40, 382
24.31	423
25.1 ff.	56
25.31 f.	305
25.34	57, 61, 95, 393, 419, 447
25.41	124, 235, 290, 300, 400, 447
25.46	164
26.20 ff.	25
26.35	255
26.38	344
26.39	144
26.64	109
26.65	152
26.66	27, 43, 58, 92
26.69 ff.	255
27.11	341
27.12	143
27.25	53, 92
27.34	153
27.40	94, 346

27.42	19, 94, 152	18.8	57
27.43	345	18.13	34, 105, 326
27.48	141	18.39	18
27.51	304	19.41	19
27.54	304	22.15	152
28.10	342	22.31 f.	226
28.13	109	22.43	385
28.18	361, 437	23.21	42, 53, 91
28.19	245 f., 324	23.31	48
28.20	54, 386	23.34	144, 153, 221, 264, 281
		23.42	114
Mark		24.1	44
1.35	21	24.18	149
3.27	53, 127	24.30 ff.	94
7.28	56	24.39	306
8.23	35		
8.33	87, 153	*John*	
15.15	341	1.1	193, 327
15.19	342	1.9	356
15.26	134	1.12	304 f.
		1.14	36, 340, 353, 427, 440
Luke		1.26	302
1.35	129, 438	1.47	221
1.38	330	2.6 ff.	229
2.29 ff.	118, 432	2.9	266
2.46 ff.	400	2.17	141, 147
3.27	415	2.18	440
4.6 ff.	54	2.19	99, 335
4.10 f.	384 f.	2.21	99, 335
4.22	147	4.7	78, 148
6.37	46	4.10	84
10.18	355	4.13 f.	103, 258
10.20	156	4.18	54
12.6	103	5.2 ff.	341
13.32 f.	88	5.22	82, 184, 295, 335
13.34	382	5.27	226
14.11	228	5.28	139
16.19 ff.	173	5.46	371
16.23	333	6.71	24
17.17 f.	85, 419	7.38	397, 435
18.1	329	8.4 f.	42

8.17	154	*Acts*	
8.25	121, 340	2.3 f.	353
8.36	263	2.4	296
8.39	146, 159	2.37	94
8.44	413	2.41	224
9.7	341	4.32	125, 163
9.29	147	5.3 f.	324
9.39	425	7.57	135
10.16	247, 436	9.1 ff.	17
10.18	82, 91, 344, 431	9.4	41, 58, 135
10.27 f.	412	9.26	135
11.11	128	10.13	60
11.35	148	10.38	6
11.48	93	13.46	339
12.24	67	23.3	129, 437 f.
12.28	359	23.5	438
13.4 f.	396		
14.6	111, 245, 326, 332	*Romans*	
14.10	35, 54, 88, 130	1.24	267, 299
14.15	441	2.12	168
14.21	386	5.3	43, 67, 72, 169
14.27	183	5.12	368
14.30	52, 145, 360	5.35	215
15.5	288	8.2	263 f.
15.16	99	8.18	85
16.15	184, 226	8.24 f.	407
16.22 f.	74	8.26	17
17.10	361, 432	8.32	155
17.25	144	8.35	400
18.5 f.	396	10.4	106, 320
18.33	25	10.10	107 f.
18.37	88, 217	11.1 f.	411
19.6	46, 143	11.6	319
19.11	112, 155, 355	11.9 f.	141
19.15	232	11.25 f.	55, 367
19.19	38	12.15	210
19.28	78		
19.30	25	*1 Corinthians*	
19.34	342	1.20	47, 310, 418
20.19	342	1.24 f.	136, 145, 246
21.18	142	1.25	439

1.27	145	12.7 ff.	442
1.31	2	12.21	5
2.7	232		
2.8	304	*Galatians*	
2.9	99, 340	4.4	201, 440
3.1 f.	104	4.19	8, 186
3.11	337, 439	6.14	378
3.17	271, 311		
4.7	57, 303	*Ephesians*	
4.8	129	1.3 f.	136
4.15	186	2.10	389
4.21	363	2.17	325
6.3	405	4.7	99, 131
6.17	87	4.8	124
7.38	237	5.8	62
8.2	164	6.12	31, 405
8.5 f.	303	6.15	68
8.6	226	6.17	56
10.1 ff.	252, 257		
10.4	71, 258	*Philippians*	
10.13	286	2.6 f.	187, 306
10.21	153	2.7 f.	327
12.8 ff.	99	2.9	40, 359, 439 f.
12.26	83, 283	2.10	158
13.4 f.	444	3.2	133
13.12	433	3.5	135
15.51	26	3.13	164
15.54	20	3.14	392
2 Corinthians		*Colossians*	
4.8 ff.	430	2.9	363
4.17	69	2.18 f.	6
5.10	98, 436		
5.19	98	*1 Thessalonians*	
5.21	145	5.5	87
6.2	148	5.16 ff.	443
6.10	158		
6.13 f.	298	*1 Timothy*	
8.9	156 f., 186	1.9	254
9.7	389	1.13	34, 319
11.23 f.	370	2.8	86

5.6	49	*1 Peter*	
6.17 f.	81	1.12	324
		4.17	65
2 Timothy			
2.5	64		
3.16	137	*2 Peter*	
4.7 f.	319	1.21	252
4.8	452		
		1 John	
Hebrews		2.18	243
1.1 ff.	18		
1.13	160, 441	*Apocalypse*	
3.2	108	1.8	141, 362
3.13	412	1.17	362
4.4	414	5.5	135, 159
9.9	269	6.10	281
9.11 f.	139	19.10	428
9.24	139, 269	19.16	232, 273
12.6	59, 363	21.6	362
		21.16	56
James		22.13	362
1.17	397	22.16	362
5.20	127		

2. AUTHORS

Adriaen, M., 504
Aetius, 501
Albinus, 491
Ambrose, 499; *Hymns*, 187 f., 229, 484
Apuleius, 497
Aristotle: *Metaphysics*, 501
Augustine, 239, 334, 365, 439, 498, 499; *Confessions*, 125, 475; *De civ. Dei*, 479; *De consensu evangelistarum*, 267, 487; *De musica*, 491; *De sermone Domini in monte*, 46; *De Trinitate*, 36, 77; *Enarr. in Ps., passim; Enchiridion*, 145; *Epp.*, 483; *Locutiones in Hept.*, 239, 485; *Tract. in ep. Ioh. ad Parthos*, 36

Bede, 460
Bernard of Clairvaux, 498
Boethius, translator of Euclid, 505; *Consolation of Philosophy*, 464, 475; *Contra Eutychen*, 481; *De musica*, 491

Candidus of Fulda, 460
Cassian, John: *Conferences*, 162, 477 f.

Cassiodorus: *De orthographia*, 499;
  Princ. geom. disc., 504; *Variae*, 505
Chadwick, H., 481, 500
Charisius, 461
Chrysostom, John: *Hom. in Ascens.*
  Domini, 207
Cicero: *De inventione*, 459, 478, 482;
  Pro Sex. Roscio, 480; *Topica*, 46,
  333
Cyprian, 192, 480
Cyril of Alexandria, 481
Cyril of Jerusalem, 479; *Cat. Lect.*,
  459

Diomedes, 461

Epiphanius, 485
Euclid, 423, 504

Fortunatianus, 483

Gaudentius, 490
Gibson, M., 500
Gregory the Great, 498

Honigmann, E., 485

Isidore: *Origines*, 475, 498

Jerome, 497, 499; *Adv. Jov.*, 481;
  Comm. in Isa., 189, 480; *Epp.*, 80,
  460; *Hebrew Names, passim*;
  Hom. in Ps., passim; *Psalt. iuxta*
  Hebr., 133, 137, 272; *Tract. de Ps.*,
  passim
Josephus: *Antiq. Jud.* 337, 488; *Bell.*
  Jud., 213, 482
Jugie, M. 481
Julian of Norwich, 498

Jungmann, J. A., 478
Justin Martyr, 504

Kirk, G. S., 501

Lanfranc, 460
Leclercq, H., 496
Leo Magnus: *Epp.*, 29, 108, 138, 188

McKay, J. W., 481
Martianus Capella, 500
Martin, J., *passim*
Montefusco, L. C., 483
Mutianus, 490

O'Meara, J. J., 484, 500
Origen: *Hexapla*, 94

Pliny the Elder, 464
Plutarch, 497

Quintilian, *passim*

Rahner, H., 480, 499
Raven, J., 501
Rogerson, J. W., 481

Sedulius: *Carmen Paschale*, 306, 492
Seneca the Younger, 479
Servius: *Ad Aen.*, 476
Stephen of Jerusalem, 243, 485
Szöverffy, J., 484

Varro, 505; *De lingua Latina, passim*

Walpole, A. S., 480, 484
William of Newburgh, 486
Winnington-Ingram, R. P., 490

3. GENERAL

Aaron, 255 f., 262 f., 440; meaning of, 249
Abel, 245
Abimelech, 1, 267
Abiron, 333
Abraham, 10, 51, 54, 82, 118, 146, 151, 173, 194, 245, 267, 335, 367 f.
Absalom, 365
abysses = mind of God, 176
Achis, 267
Adam, 77, 117, 120, 145, 175 f., 241, 245, 381, 431
Afric wind = Lord's words, 261
Agarens, meaning of, 309
ages, six, 394
allegory, use of, 8, 56, 100, 114, 121, 287, 435
Amalech, 309; meaning of, 7 f.
Amalekites, 86
Ammon, meaning of, 309
angels, good and bad, 269 f.
anger of God as metaphor, 59, 268, 311 f.
animals = Gentiles, 126
Antichrist, 1 ff., 55, 307 ff., 479
Antiochus IV Epiphanes, 275 ff., 286, 482
Antony of Egypt, 478
Apollinarius/Apollinarists, 329, 494
Apollo, 101
Arabia = men of worldly delights, 189; gold of, = wisdom, 192
Arians/Arius, 26, 35, 109, 298
arithmetic, 179, 379, 389

ark of covenant, 270 f.
arm = human power, 356; arm of God = Christ, 246, 355
arrows = hostile words, 41; = evangelists, 248; flying by day = persecutions, 382; arrows of children = Jews' aspirations, 94
Asaph, 197, 209 ff., 226, 231 ff., 283 ff., 292 ff., 301 ff.; meaning of, 196, 209, 224, 231, 238 f., 250, 275, 293, 301, 306
Ascension of Christ, 121, 131, 138
asp/asps = human race, 47; = Jews, 47; = devil, 385
Assyrians, meaning of, 231; = devil, 309
astrology condemned, 179
astronomy, 187
Athens, 361
Auster = Lord's words, 261

Babel, tower of, 22
Babylon, meaning of, 96, 339; = captivity of sin, 97, 109
Basan, meaning of, 133
basilisk = devil, 385
beasts of woods = devil and his demons, 137, 221; = wicked men, 137
beetle, symbol of Christ, 23
Benjamin, meaning of, 285; = Paul, 135
boar = Vespasian, 289; = devil, 289
borders of earth = prophets/apostles, 220

bow, appearance of = day of
Judgment, 65; bent bow = malice
of sinners, 270
bullocks = preachers, 114
bulls = heretics, 137
businessmen not condemned, 173

Caecilius, 468
calumniator = devil, 186
Calvary, 313
Canaanite woman, 133
canticle = good works, 389; = praise
of Godhead, 394
cattle = fickle women, 137; = foolish
men, 266
cedars = proud men, 288; = martyrs,
288
cedars of Libanus = just men, 392 f.
Chalcedon, Council of, 51 f., 481
Chaldaeans, 96, 415
chalice = divine law, 228
Cham, father of Canaan, 268
Cherubim, meaning of, 285, 438
Christ, distinction between natures
of, 91, 101, 183, 186, 195 f., 226, 298,
305 f., 327, 385, 396 f.; as
spokesman of members, 145;
speaks as human Person, 19 ff.,
142; as Advocate, 44, 55, 119; as
Beetle, 23; as Boy, 151 f., 335; as
Bread of angels, 261; as Day, 51; as
holy One, 245; as Husbandman,
284 ff.; as Justice, 173, 432; as King,
410; as Lamb, 29, 152; as Master,
152; as Mediator, 439 f.; as Mercy,
377; as Patience, 79; as Physician,
64, 84, 210, 227, 280, 322; as Priest,
98; as Redeemer, 29, 44, 57, 227,
360; as Saviour/Salvation, 79, 280,
386, 432; as Servant, 18; as Sun, 50
f., 154, 429; as Teacher, 151, 274,

328; as Tower, 72; as Victim, 98,
145; as Way, 44, 118, 245; as
Worm, 23
Cison, 310
Cleophas, 148
clouds = prophets/preachers, 44,
140, 248, 260, 353 f.; = angels/
saints, 139 f.
confession, twin meanings of, 16,
119, 225, 236, 388, 410, 443
Constantinople, 496; Council of,
494
Core, sons of, meaning of, 313 ff.;
also 320, 336
courts of Lord = prophets/apostles,
420; court = Catholic Church, 420
covenants, old and new, 221
cross, 421; formed by raising hands,
85 f.
Cyrus, 470
Cythera, 101

Damascus, 17
darkness = Jews, 222
darts = harsh words, 27
Dathan, 333
David, 1 ff., 7, 30, 34, 83, 196, 351, 365,
380; meanings of, 45, 63, 106, 328,
359, 394, 437; progenitor of Christ,
18, 251, 273, 328, 353; type of Christ,
38, 45, 51, 62, 70, 75, 90, 121, 141,
161, 359, 424, 447
day = lifetime, 2, 192, 330, 358; =
Christ, 256; = the just, 219
dead = non-believers, 347
deep sea = sins, 150
Delos, 471
Delphi, 101
demons defined, 417 f.; temptations
of, 451
depths = troubled people, 247

desert hills = false preachers, 228;
    desert regions = Gentiles, 104
devil, the, 2, 31 ff., 53 ff., 62, 145, 160,
    167 f., 183, 190, 199, 218 f., 321, 332,
    356, 360, 382, 385 ff., 429; images
    of, 385
Diana, 101
Dives, 333
Doech/Doeg, Edomite, 1; type of
    Antichrist, 1
dog(s) = Jews, 55 f., 60; = Paul, 60;
    in good and bad senses, 133
dog-fly = sting inflicted on wicked,
    266
Donatus/Donatists, 74 f., 119, 132,
    190, 416
doors of heaven = Scripture, 260
dove, meaning of, 21; symbolises
    Christ, 21; silvered, = Church,
    128; simplicity of, symbolises
    Spirit, 448 f.
dragon = devil, 218; heads of, =
    unclean spirits, 218
dust = understanding, 261

earth, shape of, 423, 426; = man, 102,
    126, 394, 438; = sinners, 64, 226,
    438; = repentant sinners, 420 f.;
    = Church/faithful, 107, 195, 416,
    433
east = persons of heavenly
    demeanour, 228
Edom, Edomites, meaning of, 67 f.,
    83, 309
Egypt = darkness of sin, 5, 137 f.,
    269; = demons, 251, 265, 268, 372;
    plagues of, 266 ff.
Eleazar, 276
Elias, 110
Elijah, 7
Eman, 342

Endor, 310
Enoch, 7
Ephesus, Council of, 481
Ephraim, 255, 272, 285, 440; meaning
    of, 67; sons of, 255 f.
Epicureans, 497, 501
Esau, 12
Ethan, meaning of, 219, 351; = devil,
    219
Ethiopia = blackness, 137 f.; =
    sinners, 189; = reformed sinners,
    218, 339
Eutyches/Eutychians, 195, 305 f., 481
evening = end of life, 374; =
    betrayal of Christ, 25; = time of
    suffering, 102
eyes of Christ = apostles, 346
Ezechiel, 96

fasting, metaphorical sense of, 148
feathered fowls = longings for
    heaven, 261
feet of Christ = rebukes and
    promises, 42
Felix, 468
fire = heat of evil mind, 49; =
    cupidity, 266; = anger, 271
first-born, meaning of, 361
first coming of Christ, 425
Flavian, 108
flesh = mankind, 98
food = holy communion, 103
foot = mental commitment, 198
footstool of God = Christ's body,
    440
forty, mystical sense of, 413
foundations of Jerusalem = Christ,
    337
foxes = Jews/Herod, 88
frog = loquacious heretic, 266

Galaad, meaning of, 66
gates = prophets/apostles, 338;
   Lord's gates = repentance, 338, 345
Gebal, meaning of, 309
Gentiles 417 ff.; = barbaric errors,
   269
geometry, 423, 426
Geth, meaning of, 30
goats associated with sinning, 114
God, etymology of, 400; without
   emotions, 27; knows no increase,
   164, 173; immobile and ubiquitous,
   172; eternal, 372; accorded human
   powers by metaphor, 258, 272, 328;
   physical parts denote powers, 328,
   403
gods = men, 331; = men inspired by
   grace, 302, 410; = pagan deities,
   417
Goliath, 1
Gomorrah, 267
grass in good and bad senses, 193; =
   sinners, 193, 390, 392; = human
   life, 374

hail = divine threats/rebukes, 266
haircloth = sadness of Christ, 148
hairs = apostles/true believers, 144
hammer = devil, 434
hands = activity/power, 26, 356; =
   good works, 240
harp, 177; of David, 295; = Christ's
   passion, 43; = almsgiving, 294; =
   joy of good works, 389, 433
heart in good and bad senses, 207
heavens = prophets/apostles, 352,
   421, 457
Hebrew language, initially universal,
   22
Hebrew Psalter, 19
Heli, sons of, 271

hell, upper and lower regions of, 333
heretics, 78, 132, 134, 357, 450
hermits, 444
Hermon, meaning of, 356
Hethites, 287
hills = martyrs, 105; = blessed ones
   below apostles/martyrs, 185; =
   arrogant thoughts, 270; everlasting
   hills = preachers, 233
Historia Monachorum, 478
holocaust, meaning of, 113
horn, in good and bad senses, 358; =
   strength, 358, 361; = patience, 434;
   = excuses/blasphemies, 227; of
   just and of sinners, 230; horn-
   shaped bows = malice of proud,
   233
horseback = arrogance, 235
house = Christ's tomb, 51; house of
   the Lord = Church, 125, 398, 415
hymn, defined, 116

Idithun, 75 ff., 238 ff.
incarnation, 40, 105, 178, 290, 303,
   307, 340, 358, 395, 415, 430
incense = prayers, 114
interpretations, varying, legitimate,
   13
Isaac, 82, 151, 173
Ishmaelites, meaning of, 309
islands = pure of heart, 189; =
   Churches, 425
Israel/Israelites, meaning of, 12, 232,
   270, 284 f., 342, 351, 432; =
   universal Church, 12, 139, 194; =
   believing Jews, 247

Jabin, meaning of, 310
Jacob, 59, 66, 82, 151, 230, 247, 255,
   279; meaning of, 259, 317; =
   Gentiles, 259; = Church/

Christian faithful, 12, 293, 295, 321, 402, 432, 439; sheep of, = Jews, 66; and the angel, 253

Janus, 214

Jebusites, 287

Jeremiah, 96, 224

Jericho, 295

Jerusalem, 24, 60, 96; meaning of, 136; wickedness of, 22; destruction of, 155, 210 ff.; profaned by Antiochus, 275 ff.; holy places in, 341 f.; = Church, 96; = heaven, 273, 314

Jews, chosen by God, 410 f.; condemnations of, *passim*; dispersion of, 58, 237, 367; punishment of, 24 f.; conversion of, prophesied, 13, 55, 59 f., 229 f., 367

Job, 16, 82, 113, 172 f., 267

John the Baptist, 302

Jonadab, 165; sons of, = committed faithful, 166

Jonah = type of Resurrection, 335

Jordan, 109 f., 188, 288

Joseph (O.T.), 67, 173; meaning of, 247, 272, 285, 295; children of, = believing Gentiles, 247; = faithful people, 284 f.

Joseph, spouse of Mary, 361

Judah, 15, 159, 232; meaning of, 136, 272 f.; type of Christ, 67, 135 f.; daughters of, = religious minds, 428

Judas, 23 ff., 53, 91, 346, 360

Judgment, 26 f., 89, 95, 210, 226, 235 f., 311 ff., 361, 392, 423; depicted in Ps. 52, 8; place of, 436; faithful participate in, 404 f.

Jupiter, 200, 410

Justice of the Father = Christ, 185

K, letter, = *kalumniator*, 186

kings = persons emptied of pride, 237

Laban, 66, 309

lamb, symbolises Christ's gentleness, 449

Lazarus and Dives, 333

Lazarus, brother of Martha and Mary, 139, 328

Leo, emperor, 243, 485

Libanus, 388; = Christ, 192

lightnings = divine precepts, 248; = prophets' words, 426

lion, as image of devil, 193, 385; of Jews, 41, 48

lips of God = prophets, 363

locust = malicious detraction, 266

Lot, 267; meaning of, 309

lots = two Testaments, 128

lowliness = earthly lodging, 373

Macedonian theology, 494

Madian, meaning of, 310

Magi, 192

man = devil, 31, 36

Manasses, meaning of, 66, 285

Mani/Manichees, 132, 229

manna, meaning of, 260; = holy communion, 260, 415

Mars 410; Mars Gradivus a demon, 97

martyrs, reason for seeking death, 85; sufferings of, 112 f., 133; rewards of, 407; spokesmen in Ps. 70(69), 161; Jewish, 277 ff.

Mary, Virgin, 52, 61, 111, 129, 183, 195, 243, 290, 298, 325 f., 330, 334 f., 343, 361 f., 396, 438 f.

Mathathias, 276 ff.

Matins, 170

Meleth, meaning of, 342, 350, 459

Mercury, 200
mercy of Father = Christ, 323;
  mercy and truth = N.T. and
  O.T., 325; linked with justice, 447
metaphors, 156
mire = the flesh, 143, 150; of the deep
  = Jews' guile, 143
mixture of wine = O.T. and N.T.,
  229
Moab, meaning of, 67, 309
monasteries, 444
Montanists, 133
moon = Church, 187 f., 364; =
  human body, 364; = fool, 219
morning = time of joy, 102, 388; =
  human lifespan, 374; = good
  works, 348; = indictment of
  Christ before Pilate, 25
Moses, 18, 60, 82, 126, 151, 156, 211,
  217, 230, 249, 251, 253, 255 f., 262
  ff., 295, 302, 325, 340, 413
  spokesman of Ps. 90(89), 370 ff.;
  as type of Church, 372; as priest,
  440
mother = synagogue, 147
mountains, in good and bad senses,
  435; = Christ, 122, 129 f., 192; =
  Church, 249; = prophets/
  apostles, 100, 129 f., 185, 192, 337 f.;
  = worldly powers, 411; = men in
  high positions, 427; = arrogant
  and wicked men, 435
music, divisions of, 295, 433, 436

Nathan, 365
Nathaniel, 221
Nephthali, meaning of, 135 f.
Nestorius/Nestorians, 51, 195, 305, 431
Nicaea, 478 f.
Nicodemus, 221

night = sadness/affliction, 343, 388;
  = this world, 240; = worldly
  men, 219
Noah, 82, 245
Nocturns, 170
noonday devil = persecution, 382
north = devil, 356
number, 379, 389

oaths, forbidden to man, 89, 414;
  God's swearing, 414
oil = soft words, 27
old age, meaning of, 170 f., 391 f, 393
orders in the Church, 444
Oreb, meaning of, 310
original sin, 368

palm-tree = just man, 392
Pandect, 337
Paphnutius, 173
parable defined, 148
parched places = minds of
  unbelievers, 258
passion of Christ, 38 ff., 51 ff., 59,
  90 ff., 141 ff., 179, 342 ff.
pasture = heavenly gifts, 412; =
  Scripture, 445
patience defined, 168
Paul, 267, 437 f.
Peace of Father = Saviour, 185, 224
pearl = Scripture, 13
Pelagius/Pelagians, 57, 499
Peter, 35, 60, 87, 90, 111, 142 f., 153,
  226, 255, 405
Phaenarete, 196
Pharaoh, 212, 235, 253; his magicians,
  332
Pharisees, 42, 326, 339, 346, 400
Philistines, 30
Pilate, 25, 30, 38, 45 f., 88, 112, 152 f.,
  202, 308, 341, 346

pillars = apostles, 226 f.; = Church, 441
pit, in good and bad senses, 151; = hell, 28, 344; = disaster, 345
plagues, Egyptian, 266 ff.
plains = faithful and just, 104, 422
plantation = Catholic Church, 393
poor of Christ = prophets/apostles, 186; = those despising pleasures/riches, 158
pot, in good and bad senses, 67
power of God = Christ, 136
prayer, disquisition on, 370 f.; right posture for, 412
predestination/predestined, 156, 170, 396, 415
presses, meaning of, 292, 313
princes = apostles, 134
Priscillianists, 132
proud one = devil, 355
psalm = musical instrument, 177, 336; as melody, 117; as holy activity, 43, 75, 109, 124, 294, 387
psalm-canticle, 117, 336, 342, 387
psalmody, power of, 157
psaltery, 294; = worthy manners, 388; = Christ's commands, 43
Pythagoreans, 389

Rahab, type of Church, 338
rain = menaces of Jews, 48
rams = apostles, 105, 114
razor = Antichrist's guile, 3
Red Sea, 212, 256, 372; prefigures baptism, 110, 218, 249, 296, 371
reins = mental constancy, 205
remission, of sins, 177
resurrection, 106 ff., 122, 141 ff., 179, 305, 334 f., 348, 424
riches, good and evil use of, 81

rivers = baptism, 361; = Jordan, 361; = apostles, 397; = holy men, 435
rock = Christ, 71, 258
rod = divine punishment, 362 f.; of Moses, 212
Rome, preeminent in worship, 212

Saba, 189
sabbath = future rest, 387
sacrifice, true, 16
Salathiel, 415
Salmana, meaning of, 310
Samuel, 440
sand = wisdom, 261
Satan, 29; and see devil
Saturn, 410
Saul, king, 1, 13 ff., 30, 51, 62, 295; type of Jews, 38
Saul (Paul), 17
Scriptures, peculiarity of expressions in, 28, 54, 57, 80, 87, 102, 110, 130, 138, 229, 310, 324, 331, 339, 361
sea = world, 100, 133; = nations, 361, 411; = hearts of evil men, 356, 434; = men's madness, 143
second coming, 307 ff., 415 ff., 430 ff.
seed = good actions, 159; of Christ, = all believers, 364; of David, = Christ, 362
Selmon, meaning of, 129
sepulchre = minds of unfaithful, 347
seventy and eighty = O.T. and N.T., 179, 375 f.
shadow, in good and bad senses, 345
sheep = Christians, 269, 282, 412, 445; = Jews, 211; faithful Jews, 282
shoe = gospel, 67
shoulders, Lord's = miracles, 382
Sichem, meaning of, 66

side of Christ = saints at Judgment, 383

Silo, 251, 270 f.

Simeon, 118, 221, 432

Sinai, 230; meaning of, 130

sinners, allowed to flourish, 197

Sion, position of, 159, 208, 233, 269, 317, 338, 342, 428; meanings of, 12, 97, 159, 208, 233, 338, 438; = Church, 159, 208, 251, 269, 273, 428, 438, 442; = Jerusalem, 212

Sisara, meaning of, 310

sixth day = incarnation, 398

sleep = death, 128; = life of unfaithful, 234

smoke = sinners, 122 f.

Socrates, 196

Sodom, 267

Solomon, 3, 27, 32, 37, 50, 56, 80, 120, 188, 191, 196; meaning of, 183; temple of, 213 ff., 337

Son, coeternal, consubstantial, equal with Father, 26, 35, 77, 82

Sophroniscus, 196

soul = whole man, 268; = physical life, 53

sparrows = human souls, 315

spider = barren life, 375

Spirit equal and consubstantial with Father and Son, 35 f., 77, 324; proceeds from Father and Son, 76

spring = placid faithful, 220

stars = holy men, 399

Stephen, protomartyr, 135

stool = incarnation, 439 ff.

summer = fervent faithful, 220

sun = Christ, 49 f., 186; = wise man, 219

sword = Scripture, 56

syllogisms, 8, 72, 86, 167, 429, 448

Syria, 66

Tabernacles, feast of, 490; tabernacles of Jacob = Church, 338; = Temple in earlier days, 337

table, in good and bad senses, 153 f.

Tabor, Mt., 395

Tanis, meaning of, 256, 265

tempest = rebellious madmen, 143

ten-stringed psaltery = Decalogue, 388 f.

terror of night = persuasion by heretics, 382

Tetractys, 389

Thabor, meaning of, 356

Tharsis, meaning of, 189

Thomas, apostle, 306

thief, good, 34, 114, 176

thirst of Christ, metaphorical sense of, 148

timbrels, meaning of, 294; interpretation of timbrel-players, 134

Titus, 88, 211, 289, 477

tongue = precepts of N.T., 296

Torobabel, 415

torrents = wicked men's sallies, 219

tower = Christ, 72

Transfiguration, 395

Trinity, 35, 40, 76 f., 226, 246, 264, 301, 332, 353, 373, 387, 416, 419 f.

trumpet = holy Spirit, 434

turtle = Church, 315; = human flesh, 315

Tyre, meaning of, 309, 339

unicorns = pride, 391; = single hope in Trinity, 273; = exaltation of Church's unity, 391 usury, condemned, 23; = obligations of sin, 191

valleys = humble people, 105
Venus 101; = demon, 97
Vespasian, 88, 211, 289
Vespers, 170
vineyard = Church, 287; = Jewish nation, 287
virgin birth, 187 f.
Vivarium, 490
vows, 237

waters = believers, 247 f.; = converted Gentiles, 249; = wicked, 150; = rebellion of common folk, 142
waves = persecutors, 101; = storms of world, 150
wax = wicked, 123
weapons = wicked designs, 41
west = sinners lacking truth, 228

wheel = universe, 248; = evil-minded men, 311
wilderness = Gentiles, 21
winds = fickleness of sinners, 311
wine = virtue, 64 f.; spiritual senses of, 149, 229
wings = Lord's protection, 72 f.; = prophets' warnings, 382
womb = Church, 169
wood = Gentiles, 289; of cross, 420
world, in good sense, 421; = unholy men, 435; worldly business and Christian life, 173

youth = time of attainment of divine grace, 169, 174; youth of Church = death of Christ and of early martyrs, 175

Zabulon, 135 f.
Zeb, meaning of, 310
Zebee, meaning of, 310
Ziph, meaning of, 13 ff.